ArtScroll Mishnah Series®

A rabbinic commentary to the Six Orders of the Mishnah

Rabbis Nosson Scherman / Meir Zlotowitz

General Editors

the mishnah

ARTSCROLL MISHNAH SERIES / A NEW TRANSLATION WITH A COMMENTARY **YAD AVRAHAM** ANTHOLOGIZED FROM TALMUDIC SOURCES AND CLASSIC COMMENTATORS.

Published by

Mesorah Publications, ltd

FIRST EDITION
First Impression . . . September 1980
SECOND EDITION
Revised and Corrected
Eight Impressions: May 1981 — June 1997
Ninth Impression . . . November 2000
Tenth Impression . . . December 2002

Published and Distributed by
MESORAH PUBLICATIONS, Ltd.
4401 Second Avenue
Brooklyn, New York 11232

Distributed in Europe by
LEHMANNS
Unit E, Viking Industrial Park
Rolling Mill Road
Jarrow, Tyne & Wear NE32 3DP
England

Distributed in Australia & New Zealand by
GOLDS WORLD OF JUDAICA
3-13 William Street
Balaclava, Melbourne 3183
Victoria Australia

Distributed in Israel by
SIFRIATI / A. GITLER — BOOKS
6 Hayarkon Street
Bnei Brak 51127

Distributed in South Africa by
KOLLEL BOOKSHOP
Shop 8A Norwood Hypermarket
Norwood 2196, Johannesburg, South Africa

THE ARTSCROLL MISHNAH SERIES ·
SEDER MOED Vol. III: *ROSH HASHANAH / YOMA / SUCCAH*
© Copyright 1980, 1981, 1997 by MESORAH PUBLICATIONS, Ltd.
4401 Second Avenue / Brooklyn, N.Y. 11232 / (718) 921-9000 / www.artscroll.com

---

ISBN
0-89906-256-3 (hard cover)
0-89906-257-1 (paperback)

Typography by Compuscribe at ArtScroll Studios, Ltd.
4401 Second Avenue / Brooklyn, NY 11232 / (718) 921-9000

Printed in the United States of America by Noble Book Press Corp.
Bound by Sefercraft, Quality Bookbinders, Ltd. Brooklyn, N.Y.

◈§ Seder Moed Vol. III:

Rosh Hashanah / ראש השנה

Chapters 1-3, Rabbi Yosef Rottenberg
Chapter 4, Rabbi Hersh Goldwurm

Yoma / יומא

Rabbi Hersh Goldwurm

Succah / סוכה

Rabbi Yisroel Gornish

The Publishers are grateful to
YESHIVA TORAH VODAATH AND MESIVTA
for their efforts in the publication of the
ARTSCROLL MISHNAH SERIES

This volume is dedicated to
the memory of

ר׳ יוסף שמעון בן חיים ע״ה

1st Lt. Joseph Simon Bravin ע״ה

who made the supreme sacrifice
at the age of 21 in Viet Nam

נפל בקרב בוויט נם כ״ה אלול תשכ״ח

January 10, 1947—September 18, 1968

God lent the world a treasure—but briefly.
His memory kindles flames of Torah study
to enrich generations
that never knew him.

תנצב״ה

הסכמה

Rabbi Moshe Feinstein
455 F. D. R. Drive
New York, N. Y. 10002

משה פיינשטיין
ר"מ תפארת ירושלים

בע"ה

[חתימת יד - מכתב כתב יד של הרב משה פיינשטיין]

[חתימה]

בע"ה

הנני מברך בזה את ידידי הרב הנכבד מהר"ר מאיר בן ידידי הרב הגאון ר' אהרן שליט"א
זלאטאוויץ ואת ידידי הרב הנכבד מהר"ר נתן שערמאן שליט"א שעמדו בראש הנהלת **חברת ארטסקרול**,
אשר הוציאו כבר הרבה חבורים חשובים בשפת אנגלית לזכות את הרבים, וגם הוציאו על משניות כרך
אחד ועכשיו מוציאים לאור עוד כרך שני, ויש בו לקוטים מספרי רבותינו מפרשי משניות על כל משנה
ומשנה, מלוקטים בטוב טעם ע"י תלמידי חכמים חשובים ומומחים לרבים, והוא לתועלת גדול להרבה
אינשי ממדינה זו שלא התרגלו מילדותם במשניות, וגם יש הרבה שבעזהשי"ת התקרבו לתורה ויראת
שמים שכבר נתגדלו ורוצים ללמוד, שיוכלו ללמוד משניות בנקל בשפה המורגלת להם, שלכן הם ממזכי
הרבים שזכותם גדול ואני מברכם שיצליחם השי"ת בחבור זה ובעוד כרכים.

וגם אני מברך בזה את ידידי הנכבד מאד עסקן ותומך גדול לתורה ולתעודה מוהר"ר אלעזר גליק
שליט"א אשר עזר הרבה להדפסת משניות אלו לזכר נשמת בנו המנוח החשוב מאד מר **אברהם יוסף** ז"ל
ונקרא הפירוש **יד אברהם** על שמו והוא זכות גדול לעילוי נשמתו בלמוד הרבים. יהי זכרו ברוך. וע"ז
באתי על החתום בער"ח אלול תש"מ.

משה פיינשטיין

מכתב ברכה

יעקב קמנצקי

RABBI J. KAMENECKI

38 SADDLE RIVER ROAD

MONSEY, NEW YORK 10952

בע"ה

יום ה' ערב חג השבועות תשל"ס, פה מאנסי.

כבוד הרבני איש החסד שוע ונדיב מוקיר רבנן מר אלעזר נ"י גליק
שלו' וברכת כל טוב.

מה מאד שמחתי בהודעי כי כבודו רכש לעצמו הזכות שייקרא ע"ש
בנו המנוח הפירוש מבואר על כל ששת סדרי משנה ע"י "ארטסקראל"
והנה חברה זו יצאה לה מוניטין בפירושה על תנ"ך, והנה נקוה שכשם
שהצליחה בתורה שבכתב כן תצליח בתורה שבע"פ. ובהיות שאותיות
"משנה" הן כאותיות "נשמה" לפיכך סוב עשה בכוונתו לעשות זאת לעילוי
נשמת בנו המנוח אברהם יוסף ע"ה, ומאד מתאים השם "יד אברהם" לזה
הפירוש, כדמצינו במקרא (ש"ב י"ח) כי אמר אין לי בן בעבור הזכיר
שמי וגו'. ואין לך דבר גדול מזה להפיץ ידיעת תורה שבע"פ בקרב
אחינו שאינם רגילים בלשון הקדש. וד' הסוב יהי' בעזרו ויוכל לברך
על המוגמר. וירוה רוב נחת מכל אשר אתו כנפש מברכו.

יעקב קמנצקי

מכתב ברכה

בעז״ה — ד׳ בהעלותך — לבני א״י, תשל״ט — פה קרית טלז, באה״ק

מע״כ ידידי האהובים הרב ר׳ מאיר והרב ר׳ נתן, נר״ו, שלום וברכה נצח!

אחדשה״ט באהבה ויקר,

לשמחה רבה היא לי להודע שהרחבתם גדול עבודתכם בקודש לתורה שבע״פ, בהוצאת המשנה בתרגום וביאור באנגלית, וראשית עבודתכם במס׳ מגילה.

אני תקוה שתשימו לב שיצאו הדברים מתוקנים מנקודת ההלכה, וחזקה עליכם שתוציאו דבר נאה ומתוקן.

בפנותכם לתורה שבע״פ יפתח אופק חדש בתורת ה׳ לאלה שקשה עליהם ללמוד הדברים במקורם, ואלה שכבר נתעשרו מעבודתכם במגילת אסתר יכנסו עתה לטרקלין חדש וישמשו להם הדברים דחף ללימוד המשנה, וגדול יהי׳ שכרכם.

יהא ה׳ בעזרכם בהוספת טבעת חדשה באותה שלשלת זהב של הפצת תורת ה׳ להמוני עם לקרב לב ישראל לאבינו שבשמים בתורה ואמונה טהורה.

אוהבכם מלונ״ח,
מרדכי

מכתב ברכה

RABBI SHNEUR KOTLER
BETH MEDRASH GOVOHA
LAKEWOOD, N. J.

בע"ה

שניאור קוטלר
בית מדרש גבוה
לייקוואוד, נ. דז.

[גוף המכתב בכתב יד]

בשורת התרחבות עבודתם הגדולה של סגל חבורת "ארטסקרול", המעתיקים ומפרשים, לתחומי התושבע"פ, לשים אלה המשפטים לפני הציבור ערוך ומוכן לאכול לפני האדם [ע' רש"י], ולשימה בפיהם — לפתוח אוצרות בשנות בצורה ולהשמיעם בכל לשון שהם שומעים — מבשרת צבא רב לתורה ולימודה [ע' תהלים ס"ח י"ב בתרגום יונתן], והיא מאותות ההתעוררות ללימוד התורה, וזאת התעודה על התנוצצות קיום ההבטחה "כי לא תשכח מפי זרעו". אשרי הזוכים להיות בין שלוחי ההשגחה לקיומה וביצועה.

יה"ר כי תצליח מלאכת שמים בידם, ויזכו ללמוד וללמד ולשמור מסורת הקבלה כי בהרקת המים החיים מכלי אל כלי תשתמר חיותם, יעמוד טעמם בם וריחם לא נמר. [וע' משאחז"ל בכ"מ ושמרתם זו משנה — וע' חי' מרן רי"ז הלוי עה"ת בפ' ואתחנן] ותהי' משנתם שלמה וברורה, ישמחו בעבודתם חברים ותלמידים, "ישוטטו רבים ותרבה הדעת", עד יקויים "אז אהפוך אל העמים שפה ברורה וגו' [צפני' ג' ט', עי' פי' אבן עזרא ומצודת דוד שם].

ונזכה כולנו לראות בהתכנסות הגליות בזכות המשניות כל חז"ל עפ"י הכתוב "גם כי יתנו בגוים עתה אקבצם", בגאולה השלמה בב"א.

הכו"ח לכבוד התורה, יום ו' עש"ק לס' "ויוצא פרח ויצץ ציץ ויגמל שקדים", ד' תמוז התשל"ט

יוסף חיים שניאור קוטלר
בלאאמו"ר הגר"א זצוק"ל

מכתב ברכה

ב״ה
לכבוד ידידי וידיד ישיבתנו, מהראשונים לכל דבר שבקדושה
הרבני הנדיב המפורסם ר׳ אליעזר הכהן גליק נ״י
אחדש״ה באהבה,

בשורה טובה שמעתי שכב׳ מצא את המקום המתאים לעשות יד ושם להנציח זכרו של בנו **אברהם יוסף ע״ה** שנקטף
בנעוריו. ״ונתתי להם בביתי ובחומתי יד ושם״. אין לו להקב״ה אלא ד׳ אמות של הלכה בלבד. א״כ זהו בית ד׳ לימוד
תורה שבע״פ וזהו המקום לעשות יד ושם לנשמת בנו ע״ה.

נר ד׳ נשמת אדם אמר הקב״ה נרי בידך ונרך בידי. נר מצוה ותורה אור, תורה זהו הנר של הקב״ה וכשושמרים נר של
הקב״ה שעל ידי הפירוש ״**יד אברהם**״ בשפה הלעוזית יתרבה לימוד ושקיעת התורה בבתי ישראל. ד׳ ישמור
נשמת אדם.

בנו אברהם יוסף ע״ה נתברך בהמדה שבו נכללות כל המדות, לב טוב והיה אהוב לחבריו. בלמדו בישיבתנו היה לו
הרצון לעלות במעלות התורה וכשעלה לארצנו הקדושה היתה מבקשו להמשיך בלמודיו. ביקוש זה ימצא מלואו על ידי
הרבים המבקשים דרך ד׳, שהפירוש ״**יד אברהם**״ יהא מפתח להם לים התלמוד.

התורה נקראת ״אש דת״ ונמשלה לאש יש לה הכח הכח לפעפע ברזל לפוצץ כוחות האדם, הניצוץ שהאיר בך רבנו הרב
שרגא פייוועל מנדלוביץ זצ״ל שמרת עליו, ועשה חיל. עכשיו אתה מסייע להאיר נצוצות בנשמות בני ישראל שיעשה חיל
ויהא לאור גדול.

תקותי עזה שכל התלמידי חכמים שנדבה רוח להוציא לפועל מלאכה ענקית זו לפרש המשניות כולה, יצא עבודתם
ברוך פאר והדר וכיוונו לאמיתה של תורה ויתקדש ויתרבה שם שמים על ידי מלאכה זו.
יתברך כב׳ וב׳ לראות ולרוות נחת רוח מצאצאי.

הכו״ח לכבוד התורה ותומכיה עש״ק במדבר תשל״ט

אלי׳ שווי

מכתב ברכה

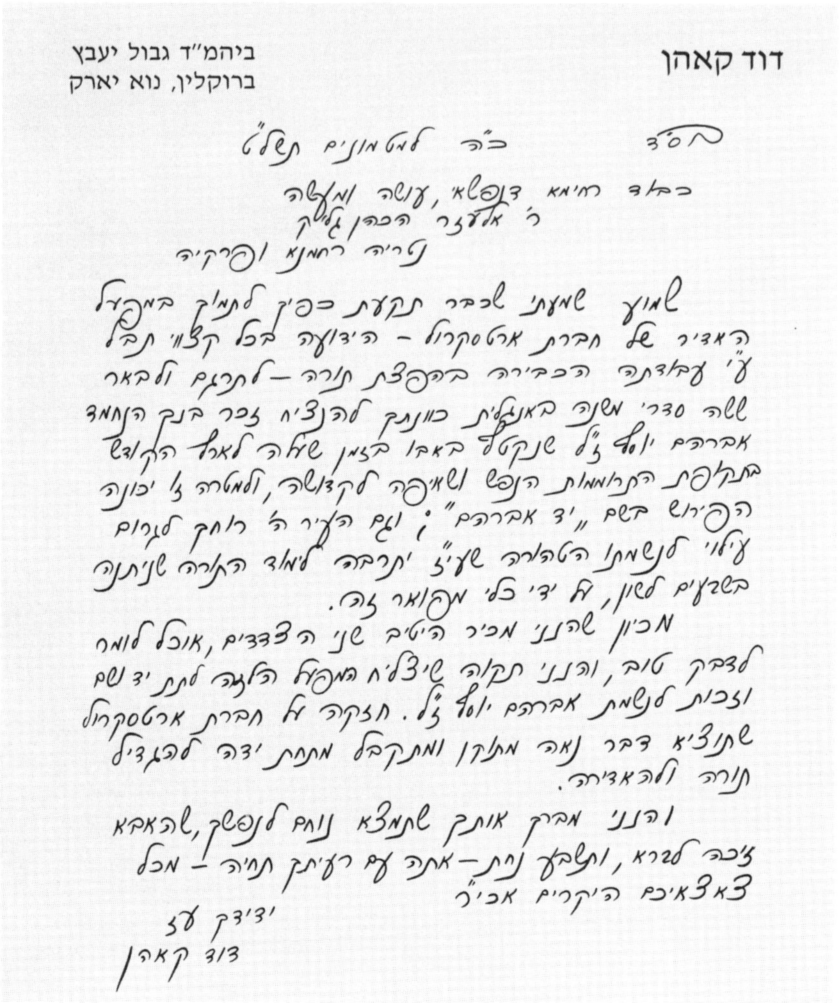

ביהמ״ד גבול יעבץ
ברוקלין, נוא יארק

דוד קאהן

[handwritten letter in Hebrew cursive]

בס״ד כ״ה למטמונים תשל״ט

כבוד רחימא דנפשאי, עושה ומעשה
ר׳ אלעזר הכהן גליק נטריה רחמנא ופרקיה

שמוע שמעתי שכבר תקעת כפיך לתמוך במפעל האדיר של חברת ארטסקרול — הידוע בכל קצווי תבל ע״י עבודתה הכבירה בהפצת תורה — לתרגם ולבאר ששה סדרי משנה באנגלית. כוונתך להנציח זכר בנך הנחמד אברהם יוסף ז״ל שנקטף באבו בזמן שעלה לארץ הקודש בתקופת התרוממות הנפש ושאיפה לקדושה, ולמטרה זו יכונה הפירוש בשם ,,**יד אברהם**״; וגם האיר פ׳ רוחך לגרום עילוי לנשמתו הטהורה שעי״ז יתרבה לימוד התורה שניתנה בשבעים לשון, על ידי כלי מפואר זה.

מכיוון שהנני מכיר היטב שני הצדדים, אוכל לומר לדבק טוב, והנני תקוה שיצליח המפעל הלזה לתת יד ושם וזכות לנשמת אברהם יוסף ז״ל. חזקה על חברת ארטסקרול שתוציא דבר נאה מתוקן ומתקבל מתחת ידה להגדיל תורה ולהאדירה.

והנני מברך אותך שתמצא נחם נחם לנפשך, שהאבא זוכה לברא, ותשבע נחת — אתה עם רעיתך תחיה — מכל צאצאיכם היקרים אכי״ר —

ידידך עז
דוד קאהן

Preface

אָמַר ר' יוֹחָנָן: לֹא כָּרַת הקב"ה בְּרִית עִם יִשְׂרָאֵל אֶלָּא עַל־תּוֹרָה
שֶׁבְּעַל־פֶּה שֶׁנֶּאֱמַר „כִּי עַל־פִּי הַדְּבָרִים הָאֵלֶּה כָּרַתִּי אִתְּךָ בְּרִית..."
R' Yochanan said: The Holy One, Blessed be He, did not seal a
covenant with Israel except because of the Oral Torah, as it is
said (Exodus 34:27): For according to these words have I sealed
a covenant with you... (Gittin 60b).

I n presenting to the Torah public this second volume of the
ARTSCROLL MISHNAH SERIES, we extend a בִּרְכַּת הוֹדָיָה, a blessing of
thanksgiving, to Hashem Yisborach for endowing Mesorah Publications with the awesome privilege of serving as His vehicle for Torah
dissemination. Simultaneous with the ongoing work on Tanach, the
Siddur, and other classics of Torah literature, the new Mishnah Series
will אי"ה be a major service to the English-speaking public that has
echoed the words of David: גַּל־עֵינַי וְאַבִּיטָה נִפְלָאוֹת מִתּוֹרָתֶךָ, Uncover
my eyes that I may see the wonders of Your Torah (Psalms 119:18).

Heretofore, there has been a serious lack of an adequate English
treatment of the Mishnah. In the view of roshei hayeshivah and
Torah scholars, there exists a need for a work that will treat the
Mishnah with depth and scope. Like the ARTSCROLL TANACH SERIES,
this new series draws upon large cross-sections of Talmudic, rabbinic,
and halachic sources. The purpose is to enable the reader to study
each mishnah as though he were sitting in the study hall, participating in the give and take of Talmudic scholarship.

Nevertheless, we must inject two words of caution. First: Although
the Mishnah, by definition, is a compendium of laws, the final
halachah does not necessarily follow the Mishnah. The development
of the final halachah proceeds through the Gemara, commentators,
codifiers, responsa, and the acknowledged Torah poskim. Even when
our commentary cites the Shulchan Aruch, the intention is to sharpen
the reader's understanding of the mishnah, but not to be a basis for
actual practice. In short, this work is meant as a study of the first step
in our recorded Oral Law — no more.

Second: As we have stressed in our other books, an ArtScroll commentary is not meant as a substitute for study of the sources. While
this commentary, like the others in the various series, will be im-
mensely useful even to accomplished scholars and will often bring to
light ideas and sources they may have overlooked, we strongly urge
those who are able to study the classic seforim in the original to do so.

In an effort to make this volume more useful to more people, we
have grouped the three tractates dealing with the festivals of the
month of Tishrei, Rosh Hashanah, Yom Kippur, and Succos. Most

editions of the Mishnah do not follow this order, nor do Rambam and Rav. However, Meiri does group them in this manner and so do most editions of the Talmud. Prominent halachic authorities concurred with the decision to combine the three tractates in this order, for the sake of utility.

The pattern of the commentary and the style of transliteration follow those of the ARTSCROLL TANACH SERIES.

Hebrew terms connoting concepts for which there are no exact English translations are defined the first time they appear and are generally transliterated thereafter.

For the reader's convenience, every word of the Mishnah has been included in the commentary headings. Therefore, the reader may study the commentary continuously without constantly referring back to the text, should he so desire.

The translation attempts to follow the text faithfully. Variations have been made when dictated by the need for clarity or English usage and syntax. Any words that have been added for the sake of flow and clarity are bracketed.

Some of the classic sources from which the commentary has been culled are, the GEMARA (abbreviated Gem.) with its commentaries, such as RASHI (1040-1105); TOSAFOS (Tos.) [Talmudic glosses by the school of scholars known collectively as Tosafists, who flourished after Rashi]; RITVA [R' Yom Tov Ishbili (1250-1330)]; RAN [R' Nissim Gerondi (mid-14th cent.)]; NIMUKEI YOSEF [R' Yosef Chaviva (early 15th cent.)]; the classical Mishnah commentators: RAMBAM (1135-1204); R' MENACHEM MEIRI (1249-1306); RAV [R' Ovadiah of Bertinoro (end of 15th cent.)]; TOSEFOS YOM TOV (Tos. Yom Tov) [R' Yom Tov Lipmann Heller (1579-1659)]; and more recent commentators: TOSEFOS R' AKIVA [R' Akiva Eiger (1761-1837); TIFERES YISRAEL (Tif. Yis.) [R' Yisrael Lipschutz (1782-1860)], and many others who wrote on individual tractates.

N o such work can serve the need for which it is intended unless the author is a talmid chochom of a very high caliber. We are particularly gratified, therefore, that we have engaged a group of authors of high scholarship and accomplishment. Although each commentary is anthologized from numerous sources, each is original in the sense that it reflects the author's own understanding, selection, and presentation.

This volume was written by RABBI HERSH GOLDWURM, RABBI YISROEL GORNISH, and RABBI YOSEF ROTTENBERG, all of them talmidei chachomim of genuine distinction. Far more than any words of ours, the quality of their work testifies to their ability. We are particularly grateful to Rabbi Goldwurm who rendered scholarly enrichment and editorial assistance in nearly every part of this sefer.

A work of such magnitude is not done singlehandedly. Though the

scholarship is that of the authors, such others as RABBI AVIE GOLD and RABBI NAFTALI KEMPLER assisted materially in producing a sefer worthy of the expectations of ArtScroll readers.

RABBI SHEA BRANDER has displayed so consistently high a standard of graphic skill, that one runs the danger of taking his artistry for granted. We do not.

We are grateful to the staff of Mesorah Publications whose diligence and dedication finds expression in this sefer: MRS. SURIE APPEL, MISS CHANEE FREIER, MISS PAULA KATZ, and MRS. FAIGIE WEINBAUM. We welcome STEPHEN BLITZ to the Mesorah staff and express our recognition of his fruitful efforts to bring Torah, in the form of the ArtScroll Series, to ever-widening circles of people who thirst for the words of Torah.

We express our thanks to RABBI DAVID FEINSTEIN שליט״א and RABBI DAVID COHEN שליט״א whose constant concern and interest throughout the history of the ArtScroll Series have been in further evidence in the course of this work.

We are deeply grateful to MR. AND MRS. HYMAN BRAVIN who have dedicated this volume in memory of their son JOSEPH SIMON ע״ה. Tradition teaches that the study of Mishnah brings elevation to the soul of a departed one — how much more so when someone's memory has been instrumental in helping tens of thousands study Mishnah!

Finally, we express our deep appreciation to MR. AND MRS. LOUIS GLICK who have dedicated the commentary of the entire ARTSCROLL MISHNAH SERIES. It bears the name YAD AVRAHAM, in memory of their son AVRAHAM YOSEF ע״ה. An appreciation of the niftar will appear in Tractate Berachos. May this dissemination of the Mishnah in his memory be a source of merit for his soul, תנצב״ה.

Both in his role as an unassuming, but outstanding, patron of Torah and as a major figure in the illustrious Yeshiva Torah Vodaath and Mesivta, Mr. Glick displays a constant and dedicated interest in our work. We are inspired by him and resolve to live up to his hopes for the ARTSCROLL MISHNAH SERIES. May he and Mrs. Glick be blessed for their generous dedication to Torah, of which this project is but one instance.

Rabbis Nosson Scherman / Meir Zlotowitz

ח׳ אלול תש״מ / August 26, 1980
Brooklyn, New York

מסכת ראש השנה

Tractate Rosh Hashanah

Translation and anthologized commentary by
Rabbi Yosef Rottenberg
Chapters 1-3

Rabbi Hersh Goldwurm
Chapter 4

Mesorah Publications, ltd

◄§ Tractate Rosh Hashanah

The tractate deals with a variety of subjects, directly or indirectly, related to the beginning of the year. However, the subjects of the Rosh Hashanah prayers and shofar blasts are not discussed until the third chapter. The tractate begins with a listing of various times that have the status of 'new year days' for particular halachic purposes regulated by temporal courts, and other times which, like the familiar Rosh Hashanah that falls on the first of Tishrei, are periods of Heavenly judgment.

Since the time of the Torah-ordained festivals is a function of the calendar, they cannot be observed unless the day of the new moon is decided and made known to the populace. The Torah requires that the New Moon [Rosh Chodesh] be designated by the *beis din* according to the testimony of witnesses who sighted the moon. That done, the news must be spread to communities far from Jerusalem or wherever else the court has its seat. Our tractate discusses in detail the position of the moon, the responsibilities and qualifications of the witnesses, their interrogation by the *beis din*, and the circumstances under which Rosh Chodesh is proclaimed.

The tractate concludes with the physical specifications of the shofar, the laws of its blowing and the particular prayers of Rosh Hashanah.

As part of the commentary and in appendices, considerable space is devoted to the uniqueness of the Jewish calendar — both as it was determined on a month-to-month basis in the time of a qualified Sanhedrin and in more recent times when the pre-ordained calendar is in use — and on the necessity of a two-day Rosh Hashanah everywhere and two-day festivals outside of *Eretz Yisrael.*

[א] **אַרְבָּעָה** רָאשֵׁי שָׁנִים הֵם: בְּאֶחָד
בְּנִיסָן רֹאשׁ הַשָּׁנָה לַמְּלָכִים
וְלָרְגָלִים.

יד אברהם

Chapter 1

1.

The first mishnah in our tractate deals with the subject of determining the beginning of the year in regard to those matters for which such determination is
halachically imperative. One might think this a simple matter — the year begins
with Rosh Hashanah (the first of Tishrei) since that is the day on which God
created the world (or Man, to be more exact). This is not, however, so. First of all,
the question of the date of Creation is itself in dispute (see *Gemara* 11b) — R' Eliezer
holds that the world was created in Tishrei, R' Joshua's view is that it was created in
Nissan. Second, and more important, with regard to many halachic matters, the
new year is not dependent on the date of Creation, but on other considerations. To
give a modern-day example, we find that although the calendar year begins on
January 1, the fiscal year may not begin until July 1, while the school year begins in
September. Although all these dates are arbitrarily chosen, while the dates in our
mishnah are based on Scripture or Rabbinic decree, nevertheless they may serve as
a helpful analogy.

אַרְבָּעָה רָאשֵׁי שָׁנִים הֵם: — *There are four
new year days:*
[Each of four separate and distinct
days in the year is the start of the new
year for a certain halachic matter or
matters. Our mishnah will enumerate
them].
The names of the Jewish months in
use today are not found in the Torah or
in the early *Prophets* and *K'suvim*
[*Hagiographa*]. Only eight of the twelve
are mentioned in the later books, among
them *Zechariah* 1:7, 7:1; *Ezra* 6:15; *Nechemiah* 1:1, 2:1, 6:15; and numerous
places in *Esther* — all of which were
written after the exile to Babylon. In
earlier books of Scripture they are referred to only as *the first month*, etc. Cf.
Ibn Ezra to *Deut.* 16:1.
Yerushalmi (*Rosh Hashanah* 1:2) explains this phenomenon by stating:
שְׁמוֹת חֳדָשִׁים עָלוּ בְּיָדָן מִבָּבֶל, *names of the
months came up with them from
Babylon.*
Ramban (comm. to *Exodus* 12:2)
elaborates on this subject and states that
the verse: הַחֹדֶשׁ הַזֶּה לָכֶם רֹאשׁ חֳדָשִׁים,
This month [Nissan] *shall be for you

the first of the months*, is a commandment to count all the months from Nissan and to refer to them by number (i.e.,
the first month, the second month, third
month, etc. from Nissan) as a constant
reminder of the great miracle of the Exodus, which occurred in Nissan (see
Gemara 7a). Therefore, Jews did not
designate special names for the months.
All this, however, changed during the
Babylonian exile. *Ramban* cites the
verse in *Jeremiah* 16:14,15 which states:
וְלֹא־יֵאָמֵר עוֹד חַי־ה' אֲשֶׁר הֶעֱלָה
בְּנֵי יִשְׂרָאֵל מֵאֶרֶץ מִצְרָיִם: כִּי אִם־חַי־ה' אֲשֶׁר
הֶעֱלָה אֶת־בְּנֵי יִשְׂרָאֵל מֵאֶרֶץ צָפוֹן, *And it
will no longer be said* [in an oath], *by
the life of HASHEM Who brought up
the Children of Israel from the land of
Egypt, but by the life of HASHEM Who
brought up the Children of Israel from
the land of the North* [Babylon]. In
other words, the miracle of the return
from Babylonian Exile will supplant the
miracle of the Exodus to some degree
(but not completely — see *Ramban*,
D'rashah LeRosh Hashanah) in the
memory of the Jewish people. This, says
Ramban, is the reason for the *Yeru-

1. **T**here are four new year days: On the first of Nissan is the new year for [reckoning the reigns of Jewish] kings and for [establishing the order of] the holidays.

YAD AVRAHAM

shalmi's statement that the names of the months are of Babylonian origin.

After the return from Babylon it was incumbent upon the Jews to remember *that* miracle by referring to the months by their Babylonian names.[1]

[The sequence of the dates in our mishnah (i.e., Nissan, Elul, Tishrei, Shevat) follows the ruling that the months are to be counted from Nissan (see *Gemara* 7a).]

בְּאֶחָד בְּנִיסָן רֹאשׁ הַשָּׁנָה לַמְּלָכִים — *On the first* [lit. *one*] *of Nissan is the new year for* [*reckoning the reigns of Jewish*] *kings*

If a king ascended the throne on any day of the year, we say that his first year ended on the last day of Adar following his accession, and that his second year is counted from the following day — the first of Nissan. His third year begins on the first day of the next Nissan, etc. Thus, if a king is crowned on the twenty-ninth of Adar, the next day, which is the first of Nissan, is reckoned as the beginning of the second year of his reign. Although it is a Rabbinic decree *(Ritva)*, this rule is derived from *I Kings* 1:6 which juxtaposes the years of

King Solomon's reign with the number of years since the Exodus from Egypt. This teaches us that a king's reign is to be reckoned from Nissan just as the Exodus occurred in Nissan *(Gemara* 2b).

The halachic application of the above rule refers to the dating of שְׁטָרוֹת, *legal documents*, such as bills of divorce, marriage contracts, deeds of sale, and loan agreements. The custom in ancient times was to date legal documents by the year of the current monarch's reign (e.g., on the third of Elul in the sixth year of King Yannai) as a sign of respect for the king *(Ran)*.

Every Jewish legal document explicitly or implicitly provides for שִׁעְבּוּד נְכָסִים, *a lien on property*, which guarantees that one's real property may be expropriated to meet the obligations incurred by the document. For example, if Reuven lent Shimon a sum of money and a document was duly written to that effect and signed by witnesses, Reuven has the right to take Shimon's real property (if Shimon defaults), even if that property had meanwhile been sold by Shimon to Levi after the loan was made. If the document were to be

---

1. A problem with *Ramban's* view is posed by the next statement of *Yerushalmi:* אַף שְׁמוֹת הַמַּלְאָכִים עָלוּ בְּיָדָן מִבָּבֶל, *The names of the angels also came up with them from Babylon.* Angels' names are not found in any Scripture text until *Daniel* (9:21, *Gavriel;* 10:21 *Michael*). *Ramban's* explanation for the change in the names of Jewish months does not seem to apply to the names of angels. In addition, the names of these two angels do not appear to be of Babylonian, but rather of Jewish, origin.

Bnei Yisas'char (Ma'amarei Chodesh Nissan 1:6) offers a different explanation of the statement regarding the names of the months. He states that the names of the months were definitely received by Moses at Sinai but fell under the category of תּוֹרָה שֶׁבְּעַל פֶּה, *Oral Law*, and were not permitted to be written down (as they are in *Zechariah, Ezra, Nechemiah*) until the Jews came to Babylon. (This may also serve as an explanation, for the angels' names). *Bnei Yisas'char* does not, however, discuss why just this part of the Oral Law was allowed to be put in writing.

(Cf. *Bereishis Rabbah* 48:9 which quotes the above *Yerushalmi*. Upon this the commentary attributed to *Rashi* states: *the names of the months came up from Babylon, etc. but before then they were not 'revealed.'* The use of the word *revealed* indicates an explanation unlike either of the above. But it can perhaps be reconciled with *Bnei Yisas'char's* view.)

predated, one who purchased property before the loan was made — but after the false date — could be swindled out of his property if the borrower defaulted. Therefore, if a king acceded to the throne in Adar, and a loan agreement was written thirteen months later in Nissan, the document must state that the loan took place in the third year of the king. If the document is dated as having been written in the *second* year of the king, it is considered predated and therefore invalid *(Rav)*. [1]

Nevertheless, while dating legal documents based on a king's reign was the method commonly used, any other dating method was also acceptable in the case of a document written under the sovereignty of a Jewish king *(Ritva)*. For non-Jewish kings, see below.

[Cf. *Rashi; Tosafos; R' Chananel;* and *Ran* for other applications of the rule of reckoning kings' reigns from the first of Nissan.]

The importance of the proper dating of legal documents notwithstanding, an explanation is still necessary for the selection of a specific date (first of Nissan) as the new year for kings. The anniversary problem of predating would seemingly be resolved even if a king's accession would be considered the new year for legal documents.

Ran explains that the selection of the first of Nissan as the new year was to provide every Jewish king with a constant זֵכֶר לִיצִיאַת מִצְרַיִם, *commemoration of the Exodus from Egypt* (which marked the beginning of Jewish sovereignty) in keeping with the verse in *I Kings* 1:6 cited above.

Meiri, however, states that the reason for not using the date of a king's accession in legal documents was because that date might be forgotten and it would then be impossible to determine whether the document was properly

dated or not. (Cf. *Rashi; Tosafos, Aruch LaNer).*

The question of the validity of a document dated in such a manner is discussed by *Tosafos* and *Meiri* who hold that the document would not be considered predated and would therefore be valid, as opposed to *Rashi* who apparently invalidates the document. (See also *Pnei Yehoshua, Sfas Emes, Aruch LaNer).*

וְלָרְגָלִים. — *and for [establishing the order of] the holidays.*

[The term רְגָלִים, refers specifically to Pesach, Shavuos, and Succos *(Exodus* 43:14).]

Pesach, the holiday which occurs in the month of Nissan, is to be considered the first holiday of the year, in keeping with *Deuteronomy* 16:16: בְּחַג הַמַּצּוֹת וּבְחַג הַשָּׁבֻעוֹת וּבְחַג הַסֻּכּוֹת, *On the festival of matzos* (i.e., Pesach) and on the festival of Shavuos and on the festival of Succos. There, the holiday of Pesach is listed first *(Rav).*

The designation of Pesach as the first holiday is relevant for the prohibition against the fulfillment of vows [בַּל תְּאַחֵר]. The Torah states כִּי תִדֹּר נֶדֶר לַה׳ אֱלֹהֶיךָ לֹא תְאַחֵר לְשַׁלְּמוֹ, *If you make a vow to HASHEM, your God, do not delay in fulfilling it* (Deut. 23:22). Referring to a person who vowed to bring a קָרְבָּן, *offering,* to God, the verse require him to bring it within a certain time limit, otherwise he transgressees the negative commandment. The duration beyond which one may not delay is the passage of three holidays from the date of the vow. Our mishnah tells us that these holidays must be in sequence from Nissan: Pesach, Shavuos, Succos. Thus if one made his vow just before Pesach, he must fulfill it within seven months before the end of Succos, the third holiday in the sequence. If,

---

1. *P'nei Yehoshua* states that according to R' Elazar who holds that thirty days is the smallest number of days that can be considered a year *(Gemara 10a),* the rule of our mishnah is applicable only if a king ascended the throne at least thirty days before the first of Nissan. *Ritva,* however, holds that R' Elazar's view applies only to matters that are דְּאוֹרַיְתָא, *Torah Law,* but not to matters of Rabbinic origin, such as the case of our mishnah (cf. *Turei Even; Sfas Emes).*

however, he made his vow between Pesach and Shavuos, his time limit would not end after three holidays (Shavuous, Succos, and Pesach) had passed, but five holidays later, after Shavuos, Succos, Pesach, Shavuos, and Succos. Only then has he transgressed, for only then have the holidays passed in the sequence required by our mishnah (Rav).[1]

In addition to the negative commandment not to delay, there is also a מִצְוַת עֲשֵׂה positive commandment, that one must offer his sacrifices on time. This is derived from וַהֲבֵאתֶם שָׁמָּה עֹלֹתֵיכֶם וְזִבְחֵיכֶם גו׳, and you shall bring there [to the Temple] your burnt offerings and your sacrifices... (Deut. 12:5). In the case of this commandment, one transgresses if he fails to bring his sacrifice by the first holiday after his vow. Our mishnah, however, is only referring to the negative commandment which one transgresses only if three holidays have passed (Rav).

The Gemara [4b] points out that our mishnah, though anonymously stated, is the view only of R' Shimon, but is disputed by other tannaim who hold that the three holidays need not be in any particular order. There are, in fact, tannaim who do not require three holidays, but state that two or even one holiday is the time limit (Rav).

[The final ruling in this dispute is in question. Rambam (Hilchos Ma'aseh Hakorbanos 14:13) and Rav rule against our mishnah and decide in favor of the tannaim who do not require the three holidays to be in order. Sefer HaMe'oros and Shiltei Gibborim rule in favor of our anonymously stated mishnah (cf. Shabbos 46a: הֲלָכָה כִּסְתַם מִשְׁנָה, the halachah follows an anonymous mishnah. For an explanation of Rambam's decision, see Kessef Mishneh).]

[See however, Teshuvos Sha'ar Efraim 32 who interprets Rambam differently and claims that Rambam rules in favor of our mishnah. Apparently Sha'ar Efraim did not see Rambam's commentary to our mishnah where he clearly states that its view is not halachically accepted.]

The reason that לַמְּלָכִים, for kings, precedes לָרְגָלִים, for festivals, in our mishnah (even though the first is by Rabbinic law while the second is by Torah law) is because the new year for kings is on the first of Nissan, while the new year for holidays is Pesach which falls on the fifteenth (Sfas Emes, Kol Haremez).

The Gemara (7a) quotes a baraisa which enumerates several other matters for which the first of Nissan is the New Year:

□ לָחֳדָשִׁים, for the months. Nissan is considered the first of the months even though the calendar year is counted from Tishrei. Thus, Tishrei is counted as the seventh month even though it begins the calendar year;

□ לְעִיבּוּרִין, for intercalations. [The addition of a thirteenth month to the year]. Once Nissan has arrived, the court may no longer intercalate a second Adar into the year;

□ לִתְרוּמַת שְׁקָלִים, for the contribution of Shekalim. All communal sacrifices that are offered after the first of Nissan must be bought with money [shekalim] that was donated for the year beginning with Nissan. See Mishnah Shekalim 1:1;

□ and some say: אַף לִשְׂכִירוּת בָּתִּים, also for the renting of houses. If one rents a house to another with the stipulation that he is renting it to him for this year, the year ends on the first of Nissan.

The Gemara (7a) offers several explanations for the omission of these matters from our mishnah.

---

1. The prohibition against delay applies not only to voluntary vows to bring a sacrifice, but also to obligatory sacrifices and to promises to dedicate donations to הֶקְדֵּשׁ, sacred, or Temple property. Its application to other matters such as תְּרוּמָה, obigatory donations of produce to a Kohen; מַעַשְׂרוֹת, tithes; donations to charity; etc. is discussed at length in Gemara 4a and 5b by almost all classic Talmudic commentators. (See also Rambam, Hilchos Ma'aseh Hakorbanos 14:13, Hilchos Matnos Aniyim 8:1; Yoreh Deah 257:3, Aruch HaShulchan HeAsid; Hilchos Ma'aseh HaKorbanos 91).

בְּאֶחָד בֶּאֱלוּל רֹאשׁ הַשָּׁנָה לְמַעְשַׂר בְּהֵמָה.
רַבִּי אֶלְעָזָר וְרַבִּי שִׁמְעוֹן אוֹמְרִים: בְּאֶחָד
בְּתִשְׁרֵי.

בְּאֶחָד בְּתִשְׁרֵי רֹאשׁ הַשָּׁנָה לַשָּׁנִים וְלַשְּׁמִטִּין

יד אברהם

בְּאֶחָד בֶּאֱלוּל רֹאשׁ הַשָּׁנָה לְמַעְשַׂר בְּהֵמָה. —
On the first of Elul is the new year for the tithe of animals.

The Torah (*Lev.* 27:32) requires the setting aside of every tenth animal from among one's flocks of sheep and goats or herds of cattle born during the year and to declare it קוֹדֶשׁ, *sanctified,* for a sacrifice to God. As the animals passed one by one through a small opening in the corral, the owner marked every tenth one and declared it *ma'aser* [tithe] (see *Rambam, Hilchos Bechoros* 7:1).

The Talmud (*Bechoros* 53b) derives from the Torah that animals born in one year cannot be counted together with those born in another year for the purpose of *ma'aser.* In other words, all the animals in the corral from among which every tenth one is declared *ma'aser,* must have been born during the same year. The mishnah here states that the year for this purpose begins on the first of Elul.

Another halachic application of our mishnah's rule is based on *Bechoros* 9:6. It is the case in which a man has a total of ten animals, five of which were born before Elul and five after Elul.

Based on our mishnah, the owner would not be required to declare *ma'aser* at all since he does not have ten animals born in one year as stated in *Bechoros* 9:6 (*Meiri*).[1]

The reason that the first of Elul is considered the new year for *ma'aser* of animals is derived by the *Gemara* (8a) from *Deut.* 14:22 where *ma'aser* of grain and *ma'aser* of animals are alluded to in the same verse. This teaches us that just as the new year for *ma'aser* of grain begins upon completion (ripening) of its coming into existence, as mentioned further in our mishnah, so does the new year for *ma'aser* of animals follow their completion (birth). Since most animals give birth in the month of Av, the new year for *ma'aser* of animals is the first of Elul (*Rav*).[2]

The *Gemara* derives this fact from a verse in *Psalms* 65:14 which indicates that the mating season for sheep and goats [בְּהֵמָה דַקָּה] is in the month of Adar. Since their gestation period is five months, they give birth in Av.

Although the gestation period for בְּהֵמָה גַסָה, *cattle,* is nine months, their mating period begins earlier with the

1. *Rambam (Hilchos Bechoros* 7:5) holds that this while it is preferable [לְבַתְּחִלָה] that animals from different years not be tithed together, if such animals had already been counted together [בְּדִעֲבַד], the *ma'aser* is valid. *Turei Even* poses the question that according to *Rambam* the mishnah should have omitted *ma'aser of animals,* since the *Gemara* (7b) declares that the mishnah mentions only matters that are invalid even *after* the fact. The problem is resolved by *Rashash* and *Sfas Emes* who maintain that *Rambam* would apply the rule of our mishnah (as *Meiri* does) to the case of five animals born before Elul and five born after Elul. There even *Rambam (ibid.* 7:6) appears to hold that the *ma'aser* is invalid even after the fact, because *neither* group, by itself, would have an obligation of *ma'aser* upon it. It is only when ten animals were born in each year that *Rambam* holds that their separation to be no more than preferable — in that case, each group of animals *does* have the obligation to be tithed. However, *Rambam's* commentary to our mishnah seems to contradict their view. (For further elaboration on this matter and for other resolutions of *Turei Even's* question see *Aruch LaNer* to 7b, *Sifsei Chachamim, Truas Melech* 13).

2. Note should be taken of this Talmudic custom of deriving facts from Biblical verses that can be ascertained by simple observation. See *Eruvin* 14a where the *Gemara* derives the ratio of the diameter of a circle to its circumference from a verse in *I Kings I* 7:23. See also *Niddah*

On the first of Elul is the new year for the tithe of animals. R' Elazar and R' Shimon say: [It is] on the first of Tishrei.

The first of Tishrei is the new year for [reckoning]

YAD AVRAHAM

result that their young are born shortly before Elul. Thus, their new year for *ma'aser* is the same as for small animals (*Tosefos Yom Tov*).

רַבִּי אֱלְעָזָר וְרַבִּי שִׁמְעוֹן אוֹמְרִים: בְּאֶחָד בְּתִשְׁרֵי. — *R' Elazar and R' Shimon say: [It is] on the first of Tishrei.*

[R' Shimon and R' Elazar disagree with the previous view (which, though quoted anonymously, is R' Meir's — see *Bechoros* 9:5), and hold that the New Year for *ma'aser* of animals is the first of *Tishrei*.]

The final ruling in this matter is in dispute among the halachic authorities. *Rambam* (*Hilchos Bechoros* 7:6) accepts the view of R' Elazar and R' Shimon, while *Rav, Meiri, Semag* (*Aseh* 212) and *Ritva* decide in favor of the first view. See *Aruch HaShulchan HeAsid, Hilchos Bechoros* 203:11.

R' Shimon and R' Elazar derive their ruling from the same verse (*Deut.* 14:2-2) as the first tanna derives his, but they interpret it differently: the comparison of the *ma'aser* of animals to the *ma'aser* of grain teaches us that just as the New Year for *ma'aser* of grain is on the first of Tishrei (as mentioned later in our mishnah), so is the new year for *ma'aser* of animals on the first of Tishrei (*Rav*).

Bechoros 9:5 gives the dates after which a newborn animal may not be eaten or sold unless *ma'aser* had been separated (*Meiri; Ritva*).

בְּאֶחָד בְּתִשְׁרֵי רֹאשׁ הַשָּׁנָה לַשָּׁנִים — *The first of Tishrei is the new year for*

[reckoning] *the years,*

The meaning of this phrase parallels לַמְלָכִים, *for reckoning the reigns of the kings* earlier in our mishnah with the same halachic implications. The only difference is that earlier the mishnah referred to Jewish kings, while here the reference is to non-Jewish kings (*Rav*).

The *Gemara* proves from *Nehemiah* 1:1 and 2:1, that the new year for non-Jewish kings cannot be the first of Nissan as it is for Jewish kings. The Sages selected the first of Tishrei to be the new year for non-Jewish kings, since it is already a new year for a number of other matters as enumerated in our mishnah (*Tos. Yom Tov*).

The reason the mishnah lists לְשָׁנִים, *for* [reckoning] *the years*, ahead of the other matters for which the first of Tishrei is the new year, is to maintain consistency with the beginning of the mishnah, where the reign of Jewish kings was mentioned first. So too, the reign of *non*-Jewish kings is listed first (*Kol Haremez*).

Rambam in his commentary to our mishnah interprets לְשָׁנִים, *for* [reckoning] *the years* as referring to the creation of the world (i.e. the years of legal documents are reckoned from the world's creation which occurred on the first of Tishrei, and are *not* reckoned by the year of the reigning non-Jewish monarch). This interpretation is based on *Rambam's* understanding of R' Zeira's view in the *Gemara* 8a (*Beis*

אֲנִי מֵבִיא לָכֶם רְאָיָה מִן הַתּוֹרָה וְאַתֶּם מְבִיאִין לִי רְאָיָה מִן הַשּׁוֹטִים 30b: *I bring you proof from the Torah, and you bring me proof from the fools!*

See, however, *Yerushalmi Terumos* 3:1 and *Challah* 1:1 which appear to be in disagreement with the above. See also *Rosh* (*Responsa* 2:19) who is perplexed by this Talmudic method.

Rabbi Moshe Heinemann quotes *R' Aharon Kotler* who explained this matter based on *Bereishis Rabbah* 1:1, הָיָה הַקָּדוֹשׁ בָּרוּךְ הוּא מַבִּיט בַּתּוֹרָה וּבוֹרֵא אֶת הָעוֹלָם, *The Holy One, Blessed be He, looked into the Torah and created the world.* In other words every phenomenon of nature is the way it is because it is so dictated by the Torah, which is the blueprint for the world. Therefore, our Sages went directly to the source of all phenomena — the Torah. They derived the ways of nature from the plan which dictated the mode of their existence.

David). Cf. *Rashi* and *Tosafos* who interpret R' Zeira's words differently. See also *Meiri, Ran, Beiur HaGra* to *Orach Chaim* 581:1; *Hagahos Ben Aryeh*.

Another interpretation of our mishnah is that of R' Nachman bar Yitzchak: לדין, *for judgment*, meaning that the first of Tishrei is the new year when God passes judgment on mankind for the coming year. [*Sifsei Chachamim* discusses the problem caused by this view with regard to the next mishnah.] The reason for dating legal documents according to the reign of non-Jewish kings is mentioned in *Gittin* (80a): מפני שלום מלכות, *in order to maintain peaceful relations with the sovereign. Ran* explains that since the non-Jews were aware of the Jewish custom of dating documents based on the accession of their kings, it would be detrimental to the maintenance of friendly relations between the king and his Jewish subjects if they neglected to do the same for non-Jewish kings. Cf. *Rashi, Tosafos, Pnei Yehoshua*.

In the case of a non-Jewish king, legal documents *must* be dated in such a way as to conform to the requirement that peaceful relations must be maintained. No other method of dating is acceptable with the exception of מנין ליצירה, *the count from Creation (Ritva)* or מנין השטרות, lit. *the count for documents.* [See *Rambam* and *Kesef Mishneh*, (*Hilchos Geirushin* 1:27) for the cases

where the problem of peace does not arise.][1]

Tosafos holds that 'peace' applies only to a גט, *bill of divorce*, since it is the most important of legal documents, but other documents need not be dated with the year of the reigning monarch. (See *Tosafos* to *Gittin* 80a).

ולשמטין — *for the Sabbatical years,*

The Sabbatical year (*Leviticus* 25:1-7), begins on the first of Tishrei. It is then prohibited by Torah law to plant or plow one's field (*Rav*). Many other laws connected with the Sabbatical year (see *Rambam, Hilchos Shemitah VeYovel* 1-9) also commence on the first of Tishrei (*Rashash*).[2]

The *Gemara* (8b) derives the rule that the first of Tishrei inaugurates the Sabbatical year from *Lev.* 25:4: וּבַשָּׁנָה הַשְּׁבִיעִית שְׁנַת שַׁבָּתוֹן יִהְיֶה לָאָרֶץ, *and in the seventh year, there shall be a year of rest for the land (Lev.* 25:4). The use of the word שָׁנָה, *year,* in this case, is considered to be similar to its use in *Deut.* 11:12, מֵרֵשִׁית הַשָּׁנָה, *from the beginning of the year,* where the first of Tishrei is meant. Similarly, in the case of *Shemitah* [the Sabbatical year], Tishrei marks the start of the year (*Tosefos Yom Tov*).

See *Torah Temimah* on this verse for a view that the omission of the *alef* from the word מרשית (which is normally spelled מראשית) indicates that Tishrei is the start of the year, since rearrangement of the letters of מרשית would read מתשרי, *from Tishrei.*

---

1. The מנין השטרות, *count for legal documents,* was reckoned from the first year of the Seleucid Empire (see *Avodah Zarah* 9a). This was in the year 3448 after Creation which corresponds to 312 B.C.E. After the Destruction of the Second Temple this remained the prevalent system for the dating of legal documents throughout the Middle East and North Africa (see *Avodah Zarah* 10a). It was abolished during the middle of the sixteenth century (except in Yemen, where it existed until modern times) by R' David ibn Zimra (*Shem HaGedolim*; cf. *Seder HaDoros* 4118). Nowadays, all halachic legal documents are dated from Creation (*Shulchan Aruch Even HaEzer* 126:5, *Choshen Mishpat* 43:2).

2. During the Temple era, these prohibitions were in force thirty days before the start of the Sabbatical year by virtue of הֲלָכָה לְמשֶׁה מִסִּינַי, *law given to Moses at Sinai* [and transmitted orally], and even before thirty days by Rabbinic decree (see *Moed Katan* 3b; *Rambam, Shemittah VeYovel* 3:1). The same Sinaitic law provides that in the absence of the Temple, work is permitted until the first of Tishrei of the Sabbatical year (*Rambam*, 3:9; cf. *Turei Even, Pnei Yehoshua, Aruch La'Ner*).]

the years, for the Sabbatical years, for the Jubilee years, for the planting [of trees], and for the vegetables.

YAD AVRAHAM

וְלַיּוֹבְלוֹת, — (and) for the Jubilee years,

Leviticus 25:8-10 commands the beis din to count seven cycles of seven years and to declare the fiftieth year as יוֹבֵל [Yovel], the Jubilee year, in which all the laws of Shemittah are in force [with the exception of the nullification of loans (Rambam Shemittah V'Yovel 10:16)] together with additional laws enumerated in Leviticus 25, e.g., the freeing of Jewish slaves, the return of lands to their original owners.

The Jubilee year as stated in our mishnah, begins on the first of Tishrei. This means, according to the Gemara, that all Jewish slaves cease working for their owners and spend the next ten days feasting and rejoicing until Yom Kippur when they are free to return home (Rambam in comm. to Mishnah). See Gemara 8b, where this view is attributed to R' Yishmael, son of R' Yochanan ben Beroka. Although other tannaim hold that Yovel begins on Yom Kippur, the halachah follows his view (Rambam, Hilchos Shemittah VeYovel 10:14).

Rav explains our mishnah as referring to the prohibition of working one's field during the Jubilee year. Kol HaRemez points out, however, that this explanation is rejected by the Gemara for the simple reason that working one's field was prohibited before the first of Tishrei in any case since the preceding year had been a Sabbatical year (see also Beis David, Poras Yosef).

לַנְּטִיעָה — for the planting [of trees],

[In Leviticus 19:23, 24, the Torah declares that if one plants a tree, it is forbidden to eat or derive any benefit from the fruit it bears during the first three years. (In fact, the fruit must be burned. See Temurah 33b). This fruit is called עָרְלָה [orlah], literally closed off from benefit. The fruit that grows during the fourth year is called רְבָעִי [revai], literally four-year-old, and must be brought to Jerusalem and eaten there.]

The first of Tishrei is the new year for reckoning the years of orlah and revai. If one planted a tree forty-five or more days[1] before the first of Tishrei, the first year of orlah is over at the end of Elul and the second year begins on the first of Tishrei. On the first of Tishrei two years later, the fourth year, revai, would be expected to begin. But by then the 'planting' has grown to the point where it is regarded as a 'tree' — and the mishnah teaches below that the new year for trees does not begin until the fifteenth of Shevat. Therefore, the young tree retains its orlah status until the fifteenth of Shevat, when it begins revai. Any fruit that grows between the fifteenth of Shevat and the following fifteenth of Shevat is considered revai (Gemara 10a).

[If one planted a tree less than forty-five days before Tishrei, the remaining days cannot be considered a year, and he must therefore count three full years from the first of Tishrei. In this instance, however, Rambam holds that orlah ends three years later and the fourth year begins on the first of Tishrei, not on the following fifteenth of Shevat. Baal HaMaor and Ran disagree and say that even in this case orlah is in force till the fifteenth of

1. [The reason for the period of at least forty-five days before Tishrei is that it takes fourteen days for the planting to take root; only then is it considered actually planted. Another thirty days are the minimum reckoned for a year according to the halachically accepted view of R' Elazar who holds that שְׁלוֹשִׁים יוֹם בְּשָׁנָה חָשׁוּב שָׁנָה, thirty days of a year are counted as an entire year (see Rambam, Hilchos Maaser Sheni 9:9, 10). Hence, there must be forty-four full days after the day of planting until Tishrei for the plant to have a year reckoned to it. See Rashash who requires only forty-three days.]

בְּאֶחָד בִּשְׁבָט רֹאשׁ הַשָּׁנָה לָאִילָן; כְּדִבְרֵי
בֵּית שַׁמַּאי. בֵּית הִלֵּל אוֹמְרִים: בַּחֲמִשָּׁה עָשָׂר
בּוֹ.

יד אברהם

Shevat (see *Shulchan Aruch, Yoreh Deah* 294:5).]

[If the planting took place between the first of Tishrei and the fifteenth of Shevat, see *Rambam, Hilchos Ma'aser Sheni* 9:12; *Raavad; Maggid Mishnah; Kesef Mishneh; Sifsei Kohen* to *Yoreh De'ah* 294:10.]

וְלַיְרָקוֹת. — *and for the vegetables.*

In the seven-year cycle which culminates in the Sabbatical year, one must tithe all his produce in the following way:

a) Each year (except the seventh) he must give a portion of his produce to a *Kohen*. This is called *terumah* [lit. *separated*] (see *Deuteronomy* 18:4).

b) From the remainder, he must then give one-tenth to a *Levi* (again, each year with the exception of the seventh year). This is called *ma'aser rishon* [*first tithe*] (see *Numbers* 18:24).

c) From the remainder of the original produce, he must separate in the first, second, fourth, and fifth years of the cycle, one-tenth which he must take to Jerusalem and eat there. This is called *ma'aser sheni* [*second tithe*] (see *Deut.* 14:22).

d) In the third and sixth years, instead of *ma'aser sheni* he must give one-tenth to the poor. This is called *ma'aser ani* [*tithe for the poor*] (see *Deut.* 14:28).

On the seventh (Sabbatical) year, all that the land produces is הֶפְקֵר,

ownerless, and no tithes are given (*Exod.* 23:11).

One may not combine the produce of one year with the produce of another for tithing purposes. In addition, the tithes *must* be given in the above order (e.g., one may not separate *ma'aser sheni* from produce of the third year or *ma'aser ani* from produce of the second year; see *Rambam, Terumos* 5:11, *Ma'aser Sheni* 1:2).

Our mishnah tells us when the year begins for tithing purposes.

The first of Tishrei is the New Year for the tithing of vegetables. Therefore, for purposes of *terumah* and *maaser rishon*, vegetables picked from the ground before Tishrei cannot be combined with vegetables picked afterwards (*Rav*).[1] In addition, vegetables picked before the first of Tishrei of the third year in the cycle must be tithed for *ma'aser sheni*, while vegetables picked afterwards must be tithed for *ma'aser ani* (*Tosefos Yom Tov*).

While the Mishnah mentions only vegetables, the same holds true for all grain (i.e., that the new year begins on the first of Tishrei). For the fruit of trees, however, the new year begins on the fifteenth of Shevat as will be mentioned below (*Tos. Yom Tov*).

The Mishnah did not use the term לְמַעֲשֵׂר, for tithing (which would include both vegetables and grain) because we might think that מַעֲשֵׂר בְּהֵמָה, tithing of animals, is included, while in reality only R' Elazar and R'

---

1. Only for vegetables does the picking determine the year of their growth. For grain, the year in which a third of its growth is attained, is its year of growth for tithing purposes. As a general rule, the tithing year for each species is determined by its עוֹנַת הַמַּעַשְׂרוֹת, *time for tithing*, mentioned in *Mishnah Ma'aseros* 1:2-4, and *Rambam, Hilchos Ma'aseros* 2:5 (cf. *Rambam, Hilchos Ma'aser Sheni* 1:2; *Tos., Rosh Hashanah* 12b; *Pnei Yehoshua; Tos. R' Akiva*).

On the first of Shevat is the new year for the tree;
according to the words of Beis Shammai. Beis Hillel
say: On the fifteenth thereof.

YAD AVRAHAM

Shimon hold that the first of Tishrei is
the date for animal tithes *(Tos. R' Akiva Eger)*.

The *Gemara* 12a,b mentions another matter for which the first of Tishrei is the new
year: לִנְדָרִים, *for vows*, meaning that if one
said, 'I vow not to derive any benefit from so
and so during *this* year,' the year ends with
the advent of Tishrei, even if the vow was
made just a day earlier.

בְּאֶחָד בִּשְׁבָט רֹאשׁ הַשָּׁנָה לָאִילָן; כְּדִבְרֵי בֵּית
שַׁמַּאי. — *On the first of Shevat is the
new year for the tree; acccording to the
words of Beis Shammai.*

Trees that blossomed [i.e. the first tiny
fruit appeared *(Meiri)*] before the first of
Shevat cannot be combined with trees
that blossomed afterwards for tithing
purposes. Also, trees that blossomed in
the third year of the Sabbatical cycle
before the first of Shevat, are treated as if
the fruit grew in the second year and
ma'aser sheni is separated, while those
that blossomed afterwards require the
separation of *ma'aser ani (Rav)*.

[In other words, everything that was
said above regarding vegetables is applicable to trees with one difference:
here the new year is in Shevat while
there it is in Tishrei.]

In addition, Shevat is the new year
for trees in regard to *orlah* and *revai* as
mentioned above, s.v. לַנְּטִיעָה, *for the
planting [of trees] (Tosefos Tom Tov)*.[1]

The *Gemara* (14a) explains that the
year of trees is reckoned from Shevat
הוֹאִיל וְיָצְאוּ רוֹב גִּשְׁמֵי שָׁנָה, *since most of
the year's rain has already ended.* Since
trees grow mainly from rain-water, that

is the normal time for blossoming
(Rashi).

Tosafos states that trees that blossomed before Shevat must have grown
because of last year's (i.e. before
Tishrei's) rain (see *Ma'adanei Yom Tov*
on *Rosh* — *Hilchos Orlah* 9 for the
halachic implications of the above two
explanations).

בֵּית הִלֵּל אוֹמְרִים: בַּחֲמִשָּׁה עָשָׂר בּוֹ. — *Beis
Hillel say: On the fifteenth thereof* [i.e.,
Shevat].

Beis Hillel claim that the new year for
trees is on the fifteenth of Shevat
regarding all the matters mentioned
above.

Their reason is either because the
normal time for blossoming is on the
fifteenth or because whatever grew
earlier was caused by last year's rain
(Tosafos 14a).

Meiri points out that the fifteenth of
Shevat is the exact middle of תְּקוּפַת טֵבֵת,
the winter season. After that date the
weather starts to warm up and the חֲנָטָה,
blossoming of trees begins in earnest.

The halachah as usual follows Beis
Hillel.

The *Gemara* (7b) mentions two more new
year days: 1) שִׁשָּׁה עָשָׂר בְּנִיסָן רֹאשׁ הַשָּׁנָה
לָעוֹמֶר, *the sixteenth of Nissan is the new
year for [the bringing of] the omer* (see *Lev.*
23:10). This means that חָדָשׁ, *new grain*, may
be eaten from that time on (see below 4: 3,
for further detail); 2) שִׁשָּׁה בְּסִיוָן רֹאשׁ הַשָּׁנָה
לִשְׁתֵּי הַלֶּחֶם, *the sixth of Sivan is the new year
for the Two Loaves* [which are offered on
Shavuos]. Until then, the new year's grain
crop could not be used for meal offerings in
the Temple.

---

1. *Sh'lah* rules that even regarding laws related to *Shemittah (the Sabbatical year)*, the New
Year for trees is *Shevat.* This is disputed, however, by most authorities, who hold that the first
of Tishrei inaugurates *Shemitah* even for trees (see R' Y.M. Tukaczinsky — *Sefer
HaShemitah*, pg. 10 note 3).

ראש השנה א/ב

[ב] **בְּאַרְבָּעָה** פְּרָקִים הָעוֹלָם נִדּוֹן: בַּפֶּסַח
עַל־הַתְּבוּאָה; בָּעֲצֶרֶת עַל־
פֵּרוֹת הָאִילָן; בְּרֹאשׁ הַשָּׁנָה כָּל־בָּאֵי הָעוֹלָם
עוֹבְרִין לְפָנָיו כִּבְנֵי מָרוֹן, שֶׁנֶּאֱמַר: ,,הַיֹּצֵר יַחַד

יד אברהם

2.

בְּאַרְבָּעָה פְּרָקִים הָעוֹלָם נִדּוֹן: — *At four junctures [of the year] the world is judged;*

[At four specific times during the year, God judges the deeds of mankind, and, based upon those deeds, makes His decisions regarding the matters enumerated in our mishnah.]

After having enumerated in mishnah 1 the four new years that are dependent on the בֵּית דִּין שֶׁל מַטָּה, *earthly court,* the tanna now enumerates the new years that are dependent on the בֵּית דִּין שֶׁל מַעֲלָה, *Heavenly Court (Meiri).*

[The sequence of this mishnah (Pesach, Shavuos, Rosh Hashanah, Succos), as in the previous mishnah, follows the rule that the months are to be counted from Nissan.]

בַּפֶּסַח עַל־הַתְּבוּאָה; — *on Pesach for the grain;*[1]

Since Pesach is the time when the grain (specifically barley) begins to ripen, God chose this time to decide whether the grain harvest of the coming

will be plentiful or meager (*Meiri; Rambam* in *comm.*).

The *Gemara* (16a) quotes a *baraisa* that God blesses the grain harvest because of the omer, a barley offering, which is brought on Pesach (*Lev.* 23:10). This is the Scriptural indication that the judgment for grain is on Pesach (*Rav*).

Sifsei Chachamim comments that on Pesach Israel is judged for adherence to the commandments relating to grain (*terumah, ma'aser, bircas hamazon,* etc.) and if these were fulfilled properly, the world is blessed with a plentiful grain harvest.

בָּעֲצֶרֶת עַל־פֵּרוֹת הָאִילָן; — *on Shavuos for the fruit of the tree;*[2]

Since Shavuos is when fruits begin to ripen on the tree, it is the proper time for God to pass judgment on the coming fruit harvest (*Meiri*).

The *Gemara* again quoted in the *baraisa* cited above (s.v. עַל התבואה) which states that the offering of שְׁתֵּי

---

1. In the Mishnah and throughout Rabbinic literature this festival is called Pesach, but Scripture always refers to it as חַג הַמַּצּוֹת, *the Festival of Matzos.* This is so because matzah is a reminder of the faith and trust of the Jews who hurriedly left Egypt and followed God into a barren wilderness without even allowing time for their dough to rise. *Pesach* (lit., *Passover*), on the other hand, is a reminder of God's kindness in 'passing over' the Jewish homes and sparing our firstborn. We, therefore, refer to the festival as Pesach, in appreciation of what God did for us, while God calls it the Festival of Matzos, in praise of the Jews (*R' Levi Yitzchok of Berdichev*). [Cf. *Berachos* 6a: the Almighty's tefillin contain verses regarding the uniqueness of the Jews, while our tefillin tell of the unity of God.]

2. *Menoras Hamaor* (ed. Jerusalem 5713 p. 295) states that Shavuos is referred to by the Sages as *Atzeres* (lit., *restraint*) in the same sense that the day after Succos is called [Shemini] Atzeres by the Torah. Both are days in which God *restrains* His people from taking leave of Jerusalem after the pilgrimage festival, and requests them to stay a while and rejoice with Him, as it were, for one more day, since parting is difficult.

[The last day of Pesach, too, is described as *Atzeres* by the Torah (*Deut.* 16:8), however, the Mishnah generally uses this title only for Shavuos. This may allude to the concept mentioned by later commentators that Shavuos, as the day the Torah was given, is the purpose and culmination of the process that began with the Exodus. Since the Mishnaic period represents

2. $\mathbf{A}$t four junctures [of the year] the world is judged: on Pesach for the grain; on Shavuos for the fruit of the tree; on Rosh Hashanah all who walk the earth pass before Him like young sheep, as

YAD AVRAHAM

הַלֶּחֶם, *the Two Loaves [of wheat]*, was brought on Shavuos (Lev. 23:17) in order to invoke God's blessing on the fruit harvest. This is the Scriptural indication that the judgment for trees takes place on *Shavuos (Rav)*.

Rav explains this *baraisa* in accord with the view of the tanna who holds that עֵץ הַדַּעַת, *the tree of knowledge*, from which Adam ate, was actually wheat (see *Sanhedrin* 70b). Since wheat is referred to by the Torah as a *tree*, the offering of a wheat sacrifice incurs blessing on all trees. Cf. *Rashi, Ran* for other explanations of this *baraisa*.

On Shavuos, Man is judged on his performance of the commandments involving fruit and trees *(orlah, revai, terumos* and *ma'aseros)*. If these were fulfilled properly, God gives his blessing to the fruit harvest *(Sifsei Chachamim)*.

בְּרֹאשׁ הַשָּׁנָה כָּל־בָּאֵי עוֹלָם עוֹבְרִין לְפָנָיו כִּבְנֵי מָרוֹן, — *on Rosh Hashanah[1] all who walk the earth pass before Him like young sheep,*

[The intent of the mishnah is to point out that every man is judged individually and none can evade God's judgment.]

All mankind passes before the Creator to be judged individually like young sheep who pass through a small opening in the corral for the purpose of tithing of animals as mentioned in the previous mishnah *(Rav)*.

In an alternate translation the *Gemara* 18a renders כִּבְנֵי מָרוֹן: like soldiers who pass in file before the king.

The fact that this judgment takes place on Rosh Hashanah is derived by the *Gemara* (8a) from *Deuteronomy* 11:12, מֵרֵשִׁית הַשָּׁנָה וְעַד אַחֲרִית שָׁנָה, *from the beginning of the year until the end of the year*, which is interpreted to mean that at the beginning of the year (i.e., the first of Tishrei) man is judged to decide what will happen to him until the end of the year *(Ran)*.

Ran poses a question: If man is judged on Rosh Hashanah and his future for the coming year is decided upon, then obviously this includes his grain and fruit harvests, and all his other matters. If so, what is the purpose

the flowering of Torah study, the Sages chose to refer to Shavuos by a name which implies its major significance. Thus, the name also implies the reason that God finds it so difficult to part from Israel after that day.]

Menoras Hamaor quotes further from *Pesikta* that in reality Shemini Atzeres should be fifty days after Succos, just as Shavuos is fifty days after Pesach. But, because of the difficulty of winter travel, God allowed it to follow Succos immediately. Shavuos, on the other hand, is during the summer when travel is easy, so God requests His people to return for one day to rejoice together before parting for the summer (cf. *Sifsei Chachamim*).

1. The term Rosh Hashanah does not appear in the Torah. Its only use in Scripture (*Ezekiel* 40:1) clearly refers to Yom Kippur (*Arachin* 12b) of the Jubilee Year which has many similarities to Rosh Hashanah (see 3:5). The sages refers to the first of Tishrei as Rosh Hashanah, based on the halachically accepted view of R' Eliezer that man was created on the first of Tishrei.

However, numerous authorities favor R' Yehoshua's view that the world was created in Nissan (see R' S.K. Mirsky, *Torah Shebe'al Peh* 7, pp. 33-39 at length.) *Tosafos* (27a) states that both views are correct in that the creation of the world was "thought" of by God in Tishrei, but was not carried out until Nissan.

For all practical purposes the controversy does not affect us. According to both views (see *Ran, Meiri*) God judges mankind on Rosh Hashanah and that is the day which inaugurates the new calendar year. Cf. *Be'ur HaGra* to *Shulchan Aruch Orach Chayim* 581:1.

ראש
השנה
א/ב

רֹאשׁ לָכֶם, הַמֵּבִין אֶל־כָּל־מַעֲשֵׂיהֶם''; וּבֶחָג נִדּוֹנִין עַל־הַמַּיִם.

יד אברהם

of the other three times of judgment mentioned in our mishnah?

Ran explains that on Pesach, Shavuos, and Succos, the world as a whole is judged and it is decided how much grain, fruit, and rain the entire world will receive. On Rosh Hashanah, however, God decides what share of these gifts each individual will receive.

Meiri explains that on Rosh Hashanah, every man is judged as to whether he will live or die, have pleasure or pain; gain profit or suffer loss. On the other matters, the judgment is not on Rosh Hashanah but on the appropriate festivals. (See *Sifsei Chachamim* for other answers to *Ran's* question.)

שֶׁנֶּאֱמַר: ,,הַיֹּצֵר יַחַד לִבָּם הַמֵּבִין אֶל־כָּל־מַעֲשֵׂיהֶם'' — *as it is said (Psalms 33:15):* Who fashions all their hearts together, Who understands all their deeds;

This verse is interpreted by the *Gemara* 18a to mean: He Who fashioned all people sees each one of them, and views the totality [*together*] of his heart and deeds.

Rashi (18a) explains that this verse should be understood in conjunction with the one preceding it: מִמְּכוֹן־שִׁבְתּוֹ הִשְׁגִּיחַ אֶל כָּל־יֹשְׁבֵי הָאָרֶץ, *from His dwelling place He oversees all inhabitants of earth.*

Rashi and *Rav* explain that although

they pass before Him one by one, God sees them all at one glance and understands all their deeds [and judges them accordingly]. (See *Tif. Yis.* and *Maharsha* for other interpretations.)

וּבֶחָג נִדּוֹנִין עַל הַמָּיִם. — *and on the Fetival* [i.e., Succos][1] *they are judged for the water.*

Since Succos is the start of the rainy season in the Holy Land, it is an appropriate time for the world to be judged on the amount of rain to fall throughout the coming year *(Meiri).*

Here, too, the *Gemara* (16a) quotes the *baraisa* which states that נִסּוּךְ הַמַּיִם, *pouring of water on the altar,* was performed on Succos (see *Succah* 4:9,10) in order to voice God's blessing on the year's rainfall. This indicates that God's judgment about water takes place on Succos *(Rav).*

Sifsei Chachamim says that Israel is judged on Succos regarding fulfillment of the commandments relating to water (מִקְוֶה, *ritual immersion;* נְטִילַת יָדַיִם, *washing hands before meals,* etc.). The performance of these commandments earns the blessing of plentiful rainfall.

[The repetition of the word נִדּוֹנִין, *they are judged,* in this final case of our mishnah, is probably because the relatively lengthy description of the judgment on Rosh Hashanah interrupted the orderly flow of words used in relation to Pesach and Shavuos.]

3.

The next seventeen mishnayos (the bulk of our tractate) are devoted to the subject of קִדּוּשׁ הַחֹדֶשׁ [*Kiddush HaChodesh*], sanctification of Rosh Chodesh [the first day of the month] based on the appearance of the new moon. A rudimentary knowledge of the subject is necessary before embarking further in our tractate.

---

1. In numerous places the Mishnah refers to Succos as חָג, *Festival,* even though the Torah uses this as a general term for all festivals (e.g., *Deut.* 16:16). *Tosefos Yom Tov* explains that one meaning of חָג is *rejoicing in dance,* and on Succos there was more rejoicing than on the other Festivals as can be seen from the use of the term זְמַן שִׂמְחָתֵנוּ, *the time of our rejoicing,* mentioned in our Succos prayers (cf. *Rambam, Hilchos Lulav* 8:12).

1
2
it is said *(Psalms* 33:15): *Who fashions all their hearts together, Who understands all their deeds;* and on the Festival they are judged for the water.

◆§ The Jewish Month

The commonly used calendar is based solely on the solar cycle in which the earth makes a complete revolution around the sum in approximately 365¼ days. The year's division into twelve months is an arbitrary method of dating events for the sake of convenience; there is no natural event that dictates which day should be the first of the month, or even that the year should be divided into twelve months rather than five, fifteen, or twenty. The lunar cycle is not a factor in the solar calendar.

Months of the Jewish calendar, however, are not arbitrary but are based on the lunar cycle in which each revolution of the moon around the sun is a month. As the Sages teach *(Succah* 29a): יִשְׂרָאֵל מוֹנִין לַלְּבָנָה וְעוֹבְדֵי כוֹכָבִים לַחַמָּה, *Jews reckon [the calendar] according to the moon and gentiles according to the sun.* This method of reckoning is ordained by the Torah, and is derived from *Exodus* 12:2 and *Numbers* 28:14 *(Rambam, Kiddush HaChodesh* 1:1).

◆§ The Lunar Cycle

The moon makes one complete revolution around the earth every 29 days, 12 hours, 44 minutes and 3⅓ seconds. Our Sages did not divide the hour into minutes and seconds, but rather into חֲלָקִים [*chalakim*], *portions,* 1080 of which constitute an hour. Each portion [*chelek*], therefore, is equal to 3 ⅓ seconds. In Rabbinic terminology, the duration of the moon's revolution is expressed as כ"ט-י"ב-תשצ"ג [29-12-793], or 29 days, 12 hours and 793 *chalakim (Rosh HaShanah* 25a; *Rambam, Kiddush HaChodesh* 6:3).

The precise moment when the moon completes its revolution of the earth to begin a new revolution, and changes from an 'old' moon to a 'new' moon is called מוֹלַד הַלְּבָנָה [*molad halevanah*], *birth of the moon,* or מוֹלָד, *molad,* for short *(Rosh Hashanah* 20b; *Rambam, Kiddush HaChodesh* 6:1). The time between one *molad* and the next, 29-12-793, is the duration of the lunar month.

Although the *molad* is an extremely important factor in the determination of the Jewish month, another factor of equal importance must be taken into account: the appearance of the first phase of the moon.

◆§ Phases of the Moon

If the moon were a luminous body, it would always appear to us as 'full' like the sun or a star — and the concept of *molad* would be meaningless. The moon, however, has no light of its own; it reflects the light it receives from the sun *(Zohar Bereishis* 135b, 249b). Depending upon its position relative to the sun and the earth during its monthly revolution around the earth, it appears to us in different phases ranging from a thin crescent to a full moon. Once a month the moon's position is between the sun and the earth, when that happens, the entire 'light' side of the moon faces the sun while the entire 'dark' side faces earth, with the result that the moon is totally invisible to us. This is the moment of the *molad;* for at precisely that instant the moon begins its movement to its next phase when it starts to be 'reborn,' or visible again. A number of hours later, as it gradually circles the earth, it reaches

a point where *some* sunlight is reflected toward the earth. Then, a small part of the moon becomes visible as a very thin crescent, which is known as the *first phase* of the moon *(Rosh Hashanah 20b; Rambam, Kiddush HaChodesh, with Lechem Mishneh; Aruch HaShulchan HeAsid, Kiddush HaChodesh 88:10-12)*. In Rabbinic terminology, this first phase is called חִדּוּשָׁה שֶׁל לְבָנָה, *renewal of the moon,* or חוֹדֶשׁ, *chodesh,* (mishnah 1:7). The word *chodesh* means not only 'month,' but 'renewal,' in the sense that the moon is 'renewed' after having disappeared. Many authorities refer to this first phase as *molad.* Though technically incorrect, it does not in any way change matters halachically.

As the moon continues to circle the earth, more and more of it becomes visible. Finally, when it has reached the half-way point in its revolution, it appears to us as a full moon. As it continues on its way, its dark side gradually turns toward earth and the size of its visible area gradually diminishes until it becomes invisible again.

The exact moment of the *molad* (and consequently of the *chodesh)* is not simultaneous throughout the earth. The *molad* and appearance of the first lunar phase in any given place are dependent upon the longitude and latitude of that place *(Rambam, Kiddush HaChodesh 18:13-16)*. However, the proclamation of Rosh Chodesh does not vary from place to place; for the purpose of *Kiddush HaChodesh,* the *molad* of Jerusalem and the moon's appearance there are the determining factors *(Rambam, Kiddush HaChodesh 11:17)*.

It would seem, based on the above, that the Jewish month should (a) always begin at the moment of the *molad* and (b) its duration should be a constant 29 days, 12 hours and 793 *chalakim.*

Neither of these conditions is possible, however. We are commanded to perform *Kiddush HaChodesh* עַל פִּי רְאִיָּה, *based on the sighting* [of the new moon] *(Rosh Hashanah 20a; Rambam, Kiddush HaChodesh 5:1)*, and, as stated above, the moon is invisible at the moment of the *molad.* Nor can months begin at constant intervals of 29-12-793, because the Torah commands that months must consist of whole days and cannot include fractions of a day; thus months cannot begin or end in the middle of the day *(Megillah 5a)*. This, then, precludes our using the moment of the *molad* or the moment of the *chodesh* as the start of the month.

One more point: the day, in Jewish law, starts at the beginning of the night and ends at sunset of the next day. When we speak of the night of the thirtieth, for example, we mean the night that precedes the thirtieth day. For different reasons, though, both the *molad* and the *chodesh* are necessary in determining the day of ראשׁ חוֹדֶשׁ, *[Rosh Chodesh] the first of the month,* as we will soon see.

◆§ The Mitzvah of Kiddush HaChodesh

הַחֹדֶשׁ הַזֶּה לָכֶם רֹאשׁ חֳדָשִׁים, *This month shall be for you the first of the months (Exodus 12:2)*. The *Gemara* (22a) interprets this verse as a מִצְוַת עֲשֵׂה, *positive commandment,* incumbent upon *beis din* to perform the *mitzvah* of *Kiddush HaChodesh* by sanctifying and declaring which day is to be Rosh Chodesh, based on certain specific criteria *(Rambam, Kiddush HaChodesh 1:7)*.

The *beis din* that has this responsibility is the Sanhedrin [Supreme Court] of seventy-one judges, any three members of which, with the participation or sanction of the *Av Beis Din* [head of Sanhedrin], may perform this *mitzvah.* However, the Sanhedrin may sanction non-members to proclaim Rosh Chodesh, provided they have the proper ordination *(Sanhedrin 2a; Rambam, Kiddush HaChodesh 1:5, 2:8)*. *Ramban* disagrees and holds that the three judges comprising the *beis din* need not be members of the Sanhedrin.

Furthermore, except under extraordinary circumstances, this *mitzvah* must be performed in *Eretz Yisrael (Berachos 63a; Rambam, Kiddush HaChodesh 1:8)*. It may be performed only during the day and not at night *(Rosh Hashanah 25b; Rambam, Kiddush HaChodesh 2:8)*.

◄§ Performance of Kiddush HaChodesh

As mentioned above, the *beis din* is commanded to sanctify the day of Rosh Chodesh: עַל פִּי רְאִיָּה, *based on the sighting* [of the new moon]. Therefore, the *beis din* must rely on the testimony of two witnesses who saw the first phase of the new moon some time after the actual *molad*. The *beis din* did not, however, completely dispense with the true astronomical calculation of the *molad*. This, along with a great deal of other astronomical calculation, was considered by the *beis din*. Thus, if the moon could not have been visible when the witnesses claimed to have seen it, or if it had to be in a different position from that to which they testified, their testimony was naturally rejected *(Rambam, Kiddush HaChodesh 1:6, 2:4)*.

After carefully screening the witnesses as to their eligibility and interrogating them to determine the reliability of their testimony, the *beis din* would then sanctify and declare the day to be Rosh Chodesh.

The time of Rosh Chodesh therefore, depended on the testimony of witnesses and their acceptance by *beis din*. But this dependence was not total. If, for example, the sky was so overcast that the moon was not seen until thirty-three days after the previous Rosh Chodesh, this did not mean that the thirty-third day was Rosh Chodesh, thus making the previous month thirty-two days long. Rosh Chodesh could be only one of two days: either on the thirtieth day from the previous Rosh Chodesh or on the thirty-first day *(Yerushalmi Shevi'is 10:1; cf. Arachin 8b-9a)*.

If the witnesses appeared on the thirtieth day, then that day was declared Rosh Chodesh. In such a case, the previous month had only twenty-nine days and was called a חָסֵר [*chasser*], *deficient* [i.e., a short month].

If they did not appear on the thirtieth day, then the next day was *automatically* Rosh Chodesh. In that case, the previous month contained thirty days and was called מָלֵא [*malei*], *full*, or מְעוּבָּר [*meubar*], literally *pregnant (Rambam, Kiddush HaChodesh 2:1-3)*.

Since either one of those two could be declared *Rosh Chodesh*, the exact date of the festivals (which are expressly dated by the Torah on specific days of specific months and hence dependent upon Rosh Chodesh) was always in doubt until *beis din* made its decision.

Beis din had to inform the people of that decision, so that they could celebrate the holy days on the proper dates. Places that could not be informed in time had to celebrate an added day, as is done today outside of *Eretz Yisrael (Rambam, Kiddush HaChodesh 5:4-6)*.

The method of *Kiddush HaChodesh* described above was in use until the year 4118 after Creation (358 C.E.). Then the entire structure of Jewish communal life in *Eretz Yisrael* was on the verge of extinction due to foreign persecution, and the very institution of the *beis din* was endangered. R' Hillel (a thirteenth generation direct descendant of Hillel the Elder), who was head of the *beis din*, instituted the current Jewish calendar and abolished קִדּוּשׁ הַחֹדֶשׁ עַל פִּי רְאִיָּה, *sanctification [of Rosh Chodesh] based on sighting*. By astronomical and halachic calculations, he and his court devised the system in use today, and sanctified every *Rosh Chodesh* until the coming of the Messiah *(Ramban, Sefer HaZechus, Gittin, ch. 4. Cf. Rambam, Kiddush HaChodesh 5:1-3; for a different interpretation of R' Hillel's enactment)*.

The above discussion was intended only to provide the information needed for a proper understanding of the following *mishnayos*. It is by no means a full study.

Based on the above, the next seventeen *mishnayos* can be classified by subject as follows: a) The coming of the witnesses — 1:4-6, 9, and 2:5;
       b) The legitimacy of the witnesses — 1:7,8, and 2:1;
       c) The interrogation of the witnesses — 2:6,8;
       d) The *beis din's* sanctification — 2:7,9,10;
       e) The notification of the *beis din's* decision — 1:3 and 2:2-4.

[ג] עַל־שִׁשָּׁה חֳדָשִׁים הַשְּׁלוּחִים יוֹצְאִין:
עַל־נִיסָן מִפְּנֵי הַפֶּסַח; עַל־
אָב מִפְּנֵי הַתַּעֲנִית; עַל־אֱלוּל מִפְּנֵי רֹאשׁ
הַשָּׁנָה; עַל־תִּשְׁרֵי מִפְּנֵי תַקָּנַת הַמּוֹעֲדוֹת; עַל־
כִּסְלֵו מִפְּנֵי חֲנֻכָּה; וְעַל־אֲדָר מִפְּנֵי הַפּוּרִים.

יד אברהם

עַל־שִׁשָּׁה חֳדָשִׁים הַשְּׁלוּחִים יוֹצְאִין: — *For six months, the messengers go forth:*

[It was incumbent upon the *beis din* to inform distant communities which of the two possible days had been declared Rosh Chodesh. As soon as Rosh Chodesh was proclaimed, they dispatched messengers throughout *Eretz Yisrael* and the Diaspora. This procedure, however, was necessary only for the six months listed below.]

The use of the plural שְׁלוּחִים, *messengers*, should not be understood to imply that the people could not trust a *single* messenger (see *Rambam, Kiddush HaChodesh* 3:14); it reflects the fact that many messengers were sent in all directions bearing the information (*Sifsei Chachamim*).

[Although this mishnah seems to belong at the end of the subject of *Kiddush HaChodesh*, it is placed here because it contains a list of months as do the previous mishnayos.]

עַל־נִיסָן מִפְּנֵי הַפֶּסַח; — *For Nissan, because of Pesach.*

The messengers had to inform the people of the day of Rosh Chodesh Nissan so that they could observe the holiday of Pesach on the proper day, the fifteenth of Nissan. There was no need to inform them about Shavuos for it is always the fiftieth day from the sixteenth of Nissan (*Leviticus* 23:15-21).

[Places not reached by the messengers in time had to observe two days because of their doubt as to the proper date. Even when they discovered the correct date of Rosh Chodesh Nissan at some time after Pesach, they were still required to observe two days of Shavuos, in order not to differentiate between the festivals (*Rambam, Kiddush HaChodesh* 3:12).

Although nowadays, after the institution of the permanent calendar, there is no longer any doubt as to the proper date of the holidays, this law of the two-day observance remains in effect. By Rabbinical decree, all places not reached by the messengers in the days of Sanhedrin must still observe two days of *Yom Tov* as did their ancestors (*Beitzah* 4b, *Rambam Kiddush HaChodesh* 5:5).

עַל־אָב מִפְּנֵי הַתַּעֲנִית; — *for Av, because of the Fast;*

The fast of Tisha B'Av was the only Rabbinically ordained fast for which messengers were dispatched. It is more important than the others because it commemorates the destruction of the Temples (*Tiferes Yisrael*; cf. *Rav, Tosefos Yom Tov*).

[Places not reached by the messengers did not observe two days of Tisha B'Av because of the extreme hardship such fasting would impose (*Pesachim* 54b). It is likely that they assumed Rosh Chodesh Av to have been declared on the day on which, by astronomical calculation, the new moon was expected to appear in *Eretz Yisrael*.[1]

עַל־אֱלוּל מִפְּנֵי רֹאשׁ הַשָּׁנָה; — *for Elul, because of Rosh Hashanah;*

---

1. *Rambam (Kiddush HaChodesh* 1:7) rules that the dissemination of the news is included in the Scriptural command to sanctify Rosh Chodesh. *Chinuch (Mitzvah* 4) and *Semag (Asin* 36, 37) disagree. In their view, though incumbent upon the *beis din*, this dissemination is not part of the *mitzvah* (see *Toledos Shmuel* 1:2).

1. *Minchas Chinuch* (301:2) proposes the novel opinion that the obligation to fast on the Seventeenth of *Tammuz*, the Ninth of Av, the Third of Tishrei and the Tenth of Teves can be

3. For six months, the messengers go forth: For Nissan, because of Pesach; for Av, because of the Fast; for Elul, because of Rosh Hashanah; for Tishrei, because of the determination of the holidays; for Kislev, because of Chanukah; for Adar, because

The people had to be informed of the day of Rosh Chodesh Elul in order to celebrate the thirtieth day as Rosh Hashanah. Although it was possible that *beis din* would decide that Elul should be *meubar*, making the thirty-first day Rosh Hashanah, the people relied on the fact that Elul was virtually always a month of twenty-nine days. Lack of knowledge of the day of Rosh Chodesh Elul might, however, result in their celebrating the twenty-ninth of Elul as Rosh Hashanah *(Rav)*.

Rashi (18a) holds that they celebrated only the thirtieth day as Rosh Hashanah, relying on the virtually invarying precedent. *Tosafos*, however, disagrees (s.v. ועל אלול), maintaining that both the thirtieth and thirty-first days were celebrated as Rosh Hashanah. (The reason Rosh Hashanah is celebrated for two days in *Eretz Yisrael* in contrast to the other holidays will be discussed later in mishnah 4:4.)

עַל־תִּשְׁרֵי מִפְּנֵי תַּקָּנַת הַמּוֹעֲדוֹת; — *for Tishrei, because of the [proper] determination of the holidays;*

Although Rosh Hashanah was celebrated, as stated above, on the assumption that it was the thirtieth day after Rosh Chodesh Elul, the slight possibility *did* exist that Elul was *meubar*. Therefore it was necessary to inform the

people of the *beis din's* decision regarding the first of Tishrei in order that they be absolutely certain of the proper dates of Yom Kippur and Succos *(Gemara,* 19b).

Those places not reached in time did not celebrate two days of Yom Kippur because of the great hardship of a two-day fast. They relied on the assumption that Elul was never thirty days *(Gemara* 21a).[1]

עַל־כִּסְלֵו מִפְּנֵי חֲנֻכָּה; — *for Kislev, because of Chanukah;*

In the places reached by the messengers Chanukah was celebrated for eight days beginning on the twenty-fifth of Kislev. Places farther away did not add an extra day to Chanukah (as they did for the Torah-ordained holidays) since Chanukah is only a Rabbinical enactment *(Pri Chadash* to *Orach Chayim* 670).

Minchas Chinuch (301:2) however, holds that when sanctification was done based on sighting all those places not notified in time celebrated nine days of Chanukah.

Arvei Nachal claims that the eight days of Chanukah already contain an additional day of observance, as the miracle lasted for only seven days (see *Turei Zahav* to *Orach Chayim* 670:1).

The views of *Minchas Chinuch* and

---

fulfilled on *any* day of their respective months. This opinion is based on the way they are listed in *Zechariah* 8:19: צוֹם הָרְבִיעִי, וְצוֹם הַחֲמִישִׁי וְצוֹם הַשְּׁבִיעִי וְצוֹם הָעֲשִׂירִי, *the fast of the fourth [month], and the fast of the fifth [month], and the fast of the seventh [month] and the fast of the tenth [month],* implying that the main consideration is the month, not the day. Initially the Rabbis decreed that the fasting should take place on the specific days mentioned above, but people unaware of the day of Rosh Chodesh were free to fast on an alternative day of those months, and thus had no problem of fasting on the wrong day.

1. R' Yaakov Emden (Glosses to *Pesachim* 54b, cf. *Lechem Shamayim)* interprets the *Gemara* differently and claims that the people *did* fast for two days. His view is rejected by all other authorities.

וּכְשֶׁהָיָה בֵּית הַמִּקְדָּשׁ קַיָּם, יוֹצְאִין אַף עַל־אִיָּר
מִפְּנֵי פֶּסַח קָטָן.

[ד] עַל שְׁנֵי חֳדָשִׁים מְחַלְּלִין אֶת־הַשַּׁבָּת:
עַל־נִיסָן וְעַל־תִּשְׁרֵי, שֶׁבָּהֶן

יד אברהם

Arvei Nachal are refuted by *Responsa Toledos Yaakov, Orach Chayim* 29,30 from *Ta'anis* 28b which states clearly that Chanukah was celebrated everywhere for eight days, whether or not notification was received. Furthermore, if Chanukah is essentially a seven-day celebration as maintained by *Arvei Nachal*, it would be only seven days long in *Eretz Yisrael*.

וְעַל־אֲדָר מִפְּנֵי הַפּוּרִים. — *for Adar, because of Purim.*

[Purim, like Chanukah a Rabbinically ordained holiday, was similarly celebrated for only *one* day, even by those whom the messengers did not reach. *Mordechai* to *Megillah* 2a offers a different reason).]

If the *beis din* decided to intercalate a month into the year [i.e., add a second Adar to the year, making it a thirteen month year], Purim is celebrated in the second Adar. Generally, the conditions requiring this intercalation were known before Adar and the *beis din* would have announced that the year would contain a thirteenth month. That being the case, it would seem necessary to dispatch messengers in the *second* Adar to inform the people concerning Purim's proper day. Nevertheless, the *Gemara* points out that the mishnah omits mention of the messengers going forth for the second Adar. This is because the mishnah follows the view that the first Adar in an intercalary year is always *meubar*. Therefore, those who are informed of the Rosh Chodesh of the first Adar, will also know the date of Rosh Chodesh of the second Adar (*Tosefos Yom Tov*). Cf. *Tosefos R' Akiva Eger* who discusses the problems involved if the decision to add a thirteenth month

was not made until after the messengers have already gone out for Adar.

[The occasional intercalary month was needed primarily in order to fulfill the Torah's injunction that Pesach be in חֹדֶשׁ הָאָבִיב, *the month of springtime*, (*Deuteronomy* 16:1) which is interpreted in *Rosh Hashanah* 21a to mean that Pesach may not be before the vernal equinox. Since the lunar year is almost eleven days shorter than the solar year, Pesach would come out earlier every year with the result that within three years it would be thirty-three days earlier. For example, if Pesach were April 12 one year, it would be April 1 the next and — in the absence of a second Adar — Pesach would be March 21 the third year, a day before the equinox. The addition of an intercalary month every two or three years moves Pesach forward to meet the above injunction. In the permanent calendar currently in use, the 3rd, 6th, 8th, 11th, 14th, 17th and 19th years of each nineteen-year cycle (for example, in the cycle beginning with 5739, the third year (5741), sixth year (5744) and so on) are intercalary years. For further deails see *Sanhedrin* 10b-13b; *Rambam, Kiddush HaChodesh* ch. 4.]

וּכְשֶׁהָיָה בֵּית הַמִּקְדָּשׁ קַיָּם, יוֹצְאִין אַף עַל־אִיָּר מִפְּנֵי פֶּסַח קָטָן. — *And when the Temple was in existence, they went forth also for [Rosh Chodesh] Iyar, because of [the] minor Pesach.*

The mishnah refers to Pesach Sheni (the Second Pesach) on the fourteenth of Iyar. Those who could not bring the קָרְבַּן פֶּסַח, *Paschal sacrifice*, the day before Pesach because they were טָמֵא, *ritually contaminated*, or because they were far from Jerusalem (see *Numbers*

of Purim. And when the Temple was in existence, they went forth also for Iyar, because of [the] minor Pesach.

4. For two months, the witnesses may desecrate the Sabbath: for Nissan, and for Tishrei, for on

YAD AVRAHAM

10:9-11; *Pesachim* 9:1) were required to bring the Paschal sacrifice on Pesach Sheni, making it necessary for them to know its exact day *(Kehati).*

Although messengers went out on Rosh Chodesh Iyar while the Temple stood, some commentators note that there was still a total of only six months that they were dispatched: Av was omitted from the list since there was no fasting on Tisha B'Av while the Temple stood *(Tos. R' Akiva Eger; Tiferes Yisrael).*

Rambam (comm.) however, states

that Tisha B'Av *was* observed even during the Temple Era.

[*Tosefos Yom Tov* states that the mishnah refers to the second Pesach as פֶּסַח קָטָן, literally, *the 'small' Pesach,* since it lasted only one day (while the first Pesach is celebrated for seven days).

[Another reason might be that the vast majority of the people offered the sacrifice on the first Pesach, leaving only a few who celebrated the second Pesach, thus allowing it to be called 'small' or 'minor'.]

4.

עַל־שְׁנֵי חֳדָשִׁים מְחַלְּלִין אֶת־הַשַּׁבָּת: — *For two months, the witnesses may desecrate the Sabbath:*

In order to travel to Jerusalem and inform the *beis din* of their sighting of the new moon, witnesses were permitted to desecrate the Sabbath if necessary *(Rav).*

The *Gemara* (see also Mishnah 1:9) derives this from the verse: אֲשֶׁר תִּקְרְאוּ אֹתָם בְּמוֹעֲדָם, *that you shall declare them in their proper time (Leviticus 23:4).* The use of the phrase *in their time* signifies that the declaration of Rosh Chodesh must be made at the proper time even if it requires חִלּוּל שַׁבָּת, *desecration of the Sabbath.* [See *Pesachim* 66a, 77a, where a similar verse teaches that the Paschal offering was brought on the Sabbath.]

This dispensation does not, however, extend to the messengers who notified the outlying populace that Rosh Chodesh had been declared; the verse mentions only *declaration* and not *notification. Aruch HaShulchan He-*

Asid (Kiddush HaChodesh 92:2) points out that travel on the Sabbath or *Yom Tov* for the purpose of notification would be an unnecessary desecration, since the people could observe festivals for two days, as did those whom the messengers never reached.

[Not *all* desecrations were permitted, however. Those that were are discussed in *comm.* to mishnah 5, s.v. בין שנראה, and in mishnah 9.]

It should be noted that מִדְּאוֹרַיְיתָא, *by Torah law,* witnesses were required to desecrate the Sabbath for *all* the months. In the absence of pilgrimage festivals and Temple offerings following the destruction of the Temple, the Sages decreed that it might be desecrated only for Nissan and Tishrei, as there was no great need to declare Rosh Chodesh correctly on the other months *(Rav; Gemara).*

עַל־נִיסָן — *for Nissan,*

In order to correctly determine the dates of Pesach and Shavuos. Shavuos

הַשְּׁלוּחִין יוֹצְאִין לְסוּרְיָא, וּבָהֶן מְתַקְּנִין אֶת־
הַמּוֹעֲדוֹת. וּכְשֶׁהָיָה בֵּית הַמִּקְדָּשׁ קַיָּם, מְחַלְּלִין
אַף עַל־כֻּלָּן מִפְּנֵי תַּקָּנַת הַקָּרְבָּן.

[ה] **בֵּין** שֶׁנִּרְאָה בַעֲלִיל, בֵּין שֶׁלֹּא נִרְאָה
בַעֲלִיל, מְחַלְּלִין עָלָיו אֶת־הַשַּׁבָּת.

יד אברהם

is exactly fifty days from the second day of Pesach, as mentioned in the previous mishnah.

וְעַל־תִּשְׁרֵי, — and for Tishrei,

In order to correctly determine the days of Rosh HaShanah, Yom Kippur, and Succos.

שֶׁבָּהֶן הַשְּׁלוּחִין יוֹצְאִין לְסוּרְיָא, — for on them the messengers go forth to Syria,

The fact that messengers were dispatched to notify the Diaspora of the sanctification of Nissan and Tishrei is an indication of the importance attached to these two months. The reason for the Sabbath desecration, as given above, is the Scriptural mandate, but the special significance of these two months helps explain why the Sages continued the Scriptural dispensation for witnesses to come on the Sabbath, even after they abolished it for other months (Rashi).

Meiri and Tiferes Yisrael give different reasons for our mishnah's mention of Syria in particular. Cf. Kol Haremez.

The Gemara (21b) notes that our mishnah seems to contradict the previous one, which stated that messengers went forth on six months. The difference, the Gemara explains, is that on the other months the messengers left as soon as they were reasonably sure when beis din would declare Rosh Chodesh. For example, if witnesses arrived on the night of the thirtieth, or if the moon was seen clearly in the sky (see 1:5), the messengers could assume that the thirtieth day would be declared Rosh Chodesh and they would depart immediately — even though beis din was not permitted to accept the witness-

es and decide the matter until morning (4:1). But for Nissan and Tishrei, they would not depart until the next day when they actually heard the beis din's proclamation. The reason for the delay on these two months was because their special importance warranted that the messengers ascertain that the witnesses not be disqualified or that beis din not decide to wait a day before declaring Rosh Chodesh.

If no witnesses appeared throughout the thirtieth day, the messengers should leave that night, knowing that the next day was automatically Rosh Chodesh (Baal HaMaor).

Tosafos disagrees. Even though the absence of witnesses on the thirtieth day guaranteed that Rosh Chodesh would be declared the next day, the messengers were not to leave until daybreak of the thirty-first. The Sages chose not to make any distinctions between the thirtieth and thirty-first to ensure that messengers would never leave earlier to announce Nissan and Tishrei (Tosefos Yom Tov).

Rashba and Baal Hamaor explain our mishnah in an entirely different way. The mishnah is not explaining why the Sages retained the permission to desecrate the Sabbath only for the sake of these two months. It merely states that Nissan and Tishrei are different from the other months in three ways:

a) Desecration is permissible on them;
b) Messengers may leave only after the beis din has declared Rosh Chodesh;
c) The proper determination of the holy days is dependent on these months.

וּבָהֶן מְתַקְּנִין אֶת הַמּוֹעֲדוֹת. — and on them, they [i.e., beis din] fix the holy days.

The primary reason for allowing

them the messengers go forth to Syria, and on them
they fix the holy days. And when the Temple was in
existence, they desecrated even for all of them
because of the determination of the sacrifice.

5. Whether it [the new moon] was clearly visible,
or whether it was not clearly visible, they
could desecrate the Sabbath because of it.

YAD AVRAHAM

desecration of the Sabbath for these two
months, is that the determination of the
days of all Torah-ordained holy days is
dependent upon the *beis din's* declaration of Rosh Chodesh Nissan and Rosh
Chodesh Tishrei *(Rav; Rashi).*

[Here is one example: the Torah ordains Yom Kippur to be *in the seventh
month, on the tenth of the month
(Leviticus 23:27).* Only after the *beis
din* declares Rosh Chodesh Tishrei *(the
seventh month)* is it possible to know
which day is *the tenth of the month.*]

וּכְשֶׁהָיָה בֵית הַמִּקְדָשׁ קַיָם, מְחַלְלִין אַף עַל-
כֻּלָן מִפְּנֵי תַקָנַת הַקָּרְבָּן. — *And when the
Temple was in existence, they
desecrated even for all of them because
of the determination [of the time] of the
sacrifice.*

On every *Rosh Chodesh* a קָרְבָּן
מוּסָף, *[Mussaf] additional sacrifice,* is
offered in the Temple *(Numbers 28:11-
15).* So that it would be offered on the
proper day, the Sabbath could be
desecrated for the sake of any month
(Rav; Rashi).

5.

בֵּין שֶׁנִּרְאָה בַעֲלִיל, — *Whether it [the new
moon] was clearly visible,*

If the moon was high above the
horizon *(Rav)* or the night was free of
clouds *(Tiferes Yisrael),* it could be assumed that the moon was seen in
Jerusalem, thus obviating the need for
desecrating the Sabbath *(Meiri).*

The desecration referred to here is the
prohibition against Sabbath travel
beyond the תְחוּם, *boundary* [i.e., 2,000
cubits out of an inhabited area *(Tiferes
Yisrael)*]. About desecrating the Sabbath in other ways see 1:9.

בֵין שֶׁלֹּא נִרְאָה בַעֲלִיל, — *[or] whether it
was not clearly visible,*

If the moon was low on the horizon
and somewhat hidden by the rays of the
setting sun *(Rav)* or the night was
cloudy *(Tiferes Yisrael),* in which cases
it very possibly was not seen in
Jerusalem ...

מְחַלְלִין עָלָיו אֶת־הַשַׁבָּת. — *they could*

desecrate the Sabbath because of it.

Even when the moon was clearly visible, witnesses who sighted it were permitted to travel to Jerusalem on the Sabbath to testify before the *beis din.*
Although their testimony was
superfluous, preventing them from
traveling might cause them to refrain
from coming in the future when their
testimony *would* be essential *(Meiri).*
[See mishnah 6 s.v. שלח לו.]

Tiferes Yisrael explains that they were
allowed to travel to Jerusalem on the
Sabbath because of the slight possibility
that the sky had been cloudy over
Jerusalem and the new moon was *not*
seen there. Thus their testimony could
be needed.

Sfas Emes wonders whether, in the
case of נִרְאָה בַעֲלִיל, a clearly visible
moon, the witnesses are *obligated* to go
and testify on the Sabbath — or whether
they are merely permitted to go, but are
under no obligation to do so.

רַבִּי יוֹסֵי אוֹמֵר: אִם נִרְאָה בַּעֲלִיל, אֵין
מְחַלְּלִין עָלָיו אֶת־הַשַּׁבָּת.

[ו] **מַעֲשֶׂה** שֶׁעָבְרוּ יוֹתֵר מֵאַרְבָּעִים זוּג,
וְעִכְּבָן רַבִּי עֲקִיבָא בְּלֹד.
שָׁלַח לוֹ רַבָּן גַּמְלִיאֵל: אִם מְעַכֵּב אַתָּה אֶת־
הָרַבִּים, נִמְצֵאתָ מַכְשִׁילָן לֶעָתִיד לָבֹא.

יד אברהם

However, *Rambam* (*Kiddush Ha-Chodesh* 3:4) quoted below clearly states that the witnesses are *obligated* to go.

רַבִּי יוֹסֵי אוֹמֵר: אִם נִרְאָה בַּעֲלִיל, אֵין מְחַלְּלִין עָלָיו אֶת־הַשַּׁבָּת. — *R' Yose says: If it was clearly visible, they could not desecrate the Sabbath because of it.*

Because it was surely seen in Jerusalem (*Rav*), as we assume that the sky was as clear in Jerusalem as it was in the place where the witnesses saw the moon (*Tiferes Yisrael*).

The halachah in this dispute favors the first *tanna*: Even if they saw it large and clearly visible to all, they should not say, 'Just as we saw it, so did others and we need not desecrate the Sabbath,' but instead whoever saw the new moon, and is fit to testify, and is within a night and a day's[1] distance from the place where the *beis din* is located, is obligated to desecrate the Sabbath and to go and testify (*Rambam, Kiddush HaChodesh* 3:4).

6.

מַעֲשֶׂה שֶׁעָבְרוּ יוֹתֵר מֵאַרְבָּעִים זוּג, — *It happened that more than forty pairs [of witnesses] passed [on their way to the beis din],*

They had sighted [a clearly visible] new moon and were traveling on Shabbos to testify before the *beis din* (*Meiri*).

[This mishnah is a continuation of the previous one, and is brought in support of the view of the *tanna kamma* [first tanna]. In the *Gemara* the two mishnayos are written as one.]

[The *beis din*, under Rabban Gamliel, was in Yavneh at this time, since Jerusalem had been destroyed.]

וְעִכְּבָן רַבִּי עֲקִיבָא בְּלֹד. — *and R'Akiva detained them in Lod.*

He followed the view of R' Yose that when the moon is clearly visible the

Sabbath may not be desecrated (*Meiri*).

Turei Even (25b) holds that this incident did not occur on the Sabbath and that R' Akiva detained them simply because there was no need for their testimony.

The *Gemara* (22a) states that it was not R' Akiva who detained them but rather an official in his district. Since he did not protest, he was blamed for their detainment (*Tosefos Yom Tov;* cf. *Shabbos* 5:4).

שָׁלַח לוֹ רַבָּן גַּמְלִיאֵל: אִם מְעַכֵּב אַתָּה אֶת־הָרַבִּים, נִמְצֵאתָ מַכְשִׁילָן לֶעָתִיד לָבֹא. — *Rabban Gamliel sent him [the following message]: If you detain the public, you are placing a stumbling-block in their path for the future.*

If they feel that their traveling is in

1. [Those living farther away *never* need come to testify, since by the time they arrive, the *beis din* will either already have declared Rosh Chodesh if witnesses appeared or, if not, will automatically declare it the next day (see mishnah 9).]

R' Yose says: If it was clearly visible, they could not desecrate the Sabbath because of it.

6. It happened that more than forty pairs [of witnesses] passed [on their way to *beis din*], and R' Akiva detained them in Lod.

Rabban Gamliel sent him [the following message]: If you detain the public, you are placing a stumbling-block in their path for the future.

YAD AVRAHAM

vain, they will refrain from coming in the future when their testimony *will* be necessary *(Meiri)*.

The halachah follows Rabban Gamliel's view as stated in the previous mishnah.

The commentators seek a halachic justification for having the witnesses desecrate the Sabbath for the sake of superfluous testimony.

— *Chasam Sofer* explains that their future reluctance to come would interfere with the proper sanctification of future months. The need to insure that such mishaps will not occur is sufficient to make their present coming a necessity, thereby permitting desecration of Shabbos (cf. *Aruch LaNer*).

— Even their *present* coming can be considered necessary, since many or most of the witnesses could be disqualified as mentioned in mishnah 1:7, thus necessitating the testimony of the last pair (cf. *Pnei Yehoshua, Mar'eh HaChodesh* 3; *Rashash* to mishnah 1:4).

[R' Akiva (or an official) held them back, for he felt that even though under Torah law they were *allowed* to travel, they ought to be prevented by Rabbinic decree, for the likelihood of their testimony being needed was remote. Rabban Gamliel, however, replied that while this might be so, such a Rabbinic enactment would prevent their coming in the future.]

◆§ **Introduction to mishnayos 7-8**

Generally, the Torah does not recognize the validity of circumstantial evidence, but requires the testimony of two eyewitnesses, as stated in *Deuteronomy* 19:15: עַל פִּי שְׁנֵי עֵדִים יָקוּם דָּבָר, *upon the testimony of two witnesses shall a matter be established* (cf. *Deuteronomy* 17:6). This rule applies to criminal cases, civil actions, the determination of marital status, and most other matters. (In other situations, some of which will be mentioned in 1:8, the testimony of one witness is sufficient.) Testimony regarding רְאִיַּת הַחֹדֶשׁ, *the sighting of the new moon*, also requires two witnesses *(Gemara* 22b).

When two witnesses are required, they must meet certain requirements before their testimony can be accepted. *Rambam (Hilchos Eidus* 9:1) lists ten categories of persons who are ineligible to testify. Anyone falling within one of those categories is ineligible to testify in the matter of *Kiddush HaChodesh*. There is no need for our mishnah to mention *all* of these categories, as their ineligibility is not limited to *Kiddush HaChodesh*, but extends to all matters of Jewish law. The following two *mishnayos* do however mention some of these categories of פְּסוּלֵי עֵדוּת, *ineligible witnesses*, for reasons which will become clear as we study these *mishnayos*.

Mishnah 7 discusses the ineligibility of קְרוֹבִים, *relatives*. *Deuteronomy* 24:16 states: לֹא יוּמְתוּ אָבוֹת עַל בָּנִים וּבָנִים לֹא יוּמְתוּ עַל אָבוֹת, *fathers shall not die because of*

[ז] **אָב** וּבְנוֹ שֶׁרָאוּ אֶת־הַחֹדֶשׁ, יֵלְכוּ. לֹא
שֶׁמִּצְטָרְפִין זֶה עִם־זֶה, אֶלָּא שֶׁאִם
יִפָּסֵל אֶחָד מֵהֶן, יִצְטָרֵף הַשֵּׁנִי עִם־אַחֵר.
רַבִּי שִׁמְעוֹן אוֹמֵר: אָב וּבְנוֹ וְכָל־הַקְּרוֹבִין
כְּשֵׁרִין לְעֵדוּת הַחֹדֶשׁ.
אָמַר רַבִּי יוֹסֵי: מַעֲשֶׂה בְּטוֹבִיָּה הָרוֹפֵא
שֶׁרָאָה אֶת־הַחֹדֶשׁ בִּירוּשָׁלַיִם הוּא וּבְנוֹ וְעַבְדּוֹ
מְשֻׁחְרָר, וְקִבְּלוּ הַכֹּהֲנִים אוֹתוֹ וְאֶת־בְּנוֹ,

יד אברהם

sons and sons shall not die because of fathers. The *Talmud* (*Sanhedrin* 27b-28a) interprets this verse to mean that fathers cannot be found guilty of a capital offense
based on the testimony of their sons and vice versa. This injunction includes close
relatives (as defined by the *Talmud ibid*) and applies not only to capital offenses but
to other cases as well. Furthermore, this injunction applies not only to perpetrators
and witnesses who are related, but also to witnesses who are related to each other,
even though they are unrelated to any of the actual participants in the case.

The ineligibility of relatives to testify is not necessarily due to the suspicion that
they may give false testimony. Their ineligibility falls under the category of גְּזֵירַת
הַכָּתוּב, a *Scriptural decree.*

Our mishnah discusses whether witnesses who are related to each other are eligible to testify in the matter of *Kiddush HaChodesh.*

7.

אָב וּבְנוֹ שֶׁרָאוּ אֶת־הַחֹדֶשׁ יֵלְכוּ. לֹא
שֶׁמִּצְטָרְפִין זֶה עִם־זֶה, אֶלָּא שֶׁאִם יִפָּסֵל אֶחָד
מֵהֶן, יִצְטָרֵף הַשֵּׁנִי עִם־אַחֵר. — *A father and
his son who saw the new moon should
go [to beis din]; not that they can be
paired together [as witnesses], but [so
that] if one of them is disqualified, the
second may be paired with another.*

[In the event a father and son or any
relatives who cannot testify together
saw the new moon, they might think it
unnecessary for both to go to *beis din*
since they cannot serve as the pair of
witnesses needed for *Kiddush HaChodesh.* Nevertheless, they all should go,
for another witness may appear with
whom one of them *can* be paired. The
reason that *both* must go is because of
the possibility that one of them may be
disqualified by reason of עֲבֵירָה, *sin*
(*Rambam; Kiddush HaChodesh* 2:1) or
by erring during בְּדִיקָה, *interrogation*
(*Rashi*).]

[This mishnah is a logical continuation of the previous one. After having
stated that *all who saw* the new moon
must come to the *beis din,* the mishnah
elaborates upon this by informing us
that even relatives must come.]

Sifsei Chachamim states that a father and
son are specified because the verse from
which we derive the ineligibility of relatives
as witnesses mentions fathers and sons.

Hon Ashir suggests that since the mishnah
relates an incident of Toviah the physician
and his son, our mishnah mentions this
relationship.

The Sages derive by Scriptural ex-
egesis that נִמְצָא אֶחָד מֵהֶם קָרוֹב אוֹ פָּסוּל
עֵדוּתָן בְּטֵלָה, *if [even] a single member of
a group of witnesses is found to be a
relative or disqualified, the testimony
[of all of them] is nullified* (*Makkos*
1:8). This being the case, how could
either the father or son offer testimony
in our case? *Meiri* explains that the

7. **A** father and his son who saw the new moon should go [to *beis din*]. Not that they can be paired together [as witnesses], but [so that] if one of them is disqualified, the second may be paired with another.

R' Shimon says: A father and his son, and all relatives are eligible for testimony about the new moon.

Said R' Yose, 'It happened that Toviah the physician saw the new moon in Jerusalem — he, his son, and his freed slave, and the *Kohanim* accepted him and his son, and disqualified his slave. But when they

YAD AVRAHAM

above dictum applies only if the relatives intended to testify *together*. In the case of our mishnah, however, the two relatives appear only to combine with others, if they are needed. (Cf. *Aruch LaNer, Turei Even*).

רַבִּי שִׁמְעוֹן אוֹמֵר: אָב וּבְנוֹ וְכָל־הַקְרוֹבִין
כְּשֵׁרִין לְעֵדוּת הַחֹדֶשׁ. — *R' Shimon says: A father and his son, and all relatives are eligible for testimony about the new moon.*

Although R' Shimon agrees that in other matters relatives are ineligible, he holds that *Kiddush HaChodesh* is different. He derives this from the verse in *Exodus* 12:1,2 וַיֹּאמֶר ה' אֶל מֹשֶׁה וְאֶל אַהֲרֹן וכו' הַחֹדֶשׁ הַזֶּה לָכֶם ..., *and God said to Moses and Aaron ... This month shall be for you ...* R' Shimon interprets this to mean: עֵדוּת זוֹ תְּהֵא כְשֵׁרָה בָּכֶם, *this testimony* (i.e., about the new moon) *is valid through you* (i.e., you — Moses and Aaron — are eligible even though you are brothers (*Rav, Gemara* 22a).

The first tanna, however, interprets this verse to mean: עֵדוּת זוֹ תְּהֵא מְסוּרָה לָכֶם, *[accepting] this testimony placed in your charge*, meaning that the *beis din* before whom the witnesses testify must be comprised of גְּדוֹלֵי הַדּוֹר, *the greatest sages of the generation*, just as Moses and Aaron were the leading sages of their time.

אָמַר רַבִּי יוֹסֵי: מַעֲשֶׂה בְּטוֹבִיָה הָרוֹפֵא שֶׁרָאָה אֶת־הַחֹדֶשׁ בִּירוּשָׁלַיִם הוּא וּבְנוֹ וְעַבְדּוֹ מְשֻׁחְרָר, — *Said R' Yose, 'It happened that Toviah the physician saw the new moon in Jerusalem — he, his son, and his freed slave,*

[The freed slave referred to here had been an עֶבֶד כְּנַעֲנִי, *gentile slave* of a Jew]. Even during his period of servitude, he had a degree of Jewishness and was obligated to perform all commandments incumbent upon Jewish women. Since his acquisition by a Jew has given him the status of a convert regarding many matters, such a slave is required to be circumcised and converted to Judaism. Nevertheless, his status as a Jew was not total: he was not permitted to marry a Jewess nor was he responsible for all *mitzvos*. Upon obtaining his freedom, his conversion was complete, and all the obligations and privileges of Jewishness devolved upon him with the sole exception of those for which Jewish lineage is a prerequisite.]

וְקִבְּלוּ הַכֹּהֲנִים אוֹתוֹ וְאֶת־בְּנוֹ, וּפָסְלוּ אֶת־עַבְדּוֹ. — *and the Kohanim accepted him and his son, and disqualified his slave.*

In accepting Toviah and his son, the *Kohanim* clearly agreed with the view of R' Shimon (*Tosefos Yom Tov*).

They disqualified his slave because the *Kohanim* held that a witness must be a מְיוּחָס, *of Jewish lineage*, in order to

וּפָסְלוּ אֶת־עַבְדּוֹ. וּכְשֶׁבָּאוּ לִפְנֵי בֵית דִּין, קִבְּלוּ
אוֹתוֹ וְאֶת־עַבְדּוֹ וּפָסְלוּ אֶת־בְּנוֹ.

[ח] **אֵלוּ** הֵן הַפְּסוּלִין: הַמְשַׂחֵק בַּקֻּבְיָא,
וּמַלְוֵי בָרִבִּית, וּמַפְרִיחֵי יוֹנִים,

יד אברהם

testify (Meiri; Tiferes Yisrael), as in Sanhedrin 4:2 which states that a judge in a capital case must be of such lineage (Tosefos Yom Tov).

[Kehati defines Kohanim as the beis din of the Kohanim. While such a beis din did exist (Eruvin 32a; Kesuvos 1:5) its main function involved matters related to Kohanim. It seems unlikely that they had any say in the matter of Kiddush HaChodesh. (See also Beis Shaul who raises other problems if a beis din is meant in this case).

It is probable that Kohanim mentioned here refers to individual Kohanim met by the witnesses on their way to the Sanhedrin [supreme Rabbinic Court], which was located in the Temple. Cf. Sifsei Chachamim; Shoshanim; LeDavid Toledos Shmuel 3:1.]

וּכְשֶׁבָּאוּ לִפְנֵי בֵית דִּין, קִבְּלוּ אוֹתוֹ וְאֶת־עַבְדּוֹ וּפָסְלוּ אֶת־בְּנוֹ. — But when they came before the beis din, they accepted him and his slave, and disqualified his son.'

[The beis din accepted the freed slave because eligibility as a witness does not require יחוס, Jewish lineage. But they disqualified Toviah's son because even Kiddush HaChodesh requires that the witnesses not be related, as stated above by the first tanna. The halachah follows this view (Rav).]

8.

◄§ Disqualification by virtue of 'wickedness.'

Mishnah 8 discusses the ineligibility of רְשָׁעִים, sinners, to testify. Exodus 23:1 states: אַל תָּשֶׁת יָדְךָ עִם רָשָׁע לִהְיֹת עֵד חָמָס, Do not collaborate with a wicked person to be a false witness. The Gemara in Sanhedrin 27a explains this verse as if it read: אַל תָּשֶׁת רָשָׁע עֵד, do not allow a wicked person to be a witness, thereby disqualifying a רָשָׁע from testifying.

The definition of 'wicked person' in this context involves numerous details. For example, which sins must one commit to fall within this category? Must the sinner know that the act is serious enough to disqualify him as a witness? A lengthy exposition of these details can be found in Rambam, Hilchos Eidus, 10:2-12:10.

In general, two categories of sinners are ineligible as witnesses: Those who are פָּסוּל מִדְּאוֹרַיְתָא, ineligible under Torah law, and those who are פָּסוּל מִדְּרַבָּנָן, ineligible under Rabbinic law. For one to be ineligible under Torah law, he must have transgressed a Torah prohibition and must also have been aware of the severity of his transgression. Those ineligible under Rabbinic law are discussed in our mishnah.

אֵלוּ הֵן הַפְּסוּלִין: — The following are ineligible [as witnesses]:

Since the previous mishnah considered the possibility of a witness being disqualified for being a sinner (according to Rambam's explanation), our mishnah proceeds to list a number of sinners who are ineligible (Rashash).

[Alternatively, since the previous mishnah required even relatives to come to beis din even if they had to profane the Sabbath to do so, our mishnah in-

came before the *beis din*, they accepted him and his slave, and disqualified his son.'

8. **T**he following are ineligible [as witnesses]: a dice-player, usurers, pigeon flyers, dealers in

YAD AVRAHAM

forms us that the following are ineligible to testify at all and need *never* come, for their coming is useless.]

The sinners mentioned in our mishnah are all eligible to testify מִדְאוֹרָיְתָא, by Torah law. They are, however, פָּסוּל מִדְרַבָּנָן, *ineligible by Rabbinic decree* (*Gemara, Rav* 22a). Even people who are only Rabbinically ineligible may not testify for *Kiddush HaChodesh* (*Tosefos Yom Tov*).

The sinners enumerated in our mishnah have transgressed prohibitions for the sake of personal gain. Having shown themselves ready to sin for profit, they are suspect of a readiness to accept bribes to testify falsely (*Rashi; Rav*).

[The mere fact that these people did not hesitate to transgress Rabbinic prohibitions does not mean that they can *be expected* to testify falsely. The rendering of false testimony is a Torah prohibition of great severity and we do not *presume* that they would be guilty of it. Nevertheless, because the *slight* suspicion does exist that they might do so, the Sages disqualified them as witnesses. Cf. *Tosefos Yom Tov, Lechem Shamayim*.]

While it is true that these sinners are ineligible to testify in all other matters, one might have assumed them eligible for *Kiddush HaChodesh*, since they are eligible by Torah law, and to reject them would delay the declaration of Rosh Chodesh and postpone the festivals by one day (*Aruch HaShulchan HeAsid, K.H.* 89:5). Our mishnah, therefore, tells us that the *beis din*, nevertheless re-

jects them.[1] Cf. *Sifsei Chachamim* and *Chiddushei Maharich* for other explanations.

הַמְשַׂחֵק בְּקֻבְיָא, — *a dice-player,*
[I.e., any sort of gambler (see *Rambam, Eidus* 10:4).]

According to R' Sheshesh (*Sanhedrin* 24b), this refers to a professional gambler. His ineligibility is caused by the fact that he does not engage in any profession of benefit to mankind, and so does not contribute to the maintenance of civilization. Such a person lacks credibility; since he is already somewhat of an outcast, he is not likely to feel embarrassment at taking a bribe to testify falsely (*Meiri*).

Rami bar Chama (*ibid*) holds that any gambler is ineligible even if he has another profession. According to this view, money won at gambling is considered stolen money and the winner a גַּזְלָן, *robber*. But he is not disqualified as a witness by Torah law since the loser pays him willingly and the gambler does not look upon his activity as robbery (*Tosafos; Rav*).

The first view is the generally accepted one. *Rambam*, however, (*Hilchos Gezeilah* 6:10, *Hilchos Eidus* 10:4 with *Kesef Mishneh*) appears to favor the second view.

וּמַלְוֵי בְרִבִּית, — *usurers,*
Both the lender and the borrower (who pays the interest) are ineligible [as the prohibition against usury applies to both] (*Sanhedrin* 25a).

Although usury is prohibited by the Torah (*Exodus* 22:24, *Leviticus* 25:36,

---

1. This is based on the rule that the Sages have the right to enact laws that conflict with Torah law, provided their enactment involves no active transgression of Torah law (see *Yevamos* 90a). The *beis din's* refusal to accept these witnesses is a passive avoidance of Torah law, and is therefore permissible.

ראש
השנה
א/ח
וְסוֹחֲרֵי שְׁבִיעִית, וַעֲבָדִים.
זֶה הַכְּלָל: כָּל־עֵדוּת שֶׁאֵין הָאִשָּׁה כְשֵׁרָה
לָהּ, אַף הֵן אֵינָן כְּשֵׁרִים לָהּ.

יד אברהם

Deuteronomy 23:20) a usurer is disqualified only under Rabbinic law. Torah law does not consider him a knowing thief since he justifies the act because the interest is given him willingly (Rav).

Others explain that the mishnah refers to usurers who practice forms of usury prohibited only under Rabbinic law (e.g., a lender who lives on the borrower's property without paying rent) [Bava Metzia 5:2], (Tiferes Yisrael).

Kol HaRemez points out that the mishnah's use of the term מַלְוֵי בְּרִבִּית, lit. lenders on interest, is meant to exclude the borrower according to the view that the borrower is not disqualified in a case of Rabbinically prohibited usury (see Shulchan Aruch Choshen Mishpat 34:10). But Sanhedrin 25b appears to contradict this explanation.

וּמַפְרִיחֵי יוֹנִים, — pigeon flyers,

One view in Sanhedrin 25a explains this to mean those who race pigeons for money, similar to the dice players mentioned above (Rav).

Another view is that it refers to people who lure pigeons from their owners' coops, thereby stealing them from their owners.

[This is not considered robbery under Torah law since the owners of the coops do not really own the pigeons, which can come and go as they please. The Sages, however, prohibited the luring away of these pigeons מִפְּנֵי דַרְכֵי שָׁלוֹם, in order to maintain the peace, between the owners and those who wish to lure them (see Chullin 139b). One who transgresses this Rabbinical prohibition is thereby disqualified as a witness.]

וְסוֹחֲרֵי שְׁבִיעִית, — (and) dealers in seventh-year [produce],

[While the produce that grows in

שְׁבִיעִית Shemittah [lit. seventh year], may be eaten, it is forbidden to engage in סְחוֹרָה, commerce, with these fruits (see Tosafos to Succah 39a for a definition of סְחוֹרָה). This is a Torah-prohibition derived from the verse in Leviticus 25b: לְאָכְלָה, for eating purposes, from which the Gemara (Avodah Zarah 62a) infers: וְלֹא לִסְחוֹרָה, but not for commercial purposes.]

Those who deal in the produce of shevi'is are disqualified as witnesses only by Rabbinic decree, although they have transgressed a Scriptural prohibition. Numerous explanations for this are given:

a) Tosafos 22a states that our mishnah is speaking of shmittah בַּזְּמַן הַזֶּה, in our days; in the absence of the Temple and the Sanhedrin, the observance of Shmittah is a Rabbinic requirement.

b) Ran explains that the dealers are unaware that they are transgressing a Torah law since they use the money gained for the purchase of food which they then eat in comformity with the halachic restrictions of Shmittah food (see Shevi'is 8:2).

c) Meiri says that since the prohibition against doing business with the produce of shevi'is is not stated clearly in the Torah but is only implied, those who transgress are treated as if they had only transgressed a Rabbinic law.

d) Rambam's interprets our mishnah with reference to people who never engage in business except during Shmittah, leading to the strong suspicion that they are engaged in forbidden commerce with the year's produce. Since, however, we cannot be certain of this, their ineligibility is only Rabbinical. Kehati points out that our mishnah's use of the term סוֹחֲרֵי שְׁבִיעִית, Shmittah dealers, and not סוֹחֲרֵי פֵּירוֹת שְׁבִיעִית, dealers in the 'produce' of

seventh-year [produce], and slaves.

This is the rule: Any testimony for which a woman is ineligible, they too are ineligible for it.

YAD AVRAHAM

Shmittah, lends support to *Rambam's* view.

וַעֲבָדִים. — *and slaves.*

Jewish-owned gentile slaves who have not been freed are ineligible to testify by Torah law as are women (*Meir;* see *Bava Kama* 88a for the derivation of slaves' ineligibility).

Though their inclusion in our mishnah is seemingly unnecessary, they are mentioned because one might think that they *should* be eligible as witnesses for *Kiddush HaChodesh,* because they have committed no sin and are not suspected of testifying falsely. This would be in accord with the view of R' Shimon in the previous mishnah who allows the testimony of relatives with regard to *Kiddush HaChodesh* (*Tosefos Yom Tov*).

זֶה הַכְּלָל: — *This is the rule:*

[Having listed witnesses who are disqualified only by Rabbinical decree, the mishnah now points out that even though they are ineligible for *Kiddush HaChodesh,* such witnesses *are* acceptable for certain other matters. To let us know for which matters they are eligible and for which they are not, a general rule is given.]

כָּל־עֵדוּת שֶׁאֵין הָאִשָּׁה כְשֵׁרָה לָהּ, — *Any testimony for which a woman is ineligible,*

The ineligibility of women as witnesses is derived in *Shevuos* 30a from *Deuteronomy* 19:17: וְעָמְדוּ שְׁנֵי הָאֲנָשִׁים, *and the two* **men** *shall stand.*

[While this verse seemingly speaks only of the litigants, and not the witnesses, the Talmudic exegesis refers it to witnesses.]

אַף הֵן אֵינָן כְּשֵׁרִים לָהּ. — *they too are ineligible for it.*

The inference is that whenever a women *is* eligible to testify, Rabbinically disqualified witness, too, are eligible. For example, a woman is eligible to testify that a man has died, thereby enabling his wife to remarry (see *Yevamos* 15:4). Another instance is the case of a woman who is suspected of adultery, in which case she must go through the procedure described in *Numbers* 5:11-31. If a single witness testifies that she committed adultery, the procedure is not performed. Such a witness may be a woman.

The testimony is not sufficient, however, to have the adulteress executed. Punishment can be administered only on the basis of testimony by two male witnesses who meet all eligibility requirements.

In both the above cases, the testimony of any of the disqualified witnesses mentioned in our mishnah is also acceptable. On the other hand, people who are considered sinners under Torah law are ineligible even in these cases (*Rav*).

9.

[The Mishnah continues to describe the circumstances whereby the Sabbath may be desecrated in order to testify about the new moon. Mishnah 4 stated that the Sabbath may be desecrated for *Kiddush HaChodesh.* Mishnah 5 added that desecration is permissible even when the new moon is clearly visible. Mishnah 6 extended this to include all witnesses who saw the new moon, and mishnah 7 included even relatives who cannot testify as a pair. Our mishnah goes even further by stating that the sick and the lame must also come, even though this requires Sabbath desecration even by non-witnesses who must accompany and aid the witness (see *Rambam, K.H.* 3:4).]

[ט] **מִי** שֶׁרָאָה אֶת־הַחֹדֶשׁ וְאֵינוֹ יָכוֹל לְהַלֵּךְ,
מוֹלִיכִין אוֹתוֹ עַל־הַחֲמוֹר, אֲפִילוּ
בְּמִטָּה. וְאִם צוֹדֶה לָהֶם, לוֹקְחִין בְּיָדָם מַקְלוֹת;
וְאִם הָיְתָה דֶרֶךְ רְחוֹקָה, לוֹקְחִין בְּיָדָם מְזוֹנוֹת.
שֶׁעַל־מַהֲלַךְ לַיְלָה וָיוֹם מְחַלְּלִין אֶת־הַשַּׁבָּת
וְיוֹצְאִין לְעֵדוּת הַחֹדֶשׁ, שֶׁנֶּאֱמַר: ,,אֵלֶּה מוֹעֲדֵי
ה'...אֲשֶׁר־תִּקְרְאוּ אֹתָם בְּמוֹעֲדָם''.

יד אברהם

מִי שֶׁרָאָה אֶת־הַחֹדֶשׁ וְאֵינוֹ יָכוֹל לְהַלֵּךְ — *If a person saw the new moon but cannot walk,*

Because he is weak or ill (*Kehati*).

If he is able to walk he must do so, for the prohibition against walking beyond the תְחוּם, *boundary* (see mishnah 5, s.v. בין שנראה) is less stringent than the prohibition of riding an animal on the Sabbath (*Tiferes Yisrael*).

מוֹלִיכִין אוֹתוֹ עַל־הַחֲמוֹר — *they may bring* [lit. *lead*] *him on a donkey,*

Even on the Sabbath (*Rashi*).

[The Sages forbade riding an animal on the Sabbath (see *Beitzah* 5:2) for one may forget it is the Sabbath and break a branch off a tree to aid in guiding the animal. Additionally, if the donkey belonged to the rider or to one of the people leading it, there would also be a Biblical prohibition of מְחַמֵּר, *leading one's loaded animal* (see *Rambam, Hilchos Shabbos* 20:1). Since Sabbath desecration for *Kiddush HaChodesh* is permitted only when necessary, it would seem preferable not to use an animal belonging to one of the travelers. Cf. *Meiri*.]

אֲפִילוּ בְּמִטָּה — [*and*] *even on a bed.*

If he is too ill to ride, he may be carried — even in a רְשׁוּת הָרַבִּים, *public domain* — on a bed (*Meiri*).

[This involves an even greater Sabbath desecration, for carrying in a public domain is one of the thirty-nine forbidden labors, for which a transgression is punishable by סְקִילָה, *stoning*.]

Although *Shabbos* 10:5 states that carrying a living person on a bed on the Sabbath is only a Rabbinic prohibition, this is true only for a person who can walk on his own (because חַי נוֹשֵׂא אֶת עַצְמוֹ, *a living person aids in his own carriage*, and the bed is subordinate to the person, thus absolving the carrier of the Torah-prohibition of carrying). But in a case such as ours in which the person being carried is helpless, to carry him is a מְלָאכָה דְאוֹרַיְתָא, *Torah-forbidden act of labor* (*Tosefos Yom Tov*).

וְאִם צוֹדֶה לָהֶם — [*And*] *If an ambush awaits them,*

It was common for the Sadducees and the Samaritans to lie in wait and ambush the witnesses to prevent their arrival at the *beis din* and to keep Rosh Chodesh from being declared on the proper day, as will be seen in the next chapter (*Rashi; Meiri*).

לוֹקְחִין בְּיָדָם מַקְלוֹת — *they may arm themselves with sticks* [lit. *take sticks in their hands*];

Or any other weapons (*Meiri*) [in order to fight off their ambushers].

Kol HaRemez infers from the use of the word בְּיָדָם, lit. *in their hands*, that they need not wear the weapons on their body — which would presumably be permissible since they would be like garments — but may carry them in their hands.

[This inference poses a difficulty. In *Shabbos* 6:4, the Sages and R' Eliezer disagree whether a man may wear weapons on the Sabbath in a public do-

9. If a person saw the new moon but cannot walk, they may bring him on a donkey, [and] even on a bed. [And] if an ambush awaits them, they may arm themselves with sticks; and if it was a distant journey, they may take food in their hands, since for a journey of a night and a day they may desecrate the Sabbath and go forth to render testimony about the new moon, as it is said *(Leviticus 23:4): These are the appointed times of HASHEM ... which you shall declare in their fixed time.*

YAD AVRAHAM

main. The ruling favors the view of the Sages that wearing the weapons is equivalent to carrying them. There is no difference, therefore, whether the weapons are worn or carried in one's hands (see *Magen Avraham, Orach Chaim* 301:10). Accordingly, the use of the word בְּיָדָם, *in their hands*, would be understood as nothing more than the mishnaic idiom, similar to its use in the next phrase of our mishnah.]

וְאִם הָיְתָה דֶרֶךְ רְחוֹקָה, לוֹקְחִין בְּיָדָם מְזוֹנוֹת. — *and if it was a distant journey, they may take food in their hands,*
And carry it with them on the Sabbath (*Meiri*).

[A question presents itself at this point. Since the mishnah has already informed us that carrying the witness on the bed is permitted on the Sabbath, even though desecration of the Sabbath is involved, why is it necessary to state that carrying weapons and food is permissible?

The likely explanation is that, while an ill witness is an *unavoidable* Sabbath desecration since there is no other way to get the witness to *beis din*, the carrying of weapons would seem unnecessary as the ambush could be fought off with bare hands or avoided or may not materialize. Carrying food would seem to be a luxury since the people would surely not starve to death by not eating even as long as a night and a day. Our mishnah tells us that both weapons and

food may be carried for if they were forbidden, the people might refrain from coming at all, similar to the law of mishnah 6.]

שֶׁעַל־מַהֲלַךְ לַיְלָה וָיוֹם — *since for a journey of a night and day*
The mishnah mentions the length of the journey to make clear why it would be important to take food (*Kol HaRemez*).

מְחַלְלִין אֶת־הַשַּׁבָּת וְיוֹצְאִין לְעֵדוּת הַחֹדֶשׁ, *they may desecrate the Sabbath and go forth to render testimony about the new moon,*
Aruch HaShulchan HeAsid (Kiddush HaChodesh 91:1) points out that the journey cannot be a *complete* night and day, but must be slightly less, because otherwise they would not arrive in time for their testimony to be of any value.

But if they saw the new moon at a place which is more than a night and day's journey to the *beis din*, they may not desecrate the Sabbath if they cannot arrive before the end of the thirtieth day. By then, either the month will have been sanctified thanks to other witnesses, or Rosh Chodesh will have been automatically deferred to the thirty-first day (*Meiri; Tosefos Yom Tov*).

שֶׁנֶּאֱמַר: ,,אֵלֶּה מוֹעֲדֵי ה'...אֲשֶׁר־תִּקְרְאוּ אֹתָם בְּמוֹעֲדָם.'' — *as it is said (Leviticus 23:4): These are the appointed times of HASHEM...which you shall declare (them) in their fixed time.*

ראש השנה ב/א

[א] **אִם** אֵינָן מַכִּירִין אוֹתוֹ, מְשַׁלְּחִין אַחֵר עִמּוֹ לְהַעִידוֹ.

יד אברהם

According to *Meiri*, this verse is cited to explain why the witnesses' arrival after the thirtieth day is useless (in which case the Sabbath may not be desecrated). The verse states that *you* shall declare, meaning that by the *beis din's* declaration that determines Rosh Chodesh — not the sighting of the witnesses. Therefore, even if they sighted the new moon on the thirtieth, Rosh Chodesh is still on the thirty-first since they did not arrive in time for the *beis din* to declare Rosh Chodesh on the thirtieth.

Most commentators, however, explain that the verse is brought as a source for permitting Sabbath desecration, in order to declare Rosh Chodesh and hence, the holy days, *in their time* (*Rambam; Rav*); see *comm.* to mishnah 4.

Aruch LaNer points out that this verse permitting Sabbath desecration is brought here and not in mishnah 4, because it was only here that the mishnah mentioned desecrating the Sabbath by *carrying*, which is a Torah prohibition, and hence requires a Torah dispensation. The earlier *mishnayos*, however, spoke only of Rabbinical prohibitions (i.e., walking outside the תְּחוּם, *boundary*).

Chapter 2

1.

The first chapter of our tractate discussed in detail the circumstances of the witnesses coming to the *beis din*. In this chapter the Mishnah goes on to discuss their arrival and the procedures followed by the *beis din*.

אִם אֵינָן מַכִּירִין אוֹתוֹ, — *If they* [the beis din] *do not know him* [i.e., the witnesses],

If the *beis din* that is to decide on *Kiddush HaChodesh* does not personally know the trustworthiness of the man who claims to have seen the new moon … (*Rashi*).

The *Gemara* (22b) explains that the use of the singular אוֹתוֹ, *him*, is not meant to imply that only one witness is sufficient for *Kiddush HaChodesh*. Rather it should be translated as *it*, referring to the collective noun הַזּוּג, *the pair* [of witnesses]. Most commentators, however, translate אוֹתוֹ as *him*, meaning that each member of the pair must be known to *beis din*, a rule with which the *Gemara* certainly agrees (see *Tosafos* 22b).

[This mishnah, which rightfully belongs in this chapter as it deals with the *beis din's* verification of witnesses, is also a continuation of the subject of the previous chapter (the witnesses coming to the *beis din*), since it goes on to say that character witnesses who are sent with the pair may also desecrate the Sabbath for this purpose.]

מְשַׁלְּחִין אַחֵר עִמּוֹ לְהַעִידוֹ. — *they* [i.e., the local *beis din*] *send another* [*pair of witnesses*] *with him to testify about him.*

The local *beis din*, whose members know him to be trustworthy, send along another pair of witnesses, known personally to the *beis din* in Jerusalem (*Tiferes Yisrael*), to testify to the trustworthiness of the witness who saw the new moon.

There was a *beis din* in practically every city and town in *Eretz Yisrael* as can be seen from *Mishnah Sanhedrin* 1:6. *Rambam* (*Kiddush HaChodesh* 2:3), however, makes no mention of a *beis din* in this connection but simply states that the townspeople would send along character witnesses.

Yerushalmi's view is that one person is sufficient to vouch for the witness

1. **I**f they [the *beis din*] do not know him, they send another [pair of witnesses] with him to testify about him.

who saw the new moon since need for a character witness is only a Rabbinic enactment; in the absence of evidence to the contrary, a witness is presumed to be qualified without outside corroboration. The halachah as always follows the view of the *Bavli* which requires two witnesses (see *Rambam, Kiddush Ha-Chodesh* 2:3).

These witnesses too were permitted to desecrate the Sabbath (*Gemara 22b*).

Since Torah law does not require these witnesses, why are they permitted to desecrate the Sabbath to comply with a Rabbinic enactment?

The Sages surely had the authority to enact a law under which witnesses not personally known to the *beis din* are not accepted (just as they had the authority to reject the testimony of witnesses whose sole ineligibility is Rabbinic as mentioned in footnote 1:8. The absence of character witnesses therefore could then result in Rosh Chodesh not being declared on the proper day. Thus, their desecration of the Sabbath is necessary to comply with the Torah law of בְּמוֹעֲדָם, *in their time.*]

The *Gemara* (22b) further states that even if only one man can be found to vouch for the witness, he may desecrate the Sabbath to accompany him on the chance that he will meet another Jew in Jerusalem who can vouch for the witness.[1]

◆§ Heretics Tamper With Rosh Chodesh

The *heretics* mentioned in our mishnah are the בַּיתוֹסִים, *Boethusians* (a branch of the heretical sect of the צְדוֹקִים, *Sadducees*) who once attempted to mislead the *beis din* by hiring false witnesses to testify that they had seen the new moon (*Gemara* 22b).

The Boethusians, like the Sadducees, rejected the validity of the Oral Law.

1. The commentator to *Ramham (Kiddush HaChodesh* 3:3) raises a question that is discussed by almost all the authorities who deal with this subject.

The Torah commands that if a boy is born on the Sabbath his circumcision must take place on the next Sabbath, even though this involves desecration of the Sabbath. If however, he was born late Friday afternoon, after sunset but before nightfall, when a halachic doubt exists whether the Sabbath has begun or not, his circumcision must be put off until Sunday (see *Mishnah, Shabbos* 19:5). Clearly, although Sabbath desecration is permitted for the sake of *milah* [*circumcision*], it is not permitted when a doubt exists on the need for that desecration.

Why then, is a single character witness permitted to desecrate the Sabbath when it is certainly likely that a second witness will not be found?

[Many authorities similarly question all the cases in the previous chapter where Sabbath desecration is permitted even when there is only a slight chance that it may be necessary (e.g. when the moon was seen clearly, when there are numerous witnesses, etc.)].

Responsa Be'er Yitzchak (*Even HaEzer* 1) explains that the very fact that the Torah permits Sabbath desecration for the sake of *Kiddush HaChodesh* is proof that this *mitzvah* overrides the Sabbath *even* in cases of uncertainty, because there can *never* be a case in which we are absolutely certain that the witnesses' desecrating the Sabbath is absolutely necessary. Even under the best of circumstances — only two witnesses saw the new moon, their eligibility is beyond doubt, and they are known to the sanctifying *beis din* — the possibility still exists that the testimony of either will be rejected because of discrepancies arising during interrogation, thereby making his coming useless. Consequently, by requiring witnesses to come on the Sabbath, the Torah is clearly allowing desecration even when its necessity is in doubt.

Other explanations are given by, among others, *Lechem Mishneh, Tosefos Yom Tov, Kol HaRemez, Beis David, Kol Sofer, Sfas Emes, Aruch HaShulchan HeAsid.*

בָּרִאשׁוֹנָה הָיוּ מְקַבְּלִין עֵדוּת הַחֹדֶשׁ מִכָּל־ רֹאשׁ
אָדָם; מִשֶּׁקִּלְקְלוּ הַמִּינִין, הִתְקִינוּ שֶׁלֹּא יְהוּ הַשָּׁנָה
מְקַבְּלִין אֶלָּא מִן־הַמַּכִּירִים. ב/ב

[ב] **בָּרִאשׁוֹנָה** הָיוּ מַשִּׂיאִין מַשּׂוּאוֹת;
מִשֶּׁקִּלְקְלוּ הַכּוּתִים,
הִתְקִינוּ שֶׁיְּהוּ שְׁלוּחִין יוֹצְאִין.

Generally, they accepted only a literal interpretation of the Torah. One major exam-ple of the many resultant halachic disputes revolved around the timing of the *Omer* offering. The Torah commands that the offering be brought מִמָּחֳרַת הַשַּׁבָּת, literally *the day after the Sabbath*. Tradition teaches that the offering is brought on the se-cond day of Pesach; in this context 'Sabbath' is interpreted as *'festival.'* The Boethusians rejected this tradition and insisted that the *Omer* must be brought on the first Sunday after the beginning of Pesach — *the day after the [Sabbath]*. A further result of their heresy would be that Shavuos (the fiftieth day from the *Omer*) would always fall on a Sunday in their calendar. (See *Leviticus* 23:11, 15, 16 and *Menachos* 65a).

One year the Boethusians attempted to deceive the *beis din*. The thirtieth of Adar was a Sabbath and the new moon had not been sighted. The Boethusians hired witnesses to testify that they had seen it, thus making that Sabbath day Rosh Chodesh Nissan, as a result of which the sixteenth of Nissan — the day when obser-vant Jews bring the *Omer* offering — would fall on a Sunday and consequently, so would Shavuos *(Rashi)*.

Their ruse was discovered, as mentioned in the *Gemara* (22b), so no actual damage was caused, but the attempt was sufficient for the Sages to enact the rule stated in our mishnah.

בָּרִאשׁוֹנָה הָיוּ מְקַבְּלִין עֵדוּת הַחֹדֶשׁ מִכָּל־ אָדָם; — *Originally they accepted testimony about the new moon from anyone,*

In earlier times, testimony about the new moon was accepted from every man whether the *beis din* knew him or not, in keeping with the rule that every Jew is assumed to be trustworthy and כָּשֵׁר לְעֵדוּת, *eligible to testify*, unless proven otherwise. The mishnah will now tell us the reason for the unusual requirement that the *beis din* must know the witnesses personally or be as-sured of their trustworthiness by the

testimony of others (*Yerushalmi*; see *Lechem Mishneh* to *Rambam, Kiddush HaChodesh* 2:2; *Yesodei haTorah* 7:7).

מִשֶּׁקִּלְקְלוּ הַמִּינִין, — *[but] after the heretics* [i.e., Boethusians] *did harm,*

As explained above, the Boethusian attempt to mislead the *beis din* was un-successful, but their near success was sufficient basis for the requirement that witnesses must henceforth be known to the *beis din*.[1]

[The mishnah text used by the *Gemara* has the term בַּיְתוֹסִים, *Boethusians*, instead of מִינִין, *heretics*. The correct version in our case is clearly בַּיְתוֹסִים for only they were in-

1. *Tosafos* raises a question: Had the Boethusians attained their goal of setting Rosh Chodesh Nissan a day sooner, would the Pesach sacrifice have been brought on the wrong day, a day too early?

Tosafos answers that this would not be a wrong day, for even if the *beis din* erred and declared Rosh Chodesh on the wrong day, their declaration stands, as stated in the *Gemara* 25a (and will be discussed in mishnah 9): אֲשֶׁר תִּקְרְאוּ אוֹתָם בְּמוֹעֲדָם, *which you will declare in*

2
2

Originally they accepted testimony about the new moon from anyone, [but] after the heretics did harm, they [the Sages] enacted that they [the *beis din*] should not accept [testimony] except from known people.

2. Originally they used to light torches; [but] after the Cutheans did harm, they enacted that messengers should go forth.

YAD AVRAHAM

terested in misleading the *beis din*, for the reason explained above. The term מִינִין or מִינִים was originally used for the early Jewish-Christian sect of heretics. Due to medieval censorship of the Talmud and other Jewish works, considerable confusion exists wherever a heretical sect is mentioned. This also holds true, in many cases, whenever the term *non-Jews* is mentioned. Because of the whims of individual censors the following terms (when not altogether omitted) are used interchangeably: נוֹצְרִי, מְשׁוּמָּד, מוּמָר, עוֹבֵד כּוֹכָבִים וּמַזָּלוֹת=עכו״ם, נָכְרִי, גּוֹי, כּוּתִי, בֵּיתוֹסִי, צְדוֹקִי, אַפִּיקוֹרוֹס, מִין, עוֹבֵד גִּילוּלִים and many more. Some modern editions of the Talmud have attempted to correct the texts but it is doubtful whether the confusion caused by the censors will ever be cleared up completely.]

הִתְקִינוּ שֶׁלֹּא יְהוּ מְקַבְּלִין אֶלָּא מִן־הַמַּכִּירִים. — *they [the Sages] enacted that they [the beis din] should not accept [testimony]*

except from known people.

[The general rule that a man is considered trustworthy unless proven otherwise was reversed by the Sages for New Moon testimony only.]

The *Yerushalmi* asks: Let this ruling apply only to Nissan but not to other months since the Boethusians had nothing to gain by misleading the *beis din* on other months. The *Yerushalmi* answers that the ruling was for *all* months to ensure that it would be observed for Nissan in which the ruling was essential.

Aruch LaNer suggests that the Boethusians were suspected of misleading the *beis din* on all months out of spite even where they gained nothing by their deception. (This answer supports *Doros HaRishonim's* thesis about the Boethusians, see above, footnote).

2.

בָּרִאשׁוֹנָה — *Originally*

[I.e., before the conspiracy described below.]

[This mishnah is out of chronological sequence, since it discusses methods of publicizing the declaration of Rosh Chodesh before the procedure for such declarations has been set forth. The mishnah is placed here because it is similar to mishnah 1 in that both deal with new rulings necessitated by the conspiracies of heretical sects.]

הָיוּ מַשִּׂיאִין מַשּׂוּאוֹת; — *they used to light torches;*

When the *beis din* accepted testimony on the thirtieth day, torches were lit the following evening (as described in the next two *mishnayos*) to notify the people that the previous month was חָסֵר, *deficient* [i.e., it contained only twenty-nine days, not thirty] and that the new month had begun on the thirtieth. (If the thirtieth day was a Friday, and

their appointed time — even if declared in error, even deliberately, the declaration of Rosh Chodesh remains valid.

This answer, however, raises a problem. If the Boethusians did not accept the validity of the Oral Law, then how could they rely on the above rule which is a product of Rabbinic exegesis — the Oral Law — and is certainly not a result of literal interpretation of the Torah?

R' Y.I. Halevy (Rabinowitz) adduces this as one of many proofs to his view that, contrary to

[ג] **כֵּיצַד** הָיוּ מַשִׂיאִין מַשׂוּאוֹת? מְבִיאִין
כְּלֻנְסָאוֹת שֶׁל אֶרֶז אֲרֻכִּין, וְקָנִים
וַעֲצֵי שֶׁמֶן וּנְעֹרֶת שֶׁל פִּשְׁתָּן. וְכוֹרֵךְ בִּמְשִׁיחָה,
וְעוֹלֶה לְרֹאשׁ הָהָר, וּמַצִּית בָּהֶן אֶת־הָאוֹר

יד אברהם

torches could not be lit at night because of the Sabbath, they lit the torches the next night). But if Rosh Chodesh was the thirty-first day, no torches were lit at all. In this way, the people in the Diaspora would know the exact day of Rosh Chodesh within a day or two after it began (*Gemara* 23a).

מִשֶּׁקִלְקְלוּ הַכּוּתִים, — [but] after the Cutheans did harm,

Who on one occasion lit torches on the night of the thirty-first even though the *beis din* had not yet declared Rosh Chodesh, and thereby misled the people of the diaspora into starting the new month a day early (*Rashi; Rav*).

[*Meiri* contends that this occurred on Rosh Hashanah. While he cites no source, it is reasonable that the Cutheans, desiring to cause as much damage as possible, would choose Rosh Hashanah to mislead the Jews. On the other months the *beis din* could have sent messengers immediately to inform the people not to rely on the torches, thereby minimizing the damage (as only those not reached by the messengers before the holidays would be misled). On Rosh Hashanah however, the entire population of the Holy Land as well as the diaspora were misled into observing the festival as soon as they sighted the torches.]

[The origin of the כותים, Cutheans, in *Eretz Yisrael* is mentioned in *II Kings* 17:24-

41. The non-Jewish citizens of Cutha were brought by the King of Assyria to settle the Samarian cities left desolate by the exile of the Ten Tribes. Although they converted to Judaism, there was considerable dispute as to the validity of their conversion (see *Kiddushin* 75b). Whatever their status, they remained a sect unto themselves — known as Samaritans because they lived in Samaria — and exhibited great animosity toward the Jews (see *Ezra* 4 for a description of their effort to prevent the construction of the Second Temple and see *Yoma* 69a for their attempt to have the Temple destroyed). It is not surprising, therefore, that they would mislead the Jews out of sheer spitefulness.]

הִתְקִינוּ שֶׁיְהוּ שְׁלוּחִין יוֹצְאִין. — they enacted that messengers should go forth.

To notify the populace of the day of Rosh Chodesh as mentioned above in 1:3.

Meiri adds that the messengers had to take along a letter from the *beis din*.

[*Meiri* does not explain the purpose of the letter, but it was obviously to ensure that the messengers were not Samaritans. From the *Gemara* 22b (which *Meiri* himself quotes earlier) however, it is clear that no such letter was needed. *Meiri* apparently assumes that only messengers who went to Syria in the period before the Samaritans required no documentation. After the Samaritans began to mislead the people, however, messengers took along a letter to confirm their reliability.

popular opinion, the Sadduccees and the Boethsians did not adhere to a philosophy of accepting the written Torah, but to one rejecting the Oral Law. The truth is they simply did not believe in the Torah at all, following the view of the Hellenists whose descendants they were. But they could not publicly reject all the commandments, as this would incur the wrath of the vast majority of the Jews among whom they had to live. In order to get by with minimal observance, they gave their disbelief a semblance of philosophical validity by claiming to adhere to the literal interpretation of the Torah which they claimed was distorted by the Sages who had "invented" the Oral Law. Accordingly, a celebration of Pesach on the wrong date was meaningless to people who would have done away with Pesach altogether had they been able to (see at length in *Doros HaRishonim*, part II, pp. 418-422).

3. How did they light the torches?

They would bring long poles of cedar-wood, reeds, balsam-wood, and fiber-chips of flax. Someone would tie them together with rope, climb to the mountaintop, set fire to them and wave [the

YAD AVRAHAM

Yerushalmi states that the practice of sending messengers was enacted by *Rabbi* (i.e., R' Yehudah HaNassi). This view is apparently contradicted by mishnah 1:3 which mentions that messengers went forth even during the time of the Temple, which had been destroyed before R' Yehudah HaNassi was born.

Meiri quotes *Raavad* who states that torches were used only to notify the Jews of Babylonia as to the proper day of Rosh Chodesh, while Jews living in Syria and other places were always notified by messengers, even before Rabbi's ruling. Mishnah

1:3 is therefore referring to the messengers who went to Syria, while our mishnah speaks of Babylonia where messengers were not sent until Rabbi abolished the use of torches.

Others explain that it was Rabban Gamliel the Elder (who lived at the time of the Temple) who abolished the use of torches. *Yerushalmi* uses the term Rabbi to refer to him, as it does elsewhere when referring to other nesi'im [heads of the Sanhedrin] besides R' Yehudah HaNassi. (*Sha'arei Toras Eretz Yisrael; Sefer Hazikaron-Doros Harishonim* p.133).]

3.

בֵּיצַד הָיוּ מַשִּׂיאִין מַשּׂוּאוֹת? — *How did they light the torches?*

[Our mishnah and the following one describe in great detail the making of the signals which were used to notify distant places of the Rosh Chodesh proclamation. Although the use of torches was abolished by Rabbinic enactment and this method had no practical halachic value, the mishnah deemed it necessary to describe the procedure since it could conceivably be adopted again. The torch method was a far quicker and more effective method of notifying vast multitudes than the dispatching of messengers, who could not reach all the people in time. Only the fear of another Samaritan conspiracy forced the *beis din* to dispense with the better method and send messengers instead. If, however, the problem of the Samaritans could be solved, the original method might be reinstituted (see *Beitzah* 4b where this is clearly stated).

Rav, (based on *Rashi*), however, says in his commentary to the previous mishnah that at first they lit torches and they did not have to hire messengers to send to the Diaspora to notify them. This implies that torches were

simply more convenient than hiring messengers, when in reality the halachically preferred method was the use of *torches*, as indicated by *Beitzah* 4b mentioned above.]

מְבִיאִין כְּלֻנְסָאוֹת שֶׁל אֶרֶז אֲרֻכִּין, — *They would bring long poles of cedarwood,*

The poles were long, so that they could be seen from afar *(Rav)*, and of cedar, a hardwood that is not consumed quickly, so that they would burn for a long time *(Tiferes Yisrael)*.

וְקָנִים וַעֲצֵי שֶׁמֶן וּנְעֹרֶת שֶׁל פִּשְׁתָּן. — *reeds, balsam-wood, fiber-chips of flax.*

These materials make the flame larger *(Rav)*.

[The *Gemara* (23a) comments that the term עֲצֵי שֶׁמֶן can be used for אַפַּרְסְמוֹן balsam-wood. *Tosafos* (s.v. עץ) points out that it sometimes means olive-wood. [In our mishnah, therefore, the reference can be to either balsam or olive wood.] Cf. *Kehati*.

וְכוֹרֵךְ בִּמְשִׁיחָה, — *Someone would tie them together with rope,*

Around the top of the pole *(Kehati)*.

וְעוֹלֶה לְרֹאשׁ הָהָר, וּמַצִּית בָּהֶן אֶת־הָאוּר,

וּמוֹלִיךְ וּמֵבִיא וּמַעֲלֶה וּמוֹרִיד, — *climb to*

וּמוֹלִיךְ וּמֵבִיא וּמַעֲלֶה וּמוֹרִיד עַד שֶׁהוּא רוֹאֶה
אֶת־חֲבֵרוֹ, שֶׁהוּא עוֹשֶׂה כֵן בְּרֹאשׁ הָהָר הַשֵּׁנִי;
וְכֵן בְּרֹאשׁ הָהָר הַשְּׁלִישִׁי.

[ד] **וּמֵאַיִן** הָיוּ מַשִּׂיאִין מַשּׂוּאוֹת? מֵהַר
הַמִּשְׁחָה לְסַרְטְבָא, וּמִסַּרְטְבָא
לִגְרוֹפִינָא, וּמִגְּרוֹפִינָא לְחַוְרָן, וּמֵחַוְרָן לְבֵית
בַּלְתִּין. וּמִבֵּית בַּלְתִּין לֹא זָזוּ מִשָּׁם, אֶלָּא מוֹלִיךְ
וּמֵבִיא וּמַעֲלֶה וּמוֹרִיד עַד שֶׁהָיָה רוֹאֶה כָל־
הַגּוֹלָה לְפָנָיו כִּמְדוּרַת הָאֵשׁ.

יד אברהם

the mountaintop, set fire to them and wave [the torch] back and forth, up and down,

This was necessary so that observers should not mistake it for a falling star which can move either vertically or horizontally but not both ways (Yerushalmi; Tosefos Yom Tov).

עַד שֶׁהוּא רוֹאֶה אֶת חֲבֵרוֹ, שֶׁהוּא עוֹשֶׂה כֵן בְּרֹאשׁ הָהָר הַשֵּׁנִי; וְכֵן בְּרֹאשׁ הָהָר הַשְּׁלִישִׁי. — until he saw his colleague doing likewise on top of the second mountain; and so, too, on top of the third mountain.

[Whereupon he could extinguish his torch.]

4.

וּמֵאַיִן הָיוּ מַשִּׂיאִין מַשּׂוּאוֹת? — And from where did they light the torches?

Upon which mountains were the torches lit? (Rashi; cf. Tosefos Yom Tov).

מֵהַר הַמִּשְׁחָה לְסַרְטְבָא, — From the Mount of Olives to Sarteva,

They began at the Mount of Olives which is right outside Jerusalem; from there they signaled to Sarteva (Rashi).

[That the first torch was lit on the Mount of Olives clearly indicates that the beis din which declared Rosh Chodesh was located in Jerusalem. This, however, was only true while the Tem-

ple was in existence. After the Destruction, the Sanhedrin was forced to move from place to place until, in the time of R' Yehudah HaNassi, it was located in Beis Shearim, then Tzipori, and finally in Tiberias (see Rashi to 31b) — all in the Galilee. Of course, it would be impossible for a beis din in Galilee, the far north, to arrange for torches to be lit first in Jerusalem.[1] This lends support to the view (mentioned in comm. to 2:2) that the torches were abolished by Rabban Gamliel the Elder who flourished some fifty years before the Temple's destruction. According to the view (cited there) that torches were still in use

1. [Tosafos (Rosh Hashanah 25a) holds, however, that in the days of R' Yehudah HaNassi, the court which decided on Kiddush HaChodesh sat in Ein Tav. While some scholars claim that Ein Tav was in Judea (e.g. Doros Harishonim part II p. 66), others place it in the Galilee (Ya'abetz, Toledos Yisrael, vol. 6, p.208). Even if we assume it to have been in Judea (Shaarei Toras Eretz Yisrael to Yerushalmi Sanhedrin 1:1 maintains that Ein Tav was in the vicinity of Lod, which though in Judea, is a day's journey from Jerusalem) it was still quite far from Jerusalem and the Mount of Olives.]

torch] back and forth, up and down , until he saw his colleague doing likewise on top of the second mountain; and so, too, on top of the third mountain.

4. **A**nd from where did they light the torches? From the Mount of Olives to Sarteva, from Sarteva to Grofina, from Grofina to Chavran, from Chavran to Beis Biltin. From Beis Biltin they did not move but [the signaler] would wave [the torch] back and forth, up and down until he saw the entire Diaspora before him as a mass of fire.

YAD AVRAHAM

in R' Yehudah HaNassi's day, our mishnah is difficult. Possibly though, our mishnah describes the original procedure, even though other mountains were used in later times. This would be in keeping with the comm. to the previous mishnah that the detailed description of the torch method in the mishnah was retained in the hope that one day it would be reinstated. This hope included not only the resolution of the problem with the Samaritans, but also the restoration of the Sanhedrin to Jerusalem.]

וּמִסַּרְטְבָא לִגְרוֹפִינָא, וּמִגְּרוֹפִינָא לְחַוְרָן, וּמֵחַוְרָן לְבֵית בִּלְתִּין. — *from Sarteva to Grofina, from Grofina to Chavran, from Chavran to Beis Biltin.*

The *Gemara* states that torches were lit also on other mountains between those mentioned above.

[Our mishnah probably lists only the major mountains that delineate the general route along which the torches were lit. The exact location of the mountains in our mishnah is the subject of a controversy among scholars (see *Kehati; R' Yitzchak Goldhar, Admas Kodesh; Atlas Carta Litekufas HaBayis*

haSheni Hamishnah VeHatalmud). In general, these mountains run in a northeasterly direction from Jerusalem toward Babylonia.]

וּמִבֵּית בִּלְתִּין לֹא זָזוּ מִשָּׁם, אֶלָּא מוֹלִיךְ וּמֵבִיא וּמַעֲלֶה וּמוֹרִיד עַד שֶׁהָיָה רוֹאֶה כָל-הַגּוֹלָה לְפָנָיו כִּמְדוּרַת הָאֵשׁ. — *From Beis Biltin they did not move but [the signaler] would wave [the torch] back and forth, up and down, until he saw the entire Diaspora before him like a mass of fire.*

Beis Biltin was located in *Eretz Yisrael* on the boundary closest to Babylonia *(Meiri),* and there the signaler would stay until each person in Pumbedisa [a border city in Babylonia *(Aruch LaNer)*] would go up to his roof and light a torch[1] *(Gemara)* making the entire city appear like a mass of fire, thereby informing the signaler at Beis Biltin that his signal had been received *(Kehati).* The message would then be relayed by torches throughout Babylonia *(Meiri).*

Aruch LaNer explains that the *Gemara's* explains *Diaspora* as referring to Pumbedisa — only one city — because the signaler could not possibly see the entire Diaspora from Beis Biltin.

1. [Pumbedisa was on the Euphrates River in whose vicinity there are no mountains from which to signal Beis Biltin that the message was received. The lighting of many torches ensured that they were seen.]

[ה] **חָצֵר** גְּדוֹלָה הָיְתָה בִירוּשָׁלַיִם, וּבֵית
יַעְזֵק הָיְתָה נִקְרֵאת, וּלְשָׁם כָּל־
הָעֵדִים מִתְכַּנְּסִים, וּבֵית דִּין בּוֹדְקִין אוֹתָם שָׁם.
וּסְעוּדוֹת גְּדוֹלוֹת עוֹשִׂין לָהֶם בִּשְׁבִיל שֶׁיִּהוּ
רְגִילִין לָבֹא.
בָּרִאשׁוֹנָה לֹא הָיוּ זָזִין מִשָּׁם כָּל־הַיּוֹם;
הִתְקִין רַבָּן גַּמְלִיאֵל הַזָּקֵן שֶׁיִּהוּ מְהַלְּכִין
אַלְפַּיִם אַמָּה לְכָל־רוּחַ.

יד אברהם

5.

**חָצֵר גְּדוֹלָה הָיְתָה בִירוּשָׁלַיִם, וּבֵית יַעְזֵק
הָיְתָה נִקְרֵאת,** — *There was a large courtyard in Jerusalem which was called Beis
Ya'azek,*

[The mishnah now returns to the
topic of our chapter, which is the recep-
tion of the witnesses by the *beis din*.]

וּלְשָׁם כָּל־הָעֵדִים מִתְכַּנְּסִים, — *and there all
the witnesses* [to the sighting of the new
moon] *gathered,*

According to *Rashi*, the witnesses
gathered in this courtyard only if they
arrived on the Sabbath (in which case
they were not permitted to roam the city
as stated further in the mishnah).

Rambam (*Kiddush HaChodesh* 2:7)
and *Meiri*, however, appear to hold that
they always gathered in Beis Ya'azek, to
facilitate the *beis din's* interrogation.

[Our mishnah's use of the words
כָּל־הָעֵדִים, *all the witnesses*, refers to the
fact that often there were numerous
witnesses to the sighting of the new
moon (see mishnah 1:6) and all were required to come and testify.]

וּבֵית דִּין בּוֹדְקִין אוֹתָם שָׁם, — *and the beis
din interrogated them there,*

The next mishnah describes the
precedure of interrogation.

Sifsei Chachamim points out that in
later years when the Sanhedrin no
longer sat in Jerusalem, the interrogation
did not necessarily take place in the
general gathering place. This can be

seen from mishnah 8 where Rabban
Gamliel (who as *nassi* lived in Yavneh
and Usha) interrogated witnesses in his
own home.

**וּסְעוּדוֹת גְּדוֹלוֹת עוֹשִׂין לָהֶם בִּשְׁבִיל שֶׁיִּהוּ
רְגִילִין לָבֹא.** — *and made them large
feasts in order that they be accustomed
to come.*

[The Sages feared that the witnesses,
seeing so many others there, might feel
they had come for nothing and refrain
from going to the trouble in the future.
Furthermore, they would be discomfited
by having to remain there all day (*Rashi*
23b s.v. סעודות). Therefore, feasts were
arranged to make the witnesses feel
appreciated.]

בָּרִאשׁוֹנָה לֹא הָיוּ זָזִין מִשָּׁם כָּל הַיּוֹם; —
*Originally they did not move from there
all day;*

If witnesses arrived on the Sabbath
from beyond the תְּחוּם, *boundary* (i.e.,
two thousand cubits outside the city)
beyond which it was forbidden to walk
on the Sabbath, they were not permitted
to leave the courtyard until after the
Sabbath. This is in keeping with the
law stated in *Eruvin* 4:1 that one who
goes beyond the boundary on the Sabbath is permitted to walk only four
cubits in every direction (*Rav*).

If, however, one finds himself inside
a walled enclosure (such as the courtyard in our case) he may walk anywhere

5. There was a large courtyard in Jerusalem which was called Beis Ya'azek, and there all the witnesses gathered, and the *beis din* interrogated them there, and made them large feasts in order that they be accustomed to come.

Originally they did not move from there all day; [then] Rabban Gamliel the Elder enacted that they should [be permitted to] walk two thousand cubits in every direction.

YAD AVRAHAM

within that enclosure *(Tos. Yom Tov).*

Tosafos explains that Jerusalem was not considered enclosed by walls (which would permit the witnesses to walk throughout the city) because at the time of our mishnah there were large breaches in the city's walls. Therefore the witnesses could not leave the confines of the courtyard.

Tosafos mentions a second possibility, that people who come from beyond the תְּחוּם, *boundary*, into a city may walk within it even if it is not enclosed by walls. If so, says *Pnei Yehoshua*, the witnesses would be permitted to walk throughout Jerusalem, and the mishnah's use of the word מִשָּׁם, *from there*, refers not to the courtyard but to the city of Jerusalem.

Aruch LaNer disagrees with *Pnei Yehoshua* and claims that it is unlikely that the mishnah refers to the entire city, and he therefore explains *Tosafos* differently. (However, *Pnei Yehoshua's* view finds support in *Meiri* who quotes a view that מִשָּׁם refers to the city.)

The ruling in the case of an unwalled city is a matter of dispute among the halachic authorities (see *Be'ur Halachah* to *Shulchan Aruch Orach Chaim* 405:6).

הִתְקִין רַבָּן גַּמְלִיאֵל הַזָּקֵן — *[then] Rabban Gamliel the Elder enacted*

[The appellation הַזָּקֵן, *the Elder*, is used to distinguish him from his grandson and namesake, Rabban Gamliel of Yavneh (mentioned in mishnah 8). Nevertheless, Rabban Gamliel the

Elder is sometimes quoted in Mishnah without the appellation הַזָּקֵן (see, for example, *Peah* 2:6; *Shekalim* 6:1).

It is usually easy to distinguish between the two, since Rabban Gamliel the Elder was *nassi* in Jerusalem before the destruction of the Temple while his grandson was *nassi* in Yavneh and Usha and is usually mentioned with his contemporaries of R' Eliezer and R' Yehoshua. Occasionally though, there is confusion as to which Rabban Gamliel is meant (see commentators to *Sanhedrin* 11b).]

שֶׁיְּהוּ מְהַלְּכִין אַלְפַּיִם אַמָּה לְכָל־רוּחַ. — *that they should [be permitted to] walk two thousand cubits in every direction.*

Since they came to Jerusalem with the permission of the *beis din*, they should be regarded like residents of the city of Jerusalem, who were permitted to walk throughout the city and in a 2000-cubit radius outside it (*Tos. Yom Tov* citing *Maggid Mishnah, Hilchos Shabbos* 27:17).

While most authorities (see *Meiri, Rambam, Hilchos Shabbos* 27:17) agree that this is the reason for Rabban Gamliel's enactment, *Tosafos* holds that it was in order that the witnesses (and the others mentioned further in the mishnah) not be discouraged from coming in the future.

Sifsei Chachamim notes that according to *Tosafos* the reason of שֶׁיְּהוּ רְגִילִין לָבֹא, *that they be in the habit of coming*, applies not only to the large feasts made for the witnesses but also to

וְלֹא אֵלּוּ בִלְבַד, אֶלָּא אַף הַחֲכָמָה הַבָּאָה לְיַלֵּד, וְהַבָּא לְהַצִּיל מִן־הַדְּלֵקָה וּמִן־הַגַּיִס וּמִן־הַנָּהָר וּמִן־הַמַּפֹּלֶת, הֲרֵי אֵלּוּ כְּאַנְשֵׁי הָעִיר, וְיֶשׁ־לָהֶם אַלְפַּיִם אַמָּה לְכָל־רוּחַ.

[ו] **כֵּיצַד** בּוֹדְקִין אֶת־הָעֵדִים? זוּג שֶׁבָּא רִאשׁוֹן, בּוֹדְקִין אוֹתוֹ רִאשׁוֹן,

יד אברהם

Rabban Gamliel's enactment. Our mishnah thus supports the view of *Tosafos*, for according to the other view, no reason is given for this enactment.

[The mishnah in *Eruvin* 4:3, however, seems to support the first view since mention is made there of leaving the תְּחוּם, boundary, "with permission."]

The length of the cubit is a matter of considerable dispute; see table in *comm.* to *Succah* 1:1.

וְלֹא אֵלּוּ בִלְבַד, — *And not only these* [witnesses],

[I.e. the above enactment was made not only for the benefit of witnesses who arrived on the Sabbath.]

אֶלָּא אַף הַחֲכָמָה הַבָּאָה לְיַלֵּד, — *but also a midwife who comes to aid a delivery,*

[I.e., a midwife who comes on the Sabbath from beyond the boundary,

which she is permitted to do since in every childbirth there is the possibility of danger to the life of both the mother and the newborn.]

וְהַבָּא לְהַצִּיל מִן־הַדְּלֵקָה וּמִן־הַגַּיִס וּמִן־הַנָּהָר וּמִן־הַמַּפֹּלֶת, — *and one who comes to rescue [people] from fire, or from an [attacking] army, or from a [flooding] river, or from a fallen building,*

[In all of these cases, desecration of the Sabbath is permitted in keeping with the rule that possible danger to life takes precedence over the Sabbath (see *Yoma* 8:6).]

הֲרֵי אֵלּוּ כְּאַנְשֵׁי הָעִיר, וְיֶשׁ־לָהֶם אַלְפַּיִם אַמָּה לְכָל־רוּחַ. — *they are considered like the people of the city and they have [the right to walk] two thousand cubits in every direction*

[For the same reasons as the witnesses.]

6.

The following mishnah discusses the questions that the beis din puts to the witnesses to determine whether they actually saw the new moon or not. These questions, as *Rambam (Kiddush HaChodesh* 2:4) points out, are based on the *beis din's* calculations of the exact position and size of the new moon at the time and place where the witnesses claim to have seen it. If the witnesses' answers do not match these astronomical facts, their testimony is rejected as either willfully false or mistaken. In addition, if the witnesses contradict each other, their testimony is invalid.

In order to understand our mishnah, we must know the astronomical principles upon which the beis din's questions are based.

The new moon receives the rays of the setting sun and reflects them back to earth in the shape of a thin crescent. The moon rises east of the sun at about the time of sunset and sets in the west not very long afterwards (see *Tosafos* 20b). Furthermore, since the crescent that we see is only that portion of the moon that is illuminated by the sun, the "horns [i.e., points]" of the crescent never point toward the sun but always point away from it.

And not only these [witnesses], but also a midwife who comes to aid a delivery, and one who comes to rescue [people] from a fire, or from an [attacking] army, or from a [flooding] river or from a fallen building — they are considered like the people of the city and they have [the right to walk] two thousand cubits in every direction.

6. How do they interrogate the witnesses? The pair that arrives first is interrogated first,

YAD AVRAHAM

While the above is true at any time of the year and at any place on Earth, the exact position of the new moon in relation to the sun and the precise direction in which the "horns" are pointed depend on the time of year and location from which the moon is observed. The reason for this is as follows:

The sun always rises in the east and sets in the west. However, the exact points of sunrise on the eastern horizon and sunset on the western horizon vary from day to day. North of the equator, where *Eretz Yisrael* is, sunrise and sunset appear further north along the eastern and western horizons respectively as summer approaches and further south with the approach of winter. Therefore, it can be said that sunset during the winter is in the southwest, while during the summer it is in the northwest. This is due to the tilt of the earth's axis in the northern hemisphere toward the sun in summer and away from it in winter. The moon, unaffected by the tilt of the earth's axis, does not change its position relative to the seasons. Therefore, during the summer the first phase of the new moon must appear south (or southeast, to be more exact) of the setting sun, while during the winter it appears to the north (or northeast) of it. The direction toward which the horns are pointed, depending as it does on the angle at which the sun's rays hit the moon, also varies accordingly (see *Rambam, Kiddush HaChodesh* 19:1-14).

כֵּיצַד בּוֹדְקִין אֶת־הָעֵדִים? — *How do they interrogate the witnesses?*

[Our mishnah mentions only the part of the interrogation that deals with the position and appearance of the moon. Undoubtedly, however, the witnesses were also asked the questions men-

tioned in *Sanhedrin* 5:1, defining the exact time and place where the witnesses claim to have seen the new moon. Otherwise some questions in *our* mishnah would be useless, since the answers to them would depend in part on the time and place of the observation.[1]]

1. Because of an apparent contradiction in the words of *Rambam* (see *Kiddush HaChodesh* 1:7 and 2:2), however, there is a disagreement whether questions defining time and place in testimony of *Kiddush HaChodesh* are required מִדְּאוֹרַיְתָא, by *Torah law*, or מִדְּרַבָּנָן, by *Rabbinic law*.

Lechem Mishneh (ibid, 2:2) holds that the interrogation is under Torah law, similar to all other cases of testimony before an ordained *beis din* (see *Sanhedrin* 4:1).

Tumim (30:3) claims that *Kiddush HaChodesh* differs from all other cases since the halachah is that even if the *beis din* declared Rosh Chodesh based on false testimony, their declaration is nevertheless valid (mishnah 2:9). Therefore, according to Torah law, there is no need to ask the witnesses any questions relating to time and place. Such questions were necessary in other matters so that it could be possible for other witnesses to contradict their

וּמַכְנִיסִין אֶת־הַגָּדוֹל שֶׁבָּהֶן, וְאוֹמְרִים לוֹ:
„אֱמֹר, כֵּיצַד רָאִיתָ אֶת־הַלְּבָנָה, לִפְנֵי הַחַמָּה
אוֹ לְאַחַר הַחַמָּה? לִצְפוֹנָהּ אוֹ לִדְרוֹמָהּ? כַּמָּה
הָיָה גָבוֹהַּ? וּלְאַיִן הָיָה נוֹטֶה? וְכַמָּה הָיָה
רָחָב?"
אִם אָמַר „לִפְנֵי הַחַמָּה", לֹא אָמַר כְּלוּם.

יד אברהם

זוּג שֶׁבָּא רִאשׁוֹן, בּוֹדְקִין אוֹתוֹ רִאשׁוֹן,
וּמַכְנִיסִין אֶת־הַגָּדוֹל שֶׁבָּהֶן, — *The pair that
arrives first is interrogated first, and the
elder is brought in*

[As in all cases of testimony before a
beis din (see *Sanhedrin* 3:6), the
witnesses are interrogated separately to
determine whether their testimony coincides. Out of respect, the elder witness
is interrogated first. This is similar to
the custom mentioned in *Gittin* 10b
regarding a legal document where the
older witness signs before the younger.]

וְאוֹמְרִים לוֹ: — *and they say to him:*
Our mishnah omits any mention of
אִיּוּם, *intimidation,* the procedure by
which the *beis din* warns the witnesses
of the consequences of testifying falsely. While this procedure was used in all
other cases (see *Mishnah Sanhedrin* 3:6,
4:5), it was unnecessary for *Kiddush
HaChodesh* since the *beis din* was not
totally dependent on their testimony
and could determine by astronomical
calculation whether or not they were
telling the truth (*Kol HaRemez*).

[It would seem, however, that our mish-
nah's failure to mention אִיּוּם, *intimidation,* is
no proof that the procedure did not take
place, as our mishnah also omits mention of
questions regarding time and place which
were certainly asked, as pointed out above
(s.v. כֵּיצַד). The fact that *Rambam* also omits

intimidation in connection with *Kiddush
HaChodesh* is no proof to *Kol HaRemez's*
contention since *Rambam* only cites laws
that are stated explicitly in the Talmud (see
S'dei Chemed K'lalei HaPoskim 5:23).

אֱמֹר, כֵּיצַד רָאִיתָ אֶת־הַלְּבָנָה, לִפְנֵי הַחַמָּה
אוֹ לְאַחַר הַחַמָּה? — *'Tell how you saw the
moon — facing the sun or away from
the sun?*

I.e., were the horns of the crescent
pointing west, toward the setting sun,
or east, away from the setting sun
(*Tiferes Yisrael*)?

לִצְפוֹנָהּ אוֹ לִדְרוֹמָהּ? — *To its north or to
its south?*

[The *Gemara* states that the correct
answer to this question depends upon
the time of year (as explained in the
preface to our mishnah) since the moon
is northeast of the sun in winter and
southeast of it in summer. If the
witness's answer contradicted this fact,
his testimony was, of course, rejected.]

כַּמָּה הָיָה גָבוֹהַּ? — *How high was it?*
I.e., how high above the horizon did
it seem to be? (*Rav; Tiferes Yisrael*).

[The commentators point out that the
witness is not expected to know the actual distance of the moon from the
earth; but its *perceived* height in human
terms (e.g. the height of a tree or a person) above the horizon. The answer to
this question varies with the time of

testimony by proving that at the time they claim to have witnessed the event they were in fact
elsewhere [עֵדוּת שֶׁאַתָּה יָכוֹל לְהַזִימָהּ] (cf. *Shach* to *Choshen Misphat* 33:16). But after the
damage caused by the Boethusians (mishnah 2:1), when the Sages ruled that testimony about
the new moon could only be accepted from witnesses known to the *beis din,* they also required
that these witnesses be interrogated (see also *Minchas Chinuch* 4:3).

Aruch HaShulchan HeAsid's view (*Kiddush HaChodesh* 89:11) is that while the questions
relating to time and place are required by Torah law, the detailed interrogation mentioned in
our mishnah is of Rabbinic origin and was instituted after the problems caused by the
Boethusians.]

and the elder is brought in and they say to him, 'Tell, how did you see the moon — facing the sun or away from the sun? To its north or to its south? How high was it? And which way was it leaning? And how wide was it?'

If he said, 'Facing the sun,' he said nothing.

YAD AVRAHAM

night that the crescent was seen and the location of the observer (see *Meiri; comm.* attributed to *Rambam, Rosh Hashanah* 24a).]

The *Gemara* notes that if the witnesses' answers to this question contradict each other only slightly, we do not reject their testimony, but attribute the contradiction to normal human error. If the contradiction is too great to be attributed to human error, the two witnesses do not comprise an acceptable pair. Nevertheless, if the testimony of a *third* witness coincides with one of them, the *beis din* accepts as valid witnesses those who agree, and ignores the testimony of the one whose answer does not match that of the others *(Rav).*

וּלְאַיִן הָיָה נוֹטֶה? — *And which way was it leaning?*

I.e., in which direction were the horns of the crescent pointed? *(Rav).*

[This question is an elaboration of the first two questions. While the moon is, for example, north of the sun in winter and its horns point away from the sun, the *exact* direction in which the horns are pointed varies from month to month and from place to place, according to the latitude from which the moon is

observed (see *Rambam, Kiddush Ha-Chodesh* 19).]

וְכַמָּה הָיָה רָחָב?" — *And how wide was it?'*

[It is not clear whether this question refers to the width of the crescent or to its length. Furthermore, as *Aruch Ha-Shulchan HeAsid (Kiddush HaChodesh* 89:12) points out, the size of the crescent is always the same at the beginning of the month.[1]

It is possible that the *beis din's* question was based on the well-known fact that the closer the moon is to the horizon, the larger it appears. The proper answer to this question would then depend on the witnesses' reply to the question: כַּמָּה הָיָה גָּבוֹהַּ?, *How high was it?* If they claimed to have seen the moon near the horizon, for example, they would have to say that it was wide (in width or length) in order for their testimony to be accepted.]

אִם אָמַר "לִפְנֵי הַחַמָּה," לֹא אָמַר כְּלוּם. — *If he said, 'Facing the sun,' he said nothing.*

If, in answer to the first question, the witness stated that the horns of the crescent had been pointing toward the sun, his testimony is invalidated, since this is

---

1. *Rambam (comm.* to Mishnah) and *Rav* state that the size of the moon depends on its distance from the sun. The commentary attributed to *Rambam (Rosh Hashanah* 24a) elaborates on this and explains that the longer the time between the *molad* (when the moon is between the sun and the earth) and the appearance of the new moon (when the moon has moved far enough from its position at the *molad* to be visible), the larger the size of the crescent. While this is undoubtedly so, the difference in size between its appearance six hours after the *molad* and its appearance twenty hours after the *molad* (see *Rambam's* example in the above *comm.*) would not be so great that a mistake or contradiction on the part of the witnesses could not be attributed to human error, thus making the question purposeless. It is possible, however, that the question was asked to eliminate an unreliable witness (who had not really seen the new moon) who would declare the size of the crescent to be so large that it could not be attributed to human error. This is similar to the question of "לִפְנֵי הַחַמָּה, *[Was it] facing the sun?,"* whose sole purpose is to weed out unreliable witnesses.

וְאַחַר־כָּךְ הָיוּ מַכְנִיסִים אֶת־הַשֵּׁנִי וּבוֹדְקִין אוֹתוֹ. אִם נִמְצְאוּ דִּבְרֵיהֶם מְכֻוָּנִים, עֵדוּתָן קַיֶּמֶת.

וּשְׁאָר כָּל־הַזּוּגוֹת שׁוֹאֲלִין אוֹתָם רָאשֵׁי דְבָרִים, לֹא שֶׁהָיוּ צְרִיכִין לָהֶן, אֶלָּא כְּדֵי שֶׁלֹּא יֵצְאוּ בְּפַחֵי נֶפֶשׁ, בִּשְׁבִיל שֶׁיְּהוּ רְגִילִים לָבֹא.

[ז] **רֹאשׁ** בֵּית דִּין אוֹמֵר: ,,מְקֻדָּשׁ!'' וְכָל הָעָם עוֹנִין אַחֲרָיו: ,,מְקֻדָּשׁ,

,,מְקֻדָּשׁ!''

יד אברהם

impossible (as explained in the introduction to our mishnah; *Tos. Yom Tov*).

The witness, of course, had to answer all the questions listed above. The mishnah mentions a wrong answer to the first question as a sample of an answer that is rejected because it contradicts astronomical facts. The proper answers to the other questions depend on time and place so the mishnah does not elaborate on them. It chose the simplest case, the one in which the correct answer is always the same (*Tiferes Yisrael; Kol HaRemez; Tos. Yom Tov*).

וְאַחַר־כָּךְ הָיוּ מַכְנִיסִים אֶת־הַשֵּׁנִי וּבוֹדְקִין אוֹתוֹ. — *Then they would have the second [witness] brought in and interrogate him.*

They asked him the same questions that they asked the first witness.

אִם נִמְצְאוּ דִּבְרֵיהֶם מְכֻוָּנִים, — *If their words are found to coincide,*

[Their testimony does not have to coincide perfectly, but must be similar enough so that a deviation can be attributed to ordinary human error.]

עֵדוּתָן קַיֶּמֶת. — *their testimony is valid.*

[And the *beis din* declares Rosh Chodesh on the thirtieth day, based on their testimony, as described in the next mishnah.]

וּשְׁאָר כָּל־הַזּוּגוֹת שׁוֹאֲלִין אוֹתָם רָאשֵׁי דְבָרִים, — *And they ask rest of the pairs [of witnesses only the] main points,*

[This is, of course, only if the testimony of the first pair was accepted. Otherwise, the next pair must undergo the thorough interrogation mentioned in our mishnah.]

לֹא שֶׁהָיוּ צְרִיכִין לָהֶן, — *not that they* [i.e., *beis din*] *needed them* [*the witnesses*],

For the testimony of the first pair of witnesses is sufficient for the *beis din* to declare Rosh Chodesh.

אֶלָּא כְּדֵי שֶׁלֹּא יֵצְאוּ בְּפַחֵי נֶפֶשׁ, — *but so that they should not leave disappointed,*

After all, they have gone to the trouble of coming to the *beis din*. Let it not be for nothing.

בִּשְׁבִיל שֶׁיְּהוּ רְגִילִים לָבֹא. — *in order that they should be accustomed to come.*

[If *beis din* were to ignore them, they might refrain from coming in the future — when their testimony might be needed — thinking that their coming is unnecessary.]

7.

רֹאשׁ בֵּית דִּין אוֹמֵר: ,,מְקֻדָּשׁ!'' — *The head of the beis din says, 'It is sanctified!'*

Our mishnah continues the previous one and teaches us that after the *beis din*

Then they would have the second [witness] brought in and interrogate him. If their words are found to coincide, their testimony is valid.

And they ask the rest of the pairs [of witnesses only the] main points, not that they [the *beis din*] needed them [the witnesses], but so that they should not leave disappointed, in order that they should be accustomed to come.

7. The head of the *beis din* says, 'It is sanctified!' And all the people respond after him, 'It is sanctified! It is sanctified!'

YAD AVRAHAM

determines that the witnesses' testimony is valid, they declare the day to be Rosh Chodesh, following the procedure mentioned here.

[*Rambam (Kiddush HaChodesh* 4:12) notes that the *head of the beis din* was known as the *Nassi*, a term we will use hereafter for the sake of brevity. The *Nassi* declares the day to be Rosh Chodesh by saying the words: 'It is sanctified!' This means that the day is sanctified as Rosh Chodesh and is considered the first day of the new month.]

[This is derived in the *Gemara* from the verse in *Leviticus* 23:44 מֹשֶׁה וַיְדַבֵּר אֶת־מֹעֲדֵי ה', *and Moses declared the holidays of HASHEM*, which teaches us that the head of the *beis din* (like Moses, who held this position) should be the one to declare the day Rosh Chodesh (*Rav*).

[While this is the preferred procedure, it is not imperative. If for some reason the *Nassi* is not present, the declaration of Rosh Chodesh may be made by someone else (see *Mishnah* 4:4, *Gemara* 25a, *Berachos* 63a, and numerous other places where someone other than the *Nassi* declared Rosh Chodesh).]

וְכָל הָעָם עוֹנִין אַחֲרָיו: ,,מְקֻדָּשׁ, מְקֻדָּשׁ!" — *And all the people respond after him, 'It is sanctified! It is sanctified!'*

The rule that the people present in the *beis din* join in the declaration is derived from *Leviticus* 23:2, אֲשֶׁר תִּקְרְאוּ אֹתָם, *that you declare them* [i.e., the holidays]. The word אֹתָם, *them*, is spelled without a *vav*, and can therefore be read אַתֶּם, *you* (plural); this teaches us that the people must also declare Rosh Chodesh. The plural expression מִקְרָאֵי קֹדֶשׁ, *declarations of sanctification*, in the above verse, implies that the people must say twice, 'It is sanctified' (*Gem.* 24a; *Rav*).

While the *Gemara* derives this entire procedure from verses in the Torah, *Ramban (Sefer HaMitzvos, Aseh* 153) maintains that if a *beis din* ignored this procedure entirely and simply ruled the day to be Rosh Chodesh on the basis of the witnesses' testimony, the decision is binding even without a formal declaration on the part of the *beis din* or the people. In *Ramban's* view, therefore, our mishnah is describing only the *preferred*, but not the *required*, procedure.

---

1. [While the mishnah mentions that the head of the *beis din* says only: 'מְקֻדָּשׁ, *It is sanctified!*', *Aruch HaShulchan HeAsid* (Kiddush HaChodesh 90:3) adds that obviously he said: מְקֻדָּשׁ הַחֹדֶשׁ, *the day of Rosh Chodesh is sanctified!* His reasoning is that the single word מְקֻדָּשׁ, *it is sanctified*, is insufficient as it does not indicate *what* is being sanctified.]

בֵּין שֶׁנִּרְאָה בִּזְמַנּוֹ בֵּין שֶׁלֹּא נִרְאָה בִּזְמַנּוֹ,
מְקַדְּשִׁין אוֹתוֹ.

רַבִּי אֶלְעָזָר בַּר־צָדוֹק אוֹמֵר: אִם לֹא נִרְאָה
בִּזְמַנּוֹ, אֵין מְקַדְּשִׁין אוֹתוֹ, שֶׁכְּבָר קִדְּשׁוּהוּ
שָׁמָיִם.

[ח] דְּמוּת צוּרוֹת לְבָנוֹת הָיוּ לוֹ לְרַבָּן
גַּמְלִיאֵל בַּטַּבְלָא וּבַכֹּתֶל

יד אברהם

Rambam (Kiddush HaChodesh 2:8) who says 'Beis din, by saying, "It is sanctified" are the ones who determine [Rosh Chodesh]', appears to disagree with Ramban. Rambam's language implies that even if the beis din decided to declare Rosh Chodesh but failed to say, "It is sanctified," the day would not be Rosh Chodesh (see Sefer Ha-Zichronos p. 39; Tos. R' Akiva Eiger to 3:1).

בֵּין שֶׁנִּרְאָה בִּזְמַנּוֹ — Whether it [the new moon] appeared at its [expected] time

I.e. the night of the thirtieth (Rav).

[That the mishnah describes the night of the thirtieth as בִּזְמַנּוֹ, at its [expected] time, does not mean that this is necessarily the normal time for the new moon to appear. In fact, it is often impossible for it to appear then as stated by Rambam (Kiddush HaChodesh 1:6). Nevertheless, because the length of the lunar cycle is twenty-nine days, twelve hours, and 44⅓ minutes, each new moon, theoretically, would fall on the thirtieth day from the last one were it not for the rule (mentioned above in Introduction to Kiddush HaChodesh) that months must consist of entire days and cannot include parts of a day. Therefore, when Rosh Chodesh does come out on the thirtieth, the mishnah refers to it as the 'expected' time. (Cf. Sifsei Chachamim).]

בֵּין שֶׁלֹּא נִרְאָה בִּזְמַנּוֹ, מְקַדְּשִׁין אוֹתוֹ. — or whether it did not appear at its [expected] time, they sanctify [the day].

Although the thirty-first is automatically Rosh Chodesh if the moon does not appear on the night of the thirtieth — nevertheless, the beis din is required to go through the above procedure in declaring the thirty-first day Rosh Chodesh (Meiri).

[In this case, however, even Rambam cited above, s.v. וכל העם would agree that if the beis din failed to make a formal declaration, the day would be Rosh Chodesh anyway.]

רַבִּי אֶלְעָזָר בַּר־צָדוֹק אוֹמֵר: אִם לֹא נִרְאָה בִּזְמַנּוֹ, אֵין מְקַדְּשִׁין אוֹתוֹ, שֶׁכְּבָר קִדְּשׁוּהוּ שָׁמָיִם. — R' Elazar ben Tzadok says: If it did not appear at its [expected] time, they do not sanctify, for it has already been sanctified by Heaven.

The thirty-first day is automatically Rosh Chodesh and therefore does not require sanctification by the beis din (Meiri).

Rav explains that R' Elazar ben Tzadok holds that the beis din is never obligated to sanctify Rosh Chodesh formally on the thirtieth day; they do so in order to publicize and give force to their decision. When Rosh Chodesh is the thirty-first day, this is not necessary, since it is automatic and not dependent on a decision by the beis din.

[Rav's explanation follows Meiri's interpretation of שֶׁכְּבָר קִדְּשׁוּהוּ שָׁמָיִם, for it has already been sanctified by Heaven, in which these words are not meant literally but are the mishnah's way of saying that the thirty-first day is auto-

Whether it [the new moon] appeared at its [expected] time or whether it did not appear at its [expected] time, they sanctify.

R' Elazar ben Tzadok says: If it did not appear at its [expected] time, they do not sanctify, for it has already been sanctified by Heaven.

8. **R**abban Gamliel had moon-shaped forms on a tablet and on the wall of his upper chamber,

YAD AVRAHAM

matically Rosh Chodesh.

Tosafos (Sanhedrin 10b) however, takes these words literally, explaining that if the *beis din* did not declare Rosh Chodesh on the thirtieth day, then the Heavenly Court does so on the morning of the the thirty-first. According to this view, verbal sanctification is *always* necessary; on the thirtieth it is done by the *beis din* on earth, and on the thirty-first, by the Heavenly Court.]

The final ruling in the dispute between the first tanna and R' Elazar

ben Tzadok favors the view of the latter *(Rav; Rambam, Kiddush HaChodesh* 2:8).

[Although the *beis din* does not follow the procedure of sanctification on the thirty-first, the fact that the day is Rosh Chodesh is publicized by having a public meal early in the morning in a specified place. It is a *mitzvah* to participate in this feast [סְעֻדַּת מִצְוָה], which is mentioned in *Sanhedrin* 8:2; (see *Rambam, Kiddush HaChodesh* 3:7; *Meiri* to *Sanhedrin* 70a).]

8.

דְּמוּת צוּרוֹת לְבָנוֹת הָיוּ לוֹ לְרַבָּן
גַּמְלִיאֵל — *Rabban Gamliel had moon-shaped forms*

These were images of the crescent in various sizes and in various positions *(Rav).*

The *Gemara* 24a raises a problem regarding these images of the moon. The Torah states *(Exodus* 20:20): לֹא תַעֲשׂוּן אִתִּי, *do not make with Me,* which is interpreted to mean: do not make images of My servants who serve before Me (lit. *with Me)* in the heavens. This is the prohibition against making images of the heavenly bodies, to which the Rabbis added a prohibition that one may not ask a gentile to make them. How then was Rabban Gamliel permitted to have images of the moon in his house?

The *Gemara* offers several answers:
— In a public place there is no fear

that such forms will be used for idolatry. Since Rabban Gamliel's home was always open to people, it was considered a public place.

— The forms used by Rabban Gamliel were made of separate pieces that were assembled as needed.

— The prohibition does not apply where the images were made for purpose of [halachic or Torah] study, as was case with Rabban Gamliel. (For further details see *Shulchan Aruch, Yoreh Deah* 141).

בְּטַבְלָא וּבַכֹּתֶל בַּעֲלִיָתוֹ, — *on a tablet and on the wall of his upper chamber,*

Tiferes Yisrael explains that Rabban Gamliel set up forms of the moon on the wall in a way that imitated its position in the heavens. The witnesses pointed out the form that most resembled what they saw. The judges had similar forms

בַּעֲלִיָתוֹ, שֶׁבָּהֶן מַרְאֶה אֶת־הַהֶדְיוֹטוֹת, וְאוֹמֵר:
„הֲכָזֶה רָאִיתָ אוֹ כָזֶה?"

מַעֲשֶׂה שֶׁבָּאוּ שְׁנַיִם וְאָמְרוּ: „רְאִינוּהוּ
שַׁחֲרִית בַּמִּזְרָח וְעַרְבִית בַּמַּעֲרָב." אָמַר רַבִּי
יוֹחָנָן בֶּן־נוּרִי: „עֵדֵי שֶׁקֶר הֵם!" כְּשֶׁבָּאוּ לְיַבְנֶה
קִבְּלָן רַבָּן גַּמְלִיאֵל.

וְעוֹד בָּאוּ שְׁנַיִם וְאָמְרוּ: „רְאִינוּהוּ בִּזְמַנּוֹ,"
וּבְלֵיל עִבּוּרוֹ לֹא נִרְאָה; וְקִבְּלָן רַבָּן גַּמְלִיאֵל.

יד אברהם

on the table in front of them, which they consulted during their interrogation and deliberation.

The "upper chamber" spoken of here is where the *beis din* usually met for *Kiddush HaChodesh* and *Ibbur HaShanah* [adding a thirteenth month to the year] as mentioned in *Sanhedrin* 11a (Tif. Yisrael).

Doros Harishonim (part I, p. 654), explains that while the lower story of a house in those days served as living quarters, the upper story was used for receiving guests and for public gatherings.

שֶׁבָּהֶן מַרְאֶה אֶת־הַהֶדְיוֹטוֹת, — *which* [lit. *with which*] *he would show the simple folk,*

They were the witnesses who could not understand the questions mentioned in mishnah 6 [or who could not verbally describe the appearance of the new moon without the aid of these images] (Tif. Yis.).

וְאוֹמֵר: „הֲכָזֶה רָאִיתָ אוֹ כָזֶה?" — *and say* [to them], *'Did you see* [the moon] *like this or like that?'*

[Rabban Gamliel would conduct the interrogation mentioned in mishnah 6 by *showing* the witnesses the different possibilities, instead of simply asking the questions enumerated there.]

מַעֲשֶׂה שֶׁבָּאוּ שְׁנַיִם וְאָמְרוּ: „רְאִינוּהוּ שַׁחֲרִית בַּמִּזְרָח וְעַרְבִית בַּמַּעֲרָב." — *It happened that two* [witnesses] *came and said, 'We saw it in the morning in the east and in*

the evening in the west.'

[The witnesses claimed to have seen the moon near the time of sunrise on the morning of the twenty-ninth and also on the same evening (the night of the thirtieth).]

Some commentators explain that they claimed to have seen the last phase of the old moon in the morning and the first phase of the new moon in the evening. Others hold that their testimony was only about the new moon which they claimed to have seen both in the morning and in the evening (*Rashi; Tosafos; Meiri; Baal HaMaor*).

[In either case, their claim was astronomically impossible as will be explained below.]

אָמַר רַבִּי יוֹחָנָן בֶּן־נוּרִי: — *R' Yochanan ben Nuri said,*

Sifsei Chachamim notes that the witnesses came first to R' Yochanan ben Nuri, who headed the *beis din* of their city because they were not known in Yavneh (the location of the *Sanhedrin*) and therefore required that their local *beis din* send along witnesses to vouch for them, in keeping with the enactment mentioned in mishnah 1.

„עֵדֵי שֶׁקֶר הֵם!" — *'They are false witnesses!'*

Because their claim is impossible (*Rav*).

— [As noted above, there are two interpretations of what their claim was. Each one is impossible:]

— To have seen the old moon in the

which he would show the simple folk, and say, 'Did you see [the moon] like this or like that?'

It happened that two [witnesses] came and said, 'We saw it in the morning in the east and in the evening in the west.' R' Yochanan ben Nuri said, 'They are false witnesses!' [But] when they came to Yavneh, Rabban Gamliel accepted them.

On another occasion two [witnesses] came and said, 'We saw it at its [expected] time,' but on the night of the added day it did not appear; [and] Rabban Gamliel accepted them.

YAD AVRAHAM

morning and the new moon in the evening is impossible because the moon is invisible for at least twenty-four hours between the final phase of the old moon and the first phase of the new one, as stated in the *Gemara* 20b (*Tos.* 24b s.v. ראינוהו).

— To have seen the new moon in the morning is equally impossible, as the new moon is *never* visible in the morning as pointed out by *Tosafos* to 20b (*Aruch LaNer*).

כְּשֶׁבָּאוּ לְיַבְנֶה קִבְּלָן רַבָּן גַּמְלִיאֵל. — [But] *when they came to Yavneh, Rabban Gamliel accepted them.*

[And declared Rosh Chodesh on the thirtieth day based on their testimony.]

Although Rabban Gamliel knew that they could not have seen the moon on both occasions as they claimed, he knew by his astronomical calculations that the new moon could have been visible on the night of the thirtieth, and therefore accepted that part of their testimony. As to their claim to have also seen the moon in the morning, as well, he disregarded it on the assumption that they must have seen a cloud which looked to them like the moon (*Rambam, comm.* to Mishnah; *Tif. Yisrael*).

[Though there are a number of other explanations of this mishnah (see *Rashi; Rav*), the above is the most astronomically valid explanation (*Tos.* 24b and see *Aruch Hashulchan HeAsid* 89:16).]

וְעוֹד בָּאוּ שְׁנַיִם וְאָמְרוּ: ,,רְאִינוּהוּ בִזְמַנּוֹ,'' וּבְלֵיל עִבּוּרוֹ לֹא נִרְאָה; — *On another occasion two came and said, 'We saw it at its [expected] time,' but on the night of the added day* [lit. *the night of its fullness*] *it did not appear;*

I.e., on the night of the thirty-first (*Rav*).

[The night of the thirty-first is called an *added day* because, if Rosh Chodesh begins that night, the previous month is thereby rendered מְעוּבָּר, *full*, in that it gains an extra, thirtieth day.]

Most commentators explain that the witnesses could not have included in their testimony that the moon was not seen on the thirty-first for that would mean that they did not arrive until the thirty-first, in which case Rosh Chodesh could surely not be on the thirtieth. They explain that the witnesses testified to seeing the new moon on the night of the thirtieth (whereupon Rabban Gamliel declared that day Rosh Chodesh) but on the next night, the *beis din* noticed that the new moon did not appear even though the sky was clear (*Rashi; Rambam, Kiddush HaChodesh* 2:6; *Tif. Yisrael; Beis David*).

Meiri, Rav and *Rambam (comm.* to Mishnah), however, appear to hold that this was part of the witnesses' testimony. The difficulty mentioned above is resolved by *Rashash* based on the view of *Rambam* (*Kiddush HaChodesh* 3:16)

אָמַר רַבִּי דוֹסָא בֶּן־הַרְכִּינַס: "עֵדֵי שֶׁקֶר הֵן! הֵיאָךְ מְעִידִים עַל־הָאִשָּׁה שֶׁיָּלְדָה, וּלְמָחָר כְּרֵסָהּ בֵּין שִׁנֶּיהָ?" אָמַר לוֹ רַבִּי יְהוֹשֻׁעַ: "רוֹאֶה אֲנִי אֶת־דְּבָרֶיךָ."

[ט] שָׁלַח לוֹ רַבָּן גַּמְלִיאֵל: "גּוֹזְרָנִי עָלֶיךָ שֶׁתָּבֹא אֶצְלִי בְּמַקֶּלְךָ וּבְמָעוֹתֶיךָ בְּיוֹם הַכִּפּוּרִים שֶׁחָל לִהְיוֹת בְּחֶשְׁבּוֹנְךָ."

יד אברהם

that if the *beis din* declared Rosh Chodesh on the thirty-first (because no witnesses appeared) and witnesses arrive later who claim to have seen the moon on the thirtieth, the *beis din* must retract its earlier declaration and consider the thirtieth day retroactively as the start of the month. Most other authorities do not agree with this view of *Rambam*.

וְקִבְּלָן רַבָּן גַּמְלִיאֵל. — *and Rabban Gamliel accepted them.*

He accepted their testimony and declared Rosh Chodesh on the thirtieth, because he knew by astronomical calculation that the moon *could* have appeared on that night. That it was not visible on the next night he attributed to a cloud that obscured it, even though the sky seemed to be clear (*Rav; Tif. Yis.*).

אָמַר רַבִּי דוֹסָא בֶּן־הַרְכִּינַס: "עֵדֵי שֶׁקֶר הֵן! — *R' Dosa ben Harkinas said, 'They are false witnesses!*

— R' Dosa ben Harkinas did not accept Rabban Gamliel's explanation of the moon's failure to appear on the

night of the thirty-first and therefore considered the witnesses' testimony to be impossible. Clearly he must also have felt that Rabban Gamliel's astronomical calculations were in error.]

הֵיאָךְ מְעִידִים עַל־הָאִשָּׁה שֶׁיָּלְדָה, וּלְמָחָר כְּרֵסָהּ בֵּין שִׁנֶּיהָ?" — *How can they testify that a woman gave birth and the next day her belly is between her teeth?'*

If a woman claims to have given birth, she cannot be visibly pregnant the next day; her physical condition belies her words. Similarly, if the moon appeared on the night of the thirtieth, as the witnesses claim, it is impossible for it not to appear the next night. Therefore, their testimony must be rejected.

אָמַר לוֹ רַבִּי יְהוֹשֻׁעַ: "רוֹאֶה אֲנִי אֶת־דְּבָרֶיךָ." — *R' Yehoshua said to him, 'I agree with your argument* [lit. *I see your words.*]'

And therefore Rosh Chodesh is on the thirty-first day. R' Yehoshua refused to accept Rabban Gamliel's declaration of Rosh Chodesh and this led to the events described in the next mishnah (*Kehati*).

9.

This mishnah is a continuation of the previous one. (In the *Gemara* the two are in fact printed as one.) When Rabban Gamliel heard that R' Yehoshua disputed his decision and decided to consider the thirty-first day *Rosh Chodesh* in defiance of his declaration, he was fearful that this would lead to a division among the people with some celebrating the holy days and festivals on one day and others on the next

R' Dosa ben Harkinas said, 'They are false witnesses. How can they testify that a woman gave birth and the next day her belly is between her teeth?'

R' Yehoshua said to him, 'I agree with your argument.'

9. **R**abban Gamliel sent [a message] to him, 'I decree upon you that you come to me with your staff and your money on the day that Yom Kippur will fall according to your reckoning.'

YAD AVRAHAM

day. Indeed, according to R' Yehoshua, Yom Kippur would fall a day later than it would according to the decision rendered by Rabban Gamliel's court. Were R' Yehoshua to observe *his* Yom Kippur, the result would be an open rift. Therefore Rabban Gamliel ordered R' Yehoshua to demonstrate publicly his acceptance of the *Nassi's* authority by treating that day as an ordinary weekday by carrying his walking stick and his money — both, of course, prohibited on Yom Kippur.[1]

שָׁלַח לוֹ רַבָּן גַּמְלִיאֵל: ,,גּוֹזְרַנִי עָלֶיךָ שֶׁתָּבֹא אֶצְלִי בְּמַקֶּלְךָ וּבִמְעוֹתֶיךָ בְּיוֹם הַכִּפּוּרִים שֶׁחָל לִהְיוֹת בְּחֶשְׁבּוֹנֶךָ." — *Rabban Gamliel sent to him* [i.e., R' Yehoshua], *'I decree upon you that you come to me with your staff and your money on the day that Yom Kippur will fall according to your reckoning.'*

[Rabban Gamliel felt compelled to assert his authority in this extreme manner in order to preserve the unity of the nation. Had R' Yehoshua been permitted to disagree in practice with the calendar as promulgated by the Sanhedrin, many others would eventually have done the same.]

There was no need to order him to fast on Rabban Gamliel's Yom Kippur. It was taken for granted that R' Yehoshua would surely observe the communal Yom Kippur; he planned only to fast two days (*Tif. Yis.*).

Several reasons are given as to why this order was sent only to R' Yehoshua and not to R' Dosa ben Harkinas (who had also disagreed with Rabban Gamliel

concerning this particular Rosh Chodesh):

1) R' Yehoshua was head of the Sanhedrin, and second to the *Nassi*, as stated in *Bava Kamma* 74b, and his dissent would cause or already caused far greater dissension among the people than that of R' Dosa ben Harkinas.

2) R' Dosa ben Harkinas, after initially disagreeing with Rabban Gamliel, retracted his opinion and accepted the *Nassi's* decision as seen below in the mishnah.

3) R' Dosa ben Harkinas was an extremely old man as mentioned in *Yevamos* 16a and Rabban Gamliel did not wish to burden him by making him travel to Yavneh (*Maharsha; Tif. Yis.*).

[Presumably it was sufficient that R' Yehoshua made a public display of carrying. That he chose to fast privately did not concern Rabban Gamliel. He did not wish to compel R' Yehoshua to eat on 'his' Yom Kippur, an act which he would regard as liable to *Kareis* (spiritual excision).]

1. [See *Bava Metzia* 59b where Rabban Gamliel had his own brother-in-law, R' Eliezer, excommunicated for defying the decision of the majority. On that occasion, Rabban Gamliel declared before God that his intent was not to uphold his own honor but to prevent a rift among the people.]

הָלַךְ וּמְצָאוֹ רַבִּי עֲקִיבָא מֵצַר, אָמַר לוֹ:
"יֵשׁ־לִי לִלְמֹד, שֶׁכָּל מַה שֶּׁעָשָׂה רַבָּן גַּמְלִיאֵל
עָשׂוּי, שֶׁנֶּאֱמַר: ,אֵלֶּה מוֹעֲדֵי ה' מִקְרָאֵי קֹדֶשׁ,
אֲשֶׁר־תִּקְרְאוּ אֹתָם' — בֵּין בִּזְמַנָּן בֵּין שֶׁלֹּא
בִזְמַנָּן, אֵין לִי מוֹעֲדוֹת אֶלָּא אֵלּוּ."
בָּא לוֹ אֵצֶל רַבִּי דּוֹסָא בֶּן הַרְכִּינַס, אָמַר לוֹ:
"אִם בָּאִין אָנוּ לָדוּן אַחַר בֵּית דִּינוֹ שֶׁל רַבָּן
גַּמְלִיאֵל, צְרִיכִין אָנוּ לָדוּן אַחַר כָּל־בֵּית דִּין
וּבֵית דִּין שֶׁעָמַד מִימוֹת מֹשֶׁה וְעַד עַכְשָׁיו;
שֶׁנֶּאֱמַר: ,וַיַּעַל מֹשֶׁה וְאַהֲרֹן נָדָב וַאֲבִיהוּא

יד אברהם

הָלַךְ וּמְצָאוֹ רַבִּי עֲקִיבָא מֵצַר, — R' Akiva
went and found him [i.e., R' Yehoshua]
troubled,

Yerushalmi states that R' Akiva was
the emissary Rabban Gamliel sent to
convey his order to R' Yehoshua.

Upon hearing the order, R' Yehoshua
declared that he would prefer to have an
affliction that would cause him to be
bedridden for a year, rather than be
forced to comply with such an order
(Gemara).

Maharsha comments that R' Yehoshua desired such an affliction for it
would render him incapable of fulfilling
Rabban Gamliel's order.

אָמַר לוֹ: "יֵשׁ לִי לִלְמֹד, שֶׁכָּל מַה שֶּׁעָשָׂה רַבָּן
גַּמְלִיאֵל עָשׂוּי, — [so] he said to him, 'I
can elucidate that whatever Rabban
Gamliel did is [validly] done,

R' Akiva had proof from the Torah
that even if the beis din erroneously
declared Rosh Chodesh on the wrong
day, the declaration is nevertheless valid
(Kehati).

[R' Akiva's statement, while halachically true, was in reality not applicable to this case. Rabban Gamliel did
not err, and his acceptance of the
witnesses was perfectly justified as set
forth by Rambam (Kiddush HaChodesh) 2:6). R' Akiva merely pointed out

to R' Yehoshua that even if the witnesses were false and Rabban Gamliel had
accepted them in error, the declaration
of Rosh Chodesh based on their
testimony was nevertheless valid.]

שֶׁנֶּאֱמַר: אֵלֶּה מוֹעֲדֵי ה' מִקְרָאֵי קֹדֶשׁ, אֲשֶׁר
תִּקְרְאוּ אֹתָם' — for it says (Leviticus
23:4): These are the holidays of
HASHEM, holy convocations, that you
shall declare them—

The declaration of the holy days is
dependent on the beis din as indicated
by the word תִּקְרְאוּ, you shall declare,
but Gemara derives from the verse the
further rule that even an erroneous
declaration is valid. The word אֹתָם,
them, can also be vocalized to read אַתֶּם,
you. This is to emphasize the power of a
beis din, as if the verse were telling the
beis din 'the festivals will be designated
whenever you choose'; the declaration
of beis din is valid even if they choose a
wrong date, willfully, by error in
calculation, or through being misled by
false witnesses. Cf. Tos. Yom Tov.

[Rambam (Kiddush HaChodesh
2:10) apparently does not agree that a
beis din can willfully declare Rosh
Chodesh on the wrong day. He does,
however, agree that an erroneous
declaration is valid. Cf. Aruch
HaShulchan HeAsid, Kiddush HaChodesh 90:12.]

R' Akiva went and found him troubled, [so] he said to him, 'I can elucidate that whatever Rabban Gamliel did is [validly] done, for it says, *(Leviticus 23:4): These are the holidays of HASHEM, holy convocations, that you shall declare them* — whether [declared] in their [expected] time or not in their [expected] time, I have no holy days but these.'

He came to R' Dosa ben Harkinas, who said to him, 'If we come to reconsider [the decisions of] Rabban Gamliel's *beis din*, then we must reconsider [the decisions of] every *beis din* that arose from the days of Moses until now; as it says *(Exodus 24:9): There went up · Moses and Aaron, Nadav and Avihu, and*

YAD AVRAHAM

בֵּין בִּזְמַנָּן בֵּין שֶׁלֹּא בִּזְמַנָּן, אֵין לִי מוֹעֲדוֹת אֶלָּא אֵלּוּ." — *whether [declared] in their [expected] time or not in their [expected] time, I have no holidays but these.'*

[It should be noted, as stated in the Introduction to *Kiddush HaChodesh* that this leeway granted to a *beis din* is limited to the thirtieth and thirtieth-first days. A declaration of Rosh Chodesh made earlier or later is definitely not valid.]

Rambam (Kiddush HaChodesh 2:10) explains the seemingly illogical halachah that a mistaken declaration must be accepted: the same One Who commanded us to observe the holidays also commanded us to rely on the *beis din* whether mistaken or not *(Tos. Yom Tov).*

בָּא לוֹ אֵצֶל רַבִּי דוֹסָא בֶּן הַרְכִּינַס, — *He* [i.e., R' Yehoshua] *came to R' Dosa ben Harkinas,*

[Who had also disagreed with Rabban Gamliel, saying that the witnesses were false.]

אָמַר לוֹ: — *who* [lit. he] *said to him,*

R' Dosa ben Harkinas accepted Rabben Gamliel's decision and consoled R' Yehoshua by telling him that in the case of *Kiddush HaChodesh* one must accept the ruling of the *beis din (Ahavas Eisan;* cf. *Tiferes Yisrael).*

אִם בָּאִין אָנוּ לָדוּן אַחַר בֵּית דִּינוֹ שֶׁל רַבָּן גַּמְלִיאֵל, — *'If we come to reconsider [the decisions of] Rabban Gamliel's beis din,*

[I.e., if we assume that they erred (and, as a result, refuse to accept their decision).]

צְרִיכִין אָנוּ לָדוּן אַחַר כָּל בֵּית דִּין וּבֵית דִּין שֶׁעָמַד מִימוֹת מֹשֶׁה וְעַד עַכְשָׁיו; — *then we must reconsider [the decisions of] every beis din that arose from the days of Moses until now;*

Of course, we do not doubt every court that ever existed, but accept their decisions. Similarly, we must follow the decisions of Rabban Gamliel's *beis din.*

[R' Dosa ben Harkinas was pointing out that if we question the authority of a *beis din* because we doubt their learning and scholarship, then we must also question the decisions of many earlier courts, some of which were not on the highest level of scholarship, as mentioned in the *Gemara* (25b) with reference to the courts of Gideon, Yiftach, and Samson.]

שֶׁנֶּאֱמַר: ,וַיַּעַל מֹשֶׁה וְאַהֲרֹן נָדָב וַאֲבִיהוּא וְשִׁבְעִים מִזִּקְנֵי יִשְׂרָאֵל.' וְלָמָּה לֹא נִתְפָּרְשׁוּ שְׁמוֹתָן שֶׁל זְקֵנִים?—אֶלָּא לְלַמֵּד, שֶׁכָּל שְׁלֹשָׁה וּשְׁלֹשָׁה שֶׁעָמְדוּ בֵית דִּין עַל־יִשְׂרָאֵל הֲרֵי הוּא כְּבֵית דִּינוֹ שֶׁל מֹשֶׁה." — *as it says (Exodus 24:9): There went up Moses and Aaron,*

וְשִׁבְעִים מִזִּקְנֵי יִשְׂרָאֵל׳. וְלָמָּה לֹא נִתְפָּרְשׁוּ שְׁמוֹתָן שֶׁל זְקֵנִים? — אֶלָּא לְלַמֵּד, שֶׁכָּל שְׁלֹשָׁה וּשְׁלֹשָׁה שֶׁעָמְדוּ בֵּית דִּין עַל־יִשְׂרָאֵל הֲרֵי הוּא כְּבֵית דִּינוֹ שֶׁל מֹשֶׁה.״

נָטַל מַקְלוֹ וּמְעוֹתָיו בְּיָדוֹ, וְהָלַךְ לְיַבְנֶה אֵצֶל רַבָּן גַּמְלִיאֵל בְּיוֹם שֶׁחָל יוֹם הַכִּפּוּרִים לִהְיוֹת בְּחֶשְׁבּוֹנוֹ.

עָמַד רַבָּן גַּמְלִיאֵל וּנְשָׁקוֹ עַל־רֹאשׁוֹ, אָמַר לוֹ: ״בּוֹא בְשָׁלוֹם, רַבִּי וְתַלְמִידִי! רַבִּי בְּחָכְמָה, וְתַלְמִידִי שֶׁקִּבַּלְתָּ דְּבָרַי.״

ג/א [א] **רָאוּהוּ** בֵּית דִּין וְכָל־יִשְׂרָאֵל, נֶחְקְרוּ הָעֵדִים, וְלֹא הִסְפִּיקוּ לוֹמַר: ״מְקֻדָּשׁ,״ עַד שֶׁחָשֵׁכָה — הֲרֵי זֶה מְעֻבָּר.

יד אברהם

Nadav and Avihu, and seventy of the elders of Israel.—Why are the names of the elders not expressly mentioned? Only to teach [us] that every three [people] that arose as a beis din for Israel are considered like the beis din of Moses.

The Torah's omission of the names of the elders of Moses' court provides an answer to those who might claim in future generations that *their* judges are not of the caliber of Moses and Aaron and need not be obeyed. One can point out to these claimants that *their* judges might be of the caliber of the seventy elders who were a part of Moses' beis din (Rav; cf. Tif. Yis.).

נָטַל מַקְלוֹ וּמְעוֹתָיו בְּיָדוֹ, וְהָלַךְ לְיַבְנֶה אֵצֶל רַבָּן גַּמְלִיאֵל בְּיוֹם שֶׁחָל יוֹם הַכִּפּוּרִים לִהְיוֹת בְּחֶשְׁבּוֹנוֹ. — [Then] he took his staff and his money in his hand and went to Yavneh to Rabban Gamliel on the day that Yom Kippur fell according to his reckoning.

After hearing the rule expounded by

R' Akiva, R' Yehoshua felt consoled *(Gemara).* His mind was further set at ease by R' Dosa's teaching and acceptance of Rabban Gamliel's ruling *(Kehati).* Thereupon R' Yehoshua set out to obey the *Nassi's* decree by a public display of voluntary subjugation: he took his money בְּיָדוֹ, *in his hand,* which he had not been ordered to do by Rabban Gamliel. He did so on his own initiative to enhance the power of the *Nassi* in the eyes of the general public *(Hon Ashir).*

עָמַד רַבָּן גַּמְלִיאֵל וּנְשָׁקוֹ עַל־רֹאשׁוֹ, אָמַר לוֹ: ״בּוֹא בְשָׁלוֹם רַבִּי וְתַלְמִידִי! רַבִּי בְּחָכְמָה וְתַלְמִידִי שֶׁקִּבַּלְתָּ דְּבָרַי.״ — *Rabban Gamliel stood up and kissed him on his head, and said to him, 'Come in peace, my master and my disciple! My master in wisdom, and my disciple in that you accepted my words.'*

In this way Rabban Gamliel himself assuaged the feelings of R' Yehoshua by declaring that although he acknowledged R' Yehoshua's superiority over

seventy of the elders of Israel. Why are the names of the elders not expressly mentioned? — Only to teach [us] that every three [people] who arose as a *beis din* for Israel are considered like the *beis din* of Moses.'

[Then] he took his staff and his money in his hand and went to Yavneh to Rabban Gamliel on the day that Yom Kippur fell according to his reckoning.

Rabban Gamliel stood up and kissed him on his head and said to him, 'Come in peace, my master and my disciple! My master in wisdom and my disciple in that you accepted my words.'

1. **I**f the *beis din* and all of Israel saw [the moon], or if the witnesses were interrogated, but they did not manage to say, 'It is sanctified,' before it grew dark — it [the month] is full.

YAD AVRAHAM

him in scholarship, and did not mean to belittle him in any way, he was forced to assert the power of his office to avoid a rift among the people *(Tif. Yis.)*.

Chapter 3

1.

Although the following chapter deals with the subject of blowing the shofar on Rosh Hashanah, the first mishnah is a continuation of the laws of *kiddush hachodesh;* accordingly it would seem to belong in the previous chapter. *Tiferes Yisrael* finds an explanation for this anomaly in the case described in the mishnah. Every thirtieth day of Elul was celebrated as Rosh Hashanah with all its attendant laws and customs (blowing the shofar, making *kiddush,* etc.) in anticipation of the witnessess' arrival later in the day. Our mishnah discusses a case where everyone saw the new moon on the thirtieth and of course treated the day as Rosh Hashanah, but the *beis din* was unable to proclaim the day as Rosh Chodesh. Nevertheless, since everyone saw the new moon and also observed the day as Rosh Hashanah we would be inclined not to invalidate the observance, and let the day stand as the New Year. Our mishnah tells us that all this notwithstanding, Rosh Hashanah must be celebrated the next day since the *beis din* failed to make the declaration until then. (Cf. *Sifsei Chachamim* who offers a homiletical explanation for the placement of this mishnah in this chapter.)

רָאוּהוּ בֵּית דִּין וְכָל יִשְׂרָאֵל, — *If the beis din and all of Israel saw [the moon],*

[This case is an elaboration of the rule stated in 2:7 which makes the date *Rosh Chodesh* dependent on the *beis din's*

proclamation מְקֻדָּשׁ, *It is sanctified.'* In our mishnah, there seems to be reason for dispensing with the rule as will be explained below.]

If the general public [or a large seg-

רָאוּהוּ בֵּית דִּין בִּלְבַד, יַעַמְדוּ שְׁנַיִם וְיָעִידוּ
בִּפְנֵיהֶם וְיֹאמְרוּ: ,,מְקֻדָּשׁ, מְקֻדָּשׁ!"
רָאוּהוּ שְׁלֹשָׁה וְהֵן בֵּית דִּין, יַעַמְדוּ הַשְּׁנַיִם

יד אברהם

ment of it (Ritva)] saw the new moon on the thirtieth day just before nightfall (Rashi).

Although beis din did not have sufficient time to complete the necessary procedures, it would already be general knowledge that the day *should* be proclaimed Rosh Chodesh. One might therefore think that today should be considered Rosh Chodesh even if the beis din failed to make the proper declaration (Gemara 25b).

Meiri notes that in this case, where the beis din itself sighted the new moon along with all of Israel, there is no need for any of the interrogations mentioned in mishnah 2:6.

Rambam and *Rav* interpret that the new moon was sighted on the night preceding the thirtieth day and the beis din's failure to sanctify the month on the next day was not due to lack of time but for some other reason.

נֶחְקְרוּ הָעֵדִים, — or if the witnesses were interrogated,

This is a new case: no one but the witnesses saw the new moon. They underwent interrogation and properly replied to the questions put to them (Gem. 25b).

וְלֹא הִסְפִּיקוּ לוֹמַר: ,,מְקֻדָּשׁ," עַד שֶׁחָשֵׁכָה — but they [beis din] did not manage to say 'It is sanctified,' before it grew dark—

The night of the thirty-first arrived (Rav). Night having fallen, beis din was powerless to continue, since the proclamation of Kiddush HaChodesh must be made during the day. Unlike other adjudications which may be completed at night if begun during the day, beis din's decision regarding the new moon must be announced during daylight (Gemara 25b). [See introduction to Kiddush HaChodesh.]

הֲרֵי זֶה מְעֻבָּר. — it [the month] is full.

The previous month contains thirty days and Rosh Chodesh does not commence until the next day.

This rule applies to both cases of our mishnah:

— Even though all Israel saw the new moon on the thirtieth, since the beis din failed to make the proclamation in time, for whatever reason, the new month does not begin until the next day, notwithstanding the fact that the general public will be confused or critical.

— In the case where the witnesses were already interrogated, one might think that since the beis din began considering the case during the day, it should be similar to דִּינֵי מָמוֹנוֹת, monetary litigations, where beis din may decide at night, provided they began their deliberations during the day (see Sanhedrin 4:1). Our mishnah states, however, that Kiddush Ha-Chodesh must be concluded before nightfall in its entirety, including beis din's declaration (Gemara 25b).

According to *Ramban* (cited in 2:7) that the statement מְקֻדָּשׁ, it is sanctified, is not necessary and the beis din's decision to declare the day Rosh Chodesh is sufficient, our mishnah's expression they did not manage to say must be understood to mean that the beis din was unable to reach its decision before nightfall (Sefer HaZichronos p.41; cf. Toledos Shmuel Kiddush HaChodesh 5:3).

רָאוּהוּ בֵּית דִּין בִּלְבַד, — If only beis din saw it,

The entire Sanhedrin of seventy-one members (Meiri), or a minor sanhedrin of twenty-three members (Tosafos) saw the new moon on the night of the thirtieth (Rav) and there were no other witnesses (Rashi).

This case is unrelated to the preceding ones and the problem here is not lack of time to declare Rosh

3
1

If only *beis din* saw it, two should stand and testify before the others, and they should say, 'It is sanctified, it is sanctified!'

If three saw it and they constitute a *beis din*, then two should stand up and set some of their colleagues

YAD AVRAHAM

Chodesh, but the court's eligibility to act as judge of a matter it had witnessed (*Rashi*).

[The question here is the application of the Talmudic rule לֹא תְהֵא שְׁמִיעָה גְדוֹלָה מֵרְאִיָּה, *hearing cannot be considered greater than seeing*. This means that although a *beis din* normally bases its decisions upon *hearing* the testimony of witnesses, it should be no less competent to render a judgment based on knowledge it acquired through *seeing*. Accordingly, logic would dictate that *beis din* could declare *Rosh Chodesh* without delay in our case since its members had themselves seen the new moon. However, as the *Gemara* (25b) explains, in our case this cannot be done, for the *beis din* witnessed the new moon at night, at which time *Rosh Chodesh* cannot be declared, therefore the procedure detailed below must be followed.[1]]

יַעַמְדוּ שְׁנַיִם וְיָעִידוּ בִּפְנֵיהֶם וְיֹאמְרוּ: ,,מְקֻדָּשׁ, מְקֻדָּשׁ!'' — *two [of them] should stand and testify before the others, and they should say, 'It is sanctified, it is sanctified!'*

Since there are no witnesses other than the members of the court, two of them must stand before their colleagues the next day and testify. The *beis din* may then declare *Rosh Chodesh*, following the procedure outlined in 2:7, with the head of the court proclaiming מְקֻדָּשׁ, *'It is sanctified'*, and the people

assembled responding מְקֻדָּשׁ, מְקֻדָּשׁ!', *It is sanctified! It is sanctified!' (Kehati)*.

This formality is necessary only because the *beis din* saw the new moon at night. If they saw it during daytime, they may declare *Rosh Chodesh* without hearing testimony (*Rambam, Meiri, et. al.*).

[Our mishnah's mention of 'standing' to testify is in keeping with the verse in *Deuteronomy* 19:17: וְעָמְדוּ שְׁנֵי הָאֲנָשִׁים, *and the two men shall stand*, which the *Gemara* (*Shavuos* 30a) interprets as a law requiring witnesses to stand while they testify.]

רָאוּהוּ שְׁלֹשָׁה וְהֵן בֵּית דִּין, — *If three saw it and they constitute a beis din*,

[The three who saw it are duly ordained and qualified to proclaim *Rosh Chodesh*.]

[This case is similar to the previous one, except that here only *three* members of the *beis din* saw the moon at night. If two of them bear witness, their colleague cannot serve as the *beis din* since *Kiddush HaChodesh* requires a *beis din* of no fewer than three members. Here, therefore, the procedure is somewhat different than in the above case.]

יַעַמְדוּ הַשְׁנַיִם וְיוֹשִׁיבוּ מֵחַבְרֵיהֶם אֵצֶל הַיָּחִיד וְיָעִידוּ בִּפְנֵיהֶם, — *then two should stand up and set some of their colleagues beside the single one and testify before them,*

Meiri argues that the three who saw the new moon must have been among

---

1. *Tosafos* explains why the *beis din* cannot simply declare *Rosh Chodesh* during the next day based on its previous night's sighting. Whenever *beis din* renders a judgment based on its own sighting of an event, it is because the sighting is equivalent to קַבָּלַת עֵדוּת, *acceptance of testimony*. But testimony only may be accepted during the day, just as a *beis din's* decision must be rendered during the day. *Tosefos R' Akiva Eiger* concludes from this that if the *beis din* saw the new moon on the evening of the thirtieth before nightfall but did not manage to declare *Rosh Chodesh* before dark, it may do so the next day without the formality of hearing testimony since its sighting — the equivalent of testimony — took place at a valid time. [See *Rashi* and *Rav* who seem to disagree. However, *Ralbach* (comm. to *Rambam, Kiddush HaChodesh* 2:9) concludes that *Rashi* agrees with *Tosafos*.]

וְיוֹשִׁיבוּ מֵחַבְרֵיהֶם אֵצֶל הַיָּחִיד וְיָעִידוּ
בִּפְנֵיהֶם, וְיֹאמְרוּ: ,,מְקֻדָּשׁ, מְקֻדָּשׁ!'' שֶׁאֵין
הַיָּחִיד נֶאֱמָן עַל־יְדֵי עַצְמוֹ.

[ב] כָּל ־הַשּׁוֹפָרוֹת כְּשֵׁרִין חוּץ מִשֶּׁל פָּרָה,
מִפְּנֵי שֶׁהוּא קֶרֶן.
אָמַר רַבִּי יוֹסֵי: וַהֲלֹא כָל הַשּׁוֹפָרוֹת נִקְרְאוּ
קֶרֶן, שֶׁנֶּאֱמַר: ,,בִּמְשֹׁךְ בְּקֶרֶן הַיּוֹבֵל''.

יד אברהם

the most illustrious members of the Sanhedrin. If not, this entire procedure would be unnecessary for all three could testify before their colleagues. But if the three are among the most illustrious it would be disrespectful to have them testify before their lesser colleagues. Consequently, one of them, the greatest of the three, should be a member of the beis din with at least two others of lesser stature, before whom the remaining judge-witnesses testify.

,,מְקֻדָּשׁ, מְקֻדָּשׁ!'' :וְיֹאמְרוּ — and they say, 'It is sanctified, it is sanctified!'

[This is the procedure mentioned in mishnah 2:7.]

Had the three seen the moon during the day, they can declare Rosh Chodesh without the following procedure unless they wish to show respect for their colleagues by seating them as the beis din (Meiri).

שֶׁאֵין הַיָּחִיד נֶאֱמָן עַל־יְדֵי עַצְמוֹ. — For an individual is not trusted alone.

The mishnah here teaches us why we add two judges to the one who saw the moon instead of allowing him to act as a one-man court. The Gemara explains that although a single properly-ordained and expert judge may try financial disputes (as mentioned in Sanhedrin 5a), a minimum beis din of three is required for Kiddush HaChodesh as derived from Exodus 12:1 where the authority to decide on Kiddush HaChodesh was not given to Moses alone but to Moses and Aaron together. Tosafos adds that although this would seem to indicate that a beis din of two is sufficient, a third judge must be added to conform to the rule mentioned in Sanhedrin 1:6 that a beis din may not contain an even number of judges.

2.

◄§ Sounding the Shofar

Having completed the subject of Kiddush HaChodesh, the remainder of our tractate is given over to the laws and regulations governing tekias shofar [blowing the shofar], the performance of which is the distinctive mitzvah of Rosh Hashanah.

Tekias shofar on Rosh Hashanah is mandated by the Torah in Numbers (29:1): יוֹם תְּרוּעָה יִהְיֶה לָכֶם, a day of shofar blowing shall it be for you. While the Torah does not explicitly state here that a shofar, as opposed to a trumpet or other instrument, must be used, the Gemara (34a) derives the need for a shofar from Leviticus 25:9 which discusses Yom Kippur of the Jubilee year (see 3:5). There the shofar is clearly mentioned as the instrument which must be blown.

The following mishnah discusses which type of shofar is valid for use on Rosh Hashanah.

beside the single one and testify before them, and say, 'It is sanctified, it is sanctified!' For an individual is not trusted alone.

2. **A**ll shofars are valid except for that of a cow, because it is called a *keren*.

R' Yose said: But are not all shofars called *keren*, as it is said (*Joshua* 6:5): *When they make a long blast with the ram's keren?*

YAD AVRAHAM

כָּל-הַשׁוֹפָרוֹת כְּשֵׁרִין — *All shofars are valid*

All animal horns that are called shofar are valid for use on Rosh Hashanah. This includes the horns of rams, ewes and goats which are curved and the horn of the wild goat (see following mishnah) which is straight (*Meiri*).

[While any of the above-mentioned horns is acceptable, the preferred horn is the subject of dispute between the tanna of the next mishnah and R' Yehudah in mishnah 5.]

Ran, pointing out that the word שׁוֹפָר has its root in the word שְׁפוֹפֶרֶת, *hollow tube*, disqualifies any horn that is not naturally hollow (e.g., deers' horns) and requires carving out to make it fit for blowing.

Ran also disqualifies horns of a non-kosher animal by analogy to the law that tefillin must be made only from the skin of a kosher animal as stated in *Shabbos* 28a.

Mishnah Berurah 586:8 notes that since there is some doubt as to *Ran's* view that the rule for tefillin also applies to shofar, one who has no other shofar but that of a non-kosher animal should blow it without reciting the blessing of shofar blowing.

חוּץ מִשֶּׁל פָּרָה, — *except for that of a cow,*

The mishnah mentions only a cow because its horns are better fit for use as a shofar than those of male cattle, but the horns of a bull or ox are equally invalid (*Meiri*).

Tosefos Yom Tov explains the

specific mention of a cow: since the verse which excludes the use of cattle horns (see below) speaks of an ox, the mishnah informs us that a cow, too, is excluded.

מִפְּנֵי שֶׁהוּא קָרֶן. — *because it is [called] a keren* [i.e., *horn*].

Deuteronomy (33:17) uses the term *keren* for cattle horns: בְּכוֹר שׁוֹרוֹ הָדָר לוֹ וְקַרְנֵי רְאֵם קַרְנָיו, *His first-born ox, majesty is his; and his horns are the horns of the wild-ox*, but on Rosh Hashanah only a horn called shofar may be used (*Rav*).

The *Gemara* mentions another reason for the disqualification of cattle horns for use in the *mitzvah* of *tekias shofar*. Since the Jews worshipped the Golden Calf, it is improper to use the horns of a calf (or any cattle) in the performance of a *mitzvah* in which we ask God to remember us with favor. This is in keeping with the dictum: אֵין קָטֵיגוֹר נַעֲשֶׂה סַנֵיגוֹר, *a prosecutor cannot become a defender.*

For the same reason, the *Kohen Gadol* [high priest] removed his *golden* vestments, made of the material used to form the Golden Calf, and wore vestments of plain white linen when performing the Yom Kippur service in the Holy of Holies (see *Rashi* to *Lev.* 16:4).

אָמַר רַבִּי יוֹסֵי: וְהָלֹא כָל הַשׁוֹפָרוֹת נִקְרְאוּ קֶרֶן, שֶׁנֶּאֱמַר: ״בִּמְשׁךְ בְּקֶרֶן הַיּוֹבֵל.״ — *R' Yose said: But are not all shofars called keren as it is said (Joshua 6:5): "When they make a long blast with the ram's keren"?*

Some readings of the mishnah have at

[ג] **שׁוֹפָר** שֶׁל רֹאשׁ הַשָּׁנָה שֶׁל יָעֵל, פָּשׁוּט,
וּפִיו מְצֻפֶּה זָהָב, וּשְׁתֵּי
חֲצוֹצְרוֹת מִן־הַצְּדָדִין.
שׁוֹפָר מַאֲרִיךְ וַחֲצוֹצְרוֹת מְקַצְּרוֹת, שֶׁמִּצְוַת
הַיּוֹם בַּשׁוֹפָר.

יד אברהם

the end of the above verse, בְּשָׁמְעֲכֶם
אֶת־קוֹל הַשּׁוֹפָר, *when you hear the sound
of the shofar (Meiri)*. At any rate, even a
ram's horn, which is called shofar is not
disqualified simply because one verse
refers to it as *keren*. Similarly, a cow's
horn is valid even though its generic
name is *keren (Meiri; Rav; cf. Rashi,
Tosafos)*.

The *Gemara* quotes the reply of the
Sages (who were the proponents of the
first view) to R' Yose: All shofars are
called both shofar and *keren*, while a
cow's horn is called only *keren*, but not
shofar. The cow's horn is disqualified,
therefore, not because it is called *keren*
but because it is never called *shofar*.
Therefore, any horn which is called by
both names is acceptable *(Meiri)*.

Yerushalmi (3:2) asks: Why do the
Sages permit the use of a wild goat's
horn (mishnah 3) — it, too, is never
called shofar? *Yerushalmi* answers that
the main reason to disqualify a calf's
horn is because of the Golden Calf.

Meiri gives a different answer to
Yerushalmi's question: Since a wild
goat's horn is called neither shofar nor
keren in Scripture, it is valid for use
because people commonly refer it as
shofar. A cow's horn, on the other
hand, which Scripture entitles *keren*,
cannot be valid, no matter what name
people give it.

Ran and *Meiri* ask further: The horn
of a he-goat is referred to in Scripture
(*Daniel* 8:5) as *keren* and never as
shofar, and it should therefore be invalid. They reply that goats and sheep
are like species and are called by the
same name in *Deut.* 14:4. The validity
of ram's horns therefore extends to include goat's horns.

The halachah favors the view of the
Sages *(Rav)* [and therefore all shofars
are acceptable (though not necessarily
preferable) except for the horns of cattle. But see *comm.* to mishnah 5 where
Rambam is quoted as having a different
view].

3.

שׁוֹפָר שֶׁל רֹאשׁ הַשָּׁנָה — *The shofar of
Rosh Hashanah*
[As opposed to the shofar used on
fast-days, discussed in the following
mishnah.]

שֶׁל יָעֵל, — *should be from a wild goat,*
While the tanna agrees with the
previous mishnah that all shofars are
valid, it is preferable in his view to use
the horn of a wild goat *(Meiri)*.

Most commentators render יָעֵל as
wild goat which is a חַיָּה, *un-
domesticated animal*, a rendering which
is based on *Onkelos* to *Deuteronomy*

14:5 which lists the kosher animals.
One of them אַקּוֹ, is translated by
Onkelos as יַעְלָא *(Rashi; Tosafos;
Meiri)*.

Aruch, however, translates יָעֵל as
young ewe, whose horns are usually
straight. Cf. *Tos. Yom Tov.*

פָּשׁוּט, — *straight,*
The horn of the wild goat is called
straight only in a relative sense, since it
is considerably less curved than that of
a sheep *(Meiri)*.

The tanna's preference for a straight
horn on Rosh Hashanah is based on the

3
3

3. The shofar of Rosh Hashanah should be from a wild goat, straight, and with a gold covered mouthpiece, and with two trumpets at the sides.

The shofar blows long and the trumpets blow short, for the commandment of the day is with the shofar.

YAD AVRAHAM

fact that it is used during prayer (*Meiri*, see mishnah 4:5), a time when one's thoughts should be simple and 'straight' (*Gemara* 26b *Rashi; Rav*), willingly accepting whatever God may decree for him *(Tif. Yis.).*

וּפִיו מְצֻפֶּה זָהָב, — *and with a gold covered mouthpiece,*

This procedure was followed only when the shofar was blown in the *Beis HaMikdash* [Holy Temple] but not anywhere else *(Rashi; Rav).*

The *Gemara* points out that the gold may not plate the part of the mouthpiece where the blower places his lips, as this would be a חֲצִיצָה, *interposition,* between his lips and the shofar (*Meiri*) and the resultant sound would be emanating through the medium of the gold and not the shofar (Rashi).

It would appear from *Rashi* that חֲצִיצָה, *interposition,* alone is not sufficient reason to disqualify such a shofar but rather the fact that the sound emanates from the gold. *Ramban* (cited by *Maggid Mishneh, Hilchos Shofar* 1:6), however, is of the opinion that interposition alone, even if the sound was unaffected, renders the shofar unfit for use. Consequently, if one blew into a shofar without his lips actually touching it, his blowing would be invalid, even though the sound comes only from the combination of his breath and the shofar *(Sifsei Chachamim).*

Rambam in describing the procedure of blowing the shofar in the Temple (*Shofar* 1:2) completely omits mention of our mishnah's statement that its mouthpiece was covered with gold. *Yom Teruah* explains that *Rambam* follows the view of the Sages in mishnah 2 who invalidate a cow's horn because

אֵין קָטֵיגוֹר נַעֲשָׂה סָנֵיגוֹר, *a prosecutor cannot turn into a defender.* For the same reason, gold should not be used (see *comm.* to above mishnah s.v. מפני). Our mishnah, which permits the use of gold on the shofar, follows the view of R' Yose who does permit the use of cow horns. The halachah does not follow R' Yose.

וּשְׁתֵּי חֲצוֹצְרוֹת מִן־הַצְּדָדִין. — *and two trumpets at the sides.*

Two men blowing silver trumpets stood on either side of the one blowing the shofar. This too, was done only in the Holy Temple and is derived by the *Gemara* from *Psalms* 98:6: בַּחֲצוֹצְרוֹת וְקוֹל שׁוֹפָר הָרִיעוּ לִפְנֵי הַמֶּלֶךְ ה', *with trumpets and shofar sound, call out before the King, HASHEM.* [The words *before the King, HASHEM* mean, in the Temple] *(Tif. Yis.).*

The shofar is placed in the center because of its importance as the commandment of the day, as the most important and distinguished of a group of people walks in the middle (*Ran; Tos. Yom Tov*).

שׁוֹפָר מַאֲרִיךְ וַחֲצוֹצְרוֹת מְקַצְּרוֹת, — *The shofar blows long and the trumpets blow short,*

After the sound of the trumpets has ceased, the shofar continues and is heard by itself, *(Meiri; Rav)* as a sign that the main obligation of the day is the shofar blowing *(Tos. Yom Tov).*

The *Gemara* raises the question that our mishnah seems to contradict the rule: תְּרֵי קָלֵי לָא מִשְׁתַּמְעֵי, *two [simultaneous] sounds cannot be distinguished,* since the shofar and trumpets are sounded together at the start in spite of the halachah that the shofar sound must

[ד] בַּתַּעֲנִיּוֹת, בְּשֶׁל זְכָרִים, כְּפוּפִין,
וּפִיהֶן מְצֻפֶּה כֶסֶף, וּשְׁתֵּי
חֲצוֹצְרוֹת בָּאֶמְצַע.
שׁוֹפָר מְקַצֵּר וַחֲצוֹצְרוֹת מַאֲרִיכוֹת, שֶׁמִּצְוַת
הַיּוֹם בַּחֲצוֹצְרוֹת.

יד אברהם

be heard from beginning to end. The *Gemara* responds that when a sound is חָבִיב, *dear*, to the listener he exerts enough concentration to distinguish the sound he is required to hear.

שֶׁמִּצְוַת הַיּוֹם בַּשׁוֹפָר. — *for the commandment of the day is with the shofar.*

Although the trumpets are also re-quired in the Temple as derived from *Psalms* 98:6 and can therefore be described as part of the *commandment of the day,* the blowing of the shofar is nevertheless of greater importance, because it is mandated by the Torah (*Numbers* 29:1) while the trumpets are mentioned only in כְּתוּבִים, *the Hagiographa (Sifsei Chachamim).*

4.

The previous mishnah having described the type of shofar preferable for use on Rosh Hashanah, and the procedure followed, this mishnah in-forms us that on fast-days a different type of shofar and procedure were used.

בַּתַּעֲנִיּוֹת, — *On fast-days,*

[A community beset by calamity is under a Rabbinic obligation to declare days of fasting and special prayer until the calamity has passed (*Rambam, Hilchos Taanis* 1:4). The types of calamity which demand the declaration of a fast are described at length in *Taanis* 1:5-7, 3:1-7 (see ArtScroll comm.). In addition to fasting, there is a Scriptural obliga-tion derived from *Numbers* 10:9 to sound the trumpets in order to stir the hearts of the people and to bring them to repentance through instilling the realization that the calamity came about because of their evil deeds (*Rambam, Taanis* 1:1-3). In the Temple, the *shofar* was blown along with the trumpets, in keeping with *Psalms* 98:6 (as mentioned in the previous mishnah).]

בְּשֶׁל זְכָרִים, כְּפוּפִין, — *they* [i.e., the shofars] *are of rams'* [horns], *curved*

The ram's horn, which is curved and bent, represents humility and subjuga-tion, which are most appropriate to a fast-day (*Gemara, 26b*).

The *Gemara* quotes a differing view that the shofar used on fast-days is a straight wild-goat's horn. *Lechem Mishneh* (based on *Rashi* 26b) in-terprets this to mean that on fast-days it does not matter what type of shofar is used — whether curved or straight. He thereby explains *Rambam's* failure to mention (in *Hilchos Taanis* 1:4) the specific type of shofar that must be blown on fast-days — for all kinds are equally permitted.

Ritva, however, quotes an opinion that on fast-days a straight horn should be used in order to differentiate between fast-days, when blowing the shofar is a Rabbinic obligation, and Rosh Hasha-nah when blowing the shofar is a Scrip-tural injunction. This opinion follows the halachically accepted view of R' Yehudah (mishnah 5) who calls for a curved shofar on Rosh Hashanah.

וּפִיהֶן מְצֻפֶּה כֶסֶף, — *and with silver-plated mouthpieces,*

4. On fast-days, they are of rams' [horns], curved, and with silver plated mouthpieces, and with two trumpets in the middle.

The shofar blows short and the trumpets blow long, for the commandment of the day is with the trumpets.

YAD AVRAHAM

The *Gemara* 27a mentions two reasons for covering the fast-day shofar with silver as opposed to the shofar of Rosh Hashanah which was gold plated.

— All horns used for gathering the populace were of silver as mentioned in *Numbers* 10:2 [and fast-days are times of communal gathering *(Tos. Yom Tov)*].

The Torah did not require Jews to go to the added expense of acquiring gold. On Rosh Hashanah, however, the honor of the day requires the use of gold.

וּשְׁתֵּי חֲצוֹצְרוֹת בָּאֶמְצַע. — *and with two trumpets in the middle.*

Two men stood in the middle blowing trumpets while to their right and left stood another two blowing shofars (Rav).

שׁוֹפָר מְקַצֵּר וַחֲצוֹצְרוֹת מַאֲרִיכוֹת, — *The shofar blows short and the trumpets blow long,*

[This is in contrast to the Temple procedure on Rosh Hashanah when the reverse was true as described in the previous mishnah.]

שֶׁמִּצְוַת הַיּוֹם בַּחֲצוֹצְרוֹת. — *for the com-*

mandment of the day is with the trumpets.

As specified in *Numbers* 10:9: עַל־הַצַּר הַצֹּרֵר אֶתְכֶם וַהֲרֵעֹתֶם בַּחֲצֹצְרֹת, [*When waging battle*] *against the enemy who oppresses you, you shall sound an alarm with trumpets (Rav).* [While the verse refers specifically to military aggression, its intent is extended to include all forms of calamity (see *Taanis* 3:8; *Rambam, Taanis* 1:1).]

While all commentators agree that our mishnah describes the fast-day procedure in the Temple, there is considerable disagreement among the authorities regarding the procedure followed outside the Temple: *Rambam* holds that only trumpets were used and the shofar was not blown at all. *Rashba's* view is that either shofars or trumpets could be used.

According to *Raavad*, trumpets were blown only during the special benedictions added to the regular prayers on a fast-day as described in the second chapter of *Taanis*. The shofar was blown throughout the rest of the day whenever prayers were said (see *Maggid Mishnah* and *Lechem Mishnah, Hilchos Taanis* 1:4).[1]

5.

The Torah (*Lev.* 25:9) ordains the blowing of the shofar on Yom Kippur of the Jubilee Year to announce the freedom of all Jewish slaves and the

return to their original owners of fields sold during the previous forty-nine years. The preceding *mishnayos* discussed the type of shofar to be used on

---

1. Nowadays, the procedure of blowing the shofar or trumpet on fast-days is no longer followed (see *Mishnah Berurah* 586:1, *Aruch HaShulchan* 586:3,4).

[ה] **שָׁוֶה** הַיּוֹבֵל לְרֹאשׁ הַשָּׁנָה לַתְּקִיעָה
וְלַבְּרָכוֹת.
רַבִּי יְהוּדָה אוֹמֵר: בְּרֹאשׁ הַשָּׁנָה תּוֹקְעִין
בְּשֶׁל זְכָרִים, וּבַיּוֹבְלוֹת בְּשֶׁל יְעֵלִים.

[ו] **שׁוֹפָר** שֶׁנִּסְדַּק וְדִבְּקוֹ, פָּסוּל. דִּבֵּק
שִׁבְרֵי שׁוֹפָרוֹת, פָּסוּל. נִקַּב

יד אברהם

Rosh Hashanah and on fast-days; the mishnah now teaches about the shofar preferable for use in the Jubilee Year.

שָׁוֶה הַיּוֹבֵל לְרֹאשׁ הַשָּׁנָה לַתְּקִיעָה — *The Jubilee Year is similar to Rosh Hashanah regarding the blowing* [of the shofar]

A straight horn of a wild goat should be used, similar to that of Rosh Hashanah, as mentioned above (mishnah 3). Although the reason for using a straight horn on Rosh Hashanah — that it is blown during prayer (see mishnah 3 s.v. פָּשׁוּט) — seems to be inapplicable to the shofar of the Jubilee year whose purpose is to announce the freeing of slaves and the return of fields to their original owners, nevertheless the tanna derives from Scripture that the same type of shofar is used in both instances (*Rav*).

Our mishnah uses the word לַתְּקִיעָה, *regarding the blowing*, to allude not only to the type of shofar, but also to the number of sounds that must be blown on *Yovel* [the Jubilee year]; they must be equal to the number blown on Rosh Hashanah as described in mishnah 4:9 (*Rav; Tif. Yis.*).

וְלַבְּרָכוֹת — *and the benedictions.*

The prayers and benedictions (described in mishnah 4:5,6) that are added to the *mussaf* [additional service] of Rosh Hashanah are also added to the *mussaf* of Yom Kippur in the Jubilee year (*Rav*).

The *Gemara* (27a) states, however, that the verse: זֶה הַיּוֹם תְּחִלַּת מַעֲשֶׂיךָ, *This day marks the start of Your crea-*tion, which is included in the Rosh Hashanah *mussaf* is *not* recited on Yom Kippur of *Yovel*, because it refers to the creation of Man which occurred on Rosh Hashanah.

רַבִּי יְהוּדָה אוֹמֵר: בְּרֹאשׁ הַשָּׁנָה תּוֹקְעִין בְּשֶׁל זְכָרִים, — *R' Yehudah says: On Rosh Hashanah [we] blow with rams' horns,*

R' Yehudah disagrees with the *tanna kamma* (and with the view mentioned in mishnah 3). He is of the opinion that even on Rosh Hashanah a curved horn is preferred, because a יוֹם הַדִּין, *day of judgment*, requires humility and subjugation, like on a fast-day (*Meiri*).

While all authorities agree that the halachah favors R' Yehudah's view, *Rambam* and most other commentators disagree regarding the proper interpretation of R' Yehudah's statement. *Rambam* (*Shofar* 1:1) holds that R' Yehudah disagrees with mishnah 2 which declared that all shofars, whether curved or straight, are valid for use on Rosh Hashanah (i.e., although one or the other may be preferable, the use of either is acceptable בְּדִיעֲבַד, *after the fact*). R' Yehudah holds that the *only* valid shofar is a curved ram's horn.

Most authorities disagree and interpret R' Yehudah's words as expressing only a *preference* for curved rams' horns — while still accepting the validity of all other horns as stated in mishnah 2 (*Ra'avad, Rosh, Ran*).

According to this view — which is the halachically accepted one (see *Orach Chaim* 586:1) — there are three levels of preference regarding the shofar to be

5. The Jubilee Year is similar to Rosh Hashanah regarding the blowing and the benedictions.

R' Yehudah says: On Rosh Hashanah [we] blow with rams' [horns], and on the Jubilee Years with wild goats' [horns].

6. A shofar that was split and he glued it together, is invalid. If he glued together broken pieces of a shofar, it is invalid. If there is a hole and he

YAD AVRAHAM

used on Rosh Hashanah.

a) All horns qualifying for the name 'shofar' are valid whether they are curved or straight. The exceptions are cattle horns, those of non-kosher animals, and horns that are not hollow as mentioned in *comm.* to mishnah 2.

b) It is preferable to use a curved horn in keeping with the view of R' Yehudah that Rosh Hashanah is a day calling for humility and submission.

c) It is especially preferable to use a curved *ram's* horn in order to invoke the merit of עֲקֵידַת יִצְחָק, *the binding of Isaac* (see *Gen.* 22:13) when Abraham sacrificed a ram in place of Isaac after having displayed his willingness to offer his own son as a a sacrifice to God (*Rosh, Ran*; cf. *Mishnah Berurah* 586:2-5).

וּבַיּוֹבְלוֹת בְּשֶׁל יְעֵלִים. — *and on the Jubilee years with wild goats' [horns].*

R' Yehudah holds that on the Jubilee, when the shofar is blown to signify freedom for slaves and the redemption of land from the ownership of strangers, a straight horn is more appropriate. Nevertheless, he agrees that in other matters (e.g., the benedictions) the Jubilee is similar to Rosh Hashanah (*Meiri; Ran; Tos. Yom Tov*).

The final ruling in regard to the Jubilee is the subject of dispute by the authorities. *Meiri* favors the view of R' Yehudah that a straight horn should be used. *Rambam (Shemitah VeYovel* 10:11) rules that the Jubilee is likened to Rosh Hashanah in all ways, including the use of a curved ram's horn.

6.

שׁוֹפָר שֶׁנִּסְדַּק — *A shofar that was split*

The mishnah refers to a crack along the length of the shofar (*Gemara* 27b), which penetrated completely the wall of the shofar. If, however, the wall is merely chipped, the shofar is not disqualified although it is preferable to have it mended prior to Rosh Hashanah (*Mishnah Berurah* 586:37, *Aruch Ha-Shulchan* 586:15).

The exact nature of this crack that invalidates the shofar is the subject of

considerable controversy:

According to *Rashi*, the shofar is completely split lengthwise into two separate pieces and its disqualification is due to the *Gemara's* (26a) rule: שׁוֹפָר אֶחָד אָמַר רַחֲמָנָא וְלֹא שְׁנַיִם וּשְׁלֹשָׁה שׁוֹפָרוֹת, *the Torah states [that the sound must emanate from] one shofar and not [from] two or three shofars.* Even if the separate pieces are glued together, the resultant shofar is still considered as a combination of two shofars.[1]

1. *Tosafos* questions *Rashi's* explanation by pointing out that according to him, the case of a split shofar is identical with the following one in the mishnah [*if he glued together...*] and one of them is therefore redundant. *Rosh* resolves the problem by explaining that in the next case, the shofar was split across the breadth; when separate pieces were attached, the sound travels from one piece to the other, thereby causing the problem of two or three shofars; in our case,

וּסְתָמוֹ: אִם מְעַכֵּב אֶת־הַתְּקִיעָה — פָּסוּל, וְאִם
לָאו — כָּשֵׁר.

יד אברהם

Tosafos holds that the shofar was split all along its length, but only on one side and is therefore still in one piece. It is disqualified because, once split, it is no longer considered a shofar but rather a piece of a shofar which one molded into an instrument similar to a shofar (*Ran*).

Maggid Mishneh (*Shofar* 1:5) maintains that if it was split along most of its length (even on only one side) it is not valid.

Rabbeinu Yonasan (quoted by *Ran*) holds that even the smallest crack along its length disqualifies it because the crack will widen (even if sealed) as the shofar is blown, and will eventually extend along the entire length of the shofar.[1] Therefore, if the shofar is tightly secured with cord to prevent further splitting, it is valid.

According to all views, our mishnah speaks only of a crack along the *length* of the shofar. A crack across its width does not disqualify it, provided the minimum length of a shofar (i.e., a *tefach* — 3-4 inches) remains whole (*Gemara* 27b).

Most authorities agree that this minimum length must extend from the mouthpiece to the crack. Otherwise the shofar is not valid (*Rosh, Ran, Meiri*).

Others validate the shofar as long as there is an entire whole *tefach* anywhere along its length, even though there is no *tefach* between the mouthpiece and the

crack (*R' Yitzchak ibn Gias*, quoted by *Ran*).

It should be noted that only if most of the shofar's circumference is cracked must the above condition be met. A smaller crack does not disqualify the shofar in any case (*Rosh*).

וְדִבְּקוֹ, — *and he glued it together,*

The mishnah means to emphasize that the shofar remains invalid even if it was repaired, but according to all the interpretations cited above, the shofar is *surely* invalid if the crack was not sealed (*Ran*).

It should be noted, however, that according to *Rashi* and *Tosafos* our mishnah speaks only of a crack that extends the entire length of the shofar. Consequently, a smaller crack (even one that runs along the majority of the shofar's length) can be sealed, rendering the shofar valid. The method of sealing is a subject of controversy. According to *Ramban*, the crack must be sealed by heating the shofar, thus causing the broken ends to weld together. Any foreign material, such as glue, may not be used, for it would mean that the sound is transmitted by means of another substance in addition to the shofar. *Ramban's* ruling is based on the third case in our mishnah, which specifies that a hole may be plugged only with shofar material (see below).

Rosh disagrees and permits the use of

however, the shofar is split lengthwise into two pieces which are attached, the sound then travels along one piece and one might think that the above invalidity is inapplicable. [The mishnah, however, disqualifies even such a shofar, for both pieces are required to produce a sound, thus bringing into play the injunction against two shofars.] Cf. *P'nei Yehoshua*.

Tosafos (27a) also disagrees with *Rashi's* view that attached pieces of a shofar fall into the category of two shofars. An example of two shofars, according to *Tosafos* would be placing two shofars one inside the other and blowing through them. The sound that emanates from the space between the two is not valid because it comes from two shofars (*Tos.* 27b אם ד"ה).

1. *Shulchan Aruch HaRav* 586:8 explains that in *Rabbenu Yonasan's* view it is not considered a *shofar* since it will eventually split completely; accordingly it is disqualified מִדְּאוֹרַיְתָא, *by Torah law. Aruch Hashulchan* 586:15 disagrees and holds that it is disqualified only by Rabbinic law because of the *possibility* that it may crack completely while being blown on Rosh Hashanah without the blower being aware of it.

sealed it: if it hinders the blowing — it is invalid, and
if not — it is valid.

YAD AVRAHAM

any sealant, differentiating between plugging a hole where the material used is visible and sealing a crack where the sealant is invisible (see *Orach Chaim* 586:8).

פָּסוּל. — *is invalid.*

Because it is considered like two shofars (*Rashi*) or because it cannot be called a shofar (*Tosafos*).

The halachah is as follows:

a) A shofar that was split along its entire length (even on one side) is not valid even if the crack was sealed by heating the shofar.

b) If most of its length is split it is not valid unless sealed (with any sealant).

c) If less than the majority is split, it should not be used (unless sealed) unless no other shofar is available, in which case it may be used even if the crack is not sealed. If the shofar is tightly bound to prevent further splitting, it may be used in any case (*Mishnah Berurah* 586:37-48).

דְּבֵק שִׁבְרֵי שׁוֹפָרוֹת, פָּסוּל. — *If he glued together broken pieces of a shofar, it is not valid.*

A shofar that had broken apart along its width in several places, resulting in two or three broken pieces is not valid after being mended because the shofar now consists of two or three shofars, in violation of the Scriptural rule that the sound must emanate from only one shofar. This disqualification exists even if each piece contains the minimum length needed for a shofar (a *tefach*) so that if the pieces had not been united, each one by itself would have been a valid shofar (*Meiri*).

Ritva quotes a more lenient view according to which our mishnah refers to broken pieces, each of which would *not* be a valid shofar by itself. [The reason

for the disqualification would be that the instrument created by such broken pieces is not considered a shofar.]

Tosafos (27a) quoted in the footnote above would appear to agree with this view.

The halachah favors the first view (*Orach Chaim* 586:10).

נֶקֶב — *If there is a hole* [*in the shofar*]

The size of this hole is less than half of the shofar, leaving most of it intact. A hole covering most of the shofar renders it invalid (*Gemara*) because it is no longer considered a shofar. Furthermore, there is no way in which this blemish can be corrected and the shofar made fit for use; for even if the hole is sealed properly, the resultant instrument is similar to one made by attaching broken fragments of a shofar, none of which is a valid shofar by itself (*Bayis Chadash* 586 s.v. ניקב; cf. *Mishnah Berurah* 586:31).

וּסְתָמוֹ: — *and he sealed it:*

Yerushalmi states that if he failed to plug the hole, the shofar is valid, notwithstanding the quality of the sound emanating from such a shofar, in keeping with the rule (*Rosh Hashanah* 27b) כָּל הַקּוֹלוֹת כְּשֵׁרִין בְּשׁוֹפָר, *all sounds* (i.e., high, low, thick, thin, soft, harsh) *emanating from a shofar are valid.* *Rama* (586:7) states, however, that it is preferable not to use a shofar with a hole in it. Cf. *Be'ur Halachah* s.v. שאין: *Aruch HaShulchan* 586:23.

Most authorities explain that the mishnah's case is one in which the hole was plugged בְּמִינוֹ, *with its own kind* (i.e., *shofar* material).[1] If the plug was שֶׁלֹא בְּמִינוֹ, *not with its own kind* (i.e., a different material), the shofar is not valid because the sound coming from it is caused by a combination the shofar and the other material, and the Torah requires a sound caused by the shofar

1. The problem of two shofars does not arise in this case since the majority of the shofar is intact. Therefore, the shofar-material used to plug the hole is בָּטל, *neutralized*, and is considered part of the larger shofar, rather than a separate entity (*Ran;* cf. *Bayis Chadash* 586 s.v. ניקב).

[ז] **הַתּוֹקֵעַ** לְתוֹךְ הַבּוֹר אוֹ לְתוֹךְ הַדּוּת אוֹ
לְתוֹךְ הַפִּטָּם: אִם קוֹל שׁוֹפָר
שָׁמַע — יָצָא; וְאִם קוֹל הֲבָרָה שָׁמַע — לֹא
יָצָא.

יד אברהם

alone (Rif; Rambam, Shofar 1:5; Ran; Rav).

Other authorities hold that the hole may be plugged with any material; as long as the sound is unaffected by the plug (see below) it is considered as if the sound was caused by the shofar alone (Tosafos; Rosh).

אִם מְעַכֵּב אֶת־הַתְּקִיעָה— — if it hinders the blowing—

If the hole was of such a nature that before it was plugged, no sound could be produced from the shofar (Meiri).

Another interpretation is that the hole hindered the blowing by weakening the sound, and plugging the hole causes the sound to return to its original quality (Yesh Meforshim quoted by Rosh).

A third view is that the quality of the sound declined after the plugging of the hole (Ramban; Ran).

פָּסוּל, — it is invalid,

According to the first two interpretations above, the disqualification is because the new sound is caused by the shofar in combination with the plug (Meiri).

According to the third explanation, because the material plugging the hole manifestly causes a change in the quality of the sound, the plug cannot be considered בָּטֵל, neutralized, and therefore does not lose its identity in the shofar (Ran).

וְאִם לָאו — כָּשֵׁר. — and if not — it is valid.

If the plug does not affect the sound of the shofar, it is considered neutral and part of the larger shofar (Kehati).

The halachah in our case is as follows:

A shofar with a plugged hole is valid if three conditions are met:

a) The hole covers less than half the shofar;

b) the shofar was sealed בְּמִינוֹ, with its own kind (i.e., shofar-material);

c) the sound of the shofar after being sealed is the same as it had been before it was pierced.

If one does not have a shofar that meets all three conditions, then a shofar that meets only conditions a) and b) or a) and c) may be used (Orach Chaim 586:7).

7.

After discussing defects that disqualify a shofar, the mishnah now turns to defective sounds emanating from a valid shofar.

הַתּוֹקֵעַ לְתוֹךְ הַבּוֹר — If a person blows [a shofar] into a pit

R' Hai Gaon explains that while our mishnah seems to be describing a rather unusual case, it was formulated at a time when foreign rulers of the Holy Land, in an attempt to eradicate the practice of Judaism, prohibited the performance of the mitzvos, thus forcing

Jews to use clandestine methods to fulfill their religious obligations (Ran).

The word לְתוֹךְ, into, implies that the one blowing the shofar is standing outside the pit and blowing into it (Derishah 585:1). Most authorities, however, explain that the blower himself was inside the pit (Rambam, Shofar 1:8; Shulchan Aruch 587:1). Practically speaking, the halachah would be the same in both cases (see Rosh 4:10; cf. Aruch Hashulchan 587:7).

Though the pit referrered to here is open on top, the possibility of an echo

7. **I**f a person blows into a pit or into a cistern or into a cask: if one heard the sound of the shofar — he has fulfilled his obligation; but if he heard the sound of an echo — he has not fulfilled his obligation.

YAD AVRAHAM

cannot be discounted. It goes without saying that the law of our mishnah certainly would apply to a cave or an underground cellar, where there is even greater likelihood of an echo (*Tif. Yisrael*; cf. *Aruch HaShulchan* 587:6).

אוֹ לְתוֹךְ הַדּוּת — *or into a cistern*

A cistern is similar to a pit, except that its walls are of stone or cement (*Rashbam* to *Bava Basra* 64a; *Tif. Yisrael*).

Others translate דּוּת as a building above the ground (*Rambam, comm.*; *Rashi; Rav*). According to this explanation the possibility of an echo would exist in any walled enclosure (*Eliyahu Rabbah* 587). *Beur Halachah* (587 s.v. אוֹ) states that even according to this translation, the major portion of the דּוּת is below ground with part of its walls extending partly above the ground. Consequently, in a building completely above ground, an echo would not be heard.

אוֹ לְתוֹךְ הַפִּטָּם: — *or into a cask:*

Rambam (*Shofar* 1:8) does not differentiate in this case (as he does in the previous cases), between those standing inside the cask and those on the outside (see below). *Kessef Mishneh* explains that this is simply because it is unlikely for anyone to be inside a cask. Therefore *Rambam* discusses the halachah as it applies to those hearing a sound deflected from the inside of a cask.

Ran, however, understands the mishnah literally, as referring to someone inside a cask. The reason for mentioning a cask, as distinct from a pit and a cistern, will be discussed below.

אִם קוֹל שׁוֹפָר שָׁמַע—יָצָא; — *if one heard the sound of the shofar — he has fulfilled his obligation;*

I.e., he heard the unadulterated sound of the shofar, without an accompanying

echo, he has fulfilled his obligation of hearing the shofar (*Kehati*).

Based on differing interpretations of the *Gemara* (27b) there is a controversy among the authorities regarding the intent of our mishnah.

Most views hold that those inside the pit are always assumed to have heard the pure sound of the shofar. Those who were outside the pit, however, must attempt to judge whether or not they heard the sound of the shofar without interference of an echo (*Rambam; Meiri; Ran; Rav*).

Rosh disagrees and holds that while those inside the pit are always assumed to have heard קוֹל שׁוֹפָר, *the sound of the shofar*, those on the outside cannot distinguish the sound of the shofar from an echo; they are always considered to have heard קוֹל הֲבָרָה, *an echo*. According to this view, אִם קוֹל שׁוֹפָר שָׁמַע, *if one heard the sound of the shofar*, is simply a reference to the people who are in the pit who are always assumed to hear the pure sound of the shofar. Those outside the the pit, however, are always assumed to have *heard the sound of an echo*.

As noted above, *Ran* differentiates between a cask and the other cases of the mishnah. Due to the nature of a cask, even someone inside it may be hearing an echo.

While the halachah follows the majority view, *Rosh's* interpretation should be taken into consideration and those outside the pit should, if possible, have the shofar blown a second time (*Mishnah Berurah* 587:7).

וְאִם קוֹל הֲבָרָה שָׁמַע—לֹא יָצָא. — *but if he heard the sound of an echo — he has not fulfilled his obligation.*

Even if he heard the sound of the shofar along with the echo, he has not discharged his obligation of hearing an

וְכֵן, מִי שֶׁהָיָה עוֹבֵר אֲחוֹרֵי בֵית הַכְּנֶסֶת, אוֹ
שֶׁהָיָה בֵיתוֹ סָמוּךְ לְבֵית הַכְּנֶסֶת, וְשָׁמַע קוֹל
שׁוֹפָר אוֹ קוֹל מְגִלָּה: אִם כִּוֵּן לִבּוֹ — יָצָא, וְאִם
לָאו — לֹא יָצָא, אַף־עַל־פִּי שֶׁזֶּה שָׁמַע וְזֶה
שָׁמַע, זֶה כִּוֵּן לִבּוֹ וְזֶה לֹא כִּוֵּן לִבּוֹ.

יד אברהם

unadulterated shofar sound (Rashi).

Even the person blowing the shofar has not fulfilled his obligation if he heard an echo, for the Torah's commandment is not to blow, but to *hear* the sound of the shofar on Rosh Hashanah. This is reflected in the blessing that is said prior to the shofar-blowing: וְצִוָּנוּ לִשְׁמֹעַ קוֹל שׁוֹפָר, *and has commanded us to* **hear** *the sound of the shofar* (Rosh 4:10; Tur 585; Rambam, Shofar 1:1; Lechem Mishneh).

וְכֵן, — *Similarly*,

The similarity between the previous case and the following one lies in the fact that in both instances the person blowing the shofar and the one listening were not together in the same location (Tos. Yom Tov).

Alternatively, in both cases we have two people hearing the same shofar being blown, yet one fulfills his obligation and the other does not (Rashash).

It should be noted, however, that in some readings of the mishnah the word וְכֵן is omitted.

מִי שֶׁהָיָה עוֹבֵר אֲחוֹרֵי בֵית הַכְּנֶסֶת, — *if one were passing behind a synagogue*,

Yerushalmi (3:7) explains the mishnah's use of the word עוֹבֵר, *passing*, to imply that if the person stopped walking as soon as he heard the sound of the shofar (Meiri), it is automatically assumed that he intended to fulfill his obligation. Therefore, if he later forgot whether he had such intent or not, he

may safely assume that he had it, and has therefore fulfilled his obligation (Magen Avraham 589:5).

אוֹ שֶׁהָיָה בֵיתוֹ סָמוּךְ לְבֵית הַכְּנֶסֶת, — *or if his house was close to a synagogue*,

In this case, too, if he stopped whatever he was doing upon hearing the sound of the shofar, he is assumed to have had the proper intent (Meiri).

וְשָׁמַע קוֹל שׁוֹפָר — *and he heard the sound of the shofar*

According to the view mentioned above (s.v. אוֹ לְתוֹךְ הֲדוּת) that the possibility of an echo exists even in buildings above ground level, the person outside the synagogue must be certain that he is hearing the pure sound of the shofar unaccompanied by an echo (Turei Zahav 587:1; cf. Beur Halachah 587 s.v. ואם).

אוֹ קוֹל מְגִלָּה: — *or the sound [of the reading] of the Megillah [i.e., Megillas Esther on Purim]*.

The mishnah mentions both the case of shofar and that of Megillah in order to teach us that although one (shofar) is a Scriptural precept and the other (Megillah) is a Rabbinic obligation, intent is required in both cases (Sifsei Chachamim).

אִם כִּוֵּן לִבּוֹ — *if he concentrated* [lit. *aimed his heart*]—

I.e., if he consciously intended to fulfill the precept of hearing the sound of the shofar or the reading of the Megillah (Gemara 28b).[1]

---

1. The source of the verb כִּוֵּן is Daniel 6:11 where the noun כַּוִּין means *windows*. Since they concentrate light into a room, כִּוֵּן in Rabbinic Hebrew is used to mean concentrate or have intent.

Additionally, while the literal meaning of לִבּוֹ is *his heart*, it is used throughout Scripture and the Talmud as referring to the mind. In fact, the Hebrew word מֹחַ, *brain* is found in Scripture only once (Job 21:24) where it means *bone-marrow*.

3
7

Similarly, if one were passing behind a synagogue, or if his house was close to a synagogue, and he heard the sound of the shofar or the sound of the *Megillah:* if he concentrated — he has fulfilled his obligation, but if not — he has not fulfilled his obligation, even though both he and someone else listened, this one concentrated but the other did not concentrate.

YAD AVRAHAM

This explanation follows the view that בַּוָנָה צְרִיכוֹת מִצְוֹת, *the fulfillment of precepts requires intent;* the person must have in mind, when performing a mitzvah, that he wishes to fulfill the obligation required by that particular mitzvah.

There is a conflicting view that holds: מִצְוֹת אֵין צְרִיכוֹת בַּוָנָה, *the fulfillment of precepts does not require intent.* Even according to this view, intent to perform the particular *act* is required, although one need not have in mind that he was doing it for the sake of a *mitzvah.* Accordingly אִם כֵּוֵן לִבּוֹ means that he meant to hear the sound of a shofar; if he thought that he was listening to the braying of a donkey or some other unrelated sound, he did not fulfill his obligation (*Gemara* 28b). Regarding the reading of the *Megillah,* the intent required is that the listener realize that the day was Purim (*Meiri*); and that the reader is not a minor or a non-Jew (*Aruch LaNer*).

For a detailed discussion of the subject of מִצְוֹת צְרִיכוֹת בַּוָנָה, see ArtScroll Mishnah, *Megillah* pp. 35-36.

יָצָא, — *he has fulfilled his obligation,*
Even though the man blowing the shofar or reading the *Megillah* was unaware of the listener's presence and had no specific intent to discharge this particular listener his obligation, the assumption is that a שְׁלִיחַ צִבּוּר, *represent-*

ative of the community [e.g., chazzan] intends to discharge any listeners, whoever they are. However, if the one blowing the shofar or reading the *Megillah* is doing so not for a community but for a private individual, then an outsider could *not* fulfill his obligation, for intent is required both on the part of the performer and the listener (*Gemara* 29a).

וְאִם לָאו— — *but if not—*
[If he did not intend to fulfill his obligation or, according to the view that such intent is unnecessary, he did not intend to hear the sound of a shofar or the reading of a *Megillah.*]

לֹא יָצָא, — *he has not fulfilled his obligation,*
However, if one entered a synagogue with the proper intent but failed to have conscious intent during the shofarblowing or *Megillah* reading, he has nevertheless fulfilled his obligation (*Magen Avraham* 589:4).

אַף־עַל־פִּי שֶׁזֶּה שָׁמַע וְזֶה שָׁמַע, זֶה כֵּוֵן לִבּוֹ וְזֶה לֹא כֵּוֵן לִבּוֹ. — *even though both he and someone else listened* [lit. *this one heard and this one heard*], *this one concentrated but the other did not concentrate.*
[I.e., even though two people both heard the same blowing of the shofar or the reading of *Megillah,* only the one with the intent fulfills his obligation.]

8.

Having discussed the halachic requirement of בַּוָנַת הַלֵּב, *concentration,* the mishnah goes on to elaborate on this subject in an Aggadic vein, and to teach us that proper concentration is of paramount importance in all matters *(Meiri).*

[ח] "וְהָיָה כַּאֲשֶׁר יָרִים משֶׁה יָדוֹ וְגָבַר יִשְׂרָאֵל" וְגוֹ'.

וְכִי־יָדָיו שֶׁל משֶׁה עוֹשׂוֹת מִלְחָמָה אוֹ שׁוֹבְרוֹת מִלְחָמָה? אֶלָּא לוֹמַר לָךְ: כָּל־זְמַן שֶׁהָיוּ יִשְׂרָאֵל מִסְתַּכְּלִים כְּלַפֵּי מַעְלָה וּמְשַׁעְבְּדִין אֶת־לִבָּם לַאֲבִיהֶם שֶׁבַּשָּׁמַיִם — הָיוּ מִתְגַּבְּרִים, וְאִם לָאו — הָיוּ נוֹפְלִין.

כַּיּוֹצֵא בַדָּבָר אַתָּה אוֹמֵר: "עֲשֵׂה לְךָ שָׂרָף וְשִׂים אֹתוֹ עַל־נֵס, וְהָיָה כָּל־הַנָּשׁוּךְ וְרָאָה אֹתוֹ וָחָי".

וְכִי־נָחָשׁ מֵמִית, אוֹ נָחָשׁ מְחַיֶּה? אֶלָּא בִזְמַן שֶׁיִּשְׂרָאֵל מִסְתַּכְּלִין כְּלַפֵּי מַעְלָה וּמְשַׁעְבְּדִין

יד אברהם

"וְהָיָה כַּאֲשֶׁר יָרִים משֶׁה יָדוֹ וְגָבַר יִשְׂרָאֵל" וגו' — And it came to pass when Moses raised his hand that Israel prevailed etc. (Exodus 17:11).

In describing Israel's battle against Amalek, the Torah states that Moses sent Joshua to lead a group of men in battle, and then ascended to the top of a hill where he raised his hands toward Heaven in prayer. While his hands were raised, Israel prevailed, but when he lowered them, Amalek prevailed. On this, our mishnah asks —

וְכִי־יָדָיו שֶׁל משֶׁה עוֹשׂוֹת מִלְחָמָה אוֹ שׁוֹבְרוֹת מִלְחָמָה? — Was it Moses' hands that won the battle or lost the battle?

Is it conceivable that the raising or lowering of Moses' hands determined the course of the battle?

While Moses undoubtedly prayed for victory as represented by the raising of his hands, the Torah states that Joshua and his men weakened Amalek, thus making it clear that the fortunes of battle depended not only on Moses (Sifsei Chachamim).

Others explain that if victory or defeat were totally dependent on Moses, then it is inconceivable that he would have lowered his hands at all no matter

how exhausted he was (Kol Haremez; Yom Teruah).

אֶלָּא לוֹמַר לָךְ: כָּל־זְמַן שֶׁהָיוּ יִשְׂרָאֵל מִסְתַּכְּלִים כְּלַפֵּי מַעְלָה, — Rather [the Torah] teaches you: As long as Israel looked heavenward,

In contrast to the normal tactics of battle, where soldiers must watch the enemy and not divert their eyes for even a moment, Israel looked to heaven, symbolizing an inner focus on God in the form of prayer (Chasam Sofer).

וּמְשַׁעְבְּדִין אֶת־לִבָּם לַאֲבִיהֶם שֶׁבַּשָּׁמַיִם—הָיוּ מִתְגַּבְּרִים, וְאִם לָאו—הָיוּ נוֹפְלִין. — and subjected their heart to their Father in Heaven — they would prevail, but when they did not — they would fall.

Thus, the raising of Moses' hands was a signal to Israel to emulate him in prayer and concentration (Tif. Yisrael).

This also explains why Moses ascended a hill to pray in seeming contradiction to the rule stated in Berachos 10b that one must not pray on a high place — he had to stand where he could be seen by all of Israel (Tos. Yom Tov; Lechem Shamayim).

Others explain the raising and lowering of Moses' hands not as a signal to Israel but rather as a reflection of the

8. **A**nd it came to pass when Moses raised his hand that Israel prevailed, etc. (Exodus 17:11).

Was it Moses' hands that won the battle or lost the battle? Rather [the Torah] teaches you: As long as Israel looked heavenward and subjected their heart to their Father in Heaven — they would prevail, but when they did not — they would fall.

In a similar matter you learn (Numbers 21:8): Make a fiery serpent and set it upon a pole, and it shall come to pass that whoever is bitten will look at it, and live.

Was it the serpent that killed or the serpent that gave life? Rather, when Israel looked heavenward

YAD AVRAHAM

prayers of the people. When they subjected their hearts to God, Moses felt strong enough to keep his hands aloft in prayer, but when they did not, his hands became weak and he was forced to lower them, causing Amalek to prevail (Maharsha; Kol Haremez; Yom Teruah).

כַּיּוֹצֵא בַדָּבָר אַתָּה אוֹמֵר: — In a similar matter you learn [lit. you say] (Numbers 21:8):

The following case proves the value of proper concentration not only as an aid to victory against an enemy, but also as an aid in combatting an affliction sent by God Himself to punish sinners (Sifsei Chachamim; cf. Tif. Yisrael).

"עֲשֵׂה לְךָ שָׂרָף וְשִׂים אֹתוֹ עַל־נֵס, וְהָיָה כָּל־הַנָּשׁוּךְ וְרָאָה אֹתוֹ וָחָי." — Make a fiery serpent and set it upon a pole, and it shall come to pass that whoever is bitten will look at it, and live.

[When the Jews, weary of their journeys in the desert, lost faith in God and began complaining of hunger and thirst, displaying ingratitude for the gift of manna that fell from heaven, they were punished by God Who sent fiery serpents to bite and kill them. After many had died, the Jews admittted their sin and asked Moses to intercede on

their behalf, whereupon God commanded Moses to make a serpent of brass and place it upon a pole where it could be seen by all. Our mishnah asks the obvious question]

וְכִי נָחָשׁ מֵמִית, אוֹ נָחָשׁ מְחַיֶּה? — Was it the serpent that killed or the serpent that gave life?

[What power can a brass serpent have to heal those who gazed upon it and not heal those who didn't?]

אֶלָּא בִּזְמַן שֶׁיִּשְׂרָאֵל מִסְתַּכְּלִין כְּלַפֵּי מַעְלָה וּמְשַׁעְבְּדִין אֶת־לִבָּם לַאֲבִיהֶן שֶׁבַּשָּׁמַיִם—הָיוּ מִתְרַפְּאִים, וְאִם־לָאו—הָיוּ נִמּוֹקִים. — Rather, when Israel looked heavenward and subjected their heart to their Father in Heaven — they were healed, but when they did not — they perished.

[The brass serpent served as a sign to Israel to repent their sins and to subject their hearts and minds in concentrated prayer to God Who dwells on high.]

[After this short digression on the subject of concentration, we return to halachic matters. The previous mishnah had indicated that one person may perform a mitzvah and thereby cause others to discharge their obligation in fulfilling it. Our mishnah now points out circumstances under which this cannot be done.]

אֶת־לִבָּם לַאֲבִיהֶן שֶׁבַּשָּׁמַיִם — הָיוּ מִתְרַפְּאִים,
וְאִם לָאו — הָיוּ נִמּוֹקִים.
חֵרֵשׁ שׁוֹטֶה וְקָטָן אֵין מוֹצִיאִין אֶת־הָרַבִּים
יְדֵי חוֹבָתָן. זֶה הַכְּלָל: כָּל־שֶׁאֵינוֹ מְחֻיָּב בַּדָּבָר,
אֵינוֹ מוֹצִיא אֶת־הָרַבִּים יְדֵי חוֹבָתָן.

[א] **יוֹם** טוֹב שֶׁל רֹאשׁ הַשָּׁנָה שֶׁחָל לִהְיוֹת
בַּשַּׁבָּת, בַּמִּקְדָּשׁ הָיוּ תוֹקְעִים, אֲבָל
לֹא בַמְּדִינָה. מִשֶּׁחָרַב בֵּית הַמִּקְדָּשׁ, הִתְקִין

יד אברהם

חֵרֵשׁ — *A deaf person,*

Although חֵרֵשׁ generally refers to a deaf-mute (see *Terumos* 1:2), in this case (i.e., blowing the shofar or reading the *Megillah*) it means even one who can speak but is merely deaf. Since we speak of shofar and *Megillah* — *mitzvos* which depend on an ability to hear, a deaf man is absolved from them. The general rule is that one cannot discharge another from an obligation from which he is himself absolved (*Tif. Yis.*).

שׁוֹטֶה — *an imbecile,*

I.e., one who is in the habit of performing senseless acts such as destroying whatever is given to him (see *Chagigah* 3b; *Rambam, Eidus* 9:9, 10; ArtScroll *Mishnayos Megillah* 2:4). Because of his limited mental capacity, he is under no obligation to perform any *mitzvos* and therefore cannot discharge others of their obligation (*Kehati*).

וְקָטָן — *and a minor*

I.e., a boy below the age of thirteen (*Meiri*). [Although he may be a קָטָן שֶׁהִגִּיעַ לְחִנּוּךְ, *minor who has attained the age of training,* who is Rabbinically obligated to perform the *mitzvos,* he cannot discharge the obligation of others who are Scripturally obligated. Cf. ArtScroll *Mishnayos Megillah* 2:4.]

אֵין מוֹצִיאִין אֶת־הָרַבִּים יְדֵי חוֹבָתָן. — *cannot discharge the obligation of the many.*

Nor can they discharge the obligation of an individual. It is possible that our

mishnah's use of the word רַבִּים, *many,* indicates that they cannot perform the *mitzvos* even for those who are not Scripturally obligated [e.g., women, who are under no obligation but are considered to have fulfilled a *mitzvah* if they hear the shofar] (*Tif. Yis;* cf. *Sifsei Chachamim*).

זֶה הַכְּלָל: כָּל־שֶׁאֵינוֹ מְחֻיָּב בַּדָּבָר, אֵינוֹ מוֹצִיא אֶת־הָרַבִּים יְדֵי חוֹבָתָן. — *This is the general rule: Whoever is not obligated [himself] in a matter [i.e., a precept] cannot discharge the obligation of the many.*

The *Gemara* (29a) explains that this refers only to a person upon whom there never was an obligation to perform the precept. One who was obligated but has already discharged his own obligation can nevertheless discharge the obligation of others because כָּל יִשְׂרָאֵל עֲרֵבִין זֶה בָּזֶה, *all Jews are responsible for each other* — i.e., every Jew is obliged to help other Jews fulfill the *mitzvos.* This obligation is sufficient to enable one to perform a *mitzvah* for others, even though he himself has already discharged his own personal obligation.

It should be noted, however, that with regard to certain *mitzvos,* such as wearing tefillin or sitting in a *succah,* one must always perform them himself, and others cannot discharge his obligation. These *mitzvos* are מִצְווֹת שֶׁבְּגוּפוֹ, *precepts involving one's body,* in which

and subjected their heart to their Father in Heaven — they were healed, but when they did not — they perished.

A deaf person, an imbecile, and a minor cannot discharge the obligation of the many. This is the general rule: Whoever is not obligated in a matter cannot discharge the obligation of the many.

1. **W**hen the Rosh Hashanah festival fell on the Sabbath, they would blow [the shofar] in the Temple, but not in the province. After the Temple

YAD AVRAHAM

the Torah requires that the *tefillin* should be on one's head and arm or that his body should be within the *succah*.

Such requirements can be met only by the individual himself (see *K'tzos Ha-Choshen* 182:1).

Chapter 4

1.

יוֹם טוֹב שֶׁל רֹאשׁ הַשָּׁנָה שֶׁחָל לִהְיוֹת בַּשַּׁבָּת, בַּמִּקְדָשׁ הָיוּ תּוֹקְעִים, — *When the Rosh Hashanah festival fell on the Sabbath, they would blow [the shofar] in the Temple,*

But not in the city of Jerusalem *(Rav; Rashi).*

Rambam (comm. to Mishnah and *Hilchos Shofar* 2:8) maintains that the term מִקְדָּשׁ, *Temple*, includes the whole of Jerusalem.

Since blowing the shofar on the Sabbath is only a שְׁבוּת, sh'vus [a category of Rabbinical prohibitions], it is permitted in the Temple because, אֵין שְׁבוּת בַּמִּקְדָּשׁ, *(Pesachim* 65a; see *Eruvin* 102b-104b): *the prohibition of sh'vus does not* [usually] *apply in the Temple (Rashi* 29b s.v גזירה; *Ritva).*

Though the Sages are empowered by the Torah to curtail or prohibit the observance of a מִצְוַת עֲשֵׂה, *positive precept* (see *Yevamos* 90a), they did not wish to eliminate entirely the *mitzvah* of blowing the shofar in a year when Rosh Hashanah fell on the Sabbath. So they exempted the Temple from their prohibition against blowing the shofar on the Sabbath *(Turei Even).*

אֲבָל לֹא בַמְּדִינָה — *but not in the province.*

This prohibition includes the city of Jerusalem as well *(Rav* citing *Rashi).*

As mentioned above, *Rambam* holds Jerusalem to have the same status as the Temple. According to his view, the term מְדִינָה, *province*, includes only the areas outside of Jerusalem.

The Sages were afraid that people, in their eagerness to fulfill the *mitzvah* of blowing the shofar, might go, shofar in hand, to an expert to be taught how to blow correctly and would inadvertently carry the shofar four cubits in the public domain [ד׳ אַמּוֹת בִּרְשׁוּת הָרַבִּים], thus transgressing a Torah prohibition. Because of this fear they forbade the fulfillment of the *mitzvah* of shofar on the Sabbath. (See also *comm.* of ArtScroll Mishnah, *Megillah* 1:2.) [The Torah empowered the Sages to preserve the Torah by forbidding the fulfillment of a מִצְוַת עֲשֵׂה, *positive precept*; see *Yevamos* 91a שֵׁב וְאַל תַּעֲשֶׂה שָׁאֲנִי] *(Rav; Gemara* 29b).

רַבָּן יוֹחָנָן בֶּן־זַכַּאי, שֶׁיִּהְיוּ תּוֹקְעִין בְּכָל־מָקוֹם
שֶׁיֶּשׁ־בּוֹ בֵּית דִּין.

אָמַר רַבִּי אֶלְעָזָר: לֹא הִתְקִין רַבָּן יוֹחָנָן בֶּן־
זַכַּאי אֶלָּא בְּיַבְנֶה בִּלְבָד.

אָמְרוּ לוֹ: אֶחָד יַבְנֶה וְאֶחָד כָּל־מָקוֹם שֶׁיֶּשׁ־
בּוֹ בֵּית דִּין.

יד אברהם

מִשֶּׁחָרַב בֵּית הַמִּקְדָּשׁ, — *After the Temple was destroyed,*

[Once the only location where the shofar was blown on the Sabbath ceased to exist, there was need to provide another place for the shofar to be blown, so that this *mitzvah* not be eliminated entirely on the Sabbath. However, according to *Rambam's* view that previously the shofar was blown throughout Jerusalem, it could have been blown in the city even in the absence of the Temple; accordingly the motive for Rabban Yochanan ben Zakkai's innovation is not clear. Perhaps the destruction of the Temple and of Jerusalem left the city in ruins and virtually uninhabited by Jews, thereby necessitating a new location for the blowing of the shofar. Moreover, *Rambam's* comments in *Hilchos Shofar* (2:8) imply that Jerusalem's special status was due to its being the seat of the Great Sanhedrin. Thus, when the Sanhedrin moved to Yavneh following the destruction of the Temple, Jerusalem lost its privileged status, necessitating a new location for blowing the shofar on the Sabbath. This view is reinforced by *Rambam* who writes that after the destruction of the Temple, the blowing of the shofar was permitted *everywhere*, but only in the *presence* of the *beis din*, whereas during the existence of the Sanhedrin, the shofar was blown throughout Jerusalem without restriction.]

הִתְקִין רַבָּן יוֹחָנָן בֶּן־זַכַּאי, שֶׁיִּהְיוּ תּוֹקְעִין בְּכָל־
מָקוֹם שֶׁיֶּשׁ־בּוֹ בֵּית דִּין. — *Rabban Yochanan ben Zakkai instituted that they blow the shofar in every place where there is a beis din.*

There was no fear that the Sabbath would be profaned, because the members of the beis din would zealously caution the people not to carry the shofar in a forbidden manner (*Rambam, Hilchos Shofar* 2:9).

The *Gemara* (29b) cites a *baraisa* which relates how Rabban Yochanan's institution came into being. Once Rosh Hashanah fell on the Sabbath and [people from] all the towns assembled [at Yavneh to hear the shofar]. R' Yochanan said to the sons of Beseira [the greatest scholars of the time (*Rashi*)], 'Let us blow the shofar.' They said to him, 'Let us consider [whether we should forbid the blowing lest people carry the shofar in a public domain' (*Rashi*)]. He answered them, 'Let us blow the shofar and then consider.' After they had blown they said to him, 'Let us consider.' He said to them, 'The horn has already been heard in Yavneh, and what has been done should not be refuted' (cf. *Sfas Emes* to 29b s.v. משחרב).

אָמַר רַבִּי אֶלְעָזָר: לֹא הִתְקִין רַבָּן יוֹחָנָן בֶּן־זַכַּאי
אֶלָּא בְּיַבְנֶה בִּלְבָד. — *R' Elazer said: Rabban Yochanan ben Zakkai instituted [this regulation] for Yavneh only.*

When Rabban Yochanan ben Zakkai instituted that the shofar may be blown before the *beis din*, he was referring only to the supreme *beis din*, the Great Sanhedrin of seventy-one sages.[1] Therefore the shofar might be blown only in Yavneh, where the Sanhedrin had its seat in his time, or wherever the

1. The *mitzvah* to appoint judges (*Deuteronomy* 16:18) consists of two parts:
   A) To appoint a supreme *beis din* — the Great Sanhedrin — of seventy-one members. Among its functions are the final resolution of halachic questions, and appointments of kings and *Kohanim Gedolim*.

was destroyed, Rabban Yochanan ben Zakkai instituted that they blow the shofar in every place where there is a *beis din*.

R' Elazar said: Rabban Yochanan ben Zakkai instituted [this regulation] for Yavneh only.

They said to him: Yavneh and any other place where there is a *beis din*.

YAD AVRAHAM

Sanhedrin were to establish itself *(Rav; Rashi; cf. Rashi cited by Ritva).*[2]

אָמְרוּ לוֹ: אֶחָד יַבְנֶה וְאֶחָד כָּל־מָקוֹם שֶׁיֵּשׁ־בּוֹ בֵּית דִּין. — *They said to him: Yavneh and any other place where there is a beis din.*

Noting that this comment seems to be redundant, the *Gemara* (29b) concludes that by comparing any other place where there is a *beis din* to Yavneh, the latter tanna indicates that any other *beis din* must resemble the *beis din* at Yavneh in permanence — it must be permanently domiciled in the locality. According to this tanna, the shofar may not be blown where a *beis din* has convened only temporarily. According to the former tanna, however, the shofar may be blown even in the presence of a temporarily convened *beis din (Rashi).*

Rambam (Hilchos Shofar 2:9 and *comm.)* interpreting the *Gemara* differently, rules that the shofar may be blown only in a בֵּית

דִּין קָבוּעַ, *permanent beis din.* (See *Rambam's comm.; Lechem Mishnah, loc. cit.)*

There is much disagreement as to the definition of the term *beis din* mentioned by the two tannaim. *Rashi* (29b s.v. אלא ביבנה) and *Rav* seem to understand this term as meaning the minor *Sanhedriyos* consisting of twenty-three members. [See footnote above.] *(Ritva* seems to have had a different version in *Rashi,* but cf., *Meiri). Rambam* and *Rif,* however, understand this term to include even a *beis din* of three. *Rambam* adds the stipulation that the members of the *beis din* must be judges who have earned סְמִיכָה [*semichah*], *ordination,* in a direct line from Moses. This line was broken during the persecutions in *Eretz Yisrael* during the fourth century C.E. See *R' Hai Gaon's* responsa cited by *Yuchasin* part II s.v. הלל הנשיא.[3]

Rif goes one step further: even an ordinary *beis din,* all of whose members lack *semichah* would be qualified. Indeed there is evidence that the shofar was blown on the Sabbath in *Rif's* presence *(Milchamos* here;

B) To appoint minor *sanhedriyos* of twenty-three members in every city and in every province. These *sanhedriyos* deal with cases whose penalty is corporal punishment. For civil cases a *beis din* of three judges is sufficient (see *Rambam, Hilchos Sanhedrin* 1:1-3 and 5:1-8).

2. The *Gemara* (31a-b) relates that the Sanhedrin moved (forty years before the destruction of the Temple; *Sanhedrin* 41a and *Avodah Zarah* 8a) from its office in the Temple Court (לִשְׁכַּת הַגָּזִית) to *Chanus* [חֲנוּת] (see *Rashi* to *Sanhedrin* 41a and *Avodah Zarah* s.v. חנות: cf. *Rashi* to *Rosh Hashanah* 31a s.v. מלשכת הגזית), from there to Jerusalem (i.e., the city proper), and from Jerusalem to Yavneh. The move to Yavneh took place while R' Yochanan ben Zakkai was נָשִׂיא, *president,* of the Sanhedrin, immediately after the destruction of Jerusalem and the Temple (cf. *Gittin* 56a-b). His predecessor in the post of *nassi* had been Rabban Shimon ben Gamliel הַנֶּהֱרָג, *the Martyr,* who was murdered by the Romans around the period of the destruction of the Temple (see *Yuchasin HaShalem,* London 5617, part I., p. 21 [year 3828] and p. 77 s.v. רבן שמעון בן גמליאל בנו של ר"ג הזקן). This is the Rabban Shimon whose tragic end is so vividly described in the *Midrashim* dealing with the famed עֲשָׂרָה הֲרוּגֵי מַלְכוּת, *Ten* [martyred] *Victims of the* [Roman] *Government,* and who are commemorated in the moving *Selichah* אֵלֶּה אֶזְכְּרָה recited in the Ashkenazic *Mussaf* service for Yom Kippur.

3. The *semichah* [ordination] discussed here joined its recipient to the long chain of tradition originating with Moses, who was ordained by God Himself; it should not be confused with

[ב] **וְעוֹד** זֹאת הָיְתָה יְרוּשָׁלַיִם יְתֵרָה עַל־ יַבְנֶה, שֶׁכָּל עִיר שֶׁהִיא רוֹאָה וְשׁוֹמַעַת וּקְרוֹבָה וִיכוֹלָה לָבֹא — תּוֹקְעִין; וּבְיַבְנֶה לֹא הָיוּ תוֹקְעִין, אֶלָּא בְּבֵית דִּין בִּלְבַד.

יד אברהם

Rosh). Though some argue *(Meromei HaSadeh* 30a) that *Rambam* concurs with *Rif, Rambam's* words indicate the opposite *(Hilchos Shofar* 2:9). *Rif's* view was not ac-

cepted in practice even by his disciples. *Shulchan Aruch (Orach Chaim* 588:4) does not even mention his view (see *Tur* and *Bais Yosef* loc. cit.).

2.

2. .יַבְנֶה עַל יְתֵרָה יְרוּשָׁלַיִם הָיְתָה זֹאת וְעוֹד — *In this [matter] too Jerusalem was superior to Yavneh,*

Yavneh was the seat of the Sanhedrin after the destruction of the Temple. Rabban Yochanan ben Zakkai was the נָשִׂיא, *president,* of the Sanhedrin during this period *(Gemara* 31a-b, *Rashi).*

The *Gemara* (30a) notes that contrary to the implication of the phrase in this too, nothing had been said earlier about the superiority of Jerusalem. It explains that although not specified, an area of Jerusalem's superiority is implied in mishnah 1.

In Jerusalem the shofar was permitted to be blown anywhere on the Sabbath, even outside the *beis din,* as implied by the fact that the words *'beis din'* are not mentioned in connection with shofar blowing. In Yavneh, however, the shofar was blown in the presence of the *beis din* [as indicated by

the phase, 'in every place where there is a *beis din'*].

Meiri points out that these two ways in which Jerusalem was superior to Yavneh are based on one underlying concept: the authority of the *beis din* in Jerusalem extended beyond its immediate proximity to all of Jerusalem and its environs, whereas in Yavneh, the *beis din's* authority applied only to its immediate presence.

According to *Rambam* (see *comm.* to 4:1 s.v. במקדש) that the term מִקְדָּשׁ, *the Temple,* includes Jerusalem, it is evident that this mishnah is merely an elaboration of mishnah 1. Where mishnah 1 had singled out only the Temple — i.e., Jerusalem — our mishnah broadens this to include its environs; our mishnah refers to the same time frame as the previous mishnah — the period before the destruction of the Temple.

According to *Rashi* (cited there) that מִקְדָּשׁ refers only to the Temple, the shofar could not be blown even in Jerusalem, let alone in its environs. This is hardly compatible with our mishnah. *Tosafos's* suggestion (29b, s.v.

the *semichah* that certifies rabbis in modern times. *Semichah* of this nature could be bestowed only by people who were themselves *semuchin* [ordained] and part of the uninterrupted chain from Moses, and it had to be bestowed by a *beis din* in *Eretz Yisrael,* whose members pronounced the candidate a *samuch* and bestowed the title 'Rabbi' upon him *(Hilchos Sanhedrin* 4:2-6). When the Jewish community in *Eretz Yisrael* was almost destroyed during the fourth century C.E., and overt religious activity was impossible, *semichah* could not be conferred. The thriving Jewish community in Babylon, though possessing scholars worthy of *semichah,* could not obtain it, because it had to bestowed by a *beis din* of *s'muchin* in *Eretz Yisrael.* As a result, the chain of *semichah* was disrupted. The *semichah* of modern times is a certification of the individual's proficiency in specific branches of Torah law, and is a comparatively recent institution thought to have originated with *R' Meir ben Baruch HaLevi* of Fulda and Vienna (whose disciples taught the famous *Maharil* of Mainz) in the 14th century C.E. Indeed when *Abarbanel* (15th century) learned of this institution (which was not practiced in his native Spain), he was amazed *(Nachalas Avos,* Chapter 6; see *Tzemach David* 5187, *Teshuvos Rivash* 268-72; *Rama* to *Tur Yoreh Deah* 242:14, *Shulchan Aruch,* loc. cit.).

4
2

2. In this matter, too, Jerusalem was superior to Yavneh, in that any town which could see [Jerusalem], and could hear, and is near, and can come [to Jerusalem on the Sabbath] — may blow [the shofar]; whereas in Yavneh they blew only before the *beis din*.

אבל) that our mishnah is referring to post-destruction Jerusalem, raises many more questions: A) After the destruction of the Temple, Jerusalem had no claim to distinction to all, just it has no such advantage to-day; B) When the mishnah uses the past tense, הָיְתָה יְרוּשָׁלַיִם יְתֵרָה, *Jerusalem was superior,* using the past tense, it implies the pre-destruction period; 3) *Rashi* himself (s.v. ועוד) clearly says that our mishnah refers to the pre-destruction era (see *Maharsha, Pnei Yehoshua, Turei Even and Aroch LaNer*).

Ritva maintains that our mishnah deals with the forty years immediately before the destruction when the Sanhedrin moved from its place in the Temple Court, first to Chanus on the Temple Mount, and then to Jerusalem proper. It was then that the shofar was blown throughout Jerusalem and its environs. This view is independently developed by *Maharsha* as well.

שֶׁבָּל עִיר שֶׁהִיא רוֹאָה — *in that any town which could see [Jerusalem],*

[I.e., every town from which Jerusalem can be seen.]

However, any town unable to view Jerusalem is not included in the privilege of blowing shofar. This is so even if the town is very close by; for example, if it is in a nearby valley and its view of Jerusalem is blocked by a wall (*Rav; Gemara* 30a).

וְשׁוֹמַעַת — *and could hear*

[The neighboring town is close enough so that the shofar being blow in in Jerusalem can be heard there.]

But if a shofar blown in Jerusalem could not be heard, even though the town was situated atop a mountain so that Jerusalem could be seen from afar, the townspeople were not entitled to the privilege of blowing the shofar on the Sabbath.

וּקְרוֹבָה — *and is near [to Jerusalem],*

[I.e., within 2,000 cubits of Jerusalem].

But if the town was situated outside the Jerusalem *t'chum* (i.e., more than 2000 cubits from the outskirts of Jerusalem; see *comm.* to *Beitzah* 5:3), it was denied this privilege even though the townspeople could 'see and hear' (*Rav; Gemara* 30a).

וִיכוֹלָה לָבֹא— *and can come [to Jerusalem on the Sabbath]*—

Even if a town possessed all the above attributes, but its citizens were prohibited to come to Jerusalem on the Sabbath — e.g., a river separated it from Jerusalem, and swimming or rowing are forbidden on the Sabbath — the townspeople were not privileged to blow the shofar on the Sabbath (*Rav; Gemara* 30a).

תּוֹקְעִין; — *may blow [the shofar on the Sabbath];*

[Any neighboring area possessing all the above attributes has Jerusalem's privileged status concerning shofar blowing on the Sabbath.]

וּבְיַבְנֶה לֹא הָיוּ תוֹקְעִין, אֶלָּא בְּבֵית דִּין בִּלְבַד. — *whereas in Yavneh they blew only before the beis din.*

[According to the first and last tannaim in the previous mishnah, the shofar could be blown in any town at its *beis din*. Since Yavneh enjoyed no advantage over any other town, the mishnah could have said simply, 'Jerusalem was superior to all other towns...' Yavneh, however, is singled out because of the prestige it enjoyed as the seat of the Sanhedrin. Additionally, by singling out Yavneh, the mishnah informs us that even R' Elazer (mishnah 1), who holds that Yavneh was privileged over other towns, concurs that it was not equal to Jerusalem.]

[ג] **בָּרִאשׁוֹנָה** הָיָה הַלּוּלָב נִטָּל בַּמִּקְדָּשׁ
שִׁבְעָה וּבַמְּדִינָה יוֹם אֶחָד.
מִשֶּׁחָרַב בֵּית הַמִּקְדָּשׁ, הִתְקִין רַבָּן יוֹחָנָן בֶּן־
זַכַּאי, שֶׁיְּהֵא לוּלָב נִטָּל בַּמְּדִינָה שִׁבְעָה זֵכֶר
לַמִּקְדָּשׁ, וְשֶׁיְּהֵא יוֹם הָנֵף כֻּלּוֹ אָסוּר.

יד אברהם

3.

Having discussed one of Rabban Yochanan ben Zakkai's innovations, the Mishnah digresses to list four others. Nowhere in the Mishnah are any other institutions attributed to R' Yochanan. However, two more institutions, which the Mishnah cites anonymously (*Ma'asar Sheni* 5:2 and *Rosh Hashanah* 1:4), are attributed to R' Yochanan in a *baraisa* (Gemara 31b) and two other institutions mentioned in *baraisos (ibid.)* are not mentioned in the Mishnah at all. These four innovations together with five listed here make a total of nine (ibid.). It is not clear why the Mishnah omits two of them altogether, and fails to mention R' Yochanan's name in connection with the other two.

בָּרִאשׁוֹנָה הָיָה הַלּוּלָב נִטָּל בַּמִּקְדָּשׁ שִׁבְעָה —
Originally the lulav was taken in the Temple [all] seven [days of Succos]

The Torah mandates: *You shall take to yourselves on the first day [of Succos] the fruit of [a citron] tree, palm branches, a twig of a myrtle tree, and willows of the stream and you shall rejoice before HASHEM your God for a seven-day period (Leviticus 23:40).* The *Sifra* (loc. cit.) and the Mishnah (*Succah* 3:9) clearly assume that the rejoicing takes place with the *lulav* and the accompanying species in one's hands, and that this must be done only *before HASHEM your God* — in the Temple — as specified in the Torah. Outside the Temple, Torah law ordains this *mitzvah* only on the first day, as spelled out in the beginning of this verse, *And you shall take to yourselves on the first day.*

Yerushalmi (here and *Succah* 3:12) cites a tannaic view that the seven-day festival was celebrated through enjoying שְׁלָמִים [shelamim], peace-offerings. If the verse ordaining joy refers to sacrifices, it cannot mean the practice of taking the *lulav* seven days in the Temple, and this *mitzvah* must therefore be of Rabbinical origin. *Bavli,* however, unequivocally (*Succah* 43b; אִי הָכִי לוּלָב נָמִי לִידְחֵי) holds the view expressed in

Sifra (see *Rashi* there s.v. לפרסמה and *Rashba-Ritva*).

Rambam (comm. to *Succah* 3:12) maintains that here, too (as in mishnah 1; see *comm.* there), the term מִקְדָּשׁ, Temple, is synonymous with Jerusalem, thus the four species had to be taken for seven days, in Jerusalem as well as in the Temple proper. But in *Mishneh Torah* (Hilchos Lulav 7:13), Rambam seems to have retracted this view as it applies to *lulav* (he wrote his comm. to the Mishnah before the *Mishneh Torah.*) Only regarding the shofar does he assign to Jerusalem the same privilege enjoyed by the Temple. Nonetheless many commentators (*Rabbeinu Manoach* loc. cit.; *Aruch LaNer* to *Succah* 41a s.v. ובמדינה; *Sefer HaMitzvos* of R' Saadiah Gaon v. 3 p. 467) maintain that the four species must be taken throughout Jerusalem by Torah law.

[See *Succah* 4:2, 4:4, and *Succah* 43a that even in the Temple, the *lulav* was taken on the Sabbath only if it was the first day of Succos. If one of the other six days fall on the Sabbath the *lulav* was not taken.]

וּבַמְּדִינָה יוֹם אֶחָד — *and in the province [the lulav was taken only] one day.*

According to the view that מִקְדָּשׁ means only the Temple, מְדִינָה includes the rest of Jerusalem as well as all of *Eretz Yisrael.*

3. **O**riginally the *lulav* was taken in the Temple [all] seven [days of Succos] and in the province [the *lulav* was taken only] one day.

After the Temple was destroyed, Rabban Yochanan ben Zakkai instituted that the *lulav* be taken in the provinces for seven [days] in remembrance of the Temple, and that the entire day of waving [the *Omer*] should be forbidden.

YAD AVRAHAM

מִשֶּׁחָרַב בֵּית הַמִּקְדָּשׁ, — *After the Temple was destroyed,*

[From then on, the *mitzvah* of taking the *lulav* seven days in the Temple could no longer be practiced. Even according to *Rambam's* definition of מִקְדָּשׁ as including Jerusalem, this *mitzvah* applied to Jerusalem only as long as the Temple stood (see *Sefer HaMitzvos*; *R' Saadiah Gaon, Mitzvos Asseh* 234).

הִתְקִין רַבָּן יוֹחָנָן בֶּן־זַכַּאי, שֶׁיְּהֵא לוּלָב נִטָּל, בַּמְּדִינָה שִׁבְעָה — *Rabban Yochanan ben Zakkai instituted that the lulav be taken in the provinces for seven [days]*

This mishnah does not mean to say that the *lulav* is taken on each of the seven days of Succos, since, after the Destruction, the four species may never be taken on the Sabbath (*Succah* 43a). Therefore, the mishnah must be understood to mean that the *mitzvah* of *lulav* is in effect *throughout* the festival (on the applicable days) rather than for only the first day, as it was (in the provinces) when the Temple stood (*Tos. Yom Tov*).

זֵכֶר לַמִּקְדָּשׁ, — *in remembrance of the Temple,*

The daily taking of the *lulav* would recall the glory of the Temple.

וְשֶׁיְּהֵא יוֹם הָנֵף כֻּלּוֹ אָסוּר. — *and that the entire day of waving [the Omer] should be forbidden.*

The Torah forbids the eating of חָדָשׁ [*chadash*], *new grain* [ie., wheat, barley, rye, oats, spelt], before the מִנְחַת הָעוֹמֶר, *Omer meal offering*, offered in the Temple on the sixteenth day of Nissan. The offering was called *Omer*

because it contained an *omer* (a measure equal to at least 86.4 fl. oz.) of freshly ground and sifted barley. Before burning this meal offering on the altar, the *kohen* lifted it up high and waved it in the four directions of the compass (see *Lev.* 23:11; *Menachos* 62a with *Rashi* s.v. מוֹלִיךְ ומביא; cf. *Rambam, Hil. T'midim U'Mussafin* 7:12). The offering is therefore called עוֹמֶר הַתְּנוּפָה, *the Omer of the Waving (Lev.* 23:15), and the sixteenth of Nissan is consequently referred to by the Torah as the *day of your waving of the Omer* (loc. cit. 23:12), and the *day of your bringing of the waved Omer* (loc. cit. 23:15). Hence our mishnah's reference to this day as the *day of waving*.

The Torah's prohibition against eating of the new grain before the *Omer* offering refers to grain that had not yet taken root at the time of the previous year's *Omer* offering (*Challah* 1:1; *Hilchos Ma'achalos Assuros* 10:4). Only five species of grain — wheat, barley, oats, rye, and spelt — are included in this prohibition (*Challah* 1:1, *Rav*). When the Temple stood, one was not permitted to partake of the new grain until after the actual offering of the *Omer* (see *Menachos* 68a; *Hilchos Ma'achalos Assuros* 10:4). Those far away from the Temple waited until noon, when they could assume that the *Omer* offering had already been completed (*Menachos* 10:5).

After the destruction of the Temple, when no *Omer* offering could be brought, Torah law permitted eating of new grain as soon as 'the horizon lit up'

[ד] **בָּרִאשׁוֹנָה** הָיוּ מְקַבְּלִין עֵדוּת הַחֹדֶשׁ
כָּל־הַיּוֹם. פַּעַם אַחַת
נִשְׁתַּהוּ הָעֵדִים מִלָּבוֹא, וְנִתְקַלְקְלוּ הַלְוִיִּם
בַּשִּׁיר, הִתְקִינוּ שֶׁלֹּא יְהוּ מְקַבְּלִין אֶלָּא עַד

יד אברהם

on the morning of the sixteenth of Nissan (Menachos 62a). Rabban Yochanan
ben Zakkai ruled that new grain was not
to be eaten the *entire* sixteenth day of
Nissan. The *Gemara* (30a) explains that
Rabban Yochanan provided for the
contingency of the Temple being rebuilt
on short notice the night just before the
sixteenth (cf. *Rashi* loc. cit.; *Succah* 41a
with *Rashi* and *Tosafos* s.v. אי נמי), in
which case it would become immediately obligatory to bring the *Omer* offering. Since the barley had to be reaped,
threshed, dried and ground, and the
meal sifted thirteen times, the offering
would not be ready before late afternoon on the sixteenth. In that case it
would be forbidden by Torah law to eat
new grain until after the offering had
been waved and offered. If the people

were in the habit of partaking of the
new grain at daybreak, they would fail
to wait for the *Omer* offering. Rabban
Yochanan therefore prohibited the use
of the new grain till nightfall to prevent
this problem from ever arising.

Yet another explanation of R' Yochanan's
ruling is given in the *Gemara*. R' Yochanan
adopted R' Yehudah's view (*Menachos* 10:5)
that in the absence of an *Omer* offering,
Chadash may not be eaten until nightfall by
Torah law. R' Yochanan did not legislate a
new institution, rather he established R'
Yehudah's view as the prevailing one by
publicizing it (וְדָרַשׁ וְהִתְקִין). This explanation
is accepted by *Rambam (comm.* to *Succah*
3:12; *Hilchos Ma'achalos Assuros* 10:2).

Tosefos Yom Tov (Succah 3:12) notes that
the grouping of these two institutions in our
mishnah indicates that they were both instituted at the same time.

4.

As explained above (preface to ch. 2), the moon's cycle is slightly longer than
29½ days; hence it became possible for witnesses to see the new moon on the thirtieth day counting from the previous new moon. Beginning at that time, the *beis din*
would be ready to accept witnesses who testified they had seen the new moon. If the
testimony was credible, the *beis din* would pronounce the thirtieth day of the cycle
Rosh Chodesh, the beginning of the new month. If no credible testimony was
received on the thirtieth day, the thirty-first day would automatically be designated
Rosh Chodesh.

As soon as the eve of the thirtieth day from Rosh Chodesh Elul arrived, people
would observe it as the *Yom Tov* of Rosh Hashanah, because of the probability that
reliable witnesses would arrive some time during the day, in which case *beis din*
would ratify this day as Rosh Hashanah, meaning that the previous night was truly
the beginning of the new year. If no witnesses arrived that day, the thirty-first day
would automatically be certified as the true Rosh Hashanah. During the entire Second Temple period this happened only once, on the first Rosh Hashanah after
Ezra's arrival in *Eretz Yisrael* (see *Gemara* 19b with *Tosafos* s.v. מימות; *Nechemiah*
8:2, 13).[1]

1. Nevertheless it appears that in the post-Mishnah era this did occur once. (See *Gemara* 21a
לוי אקלע לבבל בחדסר בתשרי with *Tosafos Yeshanim.) Rambam (Hilchos Kiddush HaChodesh*
5:8) states that even in Jerusalem *many times* they observed the *Yom Tov* Rosh Hashanah two
days, for if witnesses did not come at all on the thirtieth day [of Elul], etc.

4. Originally they accepted testimony regarding the new moon all day. Once the witnesses were delayed in arriving, and the Levites blundered in the [daily] hymn. So they ordained that they [the *beis*

YAD AVRAHAM

בָּרִאשׁוֹנָה הָיוּ מְקַבְּלִין עֵדוּת הַחֹדֶשׁ כָּל-הַיּוֹם.
— *Originally they accepted testimony regarding the new moon all day.*

[Our mishnah informs us that testimony used to be received throughout the entire day until nightfall, as is readily evident from Mishnah 3:1. Though our Mishnah says, 'They accepted testimony ... all day,' this means only that the *beis din* was prepared, if necessary, to accept testimony until nightfall. In practice, however, only once were the witnesses delayed until after the sacrifice of the תָּמִיד שֶׁל בֵּין הָעַרְבַּיִם , *daily afternoon sacrifice.* On that occasion, the lateness of the testimony caused the mishap as described below. To prevent a recurrence, the Sages instituted the rule described here.]

פַּעַם אַחַת נִשְׁתַּהוּ הָעֵדִים מִלָבוֹא, — *Once the witnesses were delayed in arriving.*

[They arrived after the completion of the daily afternoon sacrifice.]

וְנִתְקַלְקְלוּ הַלְוִיִם בַּשִׁיר, — *and the Levites blundered in the [daily] hymn,*

As explained below, the Levites sang a psalm every day in conjunction with the Temple Service. Each day and each festival had its own psalm (*Tamid* 7:4). Therefore, on the thirtieth day from Rosh Chodesh Elul, the Levites faced a dilemma — should they sing the Rosh Hashanah or the weekday psalm? On the occasion described in our mishnah, witnesses had not arrived and the service had to be performed. Consequently, the Levites sang no psalm at all (*Rav; Rashi* from *Gemara* 30b). According to this view, נִתְקַלְקְלוּ should not be understood in the positive sense that they sang the *wrong* song, rather it means that, because the Levites did not know which psalm to sing, they *blundered* in that the psalm of the day remained un-

sung. It should be noted, however, that under the circumstances, the Levites acted correctly in refraining from singing, for it is preferable to do nothing than to do the wrong thing [שֵׁב וְאַל תַּעֲשֶׂה עָדִיף].

Another opinion in the *Gemara (ibid.)* is, that assuming no witnesses would appear, the Levites sang the regular weekday psalm (see *Rashi* to *Beitzah* 5a s.v. וְנִתְקַלְקְלוּ). [Accordingly the word נִתְקַלְקְלוּ may be interpreted that they blundered in singing the weekday psalm instead of the Rosh Hashanah one.]

Yerushalmi (here) relates that a rumor went out that the witnesses had been kidnaped and would not be able to testify that day. Therefore the Levites did not wait any longer, but continued on the assumption that Rosh Hashanah would be the next day. [*Yerushalmi* clearly supports the opinion that the Levites sang the weekday psalm.]

Tosafos (30b s.v. ונתקלקלו) asks why the mishnah did not mention a [greater] problem created by the delay: Not knowing if the day was Rosh Hashanah, the *Kohanim* could not offer the *Mussaf* sacrifices, but had to omit them and offer the daily afternoon offering. After the daily afternoon offering is brought, no other offering may be sacrificed, thus effectively cancelling the Rosh Hashanah *Mussaf* offerings. *Tosafos* reply that because the *mitzvah* of sacrificing the *Mussaf* is a communal obligation (מצוה דרבים), it supersedes the prohibition against bringing offerings after the daily afternoon offering.

Rambam (Hilchos Kiddush HaChodesh 3:5) maintains that the *Kohanim* did not know whether to bring the daily afternoon offering and thus forfeit the right to offer the *Mussaf* in case witnesses arrived later, or to desist from sacrific·, the afternoon offering lest they foreclose the possibility of bringing the Rosh Hashanah *Mussaf.* Their quandary was finally resolved by the belated arrival of witnesses. In order to forestall a recurrence of this dilemma, the Sages ordained the innovation described here. The commentators are at a loss to explain why *Rambam* presents

רֹאשׁ הַמִּנְחָה. וְאִם בָּאוּ עֵדִים מִן־הַמִּנְחָה וּלְמַעְלָה — נוֹהֲגִין אוֹתוֹ הַיּוֹם קֹדֶשׁ וּלְמָחָר קֹדֶשׁ.

the problem differently than does the Mishnah (see *Tos. Yom Tov; Lechem Mishnah;* commentaries to *Gemara, Rosh HaShanah*).

◆§ The Psalm of the day

The Torah (*Numbers* 28:1-8) mandates that a מִנְחָה, *meal offering*, be brought together with each daily sacrifice (תָּמִיד) and that this be followed by a נֶסֶךְ, *wine libation*, which was poured upon the altar *(ibid.)*. As soon as the *Kohen* started to pour the wine libation *(Tamid* 7:3)], [or as the *Kohen* finished pouring it (*Hilchos T'midim U'Mussafin* 6:7; see *Ravad* there and *Meleches Shlomo* to *Tamid* 7:3), the Levites would commence to sing the psalm assigned for that day. Although all Levitical singing was accompanied by an orchestra, tannaim disagree *(Succah* 50b) whether the instrumental accompaniment to the singing was essential to the Temple singing and had to be performed on the Sabbath and on *Yom Tov*, or whether it was played only to enhance the vocal music and was not essential to the service, in which case it could not be played on the Sabbath and on *Yom Tov*. *Rambam* (*Hilchos K'lei HaMikdash* 3:3) follows the latter opinion. The Mishnah (*Tamid* 7:4; see also *Rosh Hashanah* 31a) lists the psalms which were sung every day of the week (the same psalms we recite daily in the morning prayer service). On *Yom Tov* a relevant psalm replaced the weekday psalm and was sung at both daily sacrifices.[1]

The psalm for the daily sacrifice on Rosh Hashanah was Psalm 29, but it was sung only with the daily afternoon offering. In the morning, the usual weekday psalm was sung (*Gemara* 30b). The Sages did not designate a special psalm for the morning of Rosh Hashanah because, near daybreak,

when the morning daily sacrifice was offered (see *Yoma* 3:1, *Tamid* 3:7), the *beis din* would presumably not have designated the day as Rosh Hashanah. Therefore, the morning service offered no dilemma since even on Rosh Hashanah the regular weekday psalm was sung (*Rashi*, loc. cit. s.v. שלא אמרו).

But by the time the daily afternoon offering was sacrificed, the witnesses would have already arrived so that it was known that that day was Rosh Hashanah. If they had not come by then, they would not arrive on that day at all. Therefore the special Rosh Hashanah hymn — Psalm 29 — was sung after the daily afternoon libation. After the *Mussaf* offering yet another text was sung. We have no knowledge of the texts sung after the *Mussafim* except for that of the Sabbath (portions of שירת הַאֲזִינוּ, *Ha'azinu* — *Deut.* 32) and Rosh Hashanah when Psalm 81 was sung.

הִתְקִינוּ שֶׁלֹּא יְהוּ מְקַבְּלִין אֶלָּא עַד הַמִּנְחָה. — *So they ordained that they [the beis din] accept [new moon testimony] until the Minchah;*

The daily afternoon offering was called the *Minchah* [lit. gift or offering] as evidenced in *II Kings* (16:15), *the morning burnt offering and* מִנְחַת הָעֶרֶב, *the afternoon offering,* and in *Psalms* 141:2 (see *Radak, Shorashim* s.v. נחה). By association the period in which the afternoon sacrifice was offered also acquired the name *Minchah,* as did the afternoon prayer. (See ArtScroll *comm.* to *Daniel* 9:21 for reasons why the afternoon offering and prayer are specifically called *Minchah.*)

Ramban (*Exodus* 12:6) holds that the name *Minchah* is not connected to the sacrifice, but refers to the gradual setting of the sun beginning at noon. The term *minchah* is thus derived from נחה, *to rest.*

Though the entire afternoon is referred to as *Minchah,* it is divided into two specific periods:

1) מִנְחָה גְדוֹלָה, *greater Minchah,* starting

---

1. *Turei Even* suggests that no *Yom Tov* had a unique psalm for the daily sacrifice, except for Rosh Hashanah.

din] accept [new moon testimony] only until the *Minchah*; and that if witnesses came from the *Minchah* onward — that day should be kept holy and the next day [should be kept] holy.

from one half hour after midday. This is the earliest that the afternoon offering is ever slaughtered *(Pesachim* 5:1).

2) מִנְחָה קְטַנָּה, *lesser Minchah,* beginning 3½ hours after midday; this was the usual time for the afternoon offering to be sacrificed upon the altar *(ibid.).* It was followed immediately by the rest of the service, including the libation and the singing of the daily hymn (see *Yoma* 33a אֲבַיֵי מְסָדֵר). Since the reason for the ordinance mentioned in the mishnah was to insure that the proper hymn be sung, it follows that witnesses were received even until the lesser *Minchah (Turei Even* s.v. התקינו).

In accordance with this ordinance, if witnesses, reporting a sighting of the new moon, arrived after the *Minchah* period, they would not be received. Rosh Hashanah would thus be deferred until the next day (see above 2:9). As noted above (s.v. בראשונה), during the entire Second Temple era Rosh Hashanah only once occurred on the thirty-first day from Rosh Chodesh Elul. It follows, therefore, that witnesses could not have appeared after the *Minchah* period, otherwise the proclamation of Rosh Hashanah would have been deferred. This is based on the Scriptural report *(Nehemiah* 8:2,13) of two days of Rosh Hashanah.

The wording of the mishnah, *They accepted testimony regarding the 'new moon'* — without specifying Rosh Hashanah — suggests that this ordinance was in effect on every Rosh Chodesh. The same is evident from *Tosafos* (30b s.v. ונתקלקלו—ואי"ת אמאי לא חשיב קלקול של מוסף שלא הקריב מוסף של רי"ח...). This also seems to be *Rambam's* opinion since he codifies the law of our mishnah without specifying Rosh Hashanah *(Hilchos Kiddush HaChodesh* 3:5). *R' Aharon Halevi (Beitzah* 5a) shares this opinion. *Pnei Yehoshua,* however, points out that *Rashi's* choice of language here (30b s.v. שלא אמרו; see

also *Rashi, Beitzah* 4b s.v. כל היום and 5a s.v. עד המנחה) indicates that the ruling applies only to Rosh Hashanah. This is also *Meiri's* opinion.

Turei Even (s.v. ונתקלקלו) adduces proofs that this ordinance was promulgated originally only to prevent a reoccurrence of an error in the psalm-singing on Rosh Hashanah; thus it was extended to Rosh Chodesh. *S'fas Emes,* however, suggests that once the ordinance had been promulgated originally because of Rosh Hashanah, it was decided to make no distinction between Rosh Chodesh Tishrei (Rosh Hashanah) and any other Rosh Chodesh.

וְאִם בָּאוּ עֵדִים מִן־הַמִּנְחָה וּלְמַעְלָה — *and that if witnesses came from the Minchah onward—*

[As part of their ordinance the Sages instituted that '*if witnesses came from the Minchah onward,*' an occurrence that would necessitate the deferment of Rosh Hashanah until the morrow, rendering the thirtieth day a weekday...]

נוֹהֲגִין אוֹתוֹ הַיּוֹם קֹדֶשׁ — *that day should be kept holy*

From sunset of the twenty-ninth day of Elul, the people were required to observe the day as if it were Rosh Hashanah since, from the following morning until the time of the *minchah, beis din* might accept witnesses and declare Rosh Chodesh. In fact, this happened almost invariably (see above s.v. התקינו). Therefore this day was always observed as Yom Tov; work was not done and the observances of Yom Tov were kept. After the promulgation of this ordinance, if witnesses had not arrived by *minchah* time, that thirtieth day was clearly a weekday, and Rosh Hashanah would be the next day. Nevertheless, the rest of the thirtieth day was kept as if it were Yom Tov, for

מִשֶּׁחָרַב בֵּית הַמִּקְדָּשׁ, הִתְקִין רַבָּן יוֹחָנָן בֶּן־
זַכַּאי, שֶׁיְּהוּ מְקַבְּלִין עֵדוּת הַחֹדֶשׁ כָּל־הַיּוֹם.
אָמַר רַבִּי יְהוֹשֻׁעַ בֶּן־קָרְחָה: וְעוֹד זֹאת
הִתְקִין רַבָּן יוֹחָנָן בֶּן־זַכַּאי, שֶׁאֲפִילוּ רֹאשׁ בֵּית
דִּין בְּכָל־מָקוֹם, שֶׁלֹּא יְהוּ הָעֵדִים הוֹלְכִין אֶלָּא
לִמְקוֹם הַוַּעַד.

[ה] **סֵדֶר** בְּרָכוֹת: אוֹמֵר אָבוֹת; וּגְבוּרוֹת;
וּקְדֻשַּׁת הַשֵּׁם, וְכוֹלֵל מַלְכִיּוֹת

יד אברהם

if the people were to treat it as a week-day, they would lose their reverence for this day, and would be lax in their future observance of Yom Tov on the thirtieth day (Rav; Rashi).

[Even the authorities who hold that the ordinance applied to any Rosh Chodesh must admit that this segment of the mishnah speaks about Rosh Hashanah, for there is no observance on Rosh Chodesh which can be described as 'keeping it holy'.]

וּלְמָחָר קֹדֶשׁ. — and the next day [should be kept] holy.

[The next day, the thirty-first day from Rosh Chodesh Elul, is Rosh Hashanah and observed as Yom Tov, by Torah law.]

מִשֶּׁחָרַב בֵּית הַמִּקְדָּשׁ, — After the Temple was destroyed,

[The Temple's destruction removed the reason for instituting this ordinance — to insure that the proper psalm be sung. Nevertheless, the old ordinance remained in effect until it was repealed by Rabban Yochanan ben Zakkai. It is a cardinal rule that, 'Any law enacted by an assembly of sages [דָבָר שֶׁבְּמִנְיָן], requires another assembly of equivalent sages to abrogate it (even if the reason for the original law no longer applies;

Beitzah 5a).].'

הִתְקִין רַבָּן יוֹחָנָן בֶּן־זַכַּאי, שֶׁיְּהוּ מְקַבְּלִין עֵדוּת הַחֹדֶשׁ כָּל־הַיּוֹם. — Rabban Yochanan ben Zakkai instituted that they [the beis din] accept new moon testimony all day.

אָמַר רַבִּי יְהוֹשֻׁעַ בֶּן־קָרְחָה: וְעוֹד זֹאת הִתְקִין רַבָּן יוֹחָנָן בֶּן־זַכַּאי, שֶׁאֲפִילוּ רֹאשׁ בֵּית דִּין בְּכָל־מָקוֹם, — R' Yehoshua ben Karchah said: This too [i.e., the following] did Rabban Yochanan ben Zakkai institute: that even if the head of the beis din should be in another place [lit. anywhere],

As mentioned previously (2:7), upon acceptance of the testimony, it was incumbent upon the head of the beis din to say מְקֻדָּשׁ, it is sanctified, thereby proclaiming that day Rosh Chodesh (Rav; Rashi).

שֶׁלֹּא יְהוּ הָעֵדִים הוֹלְכִין אֶלָּא לִמְקוֹם הַוַּעַד. — the witnesses should go only to the place of the assembly.

I.e., the regular meeting-place of the beis din (or Sanhedrin). In the absence of the head of the beis din, the pronouncement, 'It is sanctified' could be made by any of its members (Rav, Rashi).

5.

⤳§ מַלְכִיּוֹת זִכְרוֹנוֹת שׁוֹפָרוֹת — Kingship, Remembrances, and Shofaros

Having digressed (mishnayos 3-4) to list Rabban Yochanan's innovations, the Mishnah now returns to the original topic — the blowing of the shofar. It was blown during Mussaf in conjunction with the special liturgy of the day. The discus-

After the Temple was destroyed, Rabban Yochanan ben Zakkai instituted that they [the *beis din*] accept new moon testimony all day.

R' Yehoshua ben Karchah said: This too did Rabban Yochanan ben Zakkai institute: that even if the head of the *beis din* should be in another place, the witnesses should go only to the place of the assembly.

5. [T]his is] the order of the Blessings: He recites [the blessing called] Patriarchs; [the blessing called] Powers; [the blessing called] Holiness of the Name and includes [the] Kingship [verses] with

---

YAD AVRAHAM

sion of this mishnah focuses on the accompanying liturgy. This Rosh Hashanah liturgy, however, is an independent obligation; it is recited even in the absence of a shofar.

This liturgy takes the form of verses from the Bible attesting to מַלְכִיּוֹת, God's past and present *Kingship* and His ultimate Kingship in the future; זִכְרוֹנוֹת, *Remembrances*, God's attribute of remembering all the deeds of mankind, good and bad, and His judgment of them all on this Day of Judgment; and שׁוֹפָרוֹת, verses that mention the shofar, among them verses describing the shofar heard at Mount Sinai (*Exodus* 19:19) when God revealed Himself and gave the Torah to Israel, in order to invoke the merit of our acceptance of the Torah; we also mention the shofar which will trumpet the advent of the Messianic king. Each set of verses is introduced by a prayer that highlights the inner meaning of these verses and their connection to the Day of Judgment.

Although the *Gemara* 32a notes that the reciting of these verses is alluded to in the Torah (*Leviticus* 23:24; *Rashi* and *Sifra* there; *Numbers* 10:10, *Rashi),* the obligation to recite them is only a Rabbinical *mitzvah,* as pointed out by *Ramban* to *Leviticus* (23:24).

The sequence of the verse categories — Kingship verses, Remembrance verses, and Shofar verses — follows the rationale given by the *Gemara* 34b: '...Recite before Me Kingship [verses] so that you declare Me King over you; Remembrance [verses] so that your remembrance comes before Me for the good; and by what medium? Through the shofar' (*Rambam, comm.* to this mishnah).

סֵדֶר בְּרָכוֹת: — *The order of the Blessings:*

[I.e., of the *Shemoneh Esrei* — *Mussaf* — during which the shofar is blown.]

[It should be noted that although the respective parts of *Shemoneh Esrei* — and other sections of the liturgy as well — are called 'blessings' by the Sages, they are actually prayers. They are called blessings because they often begin, and always conclude, with blessings.]

אוֹמֵר אָבוֹת; — *He* [the *chazzan*[1]] *recites* [the blessing called] *Patriarchs,*

[The first blessing in the *Shemoneh Esrei* is called אָבוֹת, *Patriarchs,* because

---

1. There is a difference of opinion whether each individual must recite the additional blessings mentioned here (see *Baal HaMaor* and *Milchamos* toward end of fourth Perek; *Rosh* 4:4;

ראש
השנה
ד/ה
עִמָּהֶן, וְאֵינוּ תוֹקֵעַ; קְדֻשַּׁת הַיּוֹם, וְתוֹקֵעַ;
זִכְרוֹנוֹת, וְתוֹקֵעַ; שׁוֹפָרוֹת, וְתוֹקֵעַ. וְאוֹמֵר
עֲבוֹדָה, וְהוֹדָאָה, וּבִרְכַּת כֹּהֲנִים; דִּבְרֵי רַבִּי
יוֹחָנָן בֶּן־נוּרִי.

יד אברהם

in it we invoke the merit of the Patriarchs.]

Ritva and *Ran* comment that the seemingly superfluous statement, *He says* [the blessings of] *Patriarchs and Powers* implies that those sections of *Shemoneh Esrei* should be said on Rosh Hashanah in the same manner as all year round. This contradicts the almost universally held custom to interpolate זָכְרֵנוּ, *Remember us*, and מִי כָמוֹךָ, *Who is like You*, into these blessings. That the mishnah mentions only 'Kingship,' indicates opposition to including the lengthy prayers we add to the blessing (וּבְכֵן יִתְקַדֵּשׁ, וּבְכֵן תֵּן כָּבוֹד, וּבְכֵן תֵּן פַּחְדְּךָ, וּבְכֵן צַדִּיקִים, וְתִמְלֹךְ). *Ritva*, however, concludes that the implication of the mishnah can be understood to mean only that such additions to the regular formula are not *obligatory*; [indeed, if one forgets to include them he need not repeat *Shemoneh Esrei*].

וּגְבוּרוֹת; — [*the blessing called*] *Powers;*

[The second blessing of the *Shemoneh Esrei* is called *Powers* because it lists HASHEM's powers. The blessing commences appropriately with, 'You, HASHEM, are all-powerful forever ...' This is followed with a long list of HASHEM's powers as they manifest themselves in the world. Elsewhere (*Berachos* 5:2) the mishnah entitles this blessing 'Resurrection of the Dead'

(תְּחִיַּת הַמֵּתִים), after the attribute that is mentioned both at the blessing's beginning and its conclusion.]

וּקְדֻשַּׁת הַשֵּׁם, — (*and*) *the* [*blessing called*] *Holiness of the Name,*

[The third blessing of the *Shemoneh Esrei* speaks of HASHEM's holiness and of the holiness of His Name. The expression 'The Name' refers to both God Himself, Who is often called הַשֵּׁם, *The Name* (see *Deut.* 28:58; *Yoma* 3:8), and to His Holy Name which is mentioned in the blessing.][1]

וְכוֹלֵל מַלְכִיּוֹת עִמָּהֶן, — *and includes* [*the*] *Kingship* [*verses*] *with them,*

Because *Kingship* is related to the theme of the *Holiness of the Name* it is inserted into this blessing (*Aruch LaNer*). This series of verses is introduced by וְעַל כֵּן נְקַוֶּה לְךָ, *Therefore, we place our hope in You* ... and includes ten Scriptural verses which refer to God's Kingship. The blessing contains a prayer that God may reign over all the world [מְלוֹךְ עַל כָּל הָעוֹלָם כֻּלּוֹ] and concludes with a *blessing* describing Him as King of the World [מֶלֶךְ עַל כָּל הָאָרֶץ].

Since this tanna holds that Kingship is in-

Tur, Orach Chaim 591). Nowadays, these blessings are universally recited by the entire congregation (*Orach Chaim* 591:1). However, since the main purpose of our mishnah is to designate the appropriate places for the public blowing of the shofar, '*He says*' — surely refers to the *chazzan*.

According to Talmudic law, when the congregation recites the silent *Shemoneh Esrei*, the shofar is not blown. The custom in some communities to blow the shofar even during the silent *Shemoneh Esrei* is not based on halachic sources, but on Kabbalistic considerations as set forth by ARIzal (see *Orach Chaim* 592:1 with *Magen Avraham;* cf. *Aruch* s.v. ערב cited in *Tosafos Rosh Hashanah* 33b s.v. שעור and *Tur Orach Chaim* 592; *Teshuvos Avnei Nezer, Orach Chaim* 446-7).

1. *Rav* (followed by *Tiferes Yisrael*), says that קְדוּשַׁת הַשֵּׁם refers to the verse (*Isaiah* 6:3), *Holy, Holy, Holy,* ... ' which is recited by the congregation as part of the *Kedushah* during the cantor's repetition of the third blessing. But *Meleches Shlomo* (probably finding it incongruous to name the blessing for a verse that is not an integral part of it), amends *Rav* to read אַתָּה קָדוֹשׁ, *You are holy* — the opening words of the third blessing.

them, but does not blow [the shofar]; [he recites the blessing of the] Holiness of the Day, and blows; Remembrances, and blows; *Shofaros*, and blows. Then he recites the Sacrificial Service, Thanksgiving, and the Blessing of the *Kohanim*. [These are] the words of R' Yochanan ben Nuri.

YAD AVRAHAM

serted in the blessing of 'Holiness...,' we must assume that both concepts — Kingship and Holiness — are fused in the concluding blessing. That such is an accepted practice is plain from prevalent Rosh Hashanah liturgy which, unlike this tanna, includes Kingship in the fourth blessing of *Shemoneh Esrei*, the Holiness of the Day [קְדֻשַׁת הַיּוֹם]. Our concluding blessing combines *both* concepts [מֶלֶךְ עַל כָּל הָאָרֶץ ... וְיוֹם הַזִּכָּרוֹן]. We may assume that the mishnah, too, fuses both concepts in its blessing.

According to *Meiri*, the ending used for this blessing during the 'Ten days of Repentance' — הַמֶּלֶךְ הַקָּדוֹשׁ, *the Holy King* — is appropriate for the conclusion of *Kingship* as well.

[The plural form עִמָּהֶן, *with them*, obviously refers to the first three blessings of the *Shemoneh Esrei* which have all been mentioned. Though Kingship is mentioned only in the third blessing, nevertheless all three are halachically considered one unit. If one errs in the third blessing (e.g., he did not conclude that blessing with the words הַקָּדוֹשׁ הַמֶּלֶךְ during the ten days of repentance), it is not sufficient to repeat this blessing, but he must repeat all three from the beginning of the *Shemoneh Esrei* (see *Berachos* 34a; *Orach Chaim* 126:3; 114:4; 582:1).]

וְאֵינוּ תוֹקֵעַ — *but* [the person designated to blow] *does not blow the shofar;*

If the shofar were blown at the conclusion of the third blessing and not blown again until the *fifth* blessing (when the verses of Remembrance are recited), the sequence of blowing would be interrupted by the fourth blessing during which no blowing is done. However, the three sets of shofar blowing should really follow one another as closely as possible. In order to do so, the first blowing is deferred from the end of the third blessing to the end of the

fourth, the blessing of Holiness of the Day *(Turei Even; Aruch LaNer; Tif. Yis.).*

קְדֻשַׁת הַיּוֹם, וְתוֹקֵעַ — [he recites the blessing of the] *Holiness of the Day, and blows* [the shofar];

[The fourth blessing in *Shemoneh Esrei* on Sabbaths and holidays discusses the holiness of the particular day. According to R' Yochanan ben Nuri, no additional verses are added to this blessing in Rosh Hashanah; it follows the same general formula used on other holidays — beginning with אַתָּה בְחַרְתָּנוּ, *You chose us*, and ending with מְקַדֵּשׁ יִשְׂרָאֵל וְיוֹם הַזִּכָּרוֹן, *[God] Who sanctifies Israel and the day of remembrance..* As already explained, the shofar is blown at the conclusion of this blessing, and not after the third blessing, so as not to separate the first set of shofar-blowings from the succeeding two sets.]

זִכְרוֹנוֹת, וְתוֹקֵעַ — *Remembrances, and blows* [the shofar];

[The blessing beginning with אַתָּה זוֹכֵר, *You recall* ... and ends with זוֹכֵר הַבְּרִית, *Recaller of the covenant*].

שׁוֹפָרוֹת, וְתוֹקֵעַ — *Shofaros, and blows* [the shofar].

[This blessing begins with אַתָּה נִגְלֵיתָ, *You revealed Yourself*, and ends with שׁוֹמֵעַ קוֹל תְּרוּעַת עַמּוֹ יִשְׂרָאֵל בְּרַחֲמִים, *Who mercifully heeds the sound of His people Israel's blowing of shofar.*]

וְאוֹמֵר עֲבוֹדָה, — *Then he recites* [the blessing of] *the Sacrificial Service,*

[In the first of the three final blessings of every *Shemoneh Esrei*, we pray for God's acceptance of the sacrifices; in post-Temple times we pray for the ac-

אָמַר לוֹ רַבִּי עֲקִיבָא: אִם אֵינוֹ תוֹקֵעַ לַמַּלְכִיּוֹת, לָמָה הוּא מַזְכִּיר? אֶלָּא אוֹמֵר אָבוֹת; וּגְבוּרוֹת; וּקְדֻשַּׁת הַשֵּׁם; וְכוֹלֵל מַלְכִיּוֹת עִם קְדֻשַּׁת הַיּוֹם, וְתוֹקֵעַ; זִכְרוֹנוֹת, וְתוֹקֵעַ; שׁוֹפָרוֹת, וְתוֹקֵעַ. וְאוֹמֵר עֲבוֹדָה, וְהוֹדָאָה, וּבִרְכַּת כֹּהֲנִים.

[ו] **אֵין** פּוֹחֲתִין מֵעֲשָׂרָה מַלְכִיּוֹת, מֵעֲשָׂרָה זִכְרוֹנוֹת, מֵעֲשָׂרָה שׁוֹפָרוֹת. רַבִּי

יד אברהם

ceptance of our prayers which replace the sacrifices and we pray for the return to Zion of the Divine Presence and the Temple service. This blessing begins with the word רְצֵה, *Be pleased*, and concludes with הַמַּחֲזִיר שְׁכִינָתוֹ לְצִיּוֹן, *Who returns His Presence to Zion*.]

Here too, *Ritva* comments, the mishnah implies that these last three blessings should be recited in the usual way without change. See above s.v. וְאוֹמֵר אָבוֹת.

וְהוֹדָאָה, — [the blessing of] *Thanksgiving*,

[I.e., the blessing that begins מוֹדִים אֲנַחְנוּ, *We give grateful acknowledgment to You*, and concludes with וּלְךָ נָאֶה לְהוֹדוֹת, *and it is becoming to thank you*. In this blessing we thank God for all the good He grants us.]

וּבִרְכַּת כֹּהֲנִים; — *and the Blessing of the Kohanim*.

[The concluding blessing of the *Shemoneh Esrei* is given this name because the *Kohanim* bless the congregation at its beginning.]

Variant versions (cf. *Baal Halttur*) read here בִּרְכַּת כֹּהֲנִים וְשִׂים, *the Priestly Blessing and bestow peace*— i.e., the last blessing which begins with the word שִׂים (see *Shinuyei Nuschaos*).

דִּבְרֵי רַבִּי יוֹחָנָן בֶּן־נוּרִי. — [*These are*] *the words of R' Yochanan ben Nuri*.

אָמַר לוֹ רַבִּי עֲקִיבָא: אִם אֵינוֹ תוֹקֵעַ לַמַּלְכִיּוֹת, לָמָה הוּא מַזְכִּיר? — *Said R' Akiva to him.*

If he does not blow the shofar at [the blessing of] *Kingship, why does he mention* [*it* — i.e., the blessing of *Kingship*]?

The *Gemara* (32a) comments that R' Akiva's words are not meant literally, for the recital of *Kingship* is an obligation independent of the blowing of the shofar. The *Gemara* concludes that R' Akiva meant that since the recital of *Kingship* differs from the recital of *Remembrances* and *Shofaros* in that the shofar is not blown, it should also differ in the formula of the recital. Instead of the ten verses recited in the latter blessings (see mishnah 6), only nine or fewer verses should be said in the blessing of *Kingship*.

אֶלָּא אוֹמֵר אָבוֹת; וּגְבוּרוֹת; וּקְדֻשַּׁת הַשֵּׁם; — וְכוֹלֵל מַלְכִיּוֹת עִם קְדֻשַּׁת הַיּוֹם, וְתוֹקֵעַ; — *Rather, he recites* [the blessings of] *Patriarchs; Powers; and the Holiness of the Name; and includes Kingship with* [the blessing of] *the Holiness of the Day, and blows;*

R' Akiva holds that *Kingship* should be included in the fourth blessing so that it can be followed by the blowing of the shofar (*Aruch LaNer; Yom Teruah*).

זִכְרוֹנוֹת, וְתוֹקֵעַ; שׁוֹפָרוֹת, וְתוֹקֵעַ. וְאוֹמֵר — עֲבוֹדָה, וְהוֹדָאָה, וּבִרְכַּת כֹּהֲנִים. *Remembrances, and blows; Shofaros, and blows. Then he recites* [the blessing

Said R' Akiva to him: If he does not blow the shofar at Kingship, why does he mention [it]? Rather, he recites Patriarchs; Powers; and the Holiness of the Name; then includes Kingship with the Holiness of the Day, and blows; Remembrances and blows; *Shofaros*, and blows. Then he recites the Sacrificial Service, Thanksgiving, and the Blessing of the *Kohanim*.

6. They recite no fewer than ten Kingship [verses], than ten Remembrance [verses], than ten *Shofar* [verses]. R' Yochanan ben Nuri says: If he

YAD AVRAHAM

of] *the Sacrificial Service, Thanksgiving, and the Blessing of the Kohanim.* The halachah follows R' Akiva

(Rambam in comm. to Mishnah and in Seder Tefilos Kol HaShanah at the end of Sefer Ahavah).

6.

6. אֵין פּוֹחֲתִין מֵעֲשֶׂר מַלְכִיּוֹת, — *They recite no fewer than ten Kingship [verses],*

According to the prevailing custom, all members of the congregation recite these verses. The gaonic academies of Babylon, however, restricted this practice to the *chazzan*. See footnote to beginning of mishnah 5.

[As related earlier (mishnah 5) three blessings are added to the *Mussaf Shemoneh Esrei*. Each blessing comprises an introductory prayer, ten Scriptural verses referring to the theme of the respective blessing, and concludes with a brief blessing that recapitulates the theme of the full blessing.

The ten verses are selected from Scripture as follows: three from the Torah, three from *Kesuvim* [Hagiographa], three from the Prophets, and a final verse from the Torah (*Rav;* see *comm.* toward end of this mishnah).

The first blessing is based on the theme of God's Kingship. It, therefore, includes ten Scriptural verses illustrating this theme.

מֵעֲשָׂרָה זִכְרוֹנוֹת, — *than ten Remembrance [verses],*

The second blessing deals with God's Remembrance; His cognizance and recall of all human affairs. It includes ten verses on this theme.

מֵעֲשָׂרָה שׁוֹפָרוֹת. — *than ten Shofar [verses].*

The final additional blessing of the *Shemoneh Esrei* deals with *Shofaros,* the use of the shofar blast during various events. The theme is illustrated by ten Scriptural verses.

The *Gemara* (32a) gives three reasons why the Sages fixed the number of these verses at ten: (a) To correspond to the Ten Commandments; (b) To correspond to the ten times the word הַלְלוּ, *praise* [God], is repeated in the concluding chapter of *Psalms* (150), among which is the phrase, *Praise Him with shofar blowing (Psalms* 150:3). [The words *halleluyah* in the first verse and in the last verse are not counted *(Sifsei Chachamim);* (C) To correspond to the ten utterances by which God created the world (for the exact listing of these utterances, see *Gemara* 32a with *Yom*

יוֹחָנָן בֶּן־נוּרִי אוֹמֵר: אִם אָמַר שָׁלֹשׁ שָׁלֹשׁ מִכֻּלָּן, יָצָא. אֵין מַזְכִּירִין זִכְרוֹן מַלְכוּת וְשׁוֹפָר שֶׁל פֻּרְעָנוּת. מַתְחִיל בַּתּוֹרָה וּמַשְׁלִים בַּנָּבִיא. רַבִּי יוֹסֵי אוֹמֵר: אִם הִשְׁלִים בַּתּוֹרָה, יָצָא.

יד אברהם

Teruah; Aruch LaNer; and Sfas Emes; commentaries to Avos 5:1; Radal to Pirkei D'R' Eliezer 3).

רַבִּי יוֹחָנָן בֶּן נוּרִי אוֹמֵר: אִם אָמַר שָׁלֹשׁ שָׁלֹשׁ מִכֻּלָּן, — R' Yochanan ben Nuri says: If he recited three [verses] from each of them [lit. three three from them all],

[I.e., he recited three out of the ten verses in each respective set (See Gemara 32a with Rashi s.v. או דילמא).]

These three verses must include one from the Torah, one from Kesuvim (the Hagiographa), and one from the Prophets (Rashi loc. cit.; Rav; Rambam, Hilchos Shofar 3:8).

The Gemara (32a) comments that the number three corresponds to the three parts of the Bible — Torah, Prophets, and Kesuvim; and to the three-fold division of the Jewish People into Kohanim, Levites, and Israelites.

יָצָא. he has discharged his obligation.
The halachah follows R' Yochanan ben Nuri (Gemara 32a; Rambam, comm. to Mishnah and Hilchos Shofar 3:8).

However, even according to R' Yochanan ben Nuri it is preferable to include ten verses in each blessing (Hilchos Shofar 3:8; Orach Chayim 591:4; see Bais Yosef to Tur loc. cit.).

אֵין מַזְכִּירִין זִכְרוֹן מַלְכוּת וְשׁוֹפָר שֶׁל פֻּרְעָנוּת. — They should not recite [any verse of] Remembrance, Kingship, or Shofar which alludes to punishment.

[Since the goal of the day's prayers is to obtain God's mercy, it is inappropriate to cite instances of Divine retribution.]

Some examples of verse alluding to punishment are cited by the Gemara

32b: A Kingship verse is: as I live — the words of my Lord HASHEM/ELOHIM — with a strong hand and an outstretched arm and with outpoured fury אֶמְלוֹךְ, will I reign over you! (Ezekiel 20:33). A Remembrance verse is, He [God] remembered that they were but flesh ... (Psalms 78:39). A shofar verse is, Blow the shofar in Girah ... (Hosea 5:9). The chapter goes on to rebuke both the kingdom of Israel (Ephraim) and the kingdom of Judah.

[Our version of this mishnah mentions Remembrance before Kingship, unlike the order given in the first clause of the mishnah, which coincides with the order of our mussaf prayer which begins with Kingship. R' Yaakov Emden (Lechem Shamayim and Mishneh Lechem) and Tiferes Yisrael interpret the tanna's change of order as an indication that the sequence of these three additional blessings is preferred, but not absolute. Thus if one recited the Remembrance verses before the Kingship verses, the prayers need not be repeated in the proper order.]

Ran (toward the end of Rosh Hashanah), assumes that the sequence Kingship, Remembrance, Shofaros is binding, and his opinion is accepted by Magen Avraham (593:4) and Mishnah Berurah (593:5; cf. Da'as Torah loc. cit.; Teshuvos Maharsham 6:49).

Meleches Shlomo points out that the version of the mishnah found in the Yerushalmi, as well as in Rif and Rosh, had these blessings in same sequence as that of Ran and the Halachah (see also Tos. Yom Tov).

מַתְחִיל בַּתּוֹרָה וּמַשְׁלִים בַּנָּבִיא. — He begins with [verses from] the Torah and concludes with [verses from] the Prophets.

Although nothing is said in the mishnah about verses from Kesuvim, the Gemara (32a) takes it for granted that the ten verses

recited three [verses] from each of them, he has discharged his obligation.

They should not recite [any verse of] Remembrance, Kingship, or Shofar which alludes to punishment.

He begins with [verses from] the Torah and concludes with [verses from] the Prophets. R' Yose says: if he concluded with [verses from] the Torah, he has discharged his obligation.

YAD AVRAHAM

are culled from all three parts of the Bible, and the *Tosefta (Rosh HaShanah* 2:10; cited by *Ran* and *Ramban)* clearly spells out that verses from *Kesuvim* should immediately follow those from the Torah.

Oddly, *Rambam (Hilchos Shofar* 3:8), specifies that the three verses following those from the Torah are to be from *Psalms.* Although it is true that the three verses from *Kesuvim* are in fact from *Psalms,* this does not necessarily mean the rest of *Kesuvim* would be inacceptable. Indeed, a passage in the *Gemara* (32b; זִכְרָה-לִי אֱלֹהַי לְטוֹבָה *Nechemiah* 5:19) indicates that verses from elsewhere in *Kesuvim* would be acceptable.

Rosh and *Tosafos* (32a s.v. מתחיל) explain why the verses from *Kesuvim* precede those from the Prophets, despite the fact that Prophets precedes *Kesuvim* in the order of Scripture. The composer of *Psalms* (King David; see *Bava Basra* 14b) from which the *Kesuvim* verses are taken, lived before Isaiah, Jeremiah, Ezekiel, Zechariah and Obadiah — the prophets from whose books the other verses are culled (cf. *Ran).*

רַבִּי יוֹסֵי אוֹמֵר: אִם הִשְׁלִים בַּתּוֹרָה, יָצָא. — R' *Yose says: If he concluded with* [*verses from*] *the Torah he has discharged his obligation.*

On the surface R' Yose seems to agree with the first tanna that one should ideally conclude with verses from the Prophets. He seems to be adding only that if one erroneously reversed the sequence and concluded with verses from the Torah, his obligation has been discharged. However, the *Gemara* (32b)

cites a *baraisa* wherein R' Yose states that one *should* ideally conclude with Torah, but if he erred and concluded with a verse from Prophets it does not matter. Accordingly, the *Gemara* concludes that this mishnah meant to convey the same teaching. The mishnah is thus to be amended (see *R' Chananel, Rosh, Ran* and *Meiri*) to read: וּמַשְׁלִים בַּתּוֹרָה וְאִם הִשְׁלִים בַּנָּבִיא, יָצָא. *He concludes with the Torah, but if he concluded with the Prophets, he has discharged his obligation. Tosafos Yeshanim* interprets the mishnah in a manner *which* accords with the *Gemara,* but avoids textual emendation: The word יָצָא in the mishnah should be interpreted as, *He has discharged his obligation in an ideal manner.*

[The authorities (*Rashi* 33b s.v. היו משלימין בתורה; *Rosh, Ran, R' Chananel, Rambam, Hilchos Shofar* 3:8 and others) assume that according to R' Yose one should first recite three verses from the Torah, followed by three from *Kesuvim* and three from the Prophets, and conclude with a verse from the Torah. This is clearly set forth in the *Tosefta* (loc. cit). The verb, וּמַשְׁלִים, *and he concludes,* refers only to the tenth and concluding verse.

One may postulate that וּמַשְׁלִים in the first tanna's words also has this meaning. Thus according to the first tanna four verses from the Prophets are recited. This seems to have been R' Yehudah ben Berechiah's understanding (*Shitas Rivav* in the margin of *Rif* ed. Vilna; see above, s.v. ומשלים בנביא).

[ז] **הָעוֹבֵר** לִפְנֵי הַתֵּבָה בְּיוֹם טוֹב שֶׁל
רֹאשׁ הַשָּׁנָה, הַשֵּׁנִי מַתְקִיעַ;
וּבִשְׁעַת הַהַלֵּל, הָרִאשׁוֹן מַקְרֵא אֶת־הַהַלֵּל.

[ח] **שׁוֹפָר** שֶׁל רֹאשׁ הַשָּׁנָה אֵין מַעֲבִירִין
עָלָיו אֶת־הַתְּחוּם, וְאֵין מְפַקְּחִין

יד אברהם

7.

הָעוֹבֵר לִפְנֵי הַתֵּיבָה בְּיוֹם טוֹב שֶׁל רֹאשׁ
הַשָּׁנָה, — He who leads the services [lit.
he who passes before the Ark], on the
Yom Tov of Rosh Hashanah,

I.e., the *chazzan* who stands before
the Ark while leading the service. (See
comm. to *Taanis* 2:1 for an exact definition of תֵּבָה; f. *Tur Orach Chaim* 148
and 150 with *Beis Yosef* and *Bach*).]

It was customary then [as it is in most
communities today], that the *chazzan*
for *Mussaf* be someone other than the
cantor for the שַׁחֲרִית, *morning prayer*
(*Ran; Ritva* citing R' Hai Gaon).

הַשֵּׁנִי מַתְקִיעַ; — the second [chazzan]
causes the shofar to be blown;

[I.e., the second *chazzan*, the one who
leads the *Mussaf* prayer.]

[I.e., the shofar is blown during the
chazzan's recitation of the *Mussaf
Shemoneh Esrei* in the manner outlined
earlier (mishnah 5), and not during the
Shacharis Shemoneh Esrei.]

The *Gemara* (32b) comments that
ideally the shofar should be blown during *Shacharis*, the morning prayer, in
accordance with the principle of זְרִיזִים
מַקְדִּימִים לְמִצְוֹת, *the zealous hasten to
perform mitzvos*. Our mishnah's practice of blowing shofar later in the day
dates back to the time of religious
persecutions [שְׁעַת הַשְּׁמָד] by pagan
governments which forbade the blowing of the shofar. Their agents would
spy on the Jews during the morning
hours to see whether they complied.
Once the morning — the time when the
shofar was customarily blown by Jews

— had passed, this vigilance was relaxed, and the Jews were able to risk
blowing the shofar (*Rashi*).

The *Yerushalmi* gives a slightly different account. Once it happened that
the enemies, upon hearing the shofar
being blown, mistook this sound for the
signal to Jews to begin a revolt, so they
attacked and massacred the people.
Thereupon, the Sages delayed the
shofar service until *Mussaf*; when the
gentiles saw that the Jews recited
Shema, prayed the *Shacharis Shemoneh
Esrei*, read the Torah, prayed again
(*Mussaf*), and only *then* blew the
shofar, they realized that the Jews were
only performing their religious service.

Before this incident, when the shofar was
blown during the *Shacharis* prayer, it seems
reasonable to assume that the additional
blessings — Kingship, Remembrance, and
Shofaros — were said during *Shacharis*, since
as we have already seen (mishnah 5), these
blessings have a link to the shofar blowing
(see *Rashba* and *Ran* here). *Ba'al HaMaor*
(toward the end of this chapter, s.v. ואני
אומר) maintains that in Talmudic times these
three additional blessings were included in *all*
prayers, even *Maariv* and *Minchah*, but his
opinion is rejected by the other authorities;
see *Milchamos* loc. cit.]

R' Hai Gaon (cited by *Rosh* and *Ran*) comments that the הִפְעִיל, *causative*, form of the
verb וּמַתְקִיעַ, *causes ... to be blown* (instead
of תּוֹקֵעַ, *he blows*), indicates that the *chazzan*
should not blow the shofar himself. This is to
prevent the possibility that he may lose his
place in the recitation of the prayers as a
result of his preoccupation with the shofar
blowing. This applied particularly to earlier
times when prayers were recited by heart,

7. **H**e who leads the services on the *Yom Tov* of Rosh Hashanah, the second [*chazzan*] causes the shofar to be blown; but when *Hallel* is said, the first *chazzan* recites the *Hallel*.

8. **F**or the shofar of Rosh Hashanah, they may not go beyond the Sabbath boundary, nor may they

YAD AVRAHAM

but if one were confident that he would not be confused — and certainly nowadays when prayers are recited from a *machzor* — a *chazzan* may blow. In any case, there is no objection to his blowing the shofar blasts that precede *Shemoneh Esrei* (*Shulchan Aruch, Orach Chaim* 585:4).

Ritva comments that מַתְקִיעַ, *he causes the shofar to be blown*, is another way of saying מְבָרֵךְ, *he recites the [additional] blessings*. Since, as noted in mishnah 5, the shofar is to be blown during the recitation of the respective additional blessings, the *chazzan's* recitation of those blessings becomes the signal that the shofar should be blown.

וּבִשְׁעַת הַהַלֵּל — *but when Hallel is said* [lit. *at the time of Hallel*],

The *Gemara* understands this phrase to be a reference to *other* holidays when, unlike Rosh Hashanah, *Hallel* is said. From this phrase — when *Hallel* is said — rather than, *during* the recitation of *Hallel*, the *Gemara* deduces that *Hallel* is not recited on Rosh Hashanah. The ministering angels said before the Holy

One, Blessed is He, 'Master of the World, why does not Israel chant jubilant song before You on Rosh Hashanah and Yom Kippur?' He replied to them: 'With the King sitting on the throne of judgment with the books of the living and the dead open before Him, is it possible for Israel to chant jubilant song?'

הָרִאשׁוֹן מַקְרֵא אֶת־הַהַלֵּל. — *the first chazzan* [i.e.,the one who leads *Shacharis*] *recites the Hallel.*

[Talmudic custom was for the cantor to declaim the entire *Hallel* aloud, with the congregation merely listening. At the end of every phrase (see *Rambam, Hilchos Chanukah* 3:13) the congregation would respond with *Halleluyah* (see *Rashi* to *Succah* 38b s.v. הוא אומר הללו; cf. *Tosefos* there s.v. מכאן).]

Hallel is said after *Shacharis* and not after *Mussaf*, in keeping with the principle that the zealous perform *mitzvos* as early as possible (*Gemara* 32b).

8.

Mishnah 8 deals with conditions which make it impossible to fulfill the *mitzvah* of shofar without violating a Rabbinic prohibition; for example, if the shofar is located beyond the distance which the Rabbis permitted one to walk on *Yom Tov* or if it is buried under debris which one is not permitted to move on *Yom Tov*. They gave their decree the force of a Scriptural prohibition; just as it is forbidden to transgress the Torah's negative commandment to obtain a shofar, so it is forbidden to violate a Rabbinic decree for that purpose (*Ran*).

[As noted above in mishnah 1, the Sages have the authority to ordain passive non-performance of a *mitzvah*.]

שׁוֹפָר שֶׁל רֹאשׁ הַשָּׁנָה אֵין מַעֲבִירִין עָלָיו אֶת־הַתְּחוּם, — *For the shofar of Rosh Hashanah, they may not go beyond the Sabbath boundary,*

[Every Jew has a limited area, called תְּחוּם, *t'chum*, beyond which he may not go on the Sabbath or *Yom Tov*. Generally speaking, this area is two

עָלָיו אֶת־הַגַּל, לֹא עוֹלִין בָּאִילָן, וְלֹא רוֹכְבִין
עַל־גַּבֵּי בְהֵמָה, וְלֹא שָׁטִין עַל־פְּנֵי הַמַּיִם, וְאֵין
חוֹתְכִין אוֹתוֹ בֵּין בְּדָבָר שֶׁהוּא מִשּׁוּם שְׁבוּת
וּבֵין בְּדָבָר שֶׁהוּא מִשּׁוּם לֹא תַעֲשֶׂה. אֲבָל אִם
רָצָה לִתֵּן לְתוֹכוֹ מַיִם אוֹ יַיִן, יִתֵּן.
אֵין מְעַכְּבִין אֶת־הַתִּינוֹקוֹת מִלִּתְקוֹעַ, אֲבָל
מִתְעַסְּקִין עִמָּהֶן עַד שֶׁיִּלְמְדוּ.

יד אברהם

thousand cubits in all directions from the end of the inhabited area in which he is located. The *t'chum* is a Rabbinic limitation which is discussed in more detail in *Beitzah* 5:3-7.]

No Jew may violate a Rabbinic decree by leaving his *t'chum* to bring a shofar or to hear the blowing of the shofar (*Rashi; Rav*).

וְאֵין מְפַקְּחִין עָלָיו אֶת־הַגַּל — *nor may they remove a heap [of stones or debris] for it,*

[Debris may not be removed on Rosh Hashanah because it is *muktzah* [lit. *set aside*]; i.e., it serves no useful function that is permissible on *Yom Tov* and may not be moved. Thus, if the only available shofar lies buried under a pile of stones or debris, one may not transgress the Rabbinical prohibition against moving *muktzah* in order to fulfill the *mitzvah* of shofar.]

[The varieties and laws of *muktzah* are discussed in the tractate *Beitzah.*]

[The mishnah now refers to a shofar which cannot be retrieved unless one engages in activities that are Rabbinically prohibited. The general reason for the prohibitions is that these activities might cause one to unwittingly desecrate the Sabbath or festival. One who climbs a tree may tear off a branch; one who rides an animal may tear off a branch to use as a riding crop; a swimmer may construct a life preserver. These are all discussed in *Beitzah* 5:2.]

לֹא עוֹלִין בָּאִילָן — *nor may they climb a tree,*

If the shofar was atop a tree (*Meiri; Rambam, Hilchos Shofar* 1:4).

וְלֹא רוֹכְבִין עַל־גַּבֵּי בְהֵמָה, — *nor may they ride an animal,*

If a sick or weak person could not get to hear the shofar blowing unless he rode to get there (*Meiri*).

וְלֹא שָׁטִין עַל־פְּנֵי הַמַּיִם, — *nor may they swim on the water,*

If the shofar had fallen into the water (*Meiri*), or was on the other side of a river (*Rambam, loc. cit.*).

וְאֵין חוֹתְכִין אוֹתוֹ — *nor may they sever it* [i.e., the shofar]

It is forbidden to cut the shofar off the animal's head (*Tiferes Yisrael;* see also *R' Chananel* to *Gemara* 33a s.v. וְאֵין חוֹתְכִין). To do so is generally a תּוֹלָדָה, *subsidiary,* of the Torah-forbidden labor of גּוֹזֵז, *shearing* (cf. *Rambam, Hilchos Shabbos* 9:7-8), but, as the mishnah will teach, it is forbidden even if done in a manner that is forbidden only Rabbinically. Nor may one scrape clean the inside of the shofar to make it fit for blowing (*Meiri*); this is the אַב מְלָאכָה, *primary labor,* of מַכֶּה בַּפַּטִישׁ, literally *pounding with a hammer;* i.e., applying the finishing touches which make a utensil fit for use (see *Rambam, Hilchos Shabbos* 10:16).

בֵּין בְּדָבָר שֶׁהוּא מִשּׁוּם שְׁבוּת — *whether with an implement that is prohibited under Rabbinic law* [lit. *the law of rest*],

E.g., a sickle (*Gemara* 33b).

[The rule is that one is not considered to have done a Scripturally forbidden

remove a heap [of stones or debris] for it, nor may they climb a tree, nor may they ride an animal, nor may they swim on the water, nor may they sever [the shofar] whether with an implement that is prohibited under Rabbinic law or with an implement that is prohibited by the Torah. But if one wishes to put water or wine into it, he may do so.

One should not prevent the children from blowing the shofar, rather, one may occupy himself with them until they learn [to blow].

labor unless he has done it in a normal manner. If, for example, one wrote by holding a pen between his elbows instead of in his hand, he would not be considered to have transgressed under Torah law. The Rabbis, however, forbade uncommonly performed labor as well. In our case, one scraped out the inside of the horn with a sickle instead of the commonly used scraping tool (see *comm.* to *Beitzah* 5:2).]

וּבֵין בְּדָבָר שֶׁהוּא מִשּׁוּם לֹא תַעֲשֶׂה. — *or with an implement that is prohibited by the Torah* [through a negative commandment].

E.g., to cut the horn with a knife (*Gemara* 33a).

According to the *Gemara* text of *R' Chananel*, *Rif* and *Rosh*, a sickle is prohibited by Torah law and a knife is only Rabbinically prohibited. According to *Rambam* (*comm.* to Mishnah), a saw is the implement prohibited by Torah law.

The *Gemara* (33a) notes that this segment of the mishnah is superfluous: since the mishnah has previously prohibited even a Rabbinically forbidden implement, surely the Scriptural transgression remains in force.

Tosefos Yom Tov remarks that the tone of the *Gemara* implies that this superfluity does not cause any difficulty, unlike the general practice of the *Gemara* which is to find some new teaching to justify a seemingly superfluous passage. In our case, the *Gemara* is not concerned because this segment does not form a separate clause, rather it is part of a larger statement introduced by בֵּין...וּבֵין, *whether...or.*

אֲבָל אִם רָצָה לָתֵן לְתוֹכוֹ מַיִם אוֹ יַיִן, יִתֵּן. — *But if one wishes to put water or wine into it, he may do so* [lit. *he may put*].

Rinsing a shofar with water or wine enhances its' sound and makes it easier to blow. Nevertheless, doing so is not considered within the realm of the Rabbinical prohibition against repairing a utensil (*Rav; Rashi*). [This is because the *shofar* is fit for use without being rinsed. Rinsing it with water or wine only serves to *improve* its sound.]

Mishnah Berurah (586:86; *Sha'ar HaTziyun* 134) cites *Ritva's* explanation that rinsing is permitted because the improvement or 'repair' is not evident, since utensils may be rinsed on *Yom Tov* to clean them. [I have not been able to find this explanation in *Ritva.*]

אֵין מְעַכְּבִין אֶת־הַתִּינוֹקוֹת מִלִּתְקוֹעַ, — *One should not prevent the children from blowing the shofar,*

Even if Rosh Hashanah falls on the Sabbath (*Gemara* 33a).

אֲבָל מִתְעַסְּקִין עִמָּהֶן עַד שֶׁיִּלְמְדוּ. — *rather, one may occupy himself with them until they learn* [to blow].

[I.e., one may teach the children how to blow the shofar.]

R' Manoach (to *Rambam, Hilchos Shofar* 2:7) assumes that 'may occupy himself with' means that an adult may even blow the shofar in order to teach the children, but he cites a passage from *Rashi* (not in our versions) that although adults may instruct the children, they should not demonstrate by

ראש
השנה
ד/ח

וְהַמִּתְעַסֵק לֹא יָצָא, וְהַשּׁוֹמֵעַ מִן־הַמִּתְעַסֵק
לֹא יָצָא.

יד אברהם

blowing the shofar themselves (cf. *Ran* here
s.v. אפרים ר' כתב).

The *Gemara* (33a) concludes that the
mishnah's permission to teach children
refers only to a child mature enough to
be trained in the performance of the
mitzvah (לְחִינוּךְ הִגִּיעַ). A younger child
should not be taught by an adult,
although such a child need not be
stopped from blowing.[1] The above
limitation refers only to Rosh Hashanah
which falls on a Sabbath. On a weekday
Rosh Hashanah, however, even a very
young child may be taught by an adult
(see *Orach Chaim* 599 with *Beur
HaGra*).

The above is based on the version of the
Gemara accepted by *Rashi* and *Rambam*
(*comm.* to mishnah). Another version assumes that a child old enough to be trained in
the performance of *mitzvos* should have the
more stringent ruling applied to him. A
younger child may be taught even on the
Sabbath, but an older child, though he
should not be stopped from blowing himself,
may not be taught on the Sabbath. But on a
weekday *Yom Tov*, even such a child may be
taught. This is the version accepted by
Tosafos (33a, s.v. תניא); *Rosh; Rambam,
Hilchos Shofar* (2:7, according to *Maggid
Mishnah, Lechem Mishnah*). *Rif* cites both
versions and does not decide between them.

For yet a third version of the *Gemara* see
Tosafos (s.v. תניא); *Hagahos HaGra;* and
Ran.

Rambam (*Hilchos Shofar* 2:7) specifies
that this rule applies to a Sabbath which is
not Rosh Hashanah. *Rabbeinu Manoach*
(*loc. cit*) comments that this refers to the Sabbath or the two Sabbaths that precede Rosh
Hashanah [when it is timely to train a child
in the *mitzvah* of the approaching Rosh
Hashanah].

What *Rambam* holds regarding a Rosh
Hashanah that falls on the Sabbath is the
subject of controversy. In view of the fact
that the Sages specifically prohibited adults
to blow shofar on such a Sabbath (see mishnah 4), *Maggid Mishneh (loc. cit.)* assumes
that this blanket prohibition would apply
even to children. *Kessef Mishnah* and *R'
Manoach* disagree. They assume that according to *Rambam* the prohibition applies
only to adults, but children may blow on a
Sabbath Rosh Hashanah just as they could
on the Sabbath before Rosh Hashanah.

Ran holds a sharply different view. He
maintains that children may blow the shofar
only when the Sabbath and Rosh Hashanah
coincide, for then there is a Torah *mitzvah* to
blow shofar. That being the case, the Rabbis
limited their prohibition to adults only, but
did not forbid children to engage in an activity which is ordained by the Torah.[1]

וְהַמִּתְעַסֵק לֹא יָצָא, — *One who practices
[i.e., blows the shofar for practice] has
not discharged his obligation,*

The above interpretation is based
upon *Rambam (Hilchos Shofar* 1:4).
Rashi (33b s.v. מתעסק) seems to under-

---

1. *Ran,* who says that smaller children should not even be permitted to blow, has the version
noted by *Vilna Gaon* in his glosses to the *Gemara.* The conclusion given in the commentary is
based on the version printed in our edition. These versions are cited further in the commentary. See *Rosh.*

1. When the Sabbath and Rosh Hashanah coincide, adults are forbidden to blow in keeping
with the Rabbinical prohibition against performing this *mitzvah* on the Sabbath as explained
in mishnah 1 of this chapter. On other Sabbaths, when this specific prohibition does not apply, blowing the shofar is still prohibited under the general prohibition against playing instruments (see *Turei Zahav* to *Orach Chaim* 588:4; *Magen Avraham* 588:4), or because it is עוּבְדָא
דְחוֹל, weekday activity (see *Ran* to *Shabbos* 3b s.v. אמר ביבי בר אביי; also *Rif* with *Ba'al
HaMaor* and *Milchomos* there).

There is doubt whether an adult may blow the shofar needlessly on a weekday Rosh
Hashanah (see *Rama, Orach Chaim* 596:1; *Turei Zahav, Magen Avraham, Elijah Rabbah,
Shaarei Teshuvah* there; *Shaagas Aryeh* 103-4). *Birkei Yosef (loc. cit.),* however, remarks that
in practice he has not observed adherence to a ban against needless blowing.

One who practices has not discharged his obligation, and he who hears [the shofar being blown] from one who practices has not discharged his obligation.

YAD AVRAHAM

stand הַמִּתְעַסֵק to mean *one who toys;* i.e., one who is playing with the shofar and has no intention of eliciting any sound whatsoever.

The *Gemara* (33b) comments: The mishnah would seem to imply that only when someone blows with intent *to practice* does he not discharge his obligation, whereas when he blows aimlessly, without bearing in mind that he is performing a *mitzvah* he may be fulfilling the *mitzvah.* If this assumption is correct, it would prove that מִצְוֹת אֵין צְרִיכוֹת כַּוָּנָה, [*the performance of*] *mitzvos do[es] not require intent.* However, the *Gemara* concludes that this inference is not decisive — perhaps all blowing without the intent to perform a *mitzvah* may be included in the category of מִתְעַסֵק, *practice.*[1]

The halachah (*Rambam, Hilchos Shofar* 2:4; *Orach Chaim* 598:8) is that one must *intend* to perform the *mitzvah* in order to discharge his duty.

However, *Rambam's* view on the subject of intent is not clear. He rules (*Hilchos Chametz U'Matzah* 6:3) that one who ate matzah without intent *has* performed the *mitzvah.* Many authorities (*Ran* 28a; *Maggid Mishnah; Kessef Mishneh; Hilchos Shofar* 2:4) draw a distinction between *mitzvos* that involve eating (where intent is not needed) and *mitzvos* involving active participation (where intent is needed).

R' Avraham ben HaRambam (Teshuvos ed. Shulsinger 28; also *Teshuvos Birkas Avraham,* ed. Shulsinger 22) points out that close study of *Rambam's* phrasing shows that he requires intent only where someone satisfies his obligation through another person's act; i.e., he hears the shofar being blown, but does not blow it himself. Accordingly, shofar requires intent while matzah — which is eaten by the one performing the *mitzvah* — does not require intent. *Rambam,* in fact, conspicuously omits the view mentioned in the *Gemara* (33b and 28a) that תּוֹקֵעַ לְשִׁיר, *one who blows shofar* for amusement, has not performed the *mitzvah,* an indication that he does not find it consistent with the halachah.

In a similar vein, *Tosefos Yom Tov* remarks that the rule formulated here cannot be derived from the mishnah in 3:7 which states that only if he *listened* intently has he discharged his duty, for that mishnah refers to someone who does not blow, but only hears another blowing. Accordingly, we might assume that the requirement of intent would be stricter for one who merely listens.

וְהַשּׁוֹמֵעַ מִן־הַמִּתְעַסֵק לֹא יָצָא. — *and one who hears [the shofar being blown] from one who practices has not discharged his obligation.*

Even if the listener intended to perform the *mitzvah* of hearing the shofar it does not avail him, since it was not blown with valid intent (*Tos. Yom Tov*).

Because blowing the shofar is prohibited on the Sabbath, some authorities (*R' Efraim, Rif's* disciple, cited by *Ran* here and *Baal HaMaor* at the beginning of this *perek*) hold that the dispensation allowing children to blow and to be taught how to blow on the Sabbath refers only to the period when there still were בָּתֵּי דִין, *rabbinical courts,* qualified to have the shofar blown in their presence on the Sabbath (see *comm.* to mishnah 1). Nowadays, when the shofar is not blown at all on the Sabbath, even children may not blow. *Ramban (Milchamos)* disagrees and points out that all the authorities assume that this dispensation applies even in our days. It is also evident that *Rambam (Hilchos Shofar* 2:7) agrees with *Ramban.* Curiously, *R' Yosef Karo* makes no ruling on these questions in his *Shulchan Aruch,* though it is discussed in *Tur Orach Chaim* 588. *Rama* mentions obliquely in chapter 596 that teaching children to blow is permitted on *Yom Tov,* though needless blowing is prohibited; but he makes no ruling about blowing on the Sabbath.

1. [*Ran* elaborates slightly on the difference between these two cases. Cf. *Rashi* (33b s.v. וְהַמִתְעַסֵק).]

[ט] סֵדֶר תְּקִיעוֹת שָׁלשׁ שֶׁל שָׁלשׁ שָׁלשׁ. שִׁעוּר תְּקִיעָה כְּשָׁלשׁ תְּרוּעוֹת. שִׁעוּר תְּרוּעָה כְּשָׁלשׁ יַבָּבוֹת. תָּקַע בָּרִאשׁוֹנָה וּמָשַׁךְ בַּשְּׁנִיָה כִּשְׁתַּיִם — אֵין בְּיָדוֹ אֶלָּא אַחַת.

יד אברהם

9.

סֵדֶר תְּקִיעוֹת שָׁלשׁ שֶׁל שָׁלשׁ שָׁלשׁ. — *The order of the shofar blasts are three [sets] of three [blasts] each.*

Each set consists of three blasts: תְּקִיעָה, *[tekiah]* — a long, even blast; תְּרוּעָה, *[teruah]* — a wavering blast; and a final *tekiah (Rav; Rashi).*

The *Gemara* (34a) derives the obligation to blow three sets of shofar blasts from the three times *teruah* is mentioned in the Torah:

1) ... *In the seventh month* [Tishrei], *on the first of the month, there shall be a rest-day for you, a remembrance of teruah* [זִכְרוֹן תְּרוּעָה] ... *(Leviticus 23:24).*

2) ... *a day of teruah (Numbers 29:1).*

3) *And you shall proclaim with a shofar of teruah ... (Leviticus 25:9).*

Though the last verse speaks of the shofar blown on Yom Kippur of the *Yovel* (Jubilee) year, it nevertheless teaches us about Rosh Hashanah through a *gezeirah shavah.*[1]

The Torah also indicates that when a *teruah* is blown it should be bracketed by *tekios* (plural of *tekiah*). We find that the *teruah* sounded as a signal during Israel's so-journ in the wilderness had to be preceded by a *tekiah: And when you will blow a teruah* ... *(Numbers 10:5)* — the verb used for *blow* — וּתְקַעְתֶּם — is philologically related to, and is usually reserved to describe, the blowing

of a *tekiah,* as pointed out by the *Gemara.* (The grammatically perfect form would be וַהֲרֵעוֹתֶם תְּרוּעָה). It also says (*loc. cit.* verse 6), תְּרוּעָה יִתְקְעוּ ... *a teruah they shall blow* ... This indicates that the *teruah* should be followed by a *tekiah.* Here, too, a *gezeirah shavah* links the mitzvah of signaling to the mitzvah of shofar on Rosh Hashanah.

שִׁעוּר תְּקִיעָה כְּשָׁלשׁ תְּרוּעוֹת. — *The duration* [lit. *measure*] *of a tekiah is like three teruos.*

As set forth above, each set of blasts consists of a middle sound called *teruah,* preceded and followed by a *tekiah.* The *Gemara* (33b) explains our mishnah to mean that all the *tekios* together are equal to three *teruos.* What remains ambiguous — and a source of dispute among the commentators — is whether the *Gemara* refers to the length of only the introductory three *tekios,* or whether it refers to all six *tekios.* According to *Rashi* (s.v. תנא דידן) the mishnah refers only to the three *tekios* that directly precede the three *teruos.* Consequently, each *tekiah* equals one *teruah.* This opinion is also held by *Tosafos* (33b s.v. שיעור), *Rosh, Ran,*

---

1. *Gezeirah shavah* is one of the thirteen hermeneutical methods by which the Sages demonstrated the derivation of laws from the Torah. These methods were transmitted orally from generation to generation, beginning with Moses who received them from God together with the rest of the oral Torah. *Gezeirah shavah* teaches that when the same term appears in two different *mitzvos,* some or all of the laws that apply to one *mitzvah* can be applied to the other; but this method is valid only if the Sages have an oral tradition that the specific term is to be interpreted in this manner. In the chapters of both Rosh Hashanah and the Jubilee, the word שְׁבִיעִי, *seventh,* appears. The oral tradition teaches that these identical phrases are meant as a *gezeirah shavah* teaching; the Sages, therefore, elucidate that the laws of *teruah* apply cumulatively to both Rosh Hashanah and Jubilee. For the purpose of exegesis, it is considered as if the word *teruah* appears three times regarding Rosh Hashanah and three times regarding Jubilee. Consequently three sets of three blasts each are required to be blown on *Yovel* as well as on Rosh Hashanah (see above 3:5).

9. The order of the shofar blasts are three [sets] of three [blasts] each. The duration of a *tekiah* is like three *teruos*. The duration of a *teruah* is like three *quavers*.

If one blew the first [*tekiah*] and prolonged the second [*tekiah*] for the duration of two [*tekios*] — it counts as only one.

YAD AVRAHAM

Ritva, Ravad (Hilchos Shofar 3:4) *Ramban* and *Rashba. Rambam (Shofar* 3:4), however, disagrees. He maintains that the sum of the all six *tekios* equals the sum of the (three) *teruos*. Consequently a *tekiah* is equal to one half the length of a *teruah*.

שִׁעוּר תְּרוּעָה כְּשָׁלֹשׁ יַבָּבוֹת. — *The duration of a teruah is like three quavers.*

[We use the word 'quaver' in its musical sense of a very short sound.]

The translation follows *Rashi.* Consequently, since a *teruah* consists of three short sounds, a *tekiah* is as long as the combination of three quavers.

Tosafos (s.v. שִׁעוּר) maintains that each יַבָּבָה, [i.e., each of the three components of a *teruah*] is equivalent to a cluster of three quavers. Thus a *teruah* (the three יַבָּבוֹת) equals nine quavers. This opinion is shared by *Ravad* and *Rambam* (according to *Maggid Mishneh*, loc. cit.). Accordingly a *tekiah* is as long as nine quavers. According to *Rambam* (see above s.v. שִׁעוּר תקיעה) each *tekiah* must be as long as 4½ quavers.

Shulchan Aruch (Orach Chaim 590:3) cites the two opinions about the duration of the *teruah* without choosing between them. Later authorities (*Magen Avraham* 590:2; *Mishnah Berurah* 590:12) rule that though it is preferable to lengthen the *teruah* to nine quavers, if one follows *Rashi's* view and blows only three quavers for a *teruah*, he has (בְּדִיעֲבַד) discharged his obligation.

Concerning the duration of the *tekiah*, the *Shulchan Aruch* (ibid.) rules that it must equal the minimum duration of a *teruah*. *Rambam's* opinion (that it equals half a *teruah*) is not cited at all.

It is commonly accepted that the phrase three quavers or three clusters of quavers (according to *Tosafos*) describes not only the duration of the *teruah* but also its form, meaning that the *teruah* is a unit consisting of three or nine very short sounds blown in succession.

Tur (Orach Chaim 590) cites *Ba'al Halttur* who describes *teruah* as one long continuous quavering blast. He adds that this is also *Rambam's* opinion (see *Beis Yosef*). This also appears to be the opinion of the Geonim *R' Saadiah* and *R' Amram. Migdal Oz (Hilchos Shofar* 3:4) testifies that this was how the *teruah* was traditionally blown in *Eretz Yisrael* in his days. He also finds that *R' Yitzchak ibn Giath (Meah She'arim,* part I, p. 38) described the *teruah* in this manner, and that Yemenite Jews blow the *teruah* that way to this day (see *R' M. Sternbuch, Mo'adim UZemanim* 1:5). See Appendix: "The Tekios as they are performed in our Days."

תָּקַע בָּרִאשׁוֹנָה — *If one blew the first* [*tekiah*]

The *tekiah* that precedes the first of the three *teruos* was blown its usual length of time *(Rav; Rashi)*.

וּמָשַׁךְ בַּשְּׁנִיָּה כִּשְׁתַּיִם— — *and prolonged the second* [*tekiah*] *for the duration of two* [*tekios*]—

Instead of extending the concluding *tekiah* to only its minimum length [three or nine quavers, depending on the opinions given above], he extended it to twice its minimum length. In doing so, his intention was that this double-length *tekiah* should suffice for both the conclusion to the previous *teruah* and the introduction to the next *teruah* *(Rashi; Rav).*

---

1. Here even Rashi will admit that these sets were blown consecutively rather than between the additional blessings (see *Tos. Yom Tov; Meiri* with *R' A. Sofer's* notes; *Chazon Ish, Orach Chaim* 137:2).

מִי שֶׁבֵּרַךְ וְאַחַר־כָּךְ נִתְמַנָּה לוֹ שׁוֹפָר, תּוֹקֵעַ
וּמֵרִיעַ וְתוֹקֵעַ שָׁלֹשׁ פְּעָמִים.
כְּשֵׁם שֶׁשְּׁלִיחַ צִבּוּר חַיָּב, כָּךְ כָּל־יָחִיד וְיָחִיד
חַיָּב.
רַבָּן גַּמְלִיאֵל אוֹמֵר: שְׁלִיחַ צִבּוּר מוֹצִיא אֶת־
הָרַבִּים יְדֵי חוֹבָתָן.

יד אברהם

Since the intent of the blower to use this blast for two *tekios* is indicated solely by the fact that he made it twice as long as his earlier *tekiah*, the mishnah must mention that his earlier *tekiah* was of normal length (*Ramban* to 27, *Rosh* 4:8, *Tos Yom Tov*). [If the blower did not intend the second half of the *tekiah* to be used for the second set, there would be no question that it counts as only one (see *Ran* here).]

אֵין בְּיָדוֹ אֶלָּא אַחַת. — *it counts as only one* [lit. *he has only one in his hand*].

It counts as the last *tekiah* of the first set. He must blow another *tekiah* to precede the *teruah* of the second set.

[The underlying principle is that, to be valid, a *tekiah* must have a beginning and an end. Were we to divide a long *tekiah* into two, we would be left with two segments, one without an end, and the other without a beginning.[11]]

R' Yitzchak ibn Giath (*Meah Shearim* part I p. 39, cited by *Ramban* to 27a and others; cf. *Rosh*), maintains that in the case of our mishnah a long *tekiah* is not even counted as one. Since the first half of the long blast is intended as the concluding *tekiah* for the first set, it lacks an end and is therefore invalid. Similarly the second half cannot serve as the first *tekiah* of the second set because it lacks

a beginning. R' Yitzchak bases his interpretation on the *Yerushalmi*.

According to this interpretation the ruling of the mishnah, that he has only one [*tekiah*] refers not to the extra-length *tekiah* but to the *first tekiah*. Ramban (loc. cit.) strongly repudiates this opinion. Ramban's opinion is shared by *Rambam* (*Hilchos Shofar* 3:4), *Rosh*, *Rashba*, *Ritva*, and *Meiri*. However *Ran* defends R' Yitzchak's interpretation.

Shulchan Aruch (*Orach Chaim* 590:6) cites both opinions without choosing between them. *Beis Yosef* (there) rules that ideally (לְכַתְּחִלָּה) one should comply with R' Yitzchak's ruling, but if this was not done (בְּדִיעֲבַד) one has still discharged his obligation. This decision is indicated in the *Shulchan Aruch* by the manner in which these two opinions are cited. The first opinion is quoted anonymously, as if it were the general opinion, whereas R' Yitzchak's opinion is cited as, 'Some say ... '. *Mishnah Berurah* (there 25) rules like the first opinion.

מִי שֶׁבֵּרַךְ וְאַחַר־כָּךְ נִתְמַנָּה לוֹ שׁוֹפָר, — *If one recited the blessings and later a shofar became available to him,*

The congregation recited the *Mussaf* prayer and the cantor repeated the prayer, including the additional three blessings. As mentioned earlier (mish-

1. *Rashi* and *Rav* offer another reason: We cannot split a single sound into two.' According to this line of reasoning, one could discharge his obligation by hearing part of a nine-quaver segment of a *tekiah* and leaving the room while the *baal toke'a* was still blowing. Though he failed to hear the end, the 'sound was not split into two.' Though this reason is given in the *Gemara* (27a and 28a) we have omitted it because, as pointed out by *Mishnah Berurah* (590:24 with *Sha'ar HaTziyun* 22), the *Gemara's* conclusion sets forth the prinicple that one cannot discharge his obligation through hearing only a segment of a *tekiah* (see *Gemara* 28a; *Orach Chayim* 587:3). In the case of our mishnah, since one hears the entire *tekiah* from beginning to end, it does count as a single *tekiah*. *Rashi's* use of the above-cited *Gemara* does not prove that he held this reason to be ultimately valid. It is *Rashi's* practice to explain a mishnah in the simplest manner consonant with the language of the mishnah. *Rashi* relies on the student to find the conclusion in the *Gemara* and to relate it back to the mishnah (see *Tosafos Yom Tov*, *Peah* 2:2).

If one recited the blessings and later a shofar became available to him, he should blow *tekiah-teruah-tekiah* three times.

Just as the *chazzan* is obligated, so is every individual obligated.

Rabban Gamliel says: The *chazzan* discharges the congregation's obligation.

YAD AVRAHAM

nah 7) the shofar is normally blown at the conclusion of each of these blessings. Our mishnah discusses a case where a shofar did not become available until later.

תּוֹקֵעַ וּמֵרִיעַ וְתוֹקֵעַ שָׁלֹש פְּעָמִים. — *he should blow tekiah-teruah-tekiah three times.*

[He may blow the shofar without reciting the three blessings again (c.f. *Turei Even*).]

The *Gemara* (34b) deduces from this that if a *shofar* is available before the *Shemoneh Esrei* is recited, a set should be blown after each of the additional blessings.

[The *Gemara* adds that the obligation to blow the shofar during the cantor's recital of the blessings applies only to a congregation, not an individual; thus our mishnah must be speaking about a congregation. Yet the singular form of the verb בּרך and the singular pronoun לו indicates that we are speaking about an individual. It can be argued that since the shofar must be blown only during the *chazzan's* recital of the *Shemoneh Esrei*, the singular form refers to him and is perfectly appropriate.]

Kol Bo (64; cited by *Beis Yosef* to *Orach Chaim* 592) holds that the mishnah is speaking about an individual (see *Yom Teruah* who explains how the above *Gemara* is reinterpreted according to this). Thus the mishnah instructs us that if the individual had already recited the *Shemoneh Esrei* before a shofar became available, he must still blow shofar after the *Shemoneh Esrei*. Since the requirement to blow shofar is mandated by the Torah, it is not clear why the mishnah teaches us the obvious law that if one could not blow earlier he must still blow later (see *Sfas Emes* and *Turei Even*). However, we can deduce from this mishnah that the ideal procedure is for the individual

to blow shofar first and then to recite the *Mussaf Shmoneh Esrei* (see *Mishnah Berurah* 592:7 with *Sha'ar HaTziyun* 8).

[Having concluded the exposition of the laws of shofar blowing as they relate to *Shemoneh Esrei*, the mishnah goes on to the general obligation to recite this prayer.]

כְּשֵׁם שֶׁשְּׁלִיחַ צִבּוּר חַיָּב, כָּךְ כָּל־יָחִיד וְיָחִיד חַיָּב. — *Just as the chazzan* [lit. *agent of the congregation*] *is obligated, so is every individual obligated.*

Just as the *chazzan* recites *Shemoneh Esrei* silently all year round before reciting it aloud for the benefit of the congregation, so the individual must not rely on the recitation of the *chazzan* to discharge his own obligation of prayer. The *chazzan's* repeating the *Shemoneh Esrei* was instituted by the Sages solely for the benefit of those Jews who are unable to pray for themselves. Only *they* may discharge their obligation through listening to the *chazzan's* recital of the prayer (*Rav* from *Gemara* 34b).

[In Mishnaic times, the prayers were not written down and had to be learned by heart. Consequently, many people did not know the formula prescribed by the Sages.]

Though it is a universal rule that hearing a blessing is equivalent to saying it (שׁוֹמֵעַ כְּעוֹנֶה), this is not true for one who knows how to pray; insofar as possible, every individual himself should petition the Almighty for His benevolence (*Yerushalmi* cited by *Ran*).

רַבָּן גַּמְלִיאֵל אוֹמֵר: שְׁלִיחַ צִבּוּר מוֹצִיא אֶת־הָרַבִּים יְדֵי חוֹבָתָן. — *Rabban Gamliel says: The chazzan discharges the congregation's obligation.*

[It is sufficient for the congregation to listen to the *chazzan's* recital of the

prayer.] According to Rabban Gamliel, even those who are able to pray may discharge their obligation through the *chazzan* all year long as well as on Rosh Hashanah *(Rav; from Gemara 35a)*.

The *Gemara* adds that according to Rabban Gamliel, people [who do not know how to pray and are] unable even to come to the synagogue, discharge their obligation by proxy through the cantor. But those able to attend, must at least hear the recitation of the *Shemoneh Esrei* (see *Rif* and *Rosh; Rashi* 35a s.v. פוטר and אבל; *Tosafos* 34b s.v. כך;* c.f. *Rambam, Hilchos Tefillah* 8:9 with *Kessef Mishneh* and *Tur Orach Chaim* 594 with *Beis Yosef)*.

The *Gemara* (34b) explains that according to Rabban Gamliel the congregation recites the prayer first in order to give the *chazzan* a chance to review the *Shemoneh Esrei* in preparation for his recitation aloud.

The *Gemara* (35a) concludes that the halachah follows the first tanna all year round *(Rambam, Hilchos Tefillah* 8:9, *Orach Chaim* 124:1), but with regard to the *Mussaf Shemoneh Esrei* of Rosh Hashanah, people may discharge their obligation simply by listening to the *chazzan* even if they are able to pray themselves, because this *Shemoneh Esrei* has three long additional blessings — *Malchiyos, Zichronos,* and *Shofaros* (*Gemara* 35a with *Rashi* s.v. משום ראושי).

People unable to be present cannot discharge their obligation by proxy. *Rambam (Hilchos Tefillah* 8:9) omits mention of this last provision (see *Kessef Mishneh* there; *Bais Yosef* to *Tur Orach Chaim* 591). The *Shulchan Aruch* conspicuously omits all mention of this in the laws of Rosh Hashanah (though this is discussed in *Tur Orach Chaim* 591 and *Beis Yosef* there). *Tur (ibid.)* proposes that no one should rely on the cantor because it is virtually impossible to hear every word of the *chazzan's* recitation of the *Shemoneh Esrei. Magen Avraham* (beginning of 591) adds that the פיוטים, *liturgical compositions*, interspersed throughout the *chazzan's* recital of the *Shemoneh Esrei* constitute an interruption [הֶפְסֵק] in an individual's prayer, and thus precludes satisfying an individual's obligation. He also notes, that according to some authorities, one cannot rely on the cantor's recital even on Rosh Hashanah. In practice, it has become universally accepted that every individual prays for himself before the *chazzan's* recital of the *Shemoneh Esrei.*

APPENDIX

◄§ The Two-Day Yom Tov in the Diaspora

Every Yom Tov day is celebrated outside of *Eretz Yisrael* for two days. This is an outgrowth of the fact that, according to Torah law, the fixing of Rosh Chodesh was done by the *beis din* upon acceptance of the testimony of witnesses who sighted the new moon. One knew when a Yom Tov in a particular month was to be celebrated if he knew which day had been designated as Rosh Chodesh. To ensure that the public was informed, messengers were dispatched (see above 1:3) to the rest of the land as far as they could travel from Rosh Chodesh till the holiday that fell in that month. Ancient modes of transportation, did not allow them to get very far. In Tishrei since they could not travel on Rosh Hashanah, Yom Kippur, or on the Sabbath, they would generally have only ten days of travel before Succos. As a result, although the exact day of Yom Tov was known in *Eretz Yisrael*, the Diaspora would not know the exact day until the Yom Tov had already passed. The one notable exception to this was Babylon in the early days of the Second Temple, when communication from *Eretz Yisrael* was done by a simple system of signals (see above 3:3) that enabled them to convey the news of Rosh Chodesh very quickly.

Because Rosh Chodesh can only be the thirtieth or the thirty-first day from the previous Rosh Chodesh, the question of which day to observe as Yom Tov was limited to two days. For example, if the thirtieth day after Rosh Chodesh Adar was a Tuesday, the choice of Rosh Chodesh Nissan was limited to that day, Tuesday, or the next day, Wednesday. Accordingly, Jews in very distant lands knew that the first day of Pesach (the fifteenth day of Nissan) would be either Tuesday or Wednesday — but the margin of error could not be greater than that. Consequently, however, they would be forced to observe two days as the beginning of Pesach, while the Jews of *Eretz Yisrael* and the nearby Diaspora who knew which day was Pesach would celebrate only one day. By the time the next Rosh Chodesh arrived, even the people in the Diaspora would have had time to learn when the last Rosh Chodesh had been, so that the doubt never grew beyond two days.

R' Saadiah Gaon (Teshuvos HaGeonim, Mussafia 1) ascribes the obligation to celebrate two days of Yom Tov to an הֲלָכָה לְמֹשֶׁה מִסִּינַי, *oral tradition given to Moses by God on Mount Sinai. R' Hai Gaon (ibid)*, disagreeing with *R' Saadiah*, traces this practice back to an ordinance promulgated by the early prophets (גְּזֵירָה מִימוֹת נְבִיאִים רִאשׁוֹנִים) perhaps even by Joshua when he entered *Eretz Yisrael.*

As a result of Roman persecution in *Eretz Yisrael*, R' Hillel HaNassi (who lived in the fourth century C.E.), feared that the institution of *semichah* would pass into oblivion. *Semichah* was a rabbinical ordination that began with Moses and continued from teacher to student. *Semichah* was a prerequisite for the *beis din* charged with pronouncing Rosh Chodesh; without it, the months could not be consecrated and the Jewish calendar would have lost its halachic basis. R' Hillel and his court *were* properly ordained and in the year 4118 (358 C.E.) they instituted the calendar in use today (see *Ramban, Sefer HaMitzvos, Mitzvas Asseh* 153; *R' Hai Gaon* quoted by *R' Avraham ben Chiya HaNassi* in *Sefer Halbur* 3:7; *Zemach David* 4118; cf. *Rambam, Kiddush HaChodesh* 5:3).[1]

1. *R' Yitzchak HaYisraeli (Yesod Olam* 4:5) gives the date as 4260. But this must be a copyist's or typographical error. Elsewhere *(op. cit.* 4:9) he says that the calendar was adopted about 300 years after the destruction of the Temple,' which means roughly 4130 — very close the date (4118) given by *R' Hai Gaon.*

Once the calendar was adopted, the Jewish communities in the Diaspora were as well acquainted with the date of Yom Tov as those in *Eretz Yisrael*, it seemed logical that the Diaspora communities would begin observing a single Yom Tov day as in *Eretz Yisrael*.

The *beis din* of *Eretz Yisrael*, however, admonished the Diaspora 'to safeguard the custom of your fathers, (i.e., celebrate two days of Yom Tov) lest the government enact legislation forbidding Jewish observance' and the exact dates of the holy days will be widely unknown *(Beitzah* 4b). Though this reasoning applies to *Eretz Yisrael* as well, the admonition sought merely to preserve the *status quo*.

An interesting interpretation of this passage is given by *R' Hai Gaon (Teshuvos HaGeonim, Mussafia* 1). He regards it as containing *two* reasons for the observance of the two day Yom Tov: A) 'Take care to safeguard the custom of your fathers,' a self-understood declaration that the preservation of custom and tradition is a vital goal; B) 'Lest the government enact legislation forbidding Jewish observance' — which means that Jews may find themselves ignorant of the exact date.

R' Hai elucidates this further, citing the tradition that the 'early prophets' ordained that areas 'outside of the land' celebrate two days Yom Tov. As a Rabbinic ordinance it is subject to the rule that 'any law enacted by an assembly [of sages] requires another assembly [of equally qualified sages] to abrogate it' *(Beitzah* 5a). *R' Hai* modifies this with the statement that, 'The prophets commanded the Jews in the Diaspora [to celebrate two days], and we cannot presume to know the real reason for their ordinance. [Consequently] we cannot know for sure if the true cause [for the two-day celebration] has been removed' (cf. *Vilna Gaon, Ma'aseh Rav*, par. 97).

◄§ Two days Rosh Hashanah

In the pre-calendar period, when Rosh Hashanah was determined by the *beis din's* acceptance of witnesses, the exact date of Rosh Hashanah would be known only in the *beis din* and its immediate environs. Because *beis din* could not dispatch traveling emissaries on the festival, the exact date of Rosh Hashanah could become known outside the immediate area only after Rosh Hashanah, when emissaries could be dispatched. If the thirtieth day after Rosh Chodesh Elul had been declared Rosh Hashanah, the people would have observed that day and already begun celebrating a second day of Rosh Hashanah, since they could not know if the previous day had been proclaimed Rosh Hashanah or not. The Talmud *(Beitzah* 5b) states that even after Rabban Yochanan's reinstitution of the old custom (see here 4:3) that if witnesses arrived after *Minchah*, the *beis din* would accept them and proclaim that day as Rosh Hashanah, nevertheless, Rabban Yochanan still maintained that the following day should still be kept as a second day of Rosh Hashanah, as in Temple times (see *Rashi* and *Tosafos* there). *Rif (loc. cit.)* cites this as proof that even in *Eretz Yisrael*, Rosh Hashanah should be kept two days, since the people there, too, had no way of knowing whether witnesses had arrived before *Minchah*, or whether they had arrived at all. However, *R' Zerachyah HaLevi (HaMaor HaKatan* s.v. והר"יף) comments that the universal two-day observance of Rosh Hashanah was required only when Rosh Chodesh was proclaimed on the basis of witnesses testifying before *beis din*. But once the present, predetermined calendar was instituted, and everyone knew exactly when Rosh Hashanah would be, the whole of *Eretz Yisrael* fell into the category of 'the environs of the *beis din*,' which observed only one day of Rosh Hashanah when witnesses arrived before *Minchah*. *R' Zerachyah* states that, as a matter of fact, the Jewish community in *Eretz Yisrael* did not keep a two-day Rosh Hashanah until shortly before his times,

as evidenced by a responsum of *R' Hai Gaon* (see *Teshuvos HaGeonim, Musafia,* 1). *R'Zerachyah's* opinion is shared by *R' Ephraim, Rif's* famed disciple. However the unanimous consensus of other authorities agrees with *Rif,* that Rosh Hashanah must be observed for two days even in Jerusalem.

The argument is advanced *(Rosh; Rashba; Meiri)* that the reason for two days of Rosh Hashanah in the Diaspora after the adoption of the calendar — 'Safeguard the custom of your fathers lest the government enact legislation forbidding Jewish observance *(Beitzah* 4b)' — applies to *Eretz Yisrael* as well, since up to the adoption of the calendar the custom had been to keep two days even there. Even the environs of the *beis din,* which hitherto had kept only one day, were not exempted. The seat of the *beis din,* was not permanently fixed in post-Temple days (see *Rosh Hashanah* 31a; וכנגדן גלתה סנהדרין). Thus the custom of holding only one day was not linked to any specific locality, but rather to the locality where the *beis din* was sitting at the time it received witnesses. Once the calendar was adopted and there was no longer a place where *beis din* was receiving witnesses, no place qualified for a one-day observance.

R' Hai Gaon, too, in the above-cited responsum, tersely admonishes the Jewish community in *Eretz Yisrael* to 'do as their predecessors did,' and not deviate from the custom of their ancestors.[1]

Rambam (Kiddush HaChodesh 5:7) avers that because two days had previously been kept in *Eretz Yisrael,* the Sages passed an ordinance (התקינו) that even after the inception of the calendar Rosh Hashanah should be observed for two days.

◄§ Two Days Rosh Chodesh

Celebrating a two-day Rosh Chodesh six to eight times a year is a universal institution. *R' Yeshayah of Trani (Shibolei HaLeket* 162; *Teshuvos HaRid* 32:1; see also *R' Bachya* to *Exodus* 12:2) finds that it was so observed in Biblical times. The יום החדש השני, *second day of the chodesh,* mentioned in *I Samuel* (20:27) refers to the second day of Rosh Chodesh (see *Perush R' Yeshayah* to *Samuel, loc. cit.;* cf. *Rashi* and *Radak* there). This is also evident from *Targum Yonasan's* translation of this verse (see *R' Yosef Kara* there; *Teshuvos Tashbatz* 1:153). The *Yerushalmi* *(Taanis* 4:3) also understands the verse in this sense (cf. *Tzion ViYerushalayim* there).[2]

---

1. On the surface *R' Hai Gaon* seems to imply that the then-current practice of observing Rosh Hashanah for only one day was known by him to be a departure from what had been practiced by previous generations. But in light of what has been said above regarding *R' Hai's* opinion about observing two days of Yom Tov in the Diaspora, this quotation takes on a special meaning, for *R' Hai* maintains that a major factor to consider is that tradition must be preserved. We have already cited the Talmud *(Beitzah* 5b) that provides for a two-day celebration of Rosh Hashanah even when the exact date of Rosh Hashanah is known. This is no doubt a special ordinance legislated by the Sages. Thus whenever witnesses failed to arrive before *Minchah* on Rosh Hashanah, two days must be observed even if logic seems to dictate that the reason for the ordinance no longer applies. Thus, ever since the institution of *R' Hillel's* calendar, two days must always be observed. *Ramban (Milchamos* to *Beitzah* 5 s.v. ועור והרב אלפס) arrives at a similar interpretation.

2. The *Talmud (Bava Metziah* 59b), too, seems to speak about two days of Rosh Chodesh. However, *Rashi* (there s.v. בין מלא לחסר) interprets this passage in a manner that leads to a conflicting view. *Maharsha (Chiddushei Aggados)* states that, according to *Rashi,* the two-day Rosh Chodesh came into being only upon the adoption of the calendar. This contradicts the view offered here, that of *R' Yeshayah, R' Bachya* and *Tashbatz,* which rests upon the authority of *Targum Yonasan* and *Yerushalmi.*

The reason for this is that a month — the time between one new moon and the next — is not measurable in whole days, but is rather 29 days, 12 hours, and 40¹/¹⁸ minutes. Since Rosh Chodesh must start at nightfall, rather than from the instant of the new moon, the months generally alternate — one having 29 whole days, and the next 30 whole days. The possibility that the renewal of the moon will take place on the thirtieth day from the previous new moon, — in which case Rosh Chodesh had begun the previous night — is why that day is always observed as Rosh Chodesh (*Rashi* cited in *Shibolei HaLeket* 168; *R' Yeshayah of Trani*; *Rambam, Kiddush HaChodesh* 8:4). In the event Rosh Chodesh will not be until the thirty-first day, two days are observed, the first being the last day of the previous month and the second being the first of the incoming month. Festivals and dates in legal documents (e.g., divorces) are counted from that second day (*Even HaEzer* 126:6). See at length in *Beis Yosef, Even HaEzer* 126 and *Tashbatz* 1:153.

◄§ The Tekios — As they Are Performed in Our Days

Although the minimum requirements for the performance of the *mitzvah* of shofar-blowing are clearly spelled out in the mishnah (4:9), the reader will note that this description does not match what he is accustomed to hear in his synagogue during the Rosh Hashanah service. An explanation of the customary mode of performing this *mitzvah* is in order.

Although the intent of the Torah in proclaiming Rosh Hashanah *a day of Teruah* (*Numbers* 29:1) would seem to be clear — that a *teruah* be sounded — upon closer study it is not so simple. The *Gemara* (33b) notes that *Onkelos* (loc. cit.) translates *teruah*, יַבָּבָא, *yabava*, a word that appears as a verb in *Judges*. There, Scripture describes the anguish of Sisera's mother as she awaited her son who had gone to war against Israel and, unknown to her, had been killed by Yael: *Through the window she looked and* וַתְּיַבֵּב, *the mother of Sisera wept* (*Judges* 5:28). The context suggests that וַתְּיַבֵּב connotes some sort of whimpering or crying. By analogy, the *teruah* in the Torah is a shofar sound that mimics the sound of crying. The mishnah holds that *teruah-yabava* is a repetitive whimper-like sound — a series of quavers.

The *Gemara* (33a) also adduces a *baraisa* which stipulates that שְׁבָרִים, *shevarim*, moderately short blasts, be blown for *teruah*. According to that view, *yabava* is interpreted as a moan-like sound, or a drawn-out sob.

Still another view (34a) holds that *yabava* includes both of the above, with *shevarim* preceding *teruah*, because normally when calamity befalls a person, he moans first and then whimpers (ibid.). Because of these various opinions, R' Abahu (first generation of Amoraim in *Eretz Yisrael*) instituted that the shofar be blown in all the above three modes.

Thus, when the shofar is blown before the *Shemoneh Esrei*, three sets of *tekiah-shevarim-teruah-tekiah* are blown. This fulfills the requirement according to the view that *teruah* is *shevarim-teruah*. As stated in the Mishnah (4:9), three *teruos* are required, each bracketed by two *tekios*. The same is done for three sets of *shevarim* alone, and for three sets of *teruah* alone. This is the universally accepted practice.

Regarding the *tekios* blown during the *Shemoneh Esrei*, diverse customs exist. Ideally, since each of the three additional blessings should be followed by one set of the three mandated *teruos* (4:5), one set should be blown of each of the three modes. This custom is accepted in most chassidic and in a small number of Ashkenazic congregations. This custom was practiced by a small circle in *R' Nassan ben R' Yechiel's* time (Italy, 9th century of the fifth millenium, late 12th century C.E.), and with time became the custom in the Italian rite (see *Aruch* s.v. ערב cited by *Tosafos*

33b s.v. שעור; *Machzor Roma;* cf. *Shibolei HaLeket HaShalem* 301 and R' *Yeshaya MiTrani* cited there).

The custom prevalent in Gaonic and later times (*Rif; Rambam, Shofar* 3:11; *Tosafos* 33b s.v. שעור and others) was to blow only *shevarim-teruah* after the blessing of *malchiyos;* only *shevarim* after *zichronos;* and only *teruah* after *shofaros,* each bracketed by *tekios.* R' *Tam (Tosafos ibid.)* finds this peculiar, since each of these modes represents a conflicting interpretation of *teruah,* and according to any one of the above views, the other two are invalid.

Rif and *Rambam (Shofar* 3:12) anticipating this question declare that the congregation has already performed the *mitzvah* of shofar with the *tekios* that preceded the *Shemoneh Esrei.* Presumably then, any of the three possible procedures is sufficient for the *tekios* during *Shemoneh Esrei* (see *Meiri*). *Shibbolei HaLeket* (301) explains that in this view the institution of shofar-blowing before the *Shemoneh Esrei,* gave those shofar-blasts the position of prime importance in the fulfillment of the *mitzvah,* and those blown during the *Shemoneh Esrei* are relegated to a secondary position, but in R' *Tam's* view (see below) the primary fulfillment of the *mitzvah* should still be through the shofar blasts during the *Shemoneh Esrei* (see *Tosafos, Pesachim* 120a s.v. באחרונה).

R' *Tam,* in order to rectify the contradiction inherent in the prevalent custom, instituted that after each blessing one *shevarim-teruah* bracketed by *tekios* be blown. Thus since each set has *shevarim, teruah,* and *shevarim-teruah,* it would contain the sound considered a *teruah* according to every view. His solution, creates a new problem, that of הֶפְסֵק, *interruption.* For if *shevarim* is the correct method, then the *teruah* following it separates it from the *tekiah.* On the other hand, if *teruah* is the correct mode, the *shevarim* is an unnecessary interruption between it and the preceding *tekiah.* Nevertheless, the three varieties of *tekios* blown before the *Shemoneh Esrei* have already satisfied the requirement of one's Torah obligation according to all views. All that needs to be done during the *Shemoneh Esrei* is to fulfill the Rabbinical provision to blow shofar in conjunction with the three sets of verses. The problem of הֶפְסֵק, *interruption,* can be disregarded therefore.

R' *Tam's* innovation has been accepted in the Ashkenazic rite of Eastern Europe. In the German rite, however, the old custom persists.

A third custom is attested to by R' *Yosef Karo (Orach Chaim* 592:1). For *Malchiyos, shevarim-teruah* is blown three times; for *zichronos, shevarim* three times; and for *shofaros, teruah* three times. No previous source is adduced for this custom (see R' *Yeshayah Pik's* glosses there), but *Vilna Gaon* advances a halachic justification for it.

The Gaonim R' *Sherira* and R' *Hai* in a responsum quoted by many authorities (R' *Yitzchak ibn Giath, Meah Shearim* part I p. 39; *T'mim Deim* 119; *Ba'al Hamaor* here s.v. ונשתנו; *Rosh* and others) maintain that all agree that under Torah law, all modes — *teruah, shevarim,* or *shevarim-teruah* — are equally acceptable. The three varieties represent only different *customs,* not different rulings. Seeking to dispel the appearance of discord that the different customs created, R' *Abahu* instituted the universal use of all three modes during the ritual through which the community discharged its obligation under Torah law. During the *Shemoneh Esrei,* however, there is no reason to be concerned with varying customs since the Torah requirement has been fulfilled.

◄§ The Tekios Before the Shemoneh Esrei

The mishnah (4:5) discusses only the *tekios* sounded during the *Shemoneh Esrei,* and says nothing about those blown before the *Shemoneh Esrei.*

Rif remarks that the institution of tekios before the Shemoneh Esrei is only a custom, and is not mandated by either Torah or Rabbinic law. As much is evident from Rambam (Shofar 3:7 and 10). Ba'al HaMaor states that this custom originated in post-Talmudic times; earlier, the shofar was initially blown during the Shemoneh Esrei. No blessing was needed before the performance of this mitzvah; because the blessings of Malchiyos, Zichronos and Shofaros sufficed. [A parallel situation exists for the mitzvah of reciting the Shema, where the blessings that precede it replace a specific blessing for the mitzvah (see Tur Orach Chaim 235 with Beis Yosef; Ran to Succah 46a s.v. אתמר; sources cited in Da'as Torah to Orach Chaim 58:6 and 66:1; Teshuvos HaRashba 1:47 and 60).]

Ramban (Milchamos) disagrees with Ba'al HaMaor and maintains that this custom[1] was already in force during Talmudic times. He also holds that if the shofar were not blown before the Shemoneh Esrei, the blessing designed specifically for the mitzvah of shofar (אֲשֶׁר קִדְּשָׁנוּ בְּמִצְוֹתָיו וְצִוָּנוּ לִשְׁמוֹעַ קוֹל שׁוֹפָר) would be recited immediately following the blessing of Malchiyos.

---

1. It is obvious that Ramban does not relegate this usage to the category of Rabbinic law — otherwise he would surely note that he also disagrees with Rif concerning his classification of the shofar blowing before Shemoneh Esrei as custom. But all of this is academic, for a custom instituted by the Sages and universally accepted, has all the force of any Rabbinic law. Rambam (Preface to Mishneh Torah s.v. גם and ודברים; Mamrim 1:2, 2:2, 6) clearly equates customs with laws promulgated by the Sages. A large body of authorities holds that the formula recited before the performance of the mitzvos — אֲשֶׁר קִדְּשָׁנוּ בְּמִצְוֹתָיו וְצִוָּנוּ, Who has sanctified us through His mitzvos and commanded us — should be said before compliance with certain customs (see Tosafos, Succah 44b כאן; Ran there 44a s.v. אתמר; Tosafos s.v. ימים, Rosh and R' Yonah to Berachos 14a; Tur and Shulchan Aruch, Orach Chaim 422:2).

שֶׁ‎ מסכת יומא

שֶׁ‎ Tractate Yoma

Translation and anthologized commentary by
Rabbi Hersh Goldwurm

Mesorah Publications, ltd

⁊ Tractate Yoma

The word *Yoma*, Aramaic for 'day,' refers to Yom Kippur, the Day of Atonement. As unique as Yom Kippur is in present-day Jewish life, it had even greater significance when the Temple stood and the lengthy, involved ritual performed by the *Kohen Gadol* [High Priest] became the focal point of the nation. Only on Yom Kippur was a Jew, the *Kohen Gadol*, permitted to enter the Holy of Holies, only on Yom Kippur was the *Kohen Gadol* required to perform virtually the entire Temple service, and only on Yom Kippur could Israel obtain atonement for its sins of the bygone year.

The Yom Kippur Temple service takes up nearly all of our tractate; only the last of its eight chapters deals with the laws of fasting, labor, and repentance. In the course of its discussion of the service, the Mishnah digresses from time to time to elucidate general topics relating to the Temple procedure and the obigations of the *Kohanim*. Otherwise, the tractate is devoted to an elucidation of *Leviticus* 16, which is the text of the special Yom Kippur service, and, to a lesser extent, *Numbers* 29:7-11 which gives the *mussaf* [additional] offerings of Yom Kippur.

Since only the *Kohen Gadol* is eligible to perform the Yom Kippur service, the tractate begins with a description of the preparations made by him and for him during the days preceding Yom Kippur. Thereafter, the Mishnah takes us through a detailed chronological description of the day's service.

Generally, our commentary first offers the interpretation of *Rav, Rabbeinu Ovadiah of Bertinoro*, the premier commentator to Mishnah. We attempt to show *Rav's* sources for his comments, including the various discussions of the *Gemara* and the classic commentators. Where the preponderance of authorities compels us to deviate from *Rav's* interpretation, we attempt to show why. Other comments or more involved discussions are given in a smaller type size; the reader seeking only a basic understanding of the Mishnah may limit his study to the comments given in larger type.

We have placed major emphasis on *Rambam's* interpretation, as found in his *Commentary to Mishnah* and in *Mishneh Torah*, his halachic compendium. *Rambam*, of course, is the major halachic decisor regarding the Temple service and, as such, we consider it essential to incorporate his interpretation of the Mishnah in any comprehensive commentary to *Yoma*.

The *Mussaf Shemoneh Esrei* of Yom Kippur contains a summary of the Temple service, known as the *avodah*. There are several versions of the *Avodah* liturgy, all of them considered authoritative and all of them by major sages of the post-Talmudic period. Wherever relevant, we have cited the texts of the *Avodah* and attempted to show how they derive from the Mishnah and, occasionally, where problems present themselves.

Our references generally refer to the Sephardic *avodah*. A different *avodah*, though with the same name (by an anonymous author), was said in northern France during *Rashi's* time. This *avodah*, which has been preserved in the rite of some Italian communities in the Peidmont province, we refer to as אַתָּה כּוֹנַנְתָּ of אפ׳׳ם, נוּסָח אפ׳׳ם, אפ׳׳ם being an acronym for אסטי פוסאנו מנקאלוו, *Asti, Posano, Moncalvo*, the communities that used this *avodah*. The full version of this *avodah* is found in *Machzor Roma* ed. Leghorn (Livorno) 5616 (1856).

In chapter 8, which discusses halachic matters that are relevant even in the absence of the Temple, we attempt to give the interpretations that are accepted by halachah. It must be understood, however, that it is not the purpose of this work to serve as a halachah text and it should not be used for that purpose.

Although most of the sources cited in the commentary will be familiar to most scholars, some are less well known. We list them for the convenience of readers who may wish to check the original sources:

Avodas Yisrael, by **R' Yisrael Kimchi**, a commentary on the Sephardic *Avodah*.

Tashlum Abudraham, by the famed **R' David Abudraham**, a commentary on the *Avodah*.

Shifas Revivim, by **R' David Pardo**, containing the author's emended version of the *Avodah*.

Shoshanim L'David, by **R' David Pardo**, a commentary to Mishnah.

Lechem Shamayim by **R' Yaakov Emden**, a commentary to Mishnah, and the same author's *Mishneh Lechem*, glosses to *Zeraim* and *Moed*.

Kol HaRemez, by **R' Moshe Zacuta**, commentary to Mishnah.

Hon Ashir, by **R' Emanuel Chai Riki**, commentary to Mishnah.

Maasai LaMelech, by **R' Yeshayah Silberstein**, commentary to *Rambam, Sefer Avodah*.

Har HaMoriah, by **R' Meir Yonah**, commentary to *Rambam, Sefer Avodah* and *Korbanos*.

Siach Yitzchak, by **R' Yitzchak Nunez Vaez**, commentary to *Yoma*.

[א] שֶׁבְעַת יָמִים קֹדֶם יוֹם הַכִּפּוּרִים מַפְרִישִׁין כֹּהֵן גָּדוֹל מִבֵּיתוֹ לְלִשְׁכַּת פַּלְהֶדְרִין, וּמַתְקִינִין לוֹ כֹּהֵן אַחֵר

יד אברהם

Chapter 1

The special Yom Kippur Temple service may be performed only by the *Kohen Gadol (Leviticus* 16:32). Clearly, therefore, it is incumbent upon him and the community to insure that he be fit to perform the service. Furthermore, since a last minute disqualification of the *Kohen Gadol*, unlikely though this is, would make it impossible for the Yom Kippur service to be performed, those responsible for the functioning of the Temple had the further obligation to have in reserve a *Kohen* who could be appointed *Kohen Gadol* on Yom Kippur, if necessary. The primary fear of unfitness was that the *Kohen Gadol* might become טָמֵא [*tamei*], contaminated. Whenever someone is in a state of contamination [*tumah*], he is forbidden from even *entering* the Temple Courtyard; he is certainly forbidden to perform the service (*Pesachim* 67a; *Zevachim* 2:1; *Rambam, Bias HaMikdash*).

Were the *Kohen Gadol* to live with his wife in the days before Yom Kippur, it would be possible for him to contract a seven-day *tumah*, in the event they cohabited without realizing she was a נִדָּה, *menstruant*, at the time (*Yoma* 6a).

Even if he were to be isolated from her, there was no way to guarantee that he would not be *tamei* on Yom Kippur, since it is possible that on the evening of Yom Kippur, he might have a קֶרִי, *seminal emission*, or touch an object that was *tamei*. In either case, he would require immersion in a *mikveh* and remain *tamei* until the following night (*Lev.* 15:16; 17:15). In any of the above cases, the *Kohen Gadol* would be ineligible to perform the Yom Kippur service.

There is a further requirement — unrelated to the fear of contamination — that the *Kohen Gadol* withdraw from his home and be sequestered in the Temple area for seven days prior to Yom Kippur. This is derived exegetically from the Scriptural requirement (*Lev.* 8:33) that Aaron, the first *Kohen Gadol* live in the Sanctuary area for the seven days prior to the inauguration service of the Temple (*Yoma* 2a).

The first mishnah deals with the dual requirement that the *Kohen Gadol* be sequestered and that he be free from *tumah* on Yom Kippur. During his period of sequestration he is forbidden to cohabit with his wife because, as described above, such cohabitation could conceivably make him *tamei* for a full seven days, rendering him unfit for the Yom Kippur service. Furthermore, to deal with the possibility that he might become *tamei* on Yom Kippur — with the result that he could not rid himself of the *tumah* until the day was over — a substitute *Kohen Gadol* was prepared to replace him if necessary.

1.

שֶׁבְעַת יָמִים קֹדֶם יוֹם הַכִּפּוּרִים מַפְרִישִׁין כֹּהֵן גָּדוֹל — *Seven days before Yom Kippur they sequester the Kohen Gadol* [High Priest]

Since only the *Kohen Gadol* is qualified to perform the Yom Kippur service, he alone is sequestered (*Rav; Rashi*).

The *Kohen Gadol's* seclusion was not total. Although he was required to es-

tablish his residence on the Temple Mount he was allowed to leave for short periods of time. This is similar to the, *mitzvah* of *succah* which requires one to establish his domicile in the *succah*, but does not forbid him to leave it [see *Yerushalmi* cited in *Tos. Yeshanim* 6a s.v. מִבֵּיתוֹ] (*Sfas Emes*; see footnote to s.v. מִבֵּיתוֹ below).

מִבֵּיתוֹ — *from his house*

1. Seven days before Yom Kippur they sequester the *Kohen Gadol* from his house to the officials' chamber, and they prepare another *Kohen* as

YAD AVRAHAM

As noted in the prefatory remarks, the *Kohen Gadol's* sequestration from his 'house' has two connotations: A) The Torah requires him to establish his domicile in the Temple vicinity (see *Rambam, Avodas Yom HaKippurim* 1:3; *Teshuvas Tashbatz* 3:37; cf. *Lechem Shamayim*); B) he must be separated from his wife to avoid the possiblity of contracting a *tumah* of seven days duration.

Although the word מִבֵּיתוֹ is literally translated 'from his *house*' in our mishnah it has the additional meaning of 'from his *wife*'; otherwise the word מִבֵּיתוֹ is superfluous: since we are told that he is brought to *the official's chamber* he is obviously not at home. Furthermore, as the mishnah later specifies, the word בֵּיתוֹ, *his house*, in connection with the Yom Kippur service refers to the *Kohen Gadol's* **wife** (*Lev.* 16:6). Accordingly, his separation from his *wife* was a Scriptural requirement (*Tos. Rid; Meromei Sadeh*).

Chasdei David (*Tosefta* 1:1) disagrees. He suggest that the only course required by the Torah is sequestration on the Temple Mount. Theoretically, if it were possible for the *Kohen Gadol* to live in the Temple precincts without being separated from his wife, there would be no objection. [However, the very fact that he lives in the Temple area prevents cohabitation since a person in a state of *tumah* is forbidden to be in the Temple area and cohabitation causes *tumah* (see Pref. Remarks)].[1]

Meiri holds that the *only* reason for his sequestration is the fear that he may become contaminated if he lives with his wife, but not that there is an independent *mitzvah* of sequestration. *Meiri*, however, fails to account for the

text of the *Gemara* (cited above) which seems to contradict his view.

לְלִשְׁכַּת פַּלְהֶדְרִין, — *to the officials' chamber,*

[In the Talmud and in *Aruch*, the spelling is פַּרְהֶדְרִין.]

This chamber served as the *Kohen Gadol's* private office. The *Gemara* (8b) relates that it used to be called the לִשְׁכַּת בֶּלְוָטִין, *princes' chamber*, i.e., that of the *Kohanim Gedolim* [High Priests]. Later, when the office of the High Priesthood became corrupted (during the middle and late Second Temple period, as related in the *Gemara* there) and was sold to the highest bidder, the *Kohanim Gedolim* were changed every year. The chamber was renamed the לִשְׁכַּת פַּלְהֶדְרִין, *officials' chamber*, because the priesthood had become regarded as an official appointment subject to cancellation at the whim of the Hasmonean kings (see *Rashi, loc. cit.*). *Rashi* adds that not only were the *Kohanim Gedolim* frequently changed, but that the chamber itself was usually rebuilt with the advent of each subsequent *Kohen Gadol*.

The *Gemara* (19a) concludes that this chamber was on the north side of the Temple Courtyard (see *Rambam, Beis HaBechirah* 5:17 with *Mishneh LaMelech*).

According the the text of *Middos* 5:4 as it is quoted in *Gemara* 19a (as distinct from the version found in our editions of Mishnah; see commentaries there), this is the so-called לִשְׁכַּת הָעֵץ, *wood chamber*, which Abba Shaul identifies as the chamber of the *Kohen Gadol*.

Tosafos (8b s.v. דאי) poses a question: How was the *Kohen Gadol* allowed to sit and sleep in this chamber

---

1. Evidently *Chasdei David* assumes that the *Kohen Gadol's* sequestration was total; he was not allowed to leave the Temple mount. This contradicts the opinion of *Sfas Emes* cited above (s.v. שבעת ימים). See also *Gemara* 6a and *Rashi, Tosafos,* and *Tos. Yeshanim* s.v. מביתו, *Meromei Sadeh, loc. cit.*]

תַּחְתָּיו. שֶׁמָּא יֶאֱרַע בּוֹ פְּסוּל.
רַבִּי יְהוּדָה אוֹמֵר: אַף אִשָׁה אַחֶרֶת מַתְקִינִין
לוֹ, שֶׁמָּא תָמוּת אִשְׁתּוֹ שֶׁנֶּאֱמַר: וְכִפֶּר בַּעֲדוֹ
וּבְעַד בֵּיתוֹ, בֵּיתוֹ — זוֹ אִשְׁתּוֹ.

יד אברהם

which was part of the Temple Court-yard, since it is forbidden to sit in the Temple Courtyard (Gem. 25a)?

Tosafos offers two possible solutions:

A) Although this room was in the Temple Courtyard area its only door-way opened outside the enclosure. Therefore, it was not considered part of the Courtyard and was not subject to these restrictions (see *Maaser Sheni* 3:8; *Pesachim* 86a).

B) This chamber lay outside the Courtyard enclosure, however it had a door leading to the Temple Courtyard. This rendered it holy enough to be con-sidered part of the Temple Courtyard proper insofar as the *eating* of sacrifices is concerned. Therefore it was qualified to serve as the *Kohen Gadol's* domicile in these seven days, but since it was not part of the Temple Courtyard itself, and was not sanctified for the slaughtering of sacrifices, it did not fall under the restriction against sitting. [See *Zeva-chim* 56a].

וּמַתְקִינִין לוֹ כֹהֵן אַחֵר תַּחְתָּיו, — and they prepare another Kohen [to serve] as his substitute,

To be ready to serve in place of the regular *Kohen Gadol (Rav; Rashi)*.

According to R' Chanina, the *S'gan* [*Deputy*] of the *Kohanim*, the one who served as Deputy *Kohen Gadol* all year was also the substitute on Yom Kippur (Gem. 39a). This responsibility, how-ever, is omitted from *Yerushalmi's* listing of the Deputy's functions. Ac-cording to many commentators, other tannaim disagree with R' Chanina (see *Toroson shel Rishonim, Yerushalmi* 3:8; *R' Chananel* (39a); *Tos. Sotah* 42a s.v. סגן; *Tosefta* 1:4 with *Ohr HaGanuz* and commentaries). *Rambam's* code omits R' Chanina's opinion, implying that he rules otherwise.

Since the mishnah uses the verb וּמַתְקִינִין, *they prepare*, instead of וּמַפְרִישִׁין, *they sequester* (the verb used in the first part of the mishnah), we deduce that the substitute *Kohen Gadol* need not be sequestered. Although se-questration was required of the *Kohen Gadol*, he would not be *disqualified* without it; therefore, it was not imposed on the substitute (Gem. 3b).[1]

שֶׁמָּא יֶאֱרַע בּוֹ פְּסוּל. — lest he become dis-qualified [lit. maybe a disqualification would happen to him].

He may become contaminated

1. *Tosefta* (1:4), however, uses the verb מַפְרִישִׁין, *they sequestered*, in this instance too. *Kol HaRemez* deduces from *Yerushalmi* that the Deputy *Kohen Gadol*, though he did not move to the לִשְׁכַּת פַּרְהֶדְרִין, *officials' chamber*, was also separated from his wife. *Shoshanim L' David* resolves this apparent contradiction between the *Gemara* and the *Tosefta*. As mentioned above (s.v. מִבֵּיתוֹ), the sequestration of the *Kohen Gadol* had two purposes. Regarding the positive purpose of establishing residence on the Temple Mount, it can be said the the sub-stitute was absolved since non-residence would not disqualify him for service. Clearly the *Gemara* (3b) refers to this. But the second purpose, which is to separate the *Kohen Gadol* from his wife lest he become contaminated, surely applies to the substitute as well for the same reason. The substitute, too, is therefore required to take up residence in a place other than his wife's. The mishnah uses a different verb to stress the difference between the *Kohen Gadol* and his substitute. Nevertheless, the *Tosefta* uses the verb מַפְרִישִׁין, *they separate*, since it is an accurate description (see also *Chasdei David* to *Tosefta*).

Gevuras Ari wonders whether the selection of the substitute takes place seven days before Yom Kippur as the language of the mishnah seems to suggest, or whether it is sufficient to pick the substitute any time before Yom Kippur. According to the opinion just cited, he must unquestionably be selected seven days before Yom Kippur.

his substitute, lest he become disqualified.

R' Yehudah says: They also prepare another wife for him, lest his wife die, for it is said: *And he shall make atonement for himself and for his house* [*Leviticus* 16:6]; 'his house' — that is, his wife.

YAD AVRAHAM

through seminal emission [קֶרִי] or through contact with any טוּמְאָה [*tumah*], *contamination (Rav)*.

Tosefos Yom Tov (D'mai 1:1) wonders why this precaution was necessary in light of the mishnah *(Avos 5:5)* which reports ten miracles which occurred in the Holy Temple. One of the ten is that no *Kohen Gadol* ever was disqualified on Yom Kippur on account of having a seminal emission.

He answers: They did not want to rely on a miracle [אֵין סוֹמְכִין עַל הַנֵּס].

Alternatively, these ten miracles stopped after the death of Shimon Ha-Tzaddik because most *Kohanim Gedolim* after him were unworthy of miracles (see *Gem. 9a; Lechem Shamayim).* Interestingly, both of these answers are found in *Yerushalmi* (1:4). Though on the surface *Yerushalmi* seems to be dealing with a different question, *Rashbatz (Tashbatz* 3:37) understands that this question is also included.

Lechem Shamayim proposes still another answer, namely that the *Kohen Gadol* could very easily have been disqualified in another manner. If spittle from the mouth of certain טְמֵאִים, *contaminated individuals,* touched him, it would disqualify him. There was no miraculous guarantee against this contingency. He finds evidence for this in *Avos D'Rabbi Nosson* (ch. 35 cf. *Rav* to *Avos* 5:5 s.v. ולא אירע).

רַבִּי יְהוּדָה אוֹמֵר: אַף אִשָּׁה אַחֶרֶת מַתְקִינִין לוֹ, שֶׁמָּא תָמוּת אִשְׁתּוֹ, — *R' Yehudah says: They also prepare another wife for him, lest his wife die,*

The Gemara concludes that he must

actually marry her before Yom Kippur. [Otherwise, if his first wife were actually to die on Yom Kippur, he would be prohibited from marrying the second woman because of the prohibition against performing a marriage on Yom Tov (see *Beitzah* 5:2).]

This new marriage, however, causes another problem, since the *Kohen Gadol* is not allowed to have more than one wife on Yom Kippur (*Gem.* 2a). To resolve this dilemma, he gives both his wives conditional divorces, so formulated that he can annul the divorce of the first wife, and legally confirm the divorce of the second wife, if all is well. Should the first wife die during Yom Kippur day, he will confirm the first divorce and annul the second. Thus the second wife will retroactively become the *Kohen Gadol's* only wife on Yom Kippur (*Gem.* 13a,b).

Yerushalmi (cited in *Tos.* 13b s.v. חדא) holds that the *Kohen Gadol* did not actually marry the second wife. She was only *designated* to be married. Only if his first wife died on Yom Kippur would the *Kohen Gadol* wed the designee. The Rabbinic prohibition not to marry on a holiday would be suspended for such a contingency. The Babylonian Talmud, however, clearly disagrees with this.[1]

The רַבָּנָן, *Rabbis,* who disagree with R' Yehudah hold that we do not have to provide for the remote possibility that the *Kohen Gadol's* wife may die *(Gem.* 13a).

שֶׁנֶּאֱמַר: ,,וְכִפֶּר בַּעֲדוֹ וּבְעַד בֵּיתוֹ׳׳, בֵּיתוֹ—זוֹ אִשְׁתּוֹ. — *for it is said: And he shall make*

---

1. *Sfas Emes* (to *Tosafos* 13b s.v. חדא) ponders whether the חוּפָּה [*chupah*], *marriage ceremony,* held during the seven days of the *Kohen Gadol's* sequestration is valid, for it can be argued that since the wife he marries during this period must be separated from him, the *chupah* lacks the essential characteristic of enabling them to live together. If so, the preparation of the second wife would have to take place before the seven-day period.

אָמְרוּ לוֹ: אִם כֵּן, אֵין לַדָּבָר סוֹף.

[ב] **כָּל-שִׁבְעַת** הַיָּמִים הוּא זוֹרֵק אֶת־
הַדָּם, וּמַקְטִיר אֶת־
הַקְּטֹרֶת, וּמֵטִיב־אֶת הַנֵּרוֹת, וּמַקְרִיב אֶת־

יד אברהם

atonement for himself and for his house [*Leviticus* 16:6]; 'his house' — that is his wife.

Since *house* here clearly cannot mean the *building* in which he lives, it must mean the members of his *household*. All the particulars mentioned as part of the Yom Kippur service are essential to it [מְעַכְּבִין], therefore, the *Kohen Gadol* must have a *household* for which to atone. If *household* had meant his children, it would follow that their death *during* the service would disqualify him. Such a development would be against the spirit of the Torah [דְּרָכֶיהָ דַרְכֵי-נֹעַם, *its ways are pleasant ways* (Proverbs 3:17); see Yevamos 87b]. Therefore, *his household* must mean his wife. Thus, in a case of death, the *Kohen Gadol* could still serve, since by Torah law he could marry another wife (*Meshech Chochmah* to *Lev.* 16:6).

אָמְרוּ לוֹ: אִם כֵּן,— *They said to him: If so,* [If we have to provide for the remote possibility of sudden death.]

אֵין לַדָּבָר סוֹף. — *there is no end to the matter.*

For we would have to provide for the contingency that the second wife, too, might die (*Gem.* 13a).

However, R' Yehudah differentiates between the moderately remote possibility that one wife may die, and the very remote possibility that *both* wives may die suddenly (*ibid.*).

The first tanna distinguishes between a wife's possible death, a remote eventuality, for which we need not provide, and the *Kohen Gadol's* possible disqualification, a more common eventuality, for which we do have to provide (*ibid.*).

2.

Since only the *Kohen Gadol* could perform Yom Kippur service, the sages responsible for the orderly functioning of the Temple provided that he should perform much of the daily service during his week of sequestration. Thereby, he would become proficient in the various acts, thus helping insure that he would do them properly on Yom Kippur.

[In some versions this mishnah is introduced by the following: זִקְנֵי בֵית דִּין מְלַמְּדִין אוֹתוֹ סֵדֶר הַכִּפּוּרִים כָּל שִׁבְעַת הַיָּמִים, *the elders of the beis din teach him the order of the Yom Kippur (service) throughout seven days.* See *Shinuyei Nuschaos* in *Mishnayos* ed. Vilna and *Dikdukei Soferim.*]

כָּל שִׁבְעַת הַיָּמִים הוּא זוֹרֵק אֶת-הַדָּם, — *On all of these seven days he throws the blood,*

[The key service of any sacrifice is זְרִיקָה, *throwing*, the blood upon the altar.]

The blood service assigned the *Kohen Gadol* was that of the תָּמִיד, *daily offering*, so as to familiarize him with the service he would perform on Yom Kippur (*Rav*).

There were two daily offerings, morning and afternoon. During this week the *Kohen Gadol* performed the blood service of both (*Meiri*).

The mishnah does not mention that the *Kohen Gadol* performed the שְׁחִיטָה, *slaughter*, of these sacrifices, and the קַבָּלָה, *receiving* of the blood, even though he alone would have to perform both these acts as well on Yom Kippur. He did not practice

They said to him: If so, there is no end to the matter.

2. On all of these seven days he throws the blood, burns the incense, prepares the lamps, and offers the

YAD AVRAHAM

them during the seven days because the manner of their performance on Yom Kippur was different from the daily procedure. On Yom Kippur, the *Kohen Gadol* would perform *most* of the slaughter and another *Kohen* would finish the cut, while the *Kohen Gadol* received the blood (3:4). During the rest of the year, however, it is improper to slaughter this way. There would be no point in having him practice the year-round method of slaughter since this would not prepare him for the different procedure followed on Yom Kippur *(Hon Ashir)*.

However in the *Mussaf* liturgy [אַתָּה כּוֹנַנְתָּ] of some French communities [*Machzor Roma*, Leghorn 5616, v. 2, p. 214] slaughter, too, is mentioned as part of the service practiced by the *Kohen Gadol* during the seven days.

וּמַקְטִיר אֶת־הַקְּטֹרֶת, וּמֵטִיב אֶת־הַגֵּרוֹת, — *(and) burns the incense, (and) prepares* [lit. *improves*] *the lamps,*

It was a part of the daily service to rid the lamps of the ashes and to remove the old wicks *(Rav; Rashi)*.

There are four opinions as to what this service of הַטָבָה [*hatavah*], *preparing*, entailed. The controversy centers around the definition of the word בְּהֵיטִיבוֹ in *Exodus* 30:7 and the word מֵטִיב used here and elsewhere in the *Mishnah*. The first opinion, that of *Rashi* followed by *Rav*, has been cited above (see *Exodus* 30:7 with *Rashi* and *Ibn Ezra*). It follows from this that refilling the lamps and replacing the wicks do not constitute a service. Rather, they are merely necessary steps to prepare the menorah for the lighting in the evening, and consequently were not done until then. *Rashash (Tamid* 3:9) suggests this without mentioning *Rashi*. *Mikdash David (Kodashim* II, 21:2) suggests that both *Rashi* and *Rabbeinu Gershom* (to *Menachos* 100a) concur.

Rashba (Teshuvos 1:309) holds that both the cleaning and refilling of the lamps and replacing of the wicks, constituted part of the service of *hatavah* and were done during the

morning service. *Rav (Tamid* 3:9) follows this opinion.

Ramban (Milchamos, first paragraph in *Yoma)* holds that the service of *hatavah* included only filling the lamps with oil and inserting the fresh wicks, and it had to be done every morning. On Yom Kippur, it was done by the *Kohen Gadol* and he practiced on the seven preceding days. Cleaning the lamps and removing the used wicks were only preparation for the service proper — i.e., refilling the lamps and replacing the wicks — and was not done by the *Kohen Gadol.*

Rambam (T'midin U'Mussafin 3:10-12), followed by *Ritva,* holds that *hatavah* basically means to light the lamps. Accordingly, the lamps were lit not only in the afternoon but also in the morning to fulfill the obligatory service of *hatavah.* Cleaning the lamps, also part of the service, is called דִּישׁוּן [*dishun*]. Whether the *Kohen Gadol* was obliged to perform *dishun* on Yom Kippur is not clear since the mishnah (here and 3:4, and *Rambam, Avodas Yom HaKippurim* 1:5, 2:2) mentions only *hatavah.* However *Ritva* (here) states clearly that both *dishun* and *hatavah* were done by the *Kohen Gadol.* (see also *Mirkeves HaMishnah* and *Even HaAzel, T'midin U'Mussafin* 3:10).[1]

Sfas Emes asks why the mishnah does not list the *lighting* of lamps among the services practiced by the *Kohen Gadol* in anticipation of Yom Kippur. According to *Rambam,* however, this is no problem since *Rambam* defines *hatavah* as *lighting.*

◆§ **Which of the lamps were prepared by the Kohen Gadol?**

The *hatavah* of the seven lamps was not done all at once. After five lamps were prepared, another part of the service was performed, then the last two lamps were prepared. According to our mishnah, the intervening part of the service was the burning of the incense (see *Gem.* 14b and 33). Since the mishnah mentions preparing the lamps after the burning of the incense, we know

1. [*Ritva* comments that this opinion is held by most commentators; see his commentary to *Yoma* 14a and to *Shabbos,* Reichman ed., 23b].

הָרֹאשׁ וְאֶת־הָרֶגֶל; וּשְׁאָר כָּל־הַיָּמִים, אִם רָצָה
לְהַקְרִיב, מַקְרִיב, שֶׁכֹּהֵן גָּדוֹל מַקְרִיב חֵלֶק
בָּרֹאשׁ וְנוֹטֵל חֵלֶק בָּרֹאשׁ.

[ג] **מָסְרוּ** לוֹ זְקֵנִים מִזִּקְנֵי בֵית דִּין וְקוֹרִין
לְפָנָיו בְּסֵדֶר הַיּוֹם, וְאוֹמְרִים לוֹ:
אִישִׁי כֹהֵן גָּדוֹל, קְרָא אַתָּה בְּפִיךָ, שֶׁמָּא שָׁכַחְתָּ
אוֹ שֶׁמָּא לֹא לָמַדְתָּ.

יד אברהם

that the preparation referred to is that of the last two lamps (Gemara 14b). The Kohen Gadol was not obligated to perform the hatavah of the first five lamps (Tosafos 14b s.v. ההיא).

Gevuras Ari disagrees. He argues that although the mishnah refers only to the preparation of the last two lamps, this does not mean that the Kohen Gadol did not prepare the other five lamps, as well. The mishnah here lists only the services performed by the Kohen Gadol, but not all parts of each service. Since some of the lamps were prepared after the burning of the incense, this is reason enough to list the incense burning first.

Rambam (Avodas Yom HaKippurim 1:5 and 2:1) states without qualification: He [the Kohen Gadol] prepares the lamps. Rambam seems to share Gevuras Ari's opinion.

וּמַקְרִיב אֶת־הָרֹאשׁ וְאֶת־הָרֶגֶל: — and offers the head and hind leg:

[Of the קָרְבָּן תָּמִיד, daily sacrifice, whose limbs were burned on the altar. The Kohen Gadol stood at the top of the כֶּבֶשׁ, altar ramp, and the limbs of the sacrifice were brought up to him. He placed his hands on them (סְמִיכָה) and tossed them into the fire on the altar (see Tamid 7:3).]

The Mishnah mentions only the head and the hind leg, since these two limbs were always the first to be tossed onto the altar (see below 2:3). After this, he proceeded to toss all the limbs into the fire. This is also implied by Rambam (Avodas Yom HaKippurim 1:5; Tos. Yom Tov).

Meiri and Hon Ashir disagree. They maintain that since all this was needed only to familiarize the Kohen Gadol with the service, there was no need to tire him with the tossing of all the limbs.

[On Yom Kippur, though, the Kohen Gadol tossed all the limbs into the fire as is seen from mishnah 3:4.]

וּשְׁאָר כָּל הַיָּמִים, אִם רָצָה לְהַקְרִיב, מַקְרִיב. — On all other days [of the year], if he wishes to offer [any sacrifice], he may offer [it].

[The Kohanim were divided into twenty-four מִשְׁמָרוֹת, watches (i.e., shifts), which took turns performing the Temple service for one week at a time. Each watch was subdivided into בָּתֵּי אָבוֹת, family sub-units, each of which served on a specific day of the week. Only the family assigned to a specific day had the privilege of performing the service on that day (see Taanis 4:2; Rambam, Klei HaMikdash 4:3-5) See comm. to 2:1 s.v. כָּל מִי שֶׁרוֹצֶה for further discussion on this topic.]

Even though the Kohen Gadol does not belong to the family serving on a specific day (or even to the watch of the week) he may perform any service he wishes to (Rav; Rashi).

[The word לְהַקְרִיב here includes all the steps in the process of sacrificing. See Rambam, Klei HaMikdash 5:12, with Kessef Mishneh.]

שֶׁכֹּהֵן גָּדוֹל מַקְרִיב חֵלֶק בָּרֹאשׁ. — For the Kohen Gadol has the first right to offer,

He has the privilege of offering, i.e., tossing on the fire, any part of the sacrifice he may wish to (Rav; Rashi), without having to cast lots as do other kohanim (Tif. Yis.).

וְנוֹטֵל חֵלֶק בָּרֹאשׁ. — and the first right to take a portion.

He may take whichever portion he

head and the hind leg. On all the other days [of the year], if he wishes to offer [any sacrifice], he may offer it. For the *Kohen Gadol* has the first right to offer and the first right to take a portion.

3. They provide him sages from among the sages of the court who read to him about the service of the day. Then they say to him, 'My lord *Kohen Gadol*, read with your own mouth, perhaps you have forgotten or perhaps you have not learned.'

YAD AVRAHAM

wishes from the part of the sacrifice designated for the *Kohanim* (*Rashi*; *Rav*).

He need not wait until the sacrifice is divided into equal portions for all the *Kohanim*. He takes whatever he wants, even if he did not participate in the

process of sacrifice at all (*Meiri*).

[About the limitation placed on this privilege in the *Gemara* (17b), see *Meiri* there and to our mishnah; *Rambam*, *Klei HaMikdash* 5:12 with *Maasai LaMelech*, and *T'midin U'Mussafin* 4:14 with *Even HaAzel*.]

3.

מָסְרוּ לוֹ — *They provide him* [lit. *gave over to him*]

On every one of these seven days (*Tif. Yis.*).

זְקֵנִים מִזִּקְנֵי בֵית דִּין — *sages from among the sages of the court*

I.e., the *Sanhedrin* (*Tif. Yis.*), [the highest court in Jewry. It consisted of seventy-one judges and convened in one of the chambers adjacent to the Temple Courtyard (לִשְׁכַּת הַגָּזִית)].

Shoshanim L'David comments on the redundancy of the word זְקֵנִים, *sages*. It could have said מָסְרוּ לוֹ מִזִּקְנֵי בֵית דִּין, *they provided some sages from the court*. Since the word זָקֵן has two meanings: A) *a sage* — its primary meaning — and, B) *an old man*, he suggests that the mishnah repeats the word זְקֵנִים to allude to its secondary definition. Thus: *They gave over to him elders from among the sages.*

Rashash notes that the *baraisa* (4a) cites that two scholars were provided the *Kohen Gadol*. (He wonders why this is not mentioned in later sources, e.g., *Rambam*. However, *Agudah* does mention this, as does one version of the *Avodah*. [This would indicate that the use of the word זְקֵנִים, *sages*, in the mishnah follows the rule that when the

plural is used without specifying a number, the minimum, two, is meant.]

The above cited *baraisa* uses the term תַּלְמִידֵי חֲכָמִים, *scholars*, instead of זְקֵנִים which can have the dual connotation of *elders* and *sages*. This seems to contradict *Shoshanim L'David's* suggestion that old scholars are required.

וְקוֹרִין לְפָנָיו בְּסֵדֶר הַיּוֹם, — *who* [lit. *and they*] *read to him about the service of the day.*

They read the portion of the Torah (*Leviticus* 16) dealing with the service of Yom Kippur (*Rav*; *Rashi*), and elaborated upon its particulars (*Tif. Yis.*).

וְאוֹמְרִים לוֹ: אִישִׁי כֹהֵן גָּדוֹל, קְרָא אַתָּה בְּפִיךָ, — *Then they say to him, 'My lord Kohen Gadol, read with your own mouth,*

The directive is that he read the words aloud rather than content himself with listening to others or silent study. This is in accordance with the Talmudic dictum (*Eruvin* 54a), to read the verse: כִּי־חַיִּים הֵם לְמֹצְאֵיהֶם, *For they* [the words of the Torah] *are life for those who find them* (*Proverbs* 4:22), as if it read: כִּי־חַיִּים הֵם לְמוֹצָאֵיהֶם, *For they are life for those who 'enunciate' them* [lit.

עֶרֶב יוֹם הַכִּפּוּרִים שַׁחֲרִית, מַעֲמִידִין אוֹתוֹ
בְּשַׁעַר הַמִּזְרָח וּמַעֲבִירִין לְפָנָיו פָּרִים וְאֵילִים
וּכְבָשִׂים, כְּדֵי שֶׁיְּהֵא מַכִּיר וְרָגִיל בָּעֲבוֹדָה.

[ד] **כָּל־שִׁבְעַת** הַיָּמִים לֹא הָיוּ מוֹנְעִין
מִמֶּנּוּ מַאֲכָל וּמִשְׁתֶּה.

עֶרֶב יוֹם הַכִּפּוּרִים עִם—חֲשֵׁכָה לֹא הָיוּ
מַנִּיחִים אוֹתוֹ לֶאֱכוֹל הַרְבֵּה, מִפְּנֵי שֶׁהַמַּאֲכָל
מֵבִיא אֶת־הַשֵּׁנָה.

יד אברהם

bring them out with their mouths]
(Tif. Yis.; Kol HaRemez).

[See Orach Chaim 47:4 with Magen
Avraham, Be'er Heitev, and Biur
HaGra who discuss whether one fulfills
the mitzvah of Torah study by thinking
without enunciating the words. See also
Sha'arei Teshuvah (ibid) who cites
authorities that when one listens to a
Torah discourse, he is surely fulfilling a
mitzvah.]

שֶׁמָּא שָׁכַחְתָּ — perhaps you have forgotten

[Some of the rules and laws governing the Yom Kippur service.]

אוֹ שֶׁמָּא לֹא לָמַדְתָּ — or perhaps you have
not learned.'

The Gemara (18a) asks: How is it
possible for a Kohen Gadol who has
never learned to have been appointed?
The Kohen Gadol must be superior to
his fellow priests in appearance, wealth
[if he was poor it was incumbent on the
Kohanim to make him wealthy (Gem.)],
and חָכְמָה, [Torah] wisdom! The
Gemara answers that this concern over
possible ignorance by the Kohen Gadol
was present only during the Second
Temple period (after Shimon Ha-
Tzaddik) when the Hasmonean kings
sold the office of Kohen Gadol for
money (see also Gem. 9a).

עֶרֶב יוֹם הַכִּפּוּרִים שַׁחֲרִית, מַעֲמִידִין אוֹתוֹ
בְּשַׁעַר הַמִּזְרָח — On the morning of the
Eve of Yom Kippur they stand him at
the Eastern Gate

The gateway had the same lesser
degree of קְדוּשָׁה, holiness, as the Temple Mount, not the higher degree of the
Temple Courtyard (Pesachim 83b).
Yerushalmi poses the question
whether he actually stood within the
gate and did not need טְבִילָה, immersion,
for this, or whether he stood near this
gate within the Courtyard and had to
immerse himself in a mikveh prior to
this (see mishnah 3:3).

וּמַעֲבִירִין לְפָנָיו פָּרִים וְאֵילִים וּכְבָשִׂים, — and
they lead before him oxen, rams and
sheep,

He was familiarized with the species
which were to be used the next day in
the Yom Kippur service (Tif. Yis.).

Although goats, too, were sacrificed
as part of the service, they were not led
before the Kohen Gadol. The goats
which would be used in the Yom Kippur service as חַטָּאוֹת, sin offerings, to
atone for the whole populace, were
symbolic of the nation's sinfulness. To
spare the Kohen Gadol the anguish of
recalling the sins of the entire community, the goat was not shown him.
Nevertheless, he was shown oxen, even
though an ox would be a חַטָּאת, sin offering, for himself and his fellow
priests. The Kohen Gadol could be expected to know of his own and his colleagues' sins and to endeavor to spur
them to repentance. It was only the feeling of helplessness in the face of the entire people's sins which would cause
him such grief (Gemara 18a).

1
4

On the morning of the Eve of Yom Kippur they stand him at the Eastern Gate and they lead before him oxen, rams and sheep, that he should recognize [them] and be conversant in the service.

4. During the entire seven-day period, they did not withhold food and drink from him. But on the Eve of Yom Kippur toward nightfall they did not let him eat much, because food induces sleep.

YAD AVRAHAM

כְּדֵי שֶׁיְּהֵא מַכִּיר וְרָגִיל בָּעֲבוֹדָה. — *that he should recognize [them] and be conversant in the service.*

When he sees the animals he is reminded of the service that he would perform with them the next day *(Rav; Rashi).*

There were two sacrificial oxen, one an עוֹלָה, *burnt offering,* for the community and the second a חַטָּאת, *sin offering,* for the *Kohen Gadol.* It was important that he be able to distinguish between them in order to sacrifice each one for its ordained purpose. The same was true for the rams. One ram was for the public and another for the *Kohen Gadol.* Both were עוֹלוֹת, *burnt offerings.* Then there were seven sheep. All of these burnt offerings were part of the *Mussaf* service. But precautions had to be taken lest the *Kohen Gadol* confuse the sheep with their adult counterparts, the rams *(Mishneh Lechem; cf. Chiddushei Aggados Maharsha).*

4.

כָּל-שִׁבְעַת הַיָּמִים לֹא הָיוּ מוֹנְעִין מִמֶּנּוּ מַאֲכָל וּמִשְׁתֶּה. — *During the entire seven-day period, they did not withhold food and drink from him.*

They let him eat and drink whatever and as much as he wanted. They were not concerned lest he be contaminated by a seminal emission because even if this occurred he needed only טְבִילָה, *immersion,* to make him טָהוֹר [*tahor*], *cleansed,* at nightfall *(Meiri).*

עֶרֶב יוֹם הַכִּפּוּרִים עִם—חֲשֵׁכָה לֹא הָיוּ מַנִּיחִים אוֹתוֹ לֶאֱכוֹל הַרְבֵּה, — *But on the Eve of Yom Kippur toward nightfall* [lit. *darkness*] *they did not let him eat much,*

On the afternoon before Yom Kippur, it was essential to take steps that would prevent the *Kohen Gadol* from having a seminal emission during the night. Were that to happen, he could not perform the Yom Kippur service.

He was not allowed to eat any amount of foods which are likely to cause emissions, such as eggs and hot milk *(Gem. 18a),* nor was he permitted to eat excessive amounts of other foods.

מִפְּנֵי שֶׁהַמַּאֲכָל מֵבִיא אֶת-הַשֵּׁנָה. — *because food* [in excessive quantity] *induces sleep.*

[And we fear he may have an emission during his sleep, and thus be disqualified from service in the Temple until nightfall of the next day, i.e., for the whole day of Yom Kippur.]

Yerushalmi asks: One of the ten miracles which occurred in the Temple was that the *Kohen Gadol* never had an emission on Yom Kippur. Since this is so, why were they so concerned about an emission? *(Avos 5:5).*

Two answers are given: A) We do not rely on miracles [אֵין סוֹמְכִין עַל הַנֵּס] or as *Yerushalmi* puts it: לֹא תְנַסּוּ *(Deuteronomy* 6:16), *Do not test* [God] to see whether He will perform a miracle. We must do what is required of us; it is for God to decide whether a

[ה] **מְסָרוּהוּ** זִקְנֵי בֵית דִּין לְזִקְנֵי כְהֻנָּה,
וְהֶעֱלוּהוּ לַעֲלִיַּת בֵּית
אַבְטִינָס, וְהִשְׁבִּיעוּהוּ וְנִפְטְרוּ וְהָלְכוּ לָהֶם.
וְאָמְרוּ לוֹ: ,,אִישִׁי כֹהֵן גָּדוֹל, אָנוּ שְׁלוּחֵי בֵית
דִּין וְאַתָּה שְׁלוּחֵנוּ וּשְׁלִיחַ בֵּית דִּין, מַשְׁבִּיעִין

יד אברהם

miracle is warranted; B) These ten miracles occurred throughout the First Temple period, up to (and including) the time of Shimon HaTzaddik at the beginning of the Second Temple. Thereafter, the *Kohanim Gedolim* were not worthy of miracles (see above 1:1 s.v. שֶׁמָּא יֶאֱרַע).

5.

מְסָרוּהוּ זִקְנֵי בֵית דִּין לְזִקְנֵי כְהֻנָּה, — *The sages of the court put him* [i.e., the Kohen Gadol] *in the custody of the sages of the priesthood*

On Yom Kippur eve (*Rambam, Avodas Yom HaKippurim* 1:7; *Tif. Yis.*).

R' Yaakov Emden (*Mishneh Lechem*) speculates that this took place near nightfall. Is so, this mishnah follows the previous one in perfect chronological sequence.

The *avodah* [liturgical composition, describing the Temple service] כּוֹנַנְתָּ אַתָּה used in the Sephardic rite specifies, however, that this took place in the morning. But examination of the sources reveals that this opinion cannot be traced definitively to the author of this *avodah* — Yose ben Yose. Many emendations have been made in the text to adjust it to the particulars of the halachah (see *Beis Yosef* to *Orach Chaim* 621). Most of these corrections were introduced by *Chemdas Yamim* and *Shifas Reviivim*. The original text (as reproduced in *Tashlum Abudraham al HaAvodah; Seder R' Amram Gaon* ed. *Koronel* and *Seder R' Sa'adyah Gaon*) mentions nothing about the time of this oath.

The *avodah* used in the Ashkenazic rite states that the oath was administered near nightfall; it is probably *R' Yaakov Emden's* source.

וְהֶעֱלוּהוּ לַעֲלִיַּת בֵּית אַבְטִינָס, — *who* [lit. *and they*] *took him up to the Avtinas family's upper chamber,*

I.e., the sages of the court, in whose charge the *Kohen Gadol* had been previously, escorted him to the Avtinas Chamber where the sages of the priesthood were awaiting him (*Tif. Yis.*).

The Avtinas family had an עֲלִיָּה, *upper level room,* for the purpose of פִּטּוּם הַקְּטֹרֶת, *mixing the incense.* The word עֲלִיָּה, *upper chamber* or *attic*, suggests that their chamber was above another chamber on the Temple Mount. This chamber was reserved for the Avtinas family who were experts in preparing and blending the various ingredients of the incense (*Rashi*; see 3:11).

The purpose of bringing the *Kohen Gadol* here was to have the sages of the priesthood teach him how to perform חֲפִינָה, *filling the hands,* with incense (*Gem.* 19a). The *Gemara* (49b) describes this as one of the most difficult of all the Temple services. When the *Kohen Gadol* reached the Holy of Holies, holding the incense-filled ladle with his left hand, he had to grip the rim of the ladle [at the side nearer his body] with his teeth or his fingertips, tilt the ladle with his thumbs, and empty the contents into his cupped hands without spilling, or putting the ladle down (*Gem., ibid; Rambam, Avodas Yom HaKippurim* 4:1).

Before leaving the *Kohen Gadol*, the sages of the court would administer to

5. The sages of the court put him in the custody of the sages of the priesthood who took him up to the Avtinas family's upper chamber, adjured him, took their leave and went their way.

They said to him, 'My lord *Kohen Gadol*, we are emissaries of the court and you are our emissary and the emissary of the court, we adjure you by Him who

YAD AVRAHAM

him the oath described below. Then they would leave and the sages of the priesthood would instruct him in the handfilling service *(Tif. Yis.)*.

[Significantly, the oath, which referred to the details of the incense service, was administered in the chamber of the Avtinas family, the manufacturers of the incense.]

According to *Rambam*, the Avtinas chamber was situated on top of the שַׁעַר הַמַּיִם, *Water Gate*, the easternmost of three gates in the southern wall of the Temple Courtyard (see *Middos* 1:4; *Rambam, Comm.* to *Middos* 5:4). *Tiferes Yisrael* (to *Middos* 1:1) adds that a mikveh (mentioned in *Gem.* 19a) was situated next to the Avtinas chamber atop the Water Gate.

Tiferes Yisrael notes that the diagram of the Temple printed together with *Tosefos Yom Tov*, places the Avtinas Chamber *next* to the Water Gate. He concludes that this diagram was altered by the printers, and that no conclusions can be drawn from it. However, in the diagram of the Temple which is reproduced in *R' Y. Kafih's* edition of *Rambam's Commentary to Mishnah*, the Avtinas Chamber is shown next to the Water Gate. The manuscript upon which this edition is based, with the diagrams it contains, is almost unani-

mously assumed to be *Rambam's* holograph.

וְהִשְׁבִּיעוּהוּ וְנִפְטְרוּ וְהָלְכוּ לָהֶם. — *(and they) adjured him, took their leave of him and went their way.*

Before leaving, the sages of the court administered this oath to him, as can be seen from the language of the oath (see below). The only thing the sages of the priesthood did was to teach him the handfilling service *(Tos. Chadashim* citing *R' Shimshon Chasid)*.

Tiferes Yisrael adds that the *Kohen Gadol* had to respond *Amen* to the oath. This is considered as if he had uttered the oath himself (see *Shevuos* 29b). Otherwise, the mere recitation of an oath by two emissaries of the court [מוּשְׁבָּע מִפִּי אֲחֵרִים] — in the absence of an obligation to swear, as in certain monetary disputes — would have no binding power (see *ibid.*).[1]

וְאָמְרוּ לוֹ: — *(And) they said to him:*

The mishnah backtracks here and reproduces the text of the oath administered to the *Kohen Gadol (Tif. Yis.)*.

,,אִישִׁי כֹהֵן גָּדוֹל, אָנוּ שְׁלוּחֵי בֵית דִּין — 'My lord Kohen Gadol, we are emissaries of the court

And as such have the authority to force you to swear *(Tif. Yis.)*.

1. *Netziv (Meromei Sadeh, ibid)* formulates a novel concept. Anyone having some jurisdiction over another has the power to adjure him (מוּשְׁבָּע מִפִּי אֲחֵרִים). Abraham, as Eliezer's lord, was able to adjure him [וְאַשְׁבִּיעֲךָ, *I adjure you (Genesis* 24:3)]. In the same way, Joseph, as king, adjured the Children of Israel to remove his bones from Egypt [וַיַּשְׁבַּע, *he adjured (Genesis* 50:25), and הַשְׁבַּע הִשְׁבִּיעַ *(Exodus* 13:19)]. Jacob, however, lacking legal jurisdiction over Joseph, employed his moral authority and bade him to swear that he would bury Jacob in *Eretz Yisrael*: וַיֹּאמֶר הִשָּׁבְעָה לִי וַיִּשָּׁבַע לוֹ, *And He said swear to me, and he swore to him (Genesis* 47:31). The *Sanhedrin*, too, possessed jurisdiction, as demonstrated by their power to confiscate (הֶפְקֵר בֵּית דִּין הֶפְקֵר) and excommunicate (חֵרֶם). This gave them the power to adjure, i.e., to compel someone to swear a binding oath.

אָנוּ עָלֶיךָ בְּמִי שֶׁשִׁכֵּן שְׁמוֹ בַּבַּיִת הַזֶּה, שֶׁלֹּא
תְשַׁנֶּה דָּבָר מִכָּל־מַה שֶּׁאָמַרְנוּ לָךְ."
הוּא פוֹרֵשׁ וּבוֹכֶה, וְהֵן פּוֹרְשִׁין וּבוֹכִין.

[ו] **אִם** הָיָה חָכָם דּוֹרֵשׁ; וְאִם לָאו, תַּלְמִידֵי
חֲכָמִים דּוֹרְשִׁין לְפָנָיו. וְאִם רָגִיל
לִקְרוֹת, קוֹרֵא; וְאִם לָאו, קוֹרִין לְפָנָיו.

יד אברהם

וְאַתָּה שְׁלוּחֵנוּ וּשְׁלִיחַ בֵּית דִּין, — *and you are our emissary and the emissary of the court* [i.e., the *Sanhedrin*],

The apparent meaning of this phrase is that the *Kohen Gadol* performing the sacrificial service acts as an emissary of the public and of the *Sanhedrin*. He was therefore obligated to perform the service in the manner his constituents demanded. However, the *Gemara* (19a) notes that this contradicts the ruling that the priests do not serve at the pleasure of the public, but are rather the appointed emissaries of God (שְׁלוּחֵי דְּרַחֲמָנָא).

The *Gemara* concludes that they meant to tell him that the language of the oath was to be interpreted as the ad-

jurers — the sages and the *Sanhedrin* — meant it. He was their emissary insofar as the oath was concerned. This being so, he could not reinterpret the language of the oath to suit his private intentions as opposed to the purpose of the sages. [Especially since the *Kohen Gadol* only answered *Amen* he could say he had only meant to answer to the parts of the formula which did not contradict his belief. It goes without saying that legally such an excuse would be invalid. However, since the purpose of this oath was to either force the *Kohen Gadol* (if he was a secret Sadducee) to adhere to the tradition, or if he could not submit on this point, to resign from his office, the Sanhedrin made the intent of this oath crystal clear.]

◄§ Sadducean Deviations in Incense Service

At the time of the Second Temple there was a prevalent, often powerful heretical sect which called themselves צְדוֹקִים, *Sadducees*, after the name of their founder צָדוֹק, *Tzadok*, a disciple of Antigenos of Socho (*Avos* 1:3). They denied the validity of the oral tradition of the Jewish People, maintaining that only the literal sense of the Torah was binding. *Rambam (Avos* 1:3) maintains that this heresy was merely a rationale to mask their real purpose — Hellenization — total deviation from the Torah. This caused them to deviate from Jewish tradition in the Yom Kippur service. The Torah says (*Lev.* 16:2): *For with the [incense] cloud I am [allowed to be] seen on the ark-cover* (ie., in the Holy of Holies). The Sadducees interpreted the verse to mean that the *Kohen Gadol* had to place incense on the fire before he entered the Holy of Holies. But the tradition transmitted from Moses teaches that only after he enters the Holy of Holies, is the *Kohen Gadol* to place the incense on the fire as it says (*Lev.* 16:13): *And he shall put the incense on the fire 'before HASHEM'*, i.e., in the Holy of Holies. Since no one was allowed to be in the Temple while the Kohen Gadol entered the Holy of Holies (see *Leviticus* 16:17) they could not monitor his actions. Therefore, they had to administer this oath to him before Yom Kippur (*Rambam; Rav* from *Gem.* 19b).

מַשְׁבִּיעִין אָנוּ עָלֶיךָ בְּמִי שֶׁשִׁכֵּן שְׁמוֹ בַּבַּיִת הַזֶּה, שֶׁלֹּא תְשַׁנֶּה דָּבָר — *we adjure you by Him who domiciled His Name in this*

house, that you will not change anything

[The commentators ask: How was this

domiciled His Name in this House, that you will not change anything of all that we have told you.'

He would turn aside and weep, and they would turn aside and weep.

6. If he was a scholar he lectured; but if not, scholars would lecture before him. If he was accustomed to read [Scripture], he would read; but if not, they would read to him.

YAD AVRAHAM

oath binding upon the *Kohen Gadol?* If he really believed that the Torah should be interpreted as the Saducees did, then, the oath would be invalid, because, to his way of thinking, he would be swearing to transgress the Torah. Such an oath has no binding force (see *Nedarim* 2:2). Many solutions to this question have been advanced (see *Shoshanim L'David; Avodas Yisrael* p. 43, *Teshuvas Chasam Sofer, Orach Chayim* 17; *Tif. Yis.; Tos. R' Akiva* citing *Pri Chadash* and others).

Mishneh Lechem, Rashash and S'fas Emes answer that though the oath would be invalid in the *Kohen Gadol's* mind, he would nevertheless be swearing in vain, which is a grave sin (see *Shevuos* 3:8). As a Saducee, he could not — in good conscience — take God's Name in an oath which served no purpose. He would have to refuse the oath and thereby be disqualified.

מִכָּל-מַה שֶׁאָמַרְנוּ לָךְ." — *of all that we have told you.'*

For the same Sages who had read and expounded to him upon the order of the day (above mishnah 3) administered this oath *(Tos. Chad.* citing *R' Shim-*

shon Chasid).

הוא פורש ובוכה — *He* [the *Kohen Gadol] would turn aside* [lit., *separates] and weep,*

He was saddened that they suspected him of being a *Sadducee (Gem.* 19b).

וְהֵן פּורְשִׁין ובוכִין. — *and they* [the sages] *would turn aside* [lit., *separate] and weep.*

Because they suspected someone whose actions gave them no grounds for suspicion. For: 'He who suspects innocent people will be punished physically' *(Gem.* 19b).

Since it was their duty to administer the oath to the *Kohen Gadol*, why did the sages weep? They surely had not transgressed the prohibition against suspecting an innocent person. *Kol HaRemez* answers that they wept because their generation had come to such a state that even the *Kohen Gadol* on *Yom Kippur* was subject to suspicion.

6.

אם הָיָה חָכָם דּורֵשׁ; — *If he was a scholar he lectured;*

On the night of Yom Kippur precautions were taken to insure that the *Kohen Gadol* would not sleep. It was feared that if he slept he might have a seminal emission which would disqualify him for the day's service. To keep himself awake, the *Kohen Gadol* would deliver a lecture upon a point of halachah *(Rav; Rashi).*

וְאִם לָאו, תַּלְמִידֵי חֲכָמִים דּורְשִׁין לְפָנָיו. — *but if not, scholars* [lit., *disciples of scholars] would lecture before him.*

If the *Kohen Gadol* was incapable of lecturing, others would lecture for him to keep him awake.

וְאִם רָגִיל לִקְרוֹת, קורֵא; — *If he was accustomed to read* [Scripture], *he would read;*

After the halachic discourse *(Tif. Yis.).*

וּבַמֶּה קוֹרִין לְפָנָיו? בְּאִיּוֹב וּבְעֶזְרָא וּבְדִבְרֵי
הַיָּמִים.

זְכַרְיָה בֶּן־קְבוּטָל אוֹמֵר: פְּעָמִים הַרְבֵּה
קָרִיתִי לְפָנָיו בְּדָנִיֵּאל.

[ז] **בִּקֵּשׁ** לְהִתְנַמְנֵם, פִּרְחֵי כְהֻנָּה מַכִּין
לְפָנָיו בְּאֶצְבַּע צְרָדָה, וְאוֹמְרִים
לוֹ: ,,אִישִׁי כֹהֵן גָּדוֹל, עֲמֹד וְהָפֵג אַחַת עַל־
הָרִצְפָּה!'' וּמַעֲסִיקִין אוֹתוֹ עַד שֶׁיַּגִּיעַ זְמַן הַשְּׁחִיטָה.

יד אברהם

Tiferes Yisrael (Boaz 2) comments
that these three books represent three
distinct areas of interest:

Tiferes Yisrael (Boaz 2) comments
that these three books represent three
distinct areas of interest:
A) *Educational* — for this they read the
book of *Job* with its profound discourses about the purpose of life.
B) *Emotional* — for this they read *Ezra*
with its moving descriptions of the
desolation of Jerusalem and the difficulties the returnees had to overcome
to rebuild the city and the Temple. This
might inspire the *Kohen Gadol* to feel
the importance of the day's service.
C) *Diversional* — for this they read
Chronicles which highlights the important happenings of the First Temple era.

זְכַרְיָה בֶּן־קְבוּטָל אוֹמֵר: פְּעָמִים הַרְבֵּה קָרִיתִי
לְפָנָיו בְּדָנִיֵּאל. — *Zechariah ben Kevutal
says: Many times I read before him
from Daniel.*

Yerushalmi mentions that they read
to him from *Proverbs* and *Psalms*. *Rambam* (*Avodas HaKippurim* 18) says
simply, They read to him 'from the
Holy Writings.'

Shoshanim L'David suggests that
Zechariah ben Kevutal maintains that
no specific book had to be read. For this
he cites as proof that he himself read to
the *Kohen Gadol* from *Daniel*. Any
book of the Scriptures may be read. For
this reason, *Rambam* does not mention
any specific book.

וְאִם לַאו, קוֹרִין לְפָנָיו. — *but if not, they*
[the *kohanim* or the scholars] *would
read to him.*

[Scripture in those days was unvowelized
(like our Torah scrolls). Therefore one had to
be well-versed to merely read Scripture (just
as it takes much practice to read from the
Torah nowadays). The major part of the five
years that were customarily spent in study-
ing Scripture (see *Avos* 5:21) was dedicated
to learning the vocalization of the text (see
Shulchan Aruch HaRav, Talmud Torah 1:1
with *Kuntres Acharon*). Thus it was possible
for the *Kohen Gadol* not to be able to read
Scripture. Furthermore, because there were
no written commentaries to Scripture (all
commentary was oral), he might find it very
difficult to interpret many passages. If the
Kohen Gadol came from common stock he
might have difficulty even with Scriptural
language since the commonly spoken tongue
was Aramaic. All the more so if he were from
a Hellenist family and had been brought up
as a secular Jew (see above 1:5 s.v. שֶׁלֹּא
תִשְׁנֶה).]

וּבַמֶּה קוֹרִין לְפָנָיו? — *And from what did
they read to him?*

[Which books of Scripture were they
required to read?]

בְּאִיּוֹב וּבְעֶזְרָא וּבְדִבְרֵי הַיָּמִים. — *From Job,
from Ezra, and from Chronicles.*

For these discuss topics which would
draw his interest and attention and prevent him from sleeping (*Rashi; Rav*).

And from what did they read to him? From *Job*, from *Ezra*, and from *Chronicles*.

Zechariah ben Kevutal says: Many times I read before him from *Daniel*.

7. If he wished to doze, young men of the priesthood snapped before him with the index finger, and they said to him, 'My lord, *Kohen Gadol*, stand up and cool off once on the floor!'

And they kept him busy until the time for slaughtering arrived.

YAD AVRAHAM

7.

בְּקֵשׁ לְהִתְנַמְנֵם, — *If he wished to doze,*
[I.e., if they saw that he was about to doze off.]

פִּרְחֵי כְהֻנָּה — *young men* [lit. *blossoms*] *of the priesthood*
Young priests whose beards had just begun לִפְרֹחַ, *to blossom (Rav; Rashi).*

מַכִּין לְפָנָיו בְּאֶצְבַּע צְרָדָה, — *snapped before him with the index finger,*
[The translation, *index finger*, follows *Rashi's* interpretation of the *Gemara* here, *Rav* and *Rambam* in *R' Y. Kafih's* edition. The purpose of the snapping was to keep him from falling asleep.]
Tosafos (*Menachos* 35b s.v. וכמה) quotes *Aruch* (s.v. צרדה) with evidence from *Tosefta* (*Yoma* 1:9) that the middle finger is meant. *Tosafos* offers demonstrable proof: only by snapping the middle finger can a loud sound be produced. Nevertheless, variant readings in the *Tosefta* allow it to be interpreted in accord with the first opinion as well.

וְאוֹמְרִין לוֹ: "אִישִׁי כֹהֵן גָּדוֹל, עֲמֹד וְהָפֵג אַחַת עַל־הָרִצְפָּה!" — *and they said to him: 'My lord, Kohen Gadol, stand up and cool off* [lit. *dispel your warmth*] *once on the floor!'*
Because the floor was cold, he could cool his feet and dispel his drowsiness (*Rav; Rambam*).

Rashi (based on the *Gem.* 19b) interprets that they invited the *Kohen Gadol* to amuse them by performing an intricate acrobatic feat on the floor. The exercise would dispel his drowsiness. Thus, *stand up and amuse us* [lit. *dispel*, i.e., dispel your drowsiness] once on the floor.

וּמַעֲסִיקִין אוֹתוֹ — *And they kept him busy*
They said to him (*Psalms* 127:1): *If HASHEM does not build the house, in vain have its builders toiled in it* (i.e., be careful in performing the service. Do it לְשֵׁם שָׁמַיִם, *for the sake of Heaven*, so that it will be accepted. For if the sacrifices are not accepted all your labor will have been for nothing (*Gem.* 19b with *Rashi*).
Tiferes Yisrael deduces from this that they used to say all the שִׁירֵי הַמַּעֲלוֹת, *Songs of Ascents* (*Psalms* 120-134) with the *Kohen Gadol.* He notes that they did not ask the *Kohen Gadol* to read by himself since it was almost time to do the service and they wanted him to be rested.
Some versions have here (see *Shinu-yei Nuschaos*): מִיַּקִּירֵי יְרוּשָׁלַיִם לֹא הָיוּ יְשֵׁינִין כָּל־הַלַּיְלָה, כְּדֵי שֶׁיִּשְׁמַע כֹּהֵן גָּדוֹל קוֹל הֲבָרָה וְלֹא תְּהֵא שֵׁנָה חוֹטְפַתּוֹ, *Some of the prominent* [lit. *dear*] *people of Jerusalem did not sleep the entire night so that the* Kohen Gadol *should*

[ח] **בְּכָל־יוֹם** תּוֹרְמִין אֶת־הַמִּזְבֵּחַ
בִּקְרִיאַת הַגֶּבֶר אוֹ סָמוּךְ
לוֹ, בֵּין לְפָנָיו בֵּין לְאַחֲרָיו; בְּיוֹם הַכִּפּוּרִים
מֵחֲצוֹת, וּבָרְגָלִים מֵאַשְׁמוּרָה הָרִאשׁוֹנָה. וְלֹא
הָיְתָה קְרִיאַת הַגֶּבֶר מַגַּעַת עַד שֶׁהָיְתָה עֲזָרָה
מְלֵאָה מִיִּשְׂרָאֵל.

יד אברהם

hear [people] speaking and sleep should not overcome him...

This statement is also found in our versions of the *Gemara* and in *Tosefta* (1:9).

The *Gemara* mentions that even after the destruction of the Temple it was customary to remain awake at night (as

a remembrance for the Temple). This custom persists up to our days. See *Orach Chayim* 619:6.

עַד שֶׁיַּגִּיעַ זְמַן הַשְּׁחִיטָה. — *until the time for slaughtering* [the daily offering] arrived.

I.e., until daybreak (see 3:1).

8.

בְּכָל־יוֹם תּוֹרְמִין אֶת־הַמִּזְבֵּחַ — *Every day they removed* [lit. *lifted*] [ashes] *from the altar*

One of the daily services was תְּרוּמַת הַדֶּשֶׁן, *the removal of the ashes*. This is specified in the verse (*Leviticus* 6:3): *And he shall remove the ashes and he shall put them beside the altar.* The *Kohen* who won (by lot) the privilege of performing this service went up onto the altar and using a silver shovel (pan), picked up some of the burned-out coals in the center of the altar (see *comm.* to 4:3).[1] He then descended from the altar and put the ashes on the right side of the ramp leading up to the altar (*Tamid* 1:4). This service is not to be confused with הוֹצָאַת הַדֶּשֶׁן, *taking out the ashes*, i.e., ridding the altar of the accumulation of ashes. According to *Rashi* (*Leviticus* 6:4) this was done only when the accumulation of ashes necessitated it. According to *Rambam* (*T'midin U'Mussafin* 2:13) it, too, was done every day (see *Mishneh LaMelech*, loc. cit.).

בִּקְרִיאַת הַגֶּבֶר אוֹ סָמוּךְ לוֹ, בֵּין לְפָנָיו בֵּין לְאַחֲרָיו. — *at the call of the crier* [lit. *man*] *or thereabout, either before it or after it;*

One priest was appointed to wake up the *Kohanim*. The *Gemara* (20b) cites a *baraisa* that reports his formula: עִמְדוּ כֹּהֲנִים לַעֲבוֹדַתְכֶם..., *Stand up, O Kohanim, to your service, Levites* לְדוּכַנְכֶם *to your platform, and Israelites* לְמַעֲמָדְכֶם *to your station.*

An alternative meaning given in the *Gemara* (ibid.) for גֶּבֶר is *rooster*. Thus, 'at the cry of the rooster.'

Rambam (*T'midin U'Mussafin* 2:11) holds that every day this service was performed after daybreak (see *Lechem Mishneh*). *Tosafos* (*Yoma* 27b), however, rules that this service had to be performed *before* daybreak.

בְּיוֹם הַכִּפּוּרִים מֵחֲצוֹת, — *On Yom Kippur* [it was done] *from midnight,*

[Some texts read בַּחֲצוֹת, *at midnight*]. They advanced the removal of the

1. It did not matter how much was picked up as long as there was at least a fistful (*Gem.* 24a). *Rambam*, though (*Timidin U'Mussafin* 2:12) does not mention this specification as noted by *Mishneh LaMelech* (ibid) and *Tos. R'Akiva*.

8. **E**very day they removed [ashes] from the altar at the call of the crier or thereabout, either before it or after it. On Yom Kippur [it was done] from midnight, and on the festivals from the first watch. And yet before the call of the crier the Courtyard was already filled with Jews.

ashes to avoid possible חוּלְשָׁא דְכֹהֵן גָּדוֹל, *weakness of the Kohen Gadol*, for he alone had to perform the entire service of the day *(Gem. 20b)*. They were careful, therefore not to tax him unduly, especially since he was fasting *(Rashi)*.

Tosafos (s.v. משום) comments that the *Kohen Gadol* himself had to remove the ashes. From this *Tosafos* deduces that even services performed at night had to be done by the *Kohen Gadol*. This service was performed early to leave him time to rest before beginning the service of the day.

Ri (ibid.), however, maintains that this service need not be done by him. The reason it was done so early was that much time was needed to clear the center of the altar of remains of the sacrifices that were not yet fully consumed (these were placed at the sides of the altar), and to stack the wood for the fire (סִידוּר הַמַּעֲרָכָה). Had these tasks been done close to dawn, they would have extended into the morning, forcing the *Kohen Gadol* to compress the day's lengthy service into less hours. Because of the potential 'weakness of the Kohen Gadol' who had to perform the entire day's service singlehandedly while fasting, extreme caution led to having him start the service at the earliest possible moment, so that he should not be rushed in his weakened state *(Ramban, Milchamos* and *Rambam, Avodas Yom HaKippurim* 4:1 concur with *Ri)*.

וּבָרְגָלִים מֵאַשְׁמוּרָה הָרִאשׁוֹנָה. — *and on the [three] festivals [Pesach, Shevuos and Succos], from the first watch.*

From the end of the 'first watch' — i.e., at the end of the first third of the night (see *Berachos* 1:1; *Rashi*).

The *Gemara* in *Berachos* (3a) explains that the angels are divided into three (or four) מִשְׁמוּרוֹת, *groups* or *watches*, for the purpose of singing praise (שִׁירָה) to God during the night. Corresponding to this, the night is said to have three *watches*.

On the three festivals vast multitudes came to the Temple with their sacrifices. Consequently, there were many unconsumed sacrifices and much ash on the altar, that a considerable amount of time was needed to clear it. Besides, they wanted to assure the start of the morning service at the earliest possible moment *(Gem. 20b; Rav)*.

Accordingly, *Kol HaRemez* comments that they began to remove the ashes this early only beginning from the second night of the festival, for it was then that large numbers of sacrifices were being brought. But *Tosafos Yeshanim* holds that because the great throng would arrive early even on the first day, it was necessary to prepare the altar early in order not to impede the speed with which *Kohanim* could perform the services.

וְלֹא הָיְתָה קְרִיאַת הַגֶּבֶר מַגַּעַת עַד שֶׁהָיְתָה עֲזָרָה מְלֵאָה מִיִּשְׂרָאֵל. — *And yet before the call of the crier the Courtyard was already filled with Jews* [lit. *until the Courtyard was filled with Jews*].

Who arrived early on Yom Tov morning to be able to bring their sacrifices immediately after the daily sacrifice *(Rashi; Rav)*.

Tiferes Yisrael suggests that this phrase of the mishnah may refer to Yom Kippur too. The multitudes arrived in order to be able to witness the *Kohen Gadol* perform the service.

[א] **בָּרִאשׁוֹנָה,** כָּל־מִי שֶׁרוֹצֶה לִתְרוֹם
אֶת־הַמִּזְבֵּחַ, תּוֹרֵם.
וּבִזְמַן שֶׁהֵן מְרֻבִּין, רָצִין וְעוֹלִין בַּכֶּבֶשׁ, וְכָל
הַקּוֹדֵם אֶת־חֲבֵרוֹ בְּאַרְבַּע אַמּוֹת, זָכָה.
וְאִם הָיוּ שְׁנֵיהֶם שָׁוִין, הַמְמֻנֶּה אוֹמֵר לָהֶם,
,,הַצְבִּיעוּ.'' וּמָה הֵן מוֹצִיאִין? אַחַת אוֹ שְׁתַּיִם,

יד אברהם

Chapter 2

This chapter digresses from the general topic of this tractate — the Yom Kippur service. The chapter begins by elaborating on the removing of the ashes, the last topic of the previous chapter. In the course of the discussion we are told that פְּיָסוֹת, *lots*, were drawn to determine which *Kohen* won the privilege of performing the various parts of the service. Whether or not such lots were drawn on Yom Kippur as well will be examined in greater detail in the comm. to mishnah 2 (s.v. אַרְבַּע).

1.

בָּרִאשׁוֹנָה, כָּל־מִי שֶׁרוֹצֶה לִתְרוֹם אֶת־הַמִּזְבֵּחַ, תּוֹרֵם. — *At first, whoever wanted to remove [the ashes] from the altar, did so* [lit. *whoever wanted to lift the altar, lifted*].

In the early years of the Second Temple [*at first*], no lots were drawn for this service (*Rav; Rashi* from *Gem.* 22a). [Usually there was only one volunteer, if there was more than one, then a foot race decided the matter as described below. Only in the case of a tie did the racers resort to lots. This differed from the other services where selection was always by lot.]

The *Gemara* (22a) asks: 'Why did they not institute lots *at first*, as they did for the other services?' The *Gemara* answers that it was thought that most *Kohanim* would be sleeping, since this service was performed before daybreak, and there would be no need for lots. Once, a foot race between two *Kohanim* led to the accident described below; to avoid a repetition, they instituted a drawing of lots for this service too.

The only *Kohanim* eligible for the service were those who belonged to the בֵּית אָב, *family*, whose privilege it was to perform the service that day (*Rav; Rashi*).

[As already explained (comm. to 1:2; s.v. וּשְׁאָר כָּל הַיָּמִים), the *Kohanim* were divided into twenty-four groups called מִשְׁמָרוֹת, *watches*. These watches were arranged in sequence, each in turn performing the service for one week at a time. The only exceptions to this sequence were the three pilgrimage festivals (רְגָלִים) Pesach, Shavuos, and Succos, on which all *Kohanim* had the privilege of participating in the festival service, while the *Kohanim* of the watch retained the sole right to perform regular daily services. (See *Succah* 5:6-8). These watches were further subdivided into family groups (בֵּית אָב), each of which served on a particular day of the week.

It is not clear how many בָּתֵּי אָבוֹת, *family groups*, there were in each watch. Some sources say there were six, one for each weekday, while the Sabbath service was shared by the whole watch; and some say seven (see *Minchas Chinuch*, end of *mitzvah* 509; *Sh'ailos U'Teshuvos Chasam Sofer Orach Chayim* 200).

1. **A**t first, whoever wanted to remove [ashes] from the altar, did so. In case there were many, they ran and ascended the ramp, and whoever preceded his colleague into the four cubits, won.

If two of them were even, the administrator would say to them, 'Put out a finger.' What did they put

YAD AVRAHAM

וּבִזְמַן שֶׁהֵן מְרֻבִּין, — *In case* [lit. *at a time when*] *there were many,*

When there were many volunteers for this service *(Rashi; Rav).*

רָצִין וְעוֹלִין בַּכֶּבֶשׁ, — *they ran and ascended the ramp,*

Access to the roof of the altar was by way of a thirty-two cubit long ramp on its southern side.

וְכָל הַקּוֹדֵם אֶת־חֲבֵרוֹ בָּאַרְבַּע אַמּוֹת, זָכָה. — *and whoever preceded his colleague into the four cubits, won* [lit. *attained*].

Whichever *Kohen* was the first to reach the top four cubits of the ramp, was the winner of the privilege *(Rav, Rambam, Rashi).*

וְאִם הָיוּ שְׁנֵיהֶם שָׁוִין, — *If two of them were even,*

[If two reached the top of the ramp simultaneously.]

הַמְמֻנֶּה אוֹמֵר לָהֶם — *the administrator* [lit. *the appointee*] *would say to them,*

[*Shekalim* (5:1) teaches that there were various Temple departments (fifteen according to *Rambam* in *K'lei HaMikdash* 7:1), each of which was in the charge of an appointed administrator (מְמֻנֶּה). The one referred to here is the מְמֻנֶּה עַל הַגְרָלוֹת, *administrator of the lots.*]

"הַצְבִּיעוּ,, — *'Put out a finger.'*

To all of them *(Rav; Rashi)*; [not just to the winners of the footrace.]

Once, it became necessary to break a tie, the administrator would commence the following procedure: All of the *Kohanim* present, would be asked to assemble in the לִשְׁכַּת הַגָּזִית, *hewn-rock chamber* and stand in a circle around the administrator. Each would extend one

or two fingers (see below) and the administrator would remove the hat of one. The administrator would call out a random number, greater than the total of *Kohanim* present, and count the outstretched fingers, beginning with the hatless *Kohen* and going around the circle as many times as needed until he reached the designated number. The *Kohen* whose finger was counted last won the privilege of performing the service *(Rav from Gem.* 25a). This is how all the Temple lots were drawn. The lot could not be limited to the two who had tied in the foot race, since the outcome would always be obvious; if the administrator picked an odd number, the count would always end with the first *Kohen,* and if he picked an even number, the count would end with the second *Kohen (Tos. Yom Tov).*

The administrator counted only fingers, not people, because of the prohibition against counting Jews directly [*Exodus* 30:12] *(Rav; Rashi* from *Gem.* 22b).

Aruch (s.v. צבע), *Tosafos Yeshanim,* and *Ritva* hold that the number was chosen by the most eminent *Kohen* present, and it was not revealed to the administrator. *Meiri* (to 25a) holds that the number was picked by a sage of the *Sanhedrin,* which assembled in an adjoining part of the לִשְׁכַּת הַגָּזִית, *hewn-rock chamber.* The administrator then designated a *Kohen* to start the count. Such a precedure would avoid any possible suspicion of collusion.

[*Tosafos* (25a s.v. והא) holds that the hatless *Kohen* remained bareheaded until the end of the count. *Tosafos* adds that the count was not done in the Temple Courtyard proper, because it is disrespectful to stand bareheaded in the Temple Courtyard. The part of the

וְאֵין מוֹצִיאִין אֶגְדָּל בַּמִּקְדָּשׁ.

[ב] מַעֲשֶׂה שֶׁהָיוּ שְׁנֵיהֶם שָׁוִין וְרָצִין וְעוֹלִין בַּכֶּבֶשׁ, וְדָחַף אֶחָד מֵהֶן אֶת־חֲבֵרוֹ; וְנָפַל וְנִשְׁבְּרָה רַגְלוֹ. וְכֵיוָן שֶׁרָאוּ בֵּית דִּין שֶׁבָּאִין לִידֵי סַכָּנָה, הִתְקִינוּ שֶׁלֹּא יְהוּ תוֹרְמִין אֶת־הַמִּזְבֵּחַ, אֶלָּא בַּפַּיִס. אַרְבַּע פְּיָסוֹת הָיוּ שָׁם; וְזֶה הַפַּיִס הָרִאשׁוֹן.

יד אברהם

hewn-rock chamber where the count took place, though part of the Courtyard, was nevertheless of a lesser sanctity.]

Rambam (T'midin U'Mussafin 4:2) states that the Kohen's hat was lifted only momentarily, in order to designate the starting point of the count, but it was replaced immediately.

וּמָה הֵן מוֹצִיאִין? — What [i.e., how many fingers] did they put out?

[— To be counted.]

אַחַת אוֹ שְׁתַּיִם — One or two [fingers],

A Kohen who was not well, and therefore unable to control his other fingers while holding out one finger, may hold out two fingers, which were counted as only one (Rav, Rashi from Gem. 23a).

וְאֵין מוֹצִיאִין אֶגְדָּל בַּמִּקְדָּשׁ — but they did not put out a thumb in the Temple.

Because of the רַמָּאִים, impostors (Gem. 23a). A dishonest Kohen, seeing that the count would end with the next Kohen, might stretch out his thumb and make it seem to be from a different hand than his other finger. The count would then end with him. Only the thumb could be used for such deception because only it can be spread far from the other fingers (Rav; Rashi).

Tosefos Yom Tov points out that, because of the crowding, the fingers of any two Kohanim were extremely close to each other. This explains how such a deception could have been possible.

Rambam (T'midin U'Mussafin 4:3) holds that every Kohen was allowed to hold out one or two fingers as he pleased, and as many fingers as were put out were counted. Mirkeves Ha-Mishneh points out that this clarifies the difference between counting a person and counting fingers (see s.v. הצביעו). The thumb was not to be used since it could be retracted or put out without much notice because of its relative shortness. A Kohen might adjust the count to his liking by flicking his thumb out or back. [For Rambam's interpretation of the Gemara see Lechem Mishneh and Mirkeves Ha-Mishneh (loc. cit.), Teshuvas HaRambam ed. Shulsinger 232, ed. Freiman 348. See also Rambam's Commentary to the Mishnah (here). From R' Y. Kafih's edition of Rambam's Commentary to the Mishnah, it is evident that Rambam originally understood the Gemara differently from the conclusion he reached in T'midin U'Mussafin.]

2.

מַעֲשֶׂה שֶׁהָיוּ שְׁנֵיהֶם שָׁוִין וְרָצִין וְעוֹלִין בַּכֶּבֶשׁ,
— It once happened that two [lit. both] were even as they ran and ascended the ramp,

The two raced up the ramp neck and neck.

out? One or two, but they did not put out a thumb in the Temple.

2. **I**t once happened that two were even as they ran and ascended the ramp, and one of them pushed his colleague; he fell and his leg was broken. Once the Court realized that there was a danger, they instituted that they not remove [ashes] from the altar, except by lot.

There were four lots there; this is the first lot.

YAD AVRAHAM

וְדָחַף אֶחָד מֵהֶן אֶת־חֲבֵרוֹ; וְנָפַל וְנִשְׁבְּרָה רַגְלוֹ. — *and one of them pushed his colleague; he fell and his leg was broken.*

Having been unable to best his competitor in the race, one *Kohen* pushed the other, causing him to fall and break his leg.

וְכֵיוָן שֶׁרָאוּ בֵּית דִּין שֶׁבָּאִין לִידֵי סַכָּנָה, הִתְקִינוּ שֶׁלֹּא יְהוּ תוֹרְמִין אֶת־הַמִּזְבֵּחַ, אֶלָּא בְּפַיִס — *Once the Court realized that there was a danger* [lit. *they were coming into danger*], *they instituted that they not remove* [*the ashes*] *from the altar, except by lot.*

At first a lot had been drawn only in an instance where the race had ended in a dead heat. From that accident onward, a lot was always drawn. The procedure for the lot has been described in comm. to mishnah 1 (s.v. הַצְבִּיעוּ).

Meleches Shlomo suggests that פַּיִס, *lot,* is related to פִּיּוּס, *peace-making* (appeasement).

אַרְבַּע פְּיָסוֹת הָיוּ שָׁם; — *There were four lots there;*

They used to assemble four times during the day to draw lots for the services enumerated in this chapter. They did not draw all four lots at once because they wanted to summon a crowd four times during the day. It is a *glory to the King* to assemble a great multitude in the Temple as is written (*Psalms* 55:15): *in the house of God we will walk* בְּרָגֶשׁ, *tumultuously (Rav* quoting *Gem.* 24b; for similar rendi-

tions of the root רגשׁ, see comm. to ArtScroll *Daniel* 6:7, s.v. הַרְגִּשׁוּ).

◆§ Were lots drawn on Yom Kippur?

As alluded to in the preface to this chapter, a controversy surrounds this mishnah.

Baal HaMaor (to *Yoma* 26) contends that since the entire Yom Kippur service had to be performed by the *Kohen Gadol (Gem.* 32b), no lots were drawn on Yom Kippur. That most of the known *piyutim* for the *avodah* do mention lots does not deter *Baal HaMaor.* These poetic compositions were not meant to be halachically accurate (cf. *Tosafos* 8a s.v. דכולי).

Ramban contends that if *Baal HaMaor* is right this entire chapter dealing with lots does not belong in *Yoma.* He maintains that lots *were* needed for those services which, even on Yom Kippur, were not performed by the *Kohen Gadol.* In the case of the first lot, which was for the service of תְּרוּמַת הַדֶּשֶׁן, *removing of the ashes, Ramban* argues that this was not done by the *Kohen Gadol* since this service was usually done at night and only the services of the day had to be performed by the *Kohen Gadol* (see comm. to 1:8). We will comment upon each of the remaining three lots in its place.

Rambam's opinion falls between these two. As to the service of lifting the ashes from the altar he concurs with *Ramban* that lots are drawn for it, probably for the same reason — that only services of the day had to be performed by the *Kohen Gadol.*

As to the other lots, *Rambam* (according to *Tos. Yom Tov* here) maintains that lots were drawn only a second time for the service of דִּישׁוּן מִזְבַּח הַפְּנִימִי, *clearing the inner altar of ashes.* Nevertheless, *Rambam* himself (*T'midin UMussafin* 4:1) mentions only the

[ג] הַפַּיִס הַשֵּׁנִי: מִי שׁוֹחֵט; מִי זוֹרֵק; מִי מְדַשֵּׁן מִזְבֵּחַ הַפְּנִימִי; וּמִי מְדַשֵּׁן אֶת־הַמְּנוֹרָה; וּמִי מַעֲלֶה אֲבָרִים לַכֶּבֶשׁ —

יד אברהם

lots drawn for תְּרוּמַת הַדֶּשֶׁן, *removal of the ashes,* from the outer altar (see *Lechem Mishneh* there). Concerning *Rambam's* opinion about clearing the inner altar of ashes, see comm. to mishnah 3.

A variation on *Rambam's* opinion is found in *Ritva* (12b: citing *Ramban*). Though the *Kohen Gadol* was to perform even the regular daily service, this obligation was of Rabbinic origin. Therefore if the *Kohen Gadol* was weak, the daily service could be performed by the other *Kohanim.* In such an instance, lots were drawn. Therefore this chapter, dealing as it does with lots, *does* belong in *Yoma.*

וְזֶה הַפַּיִס הָרִאשׁוֹן. — *(and) this is the first lot.*

The *Kohen* who won the privilege of lifting the ashes got the additional privileges of סִידוּר הַמַּעֲרָכָה, *arranging the pyre,* on the altar and placing the שְׁנֵי גְזִירֵי עֵצִים, *two logs,* upon the pyre *(Gem.* 22a; see comm. to mishnah 5 s.v. וּשְׁנַיִם for an explanation of these two services).

Rambam (T'midin UMussafin 4:5) adds to this the privilege of taking a panful of coal from the outer altar and placing it upon the inner altar for the burning of the incense (see *Lechem Mishneh).*

3.

הַפַּיִס הַשֵּׁנִי: מִי שׁוֹחֵט; — *The second lot was* [to determine] *who slaughters;*

To choose the *Kohen* who would slaughter the תָּמִיד, *daily sacrifice (Rav; Rashi).*

Though שְׁחִיטָה, *slaughtering,* may be performed by a זָר, *non-Kohen,* it had a special attraction for the *Kohanim* because it was the first service of the day. As a result, lots were necessary *(Rav* to *Tamid* 3:1 based on *Yoma* 27b).

Meiri (25a) and *Ritva* (25a s.v. והראש) hold that although a *non-Kohen* was allowed to slaughter any sacrifice, the daily *tamid* sacrifice was an exception. Only בְּדִיעֲבַד,, *if it had already been* slaughtered by a *non-Kohen* was it considered valid, but לְבַתְחִילָה, *initially* [i.e., preferably] only a *Kohen* was to perform this service.

Rambam (Comm. to Mishnah), and *Rav* hold that the *Kohen* chosen by the second lot was given the honor of זְרִיקָה, *throwing,* the blood on the altar. The *Kohen* next in line was assigned to slaughter. *Rambam* explains that even though the slaughter was the first service of the offering, throwing the blood was more important, as evidenced by the law invalidating the throwing unless it was done by a *Kohen,* whereas slaughter has no such

restriction. Apparently, *Rambam's* text of our mishnah read מִי זוֹרֵק וּמִי שׁוֹחֵט, *who throws the blood and who slaughters.* This is borne out by the *Kafih* edition of his commentary.

[In *Mishneh Torah (T'midin UMussafin* 4:6), however, *Rambam* lists the slaughterer as the winner of the lot. We assume that *Rambam* later judged the prevalent version of the mishnah to be the correct one.]

Whoever won the privilege of performing any service for the תָּמִיד שֶׁל שַׁחַר, *daily morning sacrifice,* had the privilege of performing the same service for the תָּמִיד שֶׁל בֵּין הָעַרְבַּיִם, *daily afternoon sacrifice (Gemara* 26b).

The exception to this is the burning of the קְטֹרֶת, *incense,* for which separate lots were drawn for the קְטֹרֶת שֶׁל בֵּין הָעַרְבַּיִם, *afternoon incense.* See next mishnah.

On the Sabbath, the מִשְׁמָרוֹת, *watches,* change at midday, so that the outgoing watch served in the morning, and the incoming watch served in the afternoon. In the morning the members of the outgoing watch drew lots. Whoever performed any part of the morning service, performed the same part at the *mussaf* service. The incoming watch drew separate lots for the daily afternoon sacrifice. On festivals, too, the service of the

3. **T**he second lot was [to determine] who slaughters; who throws [the blood]; who clears the ashes from the inner altar; who clears the ashes from the menorah; and who brings the limbs [of the

תְּמִידִים, *daily sacrifices*, belonged to the watch of the day. (*Rambam, T'midin UMussafin* 4:9).

From the above, we may extrapolate that on Rosh Chodesh and Rosh HaShanah as well, whoever won the privilege of performing any service had that same privilege throughout the day, including the *mussafim*. But on the רְגָלִים, *pilgrimage festivals*, of Pesach, Shavuos, and Succos, the *mussafim* belonged to all the watches (see *Rambam, Klei HaMikdash* 4:4-5; *Deuteronomy* 18:6-8 with *Rashi*) so that all the watches, drew lots together for the *mussafim* (see *Sukkah* 5:6 with *Rav* s.v. בשמיני). But on the first seven days of Succos, no lots were necessary among the watches, because there were enough *mussafim* every day to grant each watch the privilege of sacrifices (*Succah* 5:6). [It stands to reason, though, that each watch drew lots among its members for the specific privileges.] On Shemini Atzeres, however, there was a smaller *mussaf*, so lots had to be drawn among the watches.

מִי זוֹרֵק; — *who throws [the blood]*;

This (second) drawing was also for the two additional services of קַבָּלָה, *receiving the blood*, in a holy basin and הוֹלָכָה, *bringing* it to the altar (*Rav* from *Gem.* 25b).

The *Gemara* (25b) concludes that one lot was held in which the winner and the twelve adjacent *Kohanim* were chosen for the service.

Ritva adds a novel comment: the *Kohen* who threw the blood was given the privilege of throwing any designated parts of the sacrifice on the altar fire. *Ritva* obviously interprets literally the description given in mishnah 4 of the last lot. The winner would only carry the parts up to the top of the altar, but not throw them on the fire. This is contrary to the interpretation of all the other commentators (see *Mishneh LaMelech* to *T'midin UMussafin* 4:6).

מִי מְדַשֵּׁן מִזְבֵּחַ הַפְּנִימִי; — *who clears the ashes from the inner altar*;

The מִזְבֵּחַ הַפְּנִימִי, *inner altar*, stood in the eastern hall of the Temple, in the part which was called קֹדֶשׁ, *Holy* or הֵיכָל, *Sanctuary*. It was also called the מִזְבֵּחַ הַזָּהָב, *golden altar*. No sacrifices were burned on this altar. It was reserved for the burning of the קְטֹרֶת, *incense*, twice a day and for the sprinkling of the blood of certain חַטָּאוֹת, *sin offerings*, e.g., the two *sin offerings*, of Yom Kippur (see *Zevachim* 5:1-2).

Gevuras Ari (25a) assumes that removing the ashes from the inner altar was done only once a day, in the morning (just as the ashes were removed from the outer altar only once in the morning). *Mikdash David (Kodashim* 9:2), however, points out that though *Tosafos* in two places (*Yoma* 14b s.v. ורמנהי and 33a s.v. אפילו; cf. 26a s.v. אלא) concurs with this, *Rambam* (comm. to *Tamid* 6:3; see *T'midin UMussafin* 1:10) clearly states that it was done again for the afternoon service.

וּמִי מְדַשֵּׁן אֶת־הַמְּנוֹרָה; — *and who removes the ashes from the menorah*;

[As mentioned before (1:2), *Rashi* and others understand this to mean only removal of the ashes (possibly also replacing the wick and the oil). Though this service was performed in the morning, the menorah was not lit until the afternoon. There was no reason to repeat this service in the afternoon. The lighting of the menorah in the afternoon was a separate service.

How was a *Kohen* chosen for the service of kindling the menorah? Either: A) the *Kohen* chosen for removing the ashes from the menorah was granted the privilege of lighting it (see *Rav, Tamid* 3:1; *Mefaresh* there s.v. והפיסו בואו); or B) another *Kohen* was chosen for lighting through one of the lots, but not by means of a separate drawing. This is not mentioned in our chapter because it is not part of the morning service (cf. *Tosafos* 26a s.v. אלא). There was no special פַּיִס, *lot*, for this lighting

הָרֹאשׁ וְהָרֶגֶל, וּשְׁתֵּי הַיָּדַיִם, הָעוֹקֶץ וְהָרֶגֶל,
הֶחָזֶה וְהַגֵּרָה, וּשְׁתֵּי הַדְּפָנוֹת, וְהַקְּרָבַיִם —
וְהַסֹּלֶת, וְהַחֲבִתִּין, וְהַיַּיִן. שְׁלֹשָׁה עָשָׂר כֹּהֲנִים
זָכוּ בוֹ.
אָמַר בֶּן־עַזַּאי לִפְנֵי רַבִּי עֲקִיבָא מִשּׁוּם רַבִּי
יְהוֹשֻׁעַ: דֶּרֶךְ הִלּוּכוֹ הָיָה קָרֵב.

יד אברהם

as evidenced in the *Gemara* (26a).

According to *Rambam*, the menorah was also lit in the morning, and the service of removing the ashes from the menorah, included lighting it (see *T'midin UMussafin* 4:6). Accordingly, the term *removing the ashes* is used to describe the entire menorah service because the first part of the process involved the ashes.

In the afternoon, the same *Kohen* repeated this service, like all the other *Kohanim* who repeated their services in the afternoon.

In view of the fact that the menorah service and the removal of the ash from the inner altar were done before the service of the daily offering, why were the slaughterer and thrower of the blood chosen first (see *Yoma* 33a הוה אביי ומסדר?

Tosafos Yeshanim (26a s.v. שוחט מי) answers that slaughter and throwing the blood were more important services, so lots were drawn for them first (see also *Rav* to *Tamid* 3:1).

Rashbam, cited in *Tosafos Yeshanim* (ibid.) answers that since the service of the *Tamid* had begun before daybreak, when they examined the designated sheep by torchlight for blemishes (*Tamid* 3:4), the other services of the *Tamid* were given precedence in the throwing of the lots (see also *Ravad* to *Tamid* beginning of ch.4).

Vilna Gaon (*Beur HaGra, Tamid* 3:1), cites evidence from *Tamid* 3:7 that though the removal of the ashes preceded the throwing of the blood, it did not precede the slaughtering. זורק מי, who should throw, is also in its rightful place because (as it has already pointed out [s.v. זורק מי] זורק includes receiving the blood in a basin, an act which followed immediately after slaughtering.

Though *Rashi* (33a s.v. התמיד דם) clearly disagrees with this opinion, it is held by *Rambam* (*T'midin UMussafin* 6:1-2).

וּמִי מַעֲלֶה אֲבָרִים לַכֶּבֶשׁ — *And who brings the limbs* [of the *daily burnt offering*] *to the ramp*—

The limbs were deposited on the lower half of the ramp (*Tamid* 4:3).

[This phrase introduces the rest of the mishnah. After the first four *Kohanim* won the right to perform the above-mentioned services, the next nine *Kohanim* were privileged to carry respective limbs of the sacrifice to the altar. The mishnah proceeds to enumerate the nine services they performed.]

הָרֹאשׁ וְהָרֶגֶל, — *the head and the hind leg*,

Of the nine *Kohanim* who won the privilege of carrying the parts of the sacrifice to the altar, the first brought the head and the right hind leg to the altar (the forelegs are known as יָדַיִם, lit. *hands*). [This *Kohen* was the fifth one to participate in the day's service] (*Rav*; *Rashi* from *Tamid* 4:3; see there for more details).

The *Gemara* (25b) explains that the head is always brought first because it is the first limb specified in *Leviticus* (1:8; in connection with the עוֹלָה, *burnt offering*) for burning on the altar. The rest of the limbs are arranged according to the amount of their meat. The hind leg is brought with the head because the head contains very little meat, whereas the hind leg is the meatiest of the limbs (*Rav*; *Rashi*; see *Tos. Yom Tov* citing *Mefaresh* to *Tamid* 4:3). [Of the two hind legs, the right is considered the more important because the Torah in-

2
3

daily burnt offering] to the ramp — the head and the hind leg, the two forelegs, the tail and the hind leg, the breast and the neck, the two sides, and the intestines, — the fine flour, the *chavitim* meal offering and the wine. Thirteen *Kohanim* won it.

Ben Azzai, in Rabbi Akiva's presence, quoted Rabbi Yehoshua: It was offered in the same way as it walked.

variably favors the symbolism of right over left. See *Lev.* 8:23-25, there 14:14; *Shulchan Aruch, Orach Chaim* 2:4).]

וּשְׁתֵּי הַיָּדַיִם, — *(and) the two forelegs,*
Both were brought by the sixth *Kohen (Rav, Tamid* 4:3).

הָעוֹקֶץ — *the tail (Rav; Rashi).*
Aruch (cited by *Meleches Shlomo*) translates עוֹקֶץ, *spine,* i.e., the end of the spine including the tail (cf. *Aruch* s.v. שזר). *Rashi* would probably agree that the whole tail area is included in this word as evidenced from *Tamid* 4:3. See also *Tosefos Yom Tov* to *Tamid* 3:1.

וְהָרֶגֶל, — *and the hind leg,*
I.e., the left hind leg. It and the tail were brought by the seventh *Kohen (Rav, Tamid* 4:3).

הֶחָזֶה — *the breast*
The fat facing the ground (between the ribs) which is severed from the ends of the ribs *(Rashi; Rav;* see *Tamid* 4:3).

וְהַגְּרָה, — *and the neck,*
The eighth *Kohen* brought both the breast and the neck *(ibid.).*

וּשְׁתֵּי הַדְּפָנוֹת, — *(and) the two sides,*
The ninth *Kohen* brought both sides. The sides included most of the rib cage.

וְהַקְּרָבַיִם— — *and the intestines—*
They were placed in a bowl *(Tamid* 4:3), and brought by the tenth *Kohen.*

וְהַסֹּלֶת, — *(and) the fine flour,*
For the מִנְחָה, *flour offering,* which accompanied the daily sacrifice as described in *Numbers* (28:5). It was brought by the eleventh *Kohen.*

וְהַחֲבִיתִּין, — *(and) the chavitin meal offering,*
The *Kohen Gadol* offered a daily

מִנְחָה, *meal offering,* consisting of a tenth-*ephah* of flour (equal to the volume of 43.2 eggs). It was baked in a מַחֲבַת, *shallow pan,* [hence the name חֲבִיתִין, *chavitin (Rashi; Rambam).*] From it they baked twelve loaves, half of which were offered in the morning and half in the afternoon *(Leviticus* 6:12-16 with *Rashi; Rambam, Ma'aseh HaKorbanos* 13:2-4). They were brought by the twelfth *Kohen.*

וְהַיַּיִן. — *and the wine,*
The wine was the נְסָכִים, *libation,* that accompanied the daily flour offering, and was poured upon the altar (see *Numbers* 28:7). This was brought by the thirteenth *Kohen.*
There is disagreement as to where this wine was poured. *Rambam (Ma'aseh Ha-Korbanos* 2:1) states that it was poured upon the יְסוֹד, *foundation,* of the altar (see *Middos* 3:1). *Ravad* disagrees and cites evidence from *Succos* (4:9) that it was poured into one of the two bowls built into the altar's southwestern corner. Indeed *Rambam* himself quotes this mishnah elsewhere *(T'midin U'Mussafin* 10:7). *Kessef Mishneh* suggests that normally the daily libation was poured onto the foundation of the altar. The only exception was during Succos when water was spilled into the one of the two bowls; then wine was poured into the other (see also *Lechem Mishneh* and *Mirkeves HaMishneh* to *Ma'aseh HaKorbanos* 2:1).

שְׁלֹשָׁה עָשָׂר כֹּהֲנִים זָכוּ בוֹ. — *Thirteen Kohanim won.*

אָמַר בֶּן־עַזַּאי לִפְנֵי רַבִּי עֲקִיבָא מִשּׁוּם רַבִּי יְהוֹשֻׁעַ: דֶּרֶךְ הִלּוּכוֹ הָיָה קָרֵב. — *Ben Azzai, in R' Akiva's presence, quoted R' Yehoshua: It was offered in the same way as it walked.*

R' Yehoshua, as quoted by Ben Az-

[ד] הַפַּיִס הַשְּׁלִישִׁי — ,,חֲדָשִׁים לַקְּטֹרֶת בֹּאוּ וְהָפִיסוּ."
וְהָרְבִיעִי — חֲדָשִׁים עִם יְשָׁנִים: מִי מַעֲלֶה אֵבָרִים מִן־הַכֶּבֶשׁ וְלַמִּזְבֵּחַ.

יד אברהם

zai, opposes the opinion that, after the head the sequence of offering was according to the meatiness of the limbs (see above s.v. הראש). He maintains that the limbs were offered (and the sequence of winning the privileges), following the anatomy of a walking animal. Thus, the head came first as indicated by *Lev.* 1:8 (as mentioned in the first opinion above), and it was accompanied by the right hind leg — out of sequence — for the reason given above. The neck and chest followed, then the two front legs, the two sides, left hind leg, and the intestines. The rest was as in the first opinion (*Rav* from *Gem.* 28b).

As mentioned in the Prefatory Remarks to this chapter (and mishnah 2 s.v. אַרְבַּע פְּיָסוֹת), some authorities hold that the lots were not drawn on Yom Kippur since the entire service was performed by the *Kohen Gadol*, while other authorities, headed by *Ramban*, hold that the four lots were drawn even on Yom Kippur. Although no lot was necessary for the service of the daily sacrifice, or for the offering of its parts since these services had to be performed by the *Kohen Gadol*, the lot was needed to determine who would remove the ashes from the inner altar and from the menorah. *Ramban* maintains that these were not considered full-fledged services since they were only מַכְשִׁירֵי עֲבוֹדָה, *preparations for other services* and did not have to be performed by the *Kohen Gadol*. *Ramban* even expresses doubt whether removal of the ashes from the inner altar is mandated by the Torah. It may be only a Rabbinic (דְּרַבָּנָן) requirement.

Rambam (*Avodas Yom HaKippurim*) concurs with *Ramban* (2:1 and 4:1) about removing the ashes from the inner altar.[1]

4.

הַפַּיִס הַשְּׁלִישִׁי—חֲדָשִׁים לַקְּטֹרֶת — *The third lot — [those] new to the incense.*

The third lot would be announced with the call, 'Those new ...'

Rambam (*T'midin U'Mussafin* 2:7) states that this announcement was made by the administrator mentioned above (2:1).

When possible, this lot was limited to *Kohanim* who had never yet burned the incense. Tradition taught that this service increased the wealth of the *Kohen* who performed it. Therefore, care was taken to give every *Kohen* an opportunity to burn the incense (*Rav* from *Gem.* 26a).

For the same reason, a second lot was made for the afternoon incense burning, a departure from the procedure of the other services, for which winners of the

1. It is not clear what his opinion is about removal of the ashes from the menorah. He mentions only מֵטִיב אֶת הַנֵּרוֹת which may, according to *Rambam*, mean *to light the lamps* (see *T'midin U'Mussafin* 3:10-12). Following *Ramban's* reasoning, removing the ashes from the menorah probably has the same status as removal of the ashes from the inner altar. [See *Avodas Yisrael* p. 83.]

On this basis *Tosefos Yom Tov* assumes that *Rambam* concurs with *Ramban* that the second lottery was also drawn on Yom Kippur.

Tosefos Yom Tov admits that *Rambam* does not concur completely, for according to him the third and fourth lots were surely not drawn. Moreover, *Rambam*, though he mentions the first lottery on Yom Kippur (*Avodas Yom HaKippurim* 2:1) says nothing about a second lottery. This leaves room for much speculation.

4. The third lot — 'Those new to the incense, come and draw lots!'

And the fourth [lot was for] new and old; [to determine] who takes the limbs up from the ramp to the altar.

morning lot performed the parallel afternoon services as well (see above 2:3, s.v. מִי שׁוֹחֵט).

בּוֹאוּ וְהָפִיסוּ. — 'come and draw lots.'

The controversy about whether lots were drawn on Yom Kippur has already been detailed earlier (s.v. 2:2). Ramban finds here too, a reason for a lottery on Yom Kippur: The service of burning the daily incense included many parts: the actual burning, bringing a pan of burning coals from the outer altar and placing it upon the inner altar. However only one lot was drawn for the service of burning the incense; the Kohen who won the privilege to burn the incense had the right to bring the pan with the coal as well. Usually, though, he picked a Kohen standing next to him or — according to some, any Kohen he wished — to assist him, (Gem. 25b and Tosafos s.v. תא שמע; cf. comm. to 2:2 s.v. וזה הפייס הראשון). On Yom Kippur, although the Kohen Gadol burned the daily incense, another Kohen carried the pan of coals. Lots were drawn for this privilege to prevent arguments among the ordinary Kohanim, since this was one of the few services they were permitted to perform on Yom Kippur. Besides, since part of the incense service was carrying the pan it, too, was conducive to increased wealth, which is why this service too was shared with other Kohanim (see Gem. 25b and Yerushalmi).

Rambam (Avodas Yom HaKippurim 2:5), however, maintains that on Yom Kippur even the pan for the daily incense was carried by the Kohen Gadol (Tos. Yom Tov 2:2).

[The above refers only to the coal for the daily incense, which was burned on Yom Kippur as well. But for the special Yom Kippur incense, which was burned in the Holy of Holies (5:1), only the Kohen Gadol could bring coals, because only he was permitted to enter the Holy of Holies.]

וְהָרְבִיעִי — חֲדָשִׁים עִם יְשָׁנִים; — And the fourth [lot was for] new and old;

All the Kohanim, whether they had ever performed this service or not, were included in this lot (Rav).

מִי מַעֲלֶה אֲבָרִים מִן־הַכֶּבֶשׁ וְלַמִּזְבֵּחַ. — [to determine] who takes the limbs up from the ramp to the altar.

The limbs of the daily sacrifice had been deposited (2:3) on the lower half of the ramp. The Kohen who won the fourth lot had the privilege of bringing these limbs up to the altar and tossing them onto the fire. The Kohanim who brought the limbs to the ramp were not given the privilege of bringing them to the altar and tossing them upon the fire, because בְּרָב־עָם הַדְרַת־מֶלֶךְ, the glory of the King is in [being served by] multitudes of people (Proverbs 14:28; Rav from Gem. 26a).

Rashi (26b s.v.עצמו), Tosafos (26a s.v. דתנן), and Meiri hold that a single Kohen brought all the limbs from the ramp to the altar. This seems to be Rambam's opinion too (see T'midim U'Mussafin 4:8 with Har Moriah). But Tosafos Yeshanim (26b s.v. דלא) and Ritva hold that as many Kohanim as were used to bring the limbs to the ramp were needed to bring them up to the altar. They contend that otherwise there would be no purpose in holding a fourth lottery to glorify the King with multitudes.

According to Ritva (comm. to 2:3 s.v. מי זורק) the Kohen who threw the blood on the altar also tossed the limbs onto the fire. The Kohen (or Kohanim) who won the fourth lot brought the limbs up

[ה] **תָּמִיד** קָרֵב בְּתִשְׁעָה, בַּעֲשָׂרָה, בְּאַחַד
עָשָׂר, בִּשְׁנֵים עָשָׂר, לֹא פָחוֹת
וְלֹא יוֹתֵר. כֵּיצַד? עַצְמוֹ — בְּתִשְׁעָה. בְּחַג —
בְּיַד אֶחָד צְלוֹחִית שֶׁל מַיִם; הֲרֵי כָאן עֲשָׂרָה.
בֵּין הָעַרְבַּיִם — בְּאַחַד עָשָׂר: הוּא עַצְמוֹ
בְּתִשְׁעָה, וּשְׁנַיִם בְּיָדָם שְׁנֵי גְזִירֵי עֵצִים.

יד אברהם

to the top of the altar where they handed them to the *Kohen* who had thrown the blood.

Ramban holds that this fourth lot was held on Yom Kippur too. Though there is no question that the *Kohen Gadol* himself had to burn the limbs upon the altar, this was so only for the unique Yom Kippur sacrifices. If אֵבָרִים וּפְדָרִים, *limbs and fat*, were left over from the previous day, as was common, any *Kohen* could toss them on the fire. For this the lot was drawn.

Tosefos Yom Tov (2:2) adds that the fourth lot was necessary even according to those who prohibit the burning of leftover limbs on Yom Kippur (see *Shabbos* 114a; *Rambam*, *T'midin U'Mussafin* 1:7). Though the *Kohen Gadol* himself had transported the limbs to the ramp, nevertheless, the *Kohanim* had the privilege of handing him each limb as he stood atop the altar and tossed the limbs on the fire. The same procedure was followed whenever the

Kohen Gadol chose to burn the limbs (see 1:2). For this privilege, the *Kohanim* drew lots.

⇒§ Were the four lots drawn at the same time?

One leaves these mishnayos with the impression that the four lots were all held at one assembly. A quick perusal of *Tamid* (1:2, 3:1, 5:2), however, makes it clear that this is not so. The first lot was held as soon as the administrator arrived — near daybreak. Then the ashes were lifted from the outer altar and other services were performed. After this the *Kohanim* assembled again for the second lot. *Rambam* (*T'midin U'Mussafin* 6:1) states that the first two lots were held one after the other (see *Har HaMoriyah*). The *Kohanim* then performed all the services allotted in the second lot after which they assembled for prayer (*Tamid* 5:1). Then they held the third and fourth lots, one after the other.

5.

תָּמִיד קָרֵב — *The daily sacrifice was offered*

The phrase תָּמִיד קָרֵב, *the daily sacrifice was offered*, includes all its services starting with the bringing of the limbs and including the meal offering, the libation etc. (*Rashi, Rav*).

בְּתִשְׁעָה, — *with nine [Kohanim]*,

I.e., sometimes with nine, sometimes with ten etc., as explained below. This minimum of nine *Kohanim* includes six to carry the sacrifice itself. This is the

number of *Kohanim* used wherever כְּבָשִׂים וְעִזִּים, *yearling sheep and goats* were offered. If a מִנְחַת נְסָכִים, *meal offering with wine*, was required (as with the daily sacrifice), two additional *Kohanim* were required (*Rambam, Ma'aseh HaKorbanos* 1:17).

בַּעֲשָׂרָה, בְּאַחַד עָשָׂר, בִּשְׁנֵים עָשָׂר, לֹא פָחוֹת וְלֹא יוֹתֵר. — *[or] with ten, [or] with eleven, [or] with twelve, no less and no more.*

[The mishnah will now give examples

5. The daily sacrifice was offered with nine, [or] with ten, [or] with eleven, [or] with twelve, no less and no more. How so? [The sacrifice] itself — with nine. On Succos one held a flask of water in his hand; thus we have ten. In the afternoon — with eleven: [the sacrifice] itself with nine, plus two who held two logs in their hands. On the Sabbath — with

YAD AVRAHAM

of when each of these numbers of Kohanim was needed.]

?כֵּיצַד — How so?

עַצְמוֹ — [The sacrifice] itself —

I.e., on a weekday when only the regular daily sacrifice was offered (Rav; Rashi).

בְּתִשְׁעָה. — with nine.

Six for carrying the limbs to the altar, and one each for the flour-offering appended to the daily sacrifice, the chavitin offering of the Kohen Gadol, and the wine libation described in mishnah 3 (Rav; Rashi).

Rashi points out that according to mishnah 3, nine Kohanim were needed simply to carry the offering to the ramp. A tenth Kohen was needed for the privilege of burning the limbs on the altar (the fourth lot picked the Kohen for this privilege; see mishnah 5).

Ritva answers that our mishnah omits the (tenth) Kohen who burned the limbs on the altar because there is a difference of opinion on this matter. R' Elazar ben Yaakov (Gem. 26a) maintains that the Kohanim who carried the limbs up the ramp, had the additional privilege of burning them on the altar (see also Rashi s.v. עצמו).

Tosafos (26a s.v. דתנן) answers that nine Kohanim were the minimum employed since the Kohen who won the fourth lot (ordinarily the tenth man) could conceivably be one of the nine Kohanim winning the second lot, in which case there would be a total of only nine.

בֶּחָג—בְּיָד אֶחָד צְלוֹחִית שֶׁל מַיִם; — On

Succos [lit. on the Festival] — one held a flask of water in his hand;

The pouring of water of Succos is not specified in the Torah. It is only hinted at in Numbers 29:12-35 (see Rashi, ibid.). It was commanded orally to Moses at Sinai and transmitted throughout the generations until the Mishnah was written. An extensive description of this service and the preparations for it are given in Succah (4:9; 5:2-3). The Gemara (26b) states that the water was offered after the daily sacrifice. The southwestern corner (קֶרֶן דְּרוֹמִית מַעֲרָבִית) of the altar had two built-in bowls which were punctured to allow the liquids poured into them to run into the שִׁיתִין, pits, below the altar. On Succos, while the regular נִסּוּךְ הַיַּיִן, wine libation, belonging to the daily offering had been poured into the eastern bowl, the נִסּוּךְ הַמַּיִם, water libation, was poured into the western bowl (Succah 4:9).

The Gemara (26b) proves that they poured the water only during the service of the תָּמִיד שֶׁל שַׁחַר, morning daily sacrifice, not in the afternoon.

הֲרֵי כָאן עֲשָׂרָה. — thus we have ten.

Nine for the daily sacrifice and the additional Kohen for the flask of water.

[Tosefos Yom Tov (s.v. ושנים) suggests that this privilege was awarding during the second lot to the fourteenth Kohen.]

בֵּין הָעַרְבַּיִם—בְּאֶחָד עָשָׂר: הוּא עַצְמוֹ בְּתִשְׁעָה, — In the afternoon — with eleven: [the sacrifice] itself with nine,

The תָּמִיד שֶׁל בֵּין הָעַרְבַּיִם, afternoon daily sacrifice, needed nine Kohanim as did the morning daily sacrifice.

[The Kohanim who had won these

וּבַשַׁבָּת — בְּאֶחָד עָשָׂר: הוּא עַצְמוֹ
בְּתִשְׁעָה, וּשְׁנַיִם בְּיָדָם שְׁנֵי בָזִיכֵי לְבוֹנָה שֶׁל
לֶחֶם הַפָּנִים. וּבַשַׁבָּת שֶׁבְּתוֹךְ הֶחָג — בְּיַד אֶחָד
צְלוֹחִית שֶׁל מָיִם.

[ו] אַיִל קָרֵב בְּאֶחָד עָשָׂר: הַבָּשָׂר בַּחֲמִשָּׁה,
הַקְּרָבַיִם וְהַסֹּלֶת וְהַיַּיִן בִּשְׁנַיִם
שְׁנָיִם.

יד אברהם

privileges for the morning services, had them for the afternoon services as well (see above 2:3 s.v. הַפַּיִס הַשֵּׁנִי.]

וּשְׁנַיִם בְּיָדָם שְׁנֵי גִזְירֵי עֵצִים. — *plus two who held two logs in their hands.*

In addition to the wood pyre prepared on the altar for the fire, there was an additional requirement to place two logs upon the pyre both in the morning and in the afternoon. This requirement is based on *Leviticus* 1:7: *The children* (plural) *of Aaron the Kohen shall put fire upon the altar and arrange logs upon the fire.* This is stated somewhat differently in *Leviticus* 6:5: *And the Kohen* (singular) *shall kindle wood on it every morning.*

Leviticus 6:7, which speaks about the morning service, is phrased in the singular, whereas *Leviticus* 1:7 is in the plural. The *Gemara* (26b) deduces from this that in the morning both logs were carried by one *Kohen,* whereas in the afternoon two *Kohanim* were needed (*Rav; Rashi*).

The Mishnah did not include the *Kohen* needed for the two logs in the morning service, because the logs were put in place before the slaughter of the daily sacrifice slaughter (see *Tamid* 2:3, 4:1). Our mishnah lists only the *Kohanim* needed for carrying the limbs to the altar and for later services (*Tosafos* to *Menachos* 89b s.v. תָּמִיד שֶׁל שַׁחַר cited in *Tos. R' Akiva*).

⊷§ **How were the Kohanim chosen for the afternoon wood service?**

Ritva holds that since the *Kohen* who won the first lot also gained the privilege of putting the two logs upon the fire (see 2:2 s.v.

וְזֶה הַפַּיִס הָרִאשׁוֹן), it was his privilege to do so in the afternoon as well, just as the services won in the other lot were performed by the same *Kohen* morning and afternoon (see 2:3 s.v. הַפַּיִס הַשֵּׁנִי). As we saw above, a single *Kohen* placed both morning logs while two *Kohanim* did so in the afternoon. The *Kohen* who won the privilege in the morning had the right to choose the second *kohen* for the afternoon service (see also *Tos. Yom Tov* s.v. וּשְׁנַיִם).

Tosafos (26a s.v. אלא) proposes that the fourteenth and fifteenth *Kohanim* won the privilege of performing these services. In enumerating only *thirteen* winners of the second lot, the mishnah includes only those who won parts in the morning service, but there were, indeed, two who would participate only in the afternoon. The total number of *Kohanim* involved in the afternoon service would not be larger, however, because the two *Kohanim* needed for the removal of the ashes from the inner altar and the menorah were not needed in the afternoon, when those services were not performed (see *Tos.* opinion cited above 2:3 s.v. מִי מְדַשֵּׁן מִזְבֵּחַ הַפְּנִימִי).

וּבַשַׁבָּת בְּאֶחָד עָשָׂר: הוּא עַצְמוֹ בְּתִשְׁעָה, וּשְׁנַיִם בְּיָדָם שְׁנֵי בָזִיכֵי לְבוֹנָה שֶׁל לֶחֶם הַפָּנִים. — *On the Sabbath with eleven: [the sacrifice] itself with nine, plus two who held [the] two spoons of frankincense of the Panim Bread in their hands.*

The *Panim* Breads were arranged every Sabbath in two tiers of six loaves each on the golden table in the קֹדֶשׁ, *Sanctuary.* Near each tier a spoonful of frankincense was placed. On the Sabbath when the breads were replaced with fresh breads, the frankincense was

eleven: [the sacrifice] itself with nine, plus two who held [the] two spoons of frankincense of the Panim Bread in their hands. On the Sabbath during Succos — one held a flask of water in his hand.

6. **A** ram was offered with eleven: the meat with five; the intestines, the fine flour, and the wine — with two each.

YAD AVRAHAM

burned on the outer altar (see *Leviticus* 24:5-9; and *Rambam, Klei HaMikdash* 2:11).

Ritva says that this service too was won during the second lot by the fourteenth and fifteenth *Kohanim*.

וּבַשַּׁבָּת שֶׁבְּתוֹךְ הֶחָג—בְּיַד אֶחָד צְלוֹחִית

שֶׁל מָיִם. — *On the Sabbath during Succos — one held a flask of water in his hand.*

[He was in addition to the eleven *Kohanim* used every Sabbath. This *Kohen* completed the maximum number of twelve.]

6.

אַיִל — *A ram*

[Rams were used for many sacrifices including all the *mussafim* except for that of the Sabbath. To qualify for sacrifice, a ram had to be over one year and thirty days old (see *Parah* 1:3).]

קָרֵב בְּאַחַד עָשָׂר: — *was offered with eleven:*

[How were these *Kohanim* chosen? It stands to reason that for those parts of the service where the number of *Kohanim* needed for a ram were the same as those needed for the sheep of the daily sacrifice (slaughter, tossing of the blood, bringing the limbs to the altar), these *Kohanim* who performed the services for the daily sacrifice performed the same services for the ram (see 2:3 s.v. מִי שׁוֹחֵט). Thus the bringing of the limbs, which required five *Kohanim* both for a sheep (the daily sacrifice) and for a ram, was done by the same *Kohanim* who had won these privileges for the daily sacrifice. In the case of the intestines, flour, and wine, where a ram required two *Kohanim* for each service rather than the one used for the daily sacrifice, there are three possible procedures: A) The single *Kohen*

who performed each service for the daily sacrifice picked a *Kohen* to accompany him; B) The additional *Kohanim* were picked in the second lot following the selection of usual thirteen *Kohanim*; C) Since these services were performed in a different manner than the daily sacrifice, the *Kohanim* performing them during the daily service had no claim to them (see *Tosafos'* opinion cited in comm. to 2:5). Therefore two additional *Kohanim* were picked in the second lottery for each of these services.]

הַבָּשָׂר בַּחֲמִשָּׁה, — *the meat with five,*

The procedure was the same as that for the parts of the sheep for the daily sacrifice *(Rav; Rashi)*.

הַקְּרָבַיִם — *the intestines,*

The innards of a ram are heavier than those of a sheep and therefore need an additional *Kohen (Meiri)*.

[Meiri's explanation presents some difficulty. If the extra weight of the intestines necessitated an additional *kohen*, why was this true only for the intestines? Surely if the ram's intestines were heavier, so were its limbs!]

Ritva (citing *Tosafos*) explains this dif-

[ז] פַּר קָרֵב בְּעֶשְׂרִים וְאַרְבָּעָה: הָרֹאשׁ
וְהָרֶגֶל — הָרֹאשׁ בְּאֶחָד, וְהָרֶגֶל
בִּשְׁנַיִם; הָעוֹקֶץ וְהָרֶגֶל — הָעוֹקֶץ בִּשְׁנַיִם,
וְהָרֶגֶל בִּשְׁנַיִם; הֶחָזֶה וְהַגֵּרָה — הֶחָזֶה בְּאֶחָד,
וְהַגֵּרָה בִּשְׁלֹשָׁה; שְׁתֵּי יָדַיִם בִּשְׁנַיִם; שְׁתֵּי
דְפָנוֹת בִּשְׁנַיִם; הַקְּרָבַיִם וְהַסֹּלֶת וְהַיַּיִן —
בִּשְׁלֹשָׁה שְׁלֹשָׁה.
בַּמֶּה דְבָרִים אֲמוּרִים? — בְּקָרְבְּנוֹת צִבּוּר;
אֲבָל בְּקָרְבַּן יָחִיד, אִם רָצָה לְהַקְרִיב —
מַקְרִיב.

יד אברהם

ferently. Even the intestines of a sheep were heavy, but since the *Gemara* (27a) finds an allusion in the words of the Torah to the use of six *Kohanim* for the sheep, only one *Kohen* carried the intestines. Since no such hint exists for a ram, two *Kohanim* could be used.

וְהַסֹּלֶת — *and the fine flour,*
The flour offering accompanying a ram contains twice as much flour as the daily sacrifice. See *Numbers* 15:1-10.

וְהַיַּיִן— *and the wine —*
Here too, the volume of wine for a ram is greater than that for a sheep. See *Numbers* 15:1-10. [The need for two

Kohanim was clearly not because the wine and the fine flour for the ram were too heavy for one *Kohen*. They were probably needed to draw attention to the greater volume of these offerings and to enhance the sacrifice (כְּבוֹד הַקָּרְבָּן).]

בִּשְׁנַיִם שְׁנַיִם — *with two each* [lit. *with two two*].
They did not divide the intestines, the fine flour, and the wine into two parts. They were placed in a single vessel which was carried by both *Kohanim* (*Tif. Yis.*).

7.

פַּר — *An ox*
[Oxen, too, were part of all the *mussafim* except those of the Sabbath. A calf becomes an ox when it reaches its second year (*Parah* 1:2; *Rambam*, *Ma'aseh HaKorbanos* 1:14).

קָרֵב בְּעֶשְׂרִים וְאַרְבָּעָה — *was offered with twenty-four:*
[How were they chosen? The three possibilities proposed above (2:6 s.v. קרב באחד עשר), apply here as well.]

הָרֹאשׁ וְהָרֶגֶל — *the head and the hind leg —*
[I.e., the right hind leg (see 2:3 s.v. הָרֹאשׁ וְהָרֶגֶל).]

הָרֹאשׁ בְּאֶחָד, וְהָרֶגֶל בִּשְׁנַיִם — *the head with one, and the hind leg with two;*
They were not allowed to cut the leg in two. Rather the two *Kohanim* carried it together (*Tos. Yom Tov* from *Rambam, Maaseh HaKorbanos* 6:19).
[This holds true for all the limbs carried by two *Kohanim.*]

הָעוֹקֵץ וְהָרֶגֶל—הָעוֹקֵף בִּשְׁנַיִם, וְהָרֶגֶל בִּשְׁנַיִם; הֶחָזֶה וְהַגֵּרָה הֶחָזֶה בְּאֶחָד, וְהַגֵּרָה בִּשְׁלֹשָׁה — *the tail and the hind leg — the tail with two, and the hind leg with two; the breast and the neck — the breast with one and the neck with three; [the] two forelegs with two;*
[See above mishnah 3.]

7. An ox was offered with twenty-four: the head and the hind leg — the head with one, and the hind leg with two; the tail and the hind leg — the tail with two, and the hind leg with two; the breast and the neck — the breast with one, and the neck with three; [the] two forelegs with two; [the] two sides with two; the intestines, the fine flour, and the wine — with three each.

In which cases do the above apply? — For communal sacrifices; but for personal sacrifices, if he wanted to offer — he may do so.

YAD AVRAHAM

שְׁתֵּי דְפָנוֹת בִּשְׁנָיִם; — [the] two sides with two;

[Each *Kohen* carrying one side.]

הַקְּרָבַיִם וְהַסֹּלֶת וְהַיַּיִן—בִּשְׁלֹשָׁה שְׁלֹשָׁה. — the intestines, the fine flour, and the wine — with three each [lit. with three three].

Each of these respective parts of the offering was placed in a single vessel which was carried by three *Kohanim* (*Tif. Yis.*). [The reason for this is probably the one given in mishnah 6 s.v. וְהַיַּיִן.]

בַּמֶּה דְּבָרִים אֲמוּרִים? — In which cases do the above apply [lit. when are these words said]? —

In which instances do the rulings of the above mishnayos concerning the lots and the number of *Kohanim* apply (*Rav; Rashi*).

בְּקָרְבְּנוֹת צִבּוּר. — for communal sacrifices;

[I.e., sacrifices offered on behalf of the entire nation, such as the daily sacrifices and *mussafim*.]

אֲבָל בְּקָרְבַּן יָחִיד, אִם רָצָה לְהַקְרִיב—מַקְרִיב. — but for personal sacrifices, if he wanted to offer — he may do so [lit. he offers].

If a single *Kohen* wanted to perform the whole service alone without recourse to lots (*Rav; Rashi*).

Rambam (comm. to Mishnah;

Ma'aseh HaKorbanos 6:19) seems to interpret that although lots had to be drawn, the *Kohanim* had the right to use less than the prescribed number of people to assist in the service.

[*Rambam's* view is this: Ordinarily, the *Kohen* who won the lot was awarded the privilege of slaughter. Those next in line would, in turn, be assigned other portions of the service as enumerated in the mishnah. If, however, one *Kohen* wished to perform the entire service and the others gave their consent, the procedure was permitted. True, our mishnah says אִם רָצָה, *if he* (in the singular) *wanted*, but *Rambam* understands this to mean only that an individual *Kohen* initiated the request, but logic dictates that he could not usurp the rights of the others without their consent.

[By maintaining that the agreement of the other *Kohanim* was needed, *Rambam* avoids the difficulty raised by *Tosefos Yom Tov* that to permit a unilateral decision by one *Kohen* would cause conflict.]

Mishneh LaMelech (*T'midim U'Mussafin* 4:9) raises an unresolved question: Under normal circumstances, were new lots drawn to determine which *Kohanim* were to participate in the offerings of individuals, or did the assignments remain those determined by the lots cast for the communal of-

הֶפְשֵׁטָן וְנִתּוּחָן שֶׁל אֵלּוּ וָאֵלּוּ שָׁוִין.

[א] **אָמַר** לָהֶם הַמְמֻנֶּה: ,,צְאוּ וּרְאוּ, אִם הִגִּיעַ זְמַן הַשְּׁחִיטָה.'' אִם הִגִּיעַ, הָרוֹאֶה אוֹמֵר: ,,בַּרְקַאי!'' מַתִּתְיָא בֶּן־שְׁמוּאֵל אוֹמֵר: ,,הֵאִיר פְּנֵי כָל־הַמִּזְרָח.''

יד אברהם

ferings?

Regarding the selection of a *Kohen* to service an individual's personal offering, many commentators (*R' Yechezkel Lando; R' Shimshon Chasid* in *Tosafos Chadashim; Shoshanim L' David, Kol HaRemez*) concur that the individual bringing the sacrifice had the right to pick whomever he wanted from the family on duty that day. This is the case our mishnah discusses. Some of these commentators go on to say that if the owner had no preference lots are thrown.

הֶפְשֵׁטָן וְנִתּוּחָן שֶׁל אֵלּוּ וָאֵלּוּ שָׁוִין — *The flaying and dissection of these and of those are the same.*

The flaying and dissection of communal and personal sacrifices have the same laws. A non-*kohen* may perform them (*Rav* from *Gem.* 26b).

The mishnah also means to say that the procedure for flaying and dissecting described in *Tamid* 4:2-3 and summarized here was followed for all the sacrifices. It was forbidden to dissect an personal sacrifice into more pieces than a communal one (*Gevuras Ari*).

Chapter 3

[After having digressed in the previous chapter to describe the lots drawn daily in the Temple, the mishnah returns to the original topic of this tractate — the order of the Yom Kippur service. According to those who hold that no lots were drawn on Yom Kippur, we now continue from 1:7. For those who hold that even on Yom Kippur all (or the first two) lots were drawn, the mishnah here continues from the point where the second lot had been made.]

1.

אָמַר לָהֶם הַמְמֻנֶּה: — *The administrator said to them,*

[To the assembled *Kohanim*.]

The administrator referred to here [unlike 2:1 where the *administrator* is the official in charge of the lots] is the סְגָן, *Deputy Kohen Gadol* (*Rav; Rashi;* probably derived from *Sanhedrin* 19a שמע מינה הוא ממונה הוא סגן; see *Tosafos, Sotah* 42a s.v. סגן; *Meiri* and *Ritva* concur).

They appoint another *Kohen* to act as assistant to the *Kohen Gadol*. He always stands at the *Kohen Gadol's* right, which is a great honor for the *Kohen Gadol*. All other *Kohanim* are subject to the deputy's authority (*Rambam, K'lei HaMikdosh* 4:16).

[*Rambam* seemingly understands ממונה here as *Rashi* does.]

According to some authorities, the סְגָן, *deputy,* had yet another function. He was the *Kohen* designated to serve instead of the *Kohen Gadol* if the latter was disqualified, as attested to by *R' Chanina S'gan HaKohanim*

The flaying and dissection of these and of those are the same.

1. The administrator said to them; 'Go out and see, if the time for slaughtering has arrived.' If it had arrived, the one who sees [it] says, *'Barkai!'*

Mattisya ben Shmuel says: 'The whole of the east has lit up.'

YAD AVRAHAM

(Gem. 39a; see commentary above 1:1 s.v. וּמַתְקִינִין).

Tosafos (Yoma 15b s.v. אמר, *Tosafos Yeshanim* loc. cit.; *Menachos* 100a s.v. אמר) holds that the *administrator* mentioned here is not the Deputy *Kohen Gadol. Tosefos (Menachos* loc. cit. and *Tosafos Yeshanim)* suggests that the *administrator* of our mishnah is the one in charge of the lots mentioned earlier (2:1) and in *Shekalim* (5:1).

צְאוּ וּרְאוּ, אִם הִגִּיעַ זְמַן הַשְׁחִיטָה. — *'Go out and see if the time for slaughtering has arrived.'*

Go to a high place — the roof or atop a wall — from which you can see far *(Rashi).*

There was a specially designated viewing station in the Temple where an observer went up to see whether day had dawned *(Rav; Rambam, Comm. to Mishnah).*

Meiri holds that it was the task of the announcer (גְּבִינֵי כָרוֹז; see *Shekalim* 5:1) to go up to the viewing station and call out *'Barkai!'* at daybreak. Thus the administrator told the *Kohanim* to go out and ask the announcer if the time for slaughtering had arrived.

In the Temple service, any slaughter performed at night is invalid. Day is reckoned from dawn — i.e., when the first shimmer of light is observed on the eastern horizon *(Rashi).*

אִם הִגִּיעַ, הָרוֹאֶה אוֹמֵר: בָּרְקַאי! — *If it had arrived, the one who sees [it] says, 'Barkai!'*

I.e., the בָּרָק, sheen [*of the sun*] can already be seen *(Rashi, Rav).*

According to *Meiri's* opinion, הָרוֹאֶה here refers to a *designated* viewer; the

Kohen who was assigned to make the announcement.

This shimmering of the sun is equivalent of עֲלוֹת הַשַּׁחַר, *dawn (see Megillah* 2:4). As *Tosefos Yom Tov* points out, this is *not* the rising of the morning star, Venus *(Berachos* 1:1 s.v. עמוד השחר).

מַתִּתְיָא בֶן־שְׁמוּאֵל אוֹמֵר: — *Mattisya ben Shmuel says,,*

[He was the administrator of the lots, as mentioned in *Shekalim* 5:1.]

הֵאִיר פְּנֵי כָל הַמִּזְרָח — *'the whole of the east has lit up.'*

Mattisya ben Shmuel disagrees with the first opinion. It is not enough to see light in the east in one place (i.e., עמוד השחר). The *entire* east must be lit up *(Rambam; Meiri; Rav).* This seems to be the opinion of *Rivan* cited by *Tosafos Yeshanim.*

[*Rambam* adds that the halachah follows Mattisya ben Shmuel. In *Mishneh Torah,* however, *Rambam* does not render a decision on this (see *Ma'aseh HaKorbanos* ch. 4). It would seem from this that *Rambam* retracted his view that our mishnah contains a halachic disagreement in which Mattisya holds that a sacrifice is invalid prior to the lighting of the whole east. Rather, the disagreement is one relating solely to Temple customs, therefore no halachic decision is necessary (cf. *Rashi's* interpretation below).]

Rashi (Menachos 100a s.v. מתתיא בן שמואל) and *Tosafos* (there) hold that there are not two opinions here. When the one who had seen the dawn said, *'Barkai!',* Mattisya, as administrator of the lots, asked, 'Has the whole east lit up as far as Hebron?'

„עַד שֶׁבְּחֶבְרוֹן?"
וְהוּא אוֹמֵר: „הֵן."

[ב] **וְלָמָּה** הִצְרְכוּ לְכָךְ? שֶׁפַּעַם אַחַת עָלָה
מְאוֹר הַלְּבָנָה וְדִמּוּ שֶׁהֵאִיר
מִזְרָח, וְשָׁחֲטוּ אֶת־הַתָּמִיד, וְהוֹצִיאוּהוּ לְבֵית
הַשְּׂרֵפָה.
הוֹרִידוּ כֹהֵן גָּדוֹל לְבֵית הַטְּבִילָה.
זֶה הַכְּלָל הָיָה בַּמִּקְדָּשׁ: כָּל־הַמֵּסִיךְ אֶת־

יד אברהם

"עַד שֶׁבְּחֶבְרוֹן?, — 'As far as Hebron?'
The people in the Temple asked the
observer 'As far as Hebron?' I.e., 'Did
you see the sky lit up as far as Hebron?'
(Rambam; Rav).

[According to Rashi this was a continuation of Mattisya ben Shmuel's formula.]

Yerushalmi (2:1) says that they mentioned Hebron in order to allude to the
זְכוּת אָבוֹת, merit of the Patriarchs, who
are buried there.
Rashi (Menachos 100a s.v. מתניא

בן שמואל) comments that this formula
was said only on Yom Kippur and attributes this opinion to Yerushalmi.
However, Rambam (comm. to Tamid
3:1) holds that it was said every day.
Yerushalmi contains no hint that this
was said only on Yom Kippur. Siach
Yitzchok asserts that there is a copyist's
error in Rashi (c.f. comm. below s.v.
שֶׁפַּעַם אַחַת).

וְהוּא אוֹמֵר: הֵן! — And he says, 'Yes!'.
The observer answered, 'Yes!' (Gem.
28b).

2.

וְלָמָּה הִצְרְכוּ לְכָךְ? — Why was this necessary?
Why did they have to send an
observer up to the roof to see whether
day had begun? — Surely the beginning
of daylight was obvious to everyone on
the ground! (Rashi; Rav).

Magen Avraham (Orach Chaim 89:3) understands the mishnah's question to be: Why
is it necessary for the entire east to be illuminated since the day really starts at עֲלוֹת
הַשַּׁחַר, daybreak — when light is visible only
at one point of the horizon? Meiri and
Tiferes Yisrael interpret the question of our
mishnah similarly. Accordingly, the precaution not to slaughter the daily sacrifice was
only to prevent the sort of error described
below by the mishnah. Clearly, then, if the
sacrifice were slaughtered (or prayer was
recited) before full light, it is valid so long as

it was performed after daybreak. Vilna Gaon,
however, (Shnos Eliyahu, Berachos 1:1 s.v.
רשב"ג אומר) holds that הֵאִיר פְּנֵי הַמִּזְרָח, the
east has lit up, and עֲלוֹת הַשַּׁחַר, daybreak, are
synonymous. Accordingly Mattisya ben
Shmuel and the first opinion in the mishnah
differ not about the time, but only regarding
the formula which was said. If so, the question with which our mishnah begins must be
understood as Rashi explained, see above.

שֶׁפַּעַם אַחַת עָלָה מְאוֹר הַלְּבָנָה וְדִמּוּ שֶׁהֵאִיר
מִזְרָח, — Because one time the moon's
light rose and they thought that the east
had lit up [i.e., that it was sunlight],

[They therefore instituted visual observation to ascertain that it was truly
sunlight that they were seeing. According to Magen Avraham they instituted the rule not to slaughter the

3
2

'As far as Hebron?'
And he says, 'Yes!'

2. **W**hy was this necessary? Because one time the moon's light rose and they thought that the east had lit up, so they slaughtered the daily sacrifice, and then [had to] take it out to the place of burning. They took the *Kohen Gadol* down to the mikveh. This was the rule in the Temple: Whoever moved

YAD AVRAHAM

sacrifice until the entire east was lit up.]

This incident could not have taken place on Yom Kippur, the tenth of Tishrei, since the moon never rises toward the end of the night in the first half of a month. Although the error took place only once and at the end of the month, they instituted a preventive procedure that insured against the reoccurrence of such an error. The procedure was applied uniformly to every day of the year (*Rav; Rambam*). [See further comments s.v. הורידו כהן גדול.

וְשָׁחֲטוּ אֶת־הַתָּמִיד, וְהוֹצִיאוּהוּ לְבֵית הַשְּׂרֵיפָה — *so they slaughtered the daily sacrifice, and then [had to] take it out* [lit. *took it out*] *to the place* [lit. *house*] *of burning.*

[When they realized that they had slaughtered before daybreak, they took the sacrifice to the place of burning, a special place set aside for the burning of invalidated offerings. See *Pesachim* 7:8.]

הורידו כהן גדול — *They took the Kohen Gadol down*

Here the mishnah returns to its description of the Yom Kippur service begun in mishnah 1. Once the time for slaughtering the daily sacrifice had indeed arrived, the *Kohen Gadol* was taken to the mikveh to immerse himself before the service (*Rav; Gem. 29a with Rashi*).

Rambam (comm.) holds that this segment of the mishnah is connected to the previous discussion, Why was this [visual sighting of

the sun] necessary? He explains that in addition to the misleading moonrise discussed above, the mishnah now states that once, on Yom Kippur, they misjudged the light on the horizon, thinking it was already dawn when it was still night. *Rambam's* version of the mishnah (ed. *Kafih*) reads והורידו *And they took the Kohen Gadol down*, clearly connecting this phrase, which clearly speaks only of Yom Kippur, to the previous discussion. In this instance the *Kohen Gadol* had to re-immerse himself in the mikveh, because the previous immersion, erroneously performed at night, was invalid. All the immersions for the Yom Kippur service had to be done after daybreak (see comm. ed. Kafih; cf. *Meromei HaSadeh*).

לְבֵית הַטְּבִילָה — *to the mikveh.*

[A מִקְוֶה, *mikveh*, is a body of water, such as rain or well water, not drawn by humans, and channeled into an enclosure.]

זֶה הַכְּלָל הָיָה בַמִּקְדָּשׁ: — *This was the rule in the Temple:*

[The *rule* begins here and extends into mishnah 3. Although the mishnah quotes the full rule, only the second part is to needed to explain why the *Kohen Gadol* required immersion before entering the Temple Court.]

כָּל־הַמֵּסִיךְ אֶת־רַגְלָיו טָעוּן טְבִילָה, — *Whoever moved his bowels* [lit. *covered his feet*] *needed immersion,*

Rashi points out that this euphemism is used in *Scripture*, too (*I Samuel 24:3* וַיָּבֹא שָׁאוּל לְהָסֵךְ אֶת־רַגְלָיו). Because a person crouches and modestly covers his body and feet with his clothing

רַגְלָיו טָעוּן טְבִילָה, וְכָל־הַמַּטִּיל מַיִם טָעוּן קִדּוּשׁ יָדַיִם וְרַגְלָיִם.

[ג] אֵין אָדָם נִכְנָס לָעֲזָרָה לָעֲבוֹדָה, אֲפִילוּ טָהוֹר, עַד שֶׁיִּטְבֹּל. חָמֵשׁ טְבִילוֹת וַעֲשָׂרָה קִדּוּשִׁין טוֹבֵל כֹּהֵן גָּדוֹל וּמְקַדֵּשׁ בּוֹ בַיּוֹם, וְכֻלָּן בַּקֹּדֶשׁ עַל־בֵּית הַפַּרְוָה, חוּץ מִזּוֹ בִּלְבָד.

יד אברהם

while relieving himself, the act is euphemistically called 'covering one's feet'.

וְכָל־הַמַּטִּיל מַיִם טָעוּן קִדּוּשׁ יָדַיִם וְרַגְלַיִם — *and whoever urinated needed to wash his hands and his feet* [lit. *sanctification of his hands and feet*].

Rashi adds that this washing of the hands and feet was done from the כִּיוֹר, *laver,* [which stood between the altar and the Temple entrance.]

[*Exodus* 30:17-21 specifies that the *Kohanim* are obligated to wash hands and feet before entering the Temple (אֹהֶל מוֹעֵד) (see *Tosafos* to *Yoma* 5b s.v.

להביא and *Mishneh LaMelech, Bias Mikdash* 5:1; *Sefer HaMitzvos* 24; *Minchas Chinuch* 106), or performing the service (אוֹ בְגִשְׁתָם אֶל־הַמִּזְבֵּחַ). This mishnah evidently refers to a *Kohen* who *had* washed, but then left to *perform* body functions. He had to wash again before resuming the service. *Rambam* (probably assuming that the rule on washing promulgated here is of Rabbinic origin) rules that if the *Kohen* resumes the service without washing he does not invalidate the service. But if the *Kohen* had not washed before, his service is not valid (*Bias Mikdash* 5:1-2,5).]

3.

אֵין אָדָם נִכְנָס לָעֲזָרָה לַעֲבוֹדָה, — *No person may enter the Temple Courtyard for service,*

The word *service* is not meant literally; immersion is required whenever the Courtyard is entered, whether or not service will be performed (*Rashi*).

Tosafos (30a s.v. ומה: אין) concurs, citing evidence from the *Gemara* and the *Yerushalmi. Tosafos* suggests that immersion where service is not involved may be Rabbinic in origin to avoid the possibility that the person *may forget himself* and perform a service without immersion.

Tosafos Yeshanim, however, refutes this evidence, maintaining that only a performance of service (or service-related functions) necessitates immersion. This also seems to be *Rambam's* opinion (*Bias HaMikdash* 5:4).[1]

אֲפִילוּ טָהוֹר, — *even if he is tahor,*

[*Taharah* is the absence of contamination by any of the *tumos* mentioned in the Torah, such as a human corpse, the carcass of an animal not killed through *Shechitah* (kosher slaughter), seminal fluid, menstrual blood, etc. We have not translated *tahor*

1. This controversy is reflected in the variant readings given in *Shinuyei Nuschaos.* Some manuscripts (mentioned in *Ritva*) omit the word לַעֲבוֹדָה, *for service;* accordingly, the mishnah reads simply that one may not enter without immersion. *Tosefos Rid's* reading is וְלָעֲבוֹדָה, *'and' for service,* implying that the mishnah specifies both instances: no person may enter [the Temple Court], nor [may he enter] for service...

his bowels needed immersion and whoever urinated needed to wash his hands and his feet.

3. No person may enter the Temple Courtyard for service even if he is *tahor*, until he immerses himself.

On this day, the *Kohen Gadol* immerses himself five times and washes [his hands and feet] ten times, all of them in the Holy atop the Parvah Chamber, except for this one only.

YAD AVRAHAM

as 'clean' or 'pure' since these words connote *physical* cleanliness rather than *spiritual* purity. No טָמֵא [*tamei*], *contaminated person*, was allowed to enter the Temple (see *Numbers* 5:1-5 with *Rashi*); and any Temple service performed by a *tamei* was invalid. Here, the mishnah sets forth that even a *tahor* had to immerse himself before entering the Temple grounds.]

עַד שֶׁיִּטְבֹּל. — *until he immerses himself* [*in a mikveh*].

This regulation is derived from the law mentioned below that the *Kohen Gadol* required immersions whenever he changed garments and proceeded from the עֲבוֹדַת חוּץ, *service performed* [*on Yom Kippur*] *in the Courtyard*, to עֲבוֹדַת פְּנִים, *the service performed inside the Temple*, and vice versa. Logic dictates that if a *Kohen Gadol* must immerse himself when going from one form of service to another, surely immersion is required of someone making the transition from his regular routine to God's Temple service (*Rav* from *Gem.*).

חָמֵשׁ טְבִילוֹת וַעֲשָׂרָה קִדּוּשִׁין טוֹבֵל כֹּהֵן גָּדוֹל וּמְקַדֵּשׁ בּוֹ בַיּוֹם, — *On this day, the Kohen Gadol immerses himself five times and washes* [*his hands and feet*] *ten times* [lit. *five immersions and ten sanctifications does the Kohen Gadol immerse and sanctify during this day*],

[Mishnah 2 had concluded with the requirement that the *Kohen Gadol* immerse himself on Yom Kippur. Our

mishnah then digressed to discuss some of the general laws of immersion. The Tanna now returns to the order of Yom Kippur.]

That five immersions are mandatory on Yom Kippur is derived from verses in *Leviticus* 16, the chapter dealing with the Yom Kippur. Whenever any *Kohen* embarks on the Temple service, he must immerse himself. In addition every time the *Kohen Gadol* changes from his regular (eight) priestly vestments to the four linen vestments prescribed for the special Yom Kippur service, or back from the linen vestments to the regular vestments, he must immerse himself (see *Leviticus* 16:4 and 24, *Rashi*). There were four such changes, requiring four immersions; The first immersion of the day — the one required before starting any service — brings the total to five.

[Before the *Kohen Gadol* removed either set of vestments, he required קְדּוּשׁ יָדַיִם וְרַגְלַיִם, *washing* (lit. *sanctification*) *of hands and feet* (see mishnah 6). After he donned either set of vestments he was again required to wash. Thus, the four changes of vestments required a total of eight washings. In addition he began the day's service by washing after donning his regular vestments in the morning. The tenth washing preceded the removal of his priestly vestments for the last time at the end of the day.]

וְכֻלָּן בַּקֹּדֶשׁ — *all of them in the Holy* [All these immersions were per-

[ד] **פֵּרְסוּ** סָדִין שֶׁל בּוּץ בֵּינוֹ לְבֵין הָעָם.
פָּשַׁט יָרַד וְטָבַל, עָלָה וְנִסְתַּפֵּג.
הֵבִיאוּ לוֹ בִגְדֵי זָהָב, וְלָבַשׁ; וְקִדֵּשׁ יָדָיו וְרַגְלָיו.
הֵבִיאוּ לוֹ אֶת־הַתָּמִיד. קְרָצוֹ, וּמֵרַק אַחֵר
שְׁחִיטָה עַל־יָדוֹ. קִבֵּל אֶת־הַדָּם וּזְרָקוֹ. נִכְנַס

יד אברהם

formed in the *Holy* — in the Temple Courtyard. The general rule is that immersions that were part of the Yom Kippur service had to be done in the Temple Courtyard; immersions not related to Yom Kippur could be done elsewhere as they were on other days.]

עַל־בֵּית הַפַּרְוָה, — *atop the Parvah Chamber,*

[One of the chambers situated against the southern wall and within the area of the Courtyard was the Parvah Chamber, so called after its builder — Parvah *(Gem. 35a with Rashi).*

Rabbeinu Chananel (cited in *Aruch*), *Tosafos* (35a s.v. פרווה), and *Rambam* *(comm.* to *Midos* 5:3) relate that a Persian magician named Parvah, wishing to observe the service of the *Kohen Gadol* in the קוֹדֶשׁ הַקֳּדָשִׁים, *Holy of Holies,* tunneled under the Temple to reach the Holy of Holies. As he was tunneling, he was caught by the *Kohanim*. The room that was later built over the spot was named the Parvah Chamber.

The Torah stipulates *(Leviticus* 16:24): *And he shall wash his body* [lit. *flesh*] *in a holy place;* consequently the immersion had to take place in the Temple Courtyard. Since the Parvah Cham-

ber was in the Courtyard, its rooftop mikveh satisfied the requirement of *a holy place (Rav* to mishnah 6; see *Tos.* 31a s.v. וכולן).

חוּץ מִזּוֹ בִּלְבָד. — *except for this one only.*

This first immersion of the day was performed not in the קֹדֶשׁ, *Temple Court,* but rather in the *mikveh* situated above the שַׁעַר הַמַּיִם, *Water Gate,* which was in the southern wall of the Courtyard *(Middos* 1:4) near לִשְׁכַּת פַּלְהֶדְרִין, *the Kohen Gadol's chamber.* Because it was situated *atop* the wall (rather than *within* the confines of the Courtyard), and because areas atop the wall were not sanctified *(Pesachim* 86a), this mikveh was not sanctified to the same degree as the Courtyard itself.

This first immersion, mandatory every day, is not part of the special Yom Kippur service; therefore it need not be done in the Holy as is stipulated for the special Yom Kippur immersions *(Rashi* here; *Rav* to mishnah 6; see also *Rashi* to 32b with *Tosefos R' Akiva* to mishnah 6 and *comm.* there). The subsequent four immersions, mandatory as part of the Yom Kippur service, must take place in the Holy area.

4.

פֵּרְסוּ סָדִין שֶׁל בּוּץ בֵּינוֹ לְבֵין הָעָם. — *They spread a linen sheet between him and the people.*

Linen was picked as the material for that partition to serve as a reminder to the *Kohen Gadol* that he must perform the day's special service in linen vestments *(Rav* from *Gem.* 31b).

פָּשַׁט יָרַד וְטָבַל, עָלָה וְנִסְתַּפֵּג. — *He undressed, descended* [into the *mikveh*], *immersed himself, ascended, and dried himself.*

So as not to wet his vestments *(Tiferes Yisrael).*

Mishneh LaMelech (Avodas Yom HaKippurim 2:2) suggests that because of halachic

4. **T**hey spread a linen sheet between him and the people. He undressed, descended, immersed himself, ascended, and dried himself. They brought him golden vestments, and he donned them; then he washed his hands and feet. They brought him the daily offering. He made the incision and another completed the slaughter for him. He received the blood and threw it.

consideration the Kohen Gadol was obligated to dry himself; the water might contain dirt or materials that would adhere to his body, which would constitute a חֲצִיצָה, *barrier*, if they kept the vestments from lying directly upon his flesh as required by the Torah. Therefore the *Kohen Gadol* was *obligated* to dry himself to remove any such foreign matter. It is possible, however, that the mishnah here is simply relating what was done without implying any halachic obligation to do so.

הֵבִיאוּ לוֹ בִגְדֵי זָהָב, וְלָבַשׁ — *They brought him golden vestments and he donned them;*

Because the special vestments of the *Kohen Gadol* contained gold, they were known as the golden vestments. For a detailed description of these vestments (see *Exodus* 28:1-39; comm. to 7:5).

וְקִדֵּשׁ יָדָיו וְרַגְלָיו. — *then he washed* [lit. *sanctified*] *his hands and feet.*

From the כִּיּוֹר, *laver (Rashi* and *Rav).* [See *comm.* to 3:6 s.v. קִדֵּשׁ יָדָיו וְרַגְלָיו.]

Tosefos Yom Tov notes an apparent contradiction: Mishnah 4:5 says that the *Kohen Gadol* washed his hands from a golden pitcher, not the *laver.*

Lechem Shamayim and *Kol HaRemez* understand *Rashi* to mean that the water was taken from the laver to fill the golden pitcher. *Lechem Shamayim* finds halachic grounds for this.

Many (*Siach Yitzchak; Lechem Shamayim; Avodas Yisrael* p. 27;

Shoshanim L'David) explain that the golden pitcher was used only for the nine special Yom Kippur washings. But because the first washing was done every day, it was done directly from the laver as every day (according to the first opinion in 4:5).[1]

Siach Yitzchak notes that *Yerushalmi* (4:5) records a difference of opinion whether the first washing was done from the golden pitcher or the laver.

הֵבִיאוּ לוֹ אֶת־הַתָּמִיד. קְרָצוֹ, — *they brought him the daily offering. He made the incision,*

I.e., he made an incision (שְׁחִיטָה) that severed most of the trachea and the esophagus, so that the minimum requirement of kosher slaughter would be done by the *Kohen Gadol* (*Rav* from *Gem.* 32b).

וּמֵרֵק אַחֵר שְׁחִיטָה עַל־יָדוֹ. — *and another completed the slaughter for him.*

Since all the service of the day had to be done by the *Kohen Gadol*, he had to be available immediately to receive the blood [קַבָּלַת הַדָּם]. Once he had completed enough of the slaughter to validate it, another *Kohen* completed the incision, thereby freeing the *Kohen Gadol* to receive the blood (*Rav; Rashi*).

[*Meiri* and *Ritva* (above 2:3 s.v. מִי שׁוֹחֵט) hold that the תָּמִיד, *daily offering*, had to be slaughtered by a *Kohen*. See also *Yesh Seder LaMishnah*.]

Rashi (in an alternate opinion) renders

---

1. If the golden pitcher was used for the first washing, too, it might be carried to the *Kohen Gadol* outside the Temple Courtyard. That would disqualify the water and invalidate the washing (*Lechem Shamayim*; see *Zevachim* 20b; *Rambam, Bias HaMikdash* 5:10).

לְהַקְטִיר קְטֹרֶת שֶׁל שַׁחַר, וּלְהֵטִיב אֶת־הַנֵּרוֹת. וּלְהַקְרִיב אֶת־הָרֹאשׁ וְאֶת־הָאֵבָרִים, וְאֶת־ הַחֲבִתִּין וְאֶת־הַיָּיִן.

[ה] **קְטֹרֶת** שֶׁל שַׁחַר הָיְתָה קְרֵבָה בֵּין דָּם לָאֵבָרִים; שֶׁל בֵּין הָעַרְבַּיִם — בֵּין אֵבָרִים לַנְּסָכִים.

אִם הָיָה כֹהֵן גָּדוֹל זָקֵן אוֹ אִסְטְנִיס, מְחַמִּין

יד אברהם

עַל־יָדוֹ, *close by it,* i.e., immediately following the *Kohen Gadol's* incision.[1]

The *Gemara* (33a) says that completion of the incision was necessary to facilitate the flow of blood that was to be brought to the altar by the *Kohen Gadol* (*Rashi* and *Tosafos* there).

קִבֵּל אֶת־הַדָּם וּזְרָקוֹ. — *He received the blood* [in a vessel] *and threw it.*

[He tossed the blood from the vessel onto the northeast and southwest corners of the altar. He tossed enough blood on the bottom half of each corner for the blood to spread out along both adjoining walls in order to fulfill the requirement that the blood be thrown *all around the altar* (*Leviticus* 1:5). This procedure was followed for all עוֹלוֹת, *burnt offerings.*]

נִכְנַס לְהַקְטִיר קְטֹרֶת שֶׁל שַׁחַר, — *He entered* [the Temple] *to burn the morning incense,*

[This refers not to the special Yom Kippur incense offering, but to the daily incense that was offered every morning and afternoon on the golden altar inside the Holy (see *Exodus* 30:1.]

וּלְהֵטִיב אֶת הַנֵּרוֹת. — *and to prepare the lamps* [of the menorah].

This too, was a daily service as specified in *Exodus* 30:10, *When he prepares the lamps he shall burn it* [the incense]. According to some authorities (whose opinion is reflected in the translation), this service consisted of cleaning out the lamps and inserting new oil and wicks. *Rambam* holds that הַטָבָה refers specifically to *relighting* the menorah. For a detailed discussion of whether the removal of the ashes and oil was done by the *Kohen Gadol*, see *comm.* to 1:2 s.v. וּמֵטִיב אֶת־הַנֵּרוֹת and 2:3 s.v. וּמִי מְדַשֵּׁן אֶת־הַמְּנוֹרָה.

וּלְהַקְרִיב אֶת־הָרֹאשׁ וְאֶת־הָאֵבָרִים, — *He offered* [lit. *and to offer*] *the head and the limbs,*

[After the sacrifice had been dissected and the limbs deposited as usual on the lower half of the ramp, the *Kohen Gadol* ascended the ramp and tossed the limbs upon the fire.]

[Though the mishnah does not mention that the *Kohen Gadol* had to carry the limbs, that he did so is implicit in the discussion of the commentators about the Yom Kippur lots (see prefatory comments to chapter 2). I have not found this discussed explicitly anywhere. See *Kol HaRemez* cited above 1:2 s.v. וּמַקְרִיב אֶת־הָרֹאשׁ.]

וְאֶת הַחֲבִיתִּין — *the chavitin meal offering*

[See above 2:3 s.v. חֲבִיתִּין.]

וְאֶת הַיָּיִן. — *and the wine.*

Tos. Yom Tov asks why the mishnah does not mention the meal offering that came with the daily sacrifice (see above 2:3 s. v. וְהַסֹּלֶת). *Tosafos*

1. *Chullin* 32a discusses the validity of a slaughtering which is interrupted before completion (see *Rashi* there; *Yoreh Deah* 23:5 and *Shach* there, 27).

3
5

He entered [the Temple] to burn the morning incense, and to prepare the lamps. He offered the head and the limbs, the *chavitin* meal offering and the wine.

5. The morning incense was offered between the blood and the limbs; that of the afternoon — between the limbs and the *nesachim*.

If the *Kohen Gadol* was old or delicate, they

YAD AVRAHAM

Yeshanim (32b s.v. ואת החביתין) maintains that it is included in *chavitin* which, like it, was a daily meal offering.

Rambam's (Avodas Yom HaKippurim 4:1) summary of the mishnah

substitutes נְסָכִים, *libation*, for יַיִן, *wine*. As pointed out by *Tosefos R' Akiva*, the *nesachim* of the daily sacrifice includes both the wine and the flour for the meal offering.

קְטוֹרֶת שֶׁל שַׁחַר הָיְתָה קְרֵבָה בֵּין דָם לְאֵבָרִים; — *The morning incense was offered* [every day] *between the* [throwing of the] *blood and the* [offering of the] *limbs* [of the daily offering];

Although the mishnah implies that the limbs were tossed on the fire immediately after the burning of the incense, this was not the actual practice. Following the incense offering, the lamps were prepared (הֲטָבַת הַנֵּרוֹת); only then were the limbs burned.

The intention of our mishnah is not to give the complete and exact sequence of the service. The point advanced here is that at least one service h.d to intervene between the throwing of the blood and the offering of the limbs. This minimum requirement was met by inserting the service of incense between them. In practice, however, the lamps, too, were prepared at that point (*Rav* from *Gem.* 34a).

The incense was burned before completion of the *tamid* service because of a Scriptural implication. In prescribing the time for incense the Torah uses the words (*Exod.* 30:7): בַּבֹּקֶר בַּבֹּקֶר, *every morning* [lit. *in the morning, in the morning*]. The repetition implies that the service should be done *early* in the

morning. In the case of the *tamid*, however, the Torah uses the word בַּבֹּקֶר, *in the morning*, only once (*Numbers* 28:4; *Gem.* 33b).

שֶׁל בֵּין הָעַרְבַּיִם— — *that of the afternoon*—

[The daily incense offered in the afternoon.]

בֵּין אֵבָרִים לַנְּסָכִים. — *between the* [offering of the] *limbs and the nesachim.*

The word נְסָכִים, literally *libations*, usually refers to the wine poured on the altar with sacrifices (see comm. to 2:3 s.v. וְהַיַּיִן). In this mishnah, however, the term includes the *minchah* [meal offering (called הַסֹּלֶת in 2:3)] as well as the wine (*Rambam, Ma'aseh HaKorbanos* 2:1). The incense described here preceded the libation and the flour (*Gem.* 34a), both of which are included in the term נְסָכִים. Therefore we have not used the common translation *libations.*

אִם הָיָה כֹהֵן גָּדוֹל זָקֵן אוֹ אִסְטְנִיס, — *If the Kohen Gadol was old or delicate,*

[... and so he could not bear the cold water of the *mikveh*, which came directly from the spring of Eitam.]

לוֹ חַמִּין וּמַטִּילִין לְתוֹךְ הַצּוֹנֵן, כְּדֵי שֶׁתָּפִיג צִנָּתָן.

[ו] הֱבִיאוּהוּ לְבֵית הַפַּרְוָה, וּבַקֹּדֶשׁ הָיְתָה. פֵּרְסוּ סָדִין שֶׁל בּוּץ בֵּינוֹ לְבֵין הָעָם. קִדֵּשׁ יָדָיו וְרַגְלָיו, וּפָשַׁט. רַבִּי מֵאִיר אוֹמֵר: פָּשַׁט, קִדֵּשׁ יָדָיו וְרַגְלָיו. יָרַד וְטָבַל, עָלָה וְנִסְתַּפֵּג. הֵבִיאוּ לוֹ בִגְדֵי לָבָן, לָבַשׁ וְקִדֵּשׁ יָדָיו וְרַגְלָיו.

יד אברהם

מֵחַמִּין לוֹ חַמִּין — *they warmed water* [lit. *heated hot water*] *for him*

Before Yom Kippur, since it is forbidden to cook water on Yom Kippur (*Rav*).

The *Gemara* (34b) cites R' Yehudah in the *Tosefta* who states that they

heated thick pieces of iron which they put into the water when needed.[1]

וּמַטִּילִין לְתוֹךְ הַצּוֹנֵן שֶׁתָּפִיג צִנָּתָן — *and poured it into the cold water so that it should lose* [lit. *so that you should remove*] *its chill.*

6.

הֱבִיאוּהוּ לְבֵית הַפַּרְוָה, וּבַקֹּדֶשׁ הָיְתָה. — *They brought him to the Parvah Chamber, which was in the holy area.*

[I.e., the sanctified area within the Temple Courtyard walls (see mishnah 3 s.v. עַל־בֵּית הַפַּרְוָה).]

This second immersion and those following it had to take place in the Temple Courtyard as it is written (*Leviticus* 16:20): *And he shall wash his flesh in a holy place* (*Rav* from *Rashi* to 30a s.v. חוּץ מזו; see *comm.* to mishnah 3 s.v. חוּץ מזו).

פֵּרְסוּ סָדִין שֶׁל בּוּץ בֵּינוֹ לְבֵין הָעָם. — *They spread a linen sheet between him and the people.*

[See *comm.* to mishnah 4 s.v. פֵּרְסוּ סָדִין שֶׁל בּוּץ.]

קִדֵּשׁ יָדָיו וְרַגְלָיו, וּפָשַׁט. רַבִּי מֵאִיר אוֹמֵר: פָּשַׁט, קִדֵּשׁ יָדָיו וְרַגְלָיו. — *He washed* [lit. *sanctified*] *his hands and feet, and* [then] *undressed. R' Meir said:* [First] *he undressed,* [then] *he washed his hands and feet.*

According to the opinion accepted by *Rashi* and *Tosefos Yom Tov*, the

---

1. Two approaches are found in the commentators as to the relation between the *Tosefta* and our mishnah.

Rashi and *Rav* (based on *Yerushalmi*) do not offer any interpretation for the word חַמִּין. This silence indicates that the word is used in its usual sense, *hot water* [see for example, *Shabbos* 3:1, *Maasros* 4:4]. Thus, R' Yehudah's method of using heated bars is ignored by our tanna, who disallows it. The translation follows this opinion.

Rambam, on the other hand, seems to interpret R' Yehudah's statement in the *Tosefta* as an elaboration of our mishnah, for he (ed. *Kafih*) adds: However, if hot water is sufficient … this is also permissible. Thus, *Rambam* seems to understand חַמִּין in the sense of hot *things* rather than hot *water*.

Mayim Chaim (*Avodas Yom HaKippurim* 2:4 cited in *Tos. R' Akiva*) points out that *Rambam's* opinion would explain why the mishnah mentions this method for heating the water

warmed water for him and poured it into the cold water so that it should lose its chill.

6. **T**hey brought him to the Parvah Chamber, which was in the holy area. They spread a linen sheet between him and the people. He washed his hands and feet, and undressed. R' Meir said: He undressed [then] he washed his hands and feet.

He went down and immersed himself, ascended and dried himself. They brought him white vestments, he dressed and washed his hands and feet.

YAD AVRAHAM

Gemara (31b) explains that R' Meir agrees that two washings were necessary for every change of vestments, but he disagrees about their purpose. The first tanna holds that the first washing was directly preparatory to the *Kohen Gadol's* removal of his vestments, and therefore had to be done while he was still wearing them. But R' Meir holds that the first washing was in preparation for the donning of the next set of vestments, therefore it was performed after the *Kohen Gadol* had undressed, one before the immersion, the second after donning the new vestments.

The *Gemara* adds that according to R' Meir, even when the *Kohen Gadol* changed from his personal clothes into the golden vestments in the morning (mishnah 3) two washings were needed. Accordingly, by the time he had completed the day's service and was ready to change back into his personal clothing, he had already completed the total of ten washings prescribed above

in mishnah 3, two washings for each of the five changes of vestments. According to the first tanna, however, the ten washings are: one upon donning the golden vestments in the morning; two washings for each of the four changes from one set of vestments to the other; and one more washing before removing the vestments after the service.

יָרַד וְטָבַל, — *He went down and immersed himself,*

[In the *mikveh* on the roof of the Parvah Chamber.]

עָלָה וְנִסְתַּפֵּג. הֵבִיאוּ לוֹ בִגְדֵי לָבָן, — *he ascended and dried himself. They brought him white* [i.e., linen] *vestments,*

[See *comm.* to 3:4 s.v. עָלָה וְנִסְתַּפֵּג.]

There were four linen garments: the כְּתֹנֶת, *tunic;* מִכְנָסַיִם, *pants;* מִצְנֶפֶת, *turban* (see *Rambam, Klei HaMikdash* 8:19; *Exodus* 28:4 with *Rashi* and *Ramban*), and אַבְנֵט, *belt* or *girdle* (all specified in *Leviticus* 16:4). These vest-

only with regard to the second immersion, but fails to mention it in mishnah 2 regarding the first immersion which took place early in the cool morning, when an old or delicate man would surely need warm water. The heating of the water with a hot iron involved violating a Rabbinic restriction (see *Gem.* 34b with *Tosafos* s.v. הני). Because of the rule that where circumstances so dictate: אֵין שְׁבוּת בְּמִקְדָּשׁ, *Rabbinic restrictions do not apply in the Temple,* it was permitted to warm the water for a *Kohen Gadol in* the Temple Courtyard where the last four immersions of the day took place. But the first immersion took place outside the Temple Courtyard (mishnah 3), so the Rabbinic law forbidding the heating of water with pieces of iron had to be observed despite the *Kohen Gadol's* infirmity.

Tiferes Yisrael notes that the mishnah mentions the permission to heat water only in connection with an infirm *Kohen Gadol;* even in the Temple, restrictions are relaxed only in a case of genuine need.

[ז] **בַּשַּׁחַר** הָיָה לוֹבֵשׁ פְּלוּסִין שֶׁל שְׁנַיִם
עָשָׂר מָנֶה, וּבֵין הָעַרְבַּיִם הִנְדְּוִין
שֶׁל שְׁמֹנֶה מֵאוֹת זוּז; דִּבְרֵי רַבִּי מֵאִיר.
וַחֲכָמִים אוֹמְרִים: בַּשַּׁחַר הָיָה לוֹבֵשׁ שֶׁל
שְׁמוֹנָה עָשָׂר מָנֶה, וּבֵין הָעַרְבַּיִם' שֶׁל שְׁנַיִם
עָשָׂר מָנֶה, הַכֹּל שְׁלֹשִׁים מָנֶה.
אֵלּוּ מִשֶּׁל צִבּוּר; וְאִם רָצָה לְהוֹסִיף, מוֹסִיף
מִשֶּׁלּוֹ.

יד אברהם

ments were required for the Yom Kippur services performed in the Holy and in the Holy of Holies *(Rav)*.

[They were all made of pure linen as specified in the Torah *(ibid.)*, and were called בִּגְדֵי לָבָן, *white vestments*, to distinguish them from the בִּגְדֵי זָהָב, *golden vestments* some of which contained gold thread, תְּכֵלֶת, *blue wool*; אַרְגָמָן, *purple wool*; and תּוֹלַעַת שָׁנִי, *crimson wool*; in addition to linen.]

לָבַשׁ וְקִדֵּשׁ יָדָיו וְרַגְלָיו — *he dressed and [then] washed his hands and feet.*

R' Meir agrees that the second washing takes place when the *Kohen Gadol* is already dressed. The *Gemara* (32b) derives from Scripture that the *Kohanim* (on Yom Kippur as well as all year round) must be ready for service immediately after washing. Thus they must be dressed when washing their hands and feet.

7.

בַּשַּׁחַר — *In the morning*
[He donned the linen vestments twice. Once in the morning, and again in the afternoon.]

הָיָה לוֹבֵשׁ פְּלוּסִין — *he put on Pelusian [linen]*

The garments were made of linen produced at Pelusium in Egypt, which was of the finest quality *(Rashi, Rav;* see *Mosaf HeAruch* s.v. פלס*)*. *Rav* (and *Bach*) adds that *Targum Yerushalmi* renders *Ra'amseis* (*Exodus* 1:11) פִּילוּסָא.

Aruch (s.v. פלס) and *R' Chananel* translate פְּלוּסִין, *clothing*. They seem to have been followed by *Rambam* who says *(Comm. to Mishnah)*, pelusin and hindevin are types of vestments which were known in their time. They differed from one another in cut only but their material was white linen... *Mosaf HeAruch* (s.v. הנדוי) identifies them (according to *Aruch*) as a type of tunic worn over the shirt. The closest thing to this among the white vestments is the כְּתֹנֶת.

The placement of this mishnah here indicates the *Kohen Gadol* donned this special tunic only after the second immersion. It follows that when he put on his regular priestly vestments after the first immersion, even though these included a linen tunic it was a tunic of another cut (or kind). Thus the *Kohen Gadol* wore three different tunics on Yom Kippur: one with his golden vestments, and a different one each of the two times he donned his white vestments. This resolves most of *Mishneh LaMelech's* questions *(Siach Yitzchak* p. 351 quoting *R' Benjamin Espinoza)*.

שֶׁל שְׁנַיִם עָשָׂר מָנֶה — *worth* [lit. *of*] *twelve maneh,*

[The *maneh* was a large coin worth twenty-five *sela*, each of which was equivalent to four *zuzim* or *dinarim*. According to *Rambam's* tradition (comm. to *Berachos* 8:7, see *Yoreh Deah* 305:1 with *Beur HaGra*) a פְּרוּטָה, *perutah*, equals half a barley grain of silver. A *zuz* (192 *perutos*; see *Kid-*

7. **I**n the morning he put on Pelusian linen worth twelve *maneh,* and in the afternoon, Indian [linen] worth eight hundred *zuz;* these are the words of Rabbi Meir.

But the Sages say: In the morning he donned [linen] worth eighteen *maneh,* and in the afternoon [linen] worth twelve *maneh,* all worth together thirty *maneh.*

These came from the public [treasury]; but if he wishes to add, he may do so from his own.

YAD AVRAHAM

dushin 12a) would then equal ninety-six barley grains of silver. *Chazon Ish (Yoreh Deah* 192:19) calculates this as 4.8 grams of silver, and a *maneh* is thus 480 grams or 15.5 troy ounces of silver. These vestments, at 12 *maneh,* were equivalent in value to 186 troy ounces of silver.

וּבֵין הָעַרְבַּיִם, הִנְדְּוִין — *and in the afternoon, Indian* [linen]

He wore vestments of Indian linen when he returned to the Holy of Holies to remove the vessels he had used when burning the incense *(Rashi; Rav).*

Rashi, relying on *Targum Yonasan* to *Jeremiah* 13:23, renders הִנְדְּוִין, *Ethiopian. Tosefos Yom Tov,* however, finds support for *Rav's* rendition in *Targum* to *Esther* 1:1.

Aruch here again renders *clothing.*

שֶׁל שְׁמוֹנֶה מֵאוֹת זוּז; — *worth eight hundred zuz;*

[According to *Chazon Ish's* computation this would amount to 124 troy ounces of silver.]

דִּבְרֵי רַבִּי מֵאִיר. — *these are the words of Rabbi Meir.*

וַחֲכָמִים אוֹמְרִים: בַּשַּׁחַר הָיָה לוֹבֵשׁ שֶׁל שְׁמוֹנָה עָשָׂר מָנֶה, — *But the Sages say: In the morning he donned* [linen] *worth eighteen maneh,*

[By the above calculation, 279 troy ounces.]

וּבֵין הָעַרְבַּיִם, שֶׁל שְׁנַיִם עָשָׂר מָנֶה, הַכֹּל; שְׁלֹשִׁים מָנֶה. — *and in the afternoon,* [linen] *worth twelve maneh; all worth*

together thirty maneh.

Provided the total value of the morning and afternoon vestments was this amount, the precise division of value between the two sets of vestments was immaterial *(Rav* from *Gem.* 35a).

However, the morning vestments were the more valuable of the two because the Torah places greater emphasis on them *(Gem.* 35a with *Rashi).*

אֵלוּ מִשֶּׁל צִבּוּר; — *These* [amounts] *came from the public* [treasury];

The money for the vestments came from the half-*shekels* which all Jews contributed once a year to pay for the requirements of the Temple service [תְּרוּמַת הַלִּשְׁכָּה]. They were deposited in a Temple לִשְׁכָּה, *chamber.* Three times a year a container full of money was taken from the chamber for Temple expenses (see *Shekalim* 3:1-2, 4:1). *Rambam* (based upon *Tosefta Yoma* 1:17) states that the vestments of all the *Kohanim* were purchased from these funds *(Shekalim* 4:1; see *Tos. Yom Tov* here).

וְאִם רָצָה לְהוֹסִיף, מוֹסִיף מִשֶּׁלּוֹ. — *but if he wishes to add* [to these amounts], *he may do so* [lit. *he adds*] *from his own.*

However, should he wish to do so, he must contribute his private funds' to the Temple treasury before he may use them to purchase garments for the Yom Kippur service. Since his service is for the sake of the nation, it must be done in garments belonging to the nation *(Gem.* 35b; *Rashi).*

Meiri and *Ritva* add that even where

[ח] **בָּא** לוֹ אֵצֶל פָּרוֹ, וּפָרוֹ הָיָה עוֹמֵד בֵּין הָאוּלָם וְלַמִּזְבֵּחַ, רֹאשׁוֹ לַדָּרוֹם וּפָנָיו לַמַּעֲרָב.

וְהַכֹּהֵן עוֹמֵד בַּמִּזְרָח וּפָנָיו לַמַּעֲרָב, וְסוֹמֵךְ שְׁתֵּי יָדָיו עָלָיו, וּמִתְוַדֶּה.

יד אברהם

the *Kohen Gadol* personally increased the amount used for the vestments, the

morning vestments had to be costlier, as explained above, s.v. הַכֹּל שְׁלשִׁים מָנֶה.

8.

בָּא לוֹ אֵצֶל פָּרוֹ, — He [then] comes to his ox,

[Among the Yom Kippur sacrifices was an ox designated to be a חַטָּאת, *sin offering*, for the *Kohen Gadol (Leviticus 16:3)* which was purchased with his own money (*Rashi* there) and which atoned for the him, his family, and all the *Kohanim*. The blood of this ox was sprinkled in the Holy and in the Holy of Holies. Its service, therefore, required the 'white vestments' as stipulated in *Leviticus 16:4*.]

וּפָרוֹ הָיָה עוֹמֵד בֵּין הָאוּלָם וְלַמִּזְבֵּחַ, — and his ox was standing between the antechamber and the altar,

[In front of the entrance to the Temple there was a huge room, called אוּלָם, *antechamber*, sixteen cubits wide from east to west (including the thickness of its walls), and a hundred cubits long from north to south.]

This spot was chosen for the

slaughter to minimize the distance that the *Kohen Gadol* would have to carry the vessel containing the blood for sprinkling in the Holy and the Holy of Holies. Because his fasting would weaken him, care was taken to spare him any unnecessary effort (*Rav* from *Gem.* 36a).

Certain sacrifices, such as sin offerings, guilt offerings, and burnt offerings (חַטָּאות, אֲשָׁמות, עולות), had to be slaughtered on the צָפון, *north side*, of the altar. There is disagreement in the *Gemara* (36a) about the exact boundaries of the north side for this purpose. According to R' Yose ben R' Yehudah, the 'north' is limited to the area directly opposite the altar, from it to the northern wall, but the areas to the northwest and northeast — though north of the altar — are not included because they are not opposite it. R' Elazar ben R' Shimon holds that the entire area north of the altar from the antechamber to the north wall — including the northeast — is included. Rabbi [רֵבִּי] holds that the entire northern half of the Temple Courtyard, in-

---

1. Another three-way controversy further complicates matters. R' Yose holds that the altar was entirely in the northern half of the Temple Courtyard (*Zevachim* 58a). R' Yehudah (*Zevachim* 58b) holds that the altar stood in the center of the Temple Courtyard. R' Eliezer ben Yaakov (*Zevachim* 59a) holds that the entire altar was in the southern half of the Temple Courtyard. The mishnah in *Middos* (5:2) may represent yet a fourth opinion; see *Yoma* 16b with *Rashi* and *Tosafos*.

The *Gemara* (37a) deduces that mishnah 9, which specifies that the two he-goats had to be taken to the north of the altar, is of the opinion that the altar was situated entirely in the southern half of the Temple Court. Therefore, one may not slaughter a sin offering between the altar and the antechamber as our mishnah seems to indicate. The *Gemara* concludes that our mishnah means that they stood the ox in the area *adjacent* to the space between the altar and the antechamber as near as possible to the midpoint between the northern and southern halves of the Court — i.e., northwest of the northwestern corner of the altar in front of the northern half of the antechamber entrance.

8. He [then] comes to his ox; and his ox was standing between the antechamber and the altar, its head to the south and its face to the west.

The Kohen [Gadol] stands to the east facing west, and he supports both his hands upon it, and he confesses.

YAD AVRAHAM

cluding both the northeast and northwest, is included. Our mishnah concurs with one of the latter opinions. (See diagram).

* The diagram places the altar in the southern part of the Temple Court for the purpose of illustration. The exact location of the altar is the subject of a dispute in *Zevachim* 58a-59a. (See footnote below).

רֹאשׁוֹ לַדָּרוֹם וּפָנָיו לַמַּעֲרָב. — *its head to the south* [i.e., the animal's head to the south and its body to the north] *and its face to the west* [i.e., its head was turned westward].

Ideally it should have been placed to face west, toward the Holy of Holies — i.e., to face the *Shechinah*. But this would have caused the animal's rump to be turned toward the altar, where it would cause a desecration if it were to defecate. Therefore, the animal was made to stand on a north-south line with only its face turned westward toward the Holy of Holies (*Rav* from *Gem.* 36b).

וְהַכֹּהֵן עוֹמֵד בַּמִּזְרָח וּפָנָיו לַמַּעֲרָב, — *The Kohen [Gadol] stands to the east [of the ox] facing west,*

With his back to the east (*Rashi; Rav*).

[In honor of the *Shechinah* in the Holy of Holies.]

וְסוֹמֵךְ שְׁתֵּי יָדָיו עָלָיו, — *and he supports both his hands upon it,*

The *Kohen Gadol* put his two hands between its horns and leaned on the animal. This סְמִיכָה [*semichah*], *leaning,* had to be performed upon all sacrifices brought by an individual. It was always accompanied by a confession similar to the one mentioned below. The person performing *semichah* had to push down with all his might and be sure there was no substance separating his hands from the animal's head [חֲצִיצָה] (*Gem.* 36a; *Rambam, Ma'aseh HaKorbanos* 3:6-15).

וּמִתְוַדֶּה. — *and he confesses.*

◆§ Which Area is Considered צָפוֹן, North: Three Views

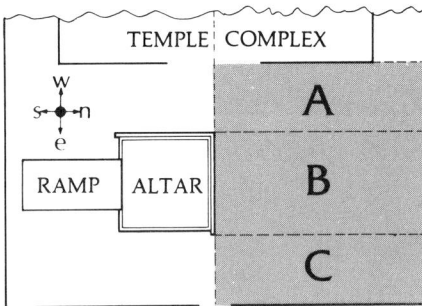

1. According to R' Yose ben R' Yehudah only area B (directly opposite the altar) is considered North;

2. According to R' Elazar ben R' Shimon areas A and B (north and northwest of the altar) are considered North;

3. According to Rabbi the entire northern half of the Inner Courtyard (areas A, B, and C) are considered North.

Shaded area indicates complete Northern half of the Inner Courtyard.

וְכָךְ הָיָה אוֹמֵר: „אָנָּא הַשֵּׁם, עָוִיתִי פָּשַׁעְתִּי חָטָאתִי לְפָנֶיךָ, אֲנִי וּבֵיתִי. אָנָּא הַשֵּׁם, כַּפֶּר־נָא לָעֲוֹנוֹת וְלַפְּשָׁעִים וְלַחֲטָאִים, שֶׁעָוִיתִי וְשֶׁפָּשַׁעְתִּי וְשֶׁחָטָאתִי לְפָנֶיךָ אֲנִי וּבֵיתִי, כַּכָּתוּב בְּתוֹרַת מֹשֶׁה עַבְדֶּךָ: „כִּי בַיּוֹם הַזֶּה יְכַפֵּר עֲלֵיכֶם וְגוֹ׳.‟

וְהֵן עוֹנִין אַחֲרָיו: „בָּרוּךְ שֵׁם כְּבוֹד מַלְכוּתוֹ לְעוֹלָם וָעֶד.‟

יד אברהם

As specified in *Leviticus* 16:6, *And he shall atone* [i.e., confess for] *himself and his family* [lit., *house*].

וְכָךְ הָיָה אוֹמֵר: „אָנָּא הַשֵּׁם, — *He would say the following: 'I beg of You, HASHEM,*

He pronounced the Four-Letter Name of God, as it is written, a pronunciation which is ordinarily forbidden. Therefore the mishnah substitutes the euphemism HASHEM (lit. *the Name*).[1]

Tur (Orach Chaim 621) cites *R' Hai Gaon's* opinion that the *Kohen Gadol* did not utter the Four-Letter Name, but the sacred Name which contains forty-two letters שֵׁם שֶׁל מ״ב; see *Kiddushin* 71a).

עָוִיתִי פָּשַׁעְתִּי חָטָאתִי לְפָנֶיךָ, — *I have acted wickedly, rebelled, and sinned before You,*

The Sages said; עֲוֹנוֹת, are *sins done*

deliberately [מֵזִיד]; פְּשָׁעִים are *sins done rebelliously* [מָרְדִים]; חֲטָאִים are *sins done through negligence* [שׁוֹגֵג] (*Gem.* 36b).

The *Gemara* cites the Sages who hold that the *Kohen Gadol* recited the confession in a sequence that placed lesser sins first — חָטָאתִי עָוִתי פָּשַׁעְתִּי, *I have sinned, acted wickedly, and rebelled.* It would be illogical for him to ask forgiveness for the lesser sins when he had already asked forgiveness for the graver sins (see *Rashi* there).

The sequence of the sins in our mishnah is R' Meir's (*ibid.*), and is based upon the verse (*Lev.* 16:21) that deals with the Yom Kippur service.[2] While R' Meir concurs with the Sages about the meaning of these terms, he maintains that their sequence need not reflect the severity of the sins but what is

1. In order to indicate the fact that the *Kohen Gadol* used this unusual pronunciation on Yom Kippur, our recitation of the סֵדֶר הָעֲבוֹדָה, *Order of the Service*, in the Yom Kippur *Mussaf* uses the word הַשֵּׁם, *the Name*, in place of God's Four-Letter Name (*Tos. Yom Tov*). However, *Bach* and others hold that in our Yom Kippur *Mussaf* God's Name should be pronounced as it usually is (*Orach Chaim* 621).

When the *Kohen Gadol* recited the words from the Torah לִפְנֵי ה׳ תִּטְהָרוּ, *before* HASHEM *you will be purified* (see below) he uttered the Name again with its unusual pronunciation. Nevertheless when the congregation recites that verse, we do not say the word HASHEM; instead we use our usual rendering of the Four-Letter Name as we always do when repeating a Scriptural verse. That this is so is indicated in 4:1 where, in quoting the verse, the Mishnah uses the usual abbreviation ה׳ rather than the word הַשֵּׁם (*Magen Avraham* to *Orach Chaim* 621:3).

2. The sequence of the *Kohen Gadol's* confession as we recite it in the Yom Kippur *Mussaf* service is the one set forth by the Sages (not that of R' Meir as in our mishnah; *Gem.* 36b; *Rashi* s.v. ההוא דנחית).

The same sequence is followed during the personal confession in all the Yom Kippur prayers (*Shulchan Aruch Orach Chaim* 621:5).

He would say the following: 'I beg of You, HASHEM, I have acted wickedly, rebelled, and sinned before You, I and my household. I beg of You, HASHEM, forgive now, the wicked acts, rebellions and sins, for I have acted wickedly, rebelled, and sinned before You, I and my household, as is written in the Torah of Your servant Moses [*Leviticus* 16:30]: "For on this day he will atone for you" ...'

And they answer after him: "Blessed is the Name — the glory of His Kingship — forever and ever."

YAD AVRAHAM

foremost in the mind of the supplant. The עֲוֹנוֹת, *deliberate sins*, because of their prevalence and frequency, concern a person more than the less prevalent פְּשָׁעִים, *rebellious sins*. The חֲטָאִים, *careless sins*, disturb him least. Only when one has purged himself of his grave sins, does he feel concern and culpability for lesser sins *(Maharsha)*.

אֲנִי וּבֵיתִי. — *I and my household* [lit. house].

[Scripture requires the *Kohen Gadol* to specify בֵּיתוֹ, *his household*, in his confession (*Lev.* 16:7). The mishnah (1:1) understands the term to refer specifically to his wife, but *Targum Onkelos* and *Yonasan* render it אֲנַשׁ בֵּיתֵהּ, literally, *the people of his house.* We may thus infer that this word can be understood in a broader sense, too.

אָנָּא הַשֵּׁם, — *I beg of You, HASHEM,*

Yerushalmi states that the text here should read בַּשֵּׁם (cf. 6:2), i.e., he recited the proper Four-Letter Name of God with the prefix בּ, *beis. Rosh* holds that although our mishnah reads הַשֵּׁם, the *Kohen Gadol* actually said בַּשֵּׁם.

Thus here we should render, *I beg of You, for the sake of Your Name. Turei Zahav* (621:2) adds that the *Kohen Gadol* prayed that the holy Four-Letter Name, which represents absolute compassion, should stand him in good stead.

The mishnah reads הַשֵּׁם because the formula people are accustomed to saying in

their prayers is אֲדֹנָי] אָנָּא הַשֵּׁם] (see *Tos. Yom Tov* 6:2 and *Tur, Orach Chaim* 621 with *Beis Yosef*).

R' Chananel (here; see *Tur Orach Chaim* 621) disagrees with *Rosh* and holds that the *Kohen Gadol* used the prefix in our version of the mishnah.

כַּפֶּר־נָא לָעֲוֹנוֹת וְלַפְּשָׁעִים וְלַחֲטָאִים, שֶׁעָוִיתִי — וְשֶׁפָּשַׁעְתִּי וְשֶׁחָטָאתִי לְפָנֶיךָ אֲנִי וּבֵיתִי, *forgive, now, the wicked acts, rebellions, and sins, for I have acted wickedly, rebelled, and sinned before You, I and my household,*

כַּכָּתוּב בְּתוֹרַת מֹשֶׁה עַבְדֶּךָ: כִּי בַיּוֹם הַזֶּה יְכַפֵּר עֲלֵיכֶם וְגו' ." — *as is written in the Torah of Your servant Moses [Leviticus* 16:30]: "For on this day he [i.e., the Kohen Gadol] will atone for you"...'

This is a verse from *Leviticus* 16:30, which the *Kohen Gadol* recited. The mishnah does not give the conclusion of the verse although the *Kohen Gadol* surely recited it in its entirety. It ends: לְטַהֵר אֶתְכֶם מִכֹּל חַטֹּאתֵיכֶם לִפְנֵי ה' תִּטְהָרוּ, *to purify you of all your sins, you shall be purified before HASHEM.* In our *Mussaf* text, we recite the complete verse as well. According to some verses cited by *Shinuyei Nuschaos,* our mishnah, too, cites the full verse.

וְהֵן עוֹנִין אַחֲרָיו: בָּרוּךְ שֵׁם כְּבוֹד מַלְכוּתוֹ לְעוֹלָם וָעֶד.'' — *And they* [all the people present] *answer after him: "Blessed is the Name — the glory of His Kingship — forever and ever."*

[Every time the *Kohen Gadol* pronounced the Name, the entire as-

[ט] **בָּא** לוֹ לְמִזְרַח הָעֲזָרָה, לִצְפוֹן הַמִּזְבֵּחַ, הַסְּגָן מִימִינוֹ וְרֹאשׁ בֵּית־אָב מִשְּׂמֹאלוֹ.

וְשָׁם שְׁנֵי שְׂעִירִים, וְקַלְפִּי הָיְתָה שָׁם וּבָהּ שְׁנֵי גוֹרָלוֹת. שֶׁל אֶשְׁכְּרוֹעַ הָיוּ, וַעֲשָׂאָן בֶּן־גַּמְלָא שֶׁל זָהָב, וְהָיוּ מַזְכִּירִין אוֹתוֹ לְשֶׁבַח.

[י] **בֶּן**־קָטִין עָשָׂה שְׁנֵים עָשָׂר דַּד לַכִּיּוֹר, שֶׁלֹּא הָיוּ לוֹ אֶלָּא שְׁנַיִם; וְאַף הוּא

יד אברהם

semblage would respond 'Blessed is...' (see *Rambam, Avodas Yom HaKippurim* 2:7).]

This formula was used instead of *Amen* as a response to all blessings in the Temple (*Taanis* 16b).

Some versions (*Rambam* ed. Kafih and others, see *Shinuyei Nuschaos*) have the text found in our versions of וְהַכֹּהֲנִים וְהָעָם הָעוֹמְדִים בָּעֲזָרָה, כְּשֶׁהָיוּ 6:2, שׁוֹמְעִין אֶת־שֵׁם הַמְפֹרָשׁ שֶׁהוּא יוֹצֵא מִפִּי כֹהֵן גָּדוֹל, הָיוּ כּוֹרְעִים וּמִשְׁתַּחֲוִים וְנוֹפְלִים עַל־פְּנֵיהֶם, וְאוֹמְרִים: ,,בָּרוּךְ שֵׁם כְּבוֹד מַלְכוּתוֹ לְעוֹלָם וָעֶד''. See comm. to 6:2.

9.

בָּא לוֹ לְמִזְרַח הָעֲזָרָה — [*Then*] *he came to the eastern part of the Courtyard*,

As the mishnah explains later (4:1), the *Kohen Gadol* would now draw lots to determine which of the two he-goats would be sacrificed and which would be sent off to Azazel. Until now he had been standing next to the אוּלָם, *antechamber*, as far west in the Temple Courtyard as possible (see above 3:8 s.v. וְלַמִּזְבֵּחַ). Now he moved to an area which, in contrast, could be called the east of the Temple Courtyard — i.e., now he stood north of the altar *itself*, not east of it.]

לִצְפוֹן הַמִּזְבֵּחַ — *north of the altar* [i.e.; directly opposite the altar],

They did not stand the he-goats between the antechamber and the altar as they did the ox (*Rashi; Rav*). Meiri adds that they stood them at the northeastern corner of the altar. They were not placed near the antechamber gate, for they would not be used until later, after the slaughter of the ox.

Therefore, the he-goats were kept as far as possible from the Temple in case they should defecate or urinate (*Tif. Yis.*).

[For further discussion of the exact position of the he-goats during the drawing of the lots, see *comm.* to 4:2 s.v. וְהֶעֱמִידוֹ and p. 68ff.]

הַסְּגָן מִימִינוֹ — *the Deputy Kohen Gadol to his right*

[See *Rambam* cited in *comm.* to 3:1 s.v. הַמְמֻנֶּה. *Meiri* here adds that the deputy replaced the *Kohen Gadol* if anything happened to him (see *comm.* to 1:1 s.v. וּמַתְקִינִין).].

וְרֹאשׁ בֵּית־אָב מִשְּׂמֹאלוֹ. — *and the head of the family to his left.*

As already mentioned (1:2 s.v. וְשָׁאַר כָּל־הַיָּמִים) the *Kohanim* were divided into מִשְׁמָרוֹת, *watches*, each of which served in rotation for a one week at a time. These watches were subdivided into בָּתֵּי אָבוֹת, *family groups*, each of which served on a specific day. Each family group chose a רֹאשׁ, *head* (see *Rambam, Klei HaMikdash* 4:11).

9. He [then] comes to the eastern part of the Courtyard north of the altar, the Deputy *Kohen Gadol* to his right and the head of the family to his left.

Two he-goats were there, and a lottery box was there in which were two lots. They [formerly] had been of boxwood, but Ben Gamla made them of gold, and they used to laud him.

10. Ben Katin made twelve spouts for the laver, for it [formerly] had only two; he also made a

YAD AVRAHAM

The sequence of watches and family groups went on even on Yom Kippur [it was partially suspended only during the three pilgrimage festivals; see *Rambam (loc cit.* 4:4)] for whatever service the *Kohen Gadol* did not perform. Thus the head of the *family* group whose turn fell on Yom Kippur had the honor of accompanying the *Kohen Gadol*.

וְשָׁם שְׁנֵי שְׂעִירִים, — *Two he-goats were there,*

One of them to be sacrificed and have its blood sprinkled in the Holy and the Holy of Holies, and the other to be sent to Azazel as described in *Leviticus* 16:7-10, 20-22.

וְקַלְפֵּי הָיְתָה שָׁם — *and a lottery box was there*

It was made of wood and was two handbreadths wide (*Rav* from *Gem.* 39a).

וּבָהּ שְׁנֵי גוֹרָלוֹת. — *in which were two lots.*

[Which of the two he-goats would be sacrificed and which sent to Azazel had not yet been determined. This had to be done by lot as specified in *Leviticus* 16:8 and described in the next chapter.]

שֶׁל אֶשְׁכְּרוֹעַ הָיוּ, — *They [formerly] had been of boxwood,*

In earlier times, the two lots had been made of boxwood [see *Aruch* s.v. אשכרע and *Rambam* ed. Kafih].

וַעֲשָׂאָן בֶּן־גַּמְלָא שֶׁל זָהָב, וְהָיוּ מַזְכִּירִין אוֹתוֹ לְשֶׁבַח. — *but Ben Gamla made them of gold, and they used to laud him* [lit., *mention him for praise*].

This is the Yehoshua ben Gamla who is mentioned elsewhere as the founder of an *elementary school* system for children (*Bava Basra* 21a with *Tosafos* s.v. זכור). His very wealthy wife paid an exorbitant amount of gold for him to be appointed *Kohen Gadol* (*Yevamos* 61a; cf. *Doros HaRishonim*). When appointed, he donated these golden lots (*Rashi; Rav*).

10.

This mishnah and the following one take up a tangential matter. Having mentioned that Ben Gamla was lauded, the *mishnah* goes on to list others who contributed to the Temple and who were either lauded or criticized.

בֶּן־קָטִין עָשָׂה שְׁנֵים עָשָׂר דַּד לַכִּיּוֹר, — *Ben Katin made twelve spouts for the laver,* Ben Katin was a Kohen Gadol who

made this improvement in the כִּיּוֹר, *laver,* used by the *Kohanim* to wash their hands and feet (*Rashi; Rav*).

עָשָׂה מוּכְנִי לַכִּיּוֹר שֶׁלֹּא יִהְיוּ מֵימָיו נִפְסָלִין
בְּלִינָה.

מֻנְבַּז הַמֶּלֶךְ הָיָה עוֹשֶׂה כָּל-יְדוֹת הַכֵּלִים שֶׁל
יוֹם הַכִּפּוּרִים שֶׁל זָהָב.

הֵילְנִי אִמּוֹ עָשְׂתָה נִבְרֶשֶׁת שֶׁל זָהָב עַל-
פִּתְחוֹ שֶׁל הֵיכָל; וְאַף הִיא עָשְׂתָה טַבְלָא שֶׁל
זָהָב, שֶׁפָּרָשַׁת סוֹטָה כְּתוּבָה עָלֶיהָ.

יד אברהם

שֶׁלֹּא הָיוּ לוֹ אֶלָּא שְׁנַיִם; — *for it [formerly]
had only two;*

He made twelve spouts so that twelve
of the thirteen *kohanim* who won the
privilege of offering the daily sacrifice
(in the second lot) could wash simultaneously without having to wait.

The thirteenth *Kohen* was the שׁוֹחֵט,
slaughterer. He did not have to wash
since even a זָר, *non-Kohen,* is permitted
to slaughter Temple offerings. Since
slaughter is not a priestly service, it does
not require priestly washing from the
laver even when it is performed by a
Kohen (*Rav* from *Gemara* 27b; see
comm. to 2:3 s.v. מִי שׁוֹחֵט).

**וְאַף הוּא עָשָׂה מוּכְנִי לַכִּיּוֹר שֶׁלֹּא יִהְיוּ מֵימָיו
נִפְסָלִין בְּלִינָה.** — *he* [Ben Katin] *also made
a machine for the laver so that its water
should not become unfit by remaining
overnight.*

[Any appropriate thing — meat,
flour, wine, blood, or water — upon be-
ing placed in a כְּלִי שָׁרֵת, *vessel used for
Temple Service,* was itself consecrated.
If it remained overnight, however, it
became פָּסוּל, *unfit* (similar to נוֹתָר; see
Rashi to *Exodus* 30:29; *Rambam, Beis
HaBechirah* 3:18).

The consecrated water in the laver
which had been drawn from the cistern
would become unfit if left standing
overnight. Although this would not affect the Temple service since the unfit
water could be drained and replaced, it
is considered a disgrace to allow any
consecrated substance, such as the
water in our case, to become unfit.

Ben Katin's machine was a wheel,

equipped with pulleys, to lower the entire laver into the בּוֹר, *cistern,* in the
Temple Courtyard overnight. When the
laver is lowered into the cistern, the unfit water becomes connected (,הַשָּׁקָה
זְרִיעָה) to the water table (מַיִם מְחֻבָּרִים)
and is considered to be of the pristine
water of the earth. Since it is regarded as
part of the earth it does not become unfit by standing overnight (*Rashi* and
Rav according to their interpretation of
Gem. 37a).

Rambam (comm. here and *Beis
HaBechirah* 3:18) interprets the
Gemara's description of מוּכְנִי [*muchni*]
differently. According to *Rambam* the
muchni was not a machine, but a kind
of reservoir which was used to store
water until it was needed for the laver.
The *muchni* was connected to a source
of water from which it was refilled
whenever water was withdrawn. It
ringed the laver and was built so that it
could be made to release water into the
laver as needed. The laver itself was
always kept empty so that no water
would become invalid overnight. When
Kohanim wished to wash at the laver,
the *muchni* was turned on to let in only
as much water as was needed. Thus, by
day's end, the *laver* was always empty.
In his commentary to *Tamid* 3:8, *Rambam* adds that the *muchni* had an ap-
paratus that raised and lowered it. [See
also *Tos. Yom Tov, Tamid* 1:4; and
Mirkeves HaMishneh to *Beis HaBechirah* 3:20.]

מֻנְבַּז הַמֶּלֶךְ — *King Monbaz*
[*Rashi, Bava Basra* 11a (s.v. מונבז

machine for the laver so that its water should not become unfit by remaining overnight.

King Monbaz made all the handles of the utensils [used] for Yom Kippur of gold.

Helene, his mother, placed a golden candelabrum over the entrance to the Holy; she also made a golden tablet, upon which the section of the suspected adulteress was written.

YAD AVRAHAM

הַמֶּלֶךְ; see glosses by *R' Mattisyahu Strashun* there) says he was one of the Hasmonean kings. This is probably derived from *Seder Olam Zuta* where Monbaz is described as the son of the Herodian king Agrifas (Agrippa) son of Hordos (Herod). *Aruch* (s.v. מלבז) concurs with *Rashi*. *Yuchasin (HaShalem,* p. 93) cites *R' Zemach Gaon* that Monbaz was the son of Herod, but strongly rejects this. Some *(Imrei Binah 52, Mosaf HeAruch)* connect Monbaz to the well-known story related by *Josephus (Antiquities* 20:2) about Helene the wife of Monobaseus, King of Adiabene (see footnote to ArtScroll *Daniel* 7:5), who, together with her son Izates, converted to Judaism shortly before the destruction of the Temple and made great gifts to the city of Jerusalem. *Bereishis Rabbah* (46:10) relates that Monbaz and his brother בזוטוס, *Bazutos* (similar to Izates) the sons of King Talmai (Ptolemy) converted to Judaism. Josephus too relates that Izates had a brother Monobaseus, but nowhere does he say that this brother converted. So even though a strong case can be made for this theory, the exact *identification* of Monbaz is still unclear.]

הָיָה עוֹשֶׂה כָּל־יְדוֹת הַכֵּלִים שֶׁל יוֹם הַכִּפּוּרִים שֶׁל זָהָב. — *made all the handles of the utensils [used] for Yom Kippur of gold.*

The *Gemara* (37b) comments that these were utensils like knives which it would be impractical to make entirely of gold. He therefore contented himself with furnishing golden handles.

Meiri adds that he made gold handles for some of the gold vessels whose handles had previously been made of other metals.

הֵילְנִי אִמּוֹ עָשְׂתָה נִבְרֶשֶׁת שֶׁל זָהָב עַל־פִּתְחוֹ שֶׁל הֵיכָל; — *Helene, his* [Monbaz's] *mother, placed* [lit. *made*] *a golden candelabrum over the entrance to the Holy* [הֵיכָל is the front chamber of the Temple — the קוֹדֶשׁ, *Holy*];

Every day of the year, the first rays of the rising sun struck the golden candelabrum, and the reflected light was visible all over Jerusalem. This informed the public that the time had come for reciting the *Shema (Gem.* 37b).

Rambam (comm. here) explains נִבְרֶשֶׁת as a pane, similar to a window pane, whose function was to reflect the first rays of the sun. Other translations (from *Yerushalmi*) are *lantern* and *lamp.*

וְאַף הִיא עָשְׂתָה טַבְלָא שֶׁל זָהָב, שֶׁפָּרְשַׁת סוֹטָה כְּתוּבָה עָלֶיהָ. — *she also made a golden tablet, upon which the section* [of the Torah] *of the suspected adulteress was written.*

Part of the procedure for a suspected adulteress (see *Numbers* 5:11-31 with *Rashi*) was to administer an oath to her (*loc. cit.* 19-22). This oath was then written on a parchment which the Kohen dipped into *bitter water* (v. 23) mixed with earth from the *soil of the tabernacle* (v. 17). In order to avoid opening a Torah scroll for the scribe to copy these oaths, Helene had the Scriptural text engraved on a golden tablet (*Rav; Rashi*).

נִקָנוֹר—נַעֲשׂוּ נִסִּים לְדַלְתוֹתָיו, וְהָיוּ
מַזְכִּירִין אוֹתוֹ לְשֶׁבַח.

[יא] **וְאֵלוּ** לִגְנַאי: שֶׁל בֵּית גַּרְמוּ לֹא רָצוּ
לְלַמֵּד עַל-מַעֲשֵׂה לֶחֶם הַפָּנִים;
שֶׁל בֵּית אַבְטִינָס לֹא רָצוּ לְלַמֵּד עַל-מַעֲשֵׂה
הַקְּטֹרֶת; הַגְרוֹס בֶּן-לֵוִי הָיָה יוֹדֵעַ פֶּרֶק בַּשִּׁיר
וְלֹא רָצָה לְלַמֵּד; בֶּן-קַמְצָר לֹא רָצָה לְלַמֵּד עַל-
מַעֲשֵׂה הַכְּתָב.
עַל-הָרִאשׁוֹנִים נֶאֱמַר: ,,זֵכֶר צַדִּיק לִבְרָכָה'',
וְעַל-אֵלוּ נֶאֱמַר: ,,וְשֵׁם רְשָׁעִים יִרְקָב''.

יד אברהם

The *Gemara* (37b) notes that it was forbidden (in their days) to write less than an entire book of the Torah. Consequently, asks the *Gemara*, how was it permitted to inscribe the text of the oath on the tablet (cf. *Yoreh Deah* 283:2 with *Shach* and *Turei Zahav*)? The *Gemara* concludes that the full Torah text was not inscribed on Helene's tablet; only the first word of each verse and the initials of the succeeding words.

נִקָנוֹר—נַעֲשׂוּ נִסִּים לְדַלְתוֹתָיו, וְהָיוּ מַזְכִּירִין אוֹתוֹ לְשֶׁבַח. — *Nikanor — miracles happened to his doors, and they used to laud him* [lit. *mention him for praise*].

The eastern entrance to the Temple Courtyard was called שַׁעַר נִקָנוֹר, *Nikanor's gate (Middos 1:4)*, because the doors for this gate were miraculously preserved for Nikanor en route to the temple (*Tif. Yis.*).

The *Gemara* (38a) relates that Nikanor went to Alexandria, Egypt to bring copper doors (*Midos 2:3*) for the Temple. While traveling home by ship, a great storm arose and the sailors, in order to lighten the burden of the ship, threw one of these heavy doors overboard. When they wished to throw the second one overboard as well, Nikanor tied himself to the remaining door, saying they would have to throw him in as well. At this the storm abated immediately. Nikanor was greatly perturbed by the loss of the first door. When they reached the port of Acco (Acre), they found that this heavy door had miraculously floated alongside the ship. Later, when all the other Temple doors were changed to gold, they left these doors of Nikanor unchanged in commemoration of the miracle.

11.

וְאֵלוּ לִגְנַאי: שֶׁל בֵּית גַּרְמוּ לֹא רָצוּ לְלַמֵּד עַל-מַעֲשֵׂה לֶחֶם הַפָּנִים; — *And these* [the following used to be mentioned] *for censure: Those of the Garmu family* [lit. *House of Garmu*] *did not want to teach* [outsiders] *about making the Panim Bread;*

Because of its shape (rectangular with two raised sides), it was difficult to remove the Bread unbroken from the pan in which it was baked. The Garmu family had a method to remove the Bread without breakage, but they refused to share their secret with others (*Gem. 38a*).

Nikanor — miracles happened to his doors, and they used to laud him.

11. And these for censure:

Those of the Garmu family did not want to teach about making the Panim Bread.

Those of the Avtinas family did not wish to teach about making the incense.

Hugros, a Levite, knew a special musical method but did not want to teach [it].

Ben Kamtzar did not want to teach the method of writing.

About the first ones it is said [*Proverbs* 10:7]: "The mention of a righteous man is for a blessing." And about the others it is said [ibid.]: "And the name of the wicked will rot."

YAD AVRAHAM

שֶׁל בֵּית אַבְטִינָס לֹא רָצוּ לְלַמֵּד עַל־מַעֲשֵׂה הַקְּטֹרֶת; — *Those of the Avtinas family did not wish to teach about making the incense;*

They knew where to find a certain herb called מַעֲלֶה עָשָׁן [lit. 'raises the smoke,'] which caused the smoke of the incense to rise up straight without any sideward dispersion.

Tosefos Yeshanim (s.v. הי"ג) adds that the species of herb was common knowledge, but only the Avtinas family could identify the superior strain of this species that caused the smoke to go straight up (see *Beis Yosef* to *Orach Chayim* 133; *Turei Zahav* there; *Mishneh LaMelech* to *Klei HaMikdash* 2:3).

הַגְרוֹס בֶּן לֵוִי הָיָה יוֹדֵעַ פֶּרֶק בְּשִׁיר וְלֹא רָצָה לְלַמֵּד; — *Hugros, a Levite, knew a special musical method* [lit. *knew a chapter of music*], *but did not want to teach* [it];

Hugros was one of those in charge of the Levite music. He had a certain method [not clearly understood] whereby he put his thumb under his tongue while singing and thereby made his singing extraordinarily pleasant (*Gem.* 38b).

Hon Ashir relates פרק to the concept of timing (as in בְּאַרְבָּעָה פְרָקִים בַּשָּׁנָה, *at four periods of the year*). Hugros had a unique way of timing his tones when he sang. He also developed a method of transcribing the music so that he could repeat all the tones and time them perfectly every time.

בֶּן־קַמְצָר לֹא רָצָה לְלַמֵּד עַל־מַעֲשֵׂה הַכְּתָב. — *Ben Kamtzar did not want to teach the method of writing* [lit. *the craft of script*].

He was able to write four different letters simultaneously by holding four pens between the five fingers of one hand. He was thus able to write all the four letters of God's name simultaneously (*Rav* from *Gem.* 38b).

It is neither permissible (nor desirable) to talk while writing the Holy Name (*Soferim* 5:6; *Yoreh Deah* 276:2). Ben Kamtzar's method reduced the time for writing and minimized the possibility of scribal interruption (*Tos. Yeshanim* s.v. לא).

It is a dishonor for the Divine Name to be in an incomplete state for even a moment (*Tosefos Yom Tov* citing *Yefei Mareh*).

[א] **טָרַף** בַּקַּלְפִּי וְהֶעֱלָה שְׁנֵי גוֹרָלוֹת; אֶחָד
כָּתוּב עָלָיו ,,לַשֵּׁם'' וְאֶחָד כָּתוּב
עָלָיו ,,לַעֲזָאזֵל.''
הַסְּגָן בִּימִינוֹ, וְרֹאשׁ בֵּית־אָב מִשְּׂמֹאלוֹ.
אִם שֶׁל שֵׁם עָלָה בִּימִינוֹ, הַסְּגָן אוֹמֵר לוֹ:
,,אִישִׁי כֹהֵן גָּדוֹל, הַגְבַּהּ יְמִינְךָ!'' וְאִם שֶׁל שֵׁם
עָלָה בִּשְׂמֹאלוֹ, רֹאשׁ בֵּית־אָב אוֹמֵר לוֹ: ,,אִישִׁי
כֹהֵן גָּדוֹל, הַגְבַּהּ שְׂמֹאלְךָ!''

יד אברהם

עַל הָרִאשׁוֹנִים נֶאֱמַר: ,,זֵכֶר צַדִּיק לִבְרָכָה'', —
About the first ones it is said: 'The men-
tion of a righteous man is for a blessing'
[*Proverbs* 10:7],

Those mentioned in mishnah 10
(Rav).

וְעַל אֵלּוּ נֶאֱמַר: ,,וְשֵׁם רְשָׁעִים יִרְקָב''. — *And*
about the others [mentioned in mish-
nah 11] *it is said* [*Proverbs* 10:7] *"And*
the name of the wicked will rot.'

The *Gemara* (38a) says that the
families of Avtinas and Garmu explained their reluctance with the argument that if their special arts became
public knowledge, people might use
them for idol-worship. *Rav* says that

the Sages did not accept their excuse
which is why the mishnah censures
them. *Yesh Seder LaMishnah* explains
that had this been their intention, they
would not have demanded double pay
for their work (as the *Gem.* 38a relates).
The *Yerushalmi*, however, says that the
Sages *did* accept their excuse.
Therefore, *Meiri* and *Tosefos Yom Tov*
say that the final curse of the mishnah
refers only to the last two people. *Meiri*,
citing a second opinion, goes even
further: When our mishnah speaks in
praise of the *first ones*, it refers to the
families of Garmu and Avtinas, who
managed to convince the Sages of the
sincerity of their intentions.

Chapter 4

Mishnah 9 of the previous chapter told how the *Kohen Gadol*, accompanied by
the Deputy *Kohen Gadol* and the head of the family on duty that day, went to the
eastern part of the Temple Courtyard where the two he-goats stood facing him. The
mishnah began to describe how the lots were drawn, and then digressed to list all
the people whose contributions to the Temple were praiseworthy or otherwise.
Now the mishnah returns to its description of the Yom Kippur service. The *Kohen
Gadol* is ready to draw the lot which would decide which of the he-goats would be
the sacrifice, and which be sent to Azazel. He proceeds to the he-goats, puts
both hands into a box which contained two lots and takes one lot in each hand. One
lot is inscribed לַשֵּׁם, *for Hashem*, and the other, לַעֲזָאזֵל, *for Azazel*. He removes
them from the box and places the lot in his right hand on the he-goat to his right,
and the lot in his left on the he-goat to his left. The he-goats are thus designated for
their respective purposes by the words written on each lot. The goat designated for
Hashem becomes the חַטָּאת, *sin offering*, whose blood will be sprinkled in the Holy
of Holies, and the he-goat designated for Azazel will be sent out to the desert and
pushed off a precipice.

1. He snatched from the lottery box and picked up two lots; one had 'For *Hashem*' inscribed on it and one had 'For *Azazel*' inscribed on it.

The Deputy *Kohen Gadol* [stood] at his right and the head of the family [on duty] at his left.

If the [lot] of *Hashem* came up in his right hand, the Deputy says to him, 'My lord *Kohen Gadol*, raise your right hand!' If that of *Hashem* came up in his left hand the head of the family says to him, 'My lord *Kohen Gadol*, raise your left hand!'

YAD AVRAHAM

1.

טָרַף בַּקַּלְפִּי, — *He* [*the Kohen Gadol*] *snatched from* [lit. *in*] *the lottery box*

The *Kohen Gadol* was required to *snatch* the lots hurriedly so that he would not be able to select the Hashem lot with his right hand. Since it was a סִימָן יָפֶה, *good omen*, if this lot came up in his right hand, he would be tempted to feel for it if he had the time to do so. Although the two lots were identical, it was possible to discern the engraved words by touch, had he not been rushed (*Rav* from *Gem.* 39a with *Rashi*).

וְהֶעֱלָה שְׁנֵי גוֹרָלוֹת; — *and picked up two lots;*

One in his right hand and one in his left. The he-goats stood facing him, one on his right hand and one on his left (*Rav; Rashi*).

[Thus the *Kohen Gadol* would place the lot in his right hand, upon the he-goat standing to his right.]

Sfas Emes comments that if the two he-goats do not stand in places corresponding to the two lots, the drawing is invalid, since the *Kohen Gadol* could then take the lot for Hashem and place it upon either he-goat.

אֶחָד כָּתוּב עָלָיו ,,לַשֵׁם'' וְאֶחָד כָּתוּב עָלָיו ,,לַעֲזָאזֵל'', — *one had 'For Hashem' inscribed on it and one had 'For Azazel' inscribed on it.*

According to *Yerushalmi*, the words had to be engraved.

[It also seems from *Yerushalmi*, as well as from *Rambam's* commentary, that the word שֵׁם, *shem* is used by our mishnah in place of the Four-Letter Name, which was inscribed on the lot.]

הַסְגָן בִּימִינוֹ וְרֹאשׁ בֵּית־אָב מִשְּׂמֹאלוֹ. — *The Deputy Kohen Gadol* [*stood*] *at his right and the head of the family* [*on duty*] *at his left.*

[Since they stood next to the *Kohen Gadol*, they were able to see immediately in which hand the lot 'For Hashem' had come up. Upon withdrawing his hands from the box, the *Kohen Gadol* probably turned the lots face up to see the writing upon them.]

This has already been mentioned earlier (in 3:9). It is parenthetically reiterated here to explain why only the Deputy *Kohen Gadol* had the privilege to say 'My lord *Kohen Gadol*, raise your right hand.' Since he stood at the *Kohen Gadol's* right side this is self-explanatory (*Tif. Yis.*).

[Many manuscripts and some printed versions lack this segment of the mishnah (from הסגן to משמאלו). See *Meleches Shlomo* and *Shinuyei Nuschaos.*]

אִם שֶׁל שֵׁם עָלָה בִּימִינוֹ, הַסְגָן אוֹמֵר לוֹ: ,,אִישִׁי כֹּהֵן גָּדוֹל, הַגְבַּהּ יְמִינְךָ!'' — *If the* [*lot*] *of Hashem came up in his right hand the Deputy says to him, 'My lord Kohen Gadol, raise your right hand!'*

To show everyone on which side the lot for Hashem came up (*Meiri*).

It was a good sign if the lot which had לַה׳, *For Hashem, written on it came up*

נָתְנוּ עַל־שְׁנֵי הַשְּׂעִירִים וְאוֹמֵר: ,,לַה'
חַטָּאת". רַבִּי יִשְׁמָעֵאל אוֹמֵר: לֹא הָיָה צָרִיךְ
לוֹמַר ,,חַטָּאת", אֶלָּא ,,לַה' ".
וְהֵן עוֹנִין אַחֲרָיו: ,,בָּרוּךְ שֵׁם כְּבוֹד מַלְכוּתוֹ
לְעוֹלָם וָעֶד".

יד אברהם

on the right. During the entire forty
years of Shimon HaTzaddik's High
Priesthood, the lot always came up in
his right hand. From then on,
sometimes it came up on the right, and
sometimes on the left (Gem. 39a).

וְאִם שֶׁל שֵׁם עָלָה בִשְׂמֹאלוֹ, רֹאשׁ בֵּית־אָב
אוֹמֵר לוֹ: ,,אִישִׁי כֹּהֵן גָּדוֹל הַגְבַּהּ שְׂמֹאלְךָ!" —
If that of Hashem came up in his left
hand, the head of the family [on duty]
says to him, 'My lord Kohen Gadol,
raise your left hand!'

So everyone can see that it contains
the lot 'For Hashem' (Meiri).

נָתְנוּ עַל־שְׁנֵי הַשְּׂעִירִים, — He puts it upon
the two he-goats,

[I.e. each lot. Many versions have
נְתָנָן, he puts 'them'.]

He placed the lot in his right hand
upon the he-goat standing at his right,
and the lot in his left hand upon the
goat standing at his left (Rashi).

[Both the drawing and the placing of
the lots upon the he-goats is described
in Leviticus 16:8.]

וְאוֹמֵר: ,,לַה' חַטָּאת!" — and [after placing
the lot which said 'For Hashem' on the
goat] says 'For Hashem — a sin offering!'

Here too he uttered the ineffable
Four-Letter Name as before (3:8; Rav;
Rambam).

The Tosefta (2:9) states that the Kohen
Gadol says לַה', For Hashem, and the סְגָן,
deputy, says חַטָּאת, sin offering. Ritva and
Smag (Mitzvas Asseh 209) cite this Tosefta.
[Rambam (Avodas Yom HaKippurim 2:6)
says: And when he puts the lot upon the he-
goat he says לְשֵׁם חַטָּאת, a sin offering for
Hashem. Siach Yitzchak takes this to mean

that the Kohen Gadol said both words. Rambam's omission of the Tosefta indicates that
he sees it as contradicting the mishnah and
therefore not acceptable as halachah.

רַבִּי יִשְׁמָעֵאל אוֹמֵר: לֹא הָיָה צָרִיךְ לוֹמַר
,,חַטָּאת," אֶלָּא ,,לַה'!" — Rabbi Yishmael
says: He did not have to say 'a sin offering', merely 'For Hashem!'

[The controversy between R' Yishmael
and the first tanna hinges upon their interpretation of the verse (Lev. 16:9)
וְהִקְרִיב ... וְעָשָׂהוּ חַטָּאת, and shall draw to him
... and he shall make it a sin offering. The
first tanna maintains that the subject of
וְעָשָׂהוּ, and he shall make it, is the Kohen
Gadol — i.e., the Kohen Gadol sanctifies the
goat as a sin offering by saying לַה' חַטָּאת,
For Hashem — a sin offering.

R' Yishmael holds that the subject is the
lot — i.e., the lot sanctifies the he-goat as a
sin offering by virtue of being placed upon
it. The ו, vav of וְעָשָׂהוּ should be considered a
וָיו הַחִיבּוּר, conjunctive vav, and the clause
would be rendered, upon which the lot had
come out and made it a sin offering. The
verb וְעָשָׂהוּ, and made it, then refers to the lot —
i.e., the lot designates the he-goat a sin offering (Malbim to Sifra loc. cit.).

[The first opinion holds that the literal interpretation renders the vav before וְעָשָׂהוּ a
ו הַמְהַפֶּכֶת, vav which changes the tense of
עָשָׂהוּ from past to future, thus, and he shall
make it a sin offering. The antecedent of he is
the Kohen Gadol who will make the he-goat
a sin offering with his pronouncement לַה'
חַטָּאת, For Hashem — a sin offering (Malbim.
See also Tos. HaRosh and Ritva).]

וְהֵן עוֹנִין אַחֲרָיו: — and they [i.e., the
Kohanim and congregation in the court-
yard] answer after him:

— When they hear him pronounce
the Name (Rashi; Rav).

He puts it upon the two he-goats, and says, 'For HASHEM — a sin offering!' Rabbi Yishmael says: He did not have to say 'a sin offering', merely, 'For HASHEM!'

And they answer after him, 'Blessed is the Name — the glory of His Kingship — forever and ever.'

YAD AVRAHAM

[This passage is not part of R' Yishmael's words. Rather the mishnah concludes by informing us how those present responded when they heard 'the Name.']

בָּרוּךְ שֵׁם כְּבוֹד מַלְכוּתוֹ לְעוֹלָם וָעֶד. — 'Blessed is the Name — the glory of His Kingship — forever and ever.'

[See comm. to 3:8.]

◄§ Did the Kohanim 'kneel and prostrate themselves' when the Kohen Gadol said חַטָּאת לַה'?

In 3:8 and 6:2 we find that the Kohanim knelt and prostrated themselves when they heard the Kohen Gadol utter the Name. There is no reason to suppose that they did not do so upon hearing this utterance. Rambam (Avodas Yom HaKippurim 7:6-7) clearly indicates that they did.

However the various Piyutim of the Avodah do not add the formula ... וְהַכֹּהֲנִים, describing the reaction of the Kohanim upon hearing 'the Name' after לַה' חַטָּאת as they do after each of the confessions.[1]

Tosefos Yom Tov (6:2) justifies this custom on the grounds that the formula וְהַכֹּהֲנִים in its entirety is out of context here. This formula ends with, 'He also timed himself to conclude "the Name" together with the blessers [i.e., when the Kohen Gadol started uttering the Name, the Kohanim

kneeled ... and said ... בָּרוּךְ שֵׁם. He timed his utterance to conclude 'the Name' as the Kohanim finished saying [בָּרוּךְ שֵׁם and said to them תִּטְהָרוּ.' Thus this formula is relevant only to an utterance of 'the Name' which occurs in the Kohen Gadol's recital of (Lev. 16:9), תִּטְהָרוּ ..., You shall be purified. Since this last segment of this formula cannot be used here, all of it is omitted.

R'Yisroel Kimchi (Avodas Yisroel p. 117) justifies the custom on other grounds. He cites the opinion of R' Sheshes (father of Rivash) that during his confessions, the Kohen Gadol cried out loudly אָנָא הַשֵּׁם (cf. Gemara 20b and 39b, וכבר אמר אנא השם ונשמע קולו ביריחו; see also Tamid 3:8 with Tos. Yom Tov and Tif. Yis.) as is fitting in a supplication to God. Here, however, since there was no prayer, only a declaration that this he-goat is a sin offering for God, there was no need to say the Name loudly. Therefore even Kohanim standing close enough to hear this utterance of the Name did not 'kneel and prostrate themselves.' R' Yisroel Kimchi finds support for this opinion in the words of Meiri. However, his view conflicts with the words of the Avodah אַמִּיץ כֹּחַ (Ashkenazic minhag), צָעַק בְּקוֹל רָם לַה' חַטָּאת, He cried out in a loud voice, 'For Hashem — a sin offering.'

The custom of omitting וְהַכֹּהֲנִים has found its way into our machzorim in a slightly varied form. It is included in אַתָּה כוֹנַנְתָּ, but the early printers inserted the instruction 'Here the congregation does not kneel.'

1. The only exception is the Avodah אַתָּה כוֹנַנְתָּ said in the Sephardic minhag (and in most chassidic congregations). But even here, this formula was not in the original Piyut as it is found in Siddur R'Saadya Gaon, Seder R'Amram Gaon, (ed. Coronel) and Tashlum Abudraham. Even R'David Pardo's emended version (Shifas Revivim found also in Tashlum Abudraham) does not have the formula וְהַכֹּהֲנִים here. Indeed Abudraham (p. 51) wonders why וְהַכֹּהֲנִים is not recited in this place. Our machzorim have been emended to remove the objections raised by Abudraham and Beis Yosef (Orach Chaim 621); much detail not found in the original has been added. Beis Yosef (ibid.) cites R'Yitzchak Arama (in Sefer Akeidah) that וְהַכֹּהֲנִים should be said here too.

[ב] **קָשַׁר** לָשׁוֹן שֶׁל זְהוֹרִית בְּרֹאשׁ שָׂעִיר
הַמִּשְׁתַּלֵּחַ וְהֶעֱמִידוֹ כְּנֶגֶד בֵּית
שִׁלּוּחוֹ. וְלַנִּשְׁחָט כְּנֶגֶד בֵּית שְׁחִיטָתוֹ.
בָּא לוֹ אֵצֶל פָּרוֹ שְׁנִיָּה, וְסוֹמֵךְ שְׁתֵּי יָדָיו
עָלָיו וּמִתְוַדֶּה.
וְכָךְ הָיָה אוֹמֵר: ,,אָנָּא הַשֵּׁם, עָוִיתִי פָּשַׁעְתִּי
חָטָאתִי לְפָנֶיךָ, אֲנִי וּבֵיתִי וּבְנֵי אַהֲרֹן עַם

יד אברהם

2.

קָשַׁר לָשׁוֹן שֶׁל זְהוֹרִית בְּרֹאשׁ שָׂעִיר הַמִּשְׁתַּלֵּחַ
— He tied a strip [lit. tongue] of red
wool to the head of the he-goat which
was sent [to Azazel]

The woolen strip was to ensure that it
would not be confused with a different
sacrificial goat. [Another he-goat was
part of the mussaf sacrifices. See
Numbers 29:11] (Gem. 41b).

What is the significance of the color
red? The Gemara (39a) relates that in
the days of Shimon HaTzaddik (the
Righteous), this strip of red wool
always turned white. This was a sign
that the sins had been forgiven, as the
prophet says (Isaiah 1:18): If your sins
will be like crimson threads they will
become white as snow ... (Rashi). After
Shimon HaTzaddik's time, it sometimes
turned white, and at other times did not
(Tif. Yis.).

[In view of the fact that the mussaf contained an ox (Numbers 28:8) as well as a
goat, why was the Kohen Gadol's ox (3:8)
not similarly identified? Nor do we find such
explicit identification at any other time,
though there were other occasions when
similar sacrifices were offered.

In every instance but that of the Yom Kippur he-goat, it was possible to delay the consecration of the prospective sacrifice until
immediately before the actual offering (see
Pesachim 66b; אָמְרוּ עָלָיו עַל הַלֵּל), thus
eliminating any possibility of confusion. In
this one instance, however, both he-goats
had to be designated for their respective purposes long before the actual service of their
sacrifice was performed. So care had to be
taken to prevent confusion.]

וְהֶעֱמִידוֹ כְּנֶגֶד בֵּית שִׁלּוּחוֹ. — and stood it
facing its destination.

To Azazel; that is, toward the eastern
gate (Rav; Rashi).

[Previously, both he-goats had been facing
west (Gem. 36a, Tosefta 2:2 with Chasdei
David, and Sifra). Now this one was turned
around to face east.]

Rosh says that he stood it in the
eastern gateway. Perhaps this is based
upon Sifra which states that the two he-
goats stood within the eastern gates
(שַׁעֲרֵי נִקָּנוֹר) during the drawing of lots.
Thus, when the he-goat was turned
eastward, facing its destination, it was
already standing within the eastern
gate. For a lengthy discussion of Sifra's
view that the drawing of the lots took
place in the eastern gates see below.

וְלַנִּשְׁחָט כְּנֶגֶד בֵּית שְׁחִיטָתוֹ. — And on the
[he-goat] that was to be slaughtered, [he
tied a strip] around its neck [lit. opposite the place of its slaughter].

The translation, following Rav and
Rashi; is based on the conclusion of the
Gemara (41b); he tied the strip around
the part of the neck where the incision
would be made. However, the Gemara
considered, and dismissed, an interpretation that the goat was placed in
the northern part of the Courtyard
where it would later be slaughtered.

[Rambam (Avodas Yom HaKappurim 3:2)
decides that בֵּית שְׁחִיטָתוֹ means the slaughtering area; i.e., the area near the altar where the
goat could be slaughtered; thus he accepts
the interpretation discarded by the Gemara.

2. He tied a strip of red wool to the head of the he-goat which was sent [to *Azazel*] and stood it facing its destination. And on the [he-goat] that was to be slaughtered, [he tied a strip] around its neck.

Then he comes to his ox a second time and leans both hands upon it and confesses.

He would say the following: 'I beg of You HASHEM, I have acted wickedly, rebelled, and sinned before You, I and my family, and the children of

YAD AVRAHAM

Mirkeves HaMishneh reconciles this view with the *Gemara* by showing that the above cited decision is not unanimous (see *Tosafos* 41b s.v. שלש). Precedents for *Rambam's* view are found in *Yose ben Yose's Avodah* אַתָּה כּוֹנַנְתָּ and in *R' Saadiah Gaon's Avodah* (in his *siddur*) (*Rosh*). *Rosh* challenges *Yose ben Yose* from the *Gemara* (Our versions of אַתָּה כּוֹנַנְתָּ have been emended to conform with the *Gemara*.) The *Avodah* אֲמִיץ כֹּחַ (Ashkenasic rite by *R' Meshulam ben R' Klonimus*) concurs with *Rambam*.]

The strip of wool tied to this he-goat was in a different place than that of the first goat so that they could be told apart. Thus the strips of wool distinguished them from other goats, and the respective locations distinguished one from the other (*Rav* from *Gem.* 41b).

בָּא לוֹ אֵצֶל פָּרוֹ שְׁנִיָּה — *Then he comes to his ox a second time*

[The *Kohen Gadol* had already encountered his ox once (3:8) and confessed upon it.]

[In *Leviticus* 16:6 we find the expression וְכִפֶּר בַּעֲדוֹ וּבְעַד בֵּיתוֹ, *and he shall atone for himself and for his house*, before the drawing of lots for the he-goats. The same expression is repeated in v. 11 after the drawing and before the slaughter of the ox. The Sages teach (*Gem.* 36b; *Sifra*, loc. cit.) that *he shall atone* means כַּפָּרַת דְּבָרִים, *verbal atonement* — i.e., confession. First the *Kohen Gadol* confessed his and his family's sins, and later he confessed the sins of his extended family, all the *Kohanim*, who are also called בֵּית אַהֲרֹן, *the house of Aaron* (Psalms 135:19 from; *Rashi's* comm. to Torah). The *Gemara* (43b) adds that it is reasonable for him to confess his own sins first and then — when he is sinfree — he confesses those of the *Kohanim*.

וְסוֹמֵךְ שְׁתֵּי יָדָיו עָלָיו וּמִתְוַדֶּה. — *and leans both hands upon it and confesses.*

— His sins, and those of his household and fellow *Kohanim*.

[This *leaning* on the ox is not specified in *Leviticus* 16. The *Talmud* (*Zevachim* 40a) does not discuss the two leanings, even though it cites a Scriptural basis for them in *Leviticus* 4:20 (see *Sifra* there and to 4:4). Perhaps the *leaning* is part of the atonement process (see *Zevachim* 6a וסמך ונרצה לכפר...), and, מעלה עליו הכתוב כאילו לא כיפר וכיפר as such, belongs together with the וידוי, *confession*. It seems from *Tosefta Menachos* (10:3) and also from *Rambam* (*Ma'aseh HaKarbonos* 3:14-15) that confession was always said during סְמִיכָה, *leaning*. Indeed *R' Shimon* (*Tosefta ibid.*) holds that it is required only with a sacrifice brought for a specific sin. Therefore, once we know that confession and leaning go together, it stands to reason that for every confession, a separate leaning was performed. See *comm.* to 3:8 s.v. וְסָמַךְ for a description of 'leaning'.]

וְכָךְ הָיָה אוֹמֵר: ,,אָנָּא הַשֵּׁם, — *He would say the following: 'I beg of You HASHEM,*

[He pronounced the Four-Letter Name as explained above 3:8.]

עָוִיתִי פָּשַׁעְתִּי חָטָאתִי לְפָנֶיךָ, — *I have acted wickedly, rebelled, and sinned before You,*

[The sequence in which the mishnah lists the sins follows *R' Meir's* opinion. The sequence held by the Sages is: חָטָאתִי עָוִיתִי פָּשַׁעְתִּי. See 3:8 for details.]

אֲנִי וּבֵיתִי וּבְנֵי אַהֲרֹן עַם קְדוֹשֶׁךָ. — *I and my family, and the children of Aaron, Your holy people.*

[In the Torah, the word עַם, *people*, is

קְדוֹשֶׁיךָ. אָנָּא הַשֵׁם, כַּפֶּר־נָא לָעֲוֹנוֹת
וְלַפְּשָׁעִים וְלַחֲטָאִים, שֶׁעָוִיתִי וְשֶׁפָּשַׁעְתִּי
וְשֶׁחָטָאתִי לְפָנֶיךָ, אֲנִי וּבֵיתִי וּבְנֵי אַהֲרֹן עַם
קְדוֹשֶׁיךָ, כַּכָּתוּב בְּתוֹרַת מֹשֶׁה עַבְדֶּךָ: ,,כִּי בַיּוֹם
הַזֶּה יְכַפֵּר עֲלֵיכֶם לְטַהֵר אֶתְכֶם מִכֹּל
חַטֹּאתֵיכֶם לִפְנֵי ה׳ תִּטְהָרוּ.״
וְהֵן עוֹנִין אַחֲרָיו: ,,בָּרוּךְ שֵׁם כְּבוֹד מַלְכוּתוֹ
לְעוֹלָם וָעֶד.״

יד אברהם

used to mean any of the twelve tribes.
See *Onkelos* and *Rashi* to *Deut.33:3;*
Rambam to *Genesis 17:6.* Aaron and his
descendants are sometimes considered a
tribe apart; see *I Chron. 23:13* and *Lev.
16:33* by implication.]

אָנָּא הַשֵׁם כַּפֶּר־נָא לָעֲוֹנוֹת וְלַפְּשָׁעִים
וְלַחֲטָאִים, שֶׁעָוִיתִי וְשֶׁפָּשַׁעְתִּי וְשֶׁחָטָאתִי
לְפָנֶיךָ, אֲנִי וּבֵיתִי וּבְנֵי אַהֲרֹן עַם קְדוֹשֶׁיךָ,
— *I beg of You HASHEM, forgive* [lit. *wipe
away*] *now the wicked acts, rebellions,
and sins, for I have acted wickedly,
rebelled, and sinned before You, I and
my family, and the children of Aaron,
Your holy people,*

Here too, the sequence follows R'
Meir's view (see above s.v. עָוִיתִי and
comm. to 3:8).

כַּכָּתוּב בְּתוֹרַת מֹשֶׁה עַבְדֶּךָ: ,,כִּי־בַיּוֹם הַזֶּה
יְכַפֵּר עֲלֵיכֶם לְטַהֵר אֶתְכֶם מִכֹּל חַטֹּאתֵיכֶם
לִפְנֵי ה׳ תִּטְהָרוּ.״ — *as is written in the
Torah of your servant Moses (Lev.
16:30): For on this day he will atone for
you to purify you before HASHEM from
all your sins shall you be purified.*

וְהֵן עוֹנִין אַחֲרָיו: ,,בָּרוּךְ שֵׁם כְּבוֹד מַלְכוּתוֹ
לְעוֹלָם וָעֶד.״ — *And they* [i.e., the
Kohanim and the congregation present]
*answer after him. 'Blessed is the Name
— the glory of His kingship — forever
and ever.'*

[See comm. to 3:8. Here too, the
audience, upon hearing 'the Name'...
knelt and bowed and prostrated
themselves. The mishnah relies on 6:2
(or on 3:8 according to the versions that

have it there) and does not repeat this
segment here.]

◆§ **Where were the he-goats standing
during the drawing of the lots?**

The mishnah (3:9) very clearly says,
He [then] *comes to the eastern part of
the Courtyard, north of the altar.* Thus,
the he-goats stood in the area directly
north of the altar, in the eastern part of
the Temple Courtyard. They could not
have been standing in the extreme
eastern portion near the eastern wall
since this would not be directly north of
the altar. Briefly, then, they stood near
the northeastern corner of the altar.

However *Rosh* says merely that the
he-goats stood in the eastern part of the
Temple Court; he conspicuously omits
the stipulation that they stand north of
the altar. Perhaps *Rosh's* opinion is
based upon *Sifra* to *Lev. 16:7* which
says that the two he-goats stood in the
eastern gateway during the drawing of
lots. (Our versions have מַעֲמִידוֹ, *he
stands it* — i.e., only the he-goat for
Azazel. But *Vilna Gaon* and *Malbim*
adopt the version מַעֲמִידָן, *he stands
them* — i.e., both he-goats.)

This contradicts mishnah 3:9, which
says that they stood north of the altar,
i.e., near the northeast corner. *Vilna
Gaon*, however, emends *Sifra* to read
לְמִזְרַח הָעֲזָרָה לְצָפוֹן הַמִּזְבֵּחַ, *to the eastern
area of the Courtyard* [and] *north of the
altar,* parallel to the mishnah. *Tosafos
Yeshanim* (37a s.v. בא לו) and *Malbim*
(seemingly) understand that there is no

Aaron, Your holy people. I beg of You HASHEM, forgive now the wicked acts, rebellions and sins, for I have acted wickedly, rebelled, and sinned before You, I and my family, and the children of Aaron, Your holy people, as is written in the Torah of Your servant Moses [*Lev.* 16:30]: *For on this day he will atone for you to purify you before HASHEM from all your sins shall you be purified.'*

And they answer after him: 'Blessed is the Name — the glory of His kingship — forever and ever.'

YAD AVRAHAM

contradiction. The he-goats stood in the part of the gate which was north of a straight line drawn from the northern side of the altar through the gate (see diagram). *Tosafos Yeshanim* cites *Rashi* (not in our versions) for this opinion. They explain that it would be an affront to bring an animal — the goat that would be sent to Azazel — near the altar and then take it away without offering it as a sacrifice. The stipulation to have the he-goats stand in the gate is probably based on the words of the Torah (*Leviticus* 16:7): וְהֶעֱמִיד אֹתָם לִפְנֵי ה' פֶּתַח אֹהֶל מוֹעֵד, *And he shall stand them before HASHEM in the door of the Sanctuary.* In the *commentary* to 3:8 we outlined three different views regarding the location of the altar in the Courtyard. The opinion advanced here is plausible only if the altar stood wholly in the southern half of the Temple Court as held by the mishnah here (*Gem.* 37a; see footnote to 3:8). If the altar stood in the center of the Temple court (*Middos* 5:2; *Rambam, Beis HaBechirah* 5:15) it was impossible to put the he-goats both in the gateway and north of the altar.

According to the opinion that the altar was in the center, there appear to be two contradictory requirements concerning the placement of the goats. Which takes precedence: that which puts the goats in the eastern gateway, or that which places them north of the altar?

According to the *Sifra*, there is no question that the *Torah* requires the he-goats to stand in the gateway. As a result, the stipulation added by the mishnah, that they stand in the north, is waived because of its impossibility. Since the northern part of the gateway was not fit for slaughtering sacrifices (see *Pesachim* 85b) the reason for placing the he-goats in the north could only have been symbolic, which is why it could be dispensed with. This may be

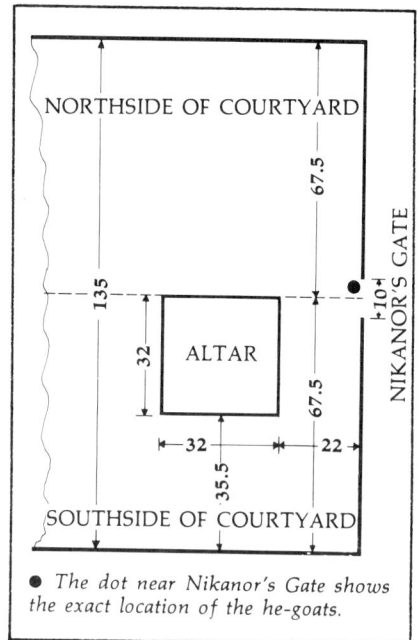

● *The dot near Nikanor's Gate shows the exact location of the he-goats.*

[ג] שְׁחָטוֹ, וְקִבֵּל בְּמִזְרָק אֶת־דָּמוֹ וּנְתָנוֹ לְמִי שֶׁהוּא מְמָרֵס בּוֹ עַל־הָרוֹבֶד הָרְבִיעִי שֶׁבַּהֵיכָל, כְּדֵי שֶׁלֹּא יִקְרֹשׁ. נָטַל מַחְתָּה וְעָלָה לְרֹאשׁ הַמִּזְבֵּחַ, וּפִנָּה גֶחָלִים אֵילֶךְ וְאֵילֶךְ, וְחוֹתֶה מִן־הַמְעֻכָּלוֹת הַפְּנִימִיּוֹת, וְיָרַד, וְהִנִּיחָהּ עַל־הָרוֹבֶד הָרְבִיעִי שֶׁבָּעֲזָרָה.

יד אברהם

the source of *Rosh's* opinion. Consequently when the he-goat was turned to the east, it was already standing within the gate. *Sifra's* version has found its way into R' David Pardo's text of אַתָּה כּוֹנַנְתָּ (although it is not in the texts of *Seder R' Amram Gaon, Avodas Yisrael,* and the standard editions). This is also how it appears in the R' *Saadiah Gaon's Siddur* and in כּוֹנַנְתָּ אַתָּה in *Machzor Roma* ed. Livorno 5616). *Rambam (Avodas Yom HaKippurim* 3:2) writes that the lots were drawn directly north of the altar.

3.

שְׁחָטוֹ, — *He slaughtered it,*

[The ox upon which he had leaned and said confession (3:8), after having leaned upon it and recited the confession a second time (mishnah 2).]

Here, too, (as in 3:4 with regard to the תָּמִיד, *daily sacrifice)* he severed only most of the trachea and esophagus — the required minimum — and let another *Kohen* complete the incision while he prepared to receive the blood [see further] *(Tos. Yom Tov; Mayim Chayim,* cited by *Siach Yitzchak).*

Kol HaRemez, Hon Ashir, and *Lechem Shamayim* disagree, arguing that the case of the daily sacrifice in 3:4 is not analogous. There, the *Kohen Gadol* was not required to complete the incision because even a *non-Kohen* was permitted to slaughter the daily sacrifice. (See *Tosafos* 32 s.v. אם; *Kessef Mishneh Avodas Yom HaKippurim* 1:2, citing *Ritva.)* The sacrifice of the ox, however, was part of the Yom Kip-

pur service, which is פָּסוּל, *not valid,* if performed by anyone except the *Kohen Gadol.* Therefore its slaughter, too, would not be valid if performed by another, hence, even the non-essential finishing of the incision had to be done by the *Kohen Gadol*[1].

וְקִבֵּל בְּמִזְרָק אֶת־דָּמוֹ — *received its blood in a basin* [lit. *a thrower* — a vessel used for throwing the blood]

וּנְתָנוֹ לְמִי שֶׁהוּא מְמָרֵס בּוֹ עַל־הָרוֹבֶד הָרְבִיעִי שֶׁבַּהֵיכָל, — *and gave it to someone [a Kohen] who would stir it on the fourth row [of pavement stones] from the Temple,*

The floor of the Temple and its Courtyard were paved with rows of marble slabs. Each row is called a רוֹבֶד *(Rashi; Rav).*

Literally, שֶׁבַּהֵיכָל should be translated *within the Temple,* implying that the blood was stirred by someone standing inside the building. The *Gemara* (43b), however, explains that this is impossible because the

---

1. See *Gemara* 42a, which cites a controversy whether slaughter of the *Kohen Gadol's* ox by a non-*Kohen* is valid. *Rambam (Pesulei HaMukdashim* 1:2) rules that it is valid. [The texts of the *Avodah* are not germane. Although the ordinary versions of כּוֹנַנְתָּ אַתָּה say that the *Kohen Gadol* did only most of the slaughter, this, like many other passages, is a later addition. It is not found in *Seder R' Amram Gaon, Abudraham,* or *Avodas Yisrael.*]

3. He slaughtered it, received its blood in a basin and gave it to someone who would stir it on the fourth row [of pavement stones] from the Temple, so that it should not coagulate.

He took a shovel and went up to the top of the altar, cleared away the coals to one side and the other, scooped up from the burned innermost [coals], descended, and put it down on the fourth row in the Courtyard.

YAD AVRAHAM

Torah decrees (Lev. 16:17): No man shall be in the Tabernacle [when the Kohen Gadol burns the incense in the Holy of Holies], meaning that no one could be in the Temple when the Kohen Gadol entered the Holy of Holies. What the mishnah must mean is the fourth row of stones in the Courtyard, counting from the gate of the Temple antechamber. The translation reflects this.

כְּדֵי שֶׁלֹּא יִקְרֹשׁ. — so that it [i.e., the blood] should not coagulate.

Between the service of receiving the blood and that of throwing it, the Kohen Gadol had to burn the incense in the Holy of Holies (below 5:1), after which he took the blood from the man who was stirring it and threw it as prescribed in 5:3. To keep the blood from coagulating during this interval, it had to be stirred (Rashi; Rav).

נָטַל מַחְתָּה — He [the Kohen Gadol] took a shovel,

[The Kohen Gadol used a small shovel with a handle to hold the coals for burning the incense.]

וְעָלָה לְרֹאשׁ הַמִּזְבֵּחַ, וּפִנָּה גֶחָלִים אֵילָךְ וְאֵילָךְ, וְחוֹתֶה מִן הַמְעֻכָּלוֹת הַפְּנִימִיּוֹת, — and went up to the top of the altar, cleared away the coals to one side and the other, scooped up from the burned innermost [coals],

[Rambam (see comm. ed. Kafih) had a shorter version, reading only וְעָלָה לְרֹאשׁ

הַמִּזְבֵּחַ וְחָתָה וְיָרַד, he went up to the top of the altar, scooped up, and descended. Furthermore, in Avodas Yom HaKippurim (4:1) he omits the specification that the Kohen Gadol take 'from the innermost coals'. He does, however, specify this for the תְּרוּמַת הַדֶּשֶׁן, removal of ashes, from the outer altar (T'midin U'Mussafin 2:12, from Tamid 1:4). There the purpose was the removal of ashes, which would naturally be most concentrated in 'the coals which had been burned in the לֵב הָאֵשׁ, heart of the fire.' For the Yom Kippur incense, however, the Torah requires גַּחֲלֵי אֵשׁ, fiery coals (Lev. 16:12); 'the innermost burned ones' would not fulfill that requirement, therefore the Kohen Gadol scooped up the uppermost, live coals.[1]

וְיָרַד, — descended [from the top of the altar to the floor of the Courtyard],

וְהִנִּיחָהּ עַל הָרוֹבֶד הָרְבִיעִי שֶׁבָּעֲזָרָה. — and put it down on the fourth row in the Courtyard.

Thus, both the shovel with the coals, and the מִזְרָק, basin, with the ox's blood were put on the same row in the Temple Court, the fourth row counting from the Temple entrance (Tos. Yom Tov citing Yerushalmi).

[Earlier, the mishnah said שֶׁבַּהֵיכָל, from the Temple, to teach us to count the rows from the Temple entrance. Here it says שֶׁבָּעֲזָרָה, in the Court, to teach us that the Temple Court is meant, not the Temple itself (as mentioned in comm. s.v. עַל־הָרוֹבֶד; Shoshanim L'David).

1. Nevertheless, in describing the procedure for the daily incense (as opposed to the Yom Kippur ritual discussed by our mishnah), Rambam writes (T'midin U'Mussafin 3:5): 'And he takes from the coals שֶׁנִּתְאַכְּלוּ, which have been burned.' Ravad comments that this is not found in the correct editions of Tamid (5:5) where the procedure for the daily incense is described. Kessef Mishneh counters that Rambam's ruling follows our versions of the

[ד] **בְּכָל־יוֹם** הָיָה חוֹתָה בְּשֶׁל כֶּסֶף
וּמְעָרֶה בְּתוֹךְ שֶׁל זָהָב,
וְהַיּוֹם חוֹתָה בְּשֶׁל זָהָב וּבָהּ הָיָה מַכְנִיס.
בְּכָל־יוֹם חוֹתָה בְּשֶׁל אַרְבַּעַת קַבִּין וּמְעָרֶה
בְּתוֹךְ שֶׁל שְׁלֹשֶׁת קַבִּין, וְהַיּוֹם חוֹתָה בְּשֶׁל
שְׁלֹשֶׁת קַבִּין וּבָהּ הָיָה מַכְנִיס.
רַבִּי יוֹסֵי אוֹמֵר: בְּכָל־יוֹם חוֹתָה בְּשֶׁל סְאָה

יד אברהם

4.

בְּכָל־יוֹם — *Every day*

Every day, except Yom Kippur, the
Kohen who won the privilege of scooping up coal for the daily incense which
was burned on the altar … (*Rav; Rashi*).

הָיָה חוֹתָה בְּשֶׁל כֶּסֶף — *he would scoop up*
[the coal] *with a silver* [shovel; lit with
one of silver]

The *Kohen* did not use a *gold* shovel
because the scooping would abrade the
gold — וְהַתּוֹרָה חָסָה עַל מָמוֹנָן שֶׁל יִשְׂרָאֵל,
*and the Torah was concerned for the
possessions* [lit. money] *of Israel* (*Gem.
44b; Rav*).

וּמְעָרֶה בְּתוֹךְ שֶׁל זָהָב, — *and empty it into
one of gold,*

[The *Kohen* emptied the coal from
the silver shovel into a gold shovel.
Then he took this coal-filled shovel into
the Temple and poured the coals onto
the inner altar. The *Kohen* who had
won the privilege of burning the incense
on that day then entered and spread the
incense over the burning coals.]

וְהַיּוֹם חוֹתָה בְּשֶׁל זָהָב — *but today* [on

Yom Kippur], *he* [the Kohen Gadol]
would scoop [the coals] *with a gold*
[shovel].

This was done to spare the *Kohen
Gadol*, who was weak from the fast, the
extra task of pouring the coals from one
shovel to another (*Gem. 44b; Rav*).

Accordingly, if this reasoning is sufficient
to permit the *Kohen Gadol's* use of a gold
shovel to scoop up coals for the special Yom
Kippur incense, it should also permit him to
use a golden shovel to scoop up coals for the
daily incense of Yom Kippur, for that, too,
had to be done by the *Kohen Gadol*.

From *Rambam's* wording in *Avodas Yom
HaKippurim* (I:5) in reformulating this passage of the mishnah, *Tosefos Yom Tov* (2:2
s.v. ארבע) deduces that the *Kohen Gadol* indeed *did* use the golden shovel on Yom Kippur for the daily incense. As much is evident
from *Meiri* (here). But *Ramban* (*Milchamos*,
first paragraph in *Yoma*) holds that the *Kohen Gadol* carried the coal himself only for
the Yom Kippur incense that was burned in
the Holy of Holies where only he might
enter. For the daily incense, however,
although he performed the burning, the coals
could be brought by a regular *Kohen* who

Mishnah exactly. (Our versions of the mishnah *Tamid* 5:5 have only וּפִנָּה גֶחָלִים אֵילָךְ וְאֵילָךְ,
[he] *cleared away the coals to one side and the other*, omitting הַפְּנִימִיּוֹת מִן־הַמְעֻכָּלוֹת [*and*
he] *scooped from the burned, innermost* [*coals*]. This concurs with *Ravad's* contention, but
some of the early versions of the Mishnah [see *Shinuyei Nuschaos* there] as well as that
printed in the editions of the Talmud, have the full version as we have it here and *Kessef
Mishneh* quotes it.

In light of *Rambam's* opinion that for the Yom Kippur incense 'burnt coals' were not
needed, why does he require such coals for the daily incense?

Tosefos Yom Tov (here) points out that though *Rambam* requires 'coals which have been
burnt for the daily incense, this is not identical to the same as the 'coals which have been
burned in the *heart of the fire*,' the kind that are necessary for removal of the ashes (*T'midin
U'Mussafin* 2:12). For the former, he requires coals that have been burned בְּלֵב הָאֵשׁ, *in the*

4. **E**very day he would scoop up [the coal] with a silver [shovel] and empty it into one of gold, but today he would scoop with a gold [shovel], and in it he would bring in [the coals].

Every day he would scoop with a four-*kab* [shovel] and empty [the contents] into one of three *kabs*, but today he would scoop with one of three *kabs* and in it he would bring in [the coals].

R' Yose says: Every day he would scoop with a one-*seah* [shovel] and empty [it] into a three-*kab*

YAD AVRAHAM

won this privilege in the third lottery. Consequently the scooping was probably done, as always, with a silver shovel. Those who hold that no third lottery was held on Yom Kippur probably hold that the *Kohen Gadol* himself carried the coals for the daily incense and used the golden shovel for scooping (*Tos. Yom Tov; ibid; see comm.* to 2:2 s.v. אַרְבַּע פִּיָסוֹת and 2:4; cf. *Mikdash David, Kadashim* 24:4).

וּבָה הָיָה מַכְנִיס. — *and in it he would bringing in* [*the coals*].

So as not to trouble the *Kohen Gadol*, who was weak from the fast, with the unnecessary task of emptying the coal from one shovel to the other (*Rav* from *Gem.* 44b). [But on other days, the coal was scooped up in a large shovel and emptied into a smaller shovel for the reason given below.]

בְּכָל־יוֹם חוֹתֶה בְּשֶׁל אַרְבַּעַת קַבִּין — *Every day he would scoop with a four-kab* [*shovel*]

[A *kab* is a measure of volume holding four לוֹגִין, *logs*, which in turn equal six בֵּיצִים, *eggs*. The volume of the average egg is about two fluid ounces. Thus one *kab*, or twenty-

four eggs, would equal forty-eight fluid ounces.; four kabs equal 192 fluid ounces or six quarts. Some authorities estimate the בֵּיצָה at about four fluid ounces. Thus all the measurements would be doubled.]

וּמְעָרֶה בְּתוֹךְ שֶׁל שְׁלֹשֶׁת קַבִּין, — *and empty* [*the contents*] *into one of three kabs,*

The extra *kab* spilled over onto the floor (*Tamid* 5:4 and *Gem.* 44b).

It was a matter of Temple etiquette [דֶּרֶךְ כָּבוֹד שֶׁל מַעֲלָה] that the shovel be filled to overflowing. The coals were therefore poured from a large shovel into a smaller one (*Rav; Tamid* 5:4).

וְהַיּוֹם חוֹתֶה בְּשֶׁל שְׁלֹשֶׁת קַבִּין וּבָה הָיָה מַכְנִיס. — *but today* [i.e., on Yom Kippur] *he* [*would*] *scoop with one of three kabs and in it he would bring in* [*the coals*].

This was done, as explained before, to lighten the *Kohen Gadol's* burden.

רַבִּי יוֹסֵי אוֹמֵר: בְּכָל־יוֹם חוֹתֶה בְּשֶׁל סְאָה וּמְעָרֶה בְּתוֹךְ שֶׁל שְׁלֹשֶׁת קַבִּין, וְהַיּוֹם חוֹתֶה בְּשֶׁל שְׁלֹשֶׁת קַבִּין, וּבָה הָיָה מַכְנִיס. — *R' Yose says: Every day he would scoop with a one-seah* [*shovel*] *and empty* [*it*]

heart of the fire, whereas for the incense, he says merely *coals that have been burned.* This suggests that coals for the daily incense though burned, were still glowing and far from becoming ashes. Only for removal of ashes did they take coals 'burned in the heart of the fire' i.e., those *totally* burned and turning to ash. *Tosefos Yom Tov* adds that (according to *Rambam*) on Yom Kippur the *Kohen Gadol* was not required to 'clear the coal to this side and to that side' in order to scoop up from the 'burned coal', so as not to burden him with additional tasks on the day when he had to perform the entire service alone while fasting.

[*Tosefos Yom Tov's* assumption that *Rambam* differentiates between coals for the ashes and for the incense is not borne out by the authoratative *Kafih* ed. According to it, the mishnah reads מְאוּכָּלוֹת הַפְּנִימִיּוֹת, *innermost, consumed,* in both *Tamid* 1:4 (removal of the ashes) and 5:5 (daily incense).]

וּמְעָרֶה בְּתוֹךְ שֶׁל שְׁלֹשֶׁת קַבִּין וְהַיּוֹם חוֹתֶה
בְּשֶׁל שְׁלֹשֶׁת קַבִּין, וּבָהּ הָיָה מַכְנִיס.
בְּכָל־יוֹם הָיְתָה כְבֵדָה, וְהַיּוֹם קַלָּה.
בְּכָל־יוֹם הָיְתָה יָדָהּ קְצָרָה, וְהַיּוֹם אֲרֻכָּה.
בְּכָל־יוֹם הָיָה זְהָבָהּ יָרֹק, וְהַיּוֹם אָדֹם; דִּבְרֵי
רַבִּי מְנַחֵם.
בְּכָל־יוֹם מַקְרִיב פְּרָס בְּשַׁחֲרִית וּפְרָס בֵּין
הָעַרְבַּיִם, וְהַיּוֹם מוֹסִיף מְלֹא חָפְנָיו.
בְּכָל־יוֹם הָיְתָה דַקָּה, וְהַיּוֹם דַּקָּה מִן־הַדַּקָּה.

יד אברהם

into a three-kab [shovel], but today [Yom Kippur] *he would scoop with a three-kab [shovel], and in it he would bring in [the coals].*

[A *seah* equals 6 kabs.]

בְּכָל־יוֹם הָיְתָה כְבֵדָה, — *Every day it [the shovel] was heavy,*

It was made of thick material (*Rav* from *Gem.* 44b).

וְהַיּוֹם קַלָּה. — *but today it was light.*

This shovel was made of thin material (*Rav* from *Gemara* 44b).

Here, too, the evident reason is to make the service easier for the *Kohen Gadol* (*Rashi*).

בְּכָל־יוֹם הָיְתָה יָדָהּ קְצָרָה, — *Every day its handle was short,*

[It was just long enough for holding.]

וְהַיּוֹם אֲרֻכָּה. — *but today it was long.*

So that the *Kohen Gadol* should be able to tuck the handle under his arm and so take some of the weight off his hands (*Rav* from *Gem.* 44b).

בְּכָל־יוֹם הָיָה זְהָבָהּ יָרֹק, — *Every day its gold was yellow,*

[יָרֹק is used in Biblical and mishnaic Hebrew for yellow, green, and blue. The translation follows the context (see *Tosafos* to *Succah* 31b s.v. ירוק).]

וְהַיּוֹם אָדֹם; — *but today it was red;*

They used gold the color of ox-blood that came from *Parvayim* (the name of a

place) (*Rav* from *Gem.* 44b).

This was one of the kinds of gold King Solomon used in the first Temple (*II Chronicles* 3:6). Our Sages said that the ox-blood color of its gold was an indication of its excellence (*Rashi* there).

Meiri and *Tiferes Yisrael* add that this gold was reserved for Yom Kippur because of its excellence.

דִּבְרֵי רַבִּי מְנַחֵם. — *[these are] the words of R' Menachem.*

[R' Menachem differentiates between the gold of the daily shovel and that of the Yom Kippur shovel.

We do not find anyone disagreeing with R' Menachem. Perhaps that is why *Rosh* cites R' Menachem's opinion. *Rambam*, however, omits it (*Avodas Yom HaKippurim* 2:5), probably on the assumption that R' Menachem's opinion is not shared by the unnamed majority (*Shoshanim L'David*).

The *Gemara* (44b) cites the *Tosefta* which adds another difference between 'every day' and 'today.' Every day the shovel did not have a נִיאֲשְׁתִּיק, but today it had a נִיאֲשְׁתִּיק.

There are several interpretations of the meaning of this word. *Rashi* renders it *a ring*; a ring hung from the handle of the Yom Kippur shovel which jingled as the *Kohen Gadol* moved, in fulfillment of the verse, *And its sound shall be heard when he comes into the Holy* (*Exodus* 28:35). *Meiri* understands נִיאֲשְׁתִּיק to mean *a base*. Every day the shovel was not put down; its contents were emptied directly onto the inner altar. But on Yom Kippur when the shovel was taken into the Holy of Holies, it was set down and then the

4
4

[shovel], but today he would scoop with a three-*kab*
[shovel], and in it he would bring in [the coals].

Every day it [the shovel] was heavy, but today it was light.

Every day, its handle was short, but today it was long.

Every day its gold was yellow, but today it was red; [these are] the words of R' Menachem.

Every day he offered a half [*maneh* of incense] in the morning, and a half [*maneh*] in the afternoon, but today he added his two cupped handfuls.

Every day it was fine, but today it was the finest of the fine.

incense was placed on the coals in the shovel. Accordingly, the Yom Kippur shovel had a base, so that it could be set down. *Aruch* (s.v. נשתק) and *Riva (Tos.* 44b s.v. בכל) explain ניאשתיק to be a נרתק, *a sleeve or covering for the handle.*

בְּכָל־יוֹם מַקְרִיב פְּרָס בְּשַׁחֲרִית וּפְרָס בֵּין הָעַרְבַּיִם, — *Every day he offered a half [maneh of incense] in the morning and a half [maneh] in the afternoon,*

[See *comm.* to 3:7 for the weight of a מָנֶה, *maneh.*]

וְהַיּוֹם מוֹסִיף מְלֹא חָפְנָיו. — *but today he added his two cupped handfuls.*

[In addition to offering the daily incense on the inner altar as usual, the *Kohen Gadol* also offered the special Yom Kippur incense, cupping his two hands together and filling them with incense, which he burned in the Holy of Holies. This is based on the verse in *Leviticus* (16:12) *And he shall take a shovelful of fiery coals from upon the*

altar, from before HASHEM, and his two cupped handfuls, of fine incense and bring it within the curtain.]

בְּכָל־יוֹם הָיְתָה דַקָּה, — *Every day it* [the incense] *was fine,*

[The daily incense (even that burned on Yom Kippur) was דַקָּה, *fine, (Kerisos* 6b; *Exodus* 30:36).]

וְהַיּוֹם דַקָּה מִן־הַדַקָּה, — *but today it* [i.e., the special Yom Kippur incense] *was the finest of the fine.*

They returned it to the mortar on Yom Kippur eve and ground it very fine so that it should be the *finest of fine (Kerisos* 5b).

Why does it say דַקָּה, *fine* (in *Lev.* 16:12 about the Yom Kippur incense), the Torah has already said (*Exodus* 30:36 regarding the daily incense), *And you shall grind it very well?* This teaches us that (for the Yom Kippur incense) the finest of fine is required (*Gem.* 45a quoted by *Rav*).

5.

Here the mishnah digresses slightly. Having mentioned the differences between Yom Kippur and other days pertaining to the service of incense, the discussion is extended to all the other differences between Yom Kippur and other days.

[ה] בְּכָל־יוֹם כֹּהֲנִים עוֹלִין בְּמִזְרָחוֹ שֶׁל כֶּבֶשׁ וְיוֹרְדִין בְּמַעֲרָבוֹ.

וְהַיּוֹם כֹּהֵן גָּדוֹל עוֹלֶה בָאֶמְצַע וְיוֹרֵד בָאֶמְצַע. רַבִּי יְהוּדָה אוֹמֵר: לְעוֹלָם כֹּהֵן גָּדוֹל עוֹלֶה בָאֶמְצַע וְיוֹרֵד בָאֶמְצַע.

בְּכָל יוֹם כֹּהֵן גָּדוֹל מְקַדֵּשׁ יָדָיו וְרַגְלָיו מִן־הַכִּיּוֹר, וְהַיּוֹם מִן־הַקִּיתוֹן שֶׁל זָהָב. רַבִּי יְהוּדָה אוֹמֵר: לְעוֹלָם כֹּהֵן גָּדוֹל מְקַדֵּשׁ יָדָיו וְרַגְלָיו מִן־הַקִּיתוֹן שֶׁל זָהָב.

[ו] בְּכָל־יוֹם הָיוּ שָׁם אַרְבַּע מַעֲרָכוֹת, וְהַיּוֹם חָמֵשׁ; דִּבְרֵי רַבִּי

יד אברהם

בְּכָל־יוֹם כֹּהֲנִים עוֹלִין בְּמִזְרָחוֹ שֶׁל כֶּבֶשׁ — *Every day the Kohanim go up [to the top of the altar] along the east side of the ramp*

Whenever a *Kohen* [including the *Kohen Gadol*] went up the ramp to the altar, he would turn to the right at the top, for 'All your turns should be to the right.' Since the ramp was on the south side of the altar, a *Kohen* going up would be facing north and when he turned right he would be facing eastward. Every *Kohen* went up on the eastern side of the ramp, 'for it was in that direction that he would turn upon arriving at the top' (*Rashi; Rav* from *Gem.* 45a).

וְיוֹרְדִין בְּמַעֲרָבוֹ — *and go down along its west,*

A *Kohen* who went up to the altar had to walk around its complete circumference before descending (see *Zevachim* 64b וּמַקִּיפִין דֶּרֶךְ שְׂמֹאל יוֹרְדִים). Thus, when they turned from the altar back onto the ramp, they would be on the west side of the ramp (*Tif. Yis.;* see *Rashi* to *Succah* 48b s.v. וּמַקִּיפִין; *Beer Sheva* to *Sotah* 15b).

וְהַיּוֹם כֹּהֵן גָּדוֹל עוֹלֶה בָאֶמְצַע וְיוֹרֵד

בָאֶמְצַע — *but today the Kohen Gadol goes up in the middle and descends in the middle.*

The *Kohen Gadol* shows the glory of his position and God's love for His nation — which the *Kohen Gadol* represents — by conducting himself on the altar like a בֶּן־בַּיִת, *member of the [King's] household (Rashi; Rav).*

[During the rest of the year the *Kohen Gadol* abided by the rules. Only on Yom Kippur did he demonstrate God's love for His nation. Thus when the mishnah says: *Every day the Kohanim, … the Kohen Gadol* is included.]

However, *Rambam (comm.;* see ed. Kafih and *Avodas Yom HaKippurim* 2:5) has the plural version וְהַיּוֹם עוֹלִים בָאֶמְצַע וְיוֹרְדִים בָאֶמְצַע, *and today they [the Kohanim] go up in the middle and they descend in the middle. Rambam* explains that to honor the *Kohen Gadol*, both he and his 'tribe' — the *Kohanim* — were allowed on Yom Kippur to disregard the usual rules for ascending and descending the ramp. *Rambam* adds that the *Kohanim* ascended the כֶּבֶשׁ, *ramp*, before the *Kohen Gadol* [as an escort] in order to honor him (*Tos. Yom Tov*).

רַבִּי יְהוּדָה אוֹמֵר: לְעוֹלָם כֹּהֵן גָּדוֹל עוֹלֶה בָאֶמְצַע וְיוֹרֵד בָאֶמְצַע. — *R' Yehudah says: The Kohen Gadol always ascends and*

5. Every day the *Kohanim* go up [to the top of the altar] along the east side of the ramp and go down along its west, but today the *Kohen Gadol* goes up in the middle and descends in the middle. R' Yehudah says: The *Kohen Gadol* always ascends and descends in the middle.

Every day the *Kohen Gadol* would wash his hands and feet from the laver, but today from the golden pitcher. R' Yehudah says: The *Kohen Gadol* would always wash his hands and feet from the golden pitcher.

6. Every day there were four pyres, but today [there were] five; these are the words of R'

YAD AVRAHAM

descends in the middle.

[Whenever he ascended to the altar.]

בְּכָל-יוֹם כֹּהֵן גָּדוֹל מְקַדֵּשׁ יָדָיו וְרַגְלָיו מִן־הַכִּיּוֹר, וְהַיּוֹם מִן־הַקִּיתוֹן שֶׁל זָהָב. — *Every day the Kohen Gadol would wash [lit. sanctified] his hands and feet from the laver, but today from the golden pitcher.*

On this day, in honor of the *Kohen Gadol*, a special vessel was designated for his use (see above 3:4 s.v. קדֵּשׁ יָדָיו

וְרַגְלָיו.)

Using the כִּיּוֹר, *laver*, for washing was not obligatory. Any vessel could be used as long as it was a כְּלִי שָׁרֵת, *sacred vessel (Tosafos 44b s.v. והיום from Zevachim 22a).*

רַבִּי יְהוּדָה אוֹמֵר: לְעוֹלָם כֹּהֵן גָּדוֹל מְקַדֵּשׁ. יָדָיו וְרַגְלָיו מִן הַקִּיתוֹן שֶׁל זָהָב. — *R' Yehudah says: The Kohen Gadol would always wash his hands and feet from the golden pitcher.*

6.

בְּכָל-יוֹם הָיוּ שָׁם אַרְבַּע מַעֲרָכוֹת, — *Every day there were four pyres,*

[Each pyre for burning offerings on the altar was called a מַעֲרָכָה, lit. *arrangement*, because of the orderly way in which the logs were piled up.]

The first pyre, called the מַעֲרָכָה גְדוֹלָה, *major pyre*, was used to burn the אֵבְרֵי הַתָּמִיד, *limbs of the daily sacrifice.* The second pyre was the מַעֲרָכָה שְׁנִיָּה שֶׁל קְטֹרֶת, *second incense pyre*, from which coals were taken to burn the daily incense. There is no disagreement about these two pyres. The third pyre (according to R' Meir and R' Yose) was for קִיּוּם הָאֵשׁ, *perpetuation of*

the fire as prescribed by the Torah (*Lev.* 6:6): *And the fire of the altar shall burn on it not to be extinguished.* The fourth pyre (according to R' Meir alone) was for the limbs and fat of the previous day's sacrifices which had not yet been consumed on the major pyre (*Rav* from *Gem.* 45a).

וְהַיּוֹם חָמֵשׁ; דִּבְרֵי רַבִּי מֵאִיר. — *but today [there were] five; these are the words of R' Meir.*

They added a fifth pyre to provide coals specifically for the Yom Kippur incense which was burned in the Holy of Holies. All the tannaim agree on the

מֵאִיר. רַבִּי יוֹסֵי אוֹמֵר: בְּכָל־יוֹם שָׁלֹשׁ, וְהַיּוֹם אַרְבַּע. רַבִּי יְהוּדָה אוֹמֵר: בְּכָל־יוֹם שְׁתַּיִם, וְהַיּוֹם שָׁלֹשׁ.

[א] **הוֹצִיאוּ** לוֹ אֶת־הַכַּף וְאֶת־הַמַּחְתָּה, וְחָפַן מְלֹא חָפְנָיו וְנָתַן לְתוֹךְ הַכַּף; הַגָּדוֹל לְפִי גָדְלוֹ, וְהַקָּטָן לְפִי קָטְנוֹ — וְכָךְ הָיְתָה מִדָּתָהּ.

יד אברהם

רַבִּי יְהוּדָה אוֹמֵר: בְּכָל־יוֹם שְׁתַּיִם; — R' Yehudah says: Every day—two;

The major pyre and the pyre for the incense sufficed. R' Yehudah maintains that there was no need for an additional pyre to perpetuate the fire. This requirement was satisfied with the two pyres (ibid.).

וְהַיּוֹם שָׁלֹשׁ. — but today—three.

A pyre was added to supply coals for the special Yom Kippur incense (ibid.).

The differences of opinions between these tannaim have their origin in their interpretations of the verses in Leviticus (6:1-6) dealing with the altar pyres (ibid.).

necessity of having a special pyre for this purpose (Rav; Gem. 45a).

רַבִּי יוֹסֵי אוֹמֵר: בְּכָל יוֹם שָׁלֹשׁ, — R' Yose says, every day [there were] three;

One for the 'major pyre' used for the daily sacrifice; the second for the daily incense; and the third for the perpetuation of the fire. R' Yose maintains that there was no need for a fourth pyre to burn the previous day's leftover sacrifices; they were burned alongside the major pyre (ibid.).

וְהַיּוֹם אַרְבַּע. — but today—four.

An additional pyre was needed to provide the coals for burning the Yom Kippur incense in the Holy of Holies (ibid.).

Chapter 5

The mishnah now returns to its description of the Yom Kippur service that had been interrupted after having described the scooping up of coal for the Yom Kippur incense (4:3). The Mishnah had digressed to list all the differences between the daily Temple service and that of Yom Kippur.

1.

הוֹצִיאוּ לוֹ — They brought him

From the לִשְׁכַּת הַכֵּלִים, chamber of the vessels (Rav; Rashi from Gem. 47a).

אֶת־הַכַּף — the ladle

A vessel for holding the incense. It was called כַּף, literally palm, because of its similarity to the palm of the hand (see Aruch s.v. כף).

וְאֶת־הַמַּחְתָּה, — and the shovel,

The shovel was brought after having been filled with incense (Tos. Yom Tov from Gem. 47a) in the לִשְׁכַּת אַבְטִינַס, Avtinus chamber, where the incense was prepared. From it the Kohen Gadol would now take incense to be deposited in the scoop, as described in our mishnah below (Gem. 47a).

[The scoopful of coal had been deposited earlier on 'the fourth row in

Meir. R' Yose says: Every day [there were] three; but today — four. R' Yehudah says: Every day — two; but today — three.

1. **T**hey brought him the ladle and the shovel, and he scooped up his cupped handfuls and placed it into the ladle; a big [*Kohen Gadol*] according to his size and a small one according to his size — and this was [the incense's required] measure.

YAD AVRAHAM

the Temple Court' (4:3). It stayed there until the *Kohen Gadol* had finished scooping the incense (see below).]

וְחָפַן מְלֹא חָפְנָיו — *and he scooped up his cupped handfuls*

[He cupped both of his hands together and scooped up as much incense as they could hold. This was a part of the service (*Gem.* 48a) and was performed in fulfillment of the Torah's prescription: *And...his two handfuls of fine incense of herbs and he shall bring it within the curtain (Leviticus* 16:12).]

וְנָתַן לְתוֹךְ הַכַּף; — *and placed it into the ladle;*

The *Gemara* (47a) explains why he could not bring the incense into the Holy of Holies in his hands. Since no one except the *Kohen Gadol* was allowed to enter the Holy of Holies, he would have to bring in the coal and then return to bring in the incense. This would contradict the procedure given in the Torah *(Lev.* 16:12) which mentions only *one* entry into the Holy of Holies. The only alternative would be to place the coal-filled shovel on top of the *Kohen Gadol's* incense-filled hands. This would require the *Kohen Gadol,* upon entering the Holy of Holies to grasp the shovel in his teeth and set it down on the floor, a procedure that would be indecorous even before a human king. So the incense was placed in a ladle, which the *Kohen Gadol* held in his left hand, while he held the coal shovel in his right. Precedent for this

use of a ladle was set by the נְשִׂיאִים, *princes,* of the tribes, when they brought incense on the occasion of the חֲנֻכַּת הַמִּשְׁכָּן. *dedication of the Tabernacle (Numbers* 7:14).

הַגָּדוֹל לְפִי גָדְלוֹ, וְהַקָּטָן לְפִי קָטְנוֹ— *a big [Kohen Gadol] according to his size* [lit. *the big one according to his bigness*], *and a small [Kohen Gadol] according to his size* [lit. *the small one according to his smallness*]—

[There was no fixed amount that had to be scooped up in the *Kohen Gadol's* hands. Each one took as much as his hands held.]

וְכָךְ הָיְתָה מִדָּתָה. — *and this was [the incense's required] measure.*

When the *Kohen Gadol* entered the Holy of Holies and emptied the contents of the ladle into his cupped hands, the amount of incense in his hands was required to be the same as it had been earlier when he scooped up the two handfuls *(Rav* from *Gem.* 47a).

[This interpretation — one of three given in the *Gemara* — is based on the premise that the *Kohen Gadol* performed חֲפִינָה, *filling his cupped hands with incense,* again in the Holy of Holies. He did *not* use a utensil to hold the incense he was to place upon the glowing coals.]

The *Gemara* (49b) cites a *Tosefta* which clearly concludes that he filled his hands again in the Holy of Holies. This is the view accepted by *Rambam* (*Avodas Yom HaKippurim* 4:1).

An alternative interpretation given in the *Gemara* is that the mishnah reiterates the

נָטַל אֶת־הַמַּחְתָּה בִּימִינוֹ וְאֶת־הַכַּף
בִּשְׂמֹאלוֹ. הָיָה מְהַלֵּךְ בַּהֵיכָל עַד שֶׁמַּגִּיעַ לְבֵין
שְׁתֵּי הַפְּרָכוֹת הַמַּבְדִּילוֹת בֵּין הַקֹּדֶשׁ וּבֵין קֹדֶשׁ
הַקֳּדָשִׁים, וּבֵינֵיהֶן אַמָּה. רַבִּי יוֹסֵי אוֹמֵר: לֹא
הָיְתָה שָׁם אֶלָּא פָרֹכֶת אַחַת בִּלְבַד, שֶׁנֶּאֱמַר:
,,וְהִבְדִּילָה הַפָּרֹכֶת לָכֶם בֵּין הַקֹּדֶשׁ וּבֵין קֹדֶשׁ
הַקֳּדָשִׁים''.

יד אברהם

measure to stress that the cupped hands of the *Kohen Gadol* had to be filled exactly, not less and not more. As a *baraisa* (48a) puts it, the handfuls were neither leveled off nor heaped up, but full, with a slight mound.

Tosafos (47a s.v. וכך) asks why the *Gemara* does not choose the obvious interpretation that וְכַךְ הָיְתָה מִדָּתָהּ, *and this was its measure*, refers to the ladle. Thus: a ladle was made to hold the exact volume he could hold in his cupped hands. (Oddly enough, this is the interpretation chosen by *Tiferes Yisrael*.)

Tosafos gives the simple answer that this would not have been practical. When the *Kohen Gadol* poured from his filled hands into the ladle, inevitably some of the incense would spill onto the floor, thus leaving less than the two handfuls in the ladle. It stands to reason, therefore, that the capacity of the ladle had to be greater than two handfuls to prevent any such loss.

נָטַל אֶת־הַמַּחְתָּה בִּימִינוֹ — *He took the shovel in his right hand*

The mishnah now speaks of the coal shovel which had been waiting on the fourth row in the Temple Court (see 4:3).

Obviously the shovel referred to here is not the one mentioned earlier in the mishnah. That shovel was used only to hold the incense from which he filled his hands (*Gem.* 47a).

וְאֶת־הַכַּף בִּשְׂמֹאלוֹ. — *and the ladle in his left.*

Because the shovelful of coal was heavy and hot, he had to hold it in his stronger, right hand, while he held the lighter ladle of incense in his left hand (*Rav* from *Gem.* 47a).

[If not for this consideration, the incense would have been in his right hand because it is the main component of this service (from *Gem., ibid*). *Rambam* (*Avodas Yom HaKippurim* 4:1) adds that were it not for the coal shovel's weight and heat, the service would have been invalid, for no Temple service may be performed with the left hand. But since it was virtually impossible for the *Kohen Gadol* to carry the coals in his left hand, the service is valid even though he transports the incense in his left. Perhaps, though, the disability of even *transporting* the incense with the right hand is of Rabbinic origin, and the Sages waived it in this case because of the difficulty involved (*Kessef Mishneh*).

הָיָה מְהַלֵּךְ בַּהֵיכָל — *He would walk through* [lit. in] *the Temple*

He entered the Temple (from the Courtyard) and advanced toward the west (i.e., toward the Holy of Holies) (*Rav; Rashi*).

עַד שֶׁמַּגִּיעַ לְבֵין שְׁתֵּי הַפְּרָכוֹת הַמַּבְדִּילוֹת בֵּין הַקֹּדֶשׁ וּבֵין קֹדֶשׁ הַקֳּדָשִׁים, — *until he reached the space between the two curtains which separated the Holy from the Holy of Holies,*

[The Temple had three chambers: The אוּלָם, antechamber, at the eastern end; the הֵיכָל, hall or קֹדֶשׁ, Holy, which was entered from the אוּלָם; and the קוֹדֶשׁ הַקֳּדָשִׁים, Holy of Holies.]

וּבֵינֵיהֶן אַמָּה. — *and between them* [the two curtains] [*was*] *a cubit.*

He took the shovel in his right hand and the ladle in his left. He would walk through the Temple until he reached the space between the two curtains which separated the Holy from the Holy of Holies, and between them [was] a cubit. R' Yose says: There was only one curtain as it says [*Exodus 26:33*]: *And the curtain shall divide for you between the Holy and the Holy of Holies.*

רַבִּי יוֹסֵי אוֹמֵר: לֹא הָיְתָה שָׁם אֶלָּא פָרֹכֶת אַחַת בִּלְבָד, שֶׁנֶּאֱמַר: ,,וְהִבְדִּילָה הַפָּרֹכֶת לָכֶם בֵּין הַקֹּדֶשׁ וּבֵין קֹדֶשׁ הַקֳּדָשִׁים." — R' *Yose says: There was only one curtain, as it says (Exodus 26:33): And the curtain shall divide for you between the Holy and the Holy of Holies.*

[Only one curtain is mentioned in the verse.]

The first tanna holds that even though the Tabernacle (to which the verse refers) had only one curtain, there were compelling reasons to have two curtains in the Second Temple.[1].

[The mishnah now returns to the majority view that there were two curtains, and explains how the *Kohen Gadol* got

into the Holy of Holies on Yom Kippur. The curtains extended all the way from the northern wall to the southern wall. To provide access to him, each curtain was folded back and pinned, as the mishnah will now describe.

However, in order to prevent the Holy of Holies from being visible to casual onlookers, the eastern curtain was folded on the south and the western curtain was folded on the north. Thus, at the point of each opening, view was blocked by the opposite curtain. As the Talmud (*Middos* 4:5; *Pesachim* 27a) teaches, precautions were taken to assure that no casual onlooker could feast his eyes on the beauty of the Holy of

1. In the First Temple there was a wall one cubit thick instead of a curtain, and the Holy of Holies was reached through a door whose opening was covered by a curtain (see *I Kings* 6:20; 8:8 with *Rashi, II Chronicles* 2:14). When the Second Temple was built, the height of its first level — forty cubits — (*Middos* 4:6) — was ten cubits higher than that of the First Temple which was thirty cubits high (*I Kings* 6:2). According to *Rashi* there (6:20) the קֹדֶשׁ(=דְּבִיר) הַקֳּדָשִׁים), *Holy of Holies*, in the First Temple was only twenty cubits high. Because the prescribed thickness of such a wall — one cubit — could not support a forty-cubit structure, they could not erect such a high wall in the Second Temple (see *Rashi* there s.v. בבנין with emendation of *Bach; Tos. Yom Tov* here). Nor could they increase the thickness of the wall, because the single cubit allotted for it, like all the dimensions of the Temple, had been divinely fixed, as King David told his son Solomon (*I Chronicles* 28:19): *Everything [I give you] in writing, from the hand of HASHEM which was upon me to enlighten me* (Rashi, *Yoma* 51b s.v. אמה טרקסין). Unable to build a wall, they had to use a curtain to divide the Holy from the Holy of Holies, as had been done in the Tabernacle. But the builders did not know whether the space upon which the wall had stood in the First Temple belonged to the Holy of Holies, or to the Holy. Not knowing where to place the curtain that had, as its stated purpose (*Exod.* 26:33), to *divide between the Holy and the Holy of Holies* (*Tos. Yom Tov; Tosafos* 51b s.v. ועבוד; cf. *Tos. Yeshanim* s.v. מספקא; *Ritva*) they hung two curtains — one, where the outer side of the wall had been; and one, where the inner side of the wall had been (*Yoma* 51b). R' Yose, however, held that no question ever arose about the status of the cubit where the wall had stood, therefore only one curtain was needed (*Rambam; Tos. Yeshanim* s.v. מספקא; *Ritva; Tos. Rid.;* cf. *Tosefta* 2:11; *Yerushalmi* 5:1). [See also *Rambam, Beis HaBechirah* 4:2, his *comm.* to *Midos* 4:7; *Teshuvas Or HaMeir* 25.]

הַחִיצוֹנָה הָיְתָה פְּרוּפָה מִן־הַדָּרוֹם,
וְהַפְּנִימִית מִן־הַצָּפוֹן. מְהַלֵּךְ בֵּינֵיהֶן, עַד
שֶׁמַּגִּיעַ לַצָּפוֹן. הִגִּיעַ לַצָּפוֹן הוֹפֵךְ פָּנָיו לַדָּרוֹם,
מְהַלֵּךְ לִשְׂמֹאלוֹ עִם־הַפָּרֹכֶת עַד־שֶׁהוּא מַגִּיעַ
לָאָרוֹן. הִגִּיעַ לָאָרוֹן, נוֹתֵן אֶת־הַמַּחְתָּה בֵּין שְׁנֵי
הַבַּדִּים. צָבַר אֶת־הַקְּטֹרֶת עַל־גַּבֵּי גֶחָלִים,

יד אברהם

Holies. *Meiri* (cf. *Tos. Yom Tov*) notes that *Kohanim* entered the Holy every day and could have seen the Holy of Holies had the curtains not blocked their view.]

הַחִיצוֹנָה הָיְתָה פְּרוּפָה מִן־הַדָּרוֹם, — *The outer [curtain] was pinned up from the south[ern side],*

The curtain was folded up on itself and its fold held in place with a gold hook to form an opening at the southern side of the Temple (*Rashi; Rav*).

Tosefos Rid suggests that it would have been unseemly for the curtain to remain open constantly. He proposes that פְּרוּפָה means that the curtain was hooked to the wall to hold it in place. The curtain was permanently attached at its top and on its northern side. On the southern side, the curtain was held in place by hooks in the wall and corresponding loops on the curtain. On Yom Kippur, the loops were disengaged to allow the *Kohen Gadol* to push the curtain aside and enter.

וְהַפְּנִימִית מִן־הַצָּפוֹן. — *and the inner one from the north[ern side].*

According to R' Yose, the opening in the one curtain was on the north (*Gem.* 51b).

Why were the curtains pinned in the manner described?

The *Gemara* (51b-52a) explains that he walked between the inner altar and the *Menorah* toward the curtain, somewhat south of the midpoint of the Temple. Upon reaching the curtain, he would turn left and walk southward until he reached the fold. Then he would enter the space between the curtains and walk all the way to the northern wall where he would turn left, entering the

Holy of Holies through the fold on that end. He would then turn left again (in effect, making a U-turn) and walk alongside the curtain until he reached the place opposite of the אָרוֹן, *Ark*, which was in the middle of the chamber.

After entering the Holy of Holies, the *Kohen Gadol* could comply with the require-

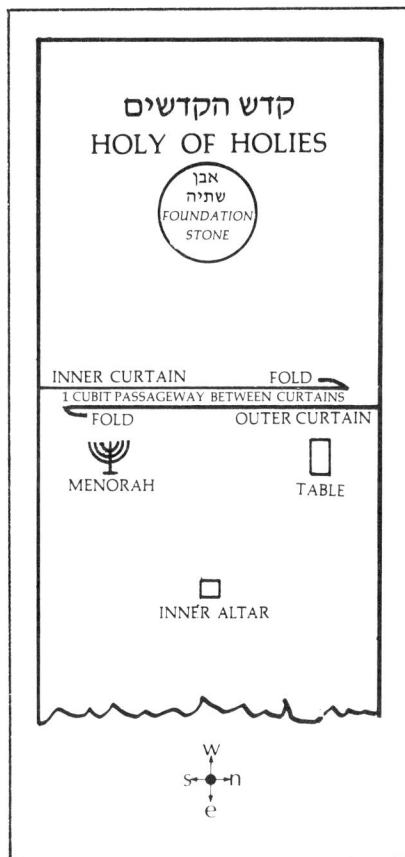

קֹדֶשׁ הַקֳּדָשִׁים
HOLY OF HOLIES

אֶבֶן שְׁתִיָּה
FOUNDATION STONE

INNER CURTAIN — FOLD
1 CUBIT PASSAGEWAY BETWEEN CURTAINS
FOLD — OUTER CURTAIN

MENORAH — TABLE

INNER ALTAR

w
s — n
e

The outer [curtain] was pinned up from the south[ern side], and the inner one from the north[ern side]. He walked between them, until he reached the north[ern side]. [When] he reached the north[ern side] he turned his face southward, walking to his left alongside the curtain until he reached the Ark. Reaching the Ark, he would put the shovel between the two poles. He heaped the incense on the burning

YAD AVRAHAM

ment that, 'Whenever you turn you should [if possible] turn to the right' (Gem. 45a, see comm. to 4:5 s.v. בְּכָל יוֹם כֹּהֲנִים עוֹלִים בְּמִזְרָחוֹ). At this point the Kohen Gadol's right side would be toward the Holy Ark and his left toward the curtain. This is preferable to the procedure that he would follow had the outer curtain been pinned from its northern and the inner curtain from its southern side. Then the requirement that one 'turn to the right would be complied with when the Kohen Gadol turned to enter between the two curtains, but not when he turned toward the Ark (Tos. Yom Tov; Tos. Yeshanim 52b citing Riva).

מְהַלֵּךְ בֵּינֵיהֶן, — He walked between them,

[He walked in the cubit-wide corridor formed by the two curtains.]

עַד שֶׁמַּגִּיעַ לַצָּפוֹן. — until he reached the north[ern side].

I.e., the northern opening — that of the inner curtain (Tiferes Yisrael).

הִגִּיעַ לַצָּפוֹן הוֹפֵךְ פָּנָיו לַדָּרוֹם, מְהַלֵּךְ לִשְׂמֹאלוֹ עִם־הַפָּרוֹכֶת — [When] he reached the north[ern side] he turned his face southward, walking to his left alongside the curtain

When one walks from north to south, east is to his left — i.e., toward the curtain (Rav; Rashi).

עַד שֶׁהוּא מַגִּיעַ לָאָרוֹן. — until he reached the Ark.

[The Ark containing the first tablets broken by Moses, the second set of tablets, and the Torah Scroll written by Moses stood in the center of the Holy of Holies (see Bava Basra 14a-b).]

Since our mishnah speaks about the Second Temple, as seen from its mention of the two curtains, it cannot literally mean the Ark, for the Ark had been hidden at the end of the First Temple period by King Yoshiyahu (see also Shekalim 6:1). What is meant is that he reached the place where the Ark had been (Gem. 52b).

הִגִּיעַ לָאָרוֹן, נוֹתֵן אֶת־הַמַּחְתָּה בֵּין שְׁנֵי הַבַּדִּים. — Reaching the Ark, he would put the shovel between the two poles.

[As it is written (Lev. 16:12): And he shall take a shovelful of coals from atop the altar, from before HASHEM [i.e., from the western portion of the altar], and two handfuls of fine incense, and he shall bring it inside the curtain.]

During the Second Temple period, this meant the place where the two poles had been when the Holy Ark stood in the Holy of Holies (Gem. 52b).

Rashi and Rav add that the during the First Temple period, the two בַּדִּים, poles, which were attached to the Ark (see Exod. 25:13) extended till they reached the curtain covering the door between the Holy and the Holy of Holies (see footnote to mishnah 1). It was between those poles that the incense was placed (Gem. 54a; see Tosafos, Menachos 98b s.v. דוחקין). Thus, the 'place' of the Ark includes all the space from the Ark to the curtain. This implies that the Kohen Gadol walked along the curtain until he reached the area between the poles, which satisfied the requirement of reaching the Ark [i.e., he did not have to walk up the actual place — in the middle of the Holy of Holies — where the Ark had stood, nor did he actually face the place of the Ark; instead, he faced southward all the while he was in the Holy of Holies.]

Meiri, however, specifies that when he reached the midpoint of the curtain, he turned to face the Ark (or its place) and advanced until he was directly in front of it.

וְנִתְמַלֵּא כָל־הַבַּיִת כֻּלּוֹ עָשָׁן.
יָצָא וּבָא לוֹ בְּדֶרֶךְ בֵּית כְּנִיסָתוֹ, וּמִתְפַּלֵּל

יד אברהם

Rambam's opinion in this matter, though on the surface similar to *Meiri's* (who was probably influenced by *Rambam*), can be understood to differ. See below s.v. יצא ובא לו for a lengthy discussion of this.

Rav's opinion is slightly ambiguous. Above, s.v. הִגִּיעַ לַצָּפוֹן, he seems to hold with *Rashi* (see also *Tos. Yom Tov* s.v. בין הבדים), but in s.v. דרך כניסתו he seems to follow *Rambam's* opinion. See below s.v. יצא ובא לו.]

צָבַר אֶת־הַקְּטֹרֶת עַל־גַּבֵּי גֶחָלִים, — *He heaped the incense on the burning coals,*

The צְדוֹקִים, *Saducees*, differed from the Sages in the method of performing this עֲבוֹדָה, *service* (see 1:5). The Sages adhered to the clear meaning of the Torah (bolstered by the Oral Tradition transmitted from Sinai) which states (*Lev.* 16:13): *And he shall put the incense upon the fire before HASHEM* — i.e., the coals were set down in the Holy of Holies and *then* the incense was burned. The Saducees held that the incense had to be put on the coals outside the Holy of Holies (*Gem.* 53a).

One view stated in the *Gemara* (49b) says that the incense was heaped in such a manner that the smoke should not rise immediately [and harm the *Kohen Gadol (Meiri)*]. Another opinion (also given in the *Gemara*) holds that the incense was spread out over the coals so that the smoke should rise quickly [not giving the *Kohen Gadol* time to 'feast his eyes' on the beauty of the Holy of Holies (*Meiri*)].

The *Gemara* (52b) also notes a difference of opinion about how the incense was put on the coals. One opinion holds that *Kohen Gadol* started on the side of the shovel nearest his body and continued heaping away from himself. The other opinion is that he began from the far end and then moved toward his body. The *Gemara* concludes that the latter opinion is more logical because

that method was used for the daily incense (*Tamid* 6:3) where the *Kohen* was warned to start from the far end lest he burn himself.

It is evident from the mishnah here that the incense was burned in the shovel. This was a departure from the procedure followed for the daily incense, where the coals were merely transported in the scoop to the inner altar and emptied on it. The incense was then burned on the altar itself (*Tamid* 6:2).

Tosafos Yeshanim (47a s.v. הכא) and *Ritva* explain that the coal shovel was necessary in the Holy of Holies where there was no altar or other vessel on which the incense could be burned. The daily incense, however, could simply be placed on the altar for burning.

וְנִתְמַלֵּא כָל־הַבַּיִת כֻּלּוֹ עָשָׁן. — *and the whole chamber filled with smoke.*

[As is written (*Lev.* 16:13): *And the smoke-cloud should cover the Ark-cover... cf. Gem.* 53a).]

The *Kohen Gadol* waited in the Holy of Holies until it was filled with smoke (*Rambam, Avodas Yom HaKippurim* 4:1).

יָצָא וּבָא לוֹ בְּדֶרֶךְ בֵּית כְּנִיסָתוֹ, — *He left, walking [backward] in the manner of his entry,*

He walked backwards, facing the place of the Ark, as a sign of humility and fear before God (*Rambam, comm.; Rav; Meiri; cf. Gemara* 53a).

The interpretation of how the *Kohen Gadol* exited hinges on where he actually burned the incense. Did he burn it 'between the poles' next to the curtain, or did he turn when he reached the place of the poles and walk right up to the place of the ark?

Rashi (52b s.v. דרך כניסתו) articulates that the Kohen Gadol simply backtracked to the entrance while continuing to face south (see above s.v. הִגִּיעַ לַצָּפוֹן and עַד שֶׁהוּא מַגִּיעַ). This

coals and the whole chamber filled with smoke.
He left, walking [backward] in the manner of his
entry, and he prayed a short prayer in the outer

YAD AVRAHAM

is consistent with his opinion *(ibid.)* that the incense was placed 'between the poles,' at a point near the curtain.

Rashi feels that this satisfies the requirement that the *Kohen Gadol* face the Ark. Thus the stipulation that the *Kohen Gadol* exit 'in the manner of his entry,' is met by his stepping backward as he continues to face southward, as he had all along.

However *Rambam (comm.* see Kafih edition) paraphrases the mishnah thus: He left walking backward, his face toward the Holy of Holies and his back toward the Holy.

Meiri's comments echo this opinion. It is difficult to describe a *Kohen Gadol* facing south as 'His face to the Holy of Holies and his back to the Holy,' but this seems to have been the *Kohen Gadol's* position as implied by the mishnah's statement that upon entering he 'turned his face southward, walking with his left side alongside the curtain' in

conjunction with the requirement that he exit, 'in the manner of his entry.'

Perhaps *Rambam* holds that when he entered the Holy of Holies on its northern side, he walked forward in a southwesterly direction (at an angle of slightly less than 45°) directly toward the Ark, in fulfillment of the statement: *He turned his face toward the south.* He walked in this direction, *until he reached the Ark.* As much can be gleaned from *Rambam's* words in *Avodas Yom HaKippurim* 4:1 where he says merely: 'He entered the Holy of Holies until he reached the Ark,' omitting the important (according to *Meiri)* stipulation that he should walk directly southward *with his left to the curtain* until he stands at the midpoint opposite

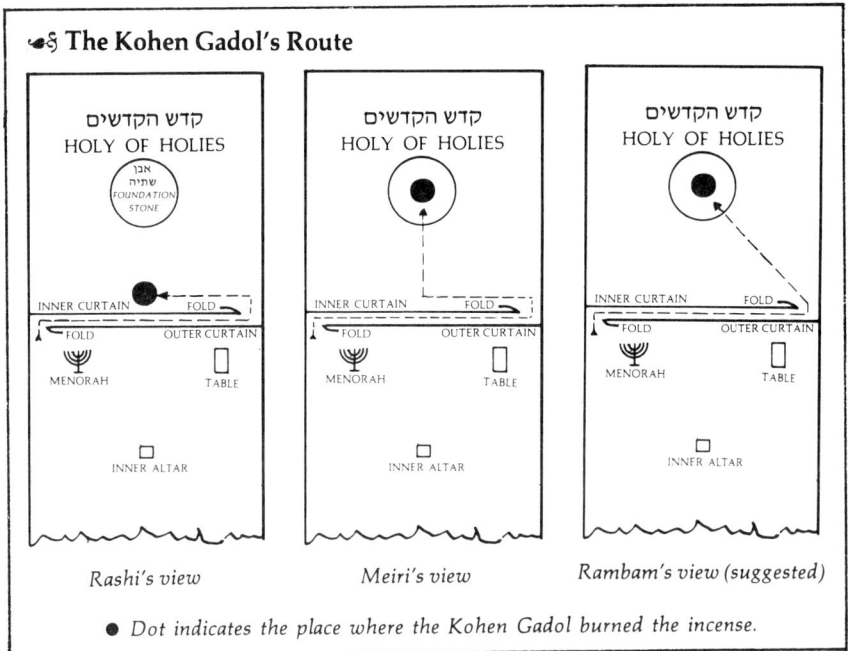

◄§ The Kohen Gadol's Route

קדש הקדשים
HOLY OF HOLIES

אבן שתיה
FOUNDATION STONE

INNER CURTAIN — FOLD
FOLD — OUTER CURTAIN
MENORAH — TABLE
INNER ALTAR

Rashi's view

קדש הקדשים
HOLY OF HOLIES

INNER CURTAIN — FOLD
FOLD — OUTER CURTAIN
MENORAH — TABLE
INNER ALTAR

Meiri's view

קדש הקדשים
HOLY OF HOLIES

INNER CURTAIN — FOLD
FOLD — OUTER CURTAIN
MENORAH — TABLE
INNER ALTAR

Rambam's view (suggested)

● *Dot indicates the place where the Kohen Gadol burned the incense.*

תְּפִלָּה קְצָרָה בַּבַּיִת הַחִיצוֹן, וְלֹא הָיָה מַאֲרִיךְ
בִּתְפִלָּתוֹ שֶׁלֹּא לְהַבְעִית אֶת־יִשְׂרָאֵל.

[ב] מִשֶּׁנִּטַּל הָאָרוֹן, אֶבֶן הָיְתָה שָׁם מִימוֹת נְבִיאִים רִאשׁוֹנִים,

יד אברהם

the Ark, and then turn and advance toward the Ark.[1]

Thus when he exited, he walked backwards along the exact diagonal path by which he had entered. However, Meiri's comments cannot be reconciled with this view. Thus *Meiri's* approach is different from both *Rashi's* and *Rambam's*.

וּמִתְפַּלֵּל תְּפִלָּה קְצָרָה בַּבַּיִת הַחִיצוֹן. — *and he prayed a short prayer in the outer chamber,*

The *Gemara* (53b) gives the text of the prayer. The standard versions of אַתָּה כוֹנַנְתָּ have additions and slight variations in wording and sequence. The *Gemara's* text is as follows:

יְהִי רָצוֹן מִלְּפָנֶיךָ ה' אֱלֹהֵינוּ וֵאלֹהֵי אֲבוֹתֵינוּ שֶׁתְּהֵא שָׁנָה הַבָּאָה עָלֵינוּ וְעַל־כָּל־עַמְּךָ בֵּית יִשְׂרָאֵל בְּכָל־מָקוֹם שֶׁהֵם אִם שְׁחוּנָה גְשׁוּמָה וְלֹא יַעֲדֵי עָבֵיד שֻׁלְטָן מִדְּבֵית יְהוּדָה וְלֹא יִהְיוּ עַמְּךָ יִשְׂרָאֵל צְרִיכִין לְפַרְנֵס זֶה מִזֶּה. וְלֹא תִכָּנֵס לְפָנֶיךָ תְּפִלַּת עוֹבְרֵי דְּרָכִים, *May it be Your will, HASHEM, our God and the God of our forefathers, that the year — coming upon us and all Your people Israel wherever they are — if it be hot, may it be rainy* [to counteract the heat] *and may sovereignty not be removed from the House of Judah,*[2] *and may Your people Israel not be required to receive sustenance from one another, and may the prayers to wayfarers not be*

permitted *to enter before You* [since travelers pray that there be no rain].

Abudraham's version of אַתָּה כוֹנַנְתָּ has this addition (found in *Yerushalmi.* See *Avodas Yisrael,* p. 169): וְעַל אֲחֵינוּ, *and* אַנְשֵׁי הַשָּׁרוֹן שֶׁלֹּא יִהְיוּ בָּתֵּיהֶם קִבְרֵיהֶם, *regarding our brothers in Samaria* [where the bricks tended to disintegrate after a few years] *let not their homes become their graves.*

(See also the יְהִי רָצוֹן toward the end of the *Avodah* אַמִּיץ כֹּחַ.) *Yerushalmi* has a much different prayer here.

Tiferes Yisrael suggests that the *Kohen Gadol* delayed this prayer until he reached the Holy, since it would have been inappropriate to pray for mundane needs in the Holy of Holies.

וְלֹא הָיָה מַאֲרִיךְ בִּתְפִלָּתוֹ שֶׁלֹּא לְהַבְעִית אֶת־יִשְׂרָאֵל. — *but he did not prolong his prayer so as not to frighten the Jews.*

Had he prolonged his stay in the Temple, the people might fear that he had died in the Holy of Holies (*Rav*).

During much of the Second Temple period when Israel was under Greek or Roman domination, the office of *Kohen Gadol* was used as a political power. Unqualified *Kohanim* would pay for the privilege of serving or be appointed in return for service rendered the government. Occasionally, Saducees gained the office. It was not uncommon for

---

1. This interpretation of *Rambam's* view is valid only if we understand him to refer to the Second Temple as does *Lechem Mishneh* s.v. יצא. Cf. *Tos. Yom Tov* to *Yoma* 5:5. During the First Temple period, however, the Kohen Gadol entered the Holy of Holies through a doorway situated directly opposite the Ark, so that he would proceed straight to the Ark without turning.

2. Yet, during the Second Temple era, the Jews in *Eretz Yisrael* were not ruled by kings of the House of Judah — the Davidic line. *Rambam's* working of this passage (*Avodas Yom HaKippurim* 4:1) leaves no doubt that *the house of Judah* is meant literally. Accordingly the prayer referred not to the rulers of *Eretz Yisrael,* but to the רֵישֵׁי גַלְוָתָא, *exilarchs* in Babylon, who were descendants of David, and enjoyed autonomy and a semi-royal status (see *Sanhedrin* 6a).

chamber, but he did not prolong his prayer so as not
to frighten the Jews.

2. After the Ark was taken away, a stone was there
from the times of the early prophets, and it

such people to die in the Holy of Holies
either because they were not worthy of
being *Kohanim Gedolim* or because
they altered the process of burning the
incense *(Rambam, comm.)*.

The *Gemara* (53b) relates that one
Kohen Gadol (Shimon HaTzaddik, ac-
cording to the *Yerushalmi* cited by *Tos.
Yeshanim*) prolonged his prayer.
Alarmed, his brethren, the *Kohanim*,

decided to enter the Temple to fetch
him. They had just started to enter
when he exited. They asked him, 'Why
did you prolong your prayer?'

He said to them, 'Does it displease
you that I prayed for you and that the
Temple should not be desolated?'

They told him, 'Do not make it a
habit to do so, for we have learned: *He
did not prolong...'*

2.

מִשֶּׁנִּטַּל הָאָרוֹן, — *After the Ark was taken
away,*

The *Gemara* (53a) comments that the
mishnah does not say מִשֶּׁנִּגְנַז הָאָרוֹן,
after the Ark was hidden, because the
tanna of the mishnah (like R' Eliezer
and R' Shimon) holds that the Ark was
not hidden by King Yoshiyahu (see
Gem. 52a), but was taken to Babylon by
King Nebuchadnezzar. Thus when
Scripture says *(II Chronicles* 36:10):
*King Nebuchadnezzar sent for and
brought· him* [King Yehoyachin] *to
Babylon with the vessels — the treasure
of the House of God,* the term *the
treasure of the House of God* refers to
the Ark.

According to another version, R'
Shimon and R' Yehudah hold that King
Yoshiyahu hid the Ark בִּמְקוֹמוֹ, *in its
place,* in order to prevent it from being
taken to Babylon *(Gemara* 52b).
Another opinion holds that it was hid-
den under the לִשְׁכַּת הָעֵצִים, *Wood
Chamber (Gem.* 54a; *Shekalim* 6:1; see
Yerushalmi).

R' Yaakov Emden (glosses to *Rambam, Beis HaBechirah* 4:1) suggests that
the Torah-ban *(Lev.* 16:2): *And he shall
not come at all times into the Holy
beyond the curtain, before the Ark-
cover which is upon the Ark, so that he*

should not die was in force only when
the Ark was inside the Holy of Holies.
Consequently when *Rambam* (apparently) rules (in *Yom HaKippurim*
1:7) that this ban applied during the
Second Temple era, he must hold that
the Ark was hidden in the Holy of
Holies. This supposition makes it difficult to understand the views of those
who hold that the Ark was taken to
Babylon or was hidden under the Wood
Chamber, for there is unanimous agreement in the Talmud that if the *Kohen
Gadol* enters the Holy of Holies without
having prepared the incense in the
prescribed manner, he violates Torah
law (see *Rambam's* commentary cited
above 5:1 s.v. וְלֹא הָיָה מַאֲרִיךְ).

In his *Mishneh Lechem,* R' Yaakov
Emden proposes a novel solution to this
problem. As known from *Rashi* to
Numbers 10:33 and *Deut.* 10:1 (see also
Tosafos, Eruvin 63b s.v. כל זמן;
Ramban to *Deut.* 4:5; *Abarbanel* to
Numbers 10:33; *Yerushalmi, Shekalim*
6:1) there were originally two Arks.
One was made in the Wilderness by
Betzalel *(Exodus* 25:10-22; 37:1-9) to
contain the Tablets and the Torah writ-
ten by Moses. This Ark later stood in
the Holy of Holies in the Temple, and is
the subject of the controversy men-

וּשְׁתִיָּה הָיְתָה נִקְרֵאת. גְּבוֹהָה מִן־הָאָרֶץ שָׁלֹשׁ
אֶצְבָּעוֹת וְעָלֶיהָ הָיָה נוֹתֵן.

[ג] נָטַל אֶת־הַדָּם מִמִּי שֶׁהָיָה מְמָרֵס בּוֹ.
נִכְנַס לַמָּקוֹם שֶׁנִּכְנַס, וְעָמַד בַּמָּקוֹם

tioned before.

The second Ark was made by Moses
to house the Tablets temporarily from
the time they were given him by God
until the dedication of the Tabernacle.
From then on Moses' Ark was used to
house the fragments of the original
stone tablets. This Ark accompanies the
Jews in their military campaigns. All
agree that at least this Ark was hidden
in the Holy of Holies.

אֶבֶן הָיְתָה שָׁם — *a stone was there*
On the place where the Ark had stood
(as evidenced from *Rambam's Beis
HaBechirah* 4:1 and *Tos. Yom Tov*).

[An alternative interpretation: On the
place where the shovel was put down. During the period of time that the Ark was in the
Holy of Holies, the *Kohen Gadol* did not
need to be directed to place the incense on
'the stone'; he would put the incense down
'between two poles' of the Ark as explained
earlier (5:1 s.v. עַד שֶׁהוּא מַגִּיעַ לָאָרוֹן). But,
after the Ark was removed, the *Kohen Gadol*
needed 'the stone to guide him to the exact
location for the incense burning.' See below
s.v. וְעָלֶיהָ הָיָה נוֹתֵן.]

Rambam (ibid.) writes: There was a stone
in the Holy of Holies — in the west[ern part]
— and upon it stood the Ark. *Tosefos Yom
Tov* asks: It is known from *Megillah* (10b
and from *Baraisa DeMeleches HaMishkan* 7)
that the Ark was placed exactly in the center
of the Holy of Holies; if so why does *Rambam* place it in the western part?

[Perhaps this can be resolved in the following manner: Megillah 10b states: 'We
have as a tradition of our fathers that the
place occupied by the Ark is not included in
the [Temple] measurements (אֵינוֹ מִן הַמִּדָּה)
מְקוֹם אָרוֹן).'

The *Talmud* elaborates: Though the
length and the breadth of the Holy of Holies
was only 20x20 cubits (*I Kings* 6:3, 20), one
could measure ten cubits from each side of
the Ark to the wall. Thus the Ark took up no

space. This was clearly a miraculous
phenomenon, illustrating that the Ark — i.e.,
the Torah — stands above this World and its
immutable natural laws. Once the Ark was
hidden or captured, this miracle ceased to be.
Consequently, the stone upon which the Ark
had stood occupied its naturally measurable
space in the Holy of Holies.

Perhaps *Rambam* locates the stone in the
western part because (according to one view)
the שְׁכִינָה, *Divine Presence*, is in the west
(*Bava Basra* 25a), and the Ark would have
been there if not for the miracle. Thus, the
distance between the curtain and the place of
the Ark — the stone — was ten cubits. When
the Ark was there, the miracle made it possible to measure ten cubits on the other sides as
well (cf. *Lechem Shamayim* here).

Tosafos (Bava Basra 25) cites *Riva* that the
Ark stood to the east. Here, too, *Tos. Yom
Tov* is at a loss to reconcile this opinion with
the *Megillah* 10b cited above. *Riva's* statement can be explained in the same manner as
Rambam's. *Riva* locates the Ark in the
eastern part of the Holy of Holies in
deference to the opinion that the שְׁכִינָה,
Divine Presence, is in the east (*Bava Basra*
25a).]

מִימוֹת נְבִיאִים רִאשׁוֹנִים, — *from the times
of the early prophets,*
David and Samuel (*Rashi*, quoting
Sotah 48b).

Tiferes Yisrael explains that they
were the discoverers of this stone [i.e.,
they knew its importance and revealed
its place].

וּשְׁתִיָּה הָיְתָה נִקְרֵאת — *and it was called
Shessiyah* [lit. *foundation*].
For from it the world was founded
(*Rashi; Rav* from *Gem.* 54b) [i.e., the
creation of the world began from this
point and this rock was the first part of
earth to be created (*Gem.* 54b).

[It is generally accepted that the great
stone in the 'Dome of the Rock' is the

was called *Shessiyah*. Its height was three fingers above the ground and upon it he would place [the shovel].

3. He took the blood from the one who was stirring it. He entered the place he had [previously] entered, stood in the place he had stood, and

YAD AVRAHAM

Shessiyah Stone *(Radbaz, Responsa* 639 and 691). See also *Ir HaKodesh Veha-Mikdash* by *R' Y.M. Tukaczinsky*, part 4 ch. 1; *Teshuvas Minchas Yitzchak* vol. 5:1).

גְּבוֹהָה מִן־הָאָרֶץ שָׁלֹשׁ אֶצְבָּעוֹת — *Its height was three fingers above the ground*

Radbaz (639) reconciles an apparent contradiction: the rock, within the Dome of the Rock is more than the 'height of two men' above the ground, whereas the mishnah says the *Shessiyah* stone was three fingers high. He points out that many other changes in the natural configuration of the Temple Mount have taken place which can be attributed to excavations made by the various peoples who occupied Jerusalem throughout the ages.

וְעָלֶיהָ הָיָה נוֹתֵן. — *and upon it he would place [the shovel]*.

[It is not clear (according to *Rambam*; see above s.v. אֶבֶן הָיְתָה שָׁם) why the shovel was placed on the *Shessiyah* Stone instead of on the area in front of the Ark, east of the stone, where it was put when the Ark was present. Perhaps *Rambam* holds that the stone was large, sprawling both eastward and westward. Although the Ark stood on the western part, the incense could be placed on the eastern part. This possibility is supported by two of *Rambam's* statements.

In *Avodas Yom HaKippurim* 4:1, he states simply that the *Kohen Gadol* burn the in-

cense on the *Shessiyah* Stone, but he fails to specify whether on the west or the east. In *Beis HaBechirah* 4:1, however, *Rambam* specifies: There was a stone in the Holy of Holies in its west, upon which the Ark was laid. The implication is that the incense could be placed on either part of the stone.

According to *Rashi* (above 5:1 s.v. עַר שֶׁהוּא מַגִּיעַ לָאָרוֹן) the *Kohen Gadol* stood near the curtain when burning the incense. Clearly then, the *Shessiyah* stone may not have been in the middle of the Holy of Holies, but near the curtain to the east. Thus the Ark which stood in the middle of the Holy of Holies *(Megillah* 10b; *Beraisa DiMeleches HaMishkan* 7) may not have stood upon the *Shessiyah* stone. In saying there was a stone *there*, the mishnah does not mean that it was on the exact site of the Ark, but rather that the stone was in the Holy of Holies or at the place of the incense burning so that the *Kohen Gadol* would know where to place the shovel as mentioned before (s.v. אֶבֶן הָיְתָה שָׁם).

This fits in with *Kaftor VaFerach* ch. 5 who, upon mentioning that *Shessiyah* means foundation, comments — And in truth — the place of the service is the foundation of the world (paraphrasing *Avos* 1:3: *The world stands upon three things... upon the* עֲבוֹדָה, *service...*). According to *Rambam*, the service was performed upon the *Shessiyah* stone only in the absence of the Ark. But if the above assumption about *Rambam's* opinion is correct, then the *Kohen Gadol* always set the scoop upon the eastern portion of the stone.]

3.

נָטַל אֶת־הַדָּם מִמִּי שֶׁהָיָה מְמָרֵס בּוֹ. — *He took the blood from the one who was stirring it*.

[Earlier (4:3) the *Kohen Gadol* had

slaughtered his ox, but instead of throwing its blood immediately, had gone to the service of burning the incense. In doing, he was following the se-

שֶׁעָמַד, וְהִזָּה מִמֶּנּוּ אַחַת לְמַעְלָה וְשֶׁבַע לְמַטָּה. וְלֹא הָיָה מִתְכַּוֵּן לְהַזּוֹת לֹא לְמַעְלָה וְלֹא לְמַטָּה, אֶלָּא כְּמַצְלִיף.

וְכָךְ הָיָה מוֹנֶה: אַחַת. אַחַת וְאַחַת. אַחַת וּשְׁתַּיִם. אַחַת וְשָׁלֹשׁ. אַחַת וְאַרְבַּע. אַחַת וְחָמֵשׁ. אַחַת וָשֵׁשׁ. אַחַת וָשֶׁבַע.

יָצָא וְהִנִּיחוֹ עַל־כַּן הַזָּהָב שֶׁבַּהֵיכָל.

יד אברהם

quence outlined in *Leviticus* (16:11, 12,14), where we read: *And he shall slaughter the ox of the sin offering which is his. And he shall take a shovelful of coals... And he shall take of the ox's blood and he shall throw...* All this time an assigned *kohen* stirred the blood to prevent it from coagulating while the *Kohen Gadol* burned the incense.]

נִכְנַס לַמָּקוֹם שֶׁנִּכְנַס — *He entered the place he had [previously] entered,*

[He now re-entered the Holy of Holies with the blood of his ox.]

וְעָמַד בַּמָּקוֹם שֶׁעָמַד, — *stood in the place he had stood,*

[Not only did he re-enter the Holy of Holies, but he also went back to the same place where he had stood — between the two poles.]

וְהִזָּה מִמֶּנּוּ אַחַת לְמַעְלָה וְשֶׁבַע לְמַטָּה. — *and sprinkled from it one [time] upward and seven [times] downward,*

[As is written (*Lev.* 16:14): *And he shall take of the ox's blood and sprinkle with his finger* (he dipped his right index finger into the blood and sprinkled it) *upon the Ark cover to the east* (upward), *and before the Ark cover shall he sprinkle seven times of the blood* (downward) *with his finger.*]

וְלֹא הָיָה מִתְכַּוֵּן לְהַזּוֹת לֹא לְמַעְלָה — *But he did not aim in sprinkling* [lit. to sprinkle] *either above*

Though he sprinkled with an upward motion (see below); he did not aim the blood to hit the top corner of the Ark cover (*Rav; Rashi*).

וְלֹא לְמַטָּה, — *or below,*

When he sprinkled with an upward motion, he did not aim for the side of the Ark cover (*Rav; Rashi*).

Teshuvos Radbaz (641) comments that after the Ark was removed, he sprinkled at the place where the Ark had been, just as the *Gemara* (52b) says that he put the incense between where the two poles had been.

אֶלָּא כְּמַצְלִיף. — *rather like one who whips.*

One who wields a whip starts with his hand held low (near his waist) and the back of his hand facing the ground, and then swings his hand above his head. Having reached a high-point, the hand is turned palm-down and the downward movement starts. Thus did the *Kohen Gadol* sprinkle upward with an upward movement, and seven downward with a downward motion. Thus *upward* and *downward* do not refer to the place where the blood fell, but to the motion with which it was sprinkled(*Aruch* s.v. מצליף and נגד cited by *Tosafos, Zevachim* 38a s.v. כמצליף and *Tos. Yeshanim, Yoma* 15a from R' Chananel).

Aruch (see other sources cited) states that all the sprinkled blood landed in the same area.

Rashi and *Rav* maintain that the

5
3

sprinkled from it one [time] upward and seven [times] downward. But he did not aim in sprinkling either above or below, rather like one who whips.

And this is how he [the *Kohen Gadol*] would count: One. One plus one. One plus two. One plus three. One plus four. One plus five. One plus six. One plus seven.

[Then] he exited and put [the vessel] on the golden stand, which was in the Holy.

blood sprinkled with the 'once upward' motion landed farthest away from the *Kohen Gadol* while that of the 'seven times downward' motions landed progressively closer to him.

Rav further explains that this is meant by the term כְּמַצְלִיף (which *Rashi* says he does not know how to explain). When one whips (a person), he starts from the top and works his way progressively down with each lash. This is also how the sprinkling was accomplished.

Meiri adds an alternate opinion that he *did* sprinkle with a forceful enough whipping motion for the blood to reach the Ark's cover, but *he did not aim* in the sense that it was not required that the blood hit a part of the Ark or even that it hit the Ark at all.

וְכָךְ הָיָה מוֹנֶה — *And this is how he* [the *Kohen Gadol*] *would count:*

[The *Kohen Gadol* counted aloud while sprinkling in order not to skip or duplicate any sprinkling.]

אַחַת. — *One.*

[When he sprinkled the 'once upward' he said אַחַת, *One*...]

אַחַת וְאַחַת. — *One plus one.*

[I.e., as he did the first downward sprinkle, he counted *one* upward plus *one* of the downward sprinklings.]

When he sprinkled the first of the 'seven downward' he did not say 'two' and continue until eight in order to emphasize the distinction between the first sprinkling, which was upward, and the group of seven which were downward *(Rav; Tosefos Yeshanim* 55a s.v. לימד*).*

If he would not specify the 'one upward' together with the seven downward, he might say 'two' for the first of the seven downward and then stop upon reaching the number 'seven', thinking he had completed the 'seven downward' when he made only six *(Rav* according to his interpretation of *Gem.* 55a; also *Tosefos Yeshanim s.v.* לומד *Rambam, Avodas Yom HaKippurim* 3:5).

אַחַת וּשְׁתַּיִם. — *One plus two.*

[By the second of the 'seven downward' he said, 'One (upward) plus two of the seven downward.]

אַחַת וְשָׁלֹשׁ. אַחַת וְאַרְבַּע. אַחַת וְחָמֵשׁ אַחַת וָשֵׁשׁ. אַחַת וְשֶׁבַע. יָצָא, וְהִנִּיחוֹ עַל-כַּן הַזָּהָב, שֶׁבַּהֵיכָל. — *One plus three. One plus four. One plus five. One plus six. One plus seven. Then he exited* [from the Holy of Holies to the Holy]. *And put (it)* [the vessel] *on the golden stand, which was in the Holy.*

[Some versions have עַל כַּן זָהָב, *on 'a' golden stand.*]

[ד] **הֱבִיאוּ** לוֹ אֶת־הַשָּׂעִיר. שְׁחָטוֹ וְקִבֵּל
בַּמִּזְרָק אֶת־דָּמוֹ. נִכְנַס לַמָּקוֹם
שֶׁנִּכְנַס, וְעָמַד בַּמָּקוֹם שֶׁעָמַד, וְהִזָּה מִמֶּנּוּ אַחַת
לְמַעְלָה וְשֶׁבַע לְמַטָּה, וְלֹא הָיָה מִתְכַּוֵּן לְהַזּוֹת
לֹא לְמַעְלָה וְלֹא לְמַטָּה, אֶלָּא כְּמַצְלִיף.
וְכָךְ הָיָה מוֹנֶה: אַחַת, אַחַת וְאַחַת, אַחַת
וּשְׁתַּיִם, וְכוּ׳. יָצָא וְהִנִּיחוֹ עַל־כַּן הַשֵּׁנִי שֶׁהָיָה
בַּהֵיכָל.
רַבִּי יְהוּדָה אוֹמֵר: לֹא הָיָה שָׁם אֶלָּא כַן אֶחָד
בִּלְבָד. נָטַל דַּם הַפָּר וְהִנִּיחַ דַּם הַשָּׂעִיר.
וְהִזָּה מִמֶּנּוּ עַל־הַפָּרֹכֶת שֶׁכְּנֶגֶד הָאָרוֹן

יד אברהם

4.

הֱבִיאוּ לוֹ אֶת־הַשָּׂעִיר. — *They brought him the he-goat.*

[He now left the Holy and went to the northern area (צָפוֹן) of the Courtyard where they brought him the he-goat upon which the lot, 'For Hashem' had fallen (above 4:1).]

שְׁחָטוֹ וְקִבֵּל בַּמִּזְרָק אֶת־דָּמוֹ. נִכְנַס לַמָּקוֹם שֶׁנִּכְנַס, — *He slaughtered it and received its blood in a basin. He entered the place where he had [previously] entered,*

[He re-entered the Holy of Holies, holding the he-goat's blood. See 4:3 s.v. שְׁחָטוֹ.]

וְעָמַד בַּמָּקוֹם שֶׁעָמַד, — *stood in the place he had stood,*

['Between the two poles,' or in front of the *Shessiyah* stone. See above mishnah 1.]

וְהִזָּה מִמֶּנּוּ אַחַת לְמַעְלָה וְשֶׁבַע לְמַטָּה, — *and sprinkled from it* [i.e., the he-goat's blood] *one [time] upward and seven [times] downward,*

As specified in *Leviticus* 16:15, *And he shall do with its* [the he-goat's] *blood as he did with the ox's blood, and he shall sprinkle it upon the Ark-cover and before the Ark-cover.*

וְלֹא הָיָה מִתְכַּוֵּן לְהַזּוֹת לֹא לְמַעְלָה וְלֹא לְמַטָּה אֶלָּא כְּמַצְלִיף, וְכָךְ הָיָה מוֹנֶה: אַחַת. אַחַת וְאַחַת. אַחַת וּשְׁתַּיִם, וְכוּ. — *but he did not aim in sprinkling either above or below, but rather like one who whips. And this is how he would count: One. One plus one. One plus two. Etc.*

I.e., he finished his count in the manner described before (mishnah 3) regarding the ox's blood.

[וכו׳ is a frequently used abbreviation for וְכוּלָּא, *and everything*, i.e., etc.] (For commentary on the foregoing see mishnah 3.)

יָצָא — *He exited*

[The Holy of Holies and entered the Holy.]

וְהִנִּיחוֹ עַל־כַּן הַשֵּׁנִי שֶׁהָיָה בַּהֵיכָל. — *and put (it)* [the vessel] *on the second stand which was in the Holy.*

[The basin with the remainder of the he-goat's blood.]

רַבִּי יְהוּדָה אוֹמֵר: לֹא הָיָה שָׁם אֶלָּא כַן אֶחָד בִּלְבָד. — *Rabbi Yehudah says: There was only one stand there.*

נָטַל דַּם הַפָּר וְהִנִּיחַ דַּם הַשָּׂעִיר. — *He took the ox's blood* [which he had left there when he finished sprinkling it in the

4. **T**hey brought him the he-goat. He slaughtered it and received its blood in a basin. He entered the place he had [previously] entered, stood in the place he had stood, and sprinkled from it one [time] upward and seven [times] downward, but he did not aim in sprinkling either above or below, rather like one who whips.

And this is how he would count: One. One plus one. One plus two. Etc. He exited and put [the vessel] on the second stand which was in the Holy.

R' Yehudah says: There was only one stand there. He took the ox's blood and put down the he-goat's blood.

He sprinkled from it at the curtain facing the Ark

YAD AVRAHAM

Holy of Holies] *and put down the he-goat's blood.*

R' Yehudah maintains that no second stand was needed. First he removed the ox's blood and then he put the he-goat's blood in its place *(Rav; Rashi).*

But according to the first opinion, he first put down the he-goat's blood and then he took the ox's blood *(Meleches Shlomo).*

According to R' Yehudah, had there been two stands it would have been possible for the *Kohen Gadol* to err and take the he-goat's blood again instead of the ox's blood *(Meiri).* Because he was weak from the fast and the service, special precautions had to be taken *(Tos. Yom Tov).*

וְהִזָּה מִמֶּנּוּ — *(And) he sprinkled from it*

[The rest of the mishnah is the mutual opinion of both the first Tanna and R' Yehudah.]

עַל-הַפָּרֹכֶת שֶׁכְּנֶגֶד הָאָרוֹן מִבַּחוּץ, — *at* [lit. *on*] *the curtain facing the Ark from the outside* [i.e., the side facing the Holy],

He sprinkled toward the portion of the curtain that was between the two poles *(Tiferes Yisrael;* see *Mishneh LaMelech* and *Har HaMoriyah* to *Ma'aseh HaKorbanos* 5:13).

[*Leviticus* (16:16) says: *And so* (as he did in the Holy of Holies) *shall he do for the Tabernacle...* (see *Gemara* 56b). It is understood that the blood sprinkled *in the Tabernacle* is sprinkled on the curtain since this is where blood is sprinkled for other sin sacrifices which have their blood sprinkled in the Holy (*Lev.* 4:6 and 17; *Malbim).*]

The *Gemara* (57a) cites the opinion of the first tanna that he sprinkled the blood only toward the curtain but not onto it. R' Elazar ben R' Yose disagrees and testified that when he visited Rome he was shown the curtain (see *Meilah* 17b) and he found many blood stains on it.

[On the surface our mishnah seem ambiguous about this question of whether or not the blood touched the curtain. The term עַל-הַפָּרֹכֶת, lit. *on the curtain,* can also be construed, *toward* the curtain (just as the term עַל-הַכַּפֹּרֶת, *on the Ark cover (Lev.* 16:15), need not mean that the blood actually landed on the Ark cover (see mishnah 3). Because the matter is not clear, the opinion of the first tanna ought to be accepted since it seems to be the majority view. Strangely, *Rambam (Ma'aseh HaKorbanos* 5:13 and *Avodas Yom HaKippurim* 4:2), does not designate either opinion. He simply quotes the mishnah וּמַזֶּה מִמֶּנּוּ עַל-הַפָּרֹכֶת, *he*

מִבַּחוּץ, אַחַת לְמַעְלָה וְשֶׁבַע לְמַטָּה, וְלֹא הָיָה מִתְכַּוֵּן וְכוּ'.

וְכָךְ הָיָה מוֹנֶה: וְכוּ'.

נָטַל דַּם הַשָּׂעִיר וְהִנִּיחַ דַּם הַפָּר, וְהִזָּה מִמֶּנּוּ עַל־הַפָּרֹכֶת שֶׁכְּנֶגֶד הָאָרוֹן מִבַּחוּץ, אַחַת לְמַעְלָה וְשֶׁבַע לְמַטָּה, וְכוּ'.

עֵרָה דַם הַפָּר לְתוֹךְ דַּם הַשָּׂעִיר. וְנָתַן אֶת־הַמָּלֵא בָּרֵיקָן.

[ה] ,,וְיָצָא אֶל־הַמִּזְבֵּחַ אֲשֶׁר לִפְנֵי־ה','' זֶה מִזְבַּח הַזָּהָב.

יד אברהם

sprinkles from it on the curtain. Perhaps he holds that the words עַל־הַפָּרֹכֶת, on the curtain clearly indicate that the mishnah accepts R' Elazar ben R' Yose's opinion that the blood was actually sprinkled onto the curtain; and *Rambam* accepted this opinion because of the rule that the decision should usually follow a סְתַם מִשְׁנָה, *anonymous mishnah*, where no opposing opinion is given. The translation preserves the ambiguity.]

אַחַת לְמַעְלָה — *one upward*
He took care that it should be thrown at least halfway up the height of the curtain (*Meiri*).

וְשֶׁבַע לְמַטָּה, — *and seven downward,*
Below the halfway point of the curtain (*Meiri*).

וְלֹא הָיָה מִתְכַּוֵּן וְכוּ'. — *but he did not aim, etc.*
[This has all been explained in *comm.* to mishnah 3 regarding the ox's blood.]

[According to the opinion of *Aruch* (cited in comm. to *mishnah* 3, s.v. אֶלָּא כְּמַצְלִיף) and others לְמַעְלָה, *upward*, and לְמַטָּה, *downward*, refer only to the direction of the sprinkling, not to where the blood landed, and all the blood fell to the ground on the same spot. It seems reasonable, accordingly, to conclude that this mishnah in saying. 'But 1e did not aim ...' holds that the blood was prinkled 'toward' not 'upon' the curtain (see bove s.v. עַל הַפָּרֹכֶת).

However, according to *Rashi* and *Rav* who understand the phrase in mishnah 3 to mean that he did not aim to hit the top corner (לְמַעְלָה) or the side (לְמַטָּה) of the Ark cover, but that he aimed his sprinkling so that each one of the drops fell closer to himself than the other, this mishnah may hold that the blood was sprinkled 'upon' the curtain (like R' Elazar ben R' Yose). *He did not aim* the blood to reach *the top* — i.e., the upper half of the curtain, *nor the bottom* — i.e., the bottom half of the curtain, *but like one who whips* — i.e., he aimed the blood so that the first drop should reach the highest (or farthest) point, the next one closer, etc.

[*Rambam* does not clarify the meaning of the phrase, 'But he did not aim ...' Thus he may agree with *Rashi*, and consequently interpret *'on the curtains* as explained above s.v. עַל הפרכת.]

וְכָךְ הָיָה מוֹנֶה: וְכוּ'. — *And this is how he would count, etc.*
[As narrated before in mishnah 3 and explained in the comm.]

נָטַל דַּם הַשָּׂעִיר — *He took the he-goat's blood*
[Which had been left standing on the golden stand, while the *Kohen Gadol* was sprinkling the ox's blood in the Holy.]

וְהִנִּיחַ דַּם הַפָּר, — *and put down the ox's blood*
[As mentioned before (s.v. נָטַל דַּם

from the outside, one upward and seven downward, but he did not aim, etc.

And this is how he would count, etc.

He took the he-goat's blood and put down the ox's blood and he sprinkled from it at the curtain facing the Ark from the outside, one upward and seven downward etc.,

He emptied the ox's blood into the he-goat's blood. And he poured the full [vessel] into the empty [vessel].

5. '**A**nd he shall go out to the altar which is before HASHEM' [Lev. 16:18] — this refers to the gold-[plated] altar [in the Holy].

YAD AVRAHAM

הַפָּר). This sequence is according to R' Yehudah who holds that there was only one stand. According to the first opinion that there were two stands, he first put down the vessel with the ox's blood, and then took the other vessel with the he-goat's blood. This is how *Rambam* (*Avodas Yom HaKippurim* 4:2) lists the sequence.]

וְהִזָּה מִמֶּנּוּ — *and he sprinkled from it* [i.e., the he-goat's blood]

עַל־הַפָּרֹכֶת שֶׁכְּנֶגֶד הָאָרוֹן מִבַּחוּץ, — *at* [lit. *on* (see above s.v. עַל־הַפָּרֹכֶת)] *the curtain facing the Ark from the outside,*

אַחַת לְמַעְלָה וְשֶׁבַע לְמַטָּה, וְכוּ׳. — *one upward and seven downward, etc.*

['Etc.' includes: 'But he did not aim...', And this is how he used to count, etc.,' as described above in mishnah 3.]

עֵירָה דַם הַפָּר לְתוֹךְ דַם הַשָּׂעִיר. — *He emp-*

tied the ox's blood into the he-goat's blood.

He did this as a preparation for the next act of the service; the sprinkling of a mixture of the two bloods on the four corners and the top of the inner altar as specified in *Leviticus* 16:18, *And he shall go out to the altar that is before HASHEM... and he shall take of the ox's blood and the he-goat's blood...* (*Rav; Rashi*).

וְנָתַן אֶת־הַמָּלֵא בָּרֵיקָן. — *And he poured* [lit. *put*] *the full* [vessel] *into the empty* [vessel].

After he had poured the ox's blood into the vessel holding the he-goat's blood he was left holding an empty vessel. He proceeded to pour the mixture back into this empty vessel to mix the two bloods [which were of different consistencies] thoroughly (*Rashi, Rav* from *Gem.* 58a).

5.

"וְיָצָא אֶל־הַמִּזְבֵּחַ אֲשֶׁר לִפְנֵי ה׳", — *'And he shall go out to the altar which is before HASHEM'* (Lev. 16:18) —

זֶה מִזְבַּח הַזָּהָב. — *this refers to the* gold[plated] *altar* [in the Holy].

The term הַמִּזְבֵּחַ אֲשֶׁר לִפְנֵי ה׳, *the altar which is before HASHEM*, refers to the gold-plated altar in the Holy (see *Exod.* 30:1-3) as indicated by the specification 'which is before HASHEM'.

Until now the *Kohen Gadol* had been

הִתְחִיל מְחַטֵּא וְיוֹרֵד. מֵהֵיכָן הוּא מַתְחִיל?
מִקֶּרֶן מִזְרָחִית־צְפוֹנִית, צְפוֹנִית־מַעֲרָבִית,
מַעֲרָבִית־דְּרוֹמִית, דְּרוֹמִית־מִזְרָחִית. מָקוֹם
שֶׁהוּא מַתְחִיל בַּחַטָּאת עַל־מִזְבֵּחַ הַחִיצוֹן,
מִשָּׁם הָיָה גוֹמֵר עַל־מִזְבֵּחַ הַפְּנִימִי.

יד אברהם

standing between the altar and the curtain. Now he had to leave this space and go to the front of the altar, standing between it and the Temple entrance. This is what the verse means when it says: *And he shall go out ... (Gem.* 58b).

הִתְחִיל מְחַטֵּא וְיוֹרֵד. — *He started to daub downward.*

[This application of the blood to the four corners of the golden altar was done in a different manner than the other thirty-nine applications of the day. In the other instances the *Kohen Gadol* dipped his finger into the blood and, with a swift motion of the hand, sprinkled it. This is indicated by the word וְהִזָּה, *he shall sprinkle,* which the Torah uses (*Lev.* 15:14,15,19) to designate these applications. Regarding this application the Torah says, *And he shall take of the ox's blood and of the he-goat's blood and he shall put it upon the corners of the altar around (Lev.* 15:18). That is why after dipping his finger into the blood he daubed the blood directly onto the altar's corners with his finger.]

[The mishnah does not tell us how far down the altar he daubed the blood. He probably daubed it from the top of each protruding corner of the altar to its bottom. The golden altar, just like the outer one, had protruding cubes on its four corners. These קְרָנוֹת, *horns,* are spelled out in *Exodus* 30:2 where it says, *From it* (the golden altar) *were* קַרְנוֹתָיו, *its horns.* This is also the term used here to designate where the blood was daubed: *And he shall put it upon* (קַרְנוֹת) *the horns of the altar around.*] I have found not found any source for the dimensions of these 'horns' (cf. *Baraisa DiMeleches HaMishkan* 11, with comm. by R'S.Y.C. Konieuski.]

The first tanna here holds that the *Kohen*

Gadol walked around the altar as he daubed the blood. He had to daub it with a downward stroke, because if he used an upward stroke, the blood might run down his hand and soil his vestments. Thus when the tanna says 'He started to daub downward,' this means that not only the first application, but also those following it, were made with downward movements *(Rav; Rashi).*

The term used for these applications מְחַטֵּא, literally means *purifies,* for these applications purified the altar (*Ritva* citing *Ramban; Tif. Yis.*).

[See *Exodus* 29:36 with *Onkelos* and *Rashi.* It is possible that in this context the word is derived from חֵטְא, *sin,* and is used here to mean *to remove* sin, similar to the way *Rashi* explains לְדַשְּׁנוֹ, [derived from דֶּשֶׁן, *ash; Exod.* 27:3 to remove the ash. See also *Radak, Shorashim* s.v. חטא.]

מֵהֵיכָן הוּא מַתְחִיל? — *Where did he start?*
[On which corner did he daub the blood first?]

מִקֶּרֶן מִזְרָחִית־צְפוֹנִית — *From the northeast [corner],*
Rashi (from *Gem.* 58b) explains why he started from this corner. This mishnah follows R' Yose (mishnah 1) who says that there was only one curtain between the Holy and the Holy of Holies and that its opening was to the north. Thus, when the *Kohen Gadol* left the Holy of Holies the first corner of the Inner Altar he passed was the northwestern one, from which he should have started the daubing according to the dictum: אֵין מַעֲבִירִין עַל הַמִּצְוֹת, *one should not bypass a mitzvah (Gem.* 33a). However, he first had to *go out* (from the space between the altar and the curtain) *to the altar which is before HASHEM,* as mentioned in the verse in *Lev.* 16:18 cited by the mishnah. When he reached the area that was no longer

5   He started to daub downward. Where did he start?
5   From the northeast corner, [to the] northwest [corner, to the] southwest [corner, to the] southeast [corner]. [At] the place from which he started [to daub] on the outer altar for a [regular] sin sacrifice — there he would finish on the inner altar.

between the altar and curtain, the nearest corner to him was the northeastern corner of the altar. According to the first tanna who says there were two curtains and the opening to the Holy was from the south, the *Kohen Gadol* began daubing from the southeastern corner because that would have been the first corner to the front.

[See also *Tos. Yom Tov; Teshuvos HaRashba* 1:388-90; and commentaries to *Rambam* loc. cit.]

Tosafos Yeshanim (59a s.v. מר) explains that this mishnah follows the opinion of the first tanna of mishnah 1 that there were two curtains. Nevertheless, the *Kohen Gadol* daubed the northeastern corner first. He was allowed to bypass the southeastern corner — despite the rule that one should not bypass a *mitzvah* — because the mishnah gives preference to the Temple rule that: All your turns should [if possible] be made to the right. Since the northeastern corner was to the right of the *Kohen Gadol*, he bypassed the southeastern corner, which he encountered first and began the daubing on the northeastern corner.

This seems also to be *Rambam's* opinion. In *Avodas Yom HaKippurim* 4:2 he rules (like our mishnah) that the *Kohen Gadol* started from the northeastern corner, although he holds *(Beis HaBechirah* 4:2) that there were two curtains *(Tos. R'Akiva).*

[This is evident from *Rambam's* own words. He says in two places *(loc. cit.* and *Maaseh HaKorbanos* 5:14) that the *Kohen* stood on the southern side (בֵּין מִזְבֵּחַ לַמְּנוֹרָה) but started offering the blood from the northeastern corner.]

On this point, our mishnah disagrees with the tanna cited in the *Gemara* (58b) who holds that the *Kohen Gadol* did indeed start from the southeastern corner.

צְפוֹנִית־מַעֲרָבִית, — [*to the*] *northwest* [*corner*],

[The second daub was on the northwestern 'horn.']

[The northwestern corner was second for two reasons. Since the *Kohen Gadol* was facing west when he began his daubing at the northeast, his right hand was to the north. Moving to the right according to the rule that all turns should be made to the right, the next corner would be the northwestern. Also, since he had been obligated to bypass the northwestern corner earlier (as mentioned before), this corner took precedence over the other ones (from *Gem.* 58b).

מַעֲרָבִית־דְּרוֹמִית, — [*to the*] *southwest* [*corner*],

[Next he daubed the southwestern 'horn' which is to the right of one facing the northwestern corner.]

דְּרוֹמִית־מִזְרָחִית. — [*to the*] *southeast* [*corner*];

[After daubing the southwestern 'horn,' he moved to the southeastern one, all the time moving to to his right.]

מָקוֹם שֶׁהוּא מַתְחִיל בְּחַטָאת עַל־מִזְבֵּחַ הַחִיצוֹן, — [*At*] *The place from which he started* [*to daub*] *on the outer altar for a* [*regular*] *sin sacrifice,*

In the case of a regular sin offering, the first application of blood was on the southeastern corner of the outer altar *(Zevachim 5:3).* The כֶּבֶש, ramp leading to the top of the altar was situated on the south side. Thus, the *Kohen* who ascended would be facing north, with this right hand toward the east. He would turn right, and begin to daub blood upon the southeastern corner.

The regular חַטָאת, *sin offering,* (brought by an individual for the inadvertent transgression of certain prohibitions), had its blood daubed on

רַבִּי אֱלִיעֶזֶר אוֹמֵר: בִּמְקוֹמוֹ הָיָה עוֹמֵד
וּמְחַטֵּא. וְעַל־כֻּלָּן הָיָה נוֹתֵן מִלְמַטָּה לְמַעְלָה,
חוּץ מִזּוּ שֶׁהָיְתָה לְפָנָיו, שֶׁעָלֶיהָ הָיָה נוֹתֵן
מִלְמַעְלָה לְמַטָּה.

[ו] **הִזָּה** עַל־טָהֳרוֹ שֶׁל מִזְבֵּחַ שֶׁבַע פְּעָמִים;
וּשְׁיָרֵי הַדָּם הָיָה שׁוֹפֵךְ עַל־יְסוֹד
מַעֲרָבִי שֶׁל מִזְבֵּחַ הַחִיצוֹן. וְשֶׁל מִזְבֵּחַ הַחִיצוֹן,
הָיָה שׁוֹפֵךְ עַל־יְסוֹד דְּרוֹמִי.

יד אברהם

the four corners of the outer altar.

מִשָּׁם הָיָה גוֹמֵר עַל־הַמִּזְבֵּחַ הַפְּנִימִי. — *there*
[lit. *from there*] *he would finish on the
inner altar.*

Some versions have שָׁם, *there* (*Tosefos
Yom Tov; Shinuyei Nuschaos*).

רַבִּי אֱלִיעֶזֶר אוֹמֵר: בִּמְקוֹמוֹ הָיָה עוֹמֵד
וּמְחַטֵּא. — *R' Eliezer says: He remained
in his place and daubed* [*the blood*].

[He did not, as the first tanna
described, walk around the altar while
applying the blood, but stood in one
place (either next to the northeastern or
the northwestern corner), and, while
standing there, applied the blood to the
four corners of the altar. He was able to
do this because this altar was only one
אַמָּה, *cubit*, square (*Exod.* 30:2).]

וְעַל־כֻּלָּן — *On all of them*
[I.e., on all the 'horns' except the one
nearest the *Kohen Gadol*.]

הָיָה נוֹתֵן מִלְמַטָּה לְמַעְלָה. — *he applied*
[*the blood*] *from the bottom to the top,*

[He started the application of the
blood from the bottom and daubed the
blood with an upward movement.]

This segment of the mishnah is the
continuation of R' Eliezer's statement.
According to him the *Kohen Gadol* was
not next to each corner when he put the
blood on it, therefore the reason for applying the blood with downward motion — so that he not soil his vestment —
does not apply (*Rav; Rashi*).

חוּץ מִזּוּ, — *except for this one*
[I.e., the corner which is the subject
of the mishnah's query: From where did
he start? — The northeastern corner.]

[Though *Rambam* rules (*Avodas
Yom HaKippurim* 4:2 and *Comm. to
Mishnah*) that the *Kohen Gadol* walked
around the altar, he maintains that only
the first application was made with a
downward movement. Evidently, he
holds that the statement at the beginning of the mishnah: *He started to daub
downward*, refers only to the first application. When the mishnah goes on to
say: *On all of them he applied* [*the
blood*] *from the bottom to the top*, it is
an opinion shared even by those who
hold that the *Kohen Gadol* walked
around the altar. This is evident from
the manuscript of *Rambam's* commentary (ed. Kafih) where *Rambam* had
originally written that this segment of
the mishnah was said by R' Eliezer, but
Rambam later crossed these words out.
Our editions of his commentary omit
this comment (see *Teshuvos HaRashba*
1:399 cited in *Kessef Mishneh; Tos.
Yom Tov; Meiri*).

שֶׁהָיְתָה לְפָנָיו, — *that was in front of him,*
[I.e., this 'horn' was in front of the
Kohen Gadol as he applied the blood to
it.]

שֶׁעָלֶיהָ הָיָה נוֹתֵן מִלְמַעְלָה לְמַטָּה. — *upon
which he applied* [*the blood*] *from the
top to the bottom.*

R' Eliezer says: He remained in his place and daubed. On all of them he applied [the blood] from the bottom to the top, except for this one that was in front of him, upon which he applied from the top to the bottom.

6. He sprinkled upon the surface of the altar seven times; and the remainder of the blood he would pour upon the western base of the outer altar. But those [sacrifices] of the outer altar, he would pour upon the southern base.

YAD AVRAHAM

6.

הַזֶּה עַל־טָהֳרוֹ שֶׁל מִזְבֵּחַ — *He sprinkled upon the surface* [lit. *purified area*] *of the altar*

First he cleared the altar of the coal and ashes (from the daily incense) and then he sprinkled blood directly upon the exposed surface of the altar *(Rav from Gem. 59a).*

שֶׁבַע פְּעָמִים; — *seven times;*

[As specified in *Leviticus* 16:19: *And he shall sprinkle upon it* (the altar) *of the blood seven times...*]

וּשְׁיָרֵי הַדָּם — *and the remainder of the blood*

[That which remained in the vessel after all the sprinkling.]

הָיָה שׁוֹפֵךְ עַל־יְסוֹד מַעֲרָבִי שֶׁל מִזְבֵּחַ הַחִיצוֹן. — *he would pour upon the western base of the outer altar.*

[The outer altar — i.e., the one in the Courtyard—was built upon a broad base which protruded beyond the altar like a step. This protrusion was called the יְסוֹד, *base.* The remaining blood was poured onto its western side.]

This was done to comply with the verse in *Leviticus* 4:7: *And all the [remaining] blood of the ox shall he pour onto the base of the altar of the burnt sacrifice* [i.e., the outer altar] *(Gem. 59a).* Though this verse does not refer directly to the Yom Kippur bull, the Sages found an allusion to the Yom

Kippur service in the redundant word הַפָּר, *the ox.* Since the ox is the subject of the whole paragraph Scripture does not have to mention it again *(Rashi citing Sifra loc. cit.* See also *Zevachim* 52a and 40a with *Tosafos* s.v. לסמיכה).

The blood was poured upon the western side of the base because it was first to be encountered by the *Kohen Gadol* as he entered the Courtyard *(Gem. 59a).*

[This rule applied to all the other sin sacrifices whose blood was sprinkled on the curtain. See *Zevachim* 5:1-2.]

וְשֶׁל מִזְבֵּחַ הַחִיצוֹן, — *But those* [sacrifices] *of the outer altar,*

[That is, those sacrifices whose blood was sprinkled *only* upon the outer altar. This includes all sacrifices except the ox and he-goat of the Yom Kippur service, the ox for the sin offering of the *Kohen Gadol* (פַּר כֹּהֵן מָשִׁיחַ), the ox for a sin committed by most of the nation (הֶעְלֵם דָּבָר שֶׁל צִבּוּר) and the he-goat for communal idolatry.]

הָיָה שׁוֹפֵךְ עַל־יְסוֹד דְּרוֹמִי. — *he would pour upon the southern base.*

[This was the first part of the base a *Kohen* encountered when he came down the ramp on the southern side of the altar *(Zevachim* 53a).]

[The base extended fully only on the altar's western and northern side. On

אֵלּוּ וָאֵלּוּ מִתְעָרְבִין בָּאַמָּה וְיוֹצְאִין לְנַחַל
קִדְרוֹן. וְנִמְכָּרִין לַגַּנָּנִין לְזֶבֶל, וּמוֹעֲלִין בָּהֶן.

[ז] כָּל־מַעֲשֵׂה יוֹם הַכִּפֻּרִים הָאָמוּר עַל־
הַסֵּדֶר, אִם הִקְדִּים
מַעֲשֶׂה לַחֲבֵרוֹ, לֹא עָשָׂה כְלוּם. הִקְדִּים דָּם

יד אברהם

the eastern and southern sides, the foundation extended only to the corners — i.e., the southwestern and northeastern corners (*Middos* 3:1).]

אֵלּוּ — *These*
[The blood of the sacrifices sprinkled in the Temple and poured out on the western foundation.]

וָאֵלּוּ — *and those*
[The blood of the sacrifices sprinkled upon the outer altar and poured out upon the southern foundation.]

מִתְעָרְבִין בָּאַמָּה — *mixed together in the canal*
A canal ran through the Courtyard through which the blood drained out. Water was channeled through it to flush it clean (see *Rashi, Pesachim* 64a s.v. אלא שהכהנים).
Rashbam (*Pesachim* 109b s.v. היכי) says it was called אַמָּה because its width was one אַמָּה, *cubit*.

On the southwestern corner of the foundation there were two holes. The blood poured upon the western and southern parts of the foundation drained through these two holes into the canal (*Middos* 3:2).

וְיוֹצְאִין לְנַחַל קִדְרוֹן. — *and flowed out to the Kidron Valley.*
The noun נַחַל, is used here to mean *valley* as in *Deut.* 21:4 (*Rashi*; see *Targum Onkelos* and *Yonasan* there; cf. *Rambam, Rotzeach; Teshuvos Maharik* 157).
[*R' Yaakov Emden* (*Sheilos Yaavetz* 1:24) suggests that two meanings — *valley* and *stream* — are implied in the word נַחַל, i.e., a valley with a stream in it. However, *Rashi's* assumption in *Deut.* that נחל means a valley, is based on *Niddah* 8b.
It seems probable that *Rashi* surmised that נַחַל here means a *valley* because otherwise how could the blood later be collected and sold (see below). *Tiferes Yisrael* also says that

---

◄§ The Altar (*viewed from above*)

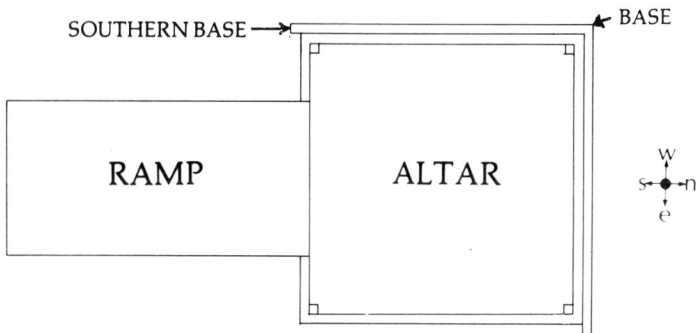

Although the base did not circle the altar on the southern side, the 1 cubit protrusion of the western base on the southern side is considered the southern base.

These and those mixed together in the canal and flowed out to the Kidron Valley. It was sold to gardeners for fertilizer, and one is liable for unauthorized use of it.

7. **T**he entire Yom Kippur service that has been listed in sequence, if he advanced one service before another, he has accomplished nothing. [For

נַחַל קִדְרוֹן here means *the valley next to the Kidron stream*. Evidence that נַחַל קִדְרוֹן refers both to the valley and to the stream can be demonstrated from *Targum Yonasan* who translates נַחַל קִדְרוֹן in *I Kings* 2:23, 15:13: נַחְלָא דְקִדְרוֹן, *the stream Kidron*, but renders the same words in *II Kings* 23:6 (where there appear twice), once נַחְלָא, *stream* and once מֵישְׁרָא, *plain* (according to the context).]

וְנִמְכָּרִין לַגַּנָּנִין לְזֶבֶל, — *It was sold to gardeners for fertilizer*,

[The Temple officials sold it to farmers with the proceeds going to the Temple treasury (הֶקְדֵּשׁ).]

וּמוֹעֲלִין בָּהֶן — *and one is liable for unauthorized use of it*.

It is forbidden to use it unless it is purchased from the Temple treasury. Once paid for, it ceases to be sacred property and may be used for private purposes. The sin of using or stealing sacred property is called מְעִילָה, *abuse* (see. *Lev.* 5:15 נֶפֶשׁ כִּי־תִמְעֹל מַעַל).]

7.

כָּל־מַעֲשֵׂה יוֹם הַכִּפֻּרִים — *The entire Yom Kippur service*

All of the services performed by the *Kohen Gadol* in his white vestments while anywhere inside the Temple, whether in the Holy of Holies or the Holy (*Rav* from *Gemara* 60a).

הָאָמוּר עַל־הַסֵּדֶר, — *that has been listed in sequence*,

In the mishnah [i.e., the order of the service as given throughout our tractate] (*Rashi; Rav*).

Meiri breaks up this phrase in the following manner כָּל־מַעֲשֵׂה יוֹם הַכִּפֻּרִים הָאָמוּר, *All of the services of Yom Kippur which have been listed* [*here*] *are* עַל הַסֵּדֶר, *in their sequence* — i.e., the mishnah lists these services in the sequence in which they have to be performed.

אִם הִקְדִּים מַעֲשֶׂה לַחֲבֵירוֹ, — *if he* [*the Kohen Gadol*] *advanced one service before another*,

[In violation of the listed sequence.]

לֹא עָשָׂה כְּלוּם. — *he has accomplished nothing*.

[The service advanced out of its proper place in the sequence is not valid. The *Kohen Gadol* continues with the sequence, and when he reaches the service which he has already done out of order, he must perform it again.]

R' Yehudah (*Gem.* 60a) specifies that only service done 'inside' is meant. *Rashi* takes this to mean the Holy of Holies. Thus the services performed only in the Holy are not included.

Rambam (*Avodas Yom HaKippurim* 5:1) understands 'inside' to mean the entire Temple building, including the Holy. Included also are services performed in the Courtyard that are necessary prerequisities for the inner rites, such as the casting of lots on the two he-goats and confession, and acts like the burning of the daily incense which he performed in his golden (regular) vestments in the Holy.

R' Nechemiah (*Gem.* 60a) holds that this rule includes all services performed in the white vestments, whether 'inside' (i.e., the Holy of Holies) or 'outside' (i.e., the Temple

הַשָּׂעִיר לְדַם הַפָּר, יַחֲזֹר וְיַזֶּה מִדַּם הַשָּׂעִיר לְאַחַר דַּם הַפָּר.

וְאִם עַד שֶׁלֹּא גָמַר אֶת־הַמַּתָּנוֹת שֶׁבִּפְנִים נִשְׁפַּךְ הַדָּם, יָבִיא דָם אַחֵר וְיַחֲזֹר וְיַזֶּה בַּתְּחִלָּה בִּפְנִים. וְכֵן בַּהֵיכָל, וְכֵן בְּמִזְבַּח הַזָּהָב, שֶׁכֻּלָּן כַּפָּרָה בִּפְנֵי עַצְמָן.

רַבִּי אֶלְעָזָר וְרַבִּי שִׁמְעוֹן אוֹמְרִים: מִמָּקוֹם שֶׁפָּסַק מִשָּׁם הוּא מַתְחִיל.

יד אברהם

Court. According to *Rashi*, 'outside' means the Holy. However, *R' Chaim HaLevi Soloveitchik* interprets R' Nechemiah to mean that only the sprinkling upon the curtain is considered *inside*, not the applications upon the golden altar (see also *Even HaAzel*).

The *Gemara* adds that slaughtering, though performed in the Courtyard, is included among the acts of service performed inside, since it is needed for the inside service [צוֹרֶךְ פְּנִים כִּפְנִים דָּמֵי]. Thus, if the he-goat were slaughtered before the ox's blood was sprinkled in the Holy of Holies (5:3,4) the *Kohen Gadol* must slaughter another he-goat after sprinkling the ox's blood.

הִקְדִּים דַּם הַשָּׂעִיר לְדַם הַפָּר, — [For example] if he advanced the he-goat's blood before the ox's blood,

[The ox's blood was always sprinkled first, whether in the Holy of Holies, or in the Holy. If the *Kohen Gadol* sprinkled the he-goat's blood first (according to *Rashi* in the Holy of Holies, and according to *Rambam* even in the Holy; see above, s.v. כָּל מַעֲשֶׂה), that service is not valid.]

יַחֲזֹר וְיַזֶּה מִדַּם הַשָּׂעִיר לְאַחַר דַּם הַפָּר. — he must again sprinkle from the he-goat's blood after [sprinkling] the ox's blood.

As pointed out before, if the he-goat was slaughtered before the *Kohen Gadol* sprinkled the ox's blood in the Holy of Holies, another he-goat has to be slaughtered. The mishnah mentions only that its *blood* must be sprinkled again — and not that a new slaughter must be done — because it discusses an instance where the he-goat was slaughtered in its rightful sequence (after the ox's blood had been sprinkled in the Holy of

Holies), but its blood was wrongly sprinkled before the ox's had been sprinkled in the Holy (*Gem.* 60a).

[According to *Rashi* the mishnah follows R' Nechemiah that any service performed in the white vestments — even in the Courtyard — is not valid if performed out of sequence (*Gevuras Ari*). But according to *Rambam* and *Rav* (see above s.v. הָאָמוּר עַל־הַסֵּדֶר) the sprinkling done in the Temple is considered בִּפְנִים, *inside*. Accordingly the mishnah can hold like R' Yehudah's opinion.]

וְאִם עַד שֶׁלֹּא גָמַר אֶת־הַמַּתָּנוֹת שֶׁבִּפְנִים נִשְׁפַּךְ הַדָּם, — And if the blood spilled before he finished the applications [of the blood] *inside*,

[Here the mishnah proceeds to a case where the service of sprinkling was performed in sequence, but could not be completed because the blood spilled.]

יָבִיא דָם אַחֵר — he [the *Kohen Gadol*] must bring other blood

[He must slaughter another animal and receive its blood.]

If the blood that spilled was the ox's, he must also repeat the filling of his hands (חֲפִינָה) with incense (see 4:3 and 5:1). This service, though performed in the Courtyard, is a necessary prerequisite for the service of burning the incense in the Holy of Holies, and as such must be done in sequence — after the slaughter of the ox (*Gem.* 60b with *Rashi*).

It seems from *Rambam* (but see *Or Sameach*) that this is so even if the *Kohen Gadol* had already finished the sprinkling in the Holy of Holies in which case the

5
7

example] if he advanced the he-goat's blood before the ox's blood, he must again sprinkle from the he-goat's blood after [sprinkling] the ox's blood.

And if the blood spilled before he finished the applications inside, he must bring other blood and he must again sprinkle inside from the beginning. The same [is true for the sprinkling] in the Holy, and the same applies to [the sprinkling on] the golden altar, because each of them is a separate atonement.

R' Elazar and R' Shimon say: From where he broke off from there he starts [again].

YAD AVRAHAM

slaughter of another ox is needed only for the sprinkling in the Holy. (Whatever service was performed with the blood before it spilled remains valid. The blood of the second ox is used only for the undone sprinklings.) *Tosefos Yeshanim* (61a s.v. בקטורת citing *Riva), Ritva* (61a), and *Meiri* hold that the incense-taking must be repeated only if the blood spilled before the sprinkling of the blood in the Holy of Holies was completed. But, if the blood spilled after the sprinkling in the Holy of Holies was completed — the incense-taking need not be redone. Patently, whenever incense had to be taken again, the whole procedure for the incense (bringing the incense into the Holy of Holies and burning it there) has to be performed again.

וְיַחֲזוֹר וְיַזֶּה בַּתְּחִלָּה בִּפְנִים. — *and he must again sprinkle inside from the beginning.*

[I.e., in the Holy of Holies.]

[Even those sprinklings which had already been done must be redone. All of the eight sprinklings in the Holy of Holies are considered one event and have to be done in sequence from the same blood.]

וְכֵן בַּהֵיכָל, — *the same [is true for the sprinkling] in the Holy,*

If the blood spilled before he finished sprinkling upon the curtain he must redo the sprinkling that had already been done. Here, however, he must redo only the sprinkling upon the curtain, not the sprinkling in the Holy of Holies *(Rav; Rash).*

וְכֵן בַּמִּזְבֵּחַ הַזָּהָב, — *and the same applies to [the sprinkling on] the golden altar,*

[If the blood spilled before he finished these applications, another ox and he-goat must be slaughtered, and their blood mixed and sprinkled.]

Even if the blood spilled after he had finished the applications on the four corners of the altar, but before he finished the sprinkling upon the top of the altar, he had to start again from the applications on the four corners of the altar, because these two groups of applications are mentioned together in the Torah *(Gevuras Ari in Miluim).*

שֶׁכֻּלָּן — *because each of them*

[Each of the groups of sprinklings mentioned before — i.e., those in the Holy of Holies, the Holy, and on the golden altar.]

כַּפָּרָה בִּפְנֵי עַצְמָן. — *is a separate* [unit of] atonement [lit. *an atonement before themselves*].

Therefore when any of these groups of sprinklings has been completed, that act of atonement has been completed and cannot be invalidated *(Rav; Rashi).*

רַבִּי אֶלְעָזָר וְרַבִּי שִׁמְעוֹן אוֹמְרִים: מִמָּקוֹם שֶׁפָּסַק מִשָּׁם הוּא מַתְחִיל. — *R' Elazar and R' Shimon say: From where he broke off from there he starts [again].*

Even if that act of atonement had not yet been completed he does not have to redo what he has already done *(Rashi, Rav).*

[א] **שְׁנֵי** שְׂעִירֵי יוֹם הַכִּפּוּרִים — מִצְוָתָן שֶׁיִּהְיוּ שְׁנֵיהֶן שָׁוִין בְּמַרְאֶה וּבְקוֹמָה וּבְדָמִים וּבִלְקִיחָתָן כְּאֶחָד. וְאַף־עַל־פִּי שֶׁאֵין שָׁוִין, כְּשֵׁרִין. לָקַח אֶחָד הַיּוֹם וְאֶחָד לְמָחָר, כְּשֵׁרִין.
מֵת אֶחָד מֵהֶן — אִם עַד שֶׁלֹּא הִגְרִיל מֵת, יִקַּח זוּג לַשֵּׁנִי; וְאִם מִשֶּׁהִגְרִיל מֵת, יָבִיא זוּג

יד אברהם

[E.g., if the blood spilled after the third sprinkling, he does not have to start from the first again. He brings other blood and starts from the fourth.]

The Halachah does not follow the view of R' Elazar and R' Shimon (Rav; Rambam, Avodas Yom HaKippurim 5:5-7).

Chapter 6

Having narrated the service performed with the *Kohen Gadol's* ox and with the he-goat designated 'For *Hashem*,' the mishnah now turns to the he-goat which had been designated 'For *Azazel*.' In a mild diversion, the mishnah discusses the laws governing the similarities between the two he-goats. Mishnayos 2-7 revert to the narration of the Yom Kippur service.

1.

שְׁנֵי שְׂעִירֵי יוֹם הַכִּפּוּרִים— — *The two he-goats of Yom Kippur—*

[Two he-goats were used in the Yom Kippur service. A drawing of lots (4:1) decided which one should be 'For *Hashem*' — it was slaughtered and its blood was sprinkled in the Holy of Holies and in the Holy (5:4,5) — and which one should be 'For *Azazel*.' The procedure followed with this second goat is described in this chapter.]

מִצְוָתָן שֶׁיִּהְיוּ שְׁנֵיהֶן שָׁוִין — *it is preferable* [lit. *their mitzvah,* i.e., the most desirable fulfillment of the commandment] that they be alike

[The word מִצְוָתָן as used in *Talmud* connotes that the action described is לְכַתְּחִלָה, *preferable,* and that its performance in that manner is a meritorious act (מִצְוָה). But a failure to perform the act in the most preferable manner does not invalidate it; it merely lacks the most desirable mode of perfor-

mance. Here too, though it is preferable that the two goats be alike, the service is valid even if they are not.]

בְּמַרְאֶה — *in color,*
They should both be either black, white, or brown (Rashi; Rav).

Sfas Emes maintains (from the version of *Rashi* found in our editions) that מַרְאֶה includes appearance, too (i.e., that one should not be fat and the other lean). But *Bach* and others emend the text so that this cannot be deduced from Rashi.

וּבְקוֹמָה וּבְדָמִים — *(and) in height, and in price;*
Scripture uses the term שְׁנֵי שְׂעִירִים, *two he-goats,* in reference to these two animals three times (*Leviticus* 16:5,7,8). The word שְׂעִירִים, *he-goats,* alone suffices to indicate that two he-goats are needed. Thus the superfluous word שְׁנֵי, *two,* is taken to mean two similar ones. The phrase is mentioned three times to

1. **T**he two he-goats of Yom Kippur — it is preferable that they be alike in color, in height and in price; and in their purchase [which should be] together. But even if they are not alike, they are valid. If he bought one today and one tomorrow, they are valid.

If one of them died — if it died before he cast the lots, he must buy a mate for the second one; but if it died after he cast the lots, he must bring another pair

YAD AVRAHAM

teach that these he-goats should be similar in three aspects (*Rav* from *Gem.* 62b according to our editions; for variant versions see *Tos. Yesh.* 62b s.v. חד).

וּבְלְקִיחָתָן כְּאֶחָד. — *and in their purchase [which should be] together* [lit. *as one*].

They should be bought from one person in a single transaction, or from two people who appoint a single representative (שָׁלִיחַ) to effect the transaction (*Tos. Yesh.* 62a s.v. ולקיחתן). The source for this is *Leviticus* 16:5, *And with the congregation of the Children of Israel's* [*funds*] *he shall buy two he-goats.* The verb יִקַּח, *he shall buy*, connotes a single transaction (*Tos. Yesh.* 62b s.v. חד).

The translation of *Leviticus* 16:5, though not literal, conforms to the exegesis of *Sifra* and *Shevuos* (14a) which understand מֵאֵת בְּנֵי יִשְׂרָאֵל to mean *and from* (with) ... *Israel's* [funds]. Consequently they render יִקַּח, *he shall buy* instead of *he shall take*.

וְאַף־עַל־פִּי שֶׁאֵין שָׁוִין, כְּשֵׁרִין. — *But even if they are not alike* [i.e., in color, height, and price], *they are valid.*

This is derived from *Leviticus* 16:9, 10, 'And Aaron shall sacrifice the שָׂעִיר, *he-goat* (singular), *upon which the lot "For HASHEM" came up and make it a sin offering. And the* שָׂעִיר *he-goat* (singular), *upon whom the lot "For Azazel" came up* ...

The word שָׂעִיר, *he-goat*, is superfluous both times. This teaches us that if the goats are not alike (i.e., they

are individuals rather than a pair) the service is valid nevertheless (*Gemara* 62b).

[Perhaps one superfluous שָׂעִיר, *he-goat*, teaches us that they may differ in the three aspects listed in the mishnah (color, height, and price), while the other superfluous word שָׂעִיר, teaches us that they may be bought separately.]

לָקַח אֶחָד הַיּוֹם וְאֶחָד לְמָחָר, כְּשֵׁרִין. — *If he bought one today and one tomorrow, they are valid.*

[The previous passage, 'But even if they are not alike, they are valid,' refers to differences in price, color, and height. This passage refers to the preference that they be bought simultaneously.]

מֵת אֶחָד מֵהֶן—אִם עַד שֶׁלֹּא הִגְרִיל מֵת, יִקַּח זוּג לַשֵּׁנִי; — *If one of them died — if it died before* [the *Kohen Gadol*] *cast the lots, he must buy a mate for the second one;*

Though the preferred process is to buy both he-goats together, the surviving goat is not disqualified (*Ritva*; cf. *Tosafos Yeshanim* 62a s.v. יקח).

וְאִם מִשֶּׁהִגְרִיל מֵת, יָבִיא זוּג אַחֵר — *but if it died after he cast the lots, he must bring another pair*

[At this point, the mere purchase of another animal will not be a remedy. The surviving animal had been designated by lot 'For *Hashem*' or 'For *Azazel*' and cannot be changed from its status; a newly purchased animal, therefore will not have been designated

אַחֵר וְיַגְרִיל עֲלֵיהֶם בַּתְּחִלָּה. וְיֹאמַר, אִם שֶׁל
שֵׁם מֵת: ,,זֶה שֶׁעָלָה עָלָיו הַגּוֹרָל ,לַשֵּׁם׳ יִתְקַיֵּם
תַּחְתָּיו׳׳; וְאִם שֶׁל עֲזָאזֵל מֵת: ,,זֶה שֶׁעָלָה עָלָיו
הַגּוֹרָל ,לַעֲזָאזֵל׳ יִתְקַיֵּם תַּחְתָּיו.׳׳ וְהַשֵּׁנִי יִרְעֶה
עַד שֶׁיִּסְתָּאֵב, וְיִמָּכֵר וְיִפְּלוּ דָמָיו לִנְדָבָה, שֶׁאֵין
חַטַּאת צִבּוּר מֵתָה. רַבִּי יְהוּדָה אוֹמֵר: תָּמוּת.
וְעוֹד אָמַר רַבִּי יְהוּדָה: נִשְׁפַּךְ הַדָּם, יָמוּת

יד אברהם

by lot as the Torah requires. Therefore, a new pair of animals must be brought to the *Kohen Gadol* and he draws lots over them.]

וְיַגְרִיל עֲלֵיהֶם בַּתְּחִלָּה. — *and he* [the *Kohen Gadol*] *cast lots upon them anew* [lit. *in the beginning*].

Some versions (see *Shinuyei Nuschaos* and *Rambam* ed. Kafih) have לְכַתְּחִלָּה (or כַּתְּחִלָּה, *Meiri*) *as at first.*

וְיֹאמַר — *(And) he is to say*

The mishnah will describe the two alternatives: if the dead goat was the one that had been designated 'For *Hashem*' or if the dead goat was the one that had been designated 'For *Azazel*. This verb *and he is to say* introduces the *Kohen Gadol's* two alternative declarations, one for each situation.

אִם שֶׁל שֵׁם מֵת: ,,זֶה שֶׁעָלָה עָלָיו הַגּוֹרָל ,לַשֵּׁם׳ יִתְקַיֵּם תַּחְתָּיו׳׳; — *if that of Hashem died, 'Let the one upon which the lot "For Hashem" fell take its place;'*

וְאִם שֶׁל עֲזָאזֵל מֵת: ,,זֶה שֶׁעָלָה עָלָיו הַגּוֹרָל ,לַעֲזָאזֵל׳ יִתְקַיֵּם תַּחְתָּיו;׳׳ — *and if that of Azazel died* [he says]: '*Let the one upon which the lot "For Azazel" fell take its place.'*

[Why should the *Kohen Gadol* have to make this declaration instead of simply taking the newly designated goat in place of the dead one without saying anything? Perhaps the term שְׁנֵי, *two* (used by the Torah for these goats as noted above s.v. וּבְקוּמָה) implies that the two he-goats are considered a pair, a unit of two goats, rather than two separate goats. Once the two goats were purchased as a unit, or even if only the lots

had been drawn simultaneously for both, the two goats became a single unit. Where one of a pair died, the *Kohen Gadol's* pronouncement turned the new he-goat and the surviving he-goat into a pair.]

וְהַשֵּׁנִי — *Then the second* [he-goat]

Now that the dead goat has been replaced, there are two goats for the one purpose: the survivor of the original pair and the second goat of the new pair. If the goat 'For *Hashem*' had died, there are now two goats 'For *Azazel*' (*Rashi; Rav*).

יִרְעֶה עַד שֶׁיִּסְתָּאֵב, — *is to graze until it becomes defective,*

[This is the only option. The superfluous goat may not be used in any secular manner since it was consecrated as a sacrifice. Nor can its sanctity be removed in any way while it is blemish-free. Therefore, it must be left to graze until it gets a defect, i.e., any wound or loss of limb that disqualifies it from being offered on the altar. See *Leviticus* 22:17-25 and *Bechoros* 6-7.]

The *Gemara* deals with the question of which goat is called 'the second' or superfluous one — the survivor of the first pair or the second goat of the new pair. Rav (the *Amora*; not the commentator to *Mishnah*) holds that it is the second goat of the new pair. The survivor is used for whatever purpose the first lot had designated it. R' Yochanan holds the opposite view; the survivor is superfluous and its place has been taken by the designee of the second lot. The controversy pivots on the question of

6
1

and he casts lots upon them anew. He is to say if that of *Hashem* died, 'Let the one upon which the lot "For *Hashem*" fell take its place'; and if that of *Azazel* died [he says], 'Let the one upon which the lot "For *Azazel*" fell take its place.' Then the second [he-goat] is to graze until it becomes defective, when it may be sold and the proceeds used for donations, for a communal sin-offering is not [left] to die. R' Yehudah says: It should [be left to] die.

R' Yehudah also said: If the blood [of the he-goat 'For *Hashem*'] spilled, [then] the one [designated] to be sent away [to *Azazel*] is left to die. If the one

whether a living sacrifice which has been disqualified can ever regain its fitness for sacrifice (בַּעֲלֵי חַיִּים נִדָּחִין). In the interval between the goat's death and the selection of its replacement, the surviving goat of the first pair was disqualified from sacrifice since only a *pair* of goats can be used for the service of Yom Kippur. Rav holds that the disqualification is not irrevocable while R' Yochanan holds it is.

וְיִמָּכֵר — *when it may be sold*

Since it now has a defect it may be sold (or redeemed) like any other animal sacrifice which becomes defective (see *Leviticus* 27:9-11 with *Rashi*).

וְיִפְּלוּ דָמָיו לִנְדָבָה, — *and the [lit. its] proceeds used [lit. will fall] for donations,*

[In terms of offerings, an animal voluntarily consecrated for sacrifice, not in order to fulfill a previous obligation (e.g., sin offering or vow), is called a קָרְבָּן נְדָבָה, *donative offering.*]

שֶׁאֵין חַטַּאת צִבּוּר מֵתָה. — *for a communal sin offering is not [left] to die.*

A personal sin offering which becomes disqualified is left to die (see *Me'ilah* 3:1). Though the he-goats of Yom Kippur, too, are sin sacrifices — *And from the congregation of the children of Israel shall he take two he-*

goats for a sin offering, (*Leviticus* 16:5) — they are not left to die because they are communal, not personal, offerings. Instead they are turned out to pasture until they become defective. The oral tradition from Sinai (see *Bava Kama* 110b; *Rambam, Pesulei HaMukdashin* 4:1) that (five) sin offerings which cannot be offered are left to die does not refer to communal sin offering (*Rav; Rashi*).

רַבִּי יְהוּדָה אוֹמֵר: תָּמוּת. — *R' Yehudah says: It* [i.e., *the 'second' he-goat*] *should [be left] to die.*

[R' Yehudah holds that the oral tradition that sin offerings which cannot be offered are left to die includes communal sin offerings too.]

R' — וְעוֹד אָמַר רַבִּי יְהוּדָה: נִשְׁפַּךְ הַדָּם, *Yehudah also said: If the blood [of the he-goat 'For Hashem'] spilled,*

If the blood spilled before the service for that he-goat was completed, then another pair of he-goats must be brought and lots drawn (*Rav; Rashi*).

יָמוּת הַמִּשְׁתַּלֵּחַ. — *[then] the one [designated] to be sent away [to Azazel] is left to die.*

The he-goat originally designated to be sent away was disqualified in the absence of its pair (see above s.v. יִרְעֶה). Even after the new he-goat 'For

הַמִּשְׁתַּלֵּחַ. מֵת הַמִּשְׁתַּלֵּחַ, יִשָּׁפֵךְ הַדָּם.

[ב] בָּא לוֹ אֵצֶל שָׂעִיר הַמִּשְׁתַּלֵּחַ וְסוֹמֵךְ
שְׁתֵּי יָדָיו עָלָיו וּמִתְוַדֶּה. וְכָךְ הָיָה
אוֹמֵר: "אָנָּא הַשֵּׁם, עָווּ, פָּשְׁעוּ, חָטְאוּ לְפָנֶיךָ
עַמְּךָ בֵּית יִשְׂרָאֵל. אָנָּא בַשֵּׁם! כַּפֶּר־נָא לַעֲוֹנוֹת

יד אברהם

Hashem' is designated, the survivor remains disqualified. R' Yehudah holds that a disqualification remains in force even after the cause of the unfitness had been removed [הוֹאִיל וְנִדְחֶה יִדָּחֶה] even if the potential sacrifice was alive [בַּעֲלֵי חַיִּים נִדְחִין] (Rav).

This runs counter to the opinion of Rav cited above (s.v. יִרְעֶה) that where one of the pair died after the drawing of lots, the survivor is sacrificed, even though it had been disqualified in the interim (Gemara 64b).

The Gemara (65a) explains that the insertion of R' Yehudah's opinion here with the introduction וְעוֹד, also, implies a connection to the previous segment of the mishnah. Previously R' Yehudah had disagreed with the first tanna and ruled that even a communal sin sacrifice is left to die. Accordingly, it would seem that the goat which the first tanna consigned 'to graze until it becomes defective,' would, according to R' Yehudah, be left to die. Since the first tanna rules that the goat of the second pair is put out to pasture, it would stand to reason that R' Yehudah would leave it to die. However, this is not true. The mishnah now adds that there is yet another disagreement between R' Yehudah and the first tanna: Although the first tanna held that the surviving goat of the first pair was used in the service, R' Yehudah cannot agree, for he holds that once the survivor became disqualified, it remains unfit and can never be used as an offering. Accordingly, R' Yehudah holds that only the second pair of goats can be used and the survivor of the first pair must be left to die. The Gemara uses this as proof for the opinion of Rav (the Amora; cited in s.v. יִרְעֶה and accepted by Rambam and Rav) that הַשֵּׁנִי, the second, in the words of the first tanna, means the extra goat of the new (second) pair (see above s.v. הַשֵּׁנִי).

מֵת הַמִּשְׁתַּלֵּחַ, — If the one which was to be sent away died,

[It died before the sprinkling of the blood of the he-goat 'For Hashem' was completed.]

יִשָּׁפֵךְ הַדָּם. — the blood [of the he-goat 'For Hashem'] must be poured out.

[And a new pair of goats must be brought, lots drawn, etc.]

The reason the goat 'For Hashem' is disqualified by the death of the other goat cannot be because the dead goat had not yet been sent to Azazel. If the death had occurred after the sin offering's blood had been sprinkled, nothing further would have to be done, since the sending of the goat need not be done by the Kohen Gadol in his white vestments; it can be done even by a non-Kohen. As such, the failure to send it does not invalidate (אֵינוֹ מְעַכֵּב) any other part of the service. The reason the goat must be replaced if it dies before the blood service is because the Torah says (Lev. 16:10): And the he-goat upon which the lot for Azazel fell shall be stood up alive before Hashem לְכַפֵּר עָלָיו, to atone for him, until he [the Kohen Gadol] atones [i.e., sprinkles the blood] for it [i.e., for the he-goat which is sent away.] Only after the blood is sprinkled can the goat be sent to Azazel. [This interpretation of the verse, which follows our Gemara, is Malbim's; Rashi's interpretation of this verse follows the tanna, R' Shimon; see Gem. 40b and Sifra.]

In this case, where the he-goat designated for Azazel dies before the blood service, all agree that the blood of the slaughtered he-goat is disqualified

which was to be sent away died, the blood [of the he-goat 'for *Hashem*] must be poured out.

2. He [then] came to the he-goat [designated] to be sent away [to *Azazel*] and he supports both of his hands on it and confesses.

And this is what he would say, 'I beg of You, HASHEM! Your nation, the Family of Israel, has acted wickedly, rebelled, and sinned before You. I pray, with Your Name! Forgive now the wicked acts, rebel-

YAD AVRAHAM

and a goat from a second pair must be slaughtered. Only in the case where the sacrificial goat was still alive when the other one died do we find the controversy discussed above whether an animal can ever become a valid sacrifice once it had been disqualified. In the case of an already slaughtered sacrifice, everyone agrees that once its blood is disqualified, the disqualification can never be removed [שְׁחוּטִין נִידָחִין] (*Rav; Meiri*).

Rambam (Avodas Yom HaKippurim 5:15) seems to disagree for he says nothing about such a case, implying that here, too, only the animal which died has to be replaced. Perhaps he holds that not all agree with the requirement that the *Azazel* he-goat be alive during the sprinkling of the other he-goat's blood. As already mentioned, R' Shimon (cited by *Rashi* to *Leviticus* 16:10 and *Sifra* there; *Gem.* 40b) has a different interpretation of the verse upon which this requirement is based, thus removing the basis for it. *Rambam* follows this opinion.

2.

Here the Mishnah returns to the narrative of the service, which had been broken off (in 5:7). The *Kohen Gadol* had finished sprinkling the ox's and the he-goat's blood, exited the Holy, and poured the remainder of the blood on the western foundation of the outer altar (*Rav*).

בָּא לוֹ אֵצֶל שָׂעִיר הַמִּשְׁתַּלֵּחַ וְסוֹמֵךְ שְׁתֵּי יָדָיו עָלָיו וּמִתְוַדֶּה. — *He [then] came to the he-goat [designated] to be sent away [to Azazel] and he supports both of his hands on it and confesses.*

[See above 3:8.]

[This was an exception. The rule is that only personal sacrifices require סְמִיכָה, *leaning*, but not communal sacrifices (Menachos 9:7). The ox upon which the *Kohen Gadol* supported his hands (3:8) while confessing is not an exception to this rule, for it is 'Aaron's' (i.e., the *Kohen Gadol's*) personal offering as is written (*Lev.* 16:6) *the ox of the sin offering which is "his"*... and he is required to purchase it with his own money (*Gem.* 51b). But the goat that is

sent away, a communal offering, is an exception to this rule for it is written (*Lev.* 16:21), *And Aaron shall support both his hands upon the hand of the live he-goat, and confess.*]

וְכָךְ הָיָה אוֹמֵר: ,,אָנָּא הַשֵּׁם! עָווּ פָּשְׁעוּ חָטְאוּ לְפָנֶיךָ עַמְּךָ בֵּית יִשְׂרָאֵל. — *And this is what he would say, 'I beg of You, HASHEM! Your nation, the Family of Israel, has acted wickedly, rebelled, and sinned before You.*

[For commentary on this confession see 3:8].

[Since this goat is the people's sacrifice, the confession mentions all the people's sins. This too is implied by the Torah which says about this confession

וְלַפְּשָׁעִים וְלַחֲטָאִים, שֶׁעָוּוּ וְשֶׁפָּשְׁעוּ וְשֶׁחָטְאוּ
לְפָנֶיךָ עַמְּךָ בֵּית יִשְׂרָאֵל, כַּכָּתוּב בְּתוֹרַת מֹשֶׁה
עַבְדֶּךָ לֵאמֹר: ,,כִּי־בַיּוֹם הַזֶּה יְכַפֵּר עֲלֵיכֶם
לְטַהֵר אֶתְכֶם מִכֹּל חַטֹּאתֵיכֶם לִפְנֵי ה'
תִּטְהָרוּ''.

וְהַכֹּהֲנִים וְהָעָם הָעוֹמְדִים בָּעֲזָרָה, כְּשֶׁהָיוּ
שׁוֹמְעִים שֵׁם הַמְפֹרָשׁ שֶׁהוּא יוֹצֵא מִפִּי כֹהֵן
גָּדוֹל, הָיוּ כּוֹרְעִים וּמִשְׁתַּחֲוִים וְנוֹפְלִים עַל־
פְּנֵיהֶם, וְאוֹמְרִים: ,,בָּרוּךְ שֵׁם כְּבוֹד מַלְכוּתוֹ
לְעוֹלָם וָעֶד''.

יד אברהם

(Lev. 16:21): *And he shall confess over it [the he-goat] all the rebellions of the children of Israel, and all their wicked acts, and all their sins.*]

אָנָּא בַשֵּׁם! — *I pray, with Your Name!*
The translation follows *Turei Zahav's* rendition of this phrase (see above 3:8) — i.e., forgive with the attribute of רַחֲמִים, *compassion* — that is represented by Your Four-Letter Name. *Tiferes Yisrael* renders, *Because of Your Name* [similar to David who prayed (Psalms 25:11): *Because of Your Name HASHEM, forgive my sin.*]

Tosefos Yom Tov notes that our copies of the mishnah are not consistent in their rendition of this part of the *Kohen Gadol's* confession. Previously (see 3:8 and 4:2) we are told that he said הַשֵּׁם (see comm. to 3:8), here the mishnah reads בַשֵּׁם. In practice, the *Kohen Gadol's* recitation of the confession was identical in all of the three times: he either said הַשֵּׁם at all times, or בַשֵּׁם.

כַּפֶּר־נָא לַעֲוֹנוֹת וְלַפְּשָׁעִים, שֶׁעָוּוּ וְשֶׁפָּשְׁעוּ וְשֶׁחָטְאוּ לְפָנֶיךָ עַמְּךָ בֵּית יִשְׂרָאֵל — *Forgive now, the wicked acts, rebellions, and the sins, for Your people, the Family of Israel, has acted wickedly, rebelled, and sinned before You,*

כַּכָּתוּב בְּתוֹרַת מֹשֶׁה עַבְדֶּךָ לֵאמֹר: כִּי בַיּוֹם הַזֶּה יְכַפֵּר עֲלֵיכֶם לְטַהֵר אֶתְכֶם מִכֹּל חַטֹּאתֵיכֶם לִפְנֵי ה' תִּטְהָרוּ'. — *as is written*

in the Torah of Your servant Moses [Lev. 16:30]: *'For on this day he [the Kohen Gadol] shall atone for you to purify you, before HASHEM shall you be purified.'*

[The punctuation given here for the Scriptural verse follows that suggested by the *trop*, *(cantillation)*.]

The following segment of this mishnah, though not found in our versions of the previous confessions (3:8 and 4:2; see comm. there) or in 4:1 when the *Kohen Gadol* said 'For Hashem, a sin sacrifice,' applies to those confessions, too (*Tos. Yom Tov*; cf. *Tif. Yis.*).

וְהַכֹּהֲנִים וְהָעָם הָעוֹמְדִים בָּעֲזָרָה, — *The Kohanim and the people who were standing in the Courtyard,*
Some versions of the mishnah do not have this segment (from והכהנים until פניהם) here nor in 3:8 nor 4:2. See *Shinuyei Nuschaos*, *Or Zorua* p.I: 281; *Teshuvos Radbaz* 810 and the gloss there. However, *Rambam* (comm. ed. Kafih) has it here and in 3:8, as does *Meiri*.]

כְּשֶׁהָיוּ שׁוֹמְעִים שֵׁם הַמְפֹרָשׁ שֶׁהוּא יוֹצֵא מִפִּי כֹהֵן גָּדוֹל, — *when they heard the Ineffable Name [lit. the explicit Name], coming out of the Kohen Gadol's mouth,*
[They heard HASHEM's Name pronounced as it is written.]
The usage of a term שֶׁהוּא יוֹצֵא, *as it came*

lions, and the sins, for Your people, the Family of Israel, has acted wickedly, rebelled, and sinned before You, as is written in the Torah of Your servant Moses [*Lev.* 16:30]: *'For on this day he* [the *Kohen Gadol*] *shall atone for you to purify you, before HASHEM shall you be purified.'*

The Kohanim and the people who were standing in the Courtyard, when they heard the Ineffable Name coming from the *Kohen Gadol's* mouth, they would kneel and prostrate themselves and fall upon their faces, and say, 'Blessed be the Name — the Glory of his Kingship — forever and ever.'

YAD AVRAHAM

out, suggests that the *Kohen Gadol* did not actually utter the Ineffable Name; it simply came out, miraculously, from his mouth (*Zera Yitzchak; Hon Ashir,* and others citing *Arizal).*

Tosefos Yom Tov deduces from the mishnah's stress on the words מִפִּי כֹהֵן גָּדוֹל, *of the Kohen Gadol's mouth,* that only when they heard the Name from *him* did they kneel and prostrate themselves. When other *Kohanim* uttered the Ineffable Name during the Priestly Blessing [בִּרְכַּת כֹּהֲנִים] (see *Sotah* 6:7) no one kneeled. This was because, as R' Moshe Kordovero writes, the pronunciation by ordinary *Kohanim* combined the consonants of the Four-Letter Name with the vowel sounds of אֲדֹנָי, *Adonai,* but the *Kohen Gadol* used a different pronunciation.

R' Hai Gaon (see *Rosh*) holds that the Name uttered by the *Kohen Gadol* was the Name consisting of forty two letters (see *Kiddushin* 70a). It was only upon hearing this Name that the *Kohanim* and people kneeled. That the people did not bow during the Priestly Blessing, when the Four-Letter Name was used, is proof of R' Hai's opinion (*Gevuras Ari).*

הָיוּ כּוֹרְעִים וּמִשְׁתַּחֲוִים וְנוֹפְלִים עַל־פְּנֵיהֶם, — *they would kneel and prostrate themselves and fall upon their faces,*

In addition to prostrating their bodies upon the ground, they bowed their faces to the ground (*Hon Ashir;* cf. *Rambam, Tefillah* 5:13, and *Berachos).*

וְאוֹמְרִים: ,,בָּרוּךְ שֵׁם כְּבוֹד מַלְכוּתוֹ לְעוֹלָם וָעֶד.'' — *and say, 'Blessed be the Name —*

the glory of His kingship — forever and ever.'

[See above 3:8.]

⚡§ How did the Kohen Gadol conceal his pronunciation of the Name?

Rambam (Avodas Yom HaKippurim 2:6 based upon the *Yerushalmi;* see *Avodas Yisrael* p. 108; cf. *Kesef Mishneh* and *Lechem Mishneh* loc. cit.) says, 'In earlier times he used to raise his voice for the Name (see *Gem.* 20b וכבר אמר אנא השם ונשמע קולו בירריחו with *Rashi; Tamid* 3:8 with commentaries). But after the wicked multiplied, he began to say it quietly and muffle it [the Name] with a sweet chant [בִּנְעִימוּת], so that even his fellow Kohanim should not recognize it.'

There are two interpretations of בִּנְעִימוּת, *with sweet chant. Lechem Mishneh* (loc. cit.) understands it to refer to the *Kohen Gadol;* — he sang while uttering the Name so that his singing would muffle his pronunciation.

Avodas Yisrael (citing *R' Moshe Nigrin*) says that the *Kohanim* and people in the Temple Court sang בָּרוּךְ שֵׁם ... , *Blessed is the Name...,'* while the *Kohen Gadol* was uttering the Name. Thus, his pronunciation of the Name was muffled by the *sweet chant* of his audience. This interpretation of *Yeru-*

[ג] **מְסָרוֹ** לְמִי שֶׁהָיָה מוֹלִיכוֹ. הַכֹּל כְּשֵׁרִין לְהוֹלִיכוֹ, אֶלָּא שֶׁעָשׂוּ הַכֹּהֲנִים גְּדוֹלִים קֶבַע, וְלֹא הָיוּ מַנִּיחִין אֶת־יִשְׂרָאֵל לְהוֹלִיכוֹ.

אָמַר רַבִּי יוֹסֵי: מַעֲשֶׂה וְהוֹלִיכוֹ עַרְסְלָא, וְיִשְׂרָאֵל הָיָה.

[ד] **וְכֶבֶשׁ** עָשׂוּ לוֹ מִפְּנֵי הַבַּבְלִיִּים שֶׁהָיוּ מְתַלְּשִׁים בִּשְׂעָרוֹ, וְאוֹמְרִים לוֹ:
,,טֹל וָצֵא, טֹל וָצֵא!"

יד אברהם

shalmi (3:7) is given by *Abudraham* (*Tashlum Abudraham* p. 50). He sees it as the source for *Rambam* (loc. cit. 2:7) who says (as do all the versions of the *Avodah*), 'He [the *Kohen Gadol*] also intended to finish [the saying of] the Name together with those blessing מַבְּרְכִים נֶגֶד — i.e., those saying ... שֵׁם בָּרוּךְ and said to them תִּטְהָרוּ, *may you be purified.* [The last word in the verse he was quoting.] *Kessef Mishneh* (and *R' Sheshes* cited in *Avodas Yisrael,* p. 109) do not give a source for this *Rambam.* According to *Abudraham* this

is inherent in the interpretation of *Rambam's* expression מַבְּלִיעוֹ בִּנְעִימוֹת, *he muffled it with a sweet chant song,* which is based on *Yerushalmi.*

[Interestingly, the *Venetian* rite in *Machzor Roma* phrase this segment of the *Avodah* as follows: אָנָּא...כַּכָּתוּב...כִּי־בַיּוֹם הַזֶּה, יְכַפֵּר עֲלֵיכֶם לְטַהֵר אֶתְכֶם לִפְנֵי־ה', omitting the word תִּטְהָרוּ. They follow this with וְהַכֹּהֲנִים וְאַף הוּא...וְאוֹמֵר לָהֶם ... When the *chazan* reaches the word תִּטְהָרוּ the congregation joins in with him to say תִּטְהָרוּ. This also seems to be *R' Saadiah Gaon's* version (see *Siddur R' Saadiah Gaon* pp. 273, 279).]

3.

מְסָרוֹ לְמִי שֶׁהָיָה מוֹלִיכוֹ — *He handed it* [the he-goat] *to the one who was to lead it* [to Azazel].

[The Torah says (Lev. 16:21): *And he shall send it by the hand of an appointed man to the desert.* Rashi (66b s.v. המוכן and loc. cit.) holds that this appointed man must be appointed before Yom Kippur. *Rambam* (*Avodas Yom HaKippurim* 3:7) says only that this man has to be someone who is מוכן, *prepared* or *appointed,* for this task, without specifying that the appointment should be made before Yom Kippur.]

הַכֹּל כְּשֵׁרִין לְהוֹלִיכוֹ — *Anyone* [even a

non-*Kohen*] *is fit to lead it,*

[The Torah does not specify what sort of person must lead the goat to Azazel.]

אֶלָּא שֶׁעָשׂוּ הַכֹּהֲנִים גְּדוֹלִים קֶבַע וְלֹא הָיוּ מַנִּיחִין אֶת־יִשְׂרָאֵל לְהוֹלִיכוֹ. — *but the Kohanim Gedolim established a rule, and did not permit an Israelite* [non-*Kohen*] *to lead it.*

Despite the fact that this task could be performed by anyone, the *Kohanim* adopted a rule that it should be assigned only to a *Kohen* (Rav).

[Some versions, *Rav's* among them, delete the word גְּדוֹלִים — i.e., the court of ordinary *Kohanim* made this rule.

3. **H**e handed it [the he-goat] to the one who was to lead it [to *Azazel*]. Anyone is fit to lead it, but the *Kohanim Gedolim* established a rule, and did not permit an Israelite to lead it.

R' Yose said: It once happened that Arsela led it, and he was an Israelite.

4. **T**hey made a ramp for it [the he-goat] because of the Babylonians who used to pull at his hair and say to him, 'Take and leave! Take and leave!'

YAD AVRAHAM

Rambam's (comm. ed. Kafiah and Avodas Yom HaKippurim 3:7) and Meiri's versions, however, are identical to ours.]

אָמַר רַבִּי יוֹסֵי: מַעֲשֶׂה וְהוֹלִיכוֹ עַרְסְלָא, וְיִשְׂרָאֵל הָיָה. — R' Yose said: It once happened [lit. an incident] that Arsela led it,

and he was an Israelite.

R' Yose disagrees and holds there was no such rule and presents as proof of his opinion the story of Arsela who was allowed to lead the he-goat to Azazel, even though he was a non-*Kohen* (R' Elyakim).

4.

וְכֶבֶשׁ עָשׂוּ לוֹ — *They made a ramp for it* [the he-goat]

They made an elevated walkway leading from the Temple-Court to outside the city (Rashi; Rav). Rambam (Shekalim 4:2) indicates that this ramp only extended to outside the Temple area.

מִפְּנֵי הַבַּבְלִיִּים — *because of the Babylonians*

The Gemara (66b) says these people were Alexandrians, but because the Jews of Eretz Yisrael disliked the Babylonians (see Rashi) they used this name as a pejorative for anyone who behaved in an uncivilized manner. R' Elyakim holds that, because the Alexandrians disliked the Babylonians (and thus resented being called Babylonians), the other Jews called them (the Alexandrians) Babylonians.

R' Isaac HaLevi proposes that it is out of character for the Mishnah to use pejorative nicknames. Indeed it is a sin to do so. He adduces Josephus Flavius' testimony that groups of Jewish brig-

ands and mercenaries from Babylonia settled in and about Alexandria. Because of their dislike for these rough and uncouth Babylonians, and to accentuate their own superiority over them, the Alexandrians called these Jews (and their descendants) Babylonians. It was these half wild 'Babylonian' Alexandrians who 'used to pull at his hair' (Doros HaRishonim, Part I, Vol. 3, pp. 115-117).

שֶׁהָיוּ מְתַלְּשִׁים בִּשְׂעָרוֹ, — *who used to pull at his hair*

The Alexandrians would taunt the man leading the goat by pulling his hair (Rashi; Meiri).

וְאוֹמְרִים לוֹ: ,,טֹל וְצֵא, טֹל וְצֵא!'' — *and say to him, 'Take and leave! Take and leave!'*

They said, 'Take away our sins and go to the wilderness; do not let our sins tarry here any longer' (Rashi, Rav, from Gemara 66b).

[As Scripture says (Lev. 16:22): And the he-goat shall carry on himself all of their rebelliousness... i.e., the final ab-

מִיַּקִּירֵי יְרוּשָׁלַיִם הָיוּ מְלַוִּין אוֹתוֹ עַד סֻכָּה
הָרִאשׁוֹנָה. עֶשֶׂר סֻכּוֹת מִירוּשָׁלַיִם וְעַד צוּק,
תִּשְׁעִים רִיס — שִׁבְעָה וּמֶחֱצָה לְכָל מִיל.

[ה] **עַל־כָּל־סֻכָּה** וְסֻכָּה אוֹמְרִים לוֹ:
,,הֲרֵי מָזוֹן וַהֲרֵי
מַיִם;'' וּמְלַוִּין אוֹתוֹ מִסֻּכָּה לְסֻכָּה, חוּץ
מֵאַחֲרוֹנָה שֶׁבָּהֶן, שֶׁאֵינוֹ מַגִּיעַ עִמּוֹ לַצוּק, אֶלָּא

יד אברהם

solution of sins depended on the he-goat reaching *Azazel.*]

מִיַּקִּירֵי יְרוּשָׁלַיִם הָיוּ מְלַוִּין אוֹתוֹ עַד סֻכָּה הָרִאשׁוֹנָה, — *Some of the eminent* [lit. *precious*] *men of Jerusalem used to accompany him to the first booth.*

[As the mishnah will now relate, booths were erected along the way for the man's benefit.]

עֶשֶׂר סֻכּוֹת מִירוּשָׁלַיִם וְעַד צוּק, — *There were ten booths from Jerusalem to* [a] *precipice;*

[The translation of צוּק follows *Rashi* and *Rav. R' Elyakim* renders it *a steep rock,* i.e., a cliff.]

תִּשְׁעִים רִיס— — [*it was*] *ninety riss—*

The total distance from Jerusalem to the precipitous mountain was 90 *riss.*

Rav gives a variant spelling רוּס, *russ,* and says that the רוּס had as many steps, or אַמּוֹת, *cubits,* as its numerical value — רוּס=266.

שִׁבְעָה וּמֶחֱצָה לְכָל מִיל. — *seven and a half* [*riss*] *to every mil.*

Thus, the distance from Jerusalem to the precipice of *Azazel* was twelve *mil* [90 *riss*÷7½ *riss* per *mil.*]. Since a *mil* is 2,000 cubits, the total distance was 24,000 cubits; approximately 7-9 miles.

According to *Rav,* who says the *riss* had 266 cubits, 7½ *riss*=1995 cubits — almost 2000 cubits or one *mil. Kol Ha-Remez* cites *Rambam* (*Rotzeach* 13:6) that the *riss* had 266²/₃ cubits, which provides exactly 2000 cubits for 7½ *riss.*

5.

עַל־כָּל־סֻכָּה וְסֻכָּה אוֹמְרִים לוֹ: ,,הֲרֵי מָזוֹן וַהֲרֵי מַיִם;'' — *At each booth they would say to him, 'Here is food and here is drink';*

In each booth, people awaited the man leading the he-goat in case he needed refreshment, so that he would not collapse from exertion of walking ninety *riss* with the he-goat (*R' Elyakim*).

[Most of this trek was under the desert sun. If the he-goat became sick, the man carried it (*Gem.* 66b).

The man was not absolved from the fast, but if he indicated that he was weak and needed to eat they gave him

food (*Rambam, Avodas Yom HaKippurim* 4:7).

The purpose of their announcement that food was available was to assure him that in case of an emergency, food was ready. This assurance would ease the fast for him and enable him to finish the fast. אֵינוֹ דוֹמֶה מִי שֶׁיֵּשׁ לוֹ פַּת בְּסַלּוֹ לְמִי שֶׁאֵין לוֹ פַּת בְּסַלּוֹ, *There is no comparison between one who has bread in his basket to one who has no bread in his basket* (*Rav* from Gemara 67a).

[This probably means that in a case where the designee could complete the fast only if he remained in the booth and rested, but not if had to continue the physical ordeal of

Some of the eminent men of Jerusalem used to accompany him to the first booth. There were ten booths from Jerusalem to [a] precipice; [it was] ninety *riss*, seven and a half [*riss*] in every *mil*.

5. **A** t each booth they would say to him, 'Here is food and here is drink'; and they would accompany him from [that] booth to [the next] booth, except for the last of them. For the [last] escort could not go with him to the precipice, but would stand

YAD AVRAHAM

walking to *Azazel* — he would be given food and drink so that he could continue his mission. Although there were other people in the booth who could carry on with leading the he-goat, the stipulation *he shall send it by the hand of an appointed man* (*Lev.* 16:21) supersedes the designee's obligation to fast. In an instance where he was so weakened by the fast that it was dangerous for him to conclude the fast even if he did not continue to *Azazel*, there would be no need for the mishnah to tell us that he was permitted to eat (*Tif. Yis;* see *Gem.* 66 s.v. עתי אפילו בטומאה and חלה משלחו ביד אחר).

The *Gemara* (67a) relates that it never happened that 'the appointed man' should need to eat.

וּמְלַוִּין אוֹתוֹ מִסֻּכָּה לְסֻכָּה, — *and they would accompany him from* [*that*] *booth to* [*the next*] *booth,*

There were ten booths along the twelve-*mil* distance to *Azazel*. He walked one *mil* until the first booth, and one *mil* from there to the second booth, and so on until the tenth booth, leaving a distance of two *mil* from the last booth to Azazel. A *mil* — 2000 אַמּוֹת, *cubits*, is equal to a תְּחוּם שַׁבָּת, *the maximum distance one is allowed to walk from one's domicile* (or from the town where one's domicile is situated) *on the Sabbath*, and on Yom Kippur. Thus, the people in the booths were allowed to accompany the designee only for 2000 cubits, one *mil*, until the next booth (*Rav; Rashi*).

One or more people spent the entire Yom Kippur in each of the booths (*Rambam, Avodas Yom HaKippurim* 3:7).

חוּץ מֵאַחֲרוֹנָה שֶׁבָּהֶן. — *except for the last of them.*

[The people in the last booth could not accompany him because the distance from their booth to the rock was more than the one-*mil* distance they were permitted to walk.]

שֶׁאֵינוֹ מַגִּיעַ עִמּוֹ לַצּוּק, — *For the* [*last*] *escort could not go with him* [all the way] *to the precipice,*

The precipice is the place referred to by the Torah (*Lev.* 16:8,10) as *Azazel*. *Rashi* (there, citing *Sifra*) and *Ramban* agree that עֲזָאזֵל means *hard* (*from* עַז, *strong* or *hard*), hence *a rock*. *Rashi* finds the stipulation that it be a high and precipitous rock (or mountain) in the term (*Lev.* 16:22) אֶרֶץ גְּזֵרָה, which he interprets (from *Yoma* 67b and *Sifra*), as חֲתוּכָה, *cut up* — i.e., precipitous.

[It seems from the *Targumim, Onkelos* and *Yonasan*, both of whom do not translate עֲזָאזֵל, that it is not a descriptive term, but the name of a specific place. Throughout the mishnah, it is never called *Azazel*, however. It may be that the exact location of the original *Azazel* was forgotten during the Babylonian exile or that the name *Rock* came into common usage with the passage of time.

Rambam, in formulating the law for this procedure (*Avodas Yom HaKippurim* 3:7 and 4:2), says merely that the he-goat is sent to 'the wilderness'. He seems to support the view of *Rashi* and *Ramban*.

Interestingly, *Targum Yonasan's* translation of the verse stipulates that the he-goat be sent to 'the desert *Tzuk*'. The word our mishnah uses for precipice is צוק, *Tzuk*. This

עוֹמֵד מֵרָחוֹק וְרוֹאֶה אֶת־מַעֲשָׂיו.

[ו] **מֶה** הָיָה עוֹשֶׂה? חוֹלֵק לָשׁוֹן שֶׁל
זְהוֹרִית; חֶצְיוֹ קָשַׁר בַּסֶּלַע וְחֶצְיוֹ
קָשַׁר בֵּין שְׁתֵּי קַרְנָיו, וּדְחָפוֹ לַאֲחוֹרָיו. וְהוּא
מִתְגַּלְגֵּל וְיוֹרֵד, וְלֹא הָיָה מַגִּיעַ לַחֲצִי הָהָר, עַד
שֶׁנַּעֲשָׂה אֵבָרִים אֵבָרִים. בָּא וְיָשַׁב לוֹ תַּחַת
סֻכָּה אַחֲרוֹנָה עַד שֶׁתֶּחְשַׁךְ.
וּמֵאֵימָתַי מְטַמֵּא בְגָדִים? מִשֶּׁיֵּצֵא חוּץ
לְחוֹמַת יְרוּשָׁלַיִם. רַבִּי שִׁמְעוֹן אוֹמֵר: מִשְׁעַת
דְּחִיָּתוֹ לַצּוּק.

יד אברהם

may mean that there was a specific place called *Tzuk* in the Judean desert.

אֶלָּא עוֹמֵד מֵרָחוֹק וְרוֹאֶה אֶת־מַעֲשָׂיו. — *but would stand from afar and observe his actions.*

The person (or people) in the last booth went along for one *mil*, the maximum distance he was allowed to walk. At that point he stopped and remained there to observe the ensuing actions (Rav; Rashi).

Tosefos Yom Tov comments that they did not erect an eleventh booth (which would enable its occupant to ac-

company the 'appointed man' all the way) for if the designee had company with him then the rock would not be considered an אֶרֶץ גְּזֵרָה, *desolate land* (Onkelos and Yonasan to Lev. 16:22).

[*Rashi* who renders אֶרֶץ גְּזֵרָה, (precipitous) land — a reference to the place's physical nature rather than its isolation — may derive the stipulation that one region must also be desolate from the specification (the only one noted by Rambam) that *he shall send the he-goat to the wilderness (Lev. 16:22).*

6.

The first part of the mishnah discusses the red wool that had been tied to the goat's horns (4:2). There was a tradition that it would turn white if God had chosen to forgive Israel's sins. This was an event that was looked upon by the people as an essential part of the day's service. Were the wool to turn white before the service of the goat had been completed, the designee might be so overcome with joy and relief that he would forget to push the goat over the precipice. To avoid this danger, the Sages introduced an innovation into the ritual.

מֶה הָיָה עוֹשֶׂה? — *What did he do?*
[What was the procedure the designee performed with the goat?]

חוֹלֵק לָשׁוֹן שֶׁל זְהוֹרִית, — *He parted the strip of red wool;*
[Earlier (4:2) after the lots were drawn, a strip of red wool was tied to the head of the goat which was to be sent away. The designee now removed this strip of wool and divided it into two parts (cf. Tosafos Yeshanim s.v. חולק; Siach Yitzchak; Gevuras Ari, Miluim).

חֶצְיוֹ קָשַׁר בַּסֶּלַע — *half of it he tied to the rock*

from afar and observe his actions.

6. **W**hat did he do? He parted the strip of red wool; half of it he tied to the rock and half he tied between its two horns, and pushed it backwards. It tumbled down, and before it reached halfway down the mountain it was torn limb from limb. He would return and sit under the [shade of the] last booth until it became dark.

And from when does he contaminate clothing? As soon as he gets outside the wall of Jerusalem. R' Shimon says: From the time he pushes him [down] to the precipice.

YAD AVRAHAM

[From which he was about to push the goat.]

וְחֶצְיוֹ קָשַׁר בֵּין שְׁתֵּי קַרְנָיו, — *and half he tied between its two horns,*

[He tied it to both horns so that the strip would be between the two of them].

He did not leave the whole strip between the goat's horns lest it turn white (as related in mishnah 8) before the goat had been pushed down the precipice, and he forget to push the goat down. Another reason he did not leave the entire strip of wool on the horns was because the goat might fall head-down, concealing the wool strip and depriving the people of this miraculous omen of Divine forgiveness. Once the designee was occupied with a detailed procedure, he would become immersed in his work and complete the ritual even if the wool were to turn white while he was busy. Only when people are inactive do we fear that they *may* forget to begin a new task (*Rav* from *Gemara* 67a).

וּדְחָפוֹ לַאֲחוֹרָיו. — *and pushed it* [the he-goat] *backwards;*

[The goat would then tumble over the precipice.]

Targum Yonasan (to *Lev.* 16:22) relates that 'a wind from before God' would push the he-goat off the precipice.

וְהוּא מִתְגַּלְגֵּל וְיוֹרֵד, וְלֹא הָיָה מַגִּיעַ לַחֲצִי

הָהָר, עַד שֶׁנַּעֲשָׂה אֵבָרִים אֵבָרִים. — *It tumbled down* [lit. *rolled and descended*], *and before it reached halfway down the mountain* [lit. *it did not reach halfway down the mountain until*], *it was torn limb from limb* [lit. *it became limbs, limbs*].

[Before the goat reached the mid-point of the mountain, it had already been torn apart by the sharp rocks and the speed of its descent.]

בָּא וְיָשַׁב לוֹ תַּחַת סֻכָּה אַחֲרוֹנָה עַד שֶׁתֶּחְשָׁךְ. — *He would return and sit under the* [*shade of the*] *last booth until it became dark.*

He was permitted to walk back two *mil*, double the maximum distance one is allowed to walk on a holiday, though this was no longer essential to the service. The Sages waived the Rabbinic prohibition against walking more than a *mil* because he might have been afraid to remain in the desert all alone, and people may be afraid to volunteer for this task in the future (*Rav; Rashi*).

וּמֵאֵימָתַי מְטַמֵּא בְגָדִים? — *And from when on does he contaminate clothing?*

The person who led the goat to Azazel becomes טָמֵא [*tamei*] contaminated, to such a degree that even his clothing becomes *tamei*, as we see from *Leviticus* (18:7): *And he who leads the*

[ז] **בָּא** לוֹ אֵצֶל פָּר וְשָׂעִיר הַנִּשְׂרָפִין. קְרָעָן
וְהוֹצִיא אֶת־אֵמוּרֵיהֶן. נְתָנָן בְּמָגִיס
וְהִקְטִירָן עַל־גַּבֵּי הַמִּזְבֵּחַ. קְלָעָן בְּמִקְלָעוֹת
וְהוֹצִיאָן לְבֵית הַשְּׂרֵפָה.
וּמֵאֵימָתַי מְטַמְּאִין בְּגָדִים? מִשֶּׁיֵּצְאוּ חוּץ
לְחוֹמַת הָעֲזָרָה. רַבִּי שִׁמְעוֹן אוֹמֵר: מִשֶּׁיַּצִּית
הָאוּר בְּרֻבָּן.

יד אברהם

he-goat to Azazel shall purify [through immersion in a mikveh] *his clothing.* The mishnah now clarifies the exact point at which the designee acquires this status.

מִשֶּׁיֵּצֵא חוּץ לְחוֹמַת יְרוּשָׁלַיִם — *As soon as he gets outside the wall of Jerusalem.*

From then on, though he has not yet reached his destination, he is considered *he who leads the he-goat 'to' Azazel.* He is already en route to his destination (*Tos. Yom Tov*).

רַבִּי שִׁמְעוֹן אוֹמֵר: מִשַּׁעַת דְּחִיָּתוֹ לַצּוּק. — *R' Shimon says: From the time he pushes him* [*down*] *to the precipice.*

R' Shimon holds that Azazel signifies the rocky slope upon which the he-goat meets its death, not the whole general area. In this sense, וְהַמְשַׁלֵּחַ אֶת־הַשָּׂעִיר לַעֲזָאזֵל (*Lev.* 16:26) should be translated, *And he who dispatches (not leads) the he-goat to Azazel...* 'Dispatches' refers to pushing the goat down the slope of the rocky mountain. Thus until the moment that he pushed the goat down, he is not considered *he who dispatches the he-goat to Azazel,* and consequently does not contaminate his clothing (*Tosefos Yom Tov*).

7.

The mishnah now reverts to the Kohen Gadol and his service in the Temple.

בָּא לוֹ אֵצֶל פָּר וְשָׂעִיר הַנִּשְׂרָפִין. — *He* [the Kohen Gadol] *came to the ox and he-goat which were to be burned.*

After the Kohen Gadol had given the he-goat 'For Azazel' to the designee (*mishnah* 3), he returned to the ox and he-goat which he had left after sprinkling their blood in the Holy of Holies and in the Holy (5:3-6). These two sacrifices were sin offerings which normally had their sacrificial parts burned on the outer altar, after which their meat was eaten by the *Kohanim* (*Zevachim* 5:3). The sin offerings of Yom Kippur, however, had their fats burned on the outer altar (like other sin offerings), but their meat could not be eaten. It was

burned in a designated place outside of Jerusalem (see *Lev.* 16:25, 27).

קְרָעָן — *He tore them*

[He opened their body cavities to gain access to the inner organs and fats which he was to burn upon the altar. The mishnah in *Pesachim* (5:10) uses identical language to describe this process in the case of the Pesach sacrifice.]

וְהוֹצִיא אֶת־אֵימוּרֵיהֶן. — *and removed their sacrificial parts.*

[From every sacrifice, certain organs (the kidneys, part of the liver, and the tail of sheep) and certain fats are offered in the altar. The mishnah calls these parts אֵימוּרִין, *emurim.*]

Rambam (preface to *Kodashim*), cited by *Tosefos Yom Tov* (*Pesachim* 5:10), relates this word to אָמוּר, *said* — i.e., these are the

7. He [the *Kohen Gadol*] came to the ox and he-goat which were to be burned. He tore them and removed their sacrificial parts. He put them in a plate and burned them upon the [outer] altar. He intertwined [the limbs of the ox and he-goat] into twists and removed them to the place of burning.

And from when do these [people] contaminate clothing? From when they go outside the wall of the Courtyard. R' Shimon says: From when the fire catches onto the greater part of [the limbs].

YAD AVRAHAM

parts which the Torah has *said* to separate from the sacrifice and burn on the altar. *Aruch* (s.v. מר 2) derives אימורין from מר, *lord.* By virtue of their being burned on the altar, these organs and parts are the *lords* of the sacrifice.

נְתָנָן בְּמָגִיס וְהִקְטִירָן עַל־גַּבֵּי הַמִּזְבֵּחַ. — *He put them in a plate and burned them upon the* [*outer*] *altar.*

The *Kohen Gadol* could not burn them on the outer altar immediately, for he was still dressed in his white vestments which were reserved for the service performed inside. Nor did he don his regular golden vestments until after he had read from the Torah (7:3). What the mishnah means is that he put the *emurin* in a plate, ready to be burned upon the altar. It is as if the mishnah had said ...וּנְתָנָן בְּמָגִיס לְהַקְטִיר, *and he put them in a plate to be burned.*

Thus the exact time for the burning of the *emurin* of these sacrifices is not spelled out in the mishnah. This gives rise to a three-way disagreement between *Rashi, Rambam* and *Tosafos* as to the exact time when this was done. See below 7:3.

קְלָעָן בְּמִקְלָעוֹת — *He intertwined* [*the limbs of the ox and he-goat*] *into twists.*

He intertwined the limbs of the slaughtered ox with those of the slaughtered he-goat. They were carried on two poles, one next to the other, and their limbs were intertwined (*Rav; Rashi*).

Rambam (comm. and *Avodas Yom HaKippurim* 3:7) says this means that the

hides of these two sacrifices were not removed, but the meat was cut up into pieces while still attached to the hide and was taken out to be burned in this state.

Aruch's version (s.v. קלע) is קְלָעָן בְּמִקְלוֹת, *he intertwined them onto poles.* He relates קְלָעָן to קְלָע, *curtain* (see *Exodus* 29:9). He intertwined the limbs of the two sacrifices onto carrying poles in such a manner that they hung from these poles like curtains.

וְהוֹצִיאָן לְבֵית הַשְּׂרֵפָה. — *And removed them to the place of burning.*

The *Kohen Gadol* appointed someone to carry the limbs to the place where they would be burned (*Avodas Yom HaKippurim* 3:7).

[The mishnah means that now the *Kohen Gadol* ordered someone to take these sacrifices to the place of burning. It is if the mishnah reads לְהוֹצִיאָן, *to remove them.*]

This place of burning was located outside of Jerusalem as specified in the Torah (*Lev.* 16:27), *And the ox sin offering and the he-goat sin offering ... shall he take to outside the camp and they shall burn* [*them*] *in fire.*

The actual burning did not take place immediately, but later, while the *Kohen Gadol* was reading from the Torah, as detailed below (7:2, *Tos. Yom Tov*).

וּמֵאֵימָתַי מְטַמְּאִין בְּגָדִים? — *And from when do these* [*people*] *contaminate clothing?*

Here, too, the Torah says (*Lev.* 16:28), *And he who burns them* [the ox and the he-goat] *shall purify his clothing* [i.e., immerse them in a

[ח] **אָמְרוּ** לוֹ לְכֹהֵן גָּדוֹל: ,,הִגִּיעַ שָׂעִיר
לַמִּדְבָּר.'' וּמִנַּיִן הָיוּ יוֹדְעִין
שֶׁהִגִּיעַ שָׂעִיר לַמִּדְבָּר? דַּרְכִּיּוֹת הָיוּ עוֹשִׁין,
וּמְנִיפִין בְּסוּדָרִין, וְיוֹדְעִין שֶׁהִגִּיעַ שָׂעִיר
לַמִּדְבָּר.

אָמַר רַבִּי יְהוּדָה: וַהֲלֹא סִמָּן גָּדוֹל הָיָה לָהֶם:
מִירוּשָׁלַיִם וְעַד בֵּית חִדּוּדוֹ שְׁלֹשָׁה מִילִין;
הוֹלְכִין מִיל, וְחוֹזְרִין מִיל, וְשׁוֹהִין כְּדֵי מִיל.
וְיוֹדְעִין שֶׁהִגִּיעַ שָׂעִיר לַמִּדְבָּר.

יד אברהם

mikveh]..., thus implying clearly that those who burn these sacrifices acquire a significant degree of contamination.

מִשֶׁיֵּצְאוּ חוּץ לְחוֹמַת הָעֲזָרָה — *From when they go outside the wall of the Courtyard.*

רַבִּי שִׁמְעוֹן אוֹמֵר: מִשֶׁיִּצִּית הָאוּר בְּרֻבָּן — *R' Shimon says: From when the fire catches onto the greater part of [the limbs].*

The first tanna's and R' Shimon's reasoning are given at length in the Gemara (68a).

8.

אָמְרוּ לוֹ לְכֹהֵן גָּדוֹל: ,,הִגִּיעַ שָׂעִיר לַמִּדְבָּר.'' — *They said to the Kohen Gadol, 'The he-goat has reached the wilderness.'*

The *Kohen Gadol* was not allowed to commence with the next phase of the service until the goat had reached the desert as is written (*Lev.* 16:22-25): *And he shall send the he-goat into the desert ... and he shall go out and perform his burnt offering ... And the fats of the sin offering shall he burn on the altar.* This teaches that only after the he-goat had been sent to the desert may the *Kohen Gadol* commence with the rest of the service (*Rav; Rashi* according to emendation cited in *Siach Yitzchak;* see *Tosefos Yom Tov*).

Although the verse speaks of the burning of the fats, the next part of the service is not that, but the reading of the Torah. However, once the Torah states that a required service may not be done before the goat reaches the desert, the concept is broadened to refer to all services which had to be performed by the *Kohen Gadol.* The *Kohen Gadol's* reading of the Torah on Yom Kippur was enjoined by

the Torah (see *Rashi* 68b s.v. בא לקרות), and it is therefore included in the rule that no service may be performed before the he-goat reaches the desert (*Siach Yitzchak*).

[Nevertheless the *Kohen Gadol* was allowed to remove the *emurin* from the animal's innards and to have the two sacrifices taken to the place of burning, since these services did not have to be performed by the *Kohen Gadol.* This is not analogous to slaughtering, which is also valid if performed by a non-*Kohen,* yet must be performed by the *Kohen Gadol* on Yom Kippur (see above 4:3 s.v. שחט) according to some authorities. The slaughtering of the ox is mentioned in the Torah (*Lev.* 16:11) as part of the Yom Kippur service, therefore it requires a *Kohen Gadol* to perform it, whereas the carving of the *emurin* is not.]

וּמִנַּיִן הָיוּ יוֹדְעִין שֶׁהִגִּיעַ שָׂעִיר לַמִּדְבָּר? דַּרְכִּיּוֹת הָיוּ עוֹשִׁין, — *And how did they know that the he-goat had reached the wilderness? They set up watch-posts*

Large boulders were set up so that watchmen standing on them could communicate with one another by waving

8. They said to the *Kohen Gadol*, 'The he-goat has reached the wilderness.' And how did they know that the he-goat had reached the wilderness? They set up watch-posts and waved cloths, and thus they knew that the he-goat had reached the wilderness.

R' Yehudah said: But they had a dependable signal: From Jerusalem to the place of the he-goat's sharp peak was three *mil;* they walked a *mil*, returned a *mil*, and tarried for a *mil*. Thus they knew that the he-goat had reached the wilderness.

YAD AVRAHAM

flags. The translation follows *Rav, Rambam, Aruch* s.v. דדכיות.

וּמְנִיפִין בְּסוּדָרִין, וְיוֹדְעִין שֶׁהִגִּיעַ שָׂעִיר לַמִּדְבָּר. — *and waved cloths, and thus they knew that the he-goat had reached the wilderness.*

[When the he-goat reached its destination, the watchman nearest the scene waved his cloth to signal the next watchman, etc.]

אָמַר רַבִּי יְהוּדָה: וַהֲלֹא סִמָּן גָּדוֹל הָיָה לָהֶם: — *R' Yehudah said: But they had a dependable* [lit. *great*] *signal:*

[They did not have to rely upon flag-waving. They had a dependable method by which they could know if the he-goat had reached the desert.]

מִירוּשָׁלַיִם וְעַד בֵּית חִדוּדוֹ — *From Jerusalem to the place of the he-goat's sharp peak*

The form of the word חִדוּדוֹ (the ו suggests possession: *its*) implies that this is not a proper name. חִדוּד means sharp; hence the translation. *Rambam's* version reads בֵּית חוֹרוֹן, Beis Choron (Tos. Yom Tov).

שְׁלֹשָׁה מִילִין; — *was three mil;*

R' Yehudah holds that once the he-goat reached the *beginning* of the desert its main purpose was accomplished and the *Kohen Gadol* could resume the service, even before it was pushed off the precipice. Thus, by using the method

described below to estimate how long it took to reach the desert, they could know when the he-goat reached the desert (*Rav; Rashi, Gemara* 68b).

הוֹלְכִין מִיל, — *they walked a mil,*

With the 'appointed man'. As related before (mishnah 4), *some of the eminent people of Jerusalem accompanied him till the first booth* which was one *mil* away (see *comm. loc. cit.; Rav; Rashi*).

וְחוֹזְרִין מִיל, — *returned a mil,*

The people accompanying the 'appointed man' to the first booth, returned to the Temple.

וְשׁוֹהִין כְּדֵי מִיל. — *and tarried for* [the time needed to walk] *a mil,*

[Since they only had to estimate only how long the 'man' needed to walk one more *mil*, they could do this quite accurately.]

וְיוֹדְעִין שֶׁהִגִּיעַ שָׂעִיר לַמִּדְבָּר. — *Thus they knew that the he-goat had reached the wilderness.*

[But the first tanna holds it was not sufficient to know whether the he-goat had reached the beginning of the wilderness. In order to resume the service, the he-goat had to reach its destination, the rock. Thus a distance of 12 *mil* had to be estimated instead of 3 *mil*. This was much more difficult to estimate with any accuracy.]

רַבִּי יִשְׁמָעֵאל אוֹמֵר: וַהֲלֹא סִמָּן אַחֵר הָיָה לָהֶם? לָשׁוֹן שֶׁל זְהוֹרִית הָיָה קָשׁוּר עַל־פִּתְחוֹ שֶׁל הֵיכָל, וּכְשֶׁהִגִּיעַ שָׂעִיר לַמִּדְבָּר הָיָה הַלָּשׁוֹן מַלְבִּין, שֶׁנֶּאֱמַר: ,,אִם־יִהְיוּ חֲטָאֵיכֶם כַּשָּׁנִים כַּשֶּׁלֶג יַלְבִּינוּ.''

[א] **בָּא** לוֹ כֹהֵן גָּדוֹל לִקְרוֹת. אִם רָצָה לִקְרוֹת בְּבִגְדֵי בוּץ, קוֹרֵא; וְאִם לֹא, קוֹרֵא בְּאִצְטְלִית לָבָן מִשֶּׁלּוֹ. חַזַּן הַכְּנֶסֶת נוֹטֵל סֵפֶר תּוֹרָה וְנוֹתְנוֹ לְרֹאשׁ הַכְּנֶסֶת; וְרֹאשׁ הַכְּנֶסֶת נוֹתְנוֹ לַסְּגָן; וְהַסְּגָן

יד אברהם

רַבִּי יִשְׁמָעֵאל אוֹמֵר: וַהֲלֹא סִמָּן אַחֵר הָיָה לָהֶם? לָשׁוֹן שֶׁל זְהוֹרִית הָיָה קָשׁוּר עַל־פִּתְחוֹ שֶׁל הֵיכָל. — R' Yishmael says: But did they not have another sign? A strip of red wool was tied atop the Temple entrance,

[In addition to those tied to 'the rock' and to the he-goat.]

וּכְשֶׁהִגִּיעַ שָׂעִיר הָיָה הַלָּשׁוֹן מַלְבִּין, — and when the he-goat reached the wilderness the strip of wool whitened,

[It miraculously changed colors from red to white.]

שֶׁנֶּאֱמַר: ,,אִם־יִהְיוּ חֲטָאֵיכֶם כַּשָּׁנִים יַלְבִּינוּ.'' — as it has been said [Isaiah 1:18]: [Even] if your sins will be like crimson threads [red symbolizes sin]

they will become white as snow.

R' Yehudah and the first *tanna* hold that they could not rely on this miraculous sign. The tying of the red strip of wool atop the Temple entrance took place only בָּרִאשׁוֹנָה, at first, in the early history of the Temple. Later on, because the people watched for this auspicious omen, and 'if it did not whiten, they were sad,' they [the Sages of those days] instituted that the strip of wool not be tied atop the Temple doors, but only 'half to the rock and half between its horns.' Thus, after this change in the place of the red strip of wool, a new sign was needed (*Tosefos Yom Tov*, based upon *Gemara* 67a).

Chapter 7

1.

בָּא לוֹ כֹהֵן גָּדוֹל לִקְרוֹת. אִם רָצָה לִקְרוֹת בְּבִגְדֵי בוּץ, קוֹרֵא; — The Kohen Gadol came to read. If he wished to read [wearing] his linen vestments, he may read;

[Once he had been informed that the goat had reached the desert (above 6:8), the Kohen Gadol came to the עֶזְרַת נָשִׁים, Women's Court] to read the portion of the Torah (Lev. 16) describing the Yom

Kippur service (Rav; Rashi).

Though the vestments were consecrated and designated for the sacrificial service, the Kohen Gadol was permitted to wear them while reading the Torah, for the Kohanim were allowed to wear their vestments or sleep in them, even after they had finished the service (Rav; Gem. 68b-70a).

וְאִם לֹא, קוֹרֵא בְּאִצְטְלִית לָבָן מִשֶּׁלּוֹ. — and

6
8   R' Yishmael says: But did they not have another sign? A strip of red wool was tied atop the Temple entrance, and when the he-goat reached the wilderness the strip of wool whitened, as it has been said [*Isaiah* 1:18]: [*Even*] *if your sins will be like crimson thread they will become white as snow.*

7
1   1. The *Kohen Gadol* came to read. If he wished to read [wearing] his linen vestments, he may read; and if not, he would read while wearing his own white robe.

The attendant of the synagogue takes a Torah Scroll and gives it to the head of the synagogue; the head of the synagogue gives it to the Deputy [*Kohen*

YAD AVRAHAM

if not, he would read while wearing his own white robe.

He was not obligated to wear his priestly vestments while reading the Torah as this was not a sacrificial service. If he preferred he could wear his own white robe, which was similar to a long shirt (*Rav; Gemara* 68b).

There is no requirement that he wear a white robe, but it was the custom (then as now) for eminent people to wear white robes on Yom Kippur (*Meiri*).

חַזַּן הַכְּנֶסֶת — *The attendant of the synagogue*

There was a synagogue on the Temple Mount near the Temple Courtyard (*Rashi*).

The man who was responsible for whatever had to be done in the synagogue, similar to today's שַׁמָּשׁ, shamash (shammes), was called חַזָּן, chazzan, in mishnaic terminology (*Rav; Rashi*). This word is derived from חָזֹה, *to see*; he was expected to 'see' what was needed and attend to it (*Tos. Yom Tov*).

[The usage of this word to denote the cantor is of later origin. *Aruch* (s.v. חזן) however, defines חַזָּן as שְׁלִיחַ צִבּוּר, cantor.]

נוֹטֵל סֵפֶר תּוֹרָה — *takes a Torah Scroll*

From the synagogue which was near

the Temple Courtyard (*Meiri*).

Rashi (Bava Basra 14a s.v. ספר העורה), assumes that the Torah Scroll written by Moses (which lay in the Ark) was used for the *Kohen Gadol's* reading, although this would have necessitated that someone enter the Holy of Holies to remove and return the Torah Scroll — an unusual course. *Rambam* makes no mention of Moses' scroll. *Shoshanim L'David* explains that *Rambam* does not necessarily disagree with *Rashi. Rambam* saw no need to mention this fact since the Torah Scroll was hidden together with the Ark before the destruction of the First Temple (see *Gem.* 53b). During the era of the Second Temple (and the end of the First), therefore, this Torah Scroll could not be used. Accordingly, since *Rambam's* description of the Yom Kippur service includes the Second Temple period, there was no need for him to mention this (see *Avodas Yisrael*, p. 206).

וְנוֹתְנוֹ לְרֹאשׁ הַכְּנֶסֶת; — *and gives it to the head of the synagogue;*

The head of the synagogue is the man who makes decisions concerning the synagogue — who should serve as cantor, who should read the Torah, who should read *maftir*, and other ceremonial matters [similar to the *gabbai* of our times] (*Rav; Rashi*).

וְרֹאשׁ הַכְּנֶסֶת נוֹתְנוֹ לַסְּגָן; וְהַסְּגָן נוֹתְנוֹ לְכֹהֵן גָּדוֹל. — *the head of the synagogue gives*

נוֹתְנוֹ לְכֹהֵן גָּדוֹל. וְכֹהֵן גָּדוֹל עוֹמֵד וּמְקַבֵּל וְקוֹרֵא עוֹמֵד.

וְקוֹרֵא ,,אַחֲרֵי מוֹת'' וְ,,אַךְ בֶּעָשׂוֹר''. וְגוֹלֵל סֵפֶר תּוֹרָה, וּמַנִּיחוֹ בְּחֵיקוֹ, וְאוֹמֵר: ,,יוֹתֵר מִמַּה שֶׁקָּרָאתִי לִפְנֵיכֶם כָּתוּב כָּאן.'' וּ,,בֶעָשׂוֹר'' שֶׁבַּחוּמֶשׁ הַפְּקוּדִים קוֹרֵא עַל־פֶּה.

יד אברהם

it to the Deputy [Kohen Gadol]; and the Deputy gives it to the Kohen Gadol.

The entire ceremony was to honor the Kohen Gadol by showing that there were many strata of officials below him (Rav; Gem. 69a).

וְכֹהֵן גָּדוֹל עוֹמֵד — The Kohen Gadol stands up,

[As the Torah Scroll was brought toward him, he arose in accord with the law that one must rise when he sees a Torah Scroll approaching (Yoreh Deah 282:3; Kiddushin 33b).]

Inferring that the Kohen Gadol had been sitting up to now, the Gemara (69a), asks how this was possible, since no one was permitted to sit in the Temple Courtyard. From this the Gemara deduces that the Kohen Gadol read the Torah in the so-called Women's Courtyard which was an enclosed area adjoining the Temple Courtyard on the east, but was really not part of it. He was therefore permitted to sit there, and rise only when the Torah Scroll approached him.

וּמְקַבֵּל וְקוֹרֵא עוֹמֵד. — accepts [the scroll] and reads while standing.

[This accords with the rule that one who reads the Torah in public should stand while doing so (see Orach Chaim 141:1; Megillah 21a).]

וְקוֹרֵא ,,אַחֲרֵי מוֹת'' — He reads [from] 'Acharei Mos' [Lev. 16]

The Kohen Gadol reads from the beginning of the Sidra Acharei Mos until the end of the segment dealing with the Yom Kippur service [Lev. 16:1-34] (Tif. Yis.).

וְ,,אַךְ בֶּעָשׂוֹר''. — and [the portion that begins] 'But on the tenth' [Lev. 23:26-32].

[This portion deals with the prohibition against doing work on Yom Kippur and with the obligation to fast.]

וְגוֹלֵל סֵפֶר תּוֹרָה, — Then he rolls up the Torah Scroll,

[I.e., having concluded this reading he closes it.]

וּמַנִּיחוֹ בְּחֵיקוֹ, — puts it in his bosom,

I.e., under his arm (Tif. Yis.).

וְאוֹמֵר: ,,יוֹתֵר מִמַּה שֶׁקָּרָאתִי לִפְנֵיכֶם כָּתוּב כָּאן.'' — and says, 'More than I have read to you is written here;'

[He tells the assemblage that the Torah contains other portions dealing with Yom Kippur.]

The Kohen Gadol said this because he was about to recite from memory a third segment of the Torah dealing with Yom Kippur (as related below). To dispel any notions that the Torah Scroll from which he had been reading was missing the passage, the Kohen Gadol made this announcement (Rav; Gem. 70a).

,,וּבֶעָשׂוֹר'' שֶׁבַּחוּמֶשׁ הַפְּקוּדִים קוֹרֵא עַל־פֶּה. — and he recites by heart from the Book of Numbers beginning 'On the tenth' [Numb. 29:7-11].

These verse describes the mussaf [additional offerings] of Yom Kippur. The passage begins, On the tenth [day] of the seventh month [Tishrei].

Today, the Book of Numbers is commonly referred to in Hebrew as בַּמִּדְבָּר, BaMidbar [lit., In the Wilderness]. In earlier generations it was called וַיְדַבֵּר, Vayedaber [lit. And he spoke; from its opening word]. In Mishnaic times it was called חֻמַּשׁ הַפְּקוּדִים. The word חוּמָשׁ, literally fifth, refers to one of the five Books of Moses. It is the forerunner of the word Chumash. פְּקוּדִים means

7
1

Gadol]; and the Deputy gives it to the *Kohen Gadol*. The *Kohen Gadol* stands up, accepts [the scroll] and reads while standing.

He reads [from] *'Acharei Mos'* [*Leviticus* 16] and [the portion that begins] *'But on the tenth'* [*Leviticus* 23:26-32]. Then he rolls up the Torah Scroll, puts it in his bosom, and says, 'More than I have read to you is written here;' and he recites by heart from the *Book of Numbers,* beginning *'On the tenth'* [*Numbers* 29:7-11].

YAD AVRAHAM

census or *numbers.* The name derives from chapters one through four and twenty-six, all of which deal with the census of Israel *(Rashi).*

Though it is not permitted to recite the Torah in public by heart (see *Orach Chayim* 49 and 144:1), an exception was made here, for otherwise the *Kohen Gadol* would not have been allowed to read this portion at all as explained below (*Magen Avraham* and *Beur HaGra* to *Orach Chayim* 144:1; see *Beis Yosef* there and *Teshuvos HaRashba;* cf. *Tos. Yesh.*).

Rabbeinu Yonah (to *Berachos* 9b s.v. לא הפסיד citing *R' Shlomo min HaHar;* also *Beis Yosef, Orach Chayim* 49) explains that any portion of Torah which one is obligated to recite is exempted from the stipulation that Torah should not be recited by heart. For example, the *Mussaf* prayer includes Torah verses dealing with the *mussaf* sacrifice, therefore the rule that Torah may not be read by heart does not apply there.

It was forbidden to bring another Torah Scroll to read this portion, because that would raise doubts whether the portion read in the second Torah was missing from the first one; otherwise why take the trouble to bring another scroll? [Our custom to take out more than one Torah does not contradict this, because we call up a different person for the reading of each section; no single person reads from more than one scroll. The rule not to read from a second scroll applies only where the person who has read from the first scroll discards it to read from a second one.]

They were also forbidden to roll the first Torah Scroll to the place in the book of *Numbers* where the *Kohen Gadol* was to read, because it would be considered an expression of disdain for the assembled people to force them to wait while this was going on. Therefore, the best course open to the *Kohen Gadol* was to recite this portion by heart (*Rav; Gem.* 70a).

But, when he read, *'But on the tenth'* from *Leviticus* 23, he was allowed to roll the Torah from his earlier reading in *Leviticus* 16, because the two chapters (*Lev.* 16 and 23) are close together, and the rolling would not keep the public waiting. In Talmudic times (a custom still maintained in Yemenite communities) every verse read in public was translated into Aramaic (see *Megillah* 4:4 ArtScroll ed., p.85). Thus, the *Kohen Gadol* was able to roll the Torah from *Leviticus* 16 to 23 while the last verse of the previous reading was being translated (*Rav; Gem.* 69b).

[The custom to translate the Torah while it is being read in public (*Rambam, Tefillah* 12:10 says it was instituted by Ezra; see *Kessef Mishneh* there) was discontinued in ancient times when the Aramaic of *Onkelos* ceased to be the vernacular. Most authorities hold that the only translation worthy of the public reading is Aramaic (see *Tur Orach Chayim* 14:5 cf. *Sefer HaEshkol* p. 2:19 p.

וּמְבָרֵךְ עָלֶיהָ שְׁמוֹנֶה בְּרָכוֹת: עַל־הַתּוֹרָה;
וְעַל־הָעֲבוֹדָה; וְעַל־הַהוֹדָאָה; וְעַל־מְחִילַת
הֶעָוֹן; וְעַל־הַמִּקְדָּשׁ בִּפְנֵי עַצְמוֹ; וְעַל־יִשְׂרָאֵל
בִּפְנֵי עַצְמָן; וְעַל־יְרוּשָׁלַיִם בִּפְנֵי עַצְמָהּ; וְעַל־
הַכֹּהֲנִים בִּפְנֵי עַצְמָן; וְעַל־שְׁאָר הַתְּפִלָּה.

יד אברהם

61; *Sefer Halttim* p. 267-8; the source for this is *Megillah* 23b; see *Tos.* there s.v. לא). Nevertheless, in many communities the custom persisted to translate into Aramaic the portion of the Torah and of the Prophets read on holidays (see *Tos. Megillah* 24a s.v. ואם; *Machzor Vitri*; *Sefer Halttim* loc. cit.; *Bach* to *Orach Chaim* 145). The Yemenite communities substituted R' Saadiah Gaon's Arabic translation *(Tafsir)* for *Onkelos* and translate the Torah in public to this day.]

וּמְבָרֵךְ עָלֶיהָ שְׁמֹנֶה בְּרָכוֹת: עַל־הַתּוֹרָה; — *Then he recites* [lit. *blesses*] *over it eight benedictions: for the Torah;*

The two benedictions that are customarily recited upon reading the Torah, one before the reading and one after *(Rav; Rambam)*.

Rashi, however, counts only the benediction said after reading the Torah. We will follow this opinion in counting these eight benedictions, because it is consistent with the version found in our *Mishnayos. Rambam's* (and *Rav's*) count of these benedictions and his version of this mishnah will be discussed below (s.v. וְעַל־שְׁאָר הַתְּפִלָּה).

The benediction recited before the reading is not counted, according to *Rashi,* because the mishnah wishes to emphasize the differences between the *Kohen Gadol's* conclusion of his Torah reading, and the procedure followed by laymen. In mishnaic times, only the first and last of the entire group of men called to read the Torah recited a benediction; the first said the benediction before the reading and the last said the benediction upon terminating the entire reading of the day *(Megillah* 4:1). [Only in later times did the Sages institute that every person called to read the Torah recite both benedictions

(*Megillah* 21b).] Since an ordinary reader would recite a single blessing, the *Kohen Gadol* is unique in that he recite an extra blessing. Consequently, the mishnah counts the concluding blessing only — the *Kohen Gadol's* additional blessing over and above what another reader would recite *(Tif. Yis.).*

וְעַל־הָעֲבוֹדָה; — *(and) for the [sacrificial] service;*

This second benediction is from the *Shemoneh Esrei.* It begins רְצֵה, *Be pleased,* and a prayer that God accept the sacrificial service of the day *(Rav; Rashi).*

Rashi gives us a more extensive version of this benediction: רְצֵה בְעַמְּךָ יִשְׂרָאֵל וְתִרְצֶה הָעֲבוֹדָה בִּדְבִיר בֵּיתֶךָ וכו' בָּרוּךְ אַתָּה ה' שֶׁאוֹתְךָ לְבַדְּךָ בְּיִרְאָה נַעֲבֹד. — *Be pleased with Your nation Israel, and be pleased with the service in the Holy of Holies of Your House etc.* [i.e., the rest of the benediction reads as in the daily prayer] *Blessed are You, HASHEM, for You alone we will serve in awe.* This חֲתִימָה, *close,* is found in *Yerushalmi* here and in *R' Chananel.* [The version we say in our *Shemoneh Esrei* was not appropriate for the Temple since a large portion of our version asks for the return to the Temple of the sacrificial service.]

וְעַל־הַהוֹדָאָה; — *(and) for the thanksgiving;*

[This is the third benediction].

The benediction is from the daily *Shemoneh Esrei* starting מוֹדִים אֲנַחְנוּ לָךְ, *We give thanks to You,* and ending with הַטּוֹב שִׁמְךָ וּלְךָ נָאֶה לְהוֹדוֹת, *Your Name is Beneficence, and it is becoming to thank you.* This sequence is based

**7
1**

Then he recites over it eight benedictions: for the Torah; for the [sacrificial] service; for the thanksgiving; for the forgiving of sins; for the Temple separately; for Israel separately; for Jerusalem separately; for the *Kohanim* separately; and for the rest of the prayer.

YAD AVRAHAM

upon the verse (*Psalms* 50:23): *He who sacrifices a thanksgiving offering should honor* (or thank) *Me*. From this we derive that sacrifice (i.e., here the benediction about the service) should be followed with thanksgiving (*Rashi*).

וְעַל־מְחִילַת הֶעָוֹן; — (*and*) *for the forgiving of sins;*
[This is the fourth benediction.]
He prays מְחוֹל לַעֲוֹנוֹתֵינוּ, *forgive our sins*. The last segment of the fourth benediction recited in every *Shemoneh Esrei* of Yom Kippur, which ends מֶלֶךְ מוֹחֵל וְסוֹלֵחַ לַעֲווֹנוֹתֵינוּ ..., *King Who forgives and pardons our sins...*, as in the Yom Kippur prayer.
Rambam (*Avodas Yom HaKippurim* 3:4) says that this benediction begins with סְלַח לָנוּ, *Forgive us*, etc. (following the formula of the daily prayer), but the end is מוֹחֵל עֲווֹנוֹת עַמּוֹ יִשְׂרָאֵל בְּרַחֲמִים, *Who forgives the sins of His people Israel with mercy* (cf. *his comm.* and *Rav*).

וְעַל־הַמִּקְדָּשׁ בִּפְנֵי עַצְמוֹ; — (*and*) *for the Temple separately* [lit. *by itself*];
[This was the fifth benediction, dealing exclusively with a request for the Temple.]
He prays that the Temple should remain standing with the שְׁכִינָה, *Divine Presence*, within it (*Rambam*, *Avodas Yom HaKippurim* 3:11).

וְעַל־יִשְׂרָאֵל בִּפְנֵי עַצְמָן; — (*and*) *for Israel separately* [lit. *by themselves*];
[This is the sixth benediction.]
He recited a separate benediction for Israel. The content of this prayer is that Hashem be satisfied with His nation Israel and that they not have their king removed. And he ends בָּרוּךְ אַתָּה ה' הַבּוֹחֵר בְּיִשְׂרָאֵל, *Blessed are You,*

HASHEM, *Who selects Israel* (*Rambam*, *Avodas Yom HaKippurim* 3:11; see *Rashi*).

וְעַל־יְרוּשָׁלַיִם בִּפְנֵי עַצְמָהּ; — (*and*) *for Jerusalem separately* [lit. *for itself*];
[He prays for the well-being of Jerusalem.]
[This phrase is found in our printed editions of the Mishnah and the Gemara. But, there is evidence that most of the early commentators, including *Rambam* (who say nothing about this), did not have it in their versions of the Mishnah (see *Shinuyei Nuschaos*). If this phrase were part of our mishnah we would have one benediction too many.]
Of the various *Avodos* the only one that lists this benediction for Jerusalem is the version of אַתָּה כוֹנַנְתָּ that is found in *Seder R' Amram Gaon*. The other authoritative versions (*Siddur R' Saadiah Gaon*; *Tashlum Abudraham*) omit it.
However, *Meiri* in his commentary to the *Avodah*, אַתָּה כוֹנַנְתָּ (*Meshiv Nefesh* or *Chibur HaTeshuvah*; see *Shinuyei Nuschaos*) says, 'There are some who add a separate benediction for Jerusalem and end it with הַבּוֹחֵר בִּירוּשָׁלַיִם, *Who chooses Jerusalem*. Those who include this blessing omit, from the total of eight, the last benediction which is a general one about all the prayers.
Tiferes Yisrael and *Meleches Shlomo* conjecture that the versions which have a separate blessing for Jerusalem omit the separate blessing for Israel; they would conclude the entire order of blessings with: עַל־יִשְׂרָאֵל וְעַל־שְׁאָר הַתְּפִלָּה, *for Israel and for the rest of the prayer*. Thus these last two could be included in one benediction (similar to *Rambam's* opinion; see s.v. וְעַל־שְׁאָר הַתְּפִלָּה).

וְעַל־הַכֹּהֲנִים בִּפְנֵי עַצְמָן; — (*and*) *for the Kohanim separately* [lit. *for themselves*];
[This is the seventh benediction.]

[ב] **הָרוֹאֶה** כֹּהֵן גָּדוֹל כְּשֶׁהוּא קוֹרֵא אֵינוֹ
רוֹאֶה פַר וְשָׂעִיר הַנִּשְׂרָפִים.
וְהָרוֹאֶה פַר וְשָׂעִיר הַנִּשְׂרָפִים אֵינוֹ רוֹאֶה כֹּהֵן
גָּדוֹל כְּשֶׁהוּא קוֹרֵא — וְלֹא מִפְּנֵי שֶׁאֵינוֹ
רַשַּׁאי, אֶלָּא שֶׁהָיְתָה דֶרֶךְ רְחוֹקָה, וּמְלֶאכֶת
שְׁנֵיהֶן שָׁוָה כְּאַחַת.

יד אברהם

According to *Rashi* this blessing ends
בָּרוּךְ אַתָּה ה' הַבּוֹחֵר בְּזַרְעוֹ שֶׁל אַהֲרֹן, *Blessed are You, HASHEM, Who chooses the
seed of Aaron.*

Rambam maintains that the blessing
is a prayer that God be pleased with the
service of the *Kohanim* and with their
deeds, and that He bless them. The
blessing ends בָּרוּךְ אַתָּה ה' מְקַדֵּשׁ הַכֹּהֲנִים,
*Blessed are You, HASHEM, Who
sanctifies the Kohanim (Avodas Yom
HaKippurim* 3:11).

וְעַל־שְׁאָר הַתְּפִלָּה. — *and for the rest of
the prayer.*

[I.e., now he recited the rest of the individual and general prayers that the
time and situation demanded. This is
the eighth benediction.]

The context of this blessing is: *Glad
song, prayer, and supplication before
You, about Your people Israel which
needs to be saved.* It ends בָּרוּךְ אַתָּה ה'
שׁוֹמֵעַ תְּפִלָּה, *Blessed are You, HASHEM,
Who hears prayer (Gem.* 70a).

The *Gemara* does not mean to specify
the exact wording of the blessing.
Rather, the *Gemara* means that the last
benediction was purposely left unfor-
mulated. It contained praise, prayer,
and supplication in whatever form and
for whichever purpose were appropriate
at the moment (from *Rambam; Meiri;*
and *Abudraham*; also from *Rashi* and
Rav to *Sotah* 7:7).

Until now we have counted these benedictions according to *Rashi's* opinion because it
coincides with our version of the mishnah.

Rambam (comm.), counts עַל־הַתּוֹרָה,
for the Torah, as two (one benediction
before and one after reading the Torah).
The other blessings follow in this sequence: 3) service; 4) thanksgiving;
5) forgiving of the sins; 6) Temple;
7) *Kohanim*; 8) the people Israel and
the rest of the prayer.

As evident from the above, *Rambam's* version of the mishnah puts
Israel next to *the rest of the prayer,*
enabling him to combine them in a
single blessing. It is also clear that his
version omits the words בִּפְנֵי עַצְמָן,
separately, next to עַל־יִשְׂרָאֵל, *for Israel.*

[However *Rambam's* own version of
the mishnah (ed. *Kafih*), though it omits
בִּפְנֵי עַצְמָן, *separately* lists עַל־הַכֹּהֲנִים
עַל־יִשְׂרָאֵל, *for the Kohanim, for Israel,*
and וְעַל־שְׁאָר הַתְּפִלָּה, *and for the rest of
the prayer,* in the same sequence as in
our version.]

In his *Mishneh Torah (Avodas Yom
HaKippurim* 3:11), however, it is clear
that he accepted the version עַל־יִשְׂרָאֵל
בִּפְנֵי עַצְמָן, *for Israel separately* (and the
sequence followed in our versions). In
order to arrive at a total of eight
benedictions he counts the benedictions
about the Torah as one (as *Rashi* does).

2.

הָרוֹאֶה כֹּהֵן גָּדוֹל כְּשֶׁהוּא קוֹרֵא אֵינוֹ
רוֹאֶה פַר וְשָׂעִיר הַנִּשְׂרָפִים. וְהָרוֹאֶה פַר
וְשָׂעִיר הַנִּשְׂרָפִים אֵינוֹ רוֹאֶה כֹּהֵן גָּדוֹל כְּשֶׁהוּא
קוֹרֵא — וְלֹא מִפְּנֵי שֶׁאֵינוֹ רַשַּׁאי, *One who*

*sees the Kohen Gadol when he reads
cannot see* [lit. *does not see*] *the ox and
the he-goat as they are burned.* [*And*]
one who sees the ox and the he-goat as

2. **O**ne who sees the *Kohen Gadol* when he reads cannot see the ox and the he-goat as they are burned. [And] one who sees the ox and the he-goat as they are burned cannot see the *Kohen Gadol* when he reads — not because he may not, but because the distance [between them] was great, and both services were performed at the same time.

YAD AVRAHAM

they are burned cannot see the Kohen Gadol when he reads—not because he may not,

This bit of information could lead to the following mistaken notion that the mishnah will soon correct: we might have though that an onlooker is *forbidden* to leave a service before it is concluded. To dispel this interpretation, the mishnah goes on to explain לֹא מִפְּנֵי שֶׁאֵינוֹ רַשַׁאי, *not because he may not do so.* The *mishnah* explicitly states that there is no such prohibition since the onlooker himself is not a participant in the service (*Rav; Gem.* 70a).

Actually, one may not leave in the middle of the Torah reading (*Berachos* 8a; *Orach Chaim* 146), but he may leave

בֵּין גַּבְרָא לְגַבְרָא, *between one reader and the next (ibid.).* In the Temple, too, one was permitted to leave when the *Kohen Gadol* finished reading *Leviticus* 16 and before he started reading *Leviticus* 23:26-32, or in the interval between the latter reading and the oral recital of *Numbers* 29:7-11 (*Tos. Yesh.; Ritva*).

אֶלָּא שֶׁהָיְתָה דֶרֶךְ רְחוֹקָה, וּמְלֶאכֶת שְׁנֵיהֶן שָׁנָה בְּאַחַת. — *but because the distance [between them] was great* [lit. *it was a far road*], *and both services were performed at the same time.*

The reason an onlooker could not see both services was because the place where the ox and the he-goat were burned was outside of Jerusalem (see above 6:4).

3.

The mishnayos up to this point have dealt with only two of the Yom Kippur sacrifices — the ox and the he-goat sin offerings whose bloods were sprinkled in the Holy of Holies and the Holy. The next two mishnayos will give us the sequence in which the other sacrifices of Yom Kippur were offered. The sacrifices of Yom Kippur are specified in two places, *Leviticus* 16 and *Numbers* 29:7.

In order to gain a fuller understanding of these complicated mishnayos, one should first familiarize himself with the different sacrifices offered on this day. Below we list the sacrifices in *Leviticus* in one column, and the *mussafim, additional offerings,* in *Numbers* in an adjacent column, so that the reader can compare the two sets of sacrifices. The תָּמִיד, *daily offering,* is omitted because we are concerned here solely with the unique Yom Kippur sacrifices. The he-goat for Azazel is omitted since it is not a sacrifice.

As can be readily seen of the sets of offerings, two of the communal sacrifices seem to be mentioned in both places — the he-goat for the people's sin offering and the ram for the people's burnt offering. (The *Kohen Gadol's personal* ram [*Lev.* 16:3], however, is not to be confused with the ram mentioned as part of the *mussafim* in *Numbers*; like all *mussafim,* that ram is a *national* sacrifice while the *Kohen Gadol's* ram is a personal one.) In the case of the he-goat, however, the Torah explicitly says that there were two *separate* goat sacrifices: the one in

[ג] **אִם** בְּבִגְדֵי בוּץ קוֹרֵא, קִדֵּשׁ יָדָיו וְרַגְלָיו, פָּשַׁט, יָרַד וְטָבַל. עָלָה וְנִסְתַּפֵּג. הֵבִיאוּ לוֹ בִגְדֵי זָהָב. וְלָבַשׁ וְקִדֵּשׁ יָדָיו וְרַגְלָיו. וְיָצָא וְעָשָׂה אֶת־אֵילוֹ וְאֶת־אֵיל הָעָם, וְאֶת־שִׁבְעַת כְּבָשִׂים תְּמִימִים בְּנֵי שָׁנָה; דִּבְרֵי רַבִּי אֱלִיעֶזֶר.

יד אברהם

Yom Kippur Sacrifices	As listed in Leviticus 16	As listed in Numbers 29
חַטָאוֹת sin offerings	The *Kohen Gadol's* ox. In the Holy of Holies and in the Holy (vs. 6, 11-20).	
	A he-goat in the Holy of Holies and in the Holy (vs. 9, 15-20).	A he-goat. On the outer altar (v. 11).
עוֹלוֹת burnt offerings	The *Kohen Gadol's* ram. On the outer altar (v. 3).	An ox. On the outer altar (v. 8).
	The people's ram. On the outer altar (v. 5).	A ram. On the outer altar (v. 8).
		Seven sheep. On the outer altar (v. 8).

Numbers is described (29:11) as, *a he-goat sin offering aside from the sin offering of* כִּפֻּרִים, *atonement*, i.e., it is not the same as the sin offering of *Leviticus*. But regarding the ram burnt offering, the Torah does not clarify whether the ram mentioned in *Numbers* is identical with that mentioned in *Leviticus*. This gives rise to a difference of opinion among tannaim. One view (R' Yehudah HaNasi) holds that both verses refer to the same sacrifice. Another opinion (R' Shimon ben Elazar) holds that two rams were brought as burnt offerings (*Gem.* 70b).

All the tannaim in our mishnah, which mentions nothing about a second ram, are assumed (*Gem.* 70b) to hold that the ram of *Leviticus* and the ram of *Numbers* are one and the same. Thus though ten sacrifices are mentioned in *Numbers* and four in *Leviticus*, their total, is thirteen, not fourteen. The service of the ox and the he-goat has been described at length in earlier chapters. The next two mishnayos will give us the sequence of the remaining eleven sacrifices.

As we shall see, in addition to the opinions of the two tannaim mentioned in the mishnah, R' Eliezer and R' Akiva, there is much difference of opinion on how to interpret their words. These disagreements are rooted in two problems. The first is at what point in the Yom Kippur service, as described in *Leviticus*, the *Kohen Gadol* offers the *mussafim* that are described in *Numbers*? The second problem lies in properly understanding the sequence of *Leviticus* 16 itself. This will be dealt with at length in the preface to the next mishnah. In the commentary to mishnah 3 we will give only the interpretation of *Rashi* and *Rav*. Two other opinions, those of *Tosafos* and *Rambam*, will be given in an appendix.

אִם בְּבִגְדֵי בוּץ קוֹרֵא, קִדֵּשׁ יָדָיו וְרַגְלָיו, — *If he read [the Torah] in the linen vest-* ments, he [then] washed [lit. sanctified] his hands and feet,

3. If he read [the Torah] in the linen vestments, he [then] washed his hands and feet, undressed, went down [into the mikveh] and immersed himself. He came up and dried himself. They brought him the golden vestments. He dressed and washed his hands and feet. Then he went out, and sacrificed his ram, and the ram of the people, and the seven unblemished male sheep in their first year; this is the opinion of R' Eliezer.

YAD AVRAHAM

[As mentioned before (mishnah 1), the *Kohen Gadol* had the option of not removing the white linen vestments he had worn while performing the service in the Holy and Holy of Holies. The mishnah explains the sequence of events if he follows this option, in which case, he is required to wash his hands and feet before removing the priestly garments (see 3:6). If, however, he had chosen to remove the vestments before reading the Torah, and read in 'his own white robe,' he would have washed his hands and feet then. He did not have to wash again upon taking off the white robe, since this change of clothing was not part of the required service of the day.]

פָּשַׁט, יָרַד וְטָבַל. עָלָה וְנִסְתַּפֵּג. — *undressed, went down [into the mikveh] and immersed himself. He came up and dried himself.*

הֵבִיאוּ לוֹ בִגְדֵי זָהָב. וְלָבַשׁ וְקִדֵּשׁ יָדָיו וְרַגְלָיו. — *They brought him the golden vestments. He dressed and washed [lit. sanctified] his hands and feet.*

[First he dressed and then he washed as set forth earlier (3:6).]

וְיָצָא — *Then he went out,*

Tiferes Yisrael understands the expression 'he went out' to mean that the *Kohen Gadol* had washed near the laver which stood between the altar and the Temple. Thus, when he went north of the altar to slaughter the sacrifices, he could be said to have gone 'out' from the area between the altar and the Temple. Though the *Kohen Gadol* washed

from a golden pitcher on Yom Kippur (4:5), rather than from the laver, *Tiferes Yisrael* holds that he washed in the area of the laver.

[However, *Tiferes Yisrael's* explanation does not explain why this term is used only here. It may be that the 'going out' is relative to where he had performed the previous service. Then, he had left the Courtyard for the first time, to read the Torah in the Women's Court. Now, he changed clothes and 'went out' from that Court to enter the Courtyard. No other change of vestments had been followed by so significant a change of location. Even in the morning the *Kohen Gadol* had come from the chamber of Sanhedrin which was within the Courtyard wall. (See comm. to 1:1.)]

וְעָשָׂה אֶת־אֵילוֹ וְאֶת־אֵיל הָעָם, — *and sacrificed [lit. did] his ram, and the ram of the people,*

[I.e., he slaughtered them, caught the blood in a basin, took the blood to the outer altar, and threw it in the manner prescribed for עוֹלוֹת, *burnt offerings* (see Lev. 1:5 with Rashi).

[These burnt offerings are those required by *Leviticus* 16:3,5. Their service is mentioned there in verse 24. According to the sequence in *Leviticus*, these sacrifices follow the sending of the he-goat to *Azazel* (v. 21-22). The reading of the Torah which separates the service of the he-goat to *Azazel* from this service is not mentioned in *Leviticus* 16 at all, therefore it is not considered a deviation from the *Leviticus*

רַבִּי עֲקִיבָא אוֹמֵר: עִם-תָּמִיד שֶׁל שַׁחַר הָיוּ
קְרֵבִין, וּפַר הָעוֹלָה. וְשָׂעִיר הַנַּעֲשֶׂה בַחוּץ הָיוּ
קְרֵבִין עִם-תָּמִיד שֶׁל בֵּין הָעַרְבַּיִם.

יד אברהם

sequence. *Leviticus* 16:23, which, according to the Oral Tradition, speaks about the service of removing the incense ladle and the coal-shovel from the Holy of Holies, is mentioned after the verses requiring sending of the he-goat to *Azazel* and before the commandment concerning these two sacrifices. However, according to the Mishnah and the Oral Tradition (mishnah 4), this service is performed not *between* these two burnt offerings, but *after* them. The reason for this change of sequence is given in the preface to the next mishnah. Thus, the placing the service of these two rams at this point following the dispatch of the goat to *Azazel* is in accord with the order laid down in *Leviticus* 16.]

וְאֶת-שִׁבְעַת כְּבָשִׂים תְּמִימִים בְּנֵי שָׁנָה; — *and the seven unblemished* [lit. *whole*] *male sheep in their first year;*

[The mishnah furnishes this information about these sheep as it appears in *Numbers* 26:8.]

These sheep are part of the *mussafim* sacrifices, required by *Numbers* 26:7-11. They are all עוֹלוֹת, *burnt offerings.*

The *Gemara* (70a) cites a *baraisa* saying that these sheep, with the other *mussafim* (the ox burnt offering and the he-goat sin offering in *Numbers* 29) were sacrificed together with the afternoon תָּמִיד, *daily offering*. According to *Rashi*, they were all offered after the *Kohen Gadol* had changed into his golden vestments for the last time. Upon doing so, he first sacrificed the *mussafim* and then the daily offering (no sacrifice was allowed after the daily offering). Prior to this last service of the day, he had worn the white vestments to remove the incense ladle and coal shovel from the Holy of Holies.

Although R' Eliezer disagrees with R' Akiva not only about the place of the

seven sheep, but also about the place of the ox and the he-goat in the sequence (see appendix, "When were the *Mussafim* sacrificed?"). R' Eliezer mentions only the sheep because there are other opinions that he wants to negate. One tanna holds (see *Gem.* 70b) that one of these seven sheep was sacrificed with the morning daily offering and the remaining six with the afternoon daily offering. Another *(ibid.)* holds that six sheep were sacrificed in the morning and the remaining one in the afternoon. By mentioning when the sheep were sacrificed, R' Eliezer expressed his differences with both R' Akiva and the other tannaim *(Tosafos ibid.).*

דִּבְרֵי רַבִּי אֱלִיעֶזֶר. — *this is the opinion* [lit. *words*] *of R' Eliezer.*

[As will be set forth below, the *Gemara* elucidates R' Eliezer's opinion at far greater length.]

רַבִּי עֲקִיבָא אוֹמֵר: עִם-תָּמִיד שֶׁל שַׁחַר הָיוּ קְרֵבִין, וּפַר הָעוֹלָה, — *R' Akiva says: They* [the seven male sheep] *were brought with the daily morning offering, as well as the ox for a burnt offering.*

[I.e., after the first immersion. In sharp contrast to R' Eliezer who holds that these *mussafim* were offered at the end of the day, R' Akiva holds that they were among the earliest parts of the service.]

Not only the sheep, but also the ox were sacrificed with the morning daily sacrifice.

The *Gemara* (70a) comments that the punctuation of the mishnah is unclear. The phrase וּפַר הָעוֹלָה, *and the ox for a burnt offering,* can be understood as we have placed it: as going together with the earlier clause, or it can be understood as the beginning of a new clause: [after telling us that the seven sheep are offered with the morning *Tamid* (daily offering), R' Akiva continues that] the ox and the he-goat are offered with the afternoon *Tamid*. Based on evidence from a

R' Akiva says: They [the seven male sheep] were brought with the daily morning offering, as well as the ox for a burnt offering. But the he-goat which is done outside were brought with the daily afternoon offering.

YAD AVRAHAM

baraisa, the Gemara adopts the first alternative, as given in our translation and commentary.

וְשָׂעִיר הַנַּעֲשָׂה בַחוּץ — But the he-goat which is done outside

This he-goat is the sin offering of the mussaf that is commanded in Numbers 29:11. Its service is performed only outside, in the Courtyard. The he-goat discussed in earlier chapters, however, is the sin offering whose blood was sprinkled inside, in the Holy of Holies and the Holy (Rav).

הָיוּ קְרֵבִין עִם־תָּמִיד שֶׁל בֵּין הָעַרְבַּיִם. — were brought with the daily afternoon offering.

Though the mishnah speaks only of one sacrifice — the he-goat which is done outside — the plural form הָיוּ, were, is used here, to include the burning of the emurim (sacrificial parts) which, like the he-goat, were offered during the same time segment as the daily afternoon sacrifice (see Tosafos 70b s.v. אחר; Tos. Yom Tov).

Here, too, the mishnah is at variance with the baraisa's version of R' Akiva's opinion (according to Rashi's interpretation). According to the baraisa the he-goat whose blood is sprinkled outside, the burnt offering, and the emurim were offered with the two rams after the third immersion, not with the afternoon daily offering as the mishnah seems to suggest. Tosefos Yom Tov submits that the phrase עִם־תָּמִיד שֶׁל בֵּין הָעַרְבַּיִם, with the daily afternoon offering, of our mishnah is meant only in a negative way — i.e., unlike the seven sheep, the he-goat which is 'done outside' is not sacrificed with the morning

daily offering after the immersion, but rather toward the end of the day, with the two rams, i.e., before them, after the third immersion.

Some versions (see Shinuyei Nuschaos) omit the words הָיוּ קְרֵבִין, were brought, thus removing the problem of plural usage for a single offering. This is Tosafos Yeshanim's version and the one adopted by Vilna Gaon (Hagahos HaGra).

R' Akiva makes no mention of the two rams that were burnt offerings, one for the Kohen Gadol and one for the people (Lev. 16:3,5). This is because there is no doubt that they were sacrificed after the third immersion. The statement at the beginning of our mishnah, and he sacrificed his ram and the people's ram, though part of R' Eliezer's statement, goes for R' Akiva as well. The only difference between them in this matter is that according to R' Eliezer the two rams follow immediately after the third immersion, whereas according to R' Akiva the immersion is followed by the he-goat sin offering, and only then are the two rams sacrificed (Tos. Yom Tov).

◆§ Elaborations on Our Mishnah

The Gemara (70a) says that our mishnah is not מְתַקַּנְתָּא, complete (in stating R' Eliezer's and R' Akiva's opinions). R' Eliezer says nothing about the burning on the outer altar of the emurim [sacrificial parts] of the ox and he-goat whose blood had been sprinkled in the Holy and Holy of Holies (6:7); nor does he make any mention of the two Mussaf offerings brought on the outer altar, the ox and the he-goat (Numbers 29:8,11). [See Appendix, "Elaborations in 7:3" for a discussion of this Gemara.]

4.

◆§ Removal of the Ladle and the Shovel

We learned in 7:3 (see prefatory remarks there) that the services described in Leviticus 16 are performed in the sequence in which they are mentioned, except for

the removal of the incense ladle and shovel from the Holy of Holies.

This service is commanded in *Leviticus* 16:23: *And Aaron shall enter the Tabernacle, and take off the linen vestments which he wore when became into the Holy, and he shall leave them there.*

The Sages (*Yoma* 32a, 71a and *Sifra*) ask, 'For what did he come?' — since he had already finished the service that was to be performed in the Holy wearing the linen vestments (*Rashi* 32a).

It is inconceivable that the *Kohen Gadol* entered the Holy to 'take off the linen vestments' and to leave them in the Holy. Firstly, it would be a sacrilege to stand undressed in the Holy. Secondly, what purpose could there be in leaving the clothing there to rot?

It can only be that he now entered the Holy to perform some service; yet it must be a service so obvious that it need not be mentioned. This can only be the removal of the ladle and the shovel which had been left in the Holy of Holies (*Ramban, Lev.* 16:23). Thus the beginning of this verse, *And Aaron shall enter the Tabernacle* (i.e., the Holy of Holies) ... is an unfinished sentence, leaving unsaid what he would do there. The rest of the verse, *and [he shall] take off ...* is a new thought describing what Aaron is to do after removing the ladle and the shovel; i.e., take off the linen vestments and *leave them there*. This was done in the privacy of one of the לשכות, *chambers*, as were all the other changes of clothing.

Furthermore, in terms of the sequence of the day's service, the commandment to remove the ladle and shovel must be regarded as out of place. According to the order as it appears in the chapter, this removal (*v.* 23) would follow the sending of the he-goat to Azazel (*vs.* 21-22) and precede the sacrifice of *his ram and the ram of the people* (*v.* 24). If that were the true order, the *Kohen Gadol* would change into his linen vestments only once throughout the day, because the entire Yom Kippur service — requiring the linen vestments — would be bunched into a single time span as it is described in *Leviticus* 16. Before beginning that order of service, he would perform the regular service in his golden vestments, and after completing it he would once again don the golden vestments to complete the day's service.

If so, there would be a total of only three changes of vestments, requiring three immersions and six washings of hands and feet (see 3:3, 6). This, however, is impossible, since there is an oral tradition from Sinai [הַלְכְּתָא גְמִירִי] that there are a total of *five* changes of vestments, necessitating five immersions and ten washings. Clearly, therefore, he had to change into his linen vestments *twice* — not once — during the day.

Accordingly, the Sages teach that the task of removing the ladle and shovel is *not* done in the order in which it appears (see below for an explanation of why the Torah inserts the verse out of sequence). Instead, after the dispatch of the goat to *Azazel* (*vs.* 21-22), the *Kohen Gadol* changed back to his golden vestments and proceeded to the 'outer service' of the two rams (*v.* 4). Later in the day, he would change back to the linen garments to remove the ladle and shovel, and then change back into his golden vestments, the fifth and last change of the day (*Yoma* 32a, 71a; *Sifra; Rashi; Ramban* to *Lev.* 16:24).

[The exact points at which these last two changes are made are discussed in mishnah 3 and the chart below.]

◈§ Vestment Changes and Services — A Summary[1]

To provide a better understanding of the Yom Kippur service, we offer a brief summary of the עֲבוֹדוֹת חוּץ, *outer services*, performed in golden vestments, and עֲבוֹדוֹת פְּנִים, *inner services*, performed in linen vestments.

---

1. [There is a controversy regarding the sacrifice of the *mussafim*. For simplicity's sake, we omit them from this summary.]

1. In the morning the *Kohen Gadol* immersed himself for the first time, dressed in his golden vestments, and the usual daily services — i.e., the daily burned offering (*Yoma* 1:8-3:5).

2. Then he took off the golden vestments, immersed himself for the second time, donned the linen vestments, performed the service outlined in *Leviticus* 16:3-22 (*Yoma* 3:6-7:3) — i.e., a slaughtering of the *Kohen Gadol's* ox, bringing the ladle and the shovel into the Holy of Holies, slaughtering of the he-goat, sprinkling the bloods of the ox and the he-goat in the Holy of Holies and the Holy, and sending the he-goat to *Azazel*.

3. The *Kohen Gadol* took off the white vestments, immersed himself for the third time, donned the golden vestments for the second time, and sacrificed the two rams (and other sacrifices, according to most opinions, as detailed in mishnah 3).

4. He undressed again, immersed himself for the fourth time, donned the white vestments for the second time, entered the Holy of Holies for the second and last time and removed the ladle and shovel.

5. He took off the linen vestments for the last time, immersed himself for the fifth time, donned the golden vestments for the third time and performed whatever remained of the services (burning the regular daily incense and lighting the *menorah* according to all opinions; see mishnah 3).

Now it can readily be seen that if the removal of the ladle and the shovel were moved up in this sequence to the place where it is listed in *Leviticus* 16 — after sending the he-goat to *Azazel* — the *Kohen Gadol* would be spared the task of changing into the linen vestments, since he would already be wearing them. Consequently, he would be able to complete the entire service following the second change into the golden vestments without needing to change again. Thus for three changes of vestments there would be only three immersions and six washings of hands.

◄§ Why is this service taken out of sequence?

Vilna Gaon (Kol Eliyahu, Chochmas Adam at the conclusion of the *sefer; Radal to VaYikra Rabbah* 21:7), suggests an ingenious answer to this question. First he poses another question. The 'ram for the people' mentioned in *Leviticus* 16:24 is identical with the ram burnt offering listed with the *mussafim* (*Numbers* 29:8. See comm. to mishnah 3). Why is this ram the only one of the *mussafim* to be listed in *Leviticus* 16 as well?

The answer is to be found in the *Vayikra Rabbah* where (according to *Vilna Gaon;* cf. *Zayis Ra'anan* to *Yalkut Lev.* 16:3) it is said that though every *Kohen Gadol* was allowed to enter the Holy of Holies only on Yom Kippur and on condition that he performed the prescribed service, Aaron himself was allowed to enter the Holy of Holies whenever he wished, provided he performed the service outlined in *Leviticus* 16 [see the justification for this in *Meshech Chochmah* to *Lev.* 16:3 s.v. זאת(ו)]).

This can be deduced from a careful reading of *Leviticus* 16. In verses 2-3 we read, *Speak to Aaron your brother! He shall not always come into the Holy ... With this* (the following order of sacrifices) *shall Aaron come into the Holy, with an ox ...* Nothing in the chapter suggests that Aaron's entry during the prescribed service is allowed only on Yom Kippur. Only at the very end of the chapter (*vs.* 29-34) is it said that this service is to be performed annually on Yom Kippur and that the *Kohen Gadol* who shall *succeed* Aaron may perform it *only* on that occasion.

This limitation applies only to the descendants of Aaron: they are required to perform the service on Yom Kippur and are forbidden to perform it at any other time. Aaron, however, could avail himself of the privilege of entering the Holy of Holies at any time, provided he performed the ritual described in ch. 16. Were he to do so, he would, indeed, follow the exact sequence of the chapter which calls for

[ד] **קָדַשׁ** יָדָיו וְרַגְלָיו, וּפָשַׁט, וְיָרַד וְטָבַל
וְעָלָה וְנִסְתַּפֵּג. הֵבִיאוּ לוֹ בִגְדֵי
לָבָן; וְלָבַשׁ, וְקִדֵּשׁ יָדָיו וְרַגְלָיו.

נִכְנַס לְהוֹצִיא אֶת־הַכַּף וְאֶת־הַמַּחְתָּה.

קִדֵּשׁ יָדָיו וְרַגְלָיו, וּפָשַׁט וְיָרַד וְטָבַל, עָלָה
וְנִסְתַּפֵּג.

הֵבִיאוּ לוֹ בִגְדֵי זָהָב; וְלָבַשׁ, וְקִדֵּשׁ יָדָיו
וְרַגְלָיו, וְנִכְנַס לְהַקְטִיר קְטֹרֶת שֶׁל בֵּין הָעַרְבַּיִם
וּלְהֵטִיב אֶת־הַנֵּרוֹת. וְקִדֵּשׁ יָדָיו וְרַגְלָיו וּפָשַׁט.

יד אברהם

only three changes of vestments and the removal of the ladle and scoop in sequence where it appears. The oral tradition calling for five changes and deferring the removal applies only to later *Kohanim Gedolim*; thus the chapter as written is precise — as it applies to Aaron.

The ram of the *mussafim* is mentioned in *Leviticus* because it — and only it — is a required part of Aaron's service even on days other than Yom Kippur.

קִדֵּשׁ יָדָיו רַגְלָיו, — *He* [the *Kohen Gadol*] *washed* [lit. *sanctified*] *his hands and feet,*

[After completing the service in the golden vestments.]

וּפָשַׁט, — *undressed* [lit. *took off*],

[He removed the golden vestments.]

וְיָרַד וְטָבַל וְעָלָה וְנִסְתַּפֵּג. — *went down* [into the mikveh] *and immersed himself, and came up and dried himself.*

הֵבִיאוּ לוֹ בִגְדֵי לָבָן; וְלָבַשׁ וְקִדֵּשׁ יָדָיו וְרַגְלָיו. — *They brought him white* [linen] *vestments; he dressed, and washed his hands and feet.*

[See above 3:6.]

נִכְנַס לְהוֹצִיא אֶת־הַכַּף וְאֶת־הַמַּחְתָּה. — *He entered* [the Holy of Holies] *to remove the ladle and the shovel.*

[Earlier in the day, the *Kohen Gadol* had brought a ladle of incense and a shovel of burning coals from the outer altar to the Holy of Holies where he had placed the shovel between the Ark poles or upon the *Shessiyah* stone, and heaped the incense upon the coal in the shovel. He had left the shovel and ladle

in the Holy of Holies while he went on with the ritual of the day. Now he returned to retrieve these utensils. The reason this service was performed at this point in the sequence is discussed at length in the preface to this mishnah.

קִדֵּשׁ יָדָיו וְרַגְלָיו, וּפָשַׁט — *He washed* [lit. *sanctified*] *his hands and feet, undressed,*

[He removed the white linen vestments.]

וְיָרַד וְטָבַל, עָלָה וְנִסְתַּפֵּג. — *went down, immersed* [himself], *came up* [from the mikveh], *and dried himself.*

[This was his fifth and final immersion.]

הֵבִיאוּ לוֹ בִגְדֵי זָהָב; וְלָבַשׁ, וְקִדֵּשׁ יָדָיו וְרַגְלָיו, — *They brought him golden vestments; he dressed, washed* [lit. *sanctified*] *his hands and feet,*

וְנִכְנַס לְהַקְטִיר קְטֹרֶת שֶׁל בֵּין הָעַרְבַּיִם — *and entered* [the Holy] *to burn the afternoon incense*

According to *Rashi* and *Tosafos* (7:3) and those following their opinion, the

4. He washed his hands and feet, undressed, went down [into the mikveh] and immersed [himself], and came up and dried himself. They brought him white [linen] vestments; he dressed, and washed his hands and feet.

He entered [the Holy of Holies] to take out the ladle and the shovel.

He washed his hands and feet, undressed, went down, immersed, came up, and dried himself.

They brought him golden vestments; he dressed, washed his hands and feet, and entered [the Holy] to burn the afternoon incense and light the lamps.

Then he washed his hands and feet and undressed.

mishnah here omits the bringing of the daily afternoon offering, which was brought after the fifth immersion and preceded the daily afternoon incense. It is omitted here because it was mentioned in mishnah 3 *(Tos.* 71a s.v. נכנס; *Tosafos Yom Tov).*

According to *Rambam* and *Ramban,* who hold that the daily afternoon sacrifice was offered after the third immersion (see above) there is no omission here *(ibid.).*

ולהטיב את־הנרות. — *and light the lamps.*

The rendering of ולהטיב here as *to light* follows *Rav.*

Elsewhere, however, (e.g. above 1:2 see comm. there; *Exodus* 30:7) this word means *to prepare* [lit. to better] i.e., to remove the ashes, old oil, and

wicks, and replace them with fresh oil and wicks. That translation does not apply here because there was no preparation of lamps in the afternoon; it had already been done in the morning *(Tos. Yom Tov).*

According to *Rambam (T'midin U'Mussafin* 3:10, 12) the lamps were cleaned and relit in the morning, and consequently had to be cleaned again in the afternoon before being lit again. Thus we can translate להטיב here, as elsewhere, *to prepare (ibid.).*[1]

קדֵש יָדָיו וְרַגְלָיו וּפָשַׁט. — *Then he washed* [lit. *sanctified*] *his hands and feet and undressed.*

[For the tenth and last time. Even though he was not going to perform any service, he had to wash his hands and

1. [However, *Rambam (ibid.)* holds that להטיב should always be rendered *to light.*] See *Kessef Mishneh* to *Avodas Yom HaKippurim* 2:2.

Tosafos (71a s.v. ולהטיב) and *Ravad (Avodas Yom HaKippurim* 2:2) hold with *Rashi* (and other authorities) that the lamps were lit only once every day — in the afternoon. Consequently the lamps were cleaned only once every day — in the morning. Still *Ravad* renders להטיב here *to prepare* as always. This does not refer to the six lamps that had already been prepared in the morning, but to the נר מַעֲרָבִי, *western lamp* (the second lamp; from the east, i.e., the first lamp to the west of another) which burned miraculously, all night and all day and was not cleaned in the morning so as not to interfere with the miracle of its constant flame (see *Shabbos* 22b with *Rashi* s.v. ובה היה מסיים: *Tamid* 3:9 with *Rav* and *comm.* above 1:2). Thus this *western lamp* was not cleaned until the afternoon, before being relit during the service of lighting the lamps. Though the mishnah mentions נרות, *lamps* (plural), it means only the cleaning of the western lamp in the afternoon, after it had burned twenty-four hours straight (this miracle stopped after the days of Shimon HaTzaddik; see above citations).]

הֵבִיאוּ לוֹ בִגְדֵי עַצְמוֹ וְלָבֵשׁ. וּמְלַוִּין אוֹתוֹ עַד
בֵּיתוֹ, וְיוֹם טוֹב הָיָה עוֹשֶׂה לְאוֹהֲבָיו בְּשָׁעָה
שֶׁיָּצָא בְשָׁלוֹם מִן־הַקֹּדֶשׁ.

[ה] **כֹּהֵן** גָּדוֹל מְשַׁמֵּשׁ בִּשְׁמוֹנָה כֵלִים
וְהֶהֶדְיוֹט בְּאַרְבָּעָה: בְּכֻתֹּנֶת
וּמִכְנָסִים וּמִצְנֶפֶת וְאַבְנֵט. מוֹסִיף עָלָיו כֹּהֵן
גָּדוֹל: חֹשֶׁן וְאֵפוֹד וּמְעִיל וְצִיץ.

יד אברהם

feet. This mishnah concurs with the first tanna of mishnah 2:6, who holds that the first of each pair of washings was required before removing vestments (*Gem.* 32a). According to R' Meir (*ibid.*) that the first washing was done while the *Kohen Gadol* was undressed, both washings in each pair were connected to the donning of the vestments. According to him, two washings were required for the first donning of the golden vestments (*ibid*). and none was required now.]

הֵבִיאוּ לוֹ בִגְדֵי עַצְמוֹ וְלָבֵשׁ. — *They brought him his personal clothing and he dressed.*

וּמְלַוִּין אוֹתוֹ עַד בֵּיתוֹ, וְיוֹם טוֹב הָיָה עוֹשֶׂה

לְאוֹהֲבָיו — *Then they* [all the people (*Meiri*)] *accompanied him to his house, and he made a feast* [lit. *holiday*] *for his friends*

Some say he made the feast at night and others say the feast was held the next day so that he could have time to prepare it (*Meiri; R' Yonason*).

בְּשָׁעָה שֶׁיָּצָא בְשָׁלוֹם מִן־הַקֹּדֶשׁ. — *for having left the Temple safely* [lit. *at the time he came out of the Holy in peace*].

The Torah warns that *He shall not come at all times to the Holy so that he will not die ... With this* [i.e. the service] *shall he come into the Holy ...* Thus if he performed any part of the service improperly, the *Kohen Gadol* was liable to lose his life.

5.

כֹּהֵן גָּדוֹל מְשַׁמֵּשׁ בִּשְׁמוֹנָה כֵלִים — *The Kohen Gadol serves in eight vestments*

[On all occasions except for those parts of the Yom Kippur service which require white linen vestments, the *Kohen Gadol* wears the eight garments that are enumerated later in the mishnah.]

וְהֶהֶדְיוֹט בְּאַרְבָּעָה: — *and the common Kohen in four:*

[These four vestments are the following:]

בְּכֻתֹּנֶת — *in a tunic,*

[The tunics of the *Kohanim* were made of linen woven in a checkered pat-

tern (*Exodus* 28:39-40). They had tight-fitting sleeves and reached almost to the heel. The tunics of the common *Kohen* and the *Kohen Gadol* were identical (*Rambam, Klei HaMikdash* 8:16-17; *Ramban* to *Exodus* 39:27). Ibn Ezra (*Exodus* 28:37) holds that only the *Kohen Gadol's* tunic was checkered (see *Mishneh LaMelech* to *Klei HaMikdash* 8:16).

וּמִכְנָסִים — *pants,*

[These pants were the same for the common *Kohen* and the *Kohen Gadol* (*Exodus* 28:42 with *Rashi; Rambam* op. cit. 28:18). They were of linen and ex-

7
5

They brought him his personal clothing and he dressed. Then they accompanied him to his house, and he made a feast for his friends for having left the Temple safely.

5. The *Kohen Gadol* serves in eight vestments and the common *Kohen* in four: in a tunic, pants, a hat, and a belt. In addition to these, the *Kohen Gadol* [wore]: a breastplate, an *ephod*, a cloak, and a [golden] plate.

tended from the waist to the knees (*ibid.*).]

וּמִצְנֶפֶת — *a hat*,

[This, too, was of linen (*Exodus* 28:39).]

The Torah refers to the hats of ordinary *Kohanim* as מִגְבָּעוֹת (*Exodus* 28:40) and to the *Kohen Gadol's* hat as מִצְנֶפֶת (28:39). However, *Rashi* (ibid. 28:4) comments that the two are identical.

The usage of language in the Mishnah differs from that of the Torah [לְשׁוֹן חֲכָמִים לְחוּד]. Where the Torah has different names for the two types of hats, the Mishnah calls them both מִצְנֶפֶת (*Tosafos* 25a s.v. נוטל; *Tos. Yom Tov*).

Tosafos (*Succah* 5a s.v. ואל) holds that the *Kohen Gadol's* hat was narrow and covered less of his head to enable him to wear the צִיץ, headband [see below, s.v. וְצִיץ], and *tefillin*. The common *Kohen's* hat covered more of his head since he needed to wear only the *tefillin*.

Ravad (*Klei HaMikdosh* 8:2) holds that the *Kohen Gadol's* hat was a long piece of cloth wound around his head like a turban. The common *Kohen* wore a narrow hat that was pointed at the top.

Rambam (loc. cit. 8:2, 19) and *Ramban* (*Exodus* 28:31) hold that both these hats were pieces of cloth sixteen cubits long, which were wound turban-fashion around the head, again and again (כְּרֶךְ עַל גַּבֵּי כְּרֶךְ). The ordinary

Kohen's turban, however, was wound in such a way that it resembled a peaked hat, whereas the *Kohen Gadol's* was wound so that it was wide and flat (see *R' Y. C. Blumenthal, Bigdei Kehunah*, pp. 38-9).

וְאַבְנֵט. — *and a belt*.

The belt worn by the *Kohen Gadol* on Yom Kippur (with his linen vestments) was linen as spelled out clearly in *Leviticus* (26:4). The belt he wore with his golden vestments was a mixture of linen; תְּכֵלֶת, blue wool; אַרְגָּמָן, purple wool; and תּוֹלַעַת שָׁנִי, red wool (*Exodus* 39:29; see *Rambam, Klei HaMikdosh* 8:13). But there is a difference of opinion about the common *Kohen's* belt. Some hold that it was made of the same mixture of materials as the belt the *Kohen Gadol* wore with his golden vestments, while some hold that the common *Kohen's* belt was of pure linen like the rest of his vestments (*Gem.* 6a). *Rambam* (*Klei HaMikdosh* 8:1) accepts the first opinion.

The belt was three fingers wide and thirty-two cubits long and he wound it around his waist (*Rambam*, ibid 8:19; see *Mishneh LaMelech* loc. cit. 8:1, 2, 19).

מוֹסִיף עָלָיו כֹּהֵן גָּדוֹל: — *In addition to these* [lit. *this*], *the Kohen Gadol* [wore];

[The *Kohen Gadol* wore all the vestments of the common *Kohen* (with slight variations as noted), plus four additional vestments.]

חֹשֶׁן — *a breastplate*,

בְּאֵלּוּ נִשְׁאָלִין בְּאוּרִים וְתֻמִּים; וְאֵין נִשְׁאָלִין אֶלָּא לְמֶלֶךְ וְלַבֵּית דִּין וּלְמִי שֶׁהַצִּבּוּר צָרִיךְ בּוֹ.

יד אברהם

The breastplate was made of a mixture of linen, blue wool, purple wool, red wool and gold threads. It was folded over and the *Urim V'Tumim* (see below) was inserted in the fold. Twelve precious stones were attached to the front of the breastplate in four rows of three stones each. Each of these stones was inscribed with the name of one of the tribes in the order of their birth (*Rambam, Klei HaMikdash* 9:7; *Rashi; Targum Yonasan* to *Exodus* 28:17-20).

Targum Yerushalmi (loc. cit.) and *Rabbeinu Tam* (*Da'as Zekeinim* to *Exodus* 28:10) hold that Leah's children were engraved first, followed by Bilhah's, by Zilpah's, and finally by Rachel's. *Targum Yonasan* (*Numbers* 2:3-25) says the names were engraved on the stones in the order of their encampment in the Wilderness. See also *Bamidbar Rabbah* 2:7 with *Rashash*.

As related below, the letters etched on the stones lit up and spelled out a message whenever the *Urim V'Tumim* was consulted. The *Gemara* (73b) notes that the letters צ, *tzadi*, and ט, *tess* (*Yerushalmi* adds ח, *chess*, and ק, *kuf*), do not appear in the names of the tribes. The *Gemara* explains that in addition to the names of the tribes, the stones were engraved with the names of the Patriarchs אַבְרָהָם יִצְחָק יַעֲקֹב, *Abraham; Isaac, Jacob*, and the phrase שִׁבְטֵי יְשֻׁרוּן, *tribes of Yeshurun* (another name for *Yisrael;* cf. *Deut.* 33:5), thus accounting for all twenty-two letters of the *Aleph Beis*.

Rambam (*Klei HaMikdash* 9:7) specifies that the names of the Patriarchs appeared before Reuben and שִׁבְטֵי יְשֻׁרוּן, after Benjamin. Some commentators (*R' Bachya; Chizkuni* and others) hold that these words were added in the following manner: Each stone had six letters on it; after each name of a tribe, letters were added from the additional five words as needed to complete the total of six letters on each stone. This is

diagramed below.

ראובנא	שמעווב	לוירהם
יהודהי	יששכרצ	זבולוח
דוקיעק	נפתליב	גדשבטי
אשרישר	יוספון	בנימין

וְאֵפוֹד — *an ephod*,

This, too, was made of gold, linen, and blue, purple, and red wools.

Rashi (*Exodus* 28:6) suggests that this was an apron-like garment that covered the *Kohen Gadol's* back from below his elbows to his heels, and was wide enough to cover the width of his back. The same description emerges from *Rambam* (*Klei HaMikdash* 9:9).

At its upper edge was a belt of the same material as the *ephod* itself and woven with it (not sewn on). The belt was long enough for both of its ends to meet in the front and to be tied (ibid.).

Two strips of cloth of the same material were sewn onto the two upper corners of the *ephod*. These כְּתֵפוֹת, *shoulder straps*, came up the *Kohen Gadol's* back, and hung down slightly over his shoulders, on to his chest. At the upper end of each shoulder strap, a precious stone (שֹׁהַם, *shoham*) was attached. The חֹשֶׁן, *breastplate*, hung from two golden chains attached to the shoulder straps. The bottom of the breastplate was also attached to the shoulder straps at the point where they were sewn to the *ephod* (*Rashi*, ibid.).

[For the sequence of the names of the twelve tribes as they are inscribed on the אַבְנֵי שֹׁהַם, *shoham stones*, see *Sotah* 36; *Yerushalmi Sotah* 7:4; *Rambam Klei*

7
5

[Wearing] these [eight vestments] they are consulted for [the decision of] the *Urim V'Tumim*. They are not consulted except for a king, the Court, or for someone whom the public needs.

YAD AVRAHAM

HaMikdash 9:9; *Or HaChaim*; *Da'as Zekeinim* and *Perush R' Avraham ben HaRambam* to *Exodus* 28:10.]

Rashbam (*Exodus* 28:7) modifies the above description in two ways: A) The *ephod* was wide enough to wrap around the *Kohen Gadol's* sides and come together in front so it covered him front and back; B) the כְּתֵפוֹת were not mere shoulder straps, but a piece of cloth which covered his entire back from above the waist of the *ephod*. At his neck, the cloth branched off into two shoulder pieces which terminated with the *shoham* stones as described before.

וּמְעִיל — *a cloak,*

This garment was made entirely of blue wool (*Exodus* 28:31). It was a four-cornered garment without sleeves (*Rambam, Klei HaMikdash* 9:3) and had a hole in the middle (like a *talis kattan*) through which the *Kohen Gadol* put his head (*Exodus* 28:32).

Rashi (*Exodus* 28:4) holds that the מְעִיל was a shirtlike garment (i.e., with sleeves, cf. *Ramban* ibid.). This seems to be *Ravad's* opinion as well (*Klei HaMikdash* 9:3; see *Kessef Mishneh* there).

On the cloak's hem were seventy-two round, pomegranate-like balls of blue, purple and red wool. There were also seventy-two golden bells hung on the hem of the cloak. After every wool pomegranate, a golden ball was hung, thirty-six in front and thirty-six in back (see *Ex.* 28:31-35 with *Rashi; Rambam,* ibid.).

Ramban (*Exodus* 28) holds that the woolen pomegranates were hollow and the bells were contained within them.

וְצִיץ — *and a [golden] plate.*

This was a gold plate worn on his forehead. It was two fingerbreadths wide and had the words קֹדֶשׁ לַה', *Holy*

to *HASHEM*, engraved on it. According to *Rashi*, it was suspended and held in place (at the hairline) by means of six threads of blue wool (*Exodus* 28:36-7). *Ramban* and *Ibn Ezra* hold there was only one thread.

[For the exact method used in engraving the Name, see *Rambam* and *Ravad, Klei HaMikdash* 1:1-2.]

The sequence of donning the vestments was as follows: pants, tunic, belt, cloak, *Ephod*, breastplate, hat, and plate (*Rambam, Klei HaMikdash* 10:1-2 based on *Exodus* 29:5-6 and *Yoma* 25a).

בָּאֵלּוּ נִשְׁאָלִין בְּאוּרִים וְתֻמִּים: — [*Wearing*] *these [eight vestments] they were asked for [the decision of] the Urim V'Tumim.*

[The Torah (*Numbers* 27:21) declares (in reference to Joshua): *And he shall stand before Elazar the Kohen and shall ask him for the decision of the Urim ...* When the *Urim* was available, many important questions were posed to the *Urim* and instruction given by it had to be followed. See Appendix.]

◆§ What were the *Urim V'Tumim*?

Rashi says that they were a slip of parchment upon which the שֵׁם הַמְפֹרָשׁ, *Ineffable Four-letter Name* was written. This was the power that lit up the letters on the breastplate. *Ramban* (to *Exodus* 28:30) adds that this Name was written by Moses in a manner entrusted by God to him alone; he wrote the letters with holiness and they were considered a heavenly handicraft. *Ritva* (73b) says that the *Urim V'Tumim* were not made by man, but were Divinely written and given to Moses.

Ibn Ezra (*loc. cit.*) suggests they were some type of golden or silver forms. *Ramban* (ibid.) rejects this vigorously.

Rambam is ambiguous. His words in *Klei HaMikdash* (10:10) and in *Beis*

יומא

[א] **יוֹם** הַכִּפּוּרִים אָסוּר בַּאֲכִילָה וּבִשְׁתִיָּה
וּבִרְחִיצָה וּבְסִיכָה וּבִנְעִילַת הַסַּנְדָּל
וּבְתַשְׁמִישׁ הַמִּטָּה.
וְהַמֶּלֶךְ וְהַכַּלָּה יִרְחֲצוּ אֶת־פְּנֵיהֶם, וְהַחַיָּה
תִּנְעֹל אֶת־הַסַּנְדָּל; דִּבְרֵי רַבִּי אֱלִיעֶזֶר. וַחֲכָמִים
אוֹסְרִין.

יד אברהם

HaBechirah (4:1 see Ravad there) sug-gest that he holds Urim V'Tumim to be synonymous with the breastplate (see Kessef Mishneh there). It is not clear how Rambam interprets the verse (Ex-odus 28:30), וְנָתַתָּ אֶל־חֹשֶׁן הַמִּשְׁפָּט אֶת־ הָאוּרִים וְאֶת־הַתֻּמִּים, and you shall insert into the breastplate of judgment the Urim and the Tumim.

Rambam's son, R' Avraham, says that the Urim V'Tumim refer to the precious stones affixed to the breast-plate (as set forth in the Torah). This would explain the plural forms of Urim and Tumim (Perush R' Avraham ben HaRambam p. 426). He would thus render Exodus 28:30: You shall affix onto the breastplate of judgment the Urim and the Tumim (cf. Abarbanel there). This may also be the opinion of Tosafos (Yoma 21b s.v. ואורים).

Why are they called Urim V'Tumim? Urim (from אוֹר, light) because they il-luminate [i.e., clarify (Rashi)] their words; Tumim (from תָּמִים, complete, i.e., fulfilled) because they fulfill their words (Gemara 73b). The Urim V'Tu-mim caused the breastplate to light up and give prophetic advice as described below.

The Kohen Gadol who consulted the Urim V'Tumim had to wear all the eight vestments (Rav; Rashi).

וְאֵין נִשְׁאָלִין, — They [i.e., the Urim V'Tumim] are not consulted [lit. asked]

The Kohanim Gedolim could not be asked to consult the Urim V'Tumim ex-cept for the following cases:

אֶלָּא לְמֶלֶךְ וּלְבֵית דִּין, — except for a king, the Court,

[I.e., the great Sanhedrin of seventy-one members; see Gem. 73b; Klei HaMikdash 10:12.]

וּלְמִי שֶׁהַצִּבּוּר צָרִיךְ בּוֹ. — or for someone whom the public needs.

The Gemara (73b) seems to suggest that this refers to the כֹּהֵן מְשׁוּחַ מִלְחָמָה, Kohen anointed to accompany the army to war (see Deut. 20:1-9; Rambam, Melachim 7:1-2; Klei HaMikdash 4:21).

However, Rambam (Klei HaMikdash 10:13) explains that this refers to the Kohen anointed for war or for someone else whose inquiry is needed for the public. The reference in Gemara to the 'anointed for war' is meant only as an example.

Chapter 8

1.

Having discussed the Temple's day service at length, the Mishnah turns to a dis-cussion of the laws of Yom Kippur that apply outside the Temple — at all times in all places.

יוֹם הַכִּפּוּרִים — [On] Yom Kippur [lit. the Day of Atonement]

[Although the Temple service first began in the morning, the laws of this chapter apply from the evening of the fast.]

1. **O**n Yom Kippur eating, drinking, washing [one's body], anointing [one's body with oil], wearing shoes, and cohabitation are prohibited.

The king and the bride may wash their faces, and a new mother may put on shoes; these are the words of R' Eliezer. But the Sages prohibit [this].

YAD AVRAHAM

אָסוּר בַּאֲכִילָה וּבִשְׁתִיָּה — *eating, drinking,*
[The prohibition against eating and drinking is discussed in mishnayos 2-6.]

וּבִרְחִיצָה וּבְסִיכָה וּבִנְעִילַת הַסַּנְדָּל וּבְתַשְׁמִישׁ הַמִּטָּה. — *washing [one's body], anointing [one's body with oil], wearing shoes, and cohabitation are prohibited.*
[The word סַנְדָּל is understood by *Mosaf HeAruch* (s.v. סנדל) to be a *sandal.* There is no question that a מִנְעָל, *shoe,* is also prohibited (see *Gem.* 78b). From *Rashi (Yevamos* 102b s.v. וארקתא) it seems that a סַנְדָּל is made of hard leather and a מִנְעָל of soft leather. This does not necessarily contradict *Mosaf HeAruch's* definition.] Only leather shoes are prohibited (*Gem.* 78; *Orach Chaim* 614:2; but see *Mishnah Berurah* there 5; *Bach* cited in *Beur Halachah).*

The *Gemara* (76a) derives the prohibition against these five pleasures (eating and drinking count as one) from the five times the Torah mentions the command to *afflict* oneself on Yom Kippur *(Lev.* 16:29,31; 23:27,29; *Numbers* 29:7). The *Gemara* (76-77) demonstrates from various Scriptural verses that abstinence from any of these five pleasures is called an עִנּוּי, *affliction.* However, only eating and drinking incur the punishment of כָּרֵת, *kares,* [*spiritual excision*] for willful transgression *(Gem.* 74a).

From the fact only eating and drinking incur *kares,* *Rambam (Comm.* to *Mishnah)* deduces that the other four prohibitions are Rabbinic injunctions for which the Rabbis find support [אַסְמַכְתָּא] in Scripture. This opinion is shared by many authorities (*R' Tam* in *Tosafos* 77a s.v. דתנן, *Ri* and *Riva* in *Rosh; Tur* 611; *Tos. Yesh.* 73b s.v. יום:

and *R'Saadiah Gaon* in *Sefer HaMitzvos, Asseh* 55).

Ran (here) and *Smag (Asseh* 32) hold that all the five prohibitions are of Torah origin, even though there is no punishment of *kareis* for the last four listed in the mishnah. Many authorities concur (see sources listed in *Sefer HaMitzvos,* of R' Saadiah, *Asseh* 55).

Concerning *Rambam's* opinion in *Hilchos Shevisas Assor* (1:5), see *Kessef Mishneh* and *Hagahos Ramach* there; cf. *R' Manoach* there.

וְהַמֶּלֶךְ וְהַכַּלָּה יִרְחֲצוּ אֶת־פְּנֵיהֶם, — *The king and the bride may wash their faces,*
The king may wash because a good outward appearance is vital to his office. A bride within thirty days of her wedding may wash that she should not appear unsightly to her new husband *(Rav; Gemara* 78b).

Chayei Adam (145:15) rules that in our days, since it is customary to spend the whole day in the synagogue praying, there is no basis for this dispensation (cf. *Mishnah Berurah* 613:26).

וְהַחַיָּה תִּנְעַל אֶת־הַסַּנְדָּל; — *and a new mother may put on shoes* [lit. *sandals*];
During the first thirty days after giving birth, the cold of the floor may harm her *(Rav; Gem.* 78b).

Similarly any sick person or one who has a wound (on his foot) and is severely affected by a cold floor may don shoes. The same applies where there is danger of being bitten by scorpions or the like *(Orach Chaim* 614:4 based on *Gem.* 78b).

דִּבְרֵי רַבִּי אֱלִיעֶזֶר, — *these are the words of R' Eliezer.*
The dispensation allowing the king,

[ב] הָאוֹכֵל כְּכוֹתֶבֶת הַגַּסָּה — כָּמוֹהָ וּכְגַרְעִינָתָה — וְהַשּׁוֹתֶה מְלֹא לֻגְמָיו חַיָּב. כָּל־הָאֳכָלִין מִצְטָרְפִין לְכַכּוֹתֶבֶת, וְכָל־הַמַּשְׁקִין מִצְטָרְפִין לִמְלֹא לֻגְמָיו, הָאוֹכֵל וְשׁוֹתֶה אֵין מִצְטָרְפִין.

יד אברהם

bride, and new mother to wash is R' Eliezer's opinion (Rav; Gem. 78b).

וַחֲכָמִים אוֹסְרִין. — But the Sages prohibit [this].

The halachah follows R' Eliezer (Rav; Rambam, Shevisas Assor 5:8 with Maggid Mishneh; see Orach Chaim 614:3-4).

[It is prohibited to wash, whether in cold or warm water. One may not even dip his finger into water (Orach Chaim 613:3). However, only pleasure-related washing is prohibited. Someone whose hands or feet (or any part of the body) are besmirched with mud, may wash it off (Gem. 77b; ibid.). In the same vein, one may wash his hands (partially) upon arising and after performing bodi-

ly functions (Orach Chaim 613:2; see Mishnah Berurah for more detail). R' Eliezer's dispensation for a bride and a king probably has its roots in this distinction between pleasure and non-pleasure-related washing.]

Anointing is prohibited whether one anoints the entire body or only a part of it (Gem. 77b; Orach Chaim 614:1). Even where the anointing is not pleasure-related, but rather to remove dirt, it is prohibited (Yerushalmi 8:5; Shulchan Aruch loc. cit.).

The ban cohabitation includes all the precautionary prohibitions one must observe with a menstruant as given in Yoreh De'ah (Orach Chaim 615:1 with Mishnah Berurah)

2.

Mishnayos 2-6 discuss the prohibition against eating and drinking. Mishnah 2 speaks of the quantity of food or drink which renders one liable to כָּרֵת, excision.

הָאוֹכֵל כְּכוֹתֶבֶת הַגַּסָּה—כָּמוֹהָ וּכְגַרְעִינָתָה— — One who eats the volume of a large date — like it and its pit —

I.e, he ate food equal in volume to a large date still containing its pit (Gem. 79a; see Tosafos s.v. כותבת). This is slightly less than the volume of an average egg (Orach Chaim 612:1; Rambam, Shevisas Assor 2:1; cf. Shinuyei Nuschaos in Rambam ed. Frankel; Rav).

The prohibition against eating on Yom Kippur differs from all the other prohibitions on foods, such as the prohibition against eating non-kosher food or leavened bread on Passover. There the volume that incurs punish-

ment if eaten is a כַּזַּיִת, equal to [the volume of] an olive, (less than a large date). This difference is attributed to a basic difference in the nature of these prohibitions. For all prohibitions other than Yom Kippur the injunction is primarily aimed against eating; the oral tradition from Sinai teaches that food the volume of an olive constitutes 'eating'. Yom Kippur, on the other hand, requires that one 'afflict' himself [עינוי]. The oral tradition teaches that eating less than a big date does not relieve the affliction of fasting (בְּצִיר מֵהָכִי לֹא מְיַיתַּב דַּעְתֵּיה; Rav; Gem. 80b). [In other words, even if one eats an amount equal to an olive on Yom Kip-

2. One who eats the volume of a large date — like it and its pit — or who drinks [the volume of] both his full cheeks is liable [for punishment]. All foods combine for the volume of a date, and all drinks combine for the volume of his cheekfuls, but food and drink do not combine.

YAD AVRAHAM

pur, he has not transgressed the obligation to afflict himself. Though he has 'eaten', he is still 'afflicted'. Only if he eats the volume of a date has he become 'a person who has not afflicted himself' and liable for *kares*.]

וְהַשּׁוֹתֶה מְלֹא לֻגְמָיו — *or who drinks [the volume of] both his full cheeks*

The *Gemara* (80a) modifies this. It is enough to drink as much as can fill *one* cheek, so that, to a person looking from the side it would seem that both cheeks are full. What the mishnah means is כִּמְלֹא לֻגְמָיו, **appearing** to fill his cheeks *(Rav)*.

If he would put it all in one side of his mouth, that side would bulge *(Rambam* in his *comm.)*.

This amount is not uniform. Each person measures according to his own cheek. For the average person this is less than a *revi'is* [quarter of a *log*], *the volume of 1½ eggs (Gem.* 80b; *Orach Chaim* 612:9).

The exact volume of the date and cheekful in modern terms is a matter of some dispute among contemporary authorities. The amounts given for a date vary from 1.1-1.7 ounces or 30-48

grams. A 'cheekful' of liquid is variously defined from 1.4-1.5 fluid ounces or 40-42 cubic centimeters.

חַיָּב. — *is liable [for punishment].*

[If he willfully ate or drank these minimum quantities or more, his punishment is *kares*. If witnesses were present and warned him beforehand, his punishment is מַלְקוּת, *(thirty-nine) lashes*. If he acted unknowingly (בְּשׁוֹגֵג) he must bring a חַטָּאת, *sin offering*.]

Although only these minimum amounts are punishable, the Torah forbade the eating and drinking of even smaller amounts *(Rav; Orach Chaim* 612:5).

כָּל-הָאֳכָלִין מִצְטָרְפִין לְכַכּוֹתֶבֶת, וְכָל-הַמַּשְׁקִין מִצְטָרְפִין לִמְלֹא לֻגְמָיו, — *All foods combine for the volume of a date, and all drinks combine for the volume of his cheekfuls,*

[E.g., if one ate a half-date of meat and another half-date of fruit he is liable for punishment.]

הָאוֹכֵל וְשׁוֹתֶה אֵין מִצְטָרְפִין. — *but food and drink do not combine.*

[If one ate a half-date of food and drank half his cheekful of liquid, he is not liable to punishment.]

3.

[As a general rule, one must bring a חַטָּאת, *sin offering*, when he transgresses a negative commandment which, if done willfully, would subject him to *kares*. He becomes liable for a sin offering if this negative commandment is transgressed during a period of הֶעְלֵם, *forgetfulness* or *ignorance*: not knowing or forgetting that the act was forbidden.

If one transgressed two different prohibitions, even during one period of forgetfulness, he is liable for separate sin offerings. Similarly, if one transgressed even the *same* prohibition twice, each time during a different period of forgetfulness, he is liable for two sin offerings. But, if he transgressed the same prohibition many times

[ג] **אָכַל** וְשָׁתָה בְּהֶעְלֵם אַחַת, אֵינוֹ חַיָּב אֶלָּא חַטָּאת אֶחָת.

אָכַל וְעָשָׂה מְלָאכָה, חַיָּב שְׁנֵי חַטָּאוֹת.

אָכַל אֳכָלִין שֶׁאֵינָן רְאוּיִין לַאֲכִילָה, וְשָׁתָה מַשְׁקִין שֶׁאֵינָן רְאוּיִין לִשְׁתִיָּה, וְשָׁתָה צִיר אוֹ מֻרְיָס, פָּטוּר.

[ד] **הַתִּינוֹקוֹת,** אֵין מְעַנִּין אוֹתָן בְּיוֹם הַכִּפּוּרִים, אֲבָל מְחַנְּכִין אוֹתָם לִפְנֵי שָׁנָה וְלִפְנֵי שְׁנָתַיִם, בִּשְׁבִיל שֶׁיִּהְיוּ רְגִילִין בַּמִּצְוֹת.

יד אברהם

during a single period of forgetfulness — for example, he forgot that it was Yom Kippur, and ate repeatedly before he was reminded — he need not bring a separate sin offering for *each* 'date' that he ate, but must bring only one sin offering. Now the mishnah clarifies what the law would be if the transgressions during a single period were not of the same nature — i.e., he ate and drank; he ate and did work.]

אָכַל וְשָׁתָה בְּהֶעְלֵם אַחַת, — *If one ate and drank in a single period of forgetfulness* [lit. *concealment*],

[Either he did not know or he forgot that it was Yom Kippur, or he did not know or forgot that eating and drinking are forbidden.]

אֵינוֹ חַיָּב אֶלָּא חַטָּאת אֶחָת. — *he is liable for only one sin offering.*

Because the prohibitions against eating and drinking derive from a single Torah prohibition — that one must afflict himself on Yom Kippur — both transgressions are regarded as one. Therefore, the superficially different acts of eating and drinking are viewed as repeated transgressions of the same prohibition — of afflicting oneself (*Rav; Rashi*).

אָכַל וְעָשָׂה מְלָאכָה, חַיָּב שְׁנֵי חַטָּאוֹת. — *If one ate and did work* [on Yom Kippur], *he is liable for two sin offerings.*

He has violated two separate prohibitions: the one against eating (*Lev.* 23:29), and that against working (*ibid* 23:30) (*Rav; Rashi*).

אָכַל אֳכָלִין שֶׁאֵינָן רְאוּיִין לַאֲכִילָה, — *If one ate foods that are not fit for consumption,*

Such as bitter herbs (*Ramban, Hilchos Shevissas Assor* 2:5); or spoiled meat (*Meiri*).

וְשָׁתָה מַשְׁקִין שֶׁאֵינָן רְאוּיִין לִשְׁתִיָּה, וְשָׁתָה צִיר אוֹ מֻרְיָס, — *or drank liquids unfit for drinking,* [for example] *he drank brine or salted fish fats,*

Brine [צִיר] is the watery liquid that oozes from salted fish while מֻרְיָס is its fatty liquid (*Tiferes Yisrael; Avodah Zarah* 9b; *Aruch* s.v. אמן).

The *Gemara* 81b explains that the second וְשָׁתָה, usually translated *'and'* he drank, should be understood in this instance as we have translated: the mishnah is listing two examples of the sort of unfit liquids discussed in this clause.

From the fact that the examples given are so salty that they are totally undrinkable, the *Gemara* deduces that our mishnah follows the opinion of R' Yehudah HaNassi, who holds that vinegar, though not a beverage, is not in

3. If one ate and drank in a single period of forgetfulness, he is liable for only one sin offering.

If one ate and did work [on Yom Kippur], he is liable for two sin offerings.

If one ate foods that are not fit for consumption, or drank liquids unfit for drinking, [for example] he drank brine or salted fish fats, he is not liable [for a sin offering].

4. We do not afflict the children on Yom Kippur, but we train them prior to the [previous] year or prior to two years, so that they should be accustomed to commandments.

YAD AVRAHAM

the category of 'undrinkable liquids' (*Hon Ashir*).

However, the *Gemara* (ibid) decides that pure undiluted vinegar is also in this category of an 'unfit' liquid. See *Rambam, Shevisas Assor* 2:5; *Orach Chaim* 612:9).

פָּטוּר. — *he is not liable [for a sin offering]*.

Nevertheless, one may not drink these liquids (*Rambam, Shevisas Assor* 2:5).

The mishnah picks these examples because these liquids were used as a sauce for dipping bread. Nevertheless, since they were not drunk by themselves, one who drinks them on Yom Kippur is not liable (*Tif. Yis.*).

4.

הַתִּינוֹקוֹת, אֵין מְעַנִּין אוֹתָן בְּיוֹם הַכִּפּוּרִים, — *We do not afflict the children on Yom Kippur,*

[Until they attain their majority, which is the beginning of the fourteenth year for a male, and the beginning of the thirteenth year for a female, they have the halachic status of *children*. Their majority is also conditional upon their exhibiting the prescribed physical symptoms — i.e., two pubic hairs. Regarding the requirement to fast on Yom Kippur, however, the presence of such hairs is not germane since people must fast as soon as they reach the *age* of majority. Once they have attained *age* of majority, they must fast even if no pubic hairs are present.]

We are not obligated to withhold food from children so that they will be

forced to fast (*Rav; Rashi*).

From *Rambam's* words in *Shevisas Assor* (2:10) it seems that we are not allowed to let them to fast (*Ran*).

אֲבָל מְחַנְּכִין אוֹתָם — *but we train them*

To fast for a few hours (*Rav; Rashi* based on R' Huna and R' Chisda in *Gem.* 82a).

Rambam (comm.) says we do not feed children being trained to fast until hunger discomforts them. However in *Shevisas Assor* 2:10 he says, 'If he was accustomed to eat at two hours into the day we feed him at three. According to the stamina of the child we have him fast additional hours.' This is based on the *Gemara*. *Orach Chaim* (616:2) accepts this latter ruling.

לִפְנֵי שָׁנָה — *prior to the [previous] year* [lit. *before a year*]

The year following a male's twelfth

[ה] **עֲבֵרָה** שֶׁהֵרִיחָה מַאֲכִילִין אוֹתָהּ עַד
שֶׁתָּשִׁיב נַפְשָׁהּ. חוֹלֶה —
מַאֲכִילִין אוֹתוֹ עַל־פִּי בְקִיאִין, וְאִם אֵין שָׁם
בְּקִיאִין, מַאֲכִילִין אוֹתוֹ עַל־פִּי עַצְמוֹ עַד
שֶׁיֹּאמַר: ,,דַּי.''

יד אברהם

birthday or a female's eleventh birthday is the year preceding majority. The training period for children begins before this period. The mishnah does not specify how long this period of training, is but R' Huna and R' Nachman (in the *Gemara*) concur that it is two years. Thus the training period starts from the tenth birthday for males and the ninth for females, who attain their majority one year earlier. (Based on *Rashi* to the *Mishnah* and *Hagahos HaGra*[1]).

[There are many other interpretations of this mishnah, but an exposition of these would be too complicated and confusing. See *Rif* with *Ran*, *Meiri*, *Rambam* (*Shevisas Assor* 2:10) with commentaries.]

The expression *prior to a year* suggests that somehow the year before majority has a status different from the training period of younger children. This is because children are trained to complete the entire fast in the year before their majority. This was known so well that the mishnah did not have to mention it explicitly (*Meiri*; cf. *Hagahos HaGra*).

וְלִפְנֵי שְׁנָתַיִם, — *or prior to two years*,
The gradual training period begins more than two years before majority; prior to the the eleventh birthday for a male and the tenth year for a female. Here, too, the duration of the training period is two years, starting from the ninth birthday for a male, and from the eighth for a female.

Noting that the mishnah says *prior to* **one** year or *prior to* **two** years, the *Gemara* asks: 'If we train [them] before two years, then we surely [train them] before one year. R' Chisda explains that

the mishnah specifies different periods depending on the health of the children involved. The term *before a year* refers to a weak child, who is not expected to complete his fast until the year immediately preceding his majority. The phrase *before two years* refers to a healthy child who completes his fast in the *two* years preceding his majority. In all cases, therefore, there is a training period of two years; when it begins depends on when a child is strong enough to fast an entire day.

בִּשְׁבִיל שֶׁיִּהְיוּ רְגִילִין בְּמִצְוֹת. — *so that they should be accustomed to commandments.*

[The above interpretation is R' Huna's and R' Chisda's in the *Gemara*. R' Yochanan disagrees and holds that we never train children to complete the fast, before their majority; prior to *bar* or *bas mitzvah* we never require a child to fast more than a few hours. The only training given is to fast those few hours. According to this, לִפְנֵי שָׁנָה is construed (or emended) to mean שָׁנָה לִפְנֵי, *during the year before* [their majority], when they are required to fast by Torah law. Thus, after a boy's twelfth birthday and a girl's eleventh, we train them to fast several hours. Similarly, the phrase לִפְנֵי שְׁנָתַיִם, is interpreted as שְׁנָתַיִם לִפְנֵי, *two years before* their majority. The mishnah's distinction between one- and two-year periods is resolved as before. A one year training period for a weak child, and the two-year period for a healthy child.

Rambam makes no differentiation between males and females, or between strong and weak children. He rules that the training period starts after the ninth birthday and extends to the eleventh birthday, and that after their eleventh birthdays all children must complete their fast. He is followed in this by R' Yosef Karo in *Shulchan Aruch* (616:2).

1. [I have not been able to reconcile *Rav's* interpretation with any of the opinions in the *Gemara* (see *Shoshanim L'David*). Perhaps there is a typographical error in his words and they should be emended to read like *Rashi's*.]

5. **I**f a pregnant woman smelled [food or drink and requested it] they feed her until she recovers. A sick person — they feed him according to [the advice of] experts, but if no experts are present, they feed him relying on his own opinion until he says, 'Enough.'

YAD AVRAHAM

Rama, citing the opinion of other authorities who rule like R' Yochanan that children should never complete the fast, concludes that these opinions can be relied upon. *Mishnah Berurah (Beur Halachah)* cites the opinion of some authorities defending the Eastern European custom that children never fast, on the grounds that in our times a general weakness has descended upon the world. Therefore, unless proven otherwise, every child is considered weak and exempt from fasting (see also *Bach*).

Whenever children are trained to fast (partially), we train them not to wash or anoint themselves the whole day *(ibid.).*

But even little children should be trained not to wear shoes on Yom Kippur *(Orach Chaim* 616:1).

5.

עֻבְּרָה שֶׁהֵרִיחָה מַאֲכִילִין אוֹתָה — *If a pregnant woman smelled [food or drink and requested it] they feed her*

Because it may be dangerous to her or her unborn child if she is denied this food *(Rav; Rashi).* [See *R' Manoach* to *Shevisas Assor* 2:9.]

The *Gemara* (82b) adds that first they should whisper to her that it is Yom Kippur today. If this does not calm her craving, they should feed her. If she turned pale and did not regain her color after being told that it is Yom Kippur, they feed her even if she protests that she does not need to eat. Otherwise, she is fed only if she says she must eat *(Rama, Orach Chaim* 617:2; *Mishnah Berura*, there).

עַד שֶׁתָּשִׁיב נַפְשָׁה. — *until she recovers* [lit. *until she restores her soul*].

[Because even the unlikely possibility of פִּקוּחַ נֶפֶשׁ, *saving of life*, supersedes the observance of Yom Kippur (and all other *mitzvos except for the three cardinal sins* — idolatry, certain forbidden cohabitation and murder).]

חוֹלֶה—מַאֲכִילִין אוֹתוֹ עַל-פִּי בְקִיאִין, — *A sick person—they feed him according to [the advice of] experts,*

— Expert physicians *(Rav; Rambam).*

[The *Gemara* (83a) explains that more than one expert is needed only if the patient and one doctor declare that he can complete the fast. In such an instance they feed him only if at least two doctors say he must eat. But if only one doctor says that the patient must eat, we abide by the majority — consisting of the patient and a single doctor, or of two doctors if the patient has no opinion. The patient himself is also considered an expert for this purpose; if he insists he must eat, he overrides the unanimous negative opinion of doctors.] [See *Darkei Moshe* to *Tur Orach Chaim* 618 and *Shulchan Aruch* 328:10 that even lay people are considered 'experts' in the absence of a doctor (see *Magen Avraham, Mishnah Berurah*, there).]

וְאִם אֵין שָׁם בְּקִיאִין, מַאֲכִילִין אוֹתוֹ עַל-פִּי עַצְמוֹ — *but if no experts are present, they feed him relying on* [lit. *according to*] *his own opinion*

The *Gemara* (83a) comments that whenever a sick person requests food we accept his opinion even over that of expert doctors. It is as if it the mishnah said, 'If the patient himself says he needs food, there are no experts [i.e., their opinion is not considered]' *(Rav).*

[Perhaps this segment of the mishnah can be interpreted: Even if there are no experts who testify that he must eat — i.e., the experts present see no need to break his fast — they feed him upon his own request.]

[ו] **מִי** שֶׁאֲחָזוֹ בֻלְמוֹס, מַאֲכִילִין אוֹתוֹ אֲפִילוּ
דְּבָרִים טְמֵאִים עַד שֶׁיֵּאוֹרוּ עֵינָיו.
מִי שֶׁנְּשָׁכוֹ כֶּלֶב שׁוֹטֶה, אֵין מַאֲכִילִין אוֹתוֹ
מֵחֲצַר כָּבֵד שֶׁלּוֹ. וְרַבִּי מַתְיָא בֶּן־חָרָשׁ מַתִּיר.
וְעוֹד אָמַר רַבִּי מַתְיָא בֶּן־חָרָשׁ: הַחוֹשֵׁשׁ
בִּגְרוֹנוֹ מַטִּילִין לוֹ סַם בְּתוֹךְ פִּיו בַּשַּׁבָּת, מִפְּנֵי
שֶׁהוּא סְפֵק נְפָשׁוֹת וְכָל סְפֵק נְפָשׁוֹת דּוֹחֶה
אֶת־הַשַּׁבָּת.

יד אברהם

An alternative interpretation: The *halachah* (based on *Gem.* 83a) is that even if the patient himself believes there is in no danger in fasting, we still feed him if an expert doctor says he must eat. Thus, 'A sick person — they feed him according to experts (regardless of the patient's opinion), but if no experts are present,' we base the decision on the patient's own request.

עַד שֶׁיֹּאמַר: "דַּי." — *until he says, 'Enough.'*

6.

מִי שֶׁאֲחָזוֹ בֻלְמוֹס — *If one* [lit. *one who*[*was seized with bulmos,*

Bulmos is a dangerous illness that results from extreme hunger. It causes paleness *(Tif. Yis.)* and weakens the patient's vision *(Rashi; Orach Chaim 618:9).*

Rambam (Comm. ed. *Kafih)* gives a similar description, adding that this sickness is accompanied by fainting. A similar description is given in *Mosaf HeAruch.*

מַאֲכִילִין אוֹתוֹ אֲפִילוּ דְּבָרִים טְמֵאִים — *they feed him even forbidden foods*

[E.g., pig's meat or נְבֵילָה, *meat from an animal that died through means other than kosher slaughter.*]

Every dangerously ill person is allowed to eat forbidden food if kosher food is not available. However, someone seized with *bulmos* differs in that he must be fed immediately. Thus, if the first food available is *trefah* [non-kosher] food, even though kosher food can be obtained easily, the patient is fed the *trefah* food in order not to lose precious time. Needless to say, kosher food should be obtained if possible without delay, even in a case of *bulmos.*

For other illnesses where immediacy is not as imperative, we wait for kosher food for as long as the patient's condition permits (from *Rambam, Shevisas Assor* 2:9; *Meiri; Rama* 618:19).

There is another distinction between *bulmos* and other illnesses. When an ill person is fed on Yom Kippur, care must be taken, whenever possible, to give him less than the minimum amount (described in mishnah 2) at one time *(Orach Chaim* 618:7-8). But this limitation does not apply to someone seized with *bulmos* (loc. cit. 9 with *Mishnah Berurah*).

עַד שֶׁיֵּאוֹרוּ עֵינָיו — *until his vision is restored* [lit. *until his eyes are lit*].

The translation is based on *Rashi, Rambam (Comm.),* and *Meiri. Rav* seems to interpret עֵינָיו as *his appearance,* but even this can be reconciled with their interpretation. See *Meiri.*

מִי שֶׁנְּשָׁכוֹ כֶּלֶב שׁוֹטֶה, — *If one was bitten by a mad dog,*

[The bite of a rabid animal poses a danger to the victim's life.]

אֵין מַאֲכִילִין אוֹתוֹ מֵחֲצַר הַכָּבֵד שֶׁלּוֹ. — *they*

6. If one was seized with *bulmos*, they feed him even forbidden foods until his vision is restored.

If one was bitten by a mad dog, they may not feed him its liver lobe. But R' Masya ben Charash permits [it].

R' Masya ben Charash also said: If one has an ailment in his throat they [may] drop medicine into his mouth on the Sabbath, because there may be a danger to life and every possible danger to life supersedes the Sabbath.

YAD AVRAHAM

may not feed him its liver lobe.

Even though ancient doctors considered this to be a cure, their opinion is not significant enough to permit transgression of the prohibition against eating non-kosher food, since it is not a proven remedy (*Rav; Rashi*).

[This segment of the mishnah applies on weekdays as well as Yom Kippur.]

וְרַבִּי מַתְיָא בֶּן־חָרָשׁ מַתִּיר. — *But R' Masya ben Charash permits [it].*

He holds this cure to be a tested method to justify eating non-kosher food (*Rav; Rashi*).

Rambam understands this difference of opinion to have broader implications than merely the question of what constitutes a remedy for the bite of a rabid animal. The disagreement concerns any method of healing not proved by logic and trial, but broadly believed to be efficacious, בְּדֶרֶךְ סְגוּלָה, *in a supernatural way.* The first tanna holds that such a cure is not deemed reliable enough to permit transgression of the Torah's prohibitions. R' Masya ben Charash permits such medical practices even where a transgression of Torah law is involved. *Rambam* concludes that the halachah does not follow R' Masya ben Charash. Curiously, though, he makes no mention of this in *Shevisas Assor* (see *Magen Avraham; Daas Torah* to 328:2; *Teshuvos Maharsham* 3:225).

וְעוֹד אָמַר רַבִּי מַתְיָא בֶּן־חָרָשׁ: הַחוֹשֵׁשׁ בְּגְרוֹנוֹ — *R' Masya ben Cheresh also*

said: If one has an ailment in his throat

Rav, Rambam, and many other texts has בְּפִיו, *in his mouth,* instead of בְּגְרוֹנוֹ (see *Shinuyei Nuschaos; Tos. Yom Tov; Mishneh Lechem*).

Rav describes this as an ailment which starts with the rotting of the gums. From there, it can spread to the palate and the throat.

Tiferes Yisrael adds that the ailment can spread to the stomach. A similar description is given by *Rambam*.

מַטִילִין לוֹ סָם בְּתוֹךְ פִּיו בַּשַׁבָּת, — *they [may] drop medicine [lit. herbs] into his mouth on the Sabbath,*

R' Masya's purpose is not simply to permit the administering of previously prepared medicine since that is permitted for sick people, even when there is no danger to life (see *Orach Chaim* 328:1 with *Mishnah Berurah*). But, if the medication had not been prepared before the Sabbath, and its preparation involves performing מְלָאכָה, *forbidden labor,* such as grinding, the preparation is permitted only where necessary to save a life (cf. *Tif. Yis.*).

[For the same reason, the mishnah does not say, 'They put medicine in his mouth on Yom Kippur,' for this would be misleading. From the term Yom Kippur, we might infer that the mishnah discusses only the 'food' aspect of the medicine; since it is unfit for normal eating, it is not forbidden on Yom Kippur by Torah law and is therefore permitted in a case of illness (see *Orach Chaim* 612:6; cf. *Yoreh Deah* 155:3). But we would not know that one may even violate Torah

[ז] **מִי** שֶׁנָּפְלָה עָלָיו מַפֹּלֶת סָפֵק הוּא שָׁם
סָפֵק אֵינוֹ שָׁם, סָפֵק חַי סָפֵק מֵת, סָפֵק
עוֹבֵד כּוֹכָבִים סָפֵק יִשְׂרָאֵל; מְפַקְּחִין עָלָיו אֶת־
הַגַּל. מְצָאוּהוּ חַי, מְפַקְּחִין עָלָיו, וְאִם מֵת
יַנִּיחוּהוּ.

[ח] **חַטָאת** וְאָשָׁם וַדַּאי מְכַפְּרִין. מִיתָה
וְיוֹם הַכִּפּוּרִים מְכַפְּרִין עִם
הַתְּשׁוּבָה.

יד אברהם

law for the sake of the patient. The insertion of the words *on the Sabbath* tells us that even though it is necessary to desecrate the Sabbath by performing prohibited work, it is still permitted to give the patient his medicine.]

מִפְּנֵי שֶׁהוּא סָפֵק נְפָשׁוֹת וְכָל סָפֵק נְפָשׁוֹת דּוֹחֶה אֶת־הַשַׁבָּת. — *because there may be a danger to life* [lit. *it is a question of lives*] *and every possible danger to life supersedes the Sabbath.*

[The saving of a life similarly takes precedence over any other prohibition of the Torah, such as eating on Yom Kippur. The only categories of prohibitions not set aside — even when there is definite danger to life — are idolatry, certain forbidden cohabitation, and murder.]

The *Gemara* (84b) comments that the mishnah reiterates 'Every possible danger to life supersedes the Sabbath' to give additional stress to this rule. Not only where the danger is immediate

does it supersede the Sabbath, but even where doctors determine that a patient must take a certain medicine for eight days in order to weather the crisis, and if he waits until the end of the Sabbath to start the medicine he will only need to desecrate one Sabbath — he is not to wait, but should start taking the medicine immediately, even though it would require the desecration of two Sabbaths (*Rav*).

Rambam (*Shabbos* 2:3) says in summary: And it is forbidden to tarry in desecration of the Sabbath on behalf of one who is dangerously ill, for it has been said (*Lev.* 18:5): [*You shall heed My laws*] *which a person shall perform and shall 'live by' them,* but not that he should die because of them. You learn from this that the laws of the Torah are not [intended for] vengeance upon the world, but rather [for] compassion, kindness, and peace upon the world.

7.

מִי שֶׁנָּפְלָה עָלָיו מַפֹּלֶת סָפֵק הוּא שָׁם סָפֵק אֵינוֹ שָׁם, — *If a building collapsed on someone* [on the Sabbath; lit. *someone upon whom there fell a collapse and*] *it is uncertain whether he is there or not,*

[I.e., it appears to the onlookers — but it is not definite — that a person was buried under the debris. Clearing away debris on the Sabbath constitutes

מְלָאכָה, *forbidden labor.*]

סָפֵק חַי סָפֵק מֵת, — [or] *it is uncertain whether he is alive or dead,*

[Even if a person is definitely trapped under the debris, it is doubtful whether our desecration of the Sabbath would be of any use, for the person may no longer be alive.]

7. **I**f a building collapsed on someone [on the Sabbath and] it is uncertain whether he is there or not, [or] it is uncertain whether he is alive or dead, [or] it is uncertain whether he is a heathen or a Jew, they [must] clear the heap [of debris] for him. If they found him alive, they [must] clear [the rest of the debris] for him, but if he is dead they leave him [there].

8. **A** sin offering and a guilt offering for a definite sin provide atonement. Death or Yom Kippur provide atonement together with repentance.

YAD AVRAHAM

סְפֵק עוֹבֵד כּוֹכָבִים סְפֵק יִשְׂרָאֵל, — [or] it is uncertain whether he is a heathen or a Jew,

[The same law pertains if there is a combination of these uncertainties; thus the situation raises many doubts as to whether desecration of the Sabbath is warranted.]

מְפַקְּחִין עָלָיו אֶת־הַגַּל. — they [must] clear [lit. open] the heap [of debris] for him.

[Even if there is only a slight chance that a life may be saved, it is required that all necessary labor must be done.]

מְצָאוּהוּ חַי, — If they found him alive,

If while digging they uncovered the person's head and saw that he was still breathing (Gemara 85a).

מְפַקְּחִין עָלָיו, — they [must] clear [the rest of the debris] for him,

Even if it is apparent that he can only live a short while, the preservation of life for a brief interval is sufficient reason to desecrate the Sabbath (Rav; Gem. 85a).

וְאִם מֵת יַנִּיחוּהוּ. — but if he is dead they leave him [there].

If they discern no sign of breathing, they may assume the person is dead (Rav; Gem. 85a; Rambam, Shabbos 2:19; Orach Chaim 329:4).

Even if they find no heartbeat, they may not stop clearing the debris. Only the cessation of breathing constitutes proof of death (ibid.).

Even though some tannaim allow saving the body of a dead person from fire, even when transgression of a Rabbinic prohibition is involved (e.g., carrying the dead man from one house to another where there is no Eruv Chatzeros), here this is not permitted. The Rabbis permitted the removal of a body from a burning building because the nature of the potential tragedy is such that people may lose themselves to their emotions and put out the fire, a prohibition whose source is in the Torah (Rav; Gem. 85a).

8.

Having concluded all of the laws concerning the Yom Kippur service, and its other observances, the mishnah turns briefly to the inner meaning of Yom Kippur — atonement. The mishnah lists the different types and degrees of atonement.

חַטָּאת — A sin offering

The sacrifice called חַטָּאת, sin offering is discussed length in Leviticus 4. It is brought to atone for the inadvertent

transgression [שׁוֹגֵג] of a negative commandment which, if violated בְּמֵזִיד, willfully, would be punished with kares [spiritual excision]. A second type of sin

תְּשׁוּבָה מְכַפֶּרֶת עַל־עֲבֵרוֹת קַלּוֹת: עַל־עֲשֵׂה וְעַל־לֹא תַעֲשֶׂה. וְעַל־הַחֲמוּרוֹת הִיא תוֹלָה עַד

יד אברהם

offering is described in *Leviticus* 5:1-13. It is brought for swearing falsely, under certain specified conditions; for entering the Temple Court while *tamei* [*contaminated*]; or for eating sacrifices while *tamei*. This sin offering is called a קָרְבָּן עוֹלֶה וְיוֹרֵד, *a graduated offering*, [lit. *a sacrifice which goes up and down*], because the monetary value of the sacrifice — whether a sheep, a pair of doves, or a meal offering — depends on the transgressor's resources.

וְאָשָׁם וַדַּאי — *and a guilt offering for a definite sin*

For three types of sins, one brings an אָשָׁם [*asham*], *guilt offering*, provided he has definitely transgressed them. In very general terms, the offerings are:

1) אֲשַׁם גְּזֵלוֹת, *guilt offering* [*asham*] *for robbery*. One had custody of someone else's movable property and, upon being asked to return it, swore that he no longer had it (*Lev.* 5:20-26 with *Rashi);*

2) אֲשַׁם מְעִילוֹת, *asham for misusing sacred property*. One inadvertently used הֶקְדֵּשׁ, *sacred property*, for his own ends (*Lev.* 5:17-19 with *Rashi*).

3) אֲשַׁם שִׁפְחָה חֲרוּפָה, *asham for cohabiting with a betrothed non-Jewish slave woman*. The cohabitation done with a non-Jewish female slave who had been immersed and was betrothed to a Jew (*Lev.* 19:20-22 with *Rashi*).

מְכַפְּרִין — *provide atonement.*

In the case of sins for which they are to be brought, complete atonement is provided by a חַטָּאת, *sin offering*, or a אָשָׁם וַדַּאי, *guilt offering for a definite sin.*

Rav adds that repentance is a prerequisite for atonement, but that the mishnah felt no need to mention it (as it does further) in the case of the atonement provided by Yom Kippur and death, since one would bring an offering only if he sincerely repented his sin.

Furthermore, סְמִיכָה, *the leaning*, of both hands on the head of the sacrifice was always accompanied by וִדּוּי, *confession* (see *Rambam, Maaseh HaKorbanos* 3:14; comm. above; *Tif. Yis.*).

There is yet another variety of *asham*, but our mishnah does *not* refer to it: אָשָׁם תָּלוּי, *a pending guilt offering*. It is brought in the event one fears that he *may* have committed a sin for which — had he committed it — he would be required to bring a חַטָּאת, *sin offering*. The function of a pending guilt offering is to prevent the possible sinner from being punished until he learns that he *did* commit the sin, in which case he must bring a sin offering. Obviously, therefore, this sort of sacrifice does not provide atonement if a sin has not been committed and therefore cannot be included with the sin and guilt offerings that do atone for sins. Moreover, on who is liable to bring a pending guilt offering is freed from his obligation if Yom Kippur intervenes. But Yom Kippur does not free someone who is required to bring one of the other offerings (*Gem.* 85b).

מִיתָה וְיוֹם הַכִּפּוּרִים מְכַפְּרִין עִם־הַתְּשׁוּבָה. — *Death or Yom Kippur provide for atonement* [*for sin*] *together with repentance.*

[As related below, in the normal course of events some sins are atoned for only by Yom Kippur. If, however, the sinner died before Yom Kippur, his death effects the same atonement as Yom Kippur. Moreover, as explained below, even Yom Kippur is not sufficient to atone for sins whose punishment is *kares*; or for the sin of הַשֵּׁם, *desecration of the Name*. But מִיתָה, *death*, always atones. The mishnah teaches us that death or יִסּוּרִים, *suffering*, like Yom Kippur, atone only in conjunction with repentance.

A person who repents on his deathbed will have his sins forgiven, for

8
8

[However] repentance [alone] atones for lesser transgressions: for positive commandments and negative commandments. But for the graver [sins], it

death combines with repentance to complete the atonement. The same is true of Yom Kippur: one achieves atonement if he repents on Yom Kippur.]

In *Rambam's* definition, repentance means that a person confesses his sins (i.e., he says· to God, חָטָאתִי, *I have sinned'*), is remorseful, and resolves never to return to that sin.

As mentioned earlier in discussing sin and guilt offerings, the mishnah omitted mention of repentance because it can be taken for granted that a sinner would not voluntarily bring a sacrifice unless he were repenting *(Rav; Rashi).*

Meiri comments that in essence it is repentance which effects forgiveness. However, the more grievous the sin, the more intense the required repentance. By their very nature, Yom Kippur, suffering, and the time of death evoke repentance of greater intensity than under normal circumstances.

Maharal (Drush for *Shabbos Teshuvah)* explains that on Yom Kippur a person elevates himself beyond the body and its needs, and dissociates himself from sin which comes to him through the body, for the soul is inherently pure. Then, the soul has the opportunity to unite with its Maker, and thus rid itself of sin, for with God there is no sin.

Michtav MeEliyahu (part 1, p. 266) suggests that on Yom Kippur the power of the יֵצֶר הָרָע, *Evil Inclination,* is muted. (The *Gemara* 20a notes that the word הַשָּׂטָן, *Satan,* has the numerical value 364, one less than the sum of days in a solar year. For on 364 days, Satan has permission to entice people to sin, but not on Yom Kippur.) On Yom Kippur, therefore, one's yearning for spiritual elevation reasserts itself after having lain dormant as a result of sin's deadening effect upon the soul [טמטום הלב]. This rejuvenation of purpose entitles the person to special consideration and forgiveness.

תְּשׁוּבָה מְכַפֶּרֶת עַל־עֲבֵירוֹת קַלּוֹת: עַל־עֲשֵׂה וְעַל־לֹא תַעֲשֶׂה. — *[However] repentance [alone] atones for lesser transgressions: for positive commandments and negative commandments.*

[Though the mishnah had said that repentance atones together with Yom Kippur, this is true only for the more grievous sins. Repentance alone suffices for קלות, *lesser transgressions,* whether they are transgressions of positive or negative commandments.]

With only two exceptions all positive commandments are regarded as *lesser,* because the Torah prescribes no specific punishment for their violation. The exceptions are the positive commandments of circumcision and of bringing the Pesach sacrifice. Willful non-performance of these commandments is punishable by *kares.* Those two, therefore, are among the graver sins for which simple repentance does not suffice.

As a general rule, negative commandments are among the grave transgressions because the willful sinner is liable for lashes or a more severe penalty such as *kares,* or death. However, negative transgressions for which there are no lashes are considered *lesser* transgressions for which repentance will suffice. Among these are transgressions that do not involve an act. For example, it is forbidden to ignore a lost article, but if one chooses to ignore it and not take steps to return it to its owner, he is not liable to corporal punishment.

The example cited by *Rav* and *Tiferes Yisrael* is לָאו הַנִּיתָּק לַעֲשֵׂה, *a negative commandment that is linked to a positive commandment.* It involves a negative commandment which, if violated, can be rectified by performing a positive commandment specifically prescribed by the Torah for that purpose. For example, the Torah forbids one to leave sacrificial meat uneaten beyond the time during which it must be eaten. If, however, it is not eaten during the prescribed time, it becomes נוֹתָר, *leftover,* and the Torah commands that

שֶׁיָּבוֹא יוֹם הַכִּפּוּרִים וִיכַפֵּר.

[ט] **הָאוֹמֵר:** ,,אֶחֱטָא וְאָשׁוּב; אֶחֱטָא וְאָשׁוּב,'' אֵין מַסְפִּיקִין בְּיָדוֹ לַעֲשׂוֹת תְּשׁוּבָה. ,,אֶחֱטָא וְיוֹם הַכִּפּוּרִים מְכַפֵּר,'' אֵין יוֹם הַכִּפּוּרִים מְכַפֵּר.

יד אברהם

it be burned. Thus, the violation of the negative commandment is *linked* to the positive one that rectifies it.

In summary, it can be said that all sins, positive and negative, are considered קַלּוֹת, *lesser*, if no punishment is prescribed for them in the Torah (see *Gevuras Ari*). For such transgressions, תְּשׁוּבָה, *repentance*, alone is sufficient.

וְעַל־הַחֲמוּרוֹת — *But for the graver [sins]*,

[Those positive or negative commandments for which the Torah enjoins punishments. As discussed above, these are the bulk of the negative commandments and circumcision and the Pesach sacrifice among the positive commandments.]

הוּא תוֹלֶה עַד שֶׁיָּבוֹא יוֹם הַכִּפּוּרִים וִיכַפֵּר. — *it* [repentance] *suspends* [punishment] *until Yom Kippur comes and provides atonement.*

[In consideration of the repentance, punishment is not meted out for his sin, but God does not forgive the sin until Yom Kippur comes. It stands to reason that if the sin was repeated before Yom Kippur and the person failed to repent, the sinner will be punished for *both* transgressions.]

The sins for which repentance and Yom Kippur suffice to bring atonement are only those for which the punishment is מַלְקוּת, [thirty-nine] *lashes.* However, the *Gemara* (86a) adds two categories of חֲמוּרוֹת, *graver sins*, that require more to achieve atonement:

A) In the case of transgressions punishable by *kares* or the death penalty, the combination of repentance

and Yom Kippur effect only תְּלִיָּה, *suspension*, of judgment and punishment. Completion of the atonement [מֵירוּק] is effected by יִסּוּרִים, *suffering.*

B) The most serious category of sin is one that causes חִלּוּל הַשֵּׁם, *desecration of the Name.* This includes any sin that causes others to emulate the sinner. For such sins, even the combination of repentance, Yom Kippur and suffering effect only suspension of punishment. Complete atonement comes only with the death of the sinner.

In summary, the levels of atonement are:

אוֹנֵס, *involuntary sins* — Where the person has in no way been negligent, there is no need for atonement (*Rambam*).

שׁוֹגֵג, *inadvertent sins* — A) Where no sacrifice need be brought, repentance is sufficient for atonement. B) Where a sacrifice must be brought, the sacrifice atones together with repentance. Yom Kippur does not eliminate the requirement of a sacrifice (*Gem.* 85b), except for a pending guilt offerng [אָשָׁם תָּלוּי].

מֵזִיד, *deliberate sins* — Here the *Gemara* list four categories of atonement (כַּפָּרָה אַרְבָּעָה חִילוּקֵי):

A) קַלּוֹת, *lesser sins*, for which the Torah prescribes no punishment. Repentance itself is sufficient atonement.

B) חֲמוּרוֹת, *grave sins*, punishable by מַלְקוּת, *lashes*. Here repentance with Yom Kippur (or death) atone.

C) חֲמוּרוֹת, *sins graver than the*

suspends [punishment] until Yom Kippur comes and provides atonement.

9. He who says, 'I will sin and repent; I will sin and repent', they do not assist him in achieving repentance.

[If he says] "I will sin and Yom Kippur will provide atonement", Yom Kippur does not provide atonement.

YAD AVRAHAM

above, which the Torah penalizes with *kares* or execution. Repentance with Yom Kippur and suffering (or death) together atone.

D) חִילוּל הַשֵּׁם, *desecration of the Divine Name* — i.e., causing others to sin. Here repentance, Yom Kippur, suffering, and death are all needed to achieve atonement.

All these distinctions are relevant only when there is no Temple. When the Holy Temple stood the service of the two he-goats was performed (together with repentance), and atoned for all sins (*Rav; Tos. Yom Tov; Shevuos* 1:6; *Rambam, Teshuvah* 1:2).

Meiri adds that the *Talmud's* enumeration of categories is intended to show the gravity of sin and thereby to influence people scrupulously to avoid sin and, if they *have* sinned, to go to extreme degrees of repentance [לְהַפְלִיג בִּתְשׁוּבָה] according to the gravity of the sin. The heavenly portals are never closed to 'total' repentance.

[Accordingly, ordinary repentance will in specific instances have to be complemented with Yom Kippur, suffering, or death in order to effect full atonement. But where a person's repentance is so intense as to equal the self-denial of Yom Kippur or the suffering of pain and death, it may no longer require them but may effect atonement by itself.]

As mentioned before the two he-goats atoned for all sins. *Sifre to Deut.* 32:2 likens the efficacy of Torah-study to that of the two he-goats: Just as the he-goats atone, so do the words of Torah (cf. *Menachos* 110a). The four categories thus relate only to people who do not apply themselves to Torah-study. It is also said in the name of R' Shalom Sharabi that prayer together with repentance can eliminate the need for the more grievous forms of atonement *(Belzer Rebbe).*

9.

הָאוֹמֵר: ,,אֶחֱטָא וְאָשׁוּב; אֶחֱטָא וְאָשׁוּב,", — *He who says, 'I will sin and repent; I will sin and repent',*

He sinned at least twice with intent to repent *(Rav from Gem. 77a).*

אֵין מַסְפִּיקִין בְּיָדוֹ לַעֲשׂוֹת תְּשׁוּבָה. — *they* [i.e., the Heavenly Court] *do not assist him in achieving repentance.*

These things [i.e., the case our mishnah and twenty-three others listed by *Rambam*] though they impede (מְעַכְּבִין) repentance do not make it impossible.

On the contrary if (despite the lack of Divine aid) a person repented, he is a בַּעַל תְּשׁוּבָה, *penitent*, and he has a share in the World to Come. The mishnah means that God will not help him repent *(Rambam, Comm. and Teshuvah* 4:1).

,,אֶחֱטָא וְיוֹם הַכִּפּוּרִים מְכַפֵּר,", אֵין יוֹם הַכִּפּוּרִים מְכַפֵּר. — *[If he says] 'I will sin and Yom Kippur will provide atonement,' Yom Kippur does not provide atonement.*

God will not assist him to repent on

עֲבֵרוֹת שֶׁבֵּין אָדָם לַמָּקוֹם, יוֹם הַכִּפּוּרִים מְכַפֵּר; עֲבֵרוֹת שֶׁבֵּין אָדָם לַחֲבֵרוֹ, אֵין יוֹם הַכִּפּוּרִים מְכַפֵּר, עַד שֶׁיְּרַצֶּה אֶת־חֲבֵרוֹ.

אֶת־זוֹ דָרַשׁ רַבִּי אֶלְעָזָר בֶּן־עֲזַרְיָה: ,,מִכֹּל חַטֹּאתֵיכֶם לִפְנֵי ה' תִּטְהָרוּ'' — עֲבֵרוֹת שֶׁבֵּין אָדָם לַמָּקוֹם, יוֹם הַכִּפּוּרִים מְכַפֵּר; עֲבֵרוֹת שֶׁבֵּין אָדָם לַחֲבֵרוֹ, אֵין יוֹם הַכִּפּוּרִים מְכַפֵּר, עַד שֶׁיְּרַצֶּה אֶת־חֲבֵרוֹ.

אָמַר רַבִּי עֲקִיבָא: אַשְׁרֵיכֶם יִשְׂרָאֵל! לִפְנֵי מִי אַתֶּם מִטַּהֲרִין? מִי מְטַהֵר אֶתְכֶם? אֲבִיכֶם שֶׁבַּשָּׁמַיִם! שֶׁנֶּאֱמַר: ,,וְזָרַקְתִּי עֲלֵיכֶם מַיִם טְהוֹרִים וּטְהַרְתֶּם''; וְאוֹמֵר: ,,מִקְוֵה יִשְׂרָאֵל ה' ''. מָה־מִקְוֶה מְטַהֵר אֶת־הַטְּמֵאִים, אַף הַקָּדוֹשׁ בָּרוּךְ הוּא מְטַהֵר אֶת־יִשְׂרָאֵל.

יד אברהם

Yom Kippur (Rambam, comm.; cf. Sefas Emes here).

עֲבֵרוֹת שֶׁבֵּין אָדָם לַמָּקוֹם, יוֹם הַכִּפּוּרִים מְכַפֵּר; — For sins between man and God [lit. the Place], Yom Kippur provides atonement;

[God is the Place of the world. The concept of God as the world's place indicates that He cannot be constrained by the limitations of space. Cf. Kuzari.]

עֲבֵרוֹת שֶׁבֵּין אָדָם לַחֲבֵרוֹ, אֵין יוֹם הַכִּפּוּרִים מְכַפֵּר, — but for sins between man and his fellow man [e.g. stealing, slandering etc.], Yom Kippur does not provide atonement,

[Even if he repents.]

עַד שֶׁיְּרַצֶּה אֶת־חֲבֵרוֹ. — until he appeases his fellow man.

Sins between a person and his fellow man ... are not forgiven until he gives his fellow man whatever he owes him, and appeases him. Even though he returned the money he owed, he must appease him and ask him to forgive

him. Even if he only angered his fellow man verbally... (Rambam, Teshuvah 2:9).

Even if one repaid whatever he owed and appeased his fellow man, he must still repent, for sins against people are double sins: First, toward the victim — this can be rectified by repaying and appeasing the agrieved party. Secondly, there is a sin toward God, Who commanded us to act equitably toward our fellow men. For this, repentance is necessary. This is evident from the mishnah which says: For the sins between man and his fellow man Yom Kippur does not provide atonement. Clearly then, for the aspect of sin that is between man and God, Yom Kippur is needed. This is also evident in Rambam (Hilchos Teshuvah 1:1) who says, 'Likewise he who hits his fellow man or damages his property, though he paid what he owed him, does not attain atonement until he confesses and repents from ever repeating an action such as this as it is said (Numbers 5:6):

8
9

For sins between man and God, Yom Kippur provides atonement; but for sins between man and his fellow man, Yom Kippur does not provide atonement, until he appeases his fellow man.

This did R' Elazar ben Azariah expound: '*From all of your sins before God shall you be cleansed* [*Lev.* 16:30] — for sins between man and God Yom Kippur provides atonement, but for sins between man and his fellow man, Yom Kippur does not provide atonement, until he appeases his fellow man.

R' Akiva said: 'Praiseworthy are you O Israel! Before Whom do you cleanse yourselves? Who cleanses you? Your Father in Heaven! As is said [*Ezekiel* 36:25]: '*And I will sprinkle pure water upon you and you shall be cleansed,*' and He also says [*Jeremiah* 17:13]: *The mikveh of Israel is HASHEM.* Just as a mikveh purifies the contaminated, so does the Holy One, Blessed is He, purify Israel.

YAD AVRAHAM

מִכָּל־חַטֹּאת הָאָדָם, *of all of the sins against men.*

אֶת־זוֹ דָּרַשׁ רַבִּי אֶלְעָזָר בֶּן־עֲזַרְיָה: ,,מִכֹּל חַטֹּאתֵיכֶם לִפְנֵי ה' תִּטְהָרוּ''—עֲבֵרוֹת שֶׁבֵּין אָדָם לַמָּקוֹם, יוֹם הַכִּפּוּרִים מְכַפֵּר; עֲבֵרוֹת שֶׁבֵּין אָדָם לַחֲבֵרוֹ, אֵין יוֹם הַכִּפּוּרִים מְכַפֵּר, עַד שֶׁיְּרַצֶּה אֶת־חֲבֵרוֹ. — *This did R' Elazar ben Azariah expound: From all of your sins before God* [i.e., between man and God] *shall you be cleansed* (*Lev.* 16:30) — [from this we derive] *for sins between man and God Yom Kippur provides atonement, but for sins between man and his fellow man, Yom Kippur does not atone, until he appeases his fellow man.*

[The cantillation [*trop*] under ה' is a *tipcha* which indicates a pause, grouping לִפְנֵי ה' together with and modifying חַטֹּאתֵיכֶם, *your sins.* Thus, the verse should be understood: *From all of your sins before God* shall you be cleansed on Yom Kippur — but from not your sins toward your fellowman.]

אָמַר רַבִּי עֲקִיבָא: אַשְׁרֵיכֶם יִשְׂרָאֵל! לִפְנֵי מִי אַתֶּם מִטַּהֲרִין? מִי מְטַהֵר אֶתְכֶם? אֲבִיכֶם שֶׁבַּשָּׁמַיִם! — *R' Akiva said: Praiseworthy are you O Israel! Before Whom do you cleanse yourselves? Who cleanses you? Your Father in Heaven!*

[Before Him you cleanse yourselves, and it is He Who reciprocates and cleanses you.]

The way to repentance is that the person himself should attempt to better his ways. This is meant by the words, *Before whom do you cleanse yourselves? Your Father in Heaven.* You purify yourselves before God. However sometimes temptation and circumstances are too strong for the person to withstand on his own. Therefore, it is necessary for God Himself to initiate the process of purification. Then, *Who cleanses you? Your Father in Heaven,* applies (*Tos. Yom Tov*).

שֶׁנֶּאֱמַר: ,,וְזָרַקְתִּי עֲלֵיכֶם מַיִם טְהוֹרִים וּטְהַרְתֶּם''; — *As is said (Ezekiel 36:25):*

'And I will sprinkle pure water upon you and you shall be cleansed;'

Sometimes God Himself initiates the process of cleansing *(Tos. Yom Tov).*

וְאוֹמֵר: ,,מִקְוֵה יִשְׂרָאֵל ה׳." — *and He* [God] *also says (Jeremiah* 17:13): *'The mikveh* [lit. *hope,* but rendered here exegetically *mikveh,* pool of water used to purify a contaminated person] *of Israel is HASHEM.'*

[We have followed those editions of the mishnah (see *Shinuyei Nuschaos)* and our editions of the *Gemara* which cite the phrase מִקְוֵה יִשְׂרָאֵל ה׳ from *Jeremiah* 17:13. Our printed editions, however, have the phrase מִקְוֵה יִשְׂרָאֵל (without the word ה׳) which is in *Jeremiah* 14:8 (see *Tos. Yom Tov).* Although we have generally followed the text as it appears in the Vilna edition containing *Tiferes Yisrael* we have deviated here because this is how this well-known mishnah is usually quoted.]

מַה־מִּקְוֶה מְטַהֵר אֶת־הַטְּמֵאִים, אַף הַקָּדוֹשׁ בָּרוּךְ הוּא מְטַהֵר אֶת־יִשְׂרָאֵל. — *Just as a mikveh purifies the contaminated, so does the Holy One, Blessed is He, purify Israel.*

Man is the main actor in the act of repentance or of purification, though he needs the helping hand of God to guide him along. When he purifies himself spiritually before his Father in Heaven, it is just like using a *mikveh.* Though the power of the *mikveh* to purify is God-given, the act of purification belongs to the person who on his own volition enters the *mikveh* to be purified *(Tosefos Yom Tov).*

Repentance and Yom Kippur alone are not sufficient where sin toward one's fellow man is concerned. The sin toward God is erased through the union of the pure soul with God just as the body attaches itself to the *mikveh* for purification. This union erases the sin which effected a barrier, between God and the soul. But sins toward one's fellow man also effect an estrangement, erect a barrier between these two human beings, and this is not eradicated through union of the soul with God *(Maharal, ibid.).*

APPENDIX I
Elaborations in 7:3

The *Gemara* (70a) says that our mishnah is not מְתַקַנְתָּא, *complete* (in stating R' Eliezer's and R' Akiva's opinions) R' Eliezer says nothing about the burning on the outer altar of the *emurim* [sacrificial parts] of the ox and he-goat whose blood had been sprinkled in the Holy and Holy of Holies (6:7); nor does he make any mention of the two *Mussaf* offerings brought on the outer altar, the ox and the he-goat (*Numbers* 29:8,11). To supply this missing information, the *Gemara* (according to *Rashi's* understanding) cites a *baraisa* that the sacrificial parts of the ox and the he-goat (of the inner service) were burned immediately following the service of the two rams discussed here. This is the right place for this service, because in *Leviticus* 16, the sacrifice of the rams (*v.* 24) is followed by the admonition: *And the fats of the sin sacrifice he shall burn upon the altar (v. 25).* The removal of the ladle and shovel, since it is not performed in the place it appears (*v.* 23; see mishnah 4), is deferred to the end of the service, after the burning of the *emurim.* The place for the service of the ox and the he-goat of the *mussafim* (an outer service) will be discussed below.

Neither R' Eliezer nor R' Akiva mentions the service of burning the *emurim* on the outer altar. The reason for this is that this service is never essential to the acceptance of a sacrifice; even if it were not done, the sacrifice would still be valid (*Tosafos* 70b s.v. ואחר).

[Perhaps another reason can be given. In *Leviticus* 16 the burning of the *emurim* is mentioned immediately after the sacrifice of the rams; thus the mishnah need not repeat the obvious. However, the mishnah *must* mention the sacrifice of the two rams, because the sequence of *Leviticus* 16, places the rams after the removal of the ladle and the shovel of the incense; but that is not the proper sequence. All of the services described previously in this tractate, though also mentioned in the Torah, nevertheless are mentioned because the mishnah supplies detail not found in the Torah. The burning of the *emurim*, by contrast, requires no elaboration.]

⋅⋅§ The Dispute between R' Eliezer and R' Akiva

R' Eliezer and R' Akiva disagree about the exact point in the sequence of the Yom Kippur service at which the *mussafim* in *Numbers* 29:7-11 are to be offered. R' Eliezer holds that, as a general rule, all sacrifices should be offered according to the order of their mention in the Torah. Accordingly, the sacrifices and services in *Leviticus* 16 should precede the *mussafim* mentioned in *Numbers* 29, just as *Leviticus* precedes *Numbers*. Thus the Yom Kippur service began with the daily morning sacrifice (nothing was permitted to be sacrificed before it) and the regular daily services (1:8-3:6) followed by the entire Yom Kippur service as set forth in *Leviticus* 16 (3:7-7:4). Then (after the removal of the ladle and the shovel and after the *Kohen Gadol's* final change into his golden vestments) came the *Mussafim* of *Numbers* 29:7-11 according to the sequence given there, first the ox, then the seven sheep, and finally the goat (the ram mentioned there had already been sacrificed as part of the service mandated by *Leviticus* 16).

Although R' Eliezer disagrees with R' Akiva about the place of the ox and the he-goat of the *mussafim*, as well as the seven sheep, he specifically mentions only the

sheep because there are other opinions among the tannaim that R' Eliezer wants to negate. One tanna holds (see *Gemara* 70b) that one of these seven sheep was sacrificed with the morning daily offering and the remaining six with the afternoon daily offering. Another *(ibid.)* holds that six sheep were sacrificed in the morning and the solitary remaining one in the afternoon. By mentioning when the sheep were sacrificed, R' Eliezer expressed his differences with R' Akiva and with the other tannaim *(Tosafos ibid.).*

◆§ When were the Mussafim sacrificed according to R' Eliezer?

Another item missing in R' Eliezer's words is the exact point at which the *mussafim* were sacrificed. All we can glean from his statement is that they were not offered following the daily morning sacrifice. On the surface, the text of the mishnah seems to suggest that they were sacrificed together with the rams of the *Kohen Gadol* and the public (i.e., after the third טְבִילָה, *immersion*). This is impossible, however since the *baraisa* cited in the *Gemara* says that they were sacrificed with the daily afternoon sacrifice, which — according to *Rashi* (and most authorities; see comm. s.v. עִם תָּמִיד שֶׁל בֵּין הָעַרְבַּיִם) — was offered after the fifth and final immersion. Thus, the *mussafim*, too, waited until after the removal of the ladle and shovel (which was done after the fourth immersion). However, this seems difficult to reconcile with the language of the mishnah.

[Since only the main points in R' Eliezer's argument with R' Akiva are mentioned (see above), perhaps it suffices to say that R' Eliezer holds that the *mussafim* were not to precede the service in *Leviticus* 16. Accordingly it can be deduced that the *mussafim* should be delayed until the whole service prescribed by *Leviticus* 16 is completed — after the removal of the ladle and the shovel, and hence after the fifth immersion. According to the opinion of *Rambam* and *Ramban* (discussed below) that the afternoon daily offering was brought after the third immersion, this passage presents no difficulties. Indeed, this passage could serve as a proof for *Rambam's* opinion.]

◆§ Tosafos's opinion

Tosafos (70b s.v. ואחר (1)) disagrees with *Rashi* on the point in the sequence where the *emurim* are burned. Instead of doing it immediately after offering the two rams (following the third immersion, as *Rashi* holds), *Tosafos* delays this service until after the fifth immersion, preceding the daily afternoon sacrifice. This opinion is shared by *Ba'al HaMaor* and *Rosh*. In their view, the text of the mishnah is read as follows: R' Akiva says: 'They were sacrificed with the daily morning offering and the burnt offering ox. But the he-goat which is done outside ... [This sentence is not completed. It is understood that the he-goat is sacrificed the next time the Kohen Gadol wears his golden vestments to offer sacrifices in the Courtyard — i.e., immediately after the third immersion — followed by the two rams.] 'They [the emurim] were offered with the daily afternoon offering.'

According to *Tosafos*, when the removal of the ladle and shovel has to be deferred from its place in the sequence (v. 23), it is moved as little as possible, and put immediately after the sacrifice of the rams (v. 24), but before the burning of the *emurim* (v. 25). The burning of the *emurim* is pushed off until after the fifth immersion before the daily afternoon sacrifices.

◆§ Rambam's opinion

Rambam (Avodas Yom HaKippurim 2:2; see *Lechem Mishneh* there and to 4:2) and *Ramban (Lev.* 16:23) disagree with all the authorities cited above. They hold

that the daily afternoon offering was brought after the third immersion. Although he admits that some sources *(Sifra)* hold with *Rashi* and the other authorities, *Ramban* nevertheless holds that the *Yerushalmi* and our mishnah (see s.v. "When were the *Mussafim* sacrificed") prove his opinion correct. Accordingly, the mishnah's statement that the he-goat that is 'done outside' is offered with the daily afternoon offering does not contradict the clear indication from the *Gemara* that this was done after the third immersion.

With the exception of the place of the daily sacrifice, *Rambam* and *Ramban* agree with *Rashi's* sequence of the day's service. *Rambam* and *Ramban* hold that the removal of the ladle and the shovel is postponed beyond the service described in *Leviticus* 16 until the entire service, including the daily offering, is concluded. The only parts of the daily service left, after the removal of the ladle and the shovel, are those that must be done in the Holy — burning the daily incense and lighting the *menorah*. It is more fitting for the *Kohen Gadol* to conclude the service in the Holy than to perform the final act of the day's service in the Holy of Holies *(Tos. Yom Tov)*.

✦§ The reason for the sequence of the sacrifices according to R' Akiva

Scripture says of the Pesach *mussafim (Numbers* 28:23): *Aside from the morning burnt offering of the daily offering* [*Tamid*], *you shall sacrifice these* [the *mussafim*]. R' Akiva interprets this as an indication that *mussafim* are to be sacrificed immediately after the morning daily offering. [Otherwise it would have sufficed to say *aside from the daily burnt offering,* as it says of all the *mussafim*. See there 28:10, 15, 31; and 29:6, 16, 19, etc.]

This rule is applicable to *all* the *mussafim*. Consequently, all the *mussafim* of the year, including those of Yom Kippur (the ox and the seven sheep), are sacrificed immediately after the daily morning offering. An exception is the *mussafim* ram that is offered after the third immersion: because it is also mentioned in *Leviticus* 16, it must follow the he-goat to *Azazel* in the sequence set forth there. The only other exception is the he-goat offered outside. Though it, too, is part of the *mussafim*, it must follow as closely as possible after the he-goat offered inside (i.e., the he-goat sin offering of *Leviticus* 16), because the Torah says (concerning the outside he-goat, *Num.* 29:11), *One he-goat, a sin offering, beside* חַטַאת הַכִּפֻּרִים, *the sin offering of atonement...* (i.e., the he-goat of *Lev.* 16:16 about which the Torah says *and he shall atone for the Holy...)* [Otherwise the phrase *aside from the sin offering of atonement...* is superfluous. The sin offering in *Numbers,* whose blood is sprinkled on the outer altar like that of all the sin offerings in Numbers 28, is surely not identical with the sin offering in *Leviticus* 16 which is sprinkled in the Holy and Holy of Holies. Cf. *Tos. Yom Tov.*] Thus the outside sin offering must be the first service after the third immersion, and it precedes even the two rams. It cannot be sacrificed earlier, because, since it is not an inside service, it must be sacrificed while the *Kohen Gadol* wears the golden vestments.

[See below for a chart listing the sequence of the services according to all the opinions mentioned here.]

✦§ The Sequence of the Kohen Gadol's Service on Yom Kippur

In order to clarify the sequence of the *Kohen Gadol's* service on Yom Kippur, we present an indexed list of the animals used in the service. Each sacrifice will be referred to in the chart by the letter ascribed to it.

§ תְּמִידִים — Daily Burnt Offering

[A] תָּמִיד שֶׁל שַׁחַר — Daily Morning Burnt Offering *(Numbers 28:1-7)*

[B] תָּמִיד שֶׁל בֵּין הָעַרְבָּיִם — Daily Afternoon Burnt Offering *(Numbers 28:8)*

§ מוּסָפִים — Mussafim

[C] פַּר — Ox burnt offering *(Numbers 29:8)*

[D] אַיִל — Ram burnt offering *(ibid.)*

[E] שִׁבְעָה כְּבָשִׂים — Seven lambs (burnt offerings) *(ibid.)*

[F] שָׂעִיר — He-goat sin offering [blood sprinkled on the outer altar] *(ibid.)*

§ עֲבוֹדַת הַיּוֹם — Special Yom Kippur Sacrifices

[G] פַּר שֶׁל כֹּהֵן גָּדוֹל — Kohen Gadol's Ox sin offering *(Leviticus 16:3, 14-19)*

[H] שָׂעִיר לה׳ — He-goat 'for Hashem' sin offering *(Leviticus 16:3, 15-19)*

[I] אַיִל שֶׁל כֹּהֵן גָּדוֹל — Kohen Gadol's Ram Burnt Offering *(16:3, 24)*

[J] אַיִל שֶׁל הָעָם — The People's Ram Burnt Offering *(16:5, 24)*. [According to our Mishnah this ram is the same ram labeled "D" above, which is mentioned in *Numbers 29:8*.]

[K] שָׂעִיר לַעֲזָאזֵל — He-goat sent to Azazel *(Leviticus 16:5, 20-22)*. This was not a קָרְבָּן, *sacrifice.*

§ The Chronological Sequence

(The numbers in parentheses indicate the relevant *Mishnayos* in *Yoma*. Shading indicates steps that are controversial.)

1. Removal of the ashes from the outer altar (1·8)[1]

2. **FIRST IMMERSION** [then donned golden vestments] (3:4)

3. Slaughter of the daily morning burnt offering [A] (3:4)

4. Receiving and throwing of its blood (3:4)[2]

5. Preparing 5 lamps of the Menorah (3:4)[3]

6. Offering the daily incense (3:5)

1. According to many authorities, this service was not performed by the *Kohen Gadol*. See *comm.* to 1:8.

2. The sequence given here is at variance with the well-known formula of Abba Shaul *(Gem.* 33a) which is recited in the daily prayers. The *Gemara* (ibid.) notes that the Mishnah (as indicated by 1:2 and 3:4) follows the view of the Rabbis who disagree with Abba Shaul.

3. *Tosafos* (14b s.v. אמר) and *Tosafos Yeshanim (loc. cit.)* hold that the *Kohen Gadol* prepared only the final two lamps. The other five lamps were prepared by a regular *Kohen*.

7. Preparing the remaining 2 lamps of the Menorah[4]

8. Burning of the limbs of the daily morning burnt offering on the outer altar (3:4)

9. The daily meal offering (3:4)

10. The *Chavitin* meal offering (3:4)

11. The wine libation (3:4)

12. According to R' Akiva most (see steps 31 and 33) of the *Mussafim* were offered here: The ox [C] and the seven lambs [E] — all burnt offerings — along with their meal offerings and wine libations. According to R' Eliezer, the entire *Mussafim* service took place later, see step 39 (7:3).

13. **SECOND IMMERSION** [then donned linen vestments] (3:6)

14 First confession on the *Kohen Gadol's* ox offering [G] (3:8)

15 Drawing lots to select the he-goats 'For Hashem' [H] and 'To Azazel' [K] (3:9, 4:1)

16 Second confession on the *Kohen Gadol's* ox sin offering [G] (4:2)

17. Slaughter of the *Kohen Gadol's* ox sin offering [G] (4:3)

18. Service of the special Yom Kippur incense: (a) scooping up of coal; (b) scooping up of incense into ladle; (c) burning of incense in the Holy of Holies. This was the *Kohen Gadol's* first entry into the Holy of Holies (4:3, 5:1-2)

19. Sprinkling the blood of the *Kohen Gadol's* ox [G] in the Holy of Holies. This was the *Kohen Gadol's* second entry into the Holy of Holies (5:3)

20. Slaughtering of the he-goat 'For Hashem' [H] (5:4)

21. Sprinkling the he-goat's blood in the Holy of Holies. This was the *Kohen Gadol's* third entry into the Holy of Holies (5:4)

22. Sprinkling the blood of the *Kohen Gadol's* ox [G] on the פָּרוֹכֶת, *curtain*, in the Holy (5:4)

23. Sprinkling of the he-goat's blood [H] on the פָּרוֹכֶת, *curtain*, in the Holy (5:4)

---

4. According to *Rambam's* view (*T'midin U'Mussafin* 3:12) that the lamps were lit in the morning as well as in the afternoon (see *comm.* to 1:2), the sequence is (assumed to be) as follows: Preparation of all seven lamps; lighting of five lamps; service of the daily incense; lighting of two lamps. According to this view, however, it is questionable whether the *Kohen Gadol* performed the preparation of the lamps.

---

24. Mixing the blood of the *Kohen Gadol's* ox [G] and the he-goat [H] (5:4)

---

25. Sprinkling the mixture on the inner altar (5:5-6)

---

26. Confession on the he-goat 'To Azazel' [K] and its presentation to the אִישׁ עִתִּי, *designated person*, for dispatch to Azazel (6:2)

---

27. Removing the entrails of the *Kohen Gadol's* ox [G] and the he-goat [H] and placing them in a utensil (6:7)

---

28. Preparing the limbs of the *Kohen Gadol's* ox [G] and the he-goat [H] for removal to the place of burning (6:7)

---

29. Reading from the Torah (7:1)

---

30. **THIRD IMMERSION** [then donned golden vestments]

---

31. According to R' Akiva the service of the he-goat sin offering of the *Mussafim* [F] took place here. According to R' Eliezer the entire *Mussafim* service took place later, see step 39 (7:3).

---

32. Offering the *Kohen Gadol's* ram [I] (7:3)

---

33. Offering the People's ram [J, D] (7:3)

---

34. Burning the entrails of the ox and he-goat (see step 27) on the outer altar (6:7)[5]

---

35. According to *Rambam* the daily afternoon burnt offering [B][6] was offered here.[7] However, according to most commentators this was performed later, see step 40 (7:3)

---

36. **FOURTH IMMERSION** [then donned linen vestments] (7:5)

---

5. *Tosafos* (70b s.v. ואחר) maintains that the removal of the ladle and coal shovel (step 37) followed immediately after the service of the people's ram burnt offering (step 33). The burning of the entrails was deferred to follow immediately after the fifth immersion (step 39), and to precede any service performed after this immersion. This is so according to both R' Eliezer and R' Akiva (see *Tosafos Yeshanim* 70b s.v. יצא). The text of the *Baraisa* cited in the *Gemara* (70a) which seems to contradict this is emended to conform to this view.

6. We have not included the services of the afternoon meal offering, *Chavitin* meal offering, and wine libation here. Neither *Rambam* (*Avodas Yom HaKippurim* 4:2), nor the Mishnah (7:3) mentions these services in connection with the *Kohen Gadol*. *Mirkeves HaMishneh* suggests that in *Rambam's* view these services were done by the *Kohen Gadol* only in the morning.

7. The above represents R' Akiva's sequence according to *Rambam*. R' Eliezer would, of course, insert the offering of the *Mussafim* (step 39) before the service of the daily burnt offering, to be followed by step 35.

37. Removal of the incense ladle and the shovel with burnt coals from the Holy of Holies. This was the *Kohen Gadol's* fourth and final entry into the Holy of Holies (7:4)

38. **FIFTH IMMERSION** [then donned golden vestments] (7:5)

39. According to R' Eliezer all the *Mussafim* [C], [E], and [F] were offered here. For R' Akiva's view, see steps 12 and 31 (7:3)

40. According to most commentators the daily afternoon burnt offering [B] was offered here, see step 35 (7:3).[8]

41. Burning the daily afternoon incense (7:4)

42. Lighting the Menorah (7:5)[8]

8. Because of many unresolved questions, I will not attempt to give a step by step account of the daily afternoon service (the meal offering, the *Chavitin*, the libation, the daily incense, and the lighting of the Menorah), because I have not been able to ascertain this sequence with any surety. The mishnah (here 7:3-4) is very brief about this segment of the service. The tractate *Tamid*, which describes the daily service in minute detail, makes no mention of the sequence to be followed in the afternoon (see *T'midim U'Mussafin* 6:11 with *Mishneh LaMelech; Pesachim* 59a; *Yoma* 3:4; *Tosefos Yom Tov* to *Tamid* 6:1).

APPENDIX II: Elaboration in 7:5

◆§ The procedure followed in inquiring of the Urim V'Tumim.

Rambam writes: The *Kohen Gadol* stands facing the Holy Ark and the inquirer stood behind him, facing the *Kohen Gadol's* back. The inquirer asks, 'Shall I go up or shall I not go up?' He does not ask loudly, nor does he think [his request] in his heart. Rather [he asks] in a low voice like one who prays alone (*Klei HaMikdash* 10:11 from *Gem.* 73a).

According to *Rashi* (73b) the inquirer stood facing the *Kohen Gadol,* and the *Kohen Gadol* stood facing the *Urim V'Tumim.* [This probably means that instead of facing straight ahead the *Kohen Gadol* bent his head to look at the breastplate.]

Rashi does not specify whether the *Kohen Gadol* faced the Holy Ark or any other direction; not even that he stood in the Temple.

R' Yaakov Emden (Lechem Shamayim) finds a source for *Rambam's* opinion (that the *Kohen Gadol* must face the Ark) in the verse (*I Samuel* 14:18) where King Saul inquired of the *Urim V'Tumim* (see *Rashi* there) and said to Achiyah (the *Kohen Gadol*):'*Bring here the Ark of HASHEM.'*

◆§ How Were Inquiries Answered by the Urim V'Tumim?

The *Gemara* (73b) cites R' Yochanan's opinion that upon the inquiry being made, certain letters on the breastplate protruded. These letters, however, were not arranged into words; only the *Kohen Gadol* could do that.

Ramban (Exod. 28:30) comments that the *Kohen Gadol* had to be worthy of prophecy, as mentioned in the *Gemara* (73b), in order to arrange the letters in the Divinely intended sequence.

Resh Lakish (there) says the letters miraculously grouped themselves, but does not explain how. This may have happened in the manner proposed by *Abarbanel (Exodus* 28), that the letters lit up and protruded in sequence. For example, when the answer was יְהוּדָה יַעֲלֶה, *Judah should advance* (cf. *Judges* 1:2) first the word יְהוּדָה, *Judah,* on the fourth stone lit up. Then a י, *yud,* appeared, then an ע, *ayin,* etc.

On the surface it seems that R' Yochanan and Resh Lakish disagree. This is *Rashi's* (s.v. בּוּלְטוֹת) understanding of it. This also seems to be *Rambam's* opinion, for in describing the process (*Klei HaMikdash* 10:11) he says only that the letters protruded, apparently ruling like R' Yochanan against Resh Lakish, as is the general rule.

Ritva offers an interesting opinion: R' Yochanan and Resh Lakish do not disagree. R' Yochanan speaks of the *Urim,* the part of the Divine Name which caused the letters to protrude. The *Kohen Gadol* first concentrated upon that (unspecified) part of the Name called *Urim,* which caused the letters to protrude. Resh Lakish speaks of the *Tumim,* another part of the Divine Name, which caused the letters to group into words.

The *Gemara (ibid.)* asks, why did the *Kohen Gadol* need to be one who speaks with רוּחַ הַקֹּדֶשׁ, *Divine Inspiration?* And the *Gemara* answers that the *Kohen Gadol* 'helped' the *Urim V'Tumim. Rashi* interprets this to mean that the *Kohen Gadol's* merit was a contributing factor in the efficacy of the *Urim V'Tumim.*

Rambam (ibid.) says that upon being asked in the proper manner, Divine Inspiration permeated the *Kohen Gadol.* He looked at the breastplate and saw in it the Divine reply as in a vision. In other words, an ordinary person would not even see the protruding letters. For this too, prophetic vision was needed.

The Urim V'Tumim in the Era of the Second Temple

The *Gemara* (21b) lists the *Urim V'Tumim* among the five things that the first Temple had and the Second Temple lacked. This needs to be clarified in light of what we know about the *Urim V'Tumim* (see above s.v. בְּאוּרִים וְתוּמִים). According to *Rambam* who understands *Urim V'Tumim* to be the breastplate itself (or the precious stones on it), it could not have been absent during the Second Temple, for without the breastplate and its stones, the *Kohen Gadol* would be מְחוּסָר בְּגָדִים *lacking vestments*, and would be unfit to perform the service (see *Mishnah Zevachim* 2:1; *Gemara* there 18a). *Rambam*, sensing this difficulty, says *(Klei HaMikdash* 10:10):

> They made an *Urim V'Tumim* during the Second Temple in order to complete [the total of] eight vestments, though they did not inquire of them. Why did they not inquire of them? Because there was no רוּחַ הַקֹּדֶשׁ, *Divine Inspiration* [i.e., there was no prophecy. Cf. *Moreh Nevuchim* 2:45], and any *Kohen* who does not speak out of Divine Inspiration [שֶׁאֵינוּ מְדַבֵּר בְּרוּחַ הַקֹּדֶשׁ] and upon whom the *Shechinah* [Divine Presence] does not rest is not inquired of.

Rambam's stipulation that 'any *Kohen*...is not inquired of' is a quotation from the *Gemara* (73b). See also *Beis HaBechirah* 4:1. This seems also to be opinion of *Tosafos* (21b s.v. אורים).

According to *Rashi* only the parchment with the Divine Name written on it was missing during the Second Temple. Thus, the *Kohen Gadol* was not lacking in vestments since the *Urim V'Tumim* was not a vestment, but something inserted *into* a vestment. *Ravad (Beis HaBechirah* 4:1) also holds that the *Urim V'Tumim* was not a vestment. According to this school of thought, why was there not an *Urim V'Tumim* during the Second Temple?

Abarbanel (to *Exodus* 28) says that when King Yoshiyahu hid the Ark *(Gem.* 52b) he also hid Moses' *Urim V'Tumim*. This is best understood according to *Ritva* (above s.v. אורים וְתמִים) that the *Urim V'Tumim* was given Moses by God, hence it was irreplaceable. According to *Ramban's* view that Moses wrote the *Urim V'Tumim*, it was replaceable, but since Moses received secret instructions on how to write the Divine Name which was the *Urim V'Tumim*, it could not be duplicated. Although *Ramban* holds that Moses revealed this secret to the greatest of the Jewish sages to whom he transmitted the סִתְרֵי תוֹרָה, *mysteries of the Torah*, it may be that with the passage of time the secret was lost and the *Urim V'Tumim* could no longer be replaced.

Abarbanel suggests another approach. Even if the *Urim V'Tumim* could have been replaced, this was not done. Their purpose was to answer the inquiries addressed to it. Since there was no רוּחַ הַקֹּדֶשׁ, *Divine Inspiration* (i.e., prophecy during the Temple, *Yoma* 21b; *Seder Olam Rabbah*, 30), — a prerequisite for the *Kohen Gadol* making the inquiry, — he could not inquire of the *Urim V'Tumim* during the Second Temple. Unable to serve its purpose the *Urim V'Tumim* was superfluous and was not replaced.

⊸§ מסכת סוכה §⊷

⊸§ Tractate Succah

Translation and anthologized commentary by
Rabbi Yisroel Gornish

Mesorah Publications, ltd

◆§ Tractate Succah

As its name implies, the tractate discusses the laws pertaining to the festival of Succos — not the laws it shares with all festivals, such as those relating to labor and food preparation, but the laws relating *only* to Succos. There are three broad subject areas dealt with in our tractate: the *succah* as a dwelling, the Four Species, and Temple ritual and rejoicing.

The *succah* itself has specific requirements regarding what materials are acceptable for its s'chach [covering], its interior and exterior size, and its walls. The Mishnah then goes on to discuss particulars about the *mitzvah* of sitting in the *succah* and conditions that may absolve one from the *mitzvah*.

The second major subject of the tractate is the Four Species: *lulav, esrog,* myrtle branches, and willow branches. Certain requirements and invalidations are shared by all four and each has its own unique characteristics. In addition to the *mitzvah* that all four be taken together, there was a ritual observed in the Temple with the willow branches, an observance that is remembered today in the form of the Hoshanah Rabbah service.

Finally, Succos was observed in the Temple by means of *mussaf* [additional] offerings far more varied and elaborate than those of the Sabbath or other festivals. Succos was also the only time of the year when a water libation was poured on the altar in addition to the regular wine libations. The Torah also ordains that Succos be celebrated as a time of joy even beyond that associated with the other festivals.

Chapter 1

◆§ The Succah

A *succah* is the temporary dwelling which a Jew establishes as his domicile during the festival of Succos. It takes its name from its סְכָךְ *covering (Rashi, 2a)* which is also its most essential feature. However, the halachah also discusses such other features of the *succah* as the composition of its walls, its dimensions, the materials that are acceptable for s'chach, and how the s'chach is to be laid. These laws are the topics of the first chapter of our tractate.

Many of the laws discussed below deal with the *succah's* measurements and are expressed in terms of cubits, handbreadths and so on. The *Talmud (Menachos* 41b) states that a handbreadth is as wide as four thumbs (of an average man) side by side at their widest point, which is equal to five forefingers or six little fingers side by side. (See also *Rambam, comm.* to *Kelayim* 6:6; *Hilchos Shabbos* 17:36).

[The codifiers do not agree on the translation of the Mishnaic measurements into contemporary terms. For example, views range from eighteen inches to a bit more than twenty-four for a cubit. Accordingly, the twenty-cubit height given in mishnah 1 could be from as little as thirty to over forty feet. For the convenience of the reader, we present the following table which presents the three most prevalent views for the finger, handbreadth and cubit. It also includes the equivalents of the twenty-cubit measure which appears in mishnah 1. It should be noted, however, that many authorities recommend that slightly larger measurements be used for safety's sake when performing a *mitzvah* that is required by the Torah.]

	אגודל Thumb	טפח Handbreadth	אמה Cubit	20 Cubits
Chazon Ish	.95 in./2.4 cm.	3.8 in./9.6 cm.	22.8 in./58 cm.	38 ft./11.6 m.
Igros Moshe	.9 in./2.25 cm.	3.75 in./9.1 cm.	21.5 in./54.6 cm.	35.83 ft./10.92 m.
R' A.C. No'eh	.8 in./2 cm.	3.2 in./8 cm.	18.9 in./48 cm.	31.5 ft./9.6m.

[א] סֻכָּה שֶׁהִיא גְבוֹהָה לְמַעְלָה מֵעֶשְׂרִים אַמָּה פְּסוּלָה. רַבִּי יְהוּדָה מַכְשִׁיר. וְשֶׁאֵינָהּ גְּבוֹהָה עֲשָׂרָה טְפָחִים, וְשֶׁאֵין לָהּ שְׁלֹשָׁה דְפָנוֹת, וְשֶׁחַמָּתָהּ מְרֻבָּה מִצִּלָּתָהּ, פְּסוּלָה.

יד אברהם

1.

סֻכָּה שֶׁהִיא גְבוֹהָה לְמַעְלָה מֵעֶשְׂרִים אַמָּה — A succah that is more than twenty cubits high

The mishnah refers to the *interior* height of the succah. The thickness of the *s'chach* is not included in this measurement (*Tif. Yis.; Orach Chaim* 633:1).

פְּסוּלָה. — *is invalid;*

If the *s'chach* is *exactly* twenty cubits above its floor, the *succah* is valid; the mishnah invalidates only a *succah* whose *s'chach* begins more than twenty cubits above the floor.

The reason for the disqualification of a higher *succah* is derived by Rava (*Gem.* 2a) from the verse (*Lev.* 23:42): בַּסֻּכֹּת תֵּשְׁבוּ שִׁבְעַת יָמִים, *you shall dwell in succos for seven days.* The word *succos* refers to buildings of a makeshift, temporary nature. Thus the implication of the commandment is that one must leave his דִּירַת קֶבַע, *permanent dwelling,* and settle in a דִּירַת עֲרַאי, *temporary dwelling.* That the *succah* is a 'temporary' dwelling means, by definition, that it need not be constructed as sturdily as a permanent structure; lightweight, flimsy walls will suffice for a *succah,* although one may build it sturdily, if he wishes (*Rashi, ibid.*).

From this duality of requirements — that its construction need not be sturdy, but that it be adequate for seven days of dwelling — the Rabbis derive that a *succah* must be strong enough to stand for the full seven days even though its walls are flimsy and makeshift enough to fit the description of דִּירַת עֲרַאי, *temporary dwelling.* Were the *succah* built taller

than twenty cubits, it could not possibly stand without a strong foundation and permanent walls to prevent it from collapsing. Construction of such a nature would remove it from the category of 'temporary dwelling' thus rendering it invalid as a *succah* (*Rav*).

The Torah cannot be interpreted to mean that even a lower structure may not be of a sturdiness that would enable it to stand for more than seven days — such an interpretation would force upon us the impossible calculation of predicting how long a given *succah* would stand. Rather, the exegesis teaches that a *succah* may not be of such a nature that it *must* be built in a permanent manner.

Walls taller than twenty cubits are generally constructed with a firmness which would make them permanent; walls of less than twenty cubits, however, can be built in a temporary manner. This is why, in Rava's view, the walls must be less than twenty cubits high; the Torah requires dimensions that will suffice for seven days regardless of how strong they are built. However, as long as a *succah* is within the twenty-cubit limit, one may build it as solidly as he pleases (*Ran; Tos. Yom Tov*).

רַבִּי יְהוּדָה מַכְשִׁיר. — R' Yehudah validates it.

R' Yehudah disagrees with the *tanna kamma* [first tanna]. He holds that one is required to erect the *succah* as a permanent structure (*Gem.* 7b). *Ramban* (*Milchamos*) explains that R' Yehudah holds there is no limitation on a *suc-*

1. **A** *succah* that is more than twenty cubits high is invalid. R' Yehudah validates it.

And [a *succah*] that is not ten handbreadths high, or [one] that does not have three walls, or [one] whose sun[ny area] is greater than its shade[d area], is invalid.

YAD AVRAHAM

cah's height. Furthermore, he recognizes no difference in the mode of construction between a high *succah* and a low one. Consequently, since a high *succah* must be built sturdily, it follows that a low one, too, must be of sturdy construction. The halachah does not follow R' Yehudah *(Rav; Tif. Yis., Orach Chaim* 613:1).

Ritva, however, understands R' Yehudah to mean that construction of a permanent nature is *permitted*, but not required. Accordingly, one may make his *succah* flimsy or sturdy, as he prefers.

וְשֶׁאֵינָה גְבוֹהָה עֲשָׂרָה טְפָחִים, — *And [a succah] that is not ten handbreadths high,*

The hollow of its interior, from floor to *s'chach*, is less than ten handbreadths high. This is a דִּירָה סְרוּחָה, *unpleasant dwelling*, for it is too confining for decent habitation *(Rav; Tif. Yis.* from *Gem.* 4a).

[The Torah requires that one 'dwell' in a *succah*. The Rabbis understand this to mean that one must consider his *succah* to be his home for the seven days of the festival. They enunciate the principle of תֵּשְׁבוּ כְּעֵין תָּדוּרוּ, *you are to dwell* (in the succah) *just as you would inhabit* (your home). By implication, in the case of conditions so unpleasant that they would cause one to abandon his own home — such as cold, a leaky roof, or the ceiling so low that one lacks even the minimal living space of ten handbreadths — such conditions free one from the obligation of remaining in the *succah*. In the case of a *succah* too small to provide the minimal space for human use, the *succah* is invalid. See 2:4.]

The *Gemara* (4a) extends the in-

validation of a *succah* lower than ten handbreadths. In the event the *s'chach* is above ten, but leaves or branches hang down so that the actual usable area within is less than ten, the *succah* is equally invalid. Conversely, if the *s'chach* is too low, and one digs a trench within it to bring the distance from the floor to the *s'chach* to the necessary ten handbreadths, the *succah* can be validated. Similarly, if the *s'chach* is more than twenty cubits high, one can validate the *succah* by building up the *succah* floor.

וְשֶׁאֵין לָהּ שְׁלֹשָׁה דְפָנוֹת, — *or [one] that does not have three walls,*

A *succah* must have a minimum of three walls. This is derived from *Leviticus* 23:42,43 where the commandment of *succah* is given. There, the Torah refers to the *succah* three times: בַּסֻּכֹּת תֵּשְׁבוּ...יֵשְׁבוּ בַסֻּכֹּת...כִּי בַסֻּכּוֹת הוֹשַׁבְתִּי אֶת־בְּנֵי יִשְׂרָאֵל, *in succos shall you dwell ... they are to dwell in succos...for I caused all the Children of Israel to dwell in succos.*

The first reference to *succah* בַּסֻּכֹּת, informs us of the *mitzvah* to dwell in a *succah*; since the word סֻכֹּת is derived from סְכָךְ, *covering* or *shade*, we know that a *succah* must have halachically acceptable *s'chach*. Thus, as we shall see below, a *succah* that fails to provide shade from the sun, is unacceptable for fulfillment of the commandment. The other two appearances of the word are vocalized the same way, although they are spelled differently: סֻכֹּת *(v.* 42) and סֻכּוֹת *(v.* 43). In its final appearance, the word is spelled מָלֵא, *full*, with a *vav*. The first, without the *vav*, can be vocalized סֻכַּת, which is singular. The second, however, because of its *vav*, can

be vocalized *only* as סְבֻּות, which is plural. The combination of the two spellings, one singular and one plural, implies that a minimum of three *succos* are suggested. From this the Rabbis deduce (*Gem.* 6b) the requirement that a *succah* must have a minimum of three walls. Two of them must have the minimum width of seven handbreadths (as mentioned above). The third wall, however, has been defined much differently in the tradition received by Moses at Sinai and transmitted orally [הֲלָכָה לְמֹשֶׁה מִסִּינַי]. In brief, it need be only slightly larger than a handbreadth, as outlined below:

If the two whole walls (7×10 handbreadths each) are at right angles to each other, the third wall can be constructed as follows: A board ten handbreadths long and a bit more than one handbreadth wide is stood on the ground slightly less than three handbreadths from the end of the walls. According to halachah, any gap of less than three handbreadths between two surfaces is considered לָבוּד [*lavud*], united, with the surfaces on either side. The concept of *lavud* means that, halachically, the entire surface is regarded as a continuous, unbroken whole. For example, a wall consisting of 3½ solid handbreadths, a 2½ handbreadth gap, and then a solid surface of four, would be regarded as an unbroken ten-handbreadth wall, rather than 7½ handbreadths of surface plus a gap of 2½. Similarly, in the case of a third, abbreviated wall of a *succah*, the board of slightly more than a handbreadth plus the gap of slightly less than three are united by means of *lavud* to form a four-handbreadth length of wall. As mentioned above, the minimum width of a *succah* wall is seven handbreadths. Thus, the four-handbreadth halachic width of the abbreviated wall constitutes a majority of the normally required size. In a case where two perpendicular walls are of the required size, the orally transmitted Law of Moses regards this abbreviated wall as adequate to satisfy the Torah's requirement of a third wall. See fig. 1.

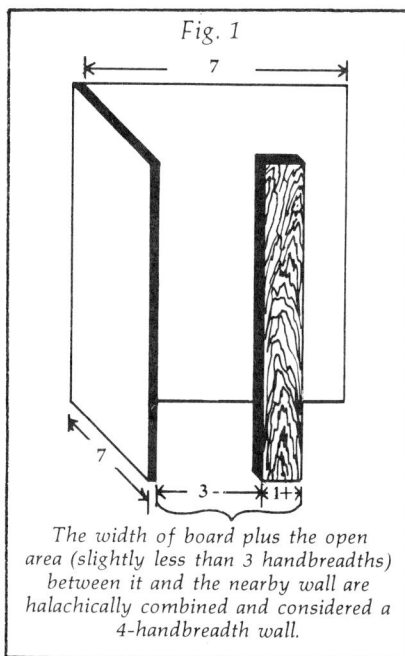

Fig. 1

The width of board plus the open area (slightly less than 3 handbreadths) between it and the nearby wall are halachically combined and considered a 4-handbreadth wall.

In practice, Rabbinic ordinance posited an additional requirement for such a situation — צוּרַת הַפֶּתַח, *an entrance frame*. In its most common application, an *entrance frame* is used to satisfy the requirement of a wall to create a רְשׁוּת הַיָּחִיד, *private domain*, for purposes of the Sabbath. It consists of two solid uprights, at least ten handbreadths high, and of any width and thickness, with a crossbar atop them of any width or thickness. The crossbar need not be solid, but may even be tautly stretched wire or cord (*Eruvin* 1:1 and *Orach Chaim* 362:1).

For the third *succah* wall described above — which is, in effect, four handbreadths wide — the Rabbis required that a צוּרַת הַפֶּתַח, *entrance frame*, be employed to extend the third wall for at least three more handbreadths, giving the wall a total width of seven handbreadths. See fig. 2.

[Some require the *entrance frame* to be four handbreadths long *(Pri Magadim).*]

In an instance where the two whole walls parallel each other, the solid part of the third wall must be slightly wider

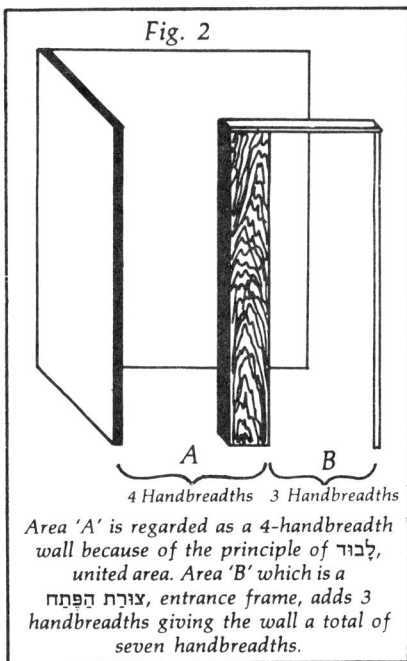

Fig. 2

Area 'A' is regarded as a 4-handbreadth wall because of the principle of לָבוּד, united area. Area 'B' which is a צוּרַת הַפֶּתַח, entrance frame, adds 3 handbreadths giving the wall a total of seven handbreadths.

4 Handbreadths   3 Handbreadths

A   B

token *lavud* wall can complete the process. Here, where the two walls are separate and achieve no independent purpose only a significant board of four handbreadths is sufficient to unify all three sections of wall to create an enclosed area.

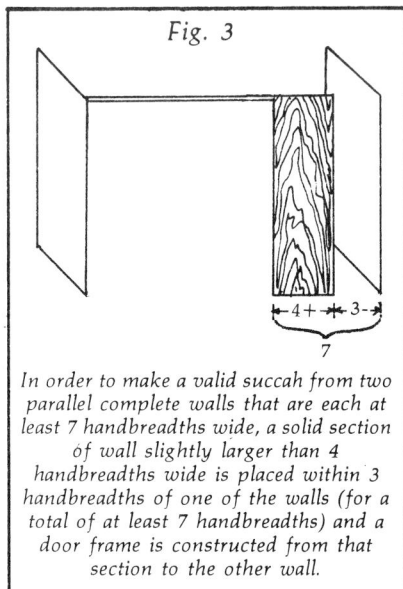

Fig. 3

←4+→←3→
7

In order to make a valid succah from two parallel complete walls that are each at least 7 handbreadths wide, a solid section of wall slightly larger than 4 handbreadths wide is placed within 3 handbreadths of one of the walls (for a total of at least 7 handbreadths) and a door frame is constructed from that section to the other wall.

than four handbreadths, and positioned within three handbreadths of one of the complete walls. The third wall will thus attain the status of a seven-handbreadth wall by adding the gap of just less than three handbreadths to just over four handbreadths of the board itself, making a total of seven[1] (*Gem.* 7a; *Rav; Tif. Yis.; Orach Chaim* 630:2). See fig. 3.

The *Gemara* (7a) teaches that in this instance the concept of *lavud* cannot be utilized to create the halachic status of a wall by positioning a board in the center of the gap with less than three handbreadths remaining on either side.

The reason is that only in the case of two valid walls, at right angles to each other can a one-handbreadth wall suffice for the third wall, because the two regulation size walls enclose an area. In such a case, the two walls serve are a unit serving the purpose of closing off entry from two sides, therefore a

וְשֶׁחַמָּתָהּ מְרֻבָּה מִצִּלָּתָהּ, — *or [one] whose sun[ny area] is greater than its shade[d area],*

[Also invalid is a *succah* whose *s'chach* permits more sunlight to filter through than it provides shade. Since, by definition, a *succah* must provide shade — *s'chach*=shelter — such a *succah* fails to perform its basic function.]

But if the sunny area and the shaded area are equal, the *succah* is valid. This refers to the sun and shade on the *succah* floor; it does not mean that the open and covered areas are equal at the top of the *succah*, for when sunlight enters through a small space it diffuses over a much larger area. Consequently, if the *s'chach* and the space amid the *s'chach*

---

1. Though *Rav* does not mention any need for an entrance frame in this case, *Rambam* (*Succah* 4:3) requires one even here. *Rosh* and *Ran* write that this question is in dispute between the authorities (*Tos. Yom Tov*).

   Shulchan Aruch (*Orach Chaim* 630:2) cites both views concerning the entrance frame. *Mishnah Berurah* (ibid. 16) quoting many authorities concludes that one should follow the stricter view, and construct an entrance frame.

סֻכָּה יְשָׁנָה — בֵּית שַׁמַּאי פּוֹסְלִין, וּבֵית הִלֵּל מַכְשִׁירִין. וְאֵיזוֹ הִיא סֻכָּה יְשָׁנָה? כָּל־שֶׁעֲשָׂאָהּ קֹדֶם לֶחָג שְׁלֹשִׁים יוֹם. אֲבָל אִם עֲשָׂאָהּ לְשֵׁם חָג, אֲפִילוּ מִתְּחִלַּת הַשָּׁנָה, כְּשֵׁרָה.

[ב] **הָעוֹשֶׂה** סֻכָּתוֹ תַּחַת הָאִילָן, כְּאִלּוּ עֲשָׂאָהּ בְּתוֹךְ הַבַּיִת.

יד אברהם

are equal, the sunny area on the floor of the *succah* will exceed the shaded patches and the *succah* will not be valid (*Rav; Tif. Yis.; Orach Chaim* 631:1).

פְּסוּלָה. — *is invalid.*

[In each of the above instances, as explained, the *succah* is not valid].

סֻכָּה יְשָׁנָה — *An old succah* —

[I.e. one which was not made expressly for the festival]. This refers only to the *s'chach* of the *succah.* As for the walls, they need not be constructed expressly for the festival (*Taz, Orach Chaim* 636:1).

בֵּית שַׁמַּאי פּוֹסְלִין, — *Beis Shammai invalidate it,*

Beis Shammai require that the *s'chach* be laid expressly for the *mitzvah* of the festival (*Rav*).

They derive their view from the verse חַג הַסֻּכֹּת תַּעֲשֶׂה לְךָ שִׁבְעַת יָמִים, *And you shall make the festival of Succos for yourself seven days* (*Deut.* 16:13). This is expounded to imply that the *succah* shall be made with the festival in mind (*Gem.* 9a).

וּבֵית הִלֵּל מַכְשִׁירִין. — *and Beis Hillel validate it.*

They do not require a *succah* to be made expressly for the festival (*Rav*).

As to the verse from which Beis Shammai derive their ruling, Beis Hillel gives it a different exegetical interpretation. They understand it to permit construction of a *succah* during the Intermediate Days (*Gem.* 9a). Beis Hillel expound the verse as follows: חַג הַסֻּכֹּת,

Succos for the sake of the festival, תַּעֲשֶׂה לְךָ שִׁבְעַת יָמִים, *you are permitted to make during* [its] *seven days* (*Rashi*). [Since construction is one of the forbidden labors of festival days, the permission to build a *succah* can refer only to the Intermediate Days.] However, one should not schedule his *succah*-building for the Intermediate Days; he may build then only if no *succah* had been made previously (*Rashi*).

Although the halachah follows Beis Hillel that the *s'chach* need not be newly laid, *Yerushalmi* teaches that it is preferable to make some minor change in the *s'chach* in honor of the festival. For this purpose it is sufficient to lift and replace an area of *s'chach* measuring a handbreadth by a handbreadth, or to lift a thin line of *s'chach* extending across the entire length or width of the *succah* (*Tosafos* 9a; *Orach Chaim* 636:1).

וְאֵיזוֹ הִיא סֻכָּה יְשָׁנָה? כָּל־שֶׁעֲשָׂאָהּ קֹדֶם לֶחָג שְׁלֹשִׁים יוֹם. — *And what is* [considered] *an 'old' succah? Whatever one built thirty days prior to the Festival.*

Throughout *Mishnayos* the festival of Succos is referred to as הֶחָג, *the Festival.*

The presumption is that a *succah* built before the festival season was made for the sake of shade, but not for the *mitzvah* of *succah.* However, if it were constructed within thirty days of the festival, when people have begun to study the laws of Succos, it is presumed to have been constructed expressly for

1
2
An old *succah* — Beis Shammai invalidate it and Beis Hillel validate it. And what is [considered] an 'old' *succah*? Whatever one built thirty days prior to the Festival. But if one built it specifically for the Festival, even [if he put it up] at the beginning of the year, it is valid.

2. **I**f one builds his *succah* under a tree, it is as though he had built it inside the house.

YAD AVRAHAM

this *mitzvah* (Rav; see also *Chok Yaakov, Orach Chaim* 429:2).

אֲבָל אִם עֲשָׂעָה לְשֵׁם חַג, אֲפִילוּ מִתְחִלַּת הַשָּׁנָה כְּשֵׁרָה. — *But if one built it specifically for the Festival, even [if he put it up] at the beginning of the year, it is valid.*

Even if he constructed it after the conclusion of the previous *Succos*, a year before the current festival, it is considered valid according to all, because he built it expressly for the sake of the *mitzvah* (*Shaar HaTziyun* 636:1:9).[1]

2.

הָעוֹשֶׂה סֻכָּתוֹ תַּחַת הָאִילָן, — *If one builds his succah under a tree,*
[I.e., the branches of the tree are directly over the *s'chach* of the *succah*. Although tree branches are valid as *s'chach*, they may be used only after being cut down. While a tree is still rooted in the earth, its branches are not valid *s'chach* (mishnah 4).]

כְּאִילוּ עֲשָׂאָהּ בְּתוֹךְ הַבַּיִת. — *it is as though he had built it inside the house.*
A *succah* built under a roof is not valid. This is derived from the verse (*Leviticus* 23:42): בַּסֻּכֹּת תֵּשְׁבוּ, *in succos shall you dwell.* Because the word בַּסֻּכֹּת, *in succos,* is spelled without a ו [*vav*], it can be read as a singular בַּסֻּכַּת, *in a succah.* By using the singular spelling, the

Torah emphasizes that one must dwell only in one *succah* — i.e., under one *s'chach*, and not in a *succah* which is covered by a tree, the roof of a house, or the *s'chach* of another *succah* (*Gem.* 9b).
From the fact that the mishnah does not say simply that a *succah* under a tree is invalid, Rava derives the underlying principle behind this invalidation. The mishnah likens this *succah* to one built inside a house: just as the roof of a house is צִלָּתָה מְרֻבָּה מֵחַמָּתָה, *its shaded area is greater than its sunny area,* so, too, the tree above invalidates the *succah* below only if the tree's shaded area is greater than the sunlit area between its branches. If, however, the trees foliage is such that חַמָּתָה

1. A *succah* which remains from year to year is considered an old *succah* even though it was originally made expressly for the festival, for once Succos passes, the purpose for which the *succah* was originally built has been fulfilled. And even though, according to the strict letter of the law a *succah* need not be made expressly for the *mitzvah* of *succah* (see *Orach Chaim* 635; *Chayei Adam* 146:38), nevertheless it is a more desirable practice [מִצְוָה מִן הַמּוּבְחָר] to construct it specifically for the forthcoming festival. Therefore, one should make some innovation even if only to lift up the *s'chach* and put it back in place; thereby he, in effect, renews the *succah* for the sake of the current Succos, making the *mitzvah* as 'desirable' as if he had built the *succah* anew (*Chayei Adam* 146:39).

סָכָּה עַל־גַּבֵּי סֻכָּה הָעֶלְיוֹנָה כְּשֵׁרָה, וְהַתַּחְתּוֹנָה פְּסוּלָה. רַבִּי יְהוּדָה אוֹמֵר: אִם אֵין דִּיּוּרִין בָּעֶלְיוֹנָה, הַתַּחְתּוֹנָה כְּשֵׁרָה.

יד אברהם

מְרֻבָּה מִצְלָתָהּ, *its sunny area is greater than its shaded area,* the *succah* below is valid (*Gem.* 9b).

Even in the event that the tree's foliage is *not* dense enough to invalidate the *succah,* Rava requires that the tree's branches be bent down and intertwined with the *s'chach.* That done, the greater amount of *s'chach* nullifies the lesser amount of the branches [בִּיטּוּל בְּרוֹב] so that the entire roof of the *succah* is regarded as one unit of valid *s'chach.*

However, the commentators disagree on the conditions requiring such inter-mingling of branches with *s'chach.*

According to *Tosafos* (9b s.v. הא), even if the *s'chach* is not thick enough to provide sufficient shade for a valid *succah,* the *succah* can be validated by intertwining branches with the *s'chach* — even though the branches are still attached to the tree. The greater amount of *s'chach* serves to nullify the branches, and the combination is regarded as a single unit of valid *s'chach.* If, however, the *s'chach* is of sufficient density to provide adequate shade, the overhanging branches can be ignored entirely — provided, of course, they are not so dense as to constitute a roof by providing more shade than sunlight.

Ran, however, disagrees. He holds that any part of the *s'chach* covered by an overhanging branch loses its halachic validity; since that part of the *succah* is shielded from the sun by a branch, the *s'chach* over that area serves no purpose and for all practical purposes is non-existent. To solve *this* problem Rava teaches that the branches must be intertwined with the *s'chach.*

Although *Ran* does not discuss a case where the *s'chach* provides less sunlight than shade, most commentators hold that *Ran* would agree with *Tosafos* that the *succah* can be validated by intertwining overhanging branches with

the *s'chach. Magen Avraham,* however, maintains that *Ran* would invalidate this procedure (see *Mishneh Berurah* to 626:1).

Whenever intertwining is permitted, it may be done as a first resort [לְכַתְּחִלָּה] (*Tos. Yom Tov*).

Rambam (*Hilchos Succah* 5:12), however, holds that simple intertwining is never sufficient; the branches must also be detached from the tree.

סֻכָּה עַל־גַּבֵּי סֻכָּה — [*If*] a *succah* [*is built*] atop another *succah*

[The *s'chach* of the lower *succah* also serves as the floor of the upper *succah.*]

הָעֶלְיוֹנָה כְּשֵׁרָה, — the upper one is valid,

It is valid only if it is not higher than twenty cubits (*Gem.* 9b; see mishnah 1). However, since the floor of the upper *succah* is the *s'chach* of the lower one, the twenty-cubit height is measured not from the ground, but from the *s'chach* of the lower *succah* (*Rashi* 10a s.v. וקיימא; *Be'ur Halachah* 628:1).

וְהַתַּחְתּוֹנָה פְּסוּלָה. — and the lower one is invalid.

For it is under two *s'chachim* and the Torah says: בַּסֻּכֹּת תֵּשְׁבוּ, *in succos shall you dwell;* i.e., under one *s'chach* (singular בַּסֻּכַּת) and not in [under] two (as explained above s.v. כאלו עשאה).

But if the upper *succah* is less than ten handbreadths high, and consequently not valid as a separate *succah* (see mishnah 1), then the two *s'chachim* are regarded as a single thick one, and the lower *succah* is valid (*Rambam, Hilchos Succah* 5:22; *Tif. Yis., Orach Chaim* 628:1).

R' Yirmiyah (*Gem.* 9b-10a) notes four possible variables in the case of upper and lower succahs:

A) If the upper *s'chach* is thick enough to provide a majority of shade, but the lower *s'chach* [in the absence of the upper *s'chach*] would permit a majority of sunlight, both

1
2

[If] a succah [is built] atop another succah the upper one is valid, and the lower one is invalid. R' Yehudah says: If there can be no tenancy in the upper one, [only] the lower one is valid.

succahs are valid in the sense that one may sit in either one. Since the lower *s'chach* is too sparse to be valid, it is halachically non-existent, with the result that the upper *s'chach* serves both. Therefore one is permitted to sit in the lower *succah*. However, the upper *s'chach* may not be higher than twenty cubits above the floor of the lower *succah*.

B) If both *succos* have sufficiently thick *s'chach*, but the upper one is higher than twenty cubits, both are invalid; the upper one because it is too high and the lower one because it has a double roof.

C) If the upper *s'chach* is too sparse to qualify on its own, but the lower *s'chach* is sufficient, the lower *succah* is valid, but not the upper one. [See *Rashi* 10a s.v. תחתינה; *Tos.* 9b s.v. הא).

D) If both *succos* had adequate *s'chach*, the lower one is invalid because it is covered by the upper, but the upper one is valid provided it is not too high.

[The *tanna kamma* (first tanna) of the mishnah has described a case where one lives on top of the lower succah, utilizing the *s'chach* of the upper *succah*. R' Yehudah will now disagree with the implication that the lower *succah* can always be considered a floor for the one above it.]

רבִּי יְהוּדָה אוֹמֵר: אִם אֵין דִּיוּרִין בָּעֶלְיוֹנָה, — *R' Yehudah says: If there can be no tenancy in the upper one,*

As noted above, when the mishnah speaks of the upper *succah*, it means that the *s'chach* of the lower one is the floor for those living above. By definition, therefore, the roof of the lower *succah* must be strong enough to bear the weight of the person living in the upper one, including whatever furnishings and floor coverings he may require. If however, it is not fit for occupancy because the *s'chach* of the lower *succah* is incapable of supporting such weight... *(Gem.* 10a; *Rav; Tif. Yis.).*

הַתַּחְתּוֹנָה כְּשֵׁרָה. — *[only] the lower one is valid.*

Since the upper *succah* has no 'floor' of its own, it has no standing as an independent dwelling.

It is axiomatic that if the lower *s'chach* is too weak to support weight, even the *tanna kamma* would agree that the upper *succah* cannot be regarded as a separate dwelling. Where, then, do the *tanna kamma* and R' Yehudah disagree? The *Gemara* (10a) explains:

A) Where the *s'chach* of the lower *succah* is very strong and can easily support a person living in the upper *succah* together with all his household items, both the *tanna kamma* and R' Yehudah agree that the lower *succah* is not valid, for it is a *succah* under a *succah*.

B) Where the *s'chach* of the lower *succah* is too weak to support a person and the utensils of the upper *succah*, both the *tanna kamma* and R' Yehudah agree that only the lower *succah* is valid. Since the upper *succah* has no floor that is capable of supporting the necessary houshold items it is not considered a separate *succah*. Therefore the lower *succah* is independently valid if it has acceptable *s'chach*, or if it lacks sufficient *s'chach* but the *s'chach* of the upper *succah* is valid *(Rashi; Rambam, Hilchos Succah* 5:22 as understood by *Kessef Mishnah; Orach Chaim* 5:22).

Even if the upper *succah* is higher than twenty cubits, the lower *succah* is *not* regarded as being under a 'roof' — only if it is under a tree or some other inherently invalid *s'chach* would the *succah* lose its acceptability, but not if it is under *true s'chach* which is too high to be usable *(Magen Avraham, Taz* to *Orach Chaim).*

The *s'chach* of the lower *succah* is too flimsy to have any standing. The result is that instead of two *succos,* one atop

[ג] **פֵּרַס** עָלֶיהָ סָדִין מִפְּנֵי הַחַמָּה, אוֹ תַחְתֶּיהָ מִפְּנֵי הַנְּשָׁר, אוֹ שֶׁפֵּרַס עַל־גַּבֵּי הַקִּינוֹף פְּסוּלָה. אֲבָל פוֹרֵס הוּא עַל־גַּבֵּי נַקְלִיטֵי הַמִּטָּה.

יד אברהם

the other, we are left with one large *succah* served by the *s'chach* of the *upper* one.

C. The dispute between the *tanna kamma* and R' Yehudah is only in a case where the *s'chach* of the lower *succah* can support the utensils of the upper one, but only with difficulty. The *tanna kamma* holds that even though the *s'chach* of the lower *succah* is very weak, so long as it supports the weight of the upper *succah's* utensils, it is con-sidered a proper *s'chach* [for a *succah* is only a temporary abode — (see comm. to mishnah 1)]. Therefore, the lower *succah* is not valid for it is a *succah* beneath a *succah*. R' Yehudah, on the other hand, holds that a permanent structure is required (see comm. to mishnah 1), and since the lower *s'chach* is too weak to qualify it as a 'permanent' floor, he disqualifies it. Thus the lower *succah* is not a *succah* beneath a *succah* (*Rav; Tos. Yom Tov*).

3.

Having discussed the size and structure of a *succah* and where it may not be placed, the mishnah now turns to the case of one who makes a shelter above or within a *succah* with material invalid for *s'chach*. As we shall see below (1:4), one of the categories not eligible to be used as *s'chach* is something which can מְקַבֵּל טֻמְאָה, *receive contamination*. Among items in this category are finished utensils, garments, and — the subject of our mishnah — sheets. It should be noted that the disqualification here under discussion is not limited to something which has actually become *tamei* [*contaminated*]; it is sufficient that the object is halachically *eligible* to become *tamei*.

פֵּרַס עָלֶיהָ סָדִין — *If one spread a sheet over* [*the s'chach*]

Since a sheet can become *tamei*, it is unfit for use as *s'chach* (*Tif. Yis.*; see mishnah 4).

מִפְּנֵי הַחַמָּה, — *because of the sun,*

Although the *succah* has sufficient *s'chach* to make it valid, enough sun comes through to discomfit the people sitting within. A sheet is draped over the *succah* to afford protection from this sunlight. Since the purpose of the sheet is for protection, it is regarded as *s'chach* — but a sheet is invalid for *s'chach* as explained above (*Rav* from *Rashi*. See *Tos. Yom Tov*).

A second interpretation maintains that the sheet is intended not to protect the people, but the *s'chach*. If the *s'chach* were to be left unshielded from the sun, its leaves would shrivel and fall off, reducing the shady area of the *succah* to the point where it would become invalid. Used in this manner, the sheet invalidates the *succah* because it becomes the only means to ensure that the *succah* maintains the required degree of shade. [Anything instrumental to the acceptability of the *s'chach* must itself be acceptable as *s'chach*, which a sheet is not] (*Rav* from *Tos.* 10a s.v. פירס).

אוֹ תַחְתֶּיהָ — *or beneath it*

Under the *s'chach* [inside the *succah*] (*Tif. Yis.*).

מִפְּנֵי הַנְּשָׁר, — *because of the falling leaves,*

To keep leaves, pine needles, and twigs from falling onto the table or into the food. Such a sheet invalidates the *succah*, as explained above, because it is susceptible to contamination (*Rav, Rashi* 10a).

1
3

3. **I**f one spread a sheet over [the *s'chach*] because of the sun, or beneath it because of the falling leaves, or if one spread it over a four-poster bed, it is invalid. However, one may spread it over a two-poster bed.

YAD AVRAHAM

According to *Tosafos* cited above, the sheet under the *s'chach* is meant to keep the *s'chach* from diminishing by preventing the drying leaves from falling down; thus the sheet will prevent the shaded area from becoming smaller than the sunny area *(Rav; Tif. Yis.)*.

R' *Tam* argues that a sheet utilized to keep out sunlight or falling leaves (*Rashi's* interpretation) — or even rain — should be acceptable. Since its only function is to minimize discomfort, it should be no different than a sheet intended to beautify the *succah*, which is permitted. The test, according to R' *Tam* is whether the sheet is necessary to maintain the validity of the *s'chach* — if so, it is not acceptable, otherwise it is permitted.

Mordechai, however, defends *Rashi* and notes a basic difference between beautification and shelter. A sheet hung as a decoration is intended to serve the *succah* and becomes a part of it, but a sheet used for shelter is, by definition, a form of *s'chach* and is, therefore, invalid (*Tos. Yom Tov*; see also *Mishnah Berurah* and *Be'ur Halachah* 629:19).

אוֹ שֶׁפֵּרַס עַל־גַּבֵּי הַקִּינוֹף, — *or if one spread it over a four-poster bed,*
The intention here was not to provide shade but to create a beautiful canopy for the bed. The canopy is not close to the *s'chach* so that it cannot be regarded as invalid *s'chach* as were the sheets in

the above cases. Nonetheless, the canopy is regarded as a separate roof, intervening between the person and the *s'chach* (*Rashi*).

פְּסוּלָה. — *it* [i.e., the *succah*] *is invalid.*
The reason for disqualifying the *succah* in the first two cases is that the sheet is subject to contamination and is therefore not valid as *s'chach* (see mishnah 4). In the third case, the *succah* is invalid because the canopy forms an אֹהֶל, *tent*, intervening between the person and the *s'chach* (*Rav*).

But if a sheet is spread inside the *succah* for decorative purposes and it is suspended within four handbreadths of the *s'chach*, the *succah* remains valid. Used this way, the sheet becomes secondary to the *s'chach* and one may sit under it.

If, however, the sheet hangs more than four handbreadths below the *s'chach*, it is considered a separate tent. Consequently, one who eats under it has failed to fulfill the *mitzvah* of eating under the *s'chach* of the *succah* (*Orach Chaim* 627:4 with *Mishnah Berurah*).[1]

אֲבָל פּוֹרֵס הוּא עַל־גַּבֵּי נַקְלִיטֵי הַמִּטָּה. — *However, one may spread it over a two-poster bed.*
I.e., a bed which has two vertical

1. *Rama (Orach Chaim* 627:4) cites *Maharil* that it is preferable to hang all נוֹיֵי סֻכָּה, *succah decorations*, within four handbreadths of the *s'chach*, so that it can be considered בָּטֵל, *secondary*, [lit. *neutralized*] to the *s'chach* and be regarded as part of it. We do not apply this regulation strictly to lamps or candelabra hung in the *succah* because the closer they are to the table the more illumination they will provide. Strictly speaking no decoration can invalidate as if it were a 'tent' unless it is four-handbreadths wide; therefore, low-hanging decorations of less than that width could not under any circumstances be considered an intervening tent. Nevertheless, as a precaution, *Maharil* ruled that all decorations (except for lamps) should be placed close to the *s'chach* (*Mishnah Berurah* ibid; *Chayei Adam* 146:36).

As explained in the commentary, in the view of *Tosafos* the mishnah invalidates only sheets whose purpose is to keep the *s'chach* from withering and falling down because such a sheet is used as *s'chach*. If, however, the sheet is used to prevent discomfort, either from the sun or from falling leaves, or if it is a decoration, it would not invalidate the *succah* as long as it is

[ד] **הִדְלָה** עָלֶיהָ אֶת־הַגֶּפֶן וְאֶת־הַדְּלַעַת
וְאֶת־הַקִּסוֹם וְסִכֵּךְ עַל־גַּבָּהּ
פְּסוּלָה. וְאִם הָיָה סִכּוּךְ הַרְבֵּה מֵהֶן, אוֹ שֶׁקְּצָצָן
כְּשֵׁרָה.
זֶה הַכְּלָל: כָּל־שֶׁהוּא מְקַבֵּל טֻמְאָה וְאֵין
גִּדּוּלוֹ מִן־הָאָרֶץ אֵין מְסַכְּכִים בּוֹ, וְכָל־דָּבָר

יד אברהם

posts, one at the head of the bed and one at its foot with a horizontal bar (or rope) connecting the tops of the two posts. A sheet draped over the horizontal pole and sloping down on either side, is not considered a tent halachically, because the peak does not have a level surface that is at least one handbreadth wide, the minimum dimension for the top of a tent or a house to be considered a 'roof.'

The slopes of the sheet are walls, not a roof. Since the sheet does not create a tent in this case, he is considered as dwelling solely under the s'chach of the succah (Rav; Tif. Yis.).

This law is stated here only in very general terms. Many other conditions are required before such a situation can be considered valid. See *Orach Chaim* 627:2; *Mishnah Berurah*, ibid; *Shaar HaTziyun*.

4.

הִדְלָה עָלֶיהָ — *If one raised onto it*

If one drew any of the following objects over the s'chach of a succah (Ran; Tos. Yom Tov).

אֶת־הַגֶּפֶן וְאֶת־הַדְּלַעַת וְאֶת־הַקִּסוֹם — *a grapevine, a gourd, or ivy,*

[Gourds and ivy grow on vines and can easily be drawn over a large area.]

וְסִכֵּךְ עַל־גַּבָּהּ — *and covered it* [i.e., the vine] *with s'chach,*

He first covered the succah with a vine and then placed valid s'chach over it (Rav; Tos. Yom Tov).

פְּסוּלָה. — *it is invalid.*

Anything still attached to the earth is not valid as s'chach. For the Scriptural source, see below s.v. מסככין בו (Rashi 11a; Rav; Tif. Yis.).

The reading of *Alfasi* and *R' Tam* is עַל גַּבָּן, *on top of them*. The implication is that the original covering of the succah was composed of *them* — i.e., the in-

eligible vine, gourd, and ivy mentioned earlier in the mishnah — and now valid s'chach was placed atop it. This being so, we may assume that the succah remains invalid only because it had originally been completed in an invalid manner, i.e., with s'chach that was still attached to the earth. But if the succah had been properly made and *afterward* was covered with vines, it would not become invalidated. This inference, however, is not compelling. The mishnah may well mean that one invalidates a succah covering it with attached vines whether or not the vines were emplaced before the s'chach (Tos. Yom Tov).

וְאִם הָיָה סִכּוּךְ הַרְבֵּה מֵהֶן, — *But if the s'chach exceeded them,*

— If the quantity of valid s'chach was greater than the amount of invalid s'chach: the vine, the gourd, or the ivy (Rav; Tif. Yis.).

within four handbreadths of the s'chach and so does not create a separate tent. Accordingly, *Magen Avraham* (Orach Chaim 629:19; 25; 640:4,8), notes if the wind is so strong as to blow out the lights in the succah and cause undue discomfort, or if it is raining so hard that the rain comes through the s'chach and ruins the food, one would ordinarily be exempt from the *mitzvah* of succah. In such instances, it is worthwhile to rely on *Tosafos'* view and spread a sheet under the s'chach (cf. *Mishnah Berurah*, ibid; *Chayei Adam* 146:37).

4. If one raised onto it a grapevine, a gourd, or ivy, and covered it with *s'chach*, it is invalid. But if the *s'chach* exceeded them, or if he detached them, it is valid.

This is the rule [regarding the validity of *s'chach*]: Whatever is susceptible to contamination or does not grow from the ground, we may not use for *s'chach*;

YAD AVRAHAM

אוֹ שֶׁקְּצָצָן — *or if he detached them,*

— He cut the vines from the ground — even if he did so after having laid them on the *succah (Rav).*

כְּשֵׁרָה. — *it is valid.*

[The *succah* is valid in either case: When the valid *s'chach* exceeds the non-valid *s'chach*, the *succah* is valid even if he does not detach the vines from the ground; or if the invalid *s'chach* exceeds the valid *s'chach*, the *succah* can be made valid by cutting the attached vines.]

If the *s'chach* exceeds the vines, one must mix the valid and invalid *s'chach* together so that the vines are not discernible. In that case, the abundant valid *s'chach* nullifies the smaller quantity of invalid *s'chach (Rav; Rashi* 11a; *Rama, Orach Chaim* 626:1).

However, as noted above in the comm. to mishnah 2, *Tosafos* hold that no intermingling is necessary if the valid *s'chach* is abundant enough to provide adequate coverage on its own. Only if the *s'chach* could not provide enough shade on its own would intermingling with the vines be necessary to validate the *succah (Tos. Yom Tov).*

In the latter case of the mishnah, after cutting the branches and vines, he must lift each vine or branch and set it down again as part of the *s'chach.* By so doing he is, in effect, putting down new, valid *s'chach* from scratch. The principle taught by this exegesis is תַּעֲשֶׂה וְלֹא מִן הֶעָשׂוּי, *you must* make [*the succah*], *but it may not come into being indirectly (Gem.* 11b). Thus, a *succah* must be valid *as constructed.* However, if it was not halachically acceptable as built, but

later had its status changed indirectly, it remains invalid. In our case, for example, the completed *succah* covered by attached vines was not valid. The subsequent severing of the vines made no physical change in the *succah* itself; the change was only an indirect one, extraneous to the building. The only recourse, therefore, is to lift the severed vines and replace them, thereby putting new, valid, *s'chach* on the *succah (Rav; Orach Chaim* 626:2).

זֶה הַכְּלָל: כָּל־שֶׁהוּא מְקַבֵּל טֻמְאָה — *This is the rule* [*regarding the validity of s'chach*]:*Whatever is susceptible to contamination*

[The concept of טֻמְאָה [*tumah*], *contamination,* is a spiritual one. A person, object, or food that is contaminated (*tamei*) can be disqualified for certain specific halachic functions and not for others. Our mishnah refers *not* to *s'chach* that has already become *tamei,* but to *s'chach* that *can* become *tamei.* As the mishnah will state, such *s'chach* is invalid.]

E.g., utensils, clothing, receptacles (*Tif. Yis.*).

[Food and drink, too, are invalid because they can become *tamei.* Materials can become *tamei* only if they have been processed into finished utensils and the like. Wood, therefore, can contract *tumah* only once it has been fashioned into a vessel, but not while it is still unfinished. Slats or bamboo, therefore, are commonly used as *s'chach.*]

וְאֵין גִּדּוּלוֹ מִן־הָאָרֶץ — *or does not grow from the ground,*

This would disqualify a hide, even if

שֶׁאֵינוֹ מְקַבֵּל טֻמְאָה וְגִדּוּלוֹ מִן־הָאָרֶץ, מְסַכְּכִין בּוֹ.

[ה] חֲבִילֵי קַשׁ וַחֲבִילֵי עֵצִים וַחֲבִילֵי זְרָדִין, אֵין מְסַכְּכִין בָּהֶן. וְכֻלָּן שֶׁהִתִּירָן כְּשֵׁרוֹת. וְכֻלָּן כְּשֵׁרוֹת לַדְּפָנוֹת.

יד אברהם

it has not yet been fashioned into a utensil or garment. Even though it is not susceptible to defilement in its raw state, its growth is not from the soil as is the growth of a tree. Also excluded are pieces of metal which have not been fashioned into utensils; though not susceptible to contamination, they do not grow. The same is true of earth or clay; although they *are* earth, they do not grow from it (*Tif. Yis.; Rama, Orach Chaim* 629:1).

אֵין מְסַכְּכִים בּוֹ, — *we may not use for s'chach;*

וְכָל־דָּבָר שֶׁאֵינוֹ מְקַבֵּל טֻמְאָה — *but whatever is not susceptible to contamination*

To be eligible as *s'chach*, a substance must be incapable of becoming *tamei*. Accordingly, such items as wooden utensils, flaxen, or cotton wearing apparel, mats etc. may not be used as *s'chach*. Even though they grow from the soil, they are not fit for *s'chach* because, as finished utensils, they are susceptible to *tumah* (*Rav*).

וְגִדּוּלוֹ מִן־הָאָרֶץ, — *and grows from the ground,*

It derives its nourishment from the soil through its roots. This excludes animals — although they derive nourishment from the earth's produce, they do not grow directly from the earth (*Tos. Yom Tov*).

מְסַכְּכִין בּוֹ. — *we may use for s'chach.*

These requirements are derived from Deuteronomy 16:13: חַג הַסֻּכֹּת תַּעֲשֶׂה לְךָ...בְּאָסְפְּךָ מִגָּרְנְךָ וּמִיִּקְבֶךָ, *A festival of Succos shall you make...with your gathering from your threshing floor and from your winepress.* The Talmud infers: What is it that you gather after the grapes are pressed and the harvest is threshed? The leftover husks and stubble, and empty vines. Thus, you make the *succah* [i.e., *s'chach*] from any material that has the characteristics of the above — it grows from the ground like them, and, like them, it does not become *tamei* (*Gem.* 12a; *Rav; Orach Chaim* 629:1).

5.

חֲבִילֵי קַשׁ וְחֲבִילֵי עֵצִים — *Bundles of straw, bundles of wood,*

They are tied together at both ends to facilitate carrying them (*Rama* 629:15).

וְחֲבִילֵי זְרָדִין, — *or bundles of fresh cane,*

This refers to a type of cane which is eaten by cattle when fresh, and is used for firewood when dry (*Rav*).

[All the above types of bundles share a characteristic: They are commonly

used for kindling. When that is the owner's intention, they are left to dry so that they will burn better. As we shall see below, this is the crucial factor in determining whether they are valid for *s'chach*.]

אֵין מְסַכְּכִין בָּהֶן. — *may not be used* [lit. *they should not use*] for *s'chach.*

Even though these materials meet the Torah's requirements for *s'chach* (mish-

1
5

but whatever is not susceptible to contamination and
grows from the ground, we may use for s'chach.

5. **B**undles of straw, bundles of wood, or bundles of fresh cane, may not be used for s'chach; but all of these are valid when they are untied. All of them are valid for the walls.

YAD AVRAHAM

nah 4), the Sages forbade their use to preclude the possiblity of a certain contingency. A man may decide to place his bundle on top of the *succah* to dry out in the sun for use later as fuel. If he later changes his mind and decides to leave his bundle as s'chach, it would not be valid because it would fall under the category of תַּעֲשֶׂה וְלֹא מִן הֶעָשׂוּי, *you must make [the succah], but it may not come into being indirectly* (see above, mishnah 4). Since his original intention in placing the bundle had not been for shade, the *s'chach* was not 'made' by him. It was only later that he changed his plans and designated the bundle for s'chach — but then no act was done to make it so. In order to avoid such an eventuality, the Sages banned the use of such bundles even if they were originally set down as s'chach (*Rav*).

Should one wish to use such materials, it is sufficient merely to untie the bundle.

Tosefos Yom Tov adds that before the absolute Rabbinic prohibition, such bundles could have been acceptable had they been placed on the *succah* for use as *shade* (but not for *s'chach*) according to Beis Hillel in mishnah 1. See *comm.* there.

Even if one used them as s'chach, in ignorance or defiance of the Rabbinic prohibition, they do not become valid after the fact, but always remain invalid (*Tos.* 12b; see *Mishnah Berurah* 40 and *Shaar HaTziyun* 61 to *Orach Chaim* 629:15).

The Sages' ban applies only to bundles that are usually intended for drying out. But a bundle of less than twenty-five pieces (e.g., twigs or husks) is not considered a 'bundle' for the purpose of this decree because such a bundle is not meant for drying out, so it is valid as s'chach in the first resort (*Tosafos* from *Yerushalmi* 12a; *Orach Chaim* 629:15).

The same applies to a cluster of twigs attached to a branch. Even though the outside ends are tied together, it is permissible to use it as s'chach without any need to break it apart because the Sages did not consider this a bundle commonly left for drying out (*Gem.* 13a; *Orach Chaim* 629:15; *Mishnah Berurah*).

וְכֻלָּן שֶׁהֱתִירָן כְּשֵׁרוֹת. — *but all of these are valid when they are untied* [lit. *when he untied them are valid*].

If he originally set the bundles in place as *s'chach* and then untied them, they are valid and he is not required to lift and replace them, even though they were Rabbinically invalid as emplaced (see comm. to mishnah 4). The reason is that the bundle is essentially valid s'chach, according to Torah law. What invalidates it is a Rabbinical ban. [In this respect they are unlike vines (mishnah 4) which must be lifted and replaced after being cut.] It is therefore sufficient for him to untie them and thereby remove the Rabbinical objection.

Only if he placed them on the *succah* in order to dry them, and then changed his mind and untied them for use as s'chach, do they remain invalid until he lifts them and sets them back in place. This was explained above s.v. אֵין מְסַכְּכִין בָּהֶן (*Orach Chaim* 629:17 and *Mishnah Berurah*).

וְכֻלָּן — *All of them*
All the aforementioned classifications

[17] **THE MISHNAH** / SUCCAH

[ו] מְסַכְּכִין בַּנְּסָרִים; דִּבְרֵי רַבִּי יְהוּדָה. וְרַבִּי מֵאִיר אוֹסֵר.

נָתַן עָלֶיהָ נֶסֶר שֶׁהוּא רָחָב אַרְבָּעָה טְפָחִים, כְּשֵׁרָה, וּבִלְבַד שֶׁלֹּא יִישַׁן תַּחְתָּיו.

יד אברהם

Torah's use of the word סֻכָּה (see comm. to mishnah 1), there is a basic difference between s'chach and walls. The word succah refers primarily to s'chach since the words are etymologically related. The exegetical reference to walls is based on allusion rather than literal definition; therefore the Scriptural reference to types of materials is taken as referring exclusively to s'chach, there are no limitations on the material eligible for use as walls (Rashi).

which are not valid as s'chach: A) attached to the ground; B) not growing from the soil; C) susceptible to tumah; and D) bundles (Rav; Tif. Yis.).

כְּשֵׁרוֹת לַדְּפָנוֹת. — are valid for the walls.
For the Scriptural word סֻכָּה [succah] primarily implies the סְכָךְ [s'chach], covering. Thus all limitations on acceptable materials (see mishnah 4) refer to the roof and not to the walls (Rav).
Although laws regarding the walls are derived from variations in the

6.

According to the guidelines laid down at the conclusion of mishnah 5, any sort of lumber would be acceptable as s'chach, for it grows from the ground and cannot become tamei in its unfinished state. That being the case, one could conceivably cover his succah with a sheet of wood four feet by eight feet. Indeed, according to Torah law, such s'chach would be valid, but the Rabbis banned the use of 'wide' boards because of גְּזֵרַת תִּקְרָה, a decree [lest a succah appear to have] a roof, like any ordinary year-round house. If such materials were permissible as s'chach some people might erroneously reason that their wooden roofs at home were equally valid as s'chach. The width of the boards covered by the ban is the subject of our mishnah.

מְסַכְּכִין בַּנְּסָרִים; דִּבְרֵי רַבִּי יְהוּדָה. וְרַבִּי מֵאִיר אוֹסֵר. — We may cover the succah with boards; these are the words of R' Yehudah. But R' Meir forbids it.
Shmuel explains (Gem. 14a) that both R' Yehudah and R' Meir agree that a board four handbreadths wide or more is not valid. The Sages banned the use of such boards מִפְּנֵי גְּזֵרַת תִּקְרָה, because of a decree [lest the succah appear to have a] roof, since such boards resemble the ceiling boards of a house, and one might see no difference between eating under the roofing of his house and that of the succah. But eating at home is clearly forbidden since the mitzvah is to leave home and live in a succah. Once the Sages prohibited the use of such boards, they applied the ban even if the boards were laid on edge so that they

covered only a narrow surface; the boards may not be used as s'chach in any manner. When boards are less than three handbreadths wide, both tannaim agree that they are valid for they are regarded as no more significant than mere sticks.
The only argument between the tannaim, continues the Gemara, is over boards between three and four handbreadths wide. R' Yehudah permits them because their size is not significant enough to cause fear that a man many decide to eat under his house ceiling. R' Meir forbids using them for s'chach because he considers their width to be significant.
R' Meir (Gem. 14a) offers the following argument in favor of his view: If the board were not there and there were an empty space

6. **W**e may cover the *succah* with boards; these are the words of R' Yehudah. But R' Meir forbids it.

If one placed atop it a board that is four handbreadths wide, [the succah] is valid, except that one may not sleep under [the board].

YAD AVRAHAM

of three handbreadths in its place, it would be forbidden to sit in that part of the *succah*. Only regarding an empty space of less than three handbreadths does the halachah say that the valid areas of *s'chach* on either side of the empty space are considered לָבוּד, *united*, with the result that the empty space is considered to be non-existent (see comm. to mishnah 1 s.v. וְשָׁאֵין לָה שָׁלֹשׁ דְּפָנוֹת). Since our board is three handbreadths wide, it *does* divide the *succah*, and has significance. Therefore the Sages found it worthy of a ban (*Rashi* 14a; *Rav*).

R' Yehudah argues that the general rule is that the minimum dimension for an area to qualify as a 'place' is four handbreadths. For example, to be considered a רְשׁוּת הַיָּחִיד, *private area*, with regard to the laws of the Sabbath, an enclosed space must be four handbreadths by four handbreadths (see *Shabbos* 5a). Therefore only a board four handbreadths wide is significant enough to be banned for use on a *succah* (ibid.).

According to the amora Rav (*Gem.* 14a), the dispute involves only boards at least four handbreadths wide; R' Meir forbids and R' Yehudah permits them; but all agree that narrower boards are permitted.

The halachah follows R' Yehudah according to Shmuel's view (*Rav*).

R' Yosef Karo states that it is our custom not to use boards for covering the *succah* even if they are less than four handbreadths wide (*Orach Chaim* 629:18), because one might cover the *succah* in a way that would allow no rain to penetrate (*Mishnah Berurah*, ibid. quoting *Sefer Mitzvos Kattan*). Others hold that smaller boards are prohibited, because nowadays it is customary for builders to make floors and ceilings from boards much narrower than the four handbreadth width that was common in Talmudic times (*op. cit.* 629:3).

נָתַן עָלֶיהָ נֶסֶר שָׁהוּא רָחָב אַרְבָּעָה
טְפָחִים —*If one placed atop it a board that is four handbreadths wide,*

[Since this clause is intended to inform us that even invalid *s'chach* does not necessarily disqualify the entire *succah*, it follows that the *s'chach* under discussion here is invalid.]

According to Shmuel's opinion (see *comm.* s.v. מסכבין) this clause of the mishnah is held by all, for even R' Yehudah agrees that a four handbreadth board is invalid. The *Gemara* (14a) comments that according to Rav's view, this clause is only according to R' Meir, but such a board is valid *s'chach* according to R' Yehudah.

כְּשֵׁרָה, — *it [the succah] is valid,*

Even though a four handbreadth board is not valid, that applies only to the board itself, but it need not disqualify the rest of the *s'chach*. If the board runs across the middle of the *succah*, it may or may not disqualify the entire *succah*, depending upon the circumstances as explained in detail further.

Rashi explains that in our mishnah, the board is placed within four cubits of one of the walls. The *succah* is valid because of the rule allowing us to regard invalid *s'chach* (up to a maximum of four cubits) placed adjacent to walls as extensions of those walls. Accordingly, the walls are regarded as bending and acting like an overhanging roof as set forth in mishnah 10. In our case, the entire width, from the wall until the end of the board, is regarded as an overhanging wall — even if part of that area is covered by valid *s'chach*. For example, adjacent to the wall are two cubits of *s'chach* and then a one-cubit board, the entire three-cubit length is regarded as an overhanging wall. This rule, aptly named דּוֹפֶן עֲקוּמָה, *bent wall*, was trans-

[ז] תִּקְרָה שֶׁאֵין עָלֶיהָ מַעֲזִיבָה — רַבִּי
יְהוּדָה אוֹמֵר: בֵּית שַׁמַּאי
אוֹמְרִים, מְפַקְפֵּק וְנוֹטֵל אַחַת מִבֵּינָתַיִם; וּבֵית

יד אברהם

mitted orally at Sinai by God to Moses (הֲלָכָה לְמֹשֶׁה מִסִּינַי).

The foregoing is true only in a *suc-cah* large enough to retain the minimum area of seven handbreadths square even after the space from the board to the ad-jacent wall is subtracted from the total area of the *succah*. Since the validity of the *succah* depends on the board being considered an extension of the wall, it follows that the area beneath it is not part of the *succah* area — it is covered by a wall rather than *s'chach* (*Orach Chaim* 632:1).

[If the board is placed over the middle of the *succah* (i.e., more than four cubits away from the walls), the *succah* may be invalidated. If the board runs across the full width of the *succah*, it must be con-sidered a barrier between the valid *s'chach* and the walls. Thus if a *succah* had three walls, and a board was placed perpendicular to its middle wall and parallel to the two flanking walls (see diagram), the *succah* has, in effect, been divided into two separate structures. The *s'chach* on either side of the

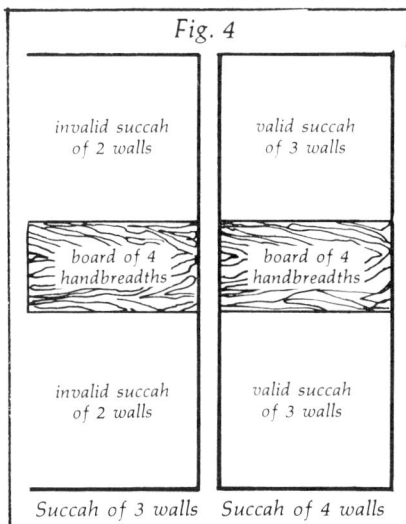

Fig. 4

board is connected to only two walls, thus invalidating both halves as *succos* (see mishnah 1). This would not apply to a four-walled *succah*, for the valid *s'chach* would still be connected to three walls, and would be valid (see *Mishnah Berurah* 632:2). If the board in discus-sion were less than four handbreadths wide there is no problem. Since such boards are halachically valid *s'chach* (see above) surely one may sleep and eat beneath them.

וּבִלְבַד שֶׁלֹּא יִישַׁן תַּחְתָּיו. — *except that one may not sleep under [the board].*

Although the rest of the *succah* re-mains valid, the board is of significant enough size to be declared a place unto itself, not to be considered part of the *s'chach* (*Mishnah Berurah* 632:6).

[Since the board itself is invalid *s'chach*, the area beneath it cannot be included in the *succah*.]

Just as one may not sleep under this board, so may he not eat, drink, or do any other act which must be done in the *succah*. The reason the mishnah speci-fies sleeping is because snacking is generally permitted outside the *succah*, whereas even napping must be done in the *succah* (*Tos. Yom Tov*; see mishnah 2:4; *Gem.* 26a; *Orach Chaim* 639:2).

[It is not fully clear what the main thrust of the mishnah is. The purpose cannot be to teach that invalid *s'chach* does not disqualify the entire *succah*, for this is true only in cir-cumstances not specified in this mishnah. Besides, this is accorded a much fuller treat-ment in mishnah 10. One cannot argue that our mishnah teaches that the invalidation of boards, being only Rabbinic, is less stringent than Scripturally invalid *s'chach*, and would not disqualify the entire *succah* under *any* circumstance, because: A) No commentators make such a distinction; they understand the mishnah to apply only to specific in-stances as outlined in the commentary; B) Such a distinction would contradict the codes (see *Orach Chaim* 629:13 and 632:1)

7. A roof that has no plaster on it — R' Yehudah says: Beis Shammai say one loosens them and removes every other board; but Beis Hillel say, he

YAD AVRAHAM

which do not differentiate between Scriptural and Rabbinic invalidations (see *Magid Mishneh* and *Kessef Mishnah* to *Hilchos Succah* 5:7; 3). *Mishnah Berurah (Sha'ar HaTziyun* 632:1) adduces a passage in *Gemara* proving that no such distinction exists.

It would seem, then, that the main point of our mishnah is the clause *except that one*

may not sleep under it! It is as if the mishnah said, *If he placed atop it a board that is four handbreadths wide* [even though the *succah* is valid, nevertheless] *one may not sleep under it.* The mishnah chose to make this point here to teach us that even boards, though their disqualification is only Rabbinic, are not considered part of the *s'chach*, and may not be slept under.]

7.

Having discussed (in mishnah 6) the laws of using individual boards for *s'chach*, the mishnah turns to the problem of how to convert a roof made of such planks into valid *s'chach*. Some authorities *(Rambam, Hilchos Succah* 5:8; *Ran; Ritva* and others) maintain that the planks under discussion in this mishnah are not of sufficient breadth to be disqualified as individual boards under the guidelines set forth in the previous mishnah — i.e., they are (at least) less than four handbreadths wide according to Shmuel whose view is adopted as halachah.

These authorities argue that it would be illogical to conceive that mishnah 6 disqualifies an individual board while our mishnah validates a board of the *same* width if it is part of a roof. Our mishnah, therefore, must speak of narrower boards.

Though individually they are not wide enough, these boards would nevertheless fall under the prohibition of the previous mishnah. For these boards, as part of a bona fide roof, should be disqualified as *s'chach* for the same reason used above to bar wider boards: lest one sit under the roof of his house. There is a further reason to disqualify the roofing boards of our mishnah. They were put down not for *s'chach*, but for roofing. Thus an *ex post facto* attempt to use them for *s'chach* should be forbidden as an indirect validation after the construction as in mishnah 4 [תַּעֲשֶׂה וְלֹא מִן הֶעָשׂוּי]. The discussion in the mishnah centers around which steps are efficacious to remove both of these disqualifications — the Torah injunction against indirectly made *s'chach*, and the Rabbinic one against boards (גְּזֵרַת תִּקְרָה).[1]

תִּקְרָה — *A roof*
Constructed of boards or planks *(Rav)*.

שֶׁאֵין עָלֶיהָ מַעֲזִיבָה— *that has no plaster on it—*
The boards that make up the roof have not yet been covered with a mixture of plaster [and pebbles *(Rama, Orach Chaim* 631:10)], the usual

method of completing a roof *(Rav; Tif. Yis.)*.

[The owner wishes to make the necessary adjustments and alter this roof into valid *s'chach*.]

רַבִּי יְהוּדָה אוֹמֵר: — *R' Yehudah says:*
[In R' Yehudah's view Beis Shammai and Beis Hillel disagree about which steps must be taken to turn the roof

---

1. Many authorities (among them *Rashi, Tosafos,* and *Rosh)* take an opposite view. Planks of less than four handbreadths would not fall under the ban against boards [גְּזֵרַת תִּקְרָה] even when they had been part of a roof. Thus the invalid planks of our mishnah would be at least four handbreadths wide. We will endeavor to present this view as fully as possible in footnotes. Our primary interpretation, however, will be the one presented above because it is simpler and because (according to *Tosefos Yom Tov)* it is adopted by *Rav,* the traditional commentator on Mishnah.

הִלֵּל אוֹמְרִים, מְפַקְפֵּק אוֹ נוֹטֵל אַחַת
מִבֵּינָתַיִם.

רַבִּי מֵאִיר אוֹמֵר: נוֹטֵל אַחַת מִבֵּינָתַיִם וְאֵין
מְפַקְפֵּק.

יד אברהם

boards into *s'chach*, and he presents their dispute.]

בֵּית שַׁמַּאי אוֹמְרִים, מְפַקְפֵּק — *Beis Shammai say one loosens them*

He frees the boards from their nails and moves them (*Rav; Rashi*).

Rosh (see *Korban Nesanel* 1) and *Tur* (631) mention only removing the nails. *Aruch* (s.v. פקפ[2]), who relates this verb to the concept of freeing, probably shares this opinion. The versions of *Rambam's* commentary that are printed in the Talmud stipulate both movement and removal (as noted by *Mishnah Berurah* 631:24) of the nails, but the authoritative *Kafih* version (based on a manuscript assumed to be in *Rambam's* own hand) mentions only removal of the nails (as noted by the translator). (*Rambam's* words in *Hilchos Succah* 5:8 are ambiguous). *Bach* (*Tur* 631) suggests that even *Rashi* means that either removal of nails or movement is sufficient. Our translation — *loosens* — reflects what appears to be the more widely held view.

Probably even the view that requires movement also does not maintain that this is included in the translation of מְפַקְפֵּק, but felt that logic requires an action which can be construed as 'making new *s'chach*', i.e., removing the planks and replacing it in the form of *s'chach*. Merely removing the nails, though surely an action, cannot be construed as 'making *s'chach*.'

This philological problem has halachic ramifications because Beis Hillel, whose opinion is the accepted one, rule that מְפַקְפֵּק is sufficient. *Mishnah Berurah* (631:24) rules that both removal of nails and movement are needed to remove the disqualification of 'indirectly-made *s'chach*' (תַּעֲשֶׂה וְלֹא מִן הֶעָשׂוּי).

וְנוֹטֵל אַחַת מִבֵּינָתַיִם; — *and removes every other board* [lit. one from between two]; He is to replace every other plank

with valid *s'chach* (*Rashi* 15a).

The *Gemara* (15a) concludes that Beis Shammai do not require both loosening the board and taking 'one from between' to validate the *succah* as the mishnah seems to imply. Rather, Beis Shammai mean to say that even if one has loosened the boards, his act is of no avail unless he also replaces every other board with *s'chach*. Only the latter course of action contributes to the validity of the *succah*; loosening the boards is not necessary where one has 'taken one from between.'

In R' Yehudah's view, Beis Shammai hold that though lifting the boards would correct the problem of indirectly-made *s'chach*, it is not sufficient to remove the disqualification based on the fear that one might consider an ordinary roof equally acceptable (גְּזֵירַת תִּקְרָה; see mishnah 6). Therefore Beis Shammai maintain that one must replace every other board with *s'chach*. This action by itself validates the *succah*: By replacing every other board with *s'chach*, the disqualification of ready-made *s'chach* is removed (cf. *Ran*). The Rabbinic ban against boards is also removed thereby for the ban applies only so long as the remaining planks can be considered part of a 'roof.' The removal of every other plank surely removes the remaining planks from the category of a 'roof.' [This is according to the view that each board is less than four handbreadths, so that no remaining board can be forbidden of itself] (see *Milchamos*).[1]

וּבֵית הִלֵּל אוֹמְרִים, מְפַקְפֵּק אוֹ נוֹטֵל אַחַת מִבֵּינָתַיִם. — *but Beis Hillel say, he*

---

1. According to *Rashi's* view that the planks discussed here are four handbreadths wide, another rationale for this remedy is needed, because even after replacing every other board, the remaining ones are still wide enough to be disqualified even had they not been part of a

1
7

[either] loosens [them] or removes every other one.
R' Meir says: He removes every other one but
does not loosen [them].

YAD AVRAHAM

[either] loosens [them] or removes every other one.

[Either loosening or replacing is sufficient.]

According to Beis Hillel, either act suffices not only to remove the disqualification of ready-made *s'chach* (a point admitted by Beis Shammai), but also to remove the prohibition against using boards. Removing every second plank is efficacious for the same reason cited above for Beis Shammai. However, Beis Hillel add that merely loosening the planks removes them from the category of a 'roof' since a permanent roof would surely have to be secured, thus the loosened planks revert to the status of simple boards, which may be used for *s'chach* if they are less than four

handbreadths wide.[1]

רַבִּי מֵאִיר אוֹמֵר: נוֹטֵל אַחַת מִבֵּינָתַיִם וְאֵין מְפַקְפֵּק. — *R' Meir says: He removes every other one but does not loosen [them].*

R' Meir holds that both Beis Shammai and Beis Hillel agree that lifting each board does not suffice, but that every other board must be replaced by *s'chach*. In this, R' Meir follows his view in mishnah 6 that boards are not acceptable as *s'chach*, even when freshly laid *(Rav; cf. Gem.).*

The halachah follows R' Yehudah *(Rav; Orach Chaim* 631:9). However, as mentioned in comm. to mishnah 6, it is not our custom to use boards as *s'chach* except in extenuating circumstances *(Mishnah Berurah* 631:26).

roof. *Rashi* (15a s.v. רבי מאיר אומר) holds that since every second plank was replaced with valid *s'chach*, it can be assumed that most (or half; see mishnah 8) of the *succah* is covered with valid *s'chach* (this assumption is made in a different instance; see *Gem.* 18a). As a consequence, the *succah* is valid in Beis Shammai's view, but one would be permitted to eat only under the area covered by the *s'chach*, and not under the remaining boards.

1. In *Rashi's* view, Beis Hillel allow the use of the loosened boards even if they are four handbreadths wide although they ordinarily forbid such boards. *Rashi* (s.v. בביטולי תקרה) explains that planks originally forming a roof are treated more favorably than ordinary boards. By loosening his roof-planks to comply with the Torah disqualification against ready-made *s'chach*, one demonstrates that he is conversant with this relatively obscure law. That being the case, he surely would be familiar with the prohibition against 'sitting under the roof of a house,' thus effectively removing the basis for the Rabbinic prohibition against using boards *(Mishnah Berurah* 631:25).

R' Yosef Karo *(Orach Chaim* 631:9) cites both views but, by referring to *Ramban* as 'some say,' seems to lean toward *Rashi*.

However, *Mishnah Berurah* (631:26) seems to assume that one should abide with the more stringent *(Ramban's)* ruling. According to *Rashi's* interpretation that the mishnah refers to four-handbreath boards, what would Beis Hillel hold if one removed every other board, but did not loosen the remaining ones? *Bach* (*Tur Orach Chaim* 637) argues that the same reasoning they apply to 'loosening' should apply here too. If so, one may sit even under the *remaining* planks; so that Beis Hillel and Beis Shammai who agree that the *succah* is valid, disagree only upon the extent of its validity: According to Beis Shammai, one may sit only under the *s'chach* replacing the removed boards, whereas Beis Hillel permit use of the entire *succah*.

Ritva as well as *Vilna Gaon* (631:13) assume that removal of every second board does not validate the remaining boards according to Beis Hillel any more than according to the Beis Shammai (see *Mishnah Berurah* 631:26). All concur, however, that in the interpretation of *Ramban's* school that the planks are less than four handbreadths wide (see the first view given in the *comm.*), removal of every second plank validates the remaining planks (see *Mishnah Berurah, ibid.).*

[ח] **הַמְקָרֶה** סִכְּתוֹ בַּשְׁפוּדִין אוֹ בַּאֲרוּכוֹת
הַמִּטָּה, אִם יֶשׁ־רֶוַח בֵּינֵיהֶן
כְּמוֹתָן, כְּשֵׁרָה.

הַחוֹטֵט בַּגָּדִישׁ לַעֲשׂוֹת בּוֹ סֻכָּה, אֵינָהּ סֻכָּה.

[ט] **הַמְשַׁלְשֵׁל** דְּפָנוֹת מִלְמַעְלָה לְמַטָּה,
אִם גָּבוֹהַ מִן־הָאָרֶץ
שְׁלֹשָׁה טְפָחִים, פְּסוּלָה; מִלְמַטָּה לְמַעְלָה, אִם
גָּבוֹהַ מִן־הָאָרֶץ עֲשָׂרָה טְפָחִים, כְּשֵׁרָה.

יד אברהם

8.

הַמְקָרֶה סִכְּתוֹ בַּשְׁפוּדִין — *If one roofs his succah with spits*

Atop his *succah*, someone laid out a framework of spits upon which he will pile *s'chach* (Rashi 15a).

Metal spits are invalid as *s'chach* because they do not grow from the ground [and because they are utensils which are susceptible to *tumah*] (*Rav*).

But wooden spits may be used, because since they are not receptacles [כְּלִי קִיבּוּל], they are not susceptible to *tumah*. It is a cardinal rule that wooden utensils, unlike utensils of other materials, do not become *tamei* unless they have the facility to 'contain' something (*Magen Avraham* 629:1; see other sources cited in *Sha'ar HaTziyun* 629:2). *Tiferes Yisrael*, however, maintains that even wooden spits may not be used as *s'chach*, because they can become *tamei* under the Rabbinic rule that any wooden utensil which serves a person through direct contact is susceptible to *tumah* even if it 'is not a container'; a spit is sometimes leaned upon by the user. Similar reasons are given by other authorities (see *Sha'ar Hatziyun ibid.*). However, *Rambam (comm.)* assumes that the mishnah refers to a metal spit.

אוֹ בַּאֲרוּכוֹת הַמִּטָּה — *or (with) bed boards* [lit. *long ones of the bed*],

These are the two wooden boards that

run the entire length of the bed and they are disqualified because they are utensils. Though such boards are not considered utensils for purposes of *tumah* unless they are part of a bed,[1] they are nevertheless invalid for *s'chach*, even when removed from the bed; once they have lost their validity as part of a bed, they remain invalid. Accordingly, even broken utensils are invalid (*Gem.* 15b; *Rambam, Hilchos Succah* 5:2; *Orach Chaim* 629:2; cf. *Rambam Comm.*; *Rav*; *Tos. Yom Tov*, and *Tos. R' Akiva*).

אִם יֶשׁ־רֶוַח בֵּינֵיהֶן כְּמוֹתָן, — *if the space between them is equal to themselves,*

[The *s'chach*-covered space left between the spits or bedboards is equal to the space covered by the spits or bedboards themselves, with the result that at least half the *succah* is covered by valid *s'chach*.]

כְּשֵׁרָה. — *it is valid.*

But the spits or headboards must not occupy any one contiguous space measuring four handbreadths (*Tif. Yis.*; *Orach Chaim* 631:8).

Rama (ibid.) points out that in the case of a small *succah* measuring only the minimum

1. An assembled bed, is susceptible to *tumah*. Though פְּשׁוּטֵי כְלֵי עֵץ, *flat wooden utensils* (i.e., having no receptacle) are not susceptible to tumah as a general rule, a bed is an exception, because it falls within the special category of utensils used for sitting or sleeping [מִדְרָס], (see *Succah* 20a; *Bava Kamma* 25b; see also *Mishnah Megillah*, preface to 1:7, ArtScroll ed.).

8. **I**f one roofs his *succah* with spits or bed boards, if the space between them is equal to themselves, it is valid.

If one hollowed out a haystack to make a *succah* inside it, it is not a *succah*.

9. **I**f one suspends the walls from above downwards, if [they are] three handbreadths above the ground, it is invalid; from below upwards, if it reaches a height of ten handbreadths from the ground, it is valid.

YAD AVRAHAM

size of seven handbreadths, the aggregate of the area covered by the spits should be less than three handbreadths, to conform with the rule outlined in *Orach Chaim* 632:1.

Theoretically the *succah* should be valid if, as stated, the spits and the air spaces are equal. But as a practical matter there will be an airspace between the *s'chach* and the spits, with the consequence that the area covered by valid *s'chach* is less than that under the spits. However, the valid *s'chach* can be placed diagonally across the spits — [(or packed tightly between them; see *Beur Halachah* 631:8)], thus eliminating all air space. Then the *succah* is valid even if the gaps and spits are exactly equal (*Gem.* 15b according to the consensus of commentators, *Orach Chaim* 631:8).

Although *Rambam* (*Comm.*; *Hilchos Succah* 5:16) rules that if the gaps and the spits

are equal, the *succah* is not valid, and *Rav* interprets the mishnah like *Rambam*, *Shulchan Aruch* (631:8) rules that if the gaps are exactly equal the *succah* is valid.

הַחוֹטֵט בְּגָדִישׁ לַעֲשׂוֹת בּוֹ סֻכָּה, — *If one hollowed out a haystack to make a succah inside it,*

He removed the straw from within, working from the bottom toward the top, until he had hollowed out a space large enough for a valid *succah* (*Rav*; *Tif. Yis.*).

אֵינָה סֻכָּה. — *it is not a succah.*

Although the top layer of hay is an acceptable material for *s'chach*, the *succah* is not valid because it was not emplaced originally for the purpose of shade; thus it is indirectly made *s'chach* [תַּעֲשֶׂה וְלֹא מִן הֶעָשׂוּי] (*Rav*; *Tif. Yis.*; *Gem.* 12a; *Orach Chaim* 635).

9.

הַמְשַׁלְשֵׁל דְּפָנוֹת מִלְמַעְלָה לְמַטָּה, — *If one suspends the walls from above downwards,*

He wove or plaited the *succah* walls working his way downwards from the *s'chach* (*Rav*; *Rashi*; *Tif. Yis.*).

אִם גָּבוֹהַּ מִן־הָאָרֶץ שְׁלֹשָׁה טְפָחִים, — *if [they are] three handbreadths above the ground,*

[If the bottom of the wall is three or more handbreadths above the ground.]

פְּסוּלָה; — *it is invalid;*

To fulfill the halachic definition of a 'wall,' the partition must be sufficient to prevent entry beneath it. Since the three-handbreadth gap between the bottom of the wall and the ground is large enough to permit the passage of goats, it lacks the halachic status of a partition (*Rashi* 16a; *Rav*).

מִלְמַטָּה לְמַעְלָה, — *from below upwards,*

[If he is building the *succah* walls from the ground up.]

אִם גָּבוֹהַּ מִן־הָאָרֶץ עֲשָׂרָה טְפָחִים, — *if it*

רַבִּי יוֹסֵי אוֹמֵר: כְּשֵׁם שֶׁמִּלְּמַטָּה לְמַעְלָה עֲשָׂרָה טְפָחִים, כָּךְ מִלְּמַעְלָה לְמַטָּה עֲשָׂרָה טְפָחִים.

הִרְחִיק אֶת־הַסְּכוּךְ מִן הַדְּפָנוֹת שְׁלֹשָׁה טְפָחִים פְּסוּלָה.

[יז] **בַּיִת** שֶׁנִּפְחַת וְסִכֵּךְ עַל־גַּבָּיו, אִם יֵשׁ מִן־ הַכֹּתֶל לַסְּכוּךְ אַרְבַּע אַמּוֹת, פְּסוּלָה. וְכֵן חָצֵר שֶׁהִיא מֻקֶּפֶת אַכְסַדְרָה.

יד אברהם

reaches a height of ten handbreadths from the ground,

[This is the minimum height for a partition in halachah (see mishnah 1).]

Orach Chaim (630:9) applies this situation even if the actual wall is only a bit larger than seven handbreadths, but begins within three handbreadths from the ground. Thus the principles of lavud (see 1:1 s.v. ושאין לה) and gud asik (see below) are utilized.

כְּשֵׁרָה. — it is valid.

This is true even if the walls do not reach the s'chach. If they are directly under the s'chach, even though there is a large gap (there are no maximum limits) from the top of the wall to the s'chach, the succah is valid. We rely on the principle גּוּד אָסִיק, gud asik (lit. pull and bring up), according to which the walls are seen as stretching upwards until the s'chach. This principle was tranmitted orally to Moses on Sinai [הֲלָכָה וְלְמֹשֶׁה מִסִּינַי] (Gem. 6b; Ritva).

If, however, the wall was not directly below the s'chach, but off to the side, the succah is still valid if the wall is within three handbreadths of the s'chach (Rav; Tif. Yis.; Orach Chaim 630:9).

רַבִּי יוֹסֵי אוֹמֵר: כְּשֵׁם שֶׁמִּלְּמַטָּה לְמַעְלָה עֲשָׂרָה טְפָחִים, — R' Yose says: Just as from below upwards ten handbreadths [suffice],

[It is considered a valid wall even

though there may be a gap larger than three handbreadths from the top of the partition to the s'chach.]

כָּךְ מִלְּמַעְלָה לְמַטָּה עֲשָׂרָה טְפָחִים. — so from above downwards ten handbreadths [suffice].

Even though there may be a gap greater than three handbreadths from the ground to the bottom of the suspended wall, R' Yose considers it valid as long as the wall is sufficiently long (as in the case of 'from below upwards'). The halachah, however, does not follow R' Yose (Rav).

The point in contention here is whether a suspended partition [וּמְחִצָּה תְּלוּיָה] can be considered as enclosing an area. R' Yose holds that it does, and therefore validates this succah, but the other sages disagree with him. They hold that since sheep can freely enter beneath the wall, it cannot be considered to act as a partition for the area.

הִרְחִיק אֶת־הַסְּכוּךְ מִן־הַדְּפָנוֹת שְׁלֹשָׁה טְפָחִים — If one moved the s'chach three handbreadths away from the walls

This does not refer to a vertical gap (as above), but to a horizontal gap between the s'chach and the wall (Rav; Tif. Yis.).

פְּסוּלָה. — it is invalid.

In a succah of three walls, an air space of three handbreadths, running between the s'chach and the wall along the entire length of the succah, invalidates it. The gap separates the s'chach from the wall and thus dis-

1
10

R' Yose says: Just as from below upwards ten handbreadths [suffice], so from above downwards ten handbreadths [suffice].

If one moved the *s'chach* three handbreadths away from the walls it is invalid.

10. **A** house that was breached and he placed *s'chach* over it, if there are four cubits from the wall to the *s'chach*, it is invalid. The same [applies to] a courtyard that is surrounded by a portico.

YAD AVRAHAM

qualifies it as a *succah* wall, thus leaving the *succah* with only two walls *(Orach Chaim* 632:2 and *Rama).*

Turei Zahav explains why we are stricter with space, where a gap of three handbreadths invalidates a *succah,* than with

boards or invalid *s'chach,* where less than four handbreadths does not disqualify the *succah* (1:6). An empty space is more easily recognized by the eye as a separation in the *s'chach* than non-valid *s'chach* which is surrounded by valid *s'chach (Orach Chaim* 632:4).

10.

בַּיִת שֶׁנִּפְחַת וְסִכֵּךְ עַל־גַּבָּיו, — *A house that was breached and he placed s'chach over it* [over the open gap] ,

If a roof was broken or its middle collapsed, leaving a large gap *(Rav; Tif. Yis.).*

אִם יֵשׁ מִן־הַכֹּתֶל לַסְּכוּךְ אַרְבַּע אַמּוֹת, — *if there are four cubits from the wall to the s'chach,*

[Since the breach is in the middle of the ceiling, leaving the remainder of the ceiling intact all around it, we measure the distance from the edges of the breach until the walls.]

פְּסוּלָה. — *it is invalid.*

[Since a distance of four cubits constitutes a separation between the *s'chach* and the wall, we do not consider the *s'chach* as having walls beneath it; nor the walls as having *s'chach* roofing them.]

If the distance between the *s'chach* and the walls is less than four cubits, the *succah* is valid. We utilize the principle of דֹּפֶן עֲקוּמָה, *bent wall,* to regard the intact sections of the ceiling as extensions of the adjacent walls. This princi-

ple was given to Moses on Sinai [הֲלָכָה לְמשֶׁה מִסִּינַי].

Nevertheless one may not eat or sleep under the intact section if it is four handbreadths wide *(Rav; Tif. Yis.; Orach Chaim* 632:1; cf. mishnah 6).

This mishnah highlights the difference between an air space between the walls and the *s'chach,* and *invalid s'chach* (i.e., a breached roof). In the former case the *s'chach* is considered sufficiently removed from the walls to disqualify the *succah,* whereas in the latter case, where the principle of *bent wall* (דֹּפֶן עֲקוּמָה) can be applied, the *s'chach* is viewed as reaching the walls. However, this does not validate the remaining part of the roof for *s'chach.* The accepted rule is *(Orach Chaim* 632:1) that one may sit and eat directly beneath invalid *s'chach* if it is less than four handbreadths wide. *Mishnah Berurah* (loc. cit. 3) cites some authorities that one should not sit and eat directly beneath invalid *s'chach* unless it is only three handbreadths or less, and adds that, ideally (לְכַתְּחִילָה), one should comply with this opinion.

Thus, in the case of the breached roof discussed here, one may not eat beneath the leftover segment of the roof if it is four handbreadths or more wide. According to

סֻכָּה גְדוֹלָה שֶׁהִקִּיפוּהָ בְּדָבָר שֶׁאֵין מְסַכְּכִים בּוֹ, אִם יֶשׁ־תַּחְתָּיו אַרְבַּע אַמּוֹת, פְּסוּלָה.

[יא] הָעוֹשֶׂה סֻכָּתוֹ כְּמִין צְרִיף, אוֹ שֶׁסְּמָכָהּ לַכֹּתֶל, רַבִּי אֱלִיעֶזֶר פּוֹסֵל, מִפְּנֵי שֶׁאֵין לָהּ גַּג; וַחֲכָמִים מַכְשִׁירִין.

מַחֲצֶלֶת קָנִים גְדוֹלָה — עֲשָׂאָהּ לִשְׁכִיבָה, מְקַבֶּלֶת טֻמְאָה וְאֵין מְסַכְּכִין בָּהּ; לְסִכּוּךְ,

יד אברהם

Mishnah Berurah, one should make sure that this segment is less than three handbreadths wide before using that area as a *succah*.

וְכֵן חָצֵר שֶׁהִיא מֻקֶּפֶת אַכְסַדְרָה — *The same [applies to] a courtyard that is surrounded by a portico.*

This refers to a courtyard surrounded on three sides by houses which open into it. From each house, a roof supported by a pillar projects toward the courtyard, shading some of it and leaving the rest exposed. If one were to lay *s'chach* over the exposed portion of the courtyard using the walls of the surrounding houses as the walls of the *succah*, the portico would separate the *s'chach* from the house walls. To determine whether that separation invalidates the structure as a *succah*, one must measure the depth of the portico roofs. Where that depth is four cubits, the *succah* is not valid, for the walls of the surrounding houses cannot be considered part of the *succah*. If less, then it is valid based on the principle of דֹּפֶן עֲקוּמָה, *bent wall* (Rashi 17a; Rav; Tif. Yis.).

Although the cases of a breached roof and a portico appear identical, there is a difference. The case of a breached ceiling teaches us that even where the walls and the ceiling are part of the same structure, if the horizontal gap between the *s'chach* and the walls is four cubits or more, the roof cannot be considered an extension of the walls. The case of the portico teaches us that even

though the house walls were not built to serve as walls for the portico, they can be combined to form a valid *succah* provided the distances are halachically correct (*Tif. Yis.*).

סֻכָּה גְדוֹלָה — *A large succah*

A large *succah* is one that retains an area of seven handbreadths square of valid *s'chach* even after the non-valid *s'chach* is removed (*Rav*).

שֶׁהִקִּיפוּהָ בְּדָבָר שֶׁאֵין מְסַכְּכִים בּוֹ — *that they ringed with material that we may not use for s'chach,*

An area of at least seven handbreadths square of valid *s'chach* was surrounded along its sides by non-valid *s'chach* which lay between it and the walls (*Rav*).

אִם יֶשׁ־תַּחְתָּיו אַרְבַּע אַמּוֹת, — *if there were four cubits beneath it,*

[We measure the space between the valid *s'chach* and the walls to see if the space, presently covered by the invalid materials, is four cubits.]

פְּסוּלָה. — *it is invalid.*

[The *succah* is not valid, because the walls are not regarded as part of the *succah*.]

This case is not similar to the two preceding ones. In the previous instances, the invalid *s'chach* was presumably made of wooden planks, material that is acceptable as *s'chach*. They are disqualified only because they were put

A large *succah* that they ringed with material that we may not use for *s'chach*, if there were four cubits beneath it, it is invalid.

11. If one makes his *succah* like a conical hut, or he leaned it against the wall, R' Eliezer invalidates it since it has no roof; but the Sages declare it valid.

A large reed mat — if made to lie upon, is susceptible to contamination and we may not use it for

YAD AVRAHAM

down to be bona fide roofs and cannot become s'chach unless they are removed and replaced as set forth in mishnah 7. In this case, however, the material separating the valid *s'chach* from the walls is not valid, so one might think that even less than four cubits of it would invalidate the *succah*. The mish-nah must teach us, therefore, that the principle of דֹּפֶן עֲקוּמָה, *bent wall*, applies in this case too (*Tif. Yis.*).

An *empty* space of three handbreadths running through the length of the *succah* invalidates the *succah* regardless of whether it is in the middle or on the side (*Rav; Orach Chaim* 632:2; see mishnah 9).

11.

הָעוֹשֶׂה סֻכָּתוֹ כְּמִין צְרִיף, — *If one makes his succah like a conical hut,*

A conical hut has no roof and the walls meet each other on top (*Rav*).

In this respect the roof and the walls are one [the walls being made of valid s'chach] (*Rashi* 19b).

אוֹ שֶׁסְּמָכָהּ לַכֹּתֶל, — *or he leaned it against the wall,*

He built a lean-to — a single wall of valid s'chach leaning against the wall of a house (*Rav; Tif. Yis.*).

רַבִּי אֱלִיעֶזֶר פּוֹסֵל, מִפְּנֵי שֶׁאֵין לָהּ גָּג; — *R' Eliezer invalidates it since it has no roof;*

In both cases one cannot distinguish between roof and wall. A *succah*, however, must be an אֹהֶל, *tent*, i.e., it must have a discernible roof at least one handbreadth wide, or have walls one handbreadth high (*Rav; Rashi; Gem.* 19b).

וַחֲכָמִים מַכְשִׁירִין. — *but the Sages declare it valid.*

The halachah follows R' Eliezer (*Rav; Orach Chaim* 631:10).

It seems odd for the halachah to follow the view of R' Eliezer who is in the minority. The

Gemara (19b) quotes a *baraisa* in which the views are reversed: R' Eliezer validates and the Sages invalidate; accordingly the *halachah* follows the majority after all (*Tos. Yom Tov*).

Why does the mishnah teach two similar cases, that of the conical hut and that of the lean-to? The first emphasizes the conviction of the Sages: even though there is no conventional wall in such a hut, they nevertheless consider it valid. In the second case the mishnah emphasizes the conviction of R' Eliezer: even though there is a conventional wall, namely, the wall of the house, he still declares it invalid (*Tif. Yis.*).

For further elucidation of how such shacks can sometimes be valid, see *Orach Chaim* 631:10 and *Rama, ibid.*

מַחֲצֶלֶת קָנִים גְּדוֹלָה—עֲשָׂאָהּ לִשְׁכִיבָה, מְקַבֶּלֶת טֻמְאָה — *A large reed mat—if made to lie upon, is susceptible to contamination*

Although such a mat is generally made for shade — in which case it may be used for s'chach — if one designated it to recline upon it loses its acceptability because it then becomes susceptible to *tumah* [the source of this disqualification was given in mishnah 4] (*Gem.* 20a; *Rav*).

מְסַכְּכִין בָּהּ וְאֵינָהּ מְקַבֶּלֶת טֻמְאָה.
רַבִּי אֱלִיעֶזֶר אוֹמֵר: אַחַת קְטַנָּה וְאַחַת
גְּדוֹלָה — עֲשָׂאָהּ לִשְׁכִיבָה, מְקַבֶּלֶת טֻמְאָה
וְאֵין מְסַכְּכִין בָּהּ; לְסִכּוּךְ, מְסַכְּכִין בָּהּ וְאֵינָהּ
מְקַבֶּלֶת טֻמְאָה.

יד אברהם

Anything made of wood (or reeds) designated for reclining is susceptible to *tumah* if reclined upon by certain specifically designated contaminated people, e.g., נִדָּה, *menstruant* (see *Rambam, M'tamei Mishkav U'Moshav 1:1*). In the case of a mat we are dealing with a wooden object lacking a receptacle [פְּשׁוּטֵי כְלֵי עֵץ], nevertheless the fact that it is used for reclining bestows susceptibility upon it (*Niddah 6:3; Gem. 20a;* footnote to mishnah 8).

וְאֵין מְסַכְּכִין בָּהּ; — *and we may not use it for s'chach;*

[According to the general rule as stated in mishnah 4.]

לְסִכּוּךְ, מְסַכְּכִין בָּהּ — *if for shade, we* [may] *use it for s'chach*

The *Gemara* (20a) explains that this segment of the mishnah refers to a small mat which is generally made for reclining. Therefore it is valid for *s'chach* only if it was designed expressly for *s'chach.*[1]

Rosh says that we may do so only if the majority of that city makes these mats for *s'chach*. If, however, the majority of the city uses such mats only for reclining, then it is not valid for *s'chach* even for an individual who made one for *s'chach*. The reason is that other people will not be aware that he made it expressly for *s'chach* and will mistaken-

ly think that all such mats are valid for *s'chach* (*Rama* quoting *Rosh; Orach Chaim* 629:6; *Mishnah Berurah, ibid.* 17).

However, in the reverse case, if most of the people make these mats for *s'chach*, and the maker intended them for reclining they are not valid (*Turei Zahav* 629:7).

According to *Rosh*, our mishnah, which distinguishes between large and small mats, speaks about a region which has clearly defined customs concerning the use of such mats. Where there is a defined usage the rule is as outlined above by *Rosh* (*Turei Zahav, ibid.*).

וְאֵינָהּ מְקַבֶּלֶת טֻמְאָה. — *and it is not susceptible to contamination.*

[For he specifically intended it for shade, and not as a mat.]

רַבִּי אֱלִיעֶזֶר אוֹמֵר: אַחַת קְטַנָּה וְאַחַת גְּדוֹלָה, עֲשָׂאָהּ לִשְׁכִיבָה, — *R' Eliezer says: Whether* [the mat is] *small or large—if he made it to lie upon,*

The *Gemara* (20a) explains that R' Eliezer disagrees with the Sages and holds that even a large mat is generally made for reclining. Therefore, the words עֲשָׂאָהּ לִשְׁכִיבָה here imply that they are *usually* made for reclining (*Rav; Tif. Yis.*).

מְקַבֶּלֶת טֻמְאָה וְאֵין מְסַכְּכִין בָּהּ; — *it is*

---

1. The *Gemara* explains why we must depart from the literal sense of the mishnah, which mentions no distinction between large and small mats. On its face, the mishnah appears to be contradictory. The first clause of the mishnah implies that only when the mat is expressly made for reclining is it disqualified; but not if it was made with no specific purpose in mind. But the second implies that only large mats *expressly* made for *s'chach* are valid; implying that those made without any intent are *not* valid. To resolve this contradiction the *Gemara* explains that the first clause speaks about large mats (as said in the mishnah). The second, more stringent clause speaks about small mats.

s'chach; if for shade, we may use it for s'chach and it is not susceptible to contamination.

R' Eliezer says: Whether [the mat is] small or large — if he made it to lie upon, it is susceptible to contamination and we may not use it as s'chach; if for s'chach, we may use it for s'chach and it is not susceptible to contamination.

YAD AVRAHAM

susceptible to contamination and we may not use it as s'chach;

[Since either is generally used for reclining, it is susceptible to tumah and not valid for s'chach.]

לִסְכּוּךְ, — if for s'chach.

He expressly designated it for s'chach [which is not its usual use] (Rav; Tif. Yis.).

מְסַכְּכִין בָּהּ וְאֵינָהּ מְקַבֶּלֶת טֻמְאָה. — we may use it for s'chach and it is not susceptible to contamination.

[Since it was made specifically for s'chach, it never attains the status of a utensil. It is, therefore, not subject to tumah and is valid as s'chach.]

The halachah does not follow R' Eliezer (Rav; Orach Chaim 629:6).

Chapter 2

Where the previous chapter discussed the laws governing the succah itself — its dimensions, the s'chach, and related matters, this chapter will discuss the manner in which one dwells in a succah — the act of performing the mitzvah. Because the mitzvah of succah requires one to sleep as well as to eat there, the mishnah will discuss several instances where there is doubt whether one has discharged his obligation to sleep in the succah.

In the temperate zones of Europe and North America, the mitzvah of sleeping in the succah has become regarded as a voluntary observance reserved for only the most devout. Far from a flouting of halachah, this apparent disregard of the law is itself based on a halachah — that of מִצְטַעֵר, feeling distressed, i.e., when climatic or other conditions are so severe that one feels a significant degree of discomfort in the succah, the mitzvah does not apply, for the succah cannot be regarded as a 'dwelling' in such circumstances. The cool evening temperatures in temperate regions makes sleeping outdoors a discomfort [מִצְטַעֵר], and consequently not obligatory. This and other reasons are given by Rama in Shulchan Aruch (Orach Chaim 639:2; cf. commentaries there) to account for the general non-compliance with this aspect of the mitzvah. Nonetheless, in the climate which serves as a setting for the mishnah, Eretz Yisrael, all these dispensations did not apply, and sleeping in the succah was viewed as no less obligatory than eating there.

Indeed the language used by the Torah to indicate the mitzvah of succah makes no specific mention of either eating or sleeping; it states generally (Lev. 23:42) In succos shall you dwell for seven days. All activities and pastimes usually taking place in the home should be done in the succah so that it becomes one's temporary abode (see Orach Chaim 639:1). However, the mishnah singles out eating and sleeping as acts requiring a succah, because these activities are, as a rule performed in the home, and must consequently be done in the temporary home for the festival — the succah.

[א] **הַיָּשֵׁן** תַּחַת הַמִּטָּה בַּסֻּכָּה לֹא יָצָא יְדֵי חוֹבָתוֹ.

אָמַר רַבִּי יְהוּדָה: נוֹהֲגִין הָיִינוּ, שֶׁהָיִינוּ יְשֵׁנִים תַּחַת הַמִּטָּה בִּפְנֵי הַזְּקֵנִים וְלֹא אָמְרוּ לָנוּ דָבָר.

אָמַר רַבִּי שִׁמְעוֹן: מַעֲשֶׂה בְטָבִי, עַבְדּוֹ שֶׁל רַבָּן גַּמְלִיאֵל, שֶׁהָיָה יָשֵׁן תַּחַת הַמִּטָּה. וְאָמַר לָהֶן רַבָּן גַּמְלִיאֵל לַזְּקֵנִים: „רְאִיתֶם טָבִי עַבְדִּי שֶׁהוּא תַּלְמִיד חָכָם וְיוֹדֵעַ שֶׁעֲבָדִים פְּטוּרִין מִן הַסֻּכָּה — לְפִיכָךְ יָשֵׁן הוּא תַּחַת הַמִּטָּה." וּלְפִי

יד אברהם

1.

הַיָּשֵׁן תַּחַת הַמִּטָּה בַּסֻּכָּה — *One who sleeps under the bed in the succah*

The *Gemara* (20b) comments that the mishnah speaks of a bed where the area beneath is ten handbreadths high so that it is considered a 'tent' by itself (*Rav; Tosafos* 20b s.v. הישן; *R' Chananel*; cf. *Rashi* s.v. הישן).

If the space beneath it was lower than ten handbreadths, it is considered to be part of the *succah* and one can discharge his obligation by sleeping there.

The stipulation that only if the bed is ten handbreadths high has one not discharged his obligation seems to contradict 1:3 that one who dwells in a *succah* under the canopy of a four-poster bed does not fulfill his obligation because the shelter of the canopy separates him from the shelter of the *succah*. There, no distinction is made between canopies of more and less than ten handbreadths, while in our case his obligation goes unfulfilled only if there are ten or more handbreadths under the bed.

Ran notes the contradiction and offers the following resolution: the purpose of a four-poster canopy is to shelter the sleeper, therefore even a height of only one handbreadth [the minimum height that can constitute a אֹהֶל, *tent*] is sufficient to qualify it as a shelter. But where there is no intention to make a shelter, as in our mishnah where the space under a bed was never meant to be a

tent — for usually no one sleeps *under* a bed — only ten handbreadths are regarded as significant enough to be considered a 'tent' within the *succah*.

לֹא יָצָא יְדֵי חוֹבָתוֹ — *has not fulfilled his obligation* [to sleep in a *succah*].

The obligation is to sleep *within* the *succah*. In this case, the bed acts as a barrier separating him from the *succah*. Consequently, when he sleeps in the 'tent' of the bed, he is not sleeping in the *succah* (*Rashi; Rav; R' Chananel; Tos.* s.v. הישן; *Orach Chaim* 627:1).

Rif, Rambam (*Comm.; Hilchos Succah* 5:23), and *Rosh* explain that a bed ten handbreadths high is regarded as a separate *succah* — with invalid *s'chach* — within a larger *succah*. Accordingly, it falls under the category of a *succah* inside another *succah* like that discussed in 1:2 (see comm. there s.v. עֲשָׂאָהּ בְּתוֹךְ הַבַּיִת). Since the space beneath the bed is ten handbreadths high, the bed itself is a *succah* (albeit with invalid *s'chach*) and should not be better than a (valid) *succah* under an (invalid) *succah* (see comm. to 1:2 s.v. בְּתוֹךְ הַבַּיִת עֲשָׂאָה כְּאִלּוּ).

אָמַר רַבִּי יְהוּדָה: נוֹהֲגִין הָיִינוּ, שֶׁהָיִינוּ יְשֵׁנִים תַּחַת הַמִּטָּה בִּפְנֵי הַזְּקֵנִים — *R' Yehudah said: We regularly slept under the bed in the presence of the Elders*

[I.e. the Sages whose disciple he was.]

1. **O**ne who sleeps under the bed in the *succah* has not fulfilled his obligation [to sleep in a *succah*].

R' Yehudah said: We regularly slept under the bed in the presence of the Elders and they said nothing to us.

R' Shimon said: There is a case of Tavi, Rabban Gamliel's slave, who used to sleep under the bed. Rabban Gamliel said to the Elders, 'Have you observed my slave Tavi? He is a scholar and knows that [gentile] slaves are exempt from [the obligation of] *succah* — that is why he sleeps under the bed.' And

YAD AVRAHAM

וְלֹא אָמְרוּ לָנוּ דָבָר. — *and they said nothing to us.*

R' Yehudah is consistent with his view (1:1) that a *succah* must be a permanent structure. Accordingly a temporary shelter, such as the area underneath a movable bed, cannot nullify the permanent shelter of the *succah* proper. [Consequently, R' Yehudah does not consider the bed a barrier between the man and the *succah*] *(Rav; Tif. Yis.; Gem.* 21b).

The halachah does not follow R' Yehudah *(Rav; Orach Chaim* 627:1).

אָמַר רַבִּי שִׁמְעוֹן: מַעֲשֶׂה בְּטָבִי, עַבְדּוֹ שֶׁל רַבָּן גַּמְלִיאֵל — *R' Shimon said: There is the case of Tavi, Rabban Gamliel's slave,*

[Tavi was scrupulous in the observance of *mitzvos* (see *Berachos* 2:1) and was also a scholar (see *Yoma* 87a).]

שֶׁהָיָה יָשֵׁן תַּחַת הַמִּטָּה. — *who used to sleep under the bed,*

[In the *succah.*]

וְאָמַר לָהֶן רַבָּן גַּמְלִיאֵל לַזְקֵנִים: ,,רְאִיתֶם טָבִי עַבְדִּי? שֶׁהוּא תַּלְמִיד חָכָם וְיוֹדֵעַ שֶׁעֲבָדִים פְּטוּרִין מִן־הַסֻּכָּה— — *Rabban Gamliel said to the Elders, 'Have you observed my slave Tavi? He is a scholar and knows that [gentile] slaves are exempt from [the obligation of] succah —*

Non-Jews who have been purchased as slaves, must, within twelve months

of their purchase, be circumcised, immersed in a *mikveh*, and accept voluntarily the *mitzvos* incumbent upon slaves owned by a Jew. In absence of any of these conditions, the owner must rid himself of this slave *(Yevamos* 48b; *Rambam, Issurei Biah* 14:9). If the slave assents to undergo conversion as above, he will have the same obligations to observe *mitzvos* as Jewish women *(Chagigah* 4a). Jewish women are exempt from all מִצְוֹת עֲשֵׂה שֶׁהַזְּמַן גְּרָמָא, *positive commandments that are dependent on a fixed time (Gem.* 28a). Since women are exempt from the *mitzvah* of *succah* because it has a fixed time (2:8), so are slaves *(Rav; Tif. Yis.).*

לְפִיכָךְ יָשֵׁן הוּא תַּחַת הַמִּטָּה.'' — *that is why he sleeps under the bed.*

[I.e., Tavi demonstrated his awareness of his exemption by sleeping under the bed, which, in accordance with the first view expressed in the mishnah, does not constitute observance of a *mitzvah* from which he is exempt. If so, why was Tavi in the *succah* at all? Probably to serve his master. Also to listen to the Torah discourses of the Sages. Presumably not wishing to take up space needed by those obligated to sleep in the *succah*, he slept under the bed (cf. *Yerushalmi* here cited by *Ran).* Implicit in the words of Rabban Gam-

דַּרְכֵּנוּ לָמַדְנוּ שֶׁהַיָּשֵׁן תַּחַת הַמִּטָּה לֹא יָצָא יְדֵי
חוֹבָתוֹ.

‏[ב] **הַסּוֹמֵךְ** סֻכָּתוֹ בְּכַרְעֵי הַמִּטָּה כְּשֵׁרָה.
רַבִּי יְהוּדָה אוֹמֵר: אִם אֵינָהּ
יְכוֹלָה לַעֲמוֹד בִּפְנֵי עַצְמָהּ, פְּסוּלָה.
סֻכָּה הַמְדֻבְלֶלֶת, וְשֶׁצִּלָּתָהּ מְרֻבָּה מֵחַמָּתָהּ,

יד אברהם

liel, 'he *slept* under the bed', is that Tavi did eat and drink in the *succah*; there was room enough for him during meals, but not for sleeping.]

וּלְפִי דַּרְכֵּנוּ לָמַדְנוּ — *And incidentally* [lit. *according to our practice*] *we deduced*

Although Rabban Gamliel mentioned Tavi's practice only in the course of general conversation in order to praise his slave, we learned a lesson (*Rav; Tif. Yis.*).

[Our practice is to derive lessons even from the casual conversation of scholars. It is axiomatic that a scholar does not make statements unless they

are well considered; therefore אֲפִילּוּ שִׂיחַת חוּלִין שֶׁל תַּלְמִידֵי חֲכָמִים צְרִיכָה לִימּוּד, *even casual conversation of Torah scholars demands study (Gem. 21b).*]

שֶׁהַיָּשֵׁן תַּחַת הַמִּטָּה לֹא יָצָא יְדֵי חוֹבָתוֹ. — *that one who sleeps under the bed does not fulfill his obligation* [to sleep in a *succah*].

R' Shimon agrees with R' Yehudah that one is obligated to construct a *succah* of a permanent nature, but unlike R' Yehudah, R' Shimon holds that a temporary shelter can nullify a permanent one (*Gem.* 21b).

2.

הַסּוֹמֵךְ סֻכָּתוֹ בְּכַרְעֵי הַמִּטָּה — *If one supports his succah on the legs of a bed*

This refers to a bed with four boards around it. The mattress is attached to the boards which extend above it for at least ten more handbreadths. *S'chach* is placed on top of these four boards, which also serve as the walls of the *succah* (*Tur; Orach Chaim* 630; *Bais Yosef* there).

כְּשֵׁרָה. — *it is valid.*

Even though when one moves the bed, he automatically moves the entire *succah* with it (*Tif. Yis.*).

רַבִּי יְהוּדָה אוֹמֵר: אִם אֵינָהּ יְכוֹלָה לַעֲמוֹד בִּפְנֵי עַצְמָהּ, — *R' Yehudah says: If it cannot stand by itself*

I.e., if the *s'chach* is not lying on an immovable frame, but will move with the bed (*Tif. Yis.*).

פְּסוּלָה. — *it is invalid.*

R' Yehudah is consistent with his view (1:1) that a *succah* must be a permanent structure; if it is movable it is invalid (*Rav; Rashi*).

The halachah does not follow R' Yehudah (*Rav; Tif. Yis.*).

In this interpretation, the fact that the halachah does not follow R' Yehudah goes without saying, for we rule against R' Yehudah wherever his opinion is based on his principle that a *succah* must be a permanent structure (see 1:1, 2:1 and 2:3 with *comm.*). This may be why *Rambam's* code omits this case.

The above cited interpretation (*Rashi's*) is based on the opinion in the *Gemara* (21b) that the reason for R' Yehudah's ruling is 'because it lacks stability (לְפִי שֶׁאֵין לָהּ קֶבַע).' However, many authorities (*Tosefos* 21b s.v. שאין; *Rif* as understood by *Ramban; Rosh; Ritva* and others) argue that mobility is no

incidentally we deduced that one who sleeps under the bed does not fulfill his obligation [to sleep in a *succah*].

2. If one supports his *succah* on the legs of a bed it is valid. R' Yehudah says: If it cannot stand by itself it is invalid.

A disarranged *succah*, or one whose shade[d area] is greater than its sun[lit area], is valid. If [the *succah*]

YAD AVRAHAM

reason for disqualification (even according to R' Yehudah). The mishnah discusses a case where the top of the *s'chach* is more than ten handbreadths above the ground, but less than ten above the mattress of the bed. As outlined in 1:1, a *succah* must have a minimum height of ten handbreadths. The *tanna kamma* rules that the presence of the bed is immaterial; since the *s'chach* is ten handbreadths above the ground, the *succah* is valid. R' Yehudah disagrees. He maintains that because the *succah* cannot stand without the bed — since it is built on the bed — its height must be measured from the level of the mattress. In that case, if there are less than ten handbreadths from the bed to the *s'chach*, the *succah* is too small to be habitable, and is, therefore, invalid. If, however, the *succah* can remain standing even if the bed is moved from beneath it, it is valid.

The authorities holding this interpretation rule like R' Yehudah. *Rosh* surmises that there is no real dissent: R' Yehudah merely articulates the anonymous opinion expressed by the first tanna.

This ruling is adopted by *Shulchan Aruch* (630:13).

The foregoing is based on the diverse interpretations of one opinion in the *Gemara*. Another opinion given in the *Gemara (ibid)* is that R' Yehudah disqualifies it because a bed is susceptible to *tumah* (see *comm.* to 1:8 s.v. הַמִּטָּה אֲרוּכוֹת בָאו) and is invalid for *s'chach*. Not only should such materials not be used for *s'chach*, but they should not even be used to support the *s'chach*. While R' Yosef Karo (*Orach Chaim* 630:13) seems to hold that such supports are acceptable (see *Mishnah Berurah* there 59), many later authorities (see *Mishnah Berurah* there and 329:22; *Bach* to *Tur* 329) rule that ideally [לְכַתְּחִילָה] one should *not* support *s'chach* with materials unfit for use as *s'chach*.

However, one may make the walls of the succah of stone and support the *s'chach* upon them. Here there is no fear that he may come to use the invalid material for *s'chach* for it is not customary to use stone as a (temporary) covering *(Ramban [Milchamos] cited by Ran)*.

סֻכָּה הַמְדֻבְלֶלֶת, — *A disarranged succah* [i.e. disarranged *s'chach*],

Some of the *s'chach* points upward and some points downward, with the result that חַמָּתָה מְרֻבָּה מִצִּלָּתָה, *its sunny area is greater than its shaded area.* The space between the pieces of *s'chach* is in no case as much as three handbreadths, so that all the *s'chach* is consequently considered as לָבוּד, *united* (2-2a, Shmuel's view; *Rav; Tif. Yis.; Orach Chaim* 631:5). See 1:9.

וְשֶׁצִּלָתָה מְרֻבָּה מֵחַמָּתָה, — *or one whose shade[d area] is greater than its sun[lit] area,*

The *s'chach* is a very thin layer and there are many air spaces between the pieces of *s'chach*, each space being less than three handbreadths. Even when all the spaces are combined, the total shaded area is greater than the sunny area *(Tif. Yis.; Orach Chaim* 631:4).

כְּשֵׁרָה. — *is valid.*

In the case of the disarranged *s'chach* (סֻכָּה הַמְדֻבְלֶלֶת), if the *s'chach* were lying evenly together, there would be more shaded area than sunny area. Since the spaces between the pieces of the disarranged *s'chach* are less than three handbreadths, we regard it as though it were all together, providing

כְּשֵׁרָה. הַמְעֻבָּה כְּמִין בַּיִת, אַף־עַל־פִּי שֶׁאֵין הַכּוֹכָבִים נִרְאִים מִתּוֹכָהּ, כְּשֵׁרָה.

[ג] הָעוֹשֶׂה סֻכָּתוֹ בְּרֹאשׁ הָעֲגָלָה אוֹ בְּרֹאשׁ הַסְּפִינָה כְּשֵׁרָה, וְעוֹלִין לָהּ בְּיוֹם טוֹב. בְּרֹאשׁ הָאִילָן אוֹ עַל־גַּבֵּי גָמָל כְּשֵׁרָה, וְאֵין עוֹלִין לָהּ בְּיוֹם טוֹב. שְׁתַּיִם בְּאִילָן וְאַחַת בִּידֵי אָדָם, אוֹ שְׁתַּיִם

יד אברהם

the necessary shade. As such it is valid (*Rashi* 22a; *Rav*).

In the case of the thinned-out s'chach, the succah's validity is based on the key that the shaded area exceeds the sunny area (*Orach Chaim* 631:4; *Tif. Yis.*).

The above commentary is based on Shmuel's view (22a). Rav (*ibid*), Shmuel's disputant, interprets the mishnah as a single case: *a meager succah* [i.e. s'chach] *whose shaded area is greater than its sun*[lit area], i.e., a very skimpy layer with patches of air less than three handbreadths in size, so long as the shaded area is greater than the sunny area, is valid (*Rashi* to 22a; *Orach Chaim* 631:4).

הַמְעֻבָּה כְּמִין בַּיִת, אַף־עַל־פִּי שֶׁאֵין הַכּוֹכָבִים נִרְאִים מִתּוֹכָהּ, כְּשֵׁרָה. — *If* [the succah] is

thickly covered like a house, even though the stars cannot be seen from inside it, it is valid.

The *succah* is valid only after the fact [בְּדִיעֲבַד]. But it is preferable [לְכַתְּחִילָה] that the s'chach be laid on so that the stars are visible through it (*Tif. Yis.; Yerushalmi* cited by *Rosh* and *Ran; Orach Chaim* 631:3).

However some authorities rule that if s'chach is so thick that a heavy rainfall cannot penetrate it, it would, in effect, be no different from a house roof and would be invalid, lest someone might just as well eat inside his house (see 1:5; *Mishnah Berurah* 631:6).

But in the event it is impossible to remove the excess s'chach, one may rely on those authorities who rule it valid (*Mishnah Berurah ibid; Shaarei Teshuvah* 631:3).

3.

הָעוֹשֶׂה סֻכָּתוֹ בְּרֹאשׁ הָעֲגָלָה — *If one makes his succah on top of a wagon*

Even though the wagon is mobile and is not stationary (*Rav*).

אוֹ בְּרֹאשׁ הַסְּפִינָה — *or on the deck of a ship*

Even if it is on the highest level of the ship where it is virtually unprotected from sea winds, which can demolish the succah (*Rashi* to 22b; *Rav*).

כְּשֵׁרָה, — *it is valid,*

Both *succos* meet the requirement of a temporary dwelling. A *succah* on the wagon is a livable abode even though it is mobile (*Rashi, ibid*).[1]

In reviewing the case of the *succah* on deck, the *Gemara* discusses the authorship of our mishnah and concludes that its author is R' Akiva, who requires that a *succah* meet only the requirements of

---

1. *Chayei Adam* (146:40) suggests that merchants who must travel on the Intermediate Days, should make a *succah* on their wagon, provided there are ten handbreadths from floor of the wagon to the s'chach.

is thickly covered like a house, even though the stars cannot be seen from inside it, it is valid.

3. If one makes his *succah* on top of a wagon or on the deck of a ship it is valid, and we may go up into it on the festival. [If he makes a *succah*] in the top of a tree or on the back of a camel it is valid, but we may not go up into it on the festival.

[If] two [walls are] in a tree and one is man-made,

YAD AVRAHAM

a temporary abode. So long as the *succah* is sturdy enough to stand up to normal *land* winds, it is a proper temporary dwelling, regardless of whether it could withstand the impact of the turbulent winds that are more common on sea than on land. The sturdiness of a *succah* as a temporary dwelling is determined by its normal location — on *land*. If, however, it cannot stand up to normal *land* winds, it is not considered a temporary dwelling by any standard, and is invalid (*Gem.* 23a; *Orach Chaim* 629:2).

וְעוֹלִין לָהּ בְּיוֹם טוֹב. — *and we may go up into it on the festival.*

This phrase is extraneous for there is no halachic reason to think that it might be forbidden to enter a ship or wagon on the festival. But since in the following case, the mishnah used the expression, *but we may not go up into it on the festival*, — and in that case, it *is* forbidden — it states here, for stylistic balance, that we *may* go up into it on the festival (*Rashi* to 22b; *Rav*).

בְּרֹאשׁ הָאִילָן — *[If he makes a succah] in the top of a tree*

He made his *succah* in a tree by erecting partitions and covering them with *s'chach* (*Rashi* to 22b; *Rav*).

According to the view (outlined in *comm.* 2:2 s.v. פְּסוּלָה) that *s'chach* should not be supported by invalid materials, the tree itself should not be used as a wall to support the *s'chach*. Rather it should be supported on poles independent of the tree (*Ran* here, cited by *Magen Avraham* 628:5; *Mishnah Berurah* 628:17; cf. *Shaar HaTziyun* there 209; see *comm.* to 2:4 s.v. וְהָאִילָנוֹת דְּפָנוֹת לָהּ).

אוֹ עַל־גַּבֵּי גָמָל — *or on the back of a camel*

He erected walls between the animal's humps and covered them with *s'chach*. But if he rested the *s'chach* on the animal's head, the *succah* is invalid even בְּדִיעֲבַד, *after the fact*; because the *s'chach* would simply fall off once the animal begins to walk (*Magen Avraham* 630:14; *Mishnah Berurah* 629:15; *Shaar HaTziyun, ibid.* 16).

כְּשֵׁרָה, וְאֵין עוֹלִין לָהּ בְּיוֹם טוֹב. — *it is valid, but we may not go up into it on the festival.*

It may be used during the Intermediate days of the festival (*Rashi* to 22b; *Rav; Ran*), but the Sages forbade making any physical use of trees or of live animals on festivals to prevent the breaking off of branches on Yom Tov (*Beitzah* 36b). In the case of climbing trees this is readily understandable; in the case of animals the fear is that he may break off a twig for use as a crop while riding the animal. However, if one *did* make use of a Rabbinically forbidden *succah* on the festival, he nevertheless fulfilled his Torah obligation of *succah* (*Rashi ibid; Rav; Meiri; Mishnah Berurah* 629:18).

שְׁתַּיִם בְּאִילָן — *[If] two [walls are] in a tree*

Most of the *succah* floor's weight rests upon the tree. Around the floor, and on the tree, he constructed two walls. (*Rashi* to 22b; *Rav; Tif. Yis.; Orach Chaim* 628:3.)

בִּידֵי אָדָם וְאַחַת בְּאִילָן כְּשֵׁרָה, וְאֵין עוֹלִין לָה בְּיוֹם טוֹב. שָׁלֹשׁ בִּידֵי אָדָם וְאַחַת בְּאִילָן כְּשֵׁרָה, וְעוֹלִין לָה בְּיוֹם טוֹב. זֶה הַכְּלָל: כָּל־שֶׁנִּטַּל הָאִילָן וִיכוֹלָה לַעֲמוֹד בִּפְנֵי עַצְמָהּ, כְּשֵׁרָה, וְעוֹלִין לָה בְּיוֹם טוֹב.

[ד] הָעוֹשֶׂה סֻכָּתוֹ בֵּין הָאִילָנוֹת, וְהָאִילָנוֹת דְּפָנוֹת לָהּ, כְּשֵׁרָה.

יד אברהם

וְאַחַת בִּידֵי אָדָם, — *and one [is] man-made,*

The rest of the *succah* floor and the third wall are supported by man-made construction. A board is set into the ground to support the part of the floor that extends beyond the tree. The third wall of the *succah* is formed by that board, or something built on it, extending upward above the floor. This wall is not supported at all by the tree. The *s'chach* is laid across the top of all three walls (*Rashi, ibid; Rav; Tif. Yis.*).

אוֹ שְׁתַּיִם בִּידֵי אָדָם וְאַחַת בְּאִילָן — *or two [are] man-made and one [is] in a tree,*

[Two walls begin on the ground and support the greater part of the *succah* floor. The third wall and the remainder of the floor are supported by the tree.]

כְּשֵׁרָה, — *it is valid,*

[The *succah* may be used during the Intermediate Days of the festival.]

וְאֵין עוֹלִין לָה בְּיוֹם טוֹב. — *but we may not go up into it on the festival.*

In either case the tree is indispensable to the *succah*, without it, the *succah* floor would collapse. Therefore, to dwell in the *succah* means to use the

tree, an act that is forbidden on festivals (*Rashi; ibid.; Rav; see comm.* above s.v. וְאֵין עוֹלִין).

Rashi (Shabbos 54b) and *Rambam (Hil. Succah* 4:6) explain this segment of the mishnah differently. *Two in a tree* refers to the walls of the *succah* — i.e. a tree or trees serve as two walls of the *succah*. The third wall is man-made, and the floor of the *succah* is the ground. Since it was customary to place things on and remove them from the *s'chach* — and this *s'chach* is supported directly by the tree — the result is that a tree will be used on Yom Tov.[1] Since use of a tree on Yom Tov is forbidden as mentioned above (comm. s.v. וְאֵין עוֹלִין לָה בְּיוֹם טוֹב), the Sages forbade the use of such a *succah* on Yom Tov as a precautionary measure, lest the *s'chach* be used as well.

שָׁלֹשׁ בִּידֵי אָדָם וְאַחַת בְּאִילָן כְּשֵׁרָה, וְעוֹלִין לָה בְּיוֹם טוֹב. — *[If] three [walls are] man-made and one [is] in a tree, it is valid, and we may go up into it on the festival.*

[This *succah* has four walls. Three of them, and the *succah* floor, are supported by man-made construction (as described earlier in the *comm.* s.v. ואחת בידי אדם), while the remaining wall and the remainder of the *succah* floor are supported by the tree.]

1. *Mishnah Berurah* (629:17) suggests that perhaps this precautionary prohibition was applicable only in early times when it was customary to hang or place things on the *s'chach*. In our times, however, since we are not accustomed to using the *s'chach* in this manner, the prohibition is not applicable. He quotes *Magen Avraham* that not withstanding this fact, tree branches should not be used to support *s'chach* because — initially [לְכַתְחִילָה] — *s'chach* should not be supported by non-valid *s'chach*.

or two [are] man-made and one [is] in a tree, it is valid, but we may not go up into it on the festival. [If] three [walls are] man-made and one [is] in a tree, it is valid, and we may go up into it on the festival.

This is the general rule: Wherever the tree can be removed and [the *succah*] can stand by itself, it is valid, and we may go up into it on the festival.

4. If one makes his *succah* between the trees, and the trees serve as its walls, it is valid.

YAD AVRAHAM

According to *Rashi (Shabbos* 154b) and *Rambam,* the *succah* is on the ground. Three of its walls are man-made and a tree is used as the fourth wall.

According to either interpretation, the tree is not an essential part of the *succah;* even without the tree, enough remains to constitute a valid *succah.*

זֶה הַכְּלָל: כָּל־שֶׁנִּטַּל הָאִילָן — *This is the general rule: Wherever the tree can be removed*

[And with it any portion of the *succah* attached to and dependent on it.]

וִיכוֹלָה לַעֲמוֹד בִּפְנֵי עַצְמָה, — *and [the succah] can stand by itself,*

[The *succah* remains standing without the support of the tree.]

כְּשֵׁרָה, — *it is valid,*

[And the support rendered by the tree is disregarded as superfluous.]

וְעוֹלִין לָהּ בְּיוֹם טוֹב. — *and we may go up into it on the festival.*

[Since the portion of the *succah* dependent on the tree is superfluous, we are not using the tree on the festival even though the tree is, in fact, bearing part of the *succah's* weight. In the implied reverse of this rule — where the *succah* cannot stand without the tree — it is valid for the Intermediate Days, the succah is also valid, but we may not go up into it on Yom Tov.]

Ran explains that this general rule is stated to allude to a case not mentioned in the mishnah: the two man-made walls are parallel to each other and the tree forms a third wall, perpendicular to the other two. Since *s'chach* lying across the two man-made walls will remain in place even if the tree were removed, one may go up into the *succah.* The case of two man-made walls that the mishnah disapproves of on Yom Tov is explained by *Ran* to refer to two perpendicular walls where the *s'chach* is supported by one man-made wall and the tree. Consequently, if the tree were removed the entire *s'chach* would fall. It is forbidden to go up into such a *succah* on Yom Tov *(Tos. Yom Tov).*

4.

הָעוֹשֶׂה סֻכָּתוֹ בֵּין הָאִילָנוֹת, וְהָאִילָנוֹת דְּפָנוֹת לָהּ, — *If one makes his succah between the trees, and the trees serve as its walls,*

But the floor of the *succah* is on the ground *(Rashi* 24b; *Ritva.* Cf. *Aruch LaNer* to *Rashi).*

[He did not support the floor of the *succah* on the trees as in the previous mishnah. Had he done so he would not be permitted to 'go up into the *succah'*

on Yom Tov. By omitting any mention of Yom Tov, the mishnah implies that the *succah* may be used even then.]

According to the view of *Rashi (Shabbos* 54b and *Rambam)* outlined in the previous mishnah (s.v. וְאֵין עוֹלִין) that a *succah* may not be used on Yom Tov if its *s'chach* rests upon trees, the *s'chach* here is supported not upon the trees, but upon poles erected near them.

The same supposition must be made ac-

שְׁלוּחֵי מִצְוָה פְּטוּרִין מִן־הַסֻּכָּה. חוּלִין וּמְשַׁמְּשֵׁיהֶן פְּטוּרִין מִן־הַסֻּכָּה. אוֹכְלִין וְשׁוֹתִין עֲרַאי חוּץ לַסֻּכָּה.

יד אברהם

cording to those who hold that one may not support s'chach with invalid materials (Meiri; cf. Milchamos and Ran to 21b; cf. Magen Avraham 628:5).

However Ravad (gloss to Rif [21b]) maintains that trees are not included in the injunction against supporting s'chach with invalid materials. Ran and Ramban (Milchamos there) disagree with this distinction.

כְּשֵׁרָה. — it is valid.

The lesson of the mishnah is that we do not fear that he will make some direct use of the tree on the festival (Meiri; Gem. 24b).

[The previous mishnah has already taught us that where 'the tree is removed and the succah can stand by itself ... we may go up into it on the festival', but this ruling is still needed. In mishnah 3, though the floor (according to Rashi in Succah) was supported by trees, it and the walls themselves were made of non-growing materials. Therefore if the support given by the trees is not needed by the floor, there is no reason for a prohibition on Yom Tov. Here, since the walls themselves are trees, the use of which is prohibited on Yom Tov, it could be argued that the continuous proximity of the trees to the person dwelling within is reason enough to prohibit use of this succah on Yom Tov. The mishnah teaches us that such a supposition is fallacious. One may indeed dwell in such a succah. However, according to the view that mishnah 3, too, refers to an instance where trees served as walls the above cannot be the lesson of the mishnah since it is already known from mishnah 3 (cf. Kol HaRemez).]

Validity of trees for succah walls is conditional upon the sturdiness of the trees themselves: they should not be swayed by normal winds; the branches should be tied together securely so that the branches do not sway in a normal wind and the intervening spaces must be filled with straw and stubble. Any partition that cannot remain rigid in the face of normal winds is not considered a partition and is invalid as a succah wall (Gem. 24b; Rav; Meiri; Orach Chaim 630:10).

שְׁלוּחֵי מִצְוָה — Those who are engaged in

the performance [lit. agents] of a mitzvah

For example: someone who is traveling to study Torah or to greet his rabbi, or is occupied with redeeming Jewish captives (Rashi to 25a; Rav).

פְּטוּרִין מִן־הַסֻּכָּה. — are exempt from the [mitzvah of] succah.

A person who is occupied with one mitzvah is exempt from another (הָעוֹסֵק בְּמִצְוָה פָּטוּר מִן־הַמִּצְוָה). This is derived from the verse which commands that the Shema must be recited בְּשִׁבְתְּךָ בְּבֵיתֶךָ, when you sit in your house (Deut. 6:7), implying that the performance of a mitzvah takes precedence over an optional activity such as merely sitting at home, but not if one is occupied with another religious commandment (Gem. 25a; Rashi, there; Rav; Orach Chaim 640:7).

There are two views concerning this exemption:

A) Rashi (ibid.), Ran, and Meiri exempt one who is involved in one mitzvah from performing a second mitzvah if performing the second mitzvah would require him to go out of his way. Consequently, people engaged in such a mission are obligated to sleep in a succah only if one is readily available. If it would be troublesome for them to build one or even look for one, they are exempt.

Following this approach but going a step further, Mordechai (740) quotes Raavyah who says that even if they can pursue their mission only by day, they are nevertheless exempt from the mitzvah of succah at night if they would be better able to continue on their mission after sleeping comfortably, rather than in a cold or uncomfortable succah. If so, restful sleep is regarded as part of accomplishing their original mitzvah mission, and supersedes the mitzvah of succah.

Those who are engaged in the performance of a *mitzvah* are exempt from the [*mitzvah* of] *succah*. Ill people and their attendants are exempt from the [*mitzvah* of] *succah*.

We may eat and drink casually outside the *succah*.

YAD AVRAHAM

B) *Tosafos* (25a s.v. שְׁלוּחֵי מִצְוָה), *Rosh* (2:6), and *Ritva* hold that one who is occupied with a *mitzvah* is exempt from another *mitzvah* only if the second one interferes with the fulfillment of the first; otherwise, he must perform both. Consequently, people on such a mission who must stop overnight are obligated to eat and sleep in a *succah* at night even if they must hunt one out or build it themselves, since the *mitzvah* of *succah* at night does not interfere with their daytime mission.

Rama (*Orach Chaim* 38:8) determines the halachah according to *Rashi, Ran,* and *Meiri.* He states that if there is a hardship involved, one is exempt; if not, one must do both *mitzvos.*

חוֹלִין וּמְשַׁמְּשֵׁיהֶן, — *Ill people and their attendants*

No danger to life is implied here. Even a person who has a headache or whose eyes are strained is exempt (*Gem.* 26a).

פְּטוּרִין מִן־הַסֻּכָּה. — *are exempt from the* [*mitzvah* of] *succah*.

The sick person is exempt because Scripture states (*Lev.* 23:42): בַּסֻּכֹּת תֵּשְׁבוּ, *In succos you shall dwell.* This teaches תֵּשְׁבוּ כְּעֵין תָּדֻרוּ, *as you are accustomed to dwell all year long at home, so are you to dwell in a succah.* But under conditions of extreme discomfort such as illness, which would cause one to leave his normal dwelling to go to a more comfortable place, he is not required to live in a *succah* (*Rav* from *Gem.* 26a).

The attendants are exempt because they are involved in the *mitzvah* of caring for the patient, and one who is involved in a *mitzvah* is exempt from

another *mitzvah* [עוֹסֵק בְּמִצְוָה פָּטוּר מִן הַמִּצְוָה] (*Levush* to *Orach Chaim* 640 *Mishnah Berurah* 640:7). [Thus this statement of the mishnah is an example of the previous dictum.]

Some authorities maintain that the attendants are exempt merely while the patient needs them. Whenever the patient does not need their aid or presence, they are obligated to fulfill the *mitzvah* of *succah* (*Orach Chaim* 640:3).

The *Gemara* (26a) also explains that those who are not ill but suffer discomfort from flies, the sun, or bad odors are also exempt from the *succah*. A person who would leave his home to escape any of the above discomforts may leave the *succah*. This exemption applies solely to the affected individual, not to his attendants (*Gem.* 26a; *Orach chaim* 640:4).

Rama (ibid.), however, cautions that on the first night of Succos, even those who suffer discomfort must eat at least כַּזַּיִת, *an olive's volume* of bread in the *succah*.

אוֹכְלִין וְשׁוֹתִין עֲרַאי חוּץ לַסֻּכָּה. — *We may eat and drink casually outside the succah*.

Ran defines עֲרַאי, *casually,* as a snack: the amount of food one might eat to take the edge off his hunger when he intends to eat a meal shortly (cf. *Daas Torah* to *Orach Chaim* 639:2).

The *Gemara* (26a) declares that a snack (אֲכִילַת עֲרַאי) is the amount of food a student might eat quickly before going off to a lecture in the study hall. *Rashi* (ibid.), and *Ran* explain that such a student eats *one mouthful* and drinks something in case the lecture will be drawn out.

Rosh (2:13) and *Tosafos* (26a) define this amount as the volume of an egg, the amount a person can swallow at one time.

[ה] **מַעֲשֶׂה** וְהֵבִיאוּ לוֹ לְרַבָּן יוֹחָנָן בֶּן־
זַכַּאי לִטְעוֹם אֶת־הַתַּבְשִׁיל,
וּלְרַבָּן גַּמְלִיאֵל שְׁתֵּי כוֹתָבוֹת וּדְלִי שֶׁל מַיִם,
וְאָמְרוּ: ,,הַעֲלוּם לַסֻּכָּה.'' וּכְשֶׁנָּתְנוּ לוֹ לְרַבִּי

יד אברהם

Rambam (Succah 6:6), says that the amount is either a little less or a little more than an egg. Obviously, he maintains, some people can swallow even more than the volume of an egg. This view is shared by *R' Yitzchak Gias (Meah Shearim p. 88)* and *Rav (2:5; see gloss in Mishnayos ed. Vilna there).*

The *Shulchan Aruch (Orach Chaim 639:2)* follows the view of *Rosh* and *Tosafos* — that up to and including an egg's volume of bread is still considered a snack. More than this is considered a meal, which must be eaten in the *succah.*

Although the mishnah also mentions שׁוֹתִין עֲרַאי, *we may drink casually*, the *Gemara* does not define 'casual' drinking. The matter is clarified by the ראשונים, *early Talmudic commentaries.*

Ran states that drinking the single drink that accompanies a snack is regarded as casual. This is implied by *Rashi (26a)* quoted in our commentary earlier: 'He takes one mouthful and drinks.'

Meiri cites the opinion of 'some' that any drinking done alone, even of wine, is defined as casual if it is not done together with food that must be eaten in the *succah.* Accordingly, the mishnah's reference to 'drinking' is probably idiomatic in the sense that we commonly refer to 'food and drink', but beverages as a separate category do not require the use of a *succah.* If the food being eaten requires a *succah,* then the accompanying drinking is considered 'fixed' (שְׁתִיַּת קֶבַע) as opposed to casual, but if the food being eaten does not require a *succah,* then the accompanying drink is also considered casual.

Rambam (Succah 6:6) defines water as the beverage meant by the term *casual drinking;* and it may be drunk

outside the *succah.* [This would seem to include other beverages that have no special significance.] Implicitly, drinking wine would be considered *fixed drinking.*

Meiri himself holds that drinking wine alone is not *fixed,* but wine with fruit is considered *fixed.* He derives his ruling from the instance when they brought Rabban Gamliel a snack of two dates and a pail of water (2:5). Their reason for bringing him so simple a snack was so that he would not have to trouble himself and go up to the *succah.* If wine is permitted out of the *succah* they certainly would have brought him some, instead of a pail of water. It is from here that *Meiri* infers that wine together with the dates would be considered a fixed meal and would not have served the purpose of freeing him from eating in the *succah.*

Some halachic authorities (*Orach Chaim 639:2*) always consider wine to be an incidental drink, holding that wine has no more significance than a fruit (*Orach Chaim 639:2; Mishnah Berurah, ibid*).

Generally, fruit and drink in any quantity may be eaten and drunk outside the *succah.* Foods made from the five grains (wheat, oats, barley, rye, and spelt), such as cake or cereal, if eaten as a fixed meal, must be eaten in the *succah (Orach Chaim 639:2). Orach Chaim 639* discusses at length the laws of the types and quantities of foods and drink that must be eaten in a *succah,* and the instances when the blessing לֵישֵׁב בַּסֻּכָּה, *to dwell in the succah,* must be recited.

Although the mishnah does not mention napping [שִׁינַת עֲרַאי], the *Gemara (26a)* quotes a *baraisa* that even napping is forbidden outside the *succah.*

The reason is given by Rabah *(ibid)*: 'There is no fixed amount for sleeping,' i.e., sometimes a person is refreshed by a short

5. Once they brought Rabban Yochanan ben Zakkai some cooked food to taste, and to Rabban Gamliel [they brought] two dates and a pail of water, and they said, 'Bring them up to the *succah.'*

YAD AVRAHAM

nap and sometimes one does not feel rested unless he sleeps many hours. Therefore, a

nap is no different from a full night's sleep in regard to the *succah* (*Rashi, ibid.*).

5.

מַעֲשֶׂה וְהֵבִיאוּ לוֹ לְרַבָּן יוֹחָנָן בֶּן־זַכַּאי לִטְעוֹם אֶת־הַתַּבְשִׁיל, — *Once they brought Rabban Yochanan ben Zakkai some cooked food to taste,*

Ran comments that the expression *to taste* implies a small amount of food — i.e. less than the amount for a סְעוּדַת קָבַע, *fixed meal.*

[According to this interpretation, the teaching derived from this story is twofold. A) He declined to taste the food outside of the *succah* even though it was less than the amount needed for a 'fixed meal'. B) Since the mishnah does not indicate that the cooked food was of the five species of grain, we may assume that it should be classified as פֵּירֵי, *fruit*, which need not be eaten in the *succah* even if they constitute the entire meal (according to most authorities even meat and fish are classified as 'fruit' in this regard). Nevertheless, Rabban Yochanan would not eat it outside the *succah.*]

Meiri suggests that the word אֶת should be translated *with.* Thus they brought him something to taste together with the cooked food. Accordingly לִטְעוֹם should be understood as *to taste,* i.e. to snack. Thus: *Once they brought Rabban Yochanan ... [a snack] together with cooked food.* It can be speculated that 'the snack' was a small amount of bread. Rabban Yochanan's refusal to eat outside of the succah can be attributed to 'the snack' which, though a small quantity, was the kind of food that must be consumed in the succah if the required amount is eaten. Thus, the second case of the mishnah — that of Rabban Gamliel who went to the *succah* for dates and water — teaches a lesson not implied by R' Yochanan: that a person is praiseworthy if he is scrupulous not to consume even fruit outside the *succah;* see *comm.* below s.v. ואמרו העלום לסוכה.

וּלְרַבָּן גַּמְלִיאֵל שְׁתֵּי כוֹתָבוֹת וּדְלִי שֶׁל מַיִם, — *and to Rabban Gamliel [they brought]*

two dates and a pail of water,

[Even a large amount of water is considered only a snack. See *comm.* to 2:4 and below s.v. ואמרו.]

וְאָמְרוּ: ,,הַעֲלוֹם לַסֻּכָּה.'' — *and they* [i.e., both Rabban Yochanan and Rabban Gamliel] *said, 'Bring them up to the succah.'*

This contradicts the previous mishnah which states that a snack may be eaten outside the *succah.* The *Gemara* (26a) resolves the contradiction by saying that our mishnah teaches that a person is not regarded as haughty if he chooses to eat even fruit and water only in the *succah.*

The *Gemara* (*Yoma* 79b) quotes a *Baraisa* which adds to the mishnah: Not because this is the halachah, but because they wished to be stricter with themselves.

Rambam (*comm.*) comments that the lesson implied by this mishnah is that one who wishes to be strict in the observance of the *mitzvos* and consequently is careful not to consume any food outside of the *succah* is praiseworthy. Though water in any amount may be drunk outside the *succah, Rambam* (*Succah* 6:6), quoted in *Orach Chaim* (639:2), states: Whoever wishes to be strict with himself and not drink even water outside the *succah,* is praiseworthy.

The Talmud (*Yoma* 79b) gives two contradictory reasons why Rabban Gamliel was not required to eat these two dates in the *succah.* A) Two pitted dates are less than an egg, the amount required for a 'fixed meal'. The implication is that had Rabban Gamliel been offered fruit equal to 'more than an egg' he

צָדוֹק אָכַל פָּחוֹת מִכַּבֵּיצָה, נְטָלוֹ בְמַפָּה וַאֲכָלוֹ חוּץ לַסֻּכָּה, וְלֹא בֵרַךְ אַחֲרָיו.

יד אברהם

would have been required to eat in the *succah*, for even fruit must be eaten in the *succah* if enough is consumed. B) Two dates are more than the normal minimum that may be eaten outside the *succah*; nevertheless they need not be eaten in the *succah* because no amount of fruit (i.e. anything not made of the five species of grain, according to most authorities) requires a succah.

Though the conclusion of the *Gemara* seems to accept the second view, *Rif* (as interpreted by *Ramban* in *Milchamos* and cited by *Ran*) adopts the first view. Virtually all of the other authorities, including *Rambam* (*Succah* 6:6) and *Shulchan Aruch* (*Orach Chaim* 639:2) adopt the second view.

וּכְשֶׁנָּתְנוּ לוֹ לְרַבִּי צָדוֹק אכֶל פָּחוֹת מִכַּבֵּיצָה, נְטָלוֹ בְמַפָּה — But when they gave R' Tzaddok food smaller than the volume of an egg, he took it with a cloth

[This food required washing of the hands before eating, i.e. it was either bread or 'something which is dipped in liquid' (דָּבָר שֶׁטִּבּוּלוֹ בְּמַשְׁקֶה) which required washing of the hands (at least in Talmudic times; see *Orach Chaim* 158:4). Nevertheless R' Tzaddok holds that food smaller than the volume of an egg does not require washing (see the discussion of the halachah below). Had he been required to wash his hands, the wrapping of food in a cloth to avoid touching it while eating would have been no substitute for washing; it is permitted only as an emergency measure when no water is to be found for a considerable distance (*Chullin* 107a; *Tosafos* here 27a s.v. הא; cf. *Orach Chaim* 163:1, with *Mishnah Berurah* 2).]

Though R' Tzaddok held that washing was not required, he held the food in a cloth for reasons of cleanliness [as explained above, wrapping the hands is no substitute where washing is required] (*Rashi*).

There are two conflicting interpretations of R' Tzaddok's action. According to one view, R' Tzaddok holds that the volume of food for which one must wash is equal to the volume for which *Bircas HaMazon* [*Grace after Meals*] must be recited. His view is that *Bircas HaMazon* is required only after eating the volume of an egg. Accordingly, since the halachah requires *Bircas HaMazon* even for the volume of an olive, washing, too, would be required for that amount. In another interpretation of R' Tzaddok's action, he holds that washing is dependent on the volume of food that is susceptible to *tumah* by Torah law — the volume of an egg. Although the Rabbis decreed that smaller amounts, too, could become *tamei*, they did not require washing for such amounts.

An amount of food sufficient to require the recitation of *Bircas HaMazon* [*Grace After Meals*] requires washing of the hands before eating. R' Tzaddok was of the opinion that the minimum amount for *Bircas HaMazon* is the 'volume of an egg' (as set forth further), consequently he did not wash his hands. According to the halachah which accepts the volume of an olive as the minimum for *Bircas HaMazon* (see below), the same quantity should be considered the minimum for washing of the hands. In order to accomodate both views, one should wash his hands, but not recite the blessing, when eating less than 'the volume of an egg (*Beur HaGra* to *Orach Chaim* 158:2; *Mishnah Berurah* ibid. 9).

From the foregoing it should be clear that less than 'the volume of an olive' should not require washing of the hands, as is clearly implied in *Orach Chaim* 158:3. However, *Magen Avraham* (158:4) rules that even smaller amounts require washing. *Mishnah Berurah* (there 10) maintains that ideally [לְכַתְּחִילָה] one should conform with this ruling. Those holding this opinion base their view upon intricate considerations of two conflicting passages of the Talmud (see *Eliyahu Rabbah* 158:3), the

But when they gave R' Tzaddok food smaller than the volume of an egg, he took it with a cloth and ate it outside the *succah*, and did not recite the benediction after it.

presentation of which is beyond the scope of this commentary.

Tosafos (Yoma 79a s.v. נטלו) and *Ran* (here) disagree with *Rashi* and hold that R' Tzaddok wrapped the food in a cloth, not for reasons of cleanliness, but because of halachic considerations. There can be two reasons for the washing of hands. A) The familiar obligation to wash the hands before eating certain foods applies to eating only. In R' Tzaddok's case, the obligation to wash before *eating* did not apply because the quantity eaten was not sufficient as explained above. B) Unwashed hands were assigned a state of contamination vis-a-vis certain categories of food as we will explain further. Where this concern is present, the hands must be washed before the mere *handling* of the food, since contact with the hands would contaminate the food. Here there would be no minimum, because food-stuffs of even *minimal* size (כל שהוא) are susceptible to contamination (albeit only by Rabbinic law according to many authorities). However there is no obligation to wash the hands when the food is wrapped in a cloth; as long as the food is untouched there is no concern.

Tosafos and *Ran* explain that R' Tzaddok was a *Kohen*, and, as such, would be the recipient of *terumah*-tithes, which are holy and must be maintained in a state of purity (*Numb.* 18:8,12). The Rabbis decreed that human hands should be regarded as contaminated [טָמֵא], since people habitually touch all sorts of things during the course of the day; and they further decreed that the hands must be cleansed before touching *terumah* (*Shabbos* 14b). Unwashed hands, regarded as *tamei*, would contaminate foods of even less than the volume of an egg (*Taharos* 2:1). As a further precaution many *Kohanim* would treat even non-sacred foods as if they were *terumah*, lest they err and contaminate *terumah*. To satisfy this requirement, it is sufficient for the *Kohen* to wrap his hands in a cloth so that he does not physically touch — and thus contaminate — the food.

When a *Kohen* eats food of less than the volume of an egg, it is sufficient for the *Kohen* to wrap his hands in a cloth or don gloves — the amount is too small to require washing preparatory to *eating*, and the hand-covering removes the danger of *tumah*. This was R' Tzaddok's situation. Being that the bread or cake brought to him was less than the volume of an egg (as mentioned in the mishnah) he wrapped his hands in a cloth in order to eat it. Had the food been the size of an egg or larger, he would have washed his hands because of the statutory obligation to do so before *eating*, which applies even where the food is not touched.

וַאֲכָלוּ חוּץ לַסֻכָּה, — *and ate it outside the succah,*

He followed the law for eating a snack (see 2:4).

Unlike his contemporaries, R' Tzaddak did not adopt the extra restriction. He demonstrated that one who is not strict with himself on this point is not to be considered careless in performing *mitzvos (Ran).*

By stating that R' Tzaddok ate *less* than an egg outside the *succah*, the mishnah implies that food whose volume *equals* an egg must be eaten in the *succah*.

The *Gemara* (26b) cites this to disprove those opinions which hold that the volume of an egg constitutes a snack and does not require a *succah*. (See *comm.* on last part of 2:4). The *Gemara* answers that even if it had been the full volume of an egg, R' Tzaddok would have eaten it outside the *succah*. The mishnah mentions the size to teach us that the small volume exempted him also from washing and from reciting *Bircas HaMazon*.

וְלֹא בֵרַךְ אַחֲרָיו. — *and did not recite the benediction after it.*

[I.e. בִּרְכַּת הַמָּזוֹן, *Grace after Meals.*]

R' Tzaddok held the view of R' Yehudah (*Berachos* 7:2) that one is obligated to recite *Bircas HaMazon* only after a meal of at least an egg's volume of bread.

[ו] **רַבִּי** אֱלִיעֶזֶר אוֹמֵר: אַרְבַּע עֶשְׂרֵה
סְעוּדוֹת חַיָּב אָדָם לֶאֱכוֹל בַּסֻּכָּה,
אַחַת בַּיּוֹם וְאַחַת בַּלַּיְלָה. וַחֲכָמִים אוֹמְרִים:
אֵין לַדָּבָר קִצְבָה, חוּץ מִלֵּילֵי יוֹם טוֹב רִאשׁוֹן
שֶׁל חַג בִּלְבָד.
וְעוֹד אָמַר רַבִּי אֱלִיעֶזֶר: מִי שֶׁלֹּא אָכַל לֵילֵי
יוֹם טוֹב הָרִאשׁוֹן, יַשְׁלִים בְּלֵילֵי יוֹם טוֹב

יד אברהם

[The halachah, however, follows R' Meir who rules that eating an olive's volume of bread obligates one in *Bircas HaMazon* (*Orach Chaim* 184:6).]

6.

רַבִּי אֱלִיעֶזֶר אוֹמֵר: אַרְבַּע עֶשְׂרֵה סְעוּדוֹת חַיָּב אָדָם לֶאֱכוֹל בַּסֻּכָּה, — *R' Eliezer says: A man is obligated to eat fourteen meals in the succah,*

Two each day for the seven days [of Succos] *(Rav).*

אַחַת בַּיּוֹם וְאַחַת בַּלַּיְלָה. — *one each* [lit. by] *day and one each* [lit. by] *night.*

R' Eliezer derives this from the verse (*Lev.* 23:42), בְּסֻכֹּת תֵּשְׁבוּ, *in succos shall you dwell,* which is interpreted to teach: תֵּשְׁבוּ כְּעֵין תָּדוּרוּ *you shall dwell* [in the succah] *just as you dwell in your own home* (see comm. on 2:4). Just as one eats a meal in the morning and a meal in the evening in his own house, he is to do the same in the *succah* (*Gem.* 27a).

וַחֲכָמִים אוֹמְרִים: אֵין לַדָּבָר קִצְבָה, — *but the Sages say: This matter has no fixed obligation,*

The Sages also agree with R' Eliezer that one should dwell in the *succah* just as he dwells at home. However, they stress that just as in one's own home if he wishes to eat he does and if not he doesn't, so it is in the *succah*: if he wants to eat he must eat in the *succah* but if not he may fast (*Gem.* 27a; *Rav*).

חוּץ מִלֵּילֵי יוֹם טוֹב רִאשׁוֹן שֶׁל חַג בִּלְבָד. — *except for the night of the first Yom Tov of the Festival only.*

I.e., the first night of Succos. The *mitzvah* of dwelling in a *succah* (*Lev.* 23:24) applies to all seven days of Suc-

cos (but not to Shimini Atzeres, the one-day festival that comes immediately after Succos), but one is not *required* to have meals in a *succah*; should he prefer to fast or eat fruit, he is free to do so. The exception to this is the first night of Succos; then, a meal must be eaten in the *succah* מִדְּאוֹרַיְתָא, *by Torah law.* This law is derived through the principle of *gezeirah shavah* [lit. *congruent expression*] one of the thirteen principles of halachic exegesis, as follows:

Regarding the festival of Succos the Torah states (*Lev.* 23:34), בַּחֲמִשָּׁה עָשָׂר יוֹם לַחֹדֶשׁ הַשְּׁבִיעִי הַזֶּה חַג הַסֻּכּוֹת, *on the fifteenth day of this seventh month is the Succos festival.*

Regarding the festival of Pesach the Torah states (*Lev.* 23:6): וּבַחֲמִשָּׁה עָשָׂר יוֹם לַחֹדֶשׁ הַזֶּה חַג הַמַּצּוֹת, *and on the fifteenth day of this month is the festival of unleavened bread.*

The Torah uses the common word *fifteenth* with relation to both festivals; the Oral Tradition teaches that the two festivals are thereby linked by a *gazeirah shavah* by means of which the distinctive laws of one festival may be applied to another. As in all cases of *gezeirah shavah*, such exegeses are not valid unless they are specifically included in the Oral Law: אֵין אָדָם דָּן גְּזֵרָה שָׁוָה מֵעַצְמוֹ, *no one may expound a gezeirah shavah on his own* (*Pesachim* 66a).

6. **R'** Eliezer says: A man is obligated to eat fourteen meals in the *succah*, one each day and one each night. But the Sages say: This matter has no fixed obligation, except for the night of the first *Yom Tov* of the Festival only.

R' Eliezer further stated: Whoever did not eat [in the *succah*] on the night of the first *Yom Tov*, must compensate for it on the night of the last *Yom Tov*.

YAD AVRAHAM

Just as Scripture mandates the eating of matzah on the first night of Pesach, so on the first night of Succos it is mandatory to eat in the *succah*. During the rest of Succos if one prefers not to eat a fixed meal, he need not eat in the *succah*. Similarly on Pesach one is not required to eat matzah after the first night (*Gemara* 27a).

Also, just as one must eat an olive's volume of matzah on the first night of Pesach, he must eat at least an olive's volume of bread in the *succah* on the first night of Succos (*Ran; Orach Chaim 639:3, Mishnah Berurah 20*). Some say that this obligation to eat in the *succah* on the first night applies even if it rains (*Ran; Rama; Orach Chaim 639:5*).

וְעוֹד אָמַר רַבִּי אֱלִיעֶזֶר: מִי שֶׁלֹּא אָכַל לֵילֵי יוֹם טוֹב הָרִאשׁוֹן, יַשְׁלִים בְּלֵילֵי יוֹם טוֹב הָאַחֲרוֹן. — *R' Eliezer further stated: Whoever did not eat [in the succah] on the night of the first Yom Tov, must compensate for it on the night of the last Yom Tov.*

The eighth festival day is Shemini Atzeres. One who failed to eat a meal in the *succah* on the first *Yom Tov* should then add food to his regular Shemini Atzeres meal to compensate for the missed meal. However, the Shemini Atzeres meal is not to be eaten in the *succah*, for the *mitzvah* of *succah* no longer applies as will be discussed below (*Rashi 27a; Rav*).

The *Gemara* (27a) queries: With what (type of food) does he compensate? If it is with bread [i.e. the bread and the foods that form the bulk of the

meal (e.g. meat and vegetables) (*Rashi*)] — he is eating the meal of the day! [This could not compensate for a missed meal for there is nothing to identify the additional food as anything more than the regular *Yom Tov* meal (*Rashi*).]

The *Gemara* concludes, he compensates with מִינֵי תַּרְגִּימָא, *minei targima*, which *Rashi* interprets as *desserts*, e.g. fruits and cakes (cf. *Tosafos* s.v. במיני).

The *Gemara* wonders at R' Eliezer: Earlier he required that fourteen meals be eaten in the *succah*. Now he states that if one missed the first meal he can eat it the night of Shemini Atzeres. How can that meal compensate for a Succos meal when it is forbidden to dwell in the *succah* on Shemini Atzeres, which is no longer the festival of Succos and to sit in a *succah* then means transgressing the prohibition of לֹא תֹסְפוּ, *you may not add* [to a *mitzvah* of the Torah (*Deut. 4:2*)]?

The *Gemara* answers that R' Eliezer changed his view about the requirement of fourteen meals in the *succah* and concurred with the Sages that there is no set number of required meals. But he disagrees with them concerning compensation for having failed to eat a meal in the *succah* on the first night. He compares eating in the *succah* to sacrifices. If one failed to bring the required sacrifices on the first *Yom Tov*, he may compensate by bringing them on the last *Yom Tov* (*Gemara* 27a following *Rashi*; but cf. *Tos.* 27a s.v. חזר בו).

Maharshal explains that once R' Eliezer retracted his opinion about eating fourteen meals in the *succah*, the question no longer remains how one can compensate on Shemini Atzeres when it is forbidden to eat in a *succah*. That is a difficulty only if the requirement is derived from the passage *in succos you shall dwell* (as explained earlier) — if so,

הָאַחֲרוֹן. וַחֲכָמִים אוֹמְרִים: אֵין לַדָּבָר
תַּשְׁלוּמִין. עַל־זֶה נֶאֱמַר: ,,מְעֻוָּת לֹא־יוּכַל
לִתְקֹן, וְחֶסְרוֹן לֹא־יוּכַל לְהִמָּנוֹת."

[ז] **מִי** שֶׁהָיָה רֹאשׁוֹ וְרֻבּוֹ בַסֻּכָּה וְשֻׁלְחָנוֹ
בְּתוֹךְ הַבַּיִת — בֵּית שַׁמַּאי פּוֹסְלִין,
וּבֵית הִלֵּל מַכְשִׁירִין.
אָמְרוּ לָהֶן בֵּית הִלֵּל לְבֵית שַׁמַּאי: ,,לֹא כָךְ
הָיָה מַעֲשֶׂה, שֶׁהָלְכוּ זִקְנֵי בֵּית שַׁמַּאי וְזִקְנֵי בֵית

יד אברהם

וַחֲכָמִים אוֹמְרִים: אֵין לַדָּבָר תַּשְׁלוּמִין. — *But the Sages say: This matter has no compensation.*

[If one missed the obligatory meal on the first night there is no way to make it up.]

עַל־זֶה נֶאֱמַר: ,,מְעֻוָּת לֹא־יוּכַל לִתְקֹן, וְחֶסְרוֹן לֹא־יוּכַל לְהִמָּנוֹת." — *About this it is said [Ecclesiastes 1:15]: A twisted thing cannot be made straight, and what is not there cannot be numbered.*

[For other applications of this verse see *Chagigah* 1:6-7; *Berachos* 26a.]

an integral part of this requirement is that one eat *in* the *succah*, something that is forbidden on Shemini Atzeres. When R' Eliezer retracted this view, and expounded that the obligation of the first meal is derived from the obligation to eat matzah, the *succah* as location of the meal becomes incidental. If it were permissible, theoretically, to eat a meal outside the *succah*, one might do so. Consequently, if it becomes necessary to compensate on Shemini Atzeres then no *succah* is needed. This, however, in no way fails to qualify as a Succos meal, since the *gezeirah shavah* — the source of the obligation — does not specify use of a *succah*.

7.

מִי שֶׁהָיָה רֹאשׁוֹ וְרֻבּוֹ בַסֻּכָּה — *A person who had his head and most of his body inside the succah*

In Talmudic times it was customary to eat in repose, lying on a couch, rather than sitting erect at a table. Thus, the mishnah discusses the case when one's head and most of his body are lying in the *succah*.

וְשֻׁלְחָנוֹ בְּתוֹךְ הַבַּיִת — *and his table inside the house —*

[Low tables were placed next to each couch. In our mishnah's case the table was not inside the *succah*, for reasons that will be discussed below.]

בֵּית שַׁמַּאי פּוֹסְלִין, וּבֵית הִלֵּל מַכְשִׁירִין. — *Beis Shammai invalidate* [the *succah*] *and Beis Hillel validate it.*

The *Gemara* (3a) states that our mish-

nah is incomplete — Beis Shammai and Beis Hillel disagree on two points of law. The circumstances of the first case are as stated in the mishnah — *a person who had his head and most of his body inside the succah and his table inside the house.* The *succah* under discussion is large enough to contain the person, his table, and even more people, but he chose to recline near the *succah* entrance and keep his table in the house (*Rashi, ibid.*). In this case Beis Shammai hold that the obligation is not fulfilled and Beis Hillel hold it is. But the language of Beis Shammai and Beis Hillel — invalid and valid — cannot be applied to this case. In the case of a large *succah* and one who chose to keep his table outside, the *succah* itself can hardly be described as invalid, for it is in no

But the Sages say: This matter has no compensation. About this matter it is said [*Ecclesiastes* 1:15]: *A twisted thing cannot be made made straight, and what is not there cannot be numbered.*

7. **A** person who had his head and most of his body inside the *succah* and his table inside the house — Beis Shammai invalidate [the *succah*] and Beis Hillel validate it.

Said Beis Hillel to Beis Shammai, 'Did it not happen that the elders of Beis Shammai and the elders of

way deficient. Rather it is the person who has been derelict in his performance of the *mitzvah*.

The second dispute between Beis Shammai and Beis Hillel is the subject of the otherwise inapplicable language of the mishnah: If the *succah* is so small that it can contain no more than his head and the greater part of his body alone [but not his table, not even if it is only one handbreadth wide], *Beis Shammai invalidate that succah and Beis Hillel validate it.*

[In summary, Beis Shammai and Beis Hillel disagree A) on the minimum size of a *succah*; and B) whether, in case of a large *succah*, one discharges his obligation if the table is not inside it.]

R' Shmuel bar Yitzchok (*Gem.* 3a) rules that a *succah* must be large enough to contain a person's head, the greater part of his body, and his table. This is measured as seven handbreadths by seven handbreadths: six handbreadths for his head and most of his body, and one for the table (*Gem.* 5a; see also *Rav* 1:1).

The *Gemara* notes that in this case the halachah follows Beis Shammai rather than Beis Hillel. *Seder* of *R' Amram* notes that this is one of only six disputes between the two schools where the halachah follows Beis Shammai (*Tosafos* 3a s.v. דְּאָמַר).

Beis Shammai's reasoning in this case is a subject of dispute among the commentaries. All agree, in the case of the large *succah* where his table is located outside the *succah* that Beis Shammai forbade it for fear שֶׁמָּא

יִמְשֵׁךְ אַחַר שֻׁלְחָנוּ, *lest he follow his table*, into the house.

As to the requirement that the *succah* contain a seventh handbreadth for a one-handbreadth table, *Rif*, *Rambam* (*Succah* 6:8), and *Rav* hold that here, too, Beis Shammai seek to keep the person from *following his table into the house*, for if the *succah* is so small, then a table will be located either outside the *succah* or in the house. Consequently, *Rif*, *Rambam* and *Rav* maintain that the halachah follows Beis Shammai in both cases.

Tosafos (3a), *Rosh* (1:1) and *Ran* explain Beis Shammai's position on the minimum size of the *succah* differently. A *succah* that has no room for a table is not even considered דִּירַת עֲרַאי, *a temporary dwelling*; the minimum requisite for any sort of dwelling being that it contain a table. A large *succah*, with a table placed outside is clearly a valid structure and the two schools disagree concerning whether we fear that one will 'follow his table.'

According to this view that Beis Shammai's reason in the case of a small *succah* is not the same as in the case of the large one, the halachah would follow Beis Shammai only in the case of a small *succah* where the *Gemara* (3a) specifically rules according to Beis Shammai, but will follow Beis Hillel (as usual) in the case of a large *succah* with its table outside (see *R' Chananel* to 3a).

The *Shulchan Aruch* concurs with *Rif*, *Rambam* and *Rav*. See Orach Chaim 634:1, 4).

אָמְרוּ לָהֶן בֵּית הִלֵּל לְבֵית שַׁמַּאי: ,,לֹא כָךְ הָיָה
מַעֲשֶׂה, שֶׁהָלְכוּ זִקְנֵי בֵית שַׁמַּאי וְזִקְנֵי בֵית הִלֵּל

הִלֵּל לְבַקֵּר אֶת־רַבִּי יוֹחָנָן בֶּן־הַחוֹרָנִי,
וּמְצָאוּהוּ שֶׁהָיָה יוֹשֵׁב רֹאשׁוֹ וְרֻבּוֹ בַסֻּכָּה
וְשֻׁלְחָנוֹ בְּתוֹךְ הַבַּיִת, וְלֹא אָמְרוּ לוֹ דָבָר?"
אָמְרוּ לָהֶן בֵּית שַׁמַּאי: "מִשָּׁם רְאָיָה? אַף הֵם
אָמְרוּ לוֹ: ,אִם כֵּן הָיִיתָ נוֹהֵג, לֹא קִיַּמְתָּ מִצְוַת
סֻכָּה מִיָּמֶיךָ'."

[ח] **נָשִׁים** וַעֲבָדִים וּקְטַנִּים פְּטוּרִים מִן־
הַסֻּכָּה. קָטָן שֶׁאֵינוֹ צָרִיךְ לְאִמּוֹ
חַיָּב בַּסֻּכָּה.

יד אברהם

לְבַקֵּר אֶת־רַבִּי יוֹחָנָן בֶּן־הַחוֹרָנִי, וּמְצָאוּהוּ
שֶׁהָיָה יוֹשֵׁב רֹאשׁוֹ וְרֻבּוֹ בַסֻּכָּה וְשֻׁלְחָנוֹ
בְּתוֹךְ הַבַּיִת, וְלֹא אָמְרוּ לוֹ דָבָר?" — *Said
Beis Hillel to Beis Shammai, 'Did it not
happen that the elders of Beis Shammai
and the elders of Beis Hillel went to visit
R' Yochanan son of the Choranite and
found him sitting with his head and
most of his body inside the succah and
his table within the house, and they said
nothing to him?'*

[A proof to the view of Beth Hillel.]

אָמְרוּ לָהֶן בֵּית שַׁמַּאי: "מִשָּׁם רְאָיָה? וְאַף הֵם
אָמְרוּ לוֹ: — *Beis Shammai replied* [lit.
said] *to them* [i.e., Beis Hillel], *'Is that
[your] proof? Actually they said to him,*

The elders of Beis Shammai *did*
protest to R' Yochanan.

Our translation follows *Rashi.
Tosefos Yom Tov* renders: *That is* [our]
proof. They actually said to him.

אִם כֵּן הָיִיתָ נוֹהֵג, לֹא קִיַּמְתָּ מִצְוַת סֻכָּה
מִיָּמֶיךָ'." — *"If this is how you have*

*[always] conducted yourself [then] you
have never in your life fulfilled the
mitzvah of succah."'*

Beis Shammai admonished R' Yochanan that since he violated the Rabbinic decree against keeping the table
outside the *succah,* he had never fulfilled the *mitzvah* properly in accordance with the regulation of the Sages,
although he had satisfied the Torah requirement *(Ritva).*

According to *Tosafos* (3a), Beis
Shammai told R' Yochanan ben Ha-
Chorani that he had never even fulfilled his Torah obligation. [Apparently
Tosafos holds that if one disregards a
Rabbinic detail of a *mitzvah* the Rabbis
have the power to nullify the entire
mitzvah. Alternatively, when the Sages
determine the details of a *mitzvah* they
define the Torah's requirement for the
mitzvah. Failure to comply with their
definition is, *ipso facto,* failure to fulfill
the *mitzvah.*]

8.

נָשִׁים וַעֲבָדִים — *Women, slaves,*

[Non-Jews sold into bondage to Jews.
See *comm.* 2:1 s.v. ויודע שעבדים.]

וּקְטַנִּים — *and minors*

[Boys under 13 years of age and girls
under 12 years are not obligated by the

Torah to perform *mitzvos*].

פְּטוּרִים מִן־הַסֻּכָּה. — *are exempt from the
succah* [i.e., from the *mitzvah* of suc-
cah].

The *Gemara* (28b) explains the mishnah's need to make this apparently ob-

Beis Hillel went to visit R' Yochanan son of the Choranite and found him sitting with his head and most of his body inside the *succah* and his table within the house, and they said nothing to him?'

Beis Shammai replied to them, 'Is that [your] proof? Actually they said to him, "If this is how you have [always] conducted yourself, [then] you have never in your life fulfilled the *mitzvah* of *succah*." '

8. **W**omen, slaves, and minors are exempt from the *succah*. A minor who does not need his mother is obligated [to dwell] in the *succah*.

YAD AVRAHAM

vious statement. Women and slaves are exempt from all מִצְוֹת עֲשֵׂה שֶׁהַזְּמַן גְּרָמָא, *mitzvos which must be performed only at specific times*, a principle that exempts them from the time-related *mitzvah* of *succah* as well. However, one might have reasoned that *succah* is an exception to the rule because of the *gezeirah shavah* from Pesach (see comm. to mishnah 6 s.v. חוץ מלילי יום טוב ראשון). Since women, like men, are obligated to fulfill all the *mitzvos* of Pesach (see *Pesachim* 43b), the same would seem to apply to the *mitzvah* of *succah* on the first night. Our mishnah is intended to disabuse us of this notion. Also the phrase בְּסֻכֹּת תֵּשְׁבוּ, *you shall dwell in succos ... (Lev.* 23:42) which teaches that a person must dwell in the *succah* in the same manner as he dwells at home (see *comm.* to mishnah 4 s.v. וחולין ומשמשיהן פטורין מן הסוכה) — this could be interpreted to mean that one's wife must join him in the *succah*, just as she does at home. The mishnah therefore teaches that women are exempt from *succah*. This is derived either from a Scriptural exemption for women (*Gemara* 28a), or by הֲלָכָה לְמֹשֶׁה מִסִּינַי, an Oral Tradition passed on to Moses at Sinai (28b).

[Because slaves have the same *mitzvah* obligations as Jewish women (see *Bava Kamma* 15a with *Rashi; Gittin*

39b), they, too, are exempt from the *mitzvah* of *succah*.]

קָטָן שֶׁאֵינוֹ צָרִיךְ לְאִמּוֹ — *A minor who does not need his mother*

The Gemara (28b) explains that this refers to a child who, when he awakens from sleep, does not call, 'mother, mother' — i.e., he is not so dependent on her that he must *continually* call her. Rather, he calls once and then remains silent (*Rashi*, ibid.).

Rambam (*Succah* 6:1) defines this age as five or six [depending on the maturity of the child]. See also *Orach Chaim* 640:2 with *Be'ur HaGra* and *Mishnah Berurah*.

חַיָּב בַּסֻּכָּה. — *is obligated [to dwell] in the succah.*

His obligation is the Rabbinical one of חִנּוּךְ, *training*, in the performance of *mitzvos*. Even so, the Sages supported this with a Scriptural basis (*Gem.* 28b).

The age of training [הִגִּיעַ לְחִנּוּךְ] is not one particular age but varies according to circumstances. When should a minor have his own *lulav*? The Sages say, (*Gem.* 42a): When he knows how to shake it properly during *Hallel*. When should he be given *tzitzis*? When he knows how to wrap himself in them. When should he be taught Torah? When he learns to speak. Circumstances determine the age of training for each particular *mitzvah* (*Tosafos* 28b; *Meiri*).

מַעֲשֶׂה וְיָלְדָה כַּלָּתוֹ שֶׁל שַׁמַּאי הַזָּקֵן וּפִחֵת אֶת־הַמַּעֲזִיבָה וְסִכֵּךְ עַל־גַּבֵּי הַמִּטָּה בִּשְׁבִיל הַקָּטָן.

[ט] **כָּל־שִׁבְעַת** הַיָּמִים אָדָם עוֹשֶׂה סֻכָּתוֹ קֶבַע וּבֵיתוֹ עֲרַאי. יָרְדוּ גְשָׁמִים, מֵאֵימָתַי מֻתָּר לְפַנּוֹת? מִשֶּׁתִּסְרַח הַמִּקְפָּה.

מָשְׁלוּ מָשָׁל: לְמָה הַדָּבָר דּוֹמֶה? לְעֶבֶד שֶׁבָּא לִמְזוֹג כּוֹס לְרַבּוֹ, וְשָׁפַךְ לוֹ קִיתוֹן עַל־פָּנָיו.

יד אברהם

מַעֲשֶׂה וְיָלְדָה כַּלָּתוֹ שֶׁל שַׁמַּאי הַזָּקֵן — *It once happened that the daughter-in-law of Shammai the Elder gave birth*

[Following the birth of her son, she was confined to her bed].

וּפִחֵת אֶת־הַמַּעֲזִיבָה — *and he removed the plaster* [roof]

Shammai removed the plastered section of roof that was over her bed (*Gemara* 28b).

וְסִכֵּךְ עַל־גַּבֵּי הַמִּטָּה בִּשְׁבִיל הַקָּטָן. — *and placed s'chach above the bed for the child.*

Shammai the Elder, disagreeing with the first tanna of our mishnah, imposes

training even upon children who still need their mothers (see comm. above). The Sages, on the other hand, maintain that since the mother is exempt from the *mitzvah* and the child needs the mother, there is no obligation to train him (*Ran*).

Rashash quoting *Maharshal* (*Yevamos* 15a) explains that Shammai surely was not training a newborn infant in the performance of *mitzvos*. His daughter-in-law had an older son who needed his mother and refused to leave her side even after she gave birth. It was not for the newborn baby that Shammai broke the ceiling, but rather for the older boy who was of the age of training.

9.

כָּל־שִׁבְעַת הַיָּמִים אָדָם עוֹשֶׂה סֻכָּתוֹ קֶבַע — *All the seven days a man must make his succah* [his] *permanent* [abode]

In what manner does a person accomplish this? If he has beautiful vessels, he should bring them into the *succah*; if he has beautiful divans, he should bring them into the *succah*; he should eat, drink and spend his leisure time in the *succah*; he should also engage in the study of Torah[1] in the *succah* (*Gemara* 28b).

וּבֵיתוֹ עֲרַאי. — *and his house* [his] *temporary* [abode].

He should do his utmost to dwell in the *succah* and use his house as infrequently as possible. He should use his house only for functional matters (e.g. cooking, etc.) whereas the succah should serve as his abode (*Rambam, Comm.*).

יָרְדוּ גְשָׁמִים, מֵאֵימָתַי מֻתָּר לְפַנּוֹת? מִשֶּׁתִּסְרַח הַמִּקְפָּה. — *If it rained* [lit. *rain*

1. If one's learning requires much concentration and it is difficult for him to concentrate in the *succah*, then he may study outside the *succah* (*Gem.* 28b; *Orach Chaim* 639:4).

It once happened that the daughter-in-law of Shammai the Elder gave birth and he removed the plaster [roof] and placed *s'chach* above the bed for the child.

9. **A**ll the seven days a man must make his *succah* [his] permanent [abode] and his house [his] temporary [abode]. If it rained, when is it permissible to leave? When the porridge becomes spoiled.

They [the Sages] illustrated this with a parable: To what is this comparable? To a slave who came to pour a cup for his master, and he poured the jug at his face.

YAD AVRAHAM

came down], when is it permissible to leave? When the porridge becomes spoiled.

מִקְפָּה (rendered here as *porridge*) is any cooked food which is neither very loose nor very thick (*Rashi* 28b; *Rav*).

The *Gemara* interprets it as a bean porridge. Most authorities *(Rashi; Rambam* in commentary; *Ritva; Rav)* understand this to be a lenient view, Even though bean porridge spoils quickly, while other foods would remain unaffected, one may leave the *succah* at this point. One need not bring such a porridge into the *succah* and wait for it to spoil; he only has to estimate the amount of time needed for it to spoil.

Meiri however, quotes authorities who understand this as a strict view, because they hold that such a porridge would take long to spoil.

The *Shulchan Aruch* follows the lenient view (*Orach Chaim* 639:5).

מָשְׁלוּ מָשָׁל: לְמָה הַדָּבָר דּוֹמֶה? — *They* [the Sages] *illustrated this with a parable: To what is this comparable?*

[I.e., being forced out of the *succah* by rain.]

לְעֶבֶד שֶׁבָּא לִמְזוֹג כּוֹס לְרַבּוֹ, — *To a slave who came to pour a cup for his master,*

[לִמְזוֹג means literally *to mix* a drink; to dilute wine with water to his master's taste.]

וְשָׁפַךְ לוֹ קִיתוֹן עַל-פָּנָיו. — *and he poured the jug at his face.*[1]

The master poured the jug into the

1. The *Vilna Gaon* explains this parable in depth. He asks why the mishnah did not simply state that a slave was coming to hand over a cup to his master and the master poured it into his face

The *Gaon* goes on to explain that Rosh Hashanah and Yom Kippur are days of judgment when many harsh punishments are decreed. Following them comes the festival of Succos with its abundance of *mitzvos: lulav, esrog*, myrtles, willows and dwelling in the *succah*. All of them are aimed at bringing out the Almighty's mercy (רַחֲמִים). By not letting us fulfill the *mitzvah* of *succah* the Almighty is telling us that he does not wish to temper His justice with mercy.

In the allegorical terminology of *Kabbalah*, wine represents harsh justice and water represents tempering mercy. The mishnah uses the term לִמְזוֹג, to indicate that the slave is coming to dilute the cup of wine held by his master. Israel seeks to dilute the severe and harsh judgments with mercy. But if the master takes the jug of water held by the slave [i.e. the tempering agent itself] and pours it into the slave's face, no dilution will take place. The Almighty, by not allowing the Jews to fulfill the *mitzvah* of *succah*, indicates that He does not wish to temper justice with mercy (*Divrei Eliyahu*).

סוכה [א] **לוּלָב** הַגָּזוּל וְהַיָּבֵשׁ פָּסוּל. שֶׁל אֲשֵׁרָה וְשֶׁל עִיר הַנִּדַּחַת פָּסוּל.

slave's face as if to say that the slave is not serving him properly, and his services are no longer desired. By causing it to rain, the Almighty is telling us that He is dissatisfied with our service and so He asks us to leave (*Rashi* 29a; *Rav*).

Chapter 3

⊷§ The Four Species

One of the central commandments connected with Succos is that of the אַרְבָּעָה מִינִים, *Four Species*. The Scriptural source of this *mitzvah, Leviticus* 23:40, reads: וּלְקַחְתֶּם לָכֶם בַּיּוֹם הָרִאשׁוֹן פְּרִי עֵץ הָדָר כַּפֹּת תְּמָרִים וַעֲנַף עֵץ־עָבֹת וְעַרְבֵי־נָחַל וּשְׂמַחְתֶּם לִפְנֵי ה׳ אֱלֹהֵיכֶם שִׁבְעַת יָמִים:

And you shall take for yourselves on the first day fruit of a beautiful tree, branches of date palms and twigs of plaited tree and willows of the brook and you shall rejoice before HASHEM your God for seven days.

Oral tradition identifies the Scriptural species as follows:
Fruit of the beautiful tree — *esrog*;
Branches of the date palm — *lulav*;
Twig of a plaited tree — *hadas* (myrtle);
Willows of the brook — *aravah*.

Each of these species is a separate component of a collective *mitzvah* but, as the *Gemara* states, אַרְבָּעָה מִינִים שֶׁבַּלּוּלָב מְעַכְּבִים זֶה אֶת זֶה, *the four species connected with the lulav are dependent upon one another*; the *mitzvah* cannot be performed in the absence of any one of them (34b; *Menachos* 27a).

As specified in the above-mentioned verse, the *mitzvah* applies only בַּיּוֹם הָרִאשׁוֹן, *on the first day* of the Succos Festival. The end of the verse, however, indicates that the Four Species are used not for only one, but for *seven* days of rejoicing. Since the Torah describes this seven-day period as being לִפְנֵי ה׳, *before HASHEM*, the Rabbis interpret that only in God's Presence, the Temple, are the Four Species taken for a full week. Thus, the *mitzvah*, as ordained by the Torah, is actually two-fold: on the first day of Succos, the obligation of taking the species applies everywhere; for the rest of the *Yom Tov*, the *mitzvah* applies only in the Temple.

After the destruction of the Second Temple, Rabban Yochanan Ben Zakkai instituted the performance of the *mitzvah* throughout Succos everywhere, in commemoration of the Temple ritual (mishnah 12). There are still differences, however, between the Sabbath and other days of Succos. See 3:12 and *Rosh Hashanah* 4:3 with commentary.

⊷§ Conditions that Invalidate the Four Species.

The initial mishnayos of this chapter offer a discussion of the various halachic invalidations of the Four Species. Some involve the physical properties or שִׁעוּר, [halachically required] *measurement*, unique to the respective species. Other invalidations, however, are common to all four.

The general invalidations fall under three categories, exegetically derived from three words in the above-mentioned verse as follows:

A) וּלְקַחְתֶּם, *And you shall take*. For the purpose of exegesis, the Rabbis interpret

1. **A** stolen *lulav* or a dry one is invalid.
[One] from an *asherah* or from a city that was led astray is invalid.

YAD AVRAHAM

this as if it were two words: וּלְקַח תָּם, *and you shall take a complete thing*, meaning שֶׁתְּהֵא לְקִיחָה תַּמָּה, *the taking must be 'complete'*. None of the species may be absent and no part of an individual species may be missing or mutilated. This invalidates any of the Four Species which are considered חָסֵר, *lacking*. For example, an *esrog* is invalid if part of its peel has been removed by a puncture or cut, no matter how minute.

B) לָכֶם, *to yourselves*. This mandates that the performance of the *mitzvah* requires legal ownership of the species; a borrowed, and certainly a stolen one, is not fit for the *mitzvah*.

C) הָדָר, *beautiful*. Although the term has specific application to the *esrog* in the context of the verse, the Sages interpret it also with reference to all four species; any one which lacks the halachic standard of beauty is invalid. Although it is meritorious that every *mitzvah* be performed in a beautiful and decorous manner, the provision that a lack of beauty invalidates the *mitzvah* is unique to the Four Species. The general principle of הִידּוּר מִצְוָה, *beautification of a mitzvah*, demands only that an effort be made to perform a *mitzvah* in such a manner, but only the Four Species are *invalid* if they lack this condition (*Tos.* 29b, s.v. בעינן).

◆§ Differences Between the First Day and the Intermediate Days

In consideration of the fact that only on the first day of Succos is the *mitzvah* ordained by Scripture, the Rabbis relaxed some of their requirements for the last six days of Succos. As the *Gemara* (29b, 36b) explains, neither the requirement of a complete species or of ownership applies after the first day of Succos, but whether or not 'beauty' is required all seven days is a matter of dispute. *Tosafos* (29b s.v. בעינן) holds that the Rabbis chose *not* to relax the latter restriction because the requirement of 'beauty' applies to *all* commandments in a general way, as explained above. *Rambam (Lulav* 8:9) holds that this requirement, too, is in effect for only the first day (see comm. to mishnah 6).

It should be noted that, in view of many commentators, the status of יוֹם טוֹב שֵׁנִי שֶׁל גָּלִיּוֹת, *the Second Day Yom Tov of the Diaspora*, is the same as that of the first day. See ch. 1 of *Rosh Hashanah*.

1.

לוּלָב הַגָּזוּל — *A stolen lulav,*

The Four Species must be the property of the one using them; a stolen *lulav*, therefore, is invalid. This will be discussed in further detail below.

S'fas Emes notes that the passive form, גָּזוּל, *stolen*, is used rather than the active הַגּוֹזֵל לוּלָב, *he who steals a lulav*. This indicates that it is the condition of the *lulav* as a stolen object that renders it invalid, not the fact that the user committed the sin of stealing. Accordingly, the *lulav* is invalid even if one did not commit the theft, but received the *lulav* from a thief, for it is a *stolen lulav* in any case.

However, *Shulchan Aruch (Orach Chaim* 649:1) cites a difference of opinion regarding whether or not a stolen *lulav* is invalid throughout the festival.

וְהַיָּבֵשׁ — *or a dry one*

Either the majority of its leaves or its spine has dried out (*Rosh* 3:2; *Tur* 645; *Orach Chaim* 645:5).

The actual degree of dryness that invalidates the *lulav* is the subject of dispute among the *rishonim* [early commentators].

Tosafos (29b) and *Rosh* (3:1) explain that *dry* means so brittle that one can

crumble it with his nail. In support of their view they cite *Berachos* (6:1) that uses this criterion with regard to the blemish of a 'dry ear' with regard to a firstborn animal.

Ravad (quoted by *Rosh, ibid.*) and *Meiri* maintain that practical experience contradicts this definition. Unlike the leaves of a myrtle that may eventually crumble (see comm. 3:2 s.v. והיבש), a *lulav* may last many years without reaching that state. In the context of *lulav*, therefore, *Ravad*, defines dryness as a total lack of greenness, where the *lulav* remains white because all its moisture is gone.[1]

Meiri cites a tradition that if one bends a leaf in half length-wise and it breaks it is considered *dry*.

Another opinion, rejected by most *rishonim* is that a year-old *lulav* is considered dried out (*Tos.* 29b explains why this is unacceptable).

The *Shulchan Aruch* (*Orach Chaim* 645:5) follows *Ravad's* view. *Rama* states that where *lulavim* were not available it was customary to rely on the more lenient view of *Tosafos* and *Rosh*.

[See comm. to 3:2 and 5 for the definition of dryness with regard to the other species.]

פָּסוּל. — *is invalid*

Although grouped together, the stolen *lulav* and the dry *lulav* are invalid for different reasons. In the case of the dry *lulav* the reason is the absence of beauty. *Rashi* and *Meiri* cite the verse: זֶה אֵלִי וְאַנְוֵהוּ, *this is my God and I will glorify Him* (Exodus 15:1), from which the Rabbis derive the dictum הִתְנָאֵה לְפָנָיו בְּמִצְוֹת, *glorify God by doing his mitzvos with beautiful articles* (see Gemara 11b and Rashi s.v. וְאַנְוֵהוּ). *Tosafos*, however, maintains that this verse means only that it is *preferable* [לְכַתְּחִלָה] that one endeavor to beautify a *mitzvah*, but not that a *mitzvah* done with an unattractive object is invalid.

That a dry *lulav* is actually rendered invalid is derived from the specific requirement that the Four Species possess הָדָר, *beauty* (Lev. 24:40), which invalidates any of the Four Species lacking this characteristic even after the fact [בְּדִעֲבַד].

The reason for the invalidity of a stolen *lulav* is the Torah's requirement that the Four Species be לָכֶם [lit. *for yourself*] which is expounded to mean מִשֶׁלָכֶם, *from your own property*. Consequently, a stolen *lulav*, which is not the property of the user, is invalid. For the same reason, even a borrowed *lulav* would be invalid.

However the unqualified statement פָּסוּל, *invalid*, indicates that the invalidation mentioned is for the entire duration of Succos, yet the requirement of ownership applies only to the first day; since a borrowed *lulav* is valid for the other six days of Succos, why should a stolen *lulav* be less so?

This leads the *Gemara* (30a) to conclude that the invalidation of a stolen *lulav* is based on the Talmudic dictum מִצְוָה הַבָּאָה בַּעֲבֵרָה, *a mitzvah made possible by a transgression*, is unacceptable. The source of this principle is *Malachi* 1:13, where God protests the bringing of unacceptable animals as offerings: וַהֲבֵאתֶם גָּזוּל וְאֶת־חַפִּסֵּחַ וְאֶת־הַחוֹלֶה, *and you have brought* [as offerings] *the stolen, the lame, and the sick*. Noting the comparison between the stolen and the lame, the *Gemara* comments that just as a lame animal is permanently invalid, so is a stolen one permanently unacceptable. This teaches that the stolen animal remains unacceptable even after a thief has acquired legal possession of it; for example, in the event of יֵאוּשׁ, [the owner's] *abandonment of hope of recovery*, which, in the view of some, entitles the thief to keep the animal though he remains obligated to pay the victim (see *Bava Kamma* 66a and *Choshen Mishpat* 353:2).

---

1. *Yerushalmi* (3:1) quotes R' Yehudah bar Pazi that total dryness connotes death. A *lulav* turning white is comparable to a corpse turning white. Such a *lulav* is therefore not valid for performing the *mitzvah* as it violates the verse (*Psalms* 115:17) לֹא הַמֵּתִים יְהַלְלוּ־יָהּ, *the dead will not praise God.*

It is this principle of מִצְוָה הַבָּאָה בַּעֲבֵירָה, a mitzvah made possible by a transgression, that distinguishes a stolen lulav from a borrowed one. Accordingly, though a borrowed lulav is unacceptable only on the first day, for its user does not own it, a stolen one is invalid for the entire Succos festival.

According to another opinion in the Gemara (30a), however, a stolen lulav is invalid only on the first day, as the disqualification of a mitzvah acquired through a transgression does not apply to a Rabbinic mitzvah (30a Tosafos s.v. מתוך). Rambam (Lulav 8:9) apparently follows this opinion, but most other authorities disagree, including Shulchan Aruch (649:1) (cf. Maggid Mishnah loc. cit. and Mishnah Berurah 649:6,8,30).

שֶׁל אֲשֵׁרָה — [One] from an asherah
I.e., a tree regarded as sacred and worshiped by idolators [Rashi 29b; Rav].
The Torah commands: וַאֲשֵׁרֵיהֶם תִּשְׂרְפוּן בָּאֵשׁ, and their sacred trees you shall burn in a fire (Deut. 12:3). As a result of the requirement that such a tree is to be burned, a lulav from it is invalid. This will be explained below.

Not every tree worshiped for idolatrous purposes is considered an asherah. According to the Gemara (31b) the asherah in our mishnah is in the category of אֲשֵׁרָה דְמֹשֶׁה, the asherah of Moses' [time], i.e., an idolatrous tree found by the Jews upon entering Eretz Yisrael in Scriptural times. Because such a tree must be burned, and its use for any purpose was forbidden, it was regarded as non-existent.

Other trees used in idol worship may, under certain circumstances, be subject to nullification by a non-Jew, in which case they would lose their status as idolatrous, forbidden objects. A lulav from such an asherah would not be invalid for the mitzvah. Even in such cases, however, a lulav that was involved in idol worship should not be used as a first resort [לְכַתְּחִלָּה] for it is distasteful to use such an object in the fulfillment of God's command (see Tosafos 31b s.v. באשרה; Orach Chaim 649:3 and Mishnah Berurah).

וְשֶׁל עִיר הַנִּדַּחַת — or from a city that was led astray
The law of this city is outlined in Deuteronomy 13:13-19. In brief, if the majority of residents in a Jewish city are persuaded by local residents to worship idols, the city is classified as an עִיר הַנִּדַּחַת, a city that was led astray, which must be totally annihilated (Rambam, Hilchos Avodah Zarah 4:2). The invalidation cited by our mishnah stems from the verse: וְשָׂרַפְתָּ בָאֵשׁ אֶת־הָעִיר וְאֶת־כָּל־שְׁלָלָהּ כָּלִיל, And you shall burn in the fire the city and all its spoil, totally (Deut. 13:17). Accordingly, the lulav from the city must be burned, and is therefore invalid as will be explained below.

פָּסוּל. — is invalid.
This invalidation is due to the failure to meet the שִׁעוּר, [the halachically prescribed] dimension of the lulav.
As both the lulav of the asherah and the lulav of the 'city' must be burned, they are considered to be lacking necessary size. This is explained in the Gemara (31b) by the Talmudic principle כָּתוּתֵי מִכַּתַּת שִׁעוּרֵיהּ, its measurements is [considered] pulverized. In the view of halachah, once an object is condemned to be burned it is considered as if it had already been burned and reduced to ashes. Thus it lacks the physical dimensions required for the respective mitzvah.

⊷§ The Pulverized Measurement

With some exceptions (Tosefos, Yevamos 103: s.v. סנדל) most Rishonim are of the opinion that this dictum applies only to the articles that must be burned, rather than those that must be buried or simply not used (Tos. 35a).

Rashi (29b) and Ritva cite the principle כָּל־הָעוֹמֵד לִשְׂרוֹף כְּשָׂרוּף דָּמֵי, anything destined to be burned is considered to have been burned, i.e., that which the halachah condemns to be burned is, in the eyes of halachah, viewed as if it is already reduced to ashes. This reasoning is based on the view of R' Shimon in Menachos 103b, that the halachic requirement is considered an accomplished fact. Accordingly, anything falling under this category is considered, in terms of halachah, non-existent. For example, a bill of divorce written on material from a 'city led astray' would be invalid, for the document would be halachically regarded as destroyed (Aruch LaNer).

נִקְטַם רֹאשׁוֹ, נִפְרְצוּ עָלָיו, פָּסוּל. נִפְרְדוּ עָלָיו כָּשֵׁר. רַבִּי יְהוּדָה אוֹמֵר: יֹאגְדֶנּוּ מִלְמָעְלָה.

יד אברהם

Many authorities disagree with this opinion, maintaining that the halachah is not like R' Shimon, but like the Sages who do not agree with the principle כָּל־הָעוֹמֵד לְשָׂרֵף כְּשָׂרוּף דָּמִי, *anything to be burned is considered to have been burned* (Beur HaGra, Even HaEzer 124:1; Shaar HaMelech, Gerushin 4:2). Ran (Gittin 21a) validates a divorce document written on material condemned to be burned, arguing that the rule of כָּתוּתֵי מִכַּתַּת שִׁעוּרֵיהּ, *its measurement is pulverized*, applies only to objects such as a lulav that require a minimum size, i.e., as a result of its condemned status, the object is considered *insignificant* although not destroyed. As a result of this insignificance the object is considered to be lacking the halachically prescribed measurement.

In the opinion of some *Rishonim* (Tos., Eruvin 80b s.v. אבל), this invalidation applies only to objects that are required to be one organic unit (e.g. lulav or a shofar). If the *mitzvah* can be performed with an aggregate of small particles as in the case of s'chach, even material from an asherah tree would be valid, as if an infinite number of leaves combined to cover the succah (Meiri, Eruvin 14b; Bikkurei Yaakov 530:1). Their reasoning is that effect of the rule of pulverized measurement is that the object is considered *disintegrated*, a condition that affects only a lulav or shofar, for example, which must be a unit; obviously it is not applicable to s'chach which may consist of many small particles as long as it provides shade (see Chiddushei R' Chaim HaLevi, Shabbos 17, for an elaboration of this view).

◂§ The Lulav

Halachic discussion of the invalidation of the lulav makes mention of its three basic physical features: שִׁדְרָה, spine; עָלִים, leaves; and תִּיוֹמֶת, twin-leaf.

The spine is the thick green core which serves as the *lulav's* center. The leaves grow out of the spine and constitute the bulk of the *lulav*. According to most commentators, the *twin-leaf* refers to the uppermost double leaf growing from the top of the *lulav* and forming its tip (Tosafos; Rosh; Rama, Orach Chaim 645:3). According to Rambam (Lulav 8:4) and Shulchan Aruch (ibid.), each of the *lulav's* leaves are referred to as a *twin-leaf*, for each is composed of two connected leaves.

There is a difference of opinion among the *Rishonim*, as to which leaves of the *lulav* the mishnah refers to as רֹאשׁוֹ, *its top*:

— Ravad holds that all the invalidations of the mishnah refer only to the spinal *core* of the *lulav*, but the leaves are halachically unessential. Accordingly, in our mishnah, נִקְטַם רֹאשׁוֹ means *the tip of its spine is broken off*.

— Rosh maintains that the *leaves* of the *lulav* are considered the *lulav* proper; accordingly, the top of the *lulav* means the top of the majority of its upper leaves.

— Ran and Maggid Mishnah (8:3) hold that the top of the *lulav* is the tip of the middle leaf (תִּיוֹמֶת) only, which, if broken off, is sufficient reason to invalidate the *lulav*.

— Shulchan Aruch (Orach Chaim 645:6) follows the view of Rosh. Rama (ibid) adds that we should be strict and follow the views of Ran and Maggid Mishnah, but, he says if the only available *lulav* is one whose middle leaf had its tip broken off, one may recite a

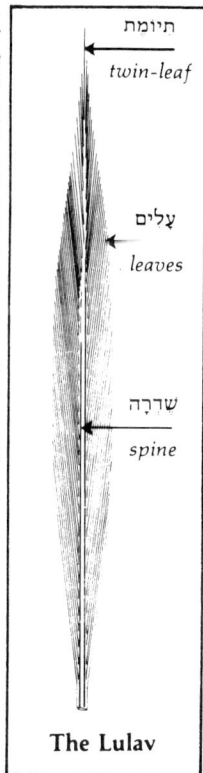

תִּיוֹמֶת

twin-leaf

עָלִים

leaves

שִׁדְרָה

spine

The Lulav

If its top was broken off, [or] its leaves severed, it is invalid.

If its leaves spread apart it is valid. R' Yehudah says: He should tie them together at the top.

blessing over it.

Other authorities disagree with this ruling. See *Biur Halachah, ibid.*

The commentators disagree on the amount of the *lulav* that must be broken to invalidate it. *Ritva*, quoting *Rabbeinu Yonah*, says that the mishnah means the greater part of the middle leaf (תִּיוֹמֶת). Nevertheless, *Ritva*, speaking for himself and his masters, takes a stricter view and interprets the mishnah to mean even a tiny piece of the top of the middle leaf is broken off.

Vilna Gaon follows this opinion but others are uncertain about this point (*Mishnah Berurah* 645:28, see *Shaar HaTziyun*).

נִקְטַם רֹאשׁ, — *If its top was broken off,*

The reason for this invalidation is failure to meet the requirements of הָדָר, beauty (*Rav*).

נִפְרְצוּ עָלָיו, — *[or] its leaves severed,*

The *Gemara* (32a) compares the leaves of this *lulav* to the leaves of a broom. The commentaries differ in their understanding of this description.

Our translation follows *Rashi* (29a) according to whom the *lulav's* leaves are completely severed from its spine and are tied to it like an old-fashioned broom (*Rav*).

Rif and *Rambam* (8:3) understand that the leaves are partially torn from the spine but are still dangling from it, thus resembling the leaves that are used in fashioning a broom.

According to *Tosafos* (29b) and *Ravad* the mishnah does not mean severed at all, but rather *split*. Noting

that each leaf is actually a double leaf folded over on itself and attached at its bottom to the spine, they explain that the leaves are still attached, but are split down their fold into two leaves. This is the same procedure used in preparing the leaves to make a broom.

Shulchan Aruch (*Orach Chaim* 645:2) follows the view of *Rif* and *Rambam* (ibid).

Rosh (3:3) and *Ran* add that the majority of the leaves must be severed to invalidate the *lulav*.

פָּסוּל. — *it is invalid.*

In both cases this is due to a lack of הָדָר, beauty (see *comm.* above s.v. וְהַיָּבֵשׁ) as this is certainly not a beautiful *lulav* (*Rashi* 29b).[1]

נִפְרְדוּ עָלָיו — *If its leaves spread apart*

I.e., they are fully attached to the spine but are spread apart on top like the branches of a tree (*Rashi* 29b; *Rav*).

Although it is common for palm branches to spread out in this fashion as they mature, a *lulav* must be used in its earlier stage when it is still straight like a rod or a scepter (*Rambam, Lulav* 7:1). This halachah is based on the Torah's reference to it as כַּפּוֹת, branches, a word which can be vocalized כָּפוּת, bound, i.e., with all the leaves together as if bound (*Ran*).

כָּשֵׁר. — *it is valid.*

Although the leaves are spread apart, the *lulav* is valid. The Torah's requirement that the leaves be *bound* means that the *lulav* be *capable* of appearing bound, i.e., if the leaves are flexible enough to be bent back and tied to the

---

1. Other related laws concerning the invalidation of the *lulav* emerge from the *Gemara* and the ensuing discussion among the *Rishonim* and *Poskim*. Some brief highlights follow:

□ Split *lulav*: If, at the top of the *lulav*, the leaves are separated, giving the *lulav* a forked appearance, then the *lulav* is invalid even if all the leaves are intact. This is called עֲשׂוּיָה כְּהֶמְנִיק, it resembles a fork [or a stylus (*Rashi*)] (*Gem.* 32a, *Orach Chaim* 645:7). It is possible for a

צִנֵּי הַר הַבַּרְזֶל כְּשֵׁרוֹת. לוּלָב שֶׁיֵּשׁ־בּוֹ שְׁלֹשָׁה טְפָחִים כְּדֵי לְנַעֲנֵעַ בּוֹ, כָּשֵׁר.

יד אברהם

spine, the *lulav* is valid. The exclusion is meant for the branches of a mature date palm whose spreading leaves are rigid and cannot be bent back and tied to the spine *(Ran)*.

רַבִּי יְהוּדָה אוֹמֵר: יֵאָגְדֶנּוּ מִלְמַעְלָה. — R' *Yehudah says: He should tie them together at the top.*

R' Yehudah interprets the word *bound* literally: if the leaves are spread apart they must be tied to the spine or the *lulav* is not valid *(Ran)*.

The halachah does not follow R' Yehudah *(Rav)*.

צִנֵּי הַר הַבַּרְזֶל — *The thorn palms of the Iron Mountain,*

Rambam writes in his *Commentary:* 'There are palm trees growing in a particular section of *Eretz Yisrael* whose *lulavim* grow in an unusual manner. The tip of each leaf reaches only to the base of its neighbor and they do not intermingle as do other *lulav* leaves. [Rambam mentions כְּזוֹ הַצּוּרָה, *like this diagram,'* but no diagram appears in our printed editions.] These are called צִנֵּי הַר הַבַּרְזֶל, *the thorn palms of the Iron Mountain.'*

The spines of these palm branches are very sparsely covered with short leaves. In some such branches, the top of the lower leaf does not reach even as far as

the beginning of the one above it *(Rashi 32a; Ran; Rav)*.

Trees that grow on rocky mountains rather than on fertile soil, have short leaves *(Tif. Yis.)* and the *lulav* itself is hard *(Ran)*.

כְּשֵׁרוֹת. — *are valid.*

Only if the top of one leaf reaches the base of the next one is the *lulav* acceptable. If, however, the leaves are so short that each one does not reach the one above it, it is invalid *(Gem. 32a; Orach Chaim 645:4)*.

לוּלָב שֶׁיֵּשׁ־בּוֹ שְׁלֹשָׁה טְפָחִים — *A lulav that is three handbreadths long*

Three handbreadths is the minimum measurement of the *lulav*. This applies to the myrtle and the willow twigs as well *(Gem. 3b)*.

כְּדֵי לְנַעֲנֵעַ בּוֹ, — *[long] enough to wave,*

The *Gemara* (32b) emends this statement to read וּכְדֵי לְנַעֲנֵעַ בּוֹ, *and long enough to wave*. This means the *lulav* must be three handbreadths long — the length of the myrtle and willow twigs — plus another handbreadth for waving. (See mishnah 9 and comm.). Thus, in total, the *lulav* must be at least *four* handbreadths long, while the myrtle and willow twigs need be only three. There is no maximum length to any of

very small split at the top of the *lulav* to invalidate the *lulav* for this reason, if the separation is readily apparent *(Pri Megadim; Mishnah Berurah 645:32)*.

□ Even if the *lulav* as a whole does not have a forked appearance, it is still subject to invalidation if the middle leaf is in actuality split. This is called נֶחְלְקָה הַתְּיוֹמֶת, *the twin leaf is split* [see comm. s.v. נִקְטַם רֹאשׁוֹ] *(Gem. 32a; Ramah 645:3)*. There is a disagreement among the commentators whether this means the entire leaf (till the spine), a major portion of it, a handbreath or even less, so a *lulav* with the middle leaf completely intact is preferable (see *Mishnah Berurah* 16, 18). This invalidation, however, applies only on the first day *(Magen Avraham; Mishnah Berurah 17)*.

□ *Hooked Lulav:* If the spine of the *lulav* is hooked and/or the entire *lulav* has a bent or hunched appearance then the *lulav* is invalid for reasons of הָדָר (i.e., for all of Succos) *(Gem. 32a; Orach Chaim 645:9)*. If, however, only the top leaves are crooked as is common, then it is valid and even preferred by some *Poskim*, for it is less likely to develop a split *(Rosh; Orach Chaim, ibid.)*. Some authorities disagree (see *Mishnah Berurah 45; Shaar HaTziyun 43)*.

The thorn palms of the Iron Mountain are valid.
A *lulav* that is three handbreadths long, [long]
enough to wave, is valid.

the species; but some hold that in all cases the *lulav* must extend one handbreadth beyond the other species *(Ran)*.

The *Gemara* records a dispute whether this fourth handbreadth is of the leaves or of the spine itself. *Shulchan Aruch (Orach Chaim 650:1)*

rules that the spine itself must extend a handbreadth beyond the other two species.

כָּשֵׁר. — *is valid.*

[Not only as a last resort (בְּדִיעֲבַד) but even initially (לְכַתְּחִלָה) one may use such a short *lulav* to fulfill the *mitzvah*.]

2.

⊷§ **The Hadas**

A full understanding of our mishnah and the laws of the *hadas* [myrtle] in general must take into account the requirement that the *hadas* be עֲבוֹת, *plaited*, i.e., covered with leaves in a fashion that resembles a plait or braid. This is derived from the Scriptural description *(Lev.* 23:40) of the *hadas as* עֲנַף עֵץ־עָבֹת, *twig of a plaited tree (Rambam, Lulav 7:2).*

The *Gemara* (32b) stipulates that the leaves of the *hadas* should grow in clusters of at least three — either from central points on the twig, or from three points on one level. A *hadas* whose growth forms a pattern of two leaves growing from one level and a third growing from above them is called a הֲדַס שׁוֹטֶה, *a wild hadas*, and is invalid. [It is quite common to find myrtle twigs growing in this fashion. The manifestations of this halachah are discussed in greater detail in *Orach Chaim* 645:3].

As noted in commentary to mishnah 1 (s.v. לולב שיבשו) the myrtle must have a minimum length of three handbreadths. According to the *Gaonim*, this entire length must be covered by leaves growing from one point. *Rosh* quotes *Ravad* that although such a *hadas* is preferable, one with such covering over more than half its minimum required length is considered valid. [See *Orach Chaim* 645:5 for the halachah.]

What if the leaves of the *hadas* grew properly, but afterwards the twig lost some of its leaves? The *Gemara* cites the halachah that even if a twig has lost most of its leaves it remains valid as long as it retains its plaited appearance. This, the *Gemara* explains, is possible only if the *hadas* is of the species which grows seven or more leaves from each point. Then, even if four leaves fall off, the remaining three will appear plaited.

In explaining the law of our mishnah that a *hadas* whose leaves were severed is invalid, *Rosh* concludes that it is not the loss of leaves that invalidates it (as in the use of the *lulav*) but the absence of its required plaited appearance. This is true, according to *Rosh*, only if the twig lost two of its three leaves for the full length of its halachically required size. *Ran* invalidates the *hadas* if only one of the leaves is missing for the length of its required size, for anything less than three leaves is no longer considered plaited. [See *Mishnah Berurah* 645:18 for the halachah.]

The law of the dry *hadas* mentioned in our mishnah is also affected by the requirement of עֲבוֹת, *plaited*. The *Gemara* (33a) says that even if only three fresh leaves remain, the *hadas* is considered valid for it maintains the semblance of a plaited twig. See *Orach Chaim* 646:8 and *Mishnah Berurah*, 21-23 for a full discussion of this halachah.

[ב] **הֲדַס** הַגָּזוּל וְהַיָּבֵשׁ פָּסוּל. שֶׁל אֲשֵׁרָה וְשֶׁל עִיר הַנִּדַּחַת פָּסוּל. נִקְטַם רֹאשׁוֹ, נִפְרְצוּ עָלָיו, אוֹ שֶׁהָיוּ עֲנָבָיו מְרֻבּוֹת מֵעָלָיו, פָּסוּל. וְאִם מִעֲטָן כָּשֵׁר, וְאֵין מְמַעֲטִין בְּיוֹם טוֹב.

יד אברהם

הֲדַס הַגָּזוּל — *A stolen myrtle twig*
The stolen myrtle is invalid for the same reason as the stolen *lulav* in mishnah 1. *Sfas Emes* (29b) suggests that the mishnah repeats the invalidations for each of the species individually to teach that even if only *one* of the species is stolen, it is considered as if he did not perform the *mitzvah* with *any* of them.

וְהַיָּבֵשׁ — *or a dry one*
[See comm. to previous mishnah s.v. והיבש.]
As in the case of the dry *lulav*, the degree of dryness is subject to question.

Tosafos, Rosh, and *Meiri* hold that the sign of a dry myrtle is if one can crumble it with one's fingers. (See comm. to mishnah 1 s.v. והיבש.)

Ravad, however, differs with this interpretation, because even when the myrtle withers to the point where it can crumble, it can be restored to its former moist state through soaking in water for a day or two. Therefore, *Ravad* maintains that the myrtle is dried out only when it turns white. At this stage, the moisture is gone and cannot be restored (*Tur, Orach Chaim* 646).

The Hadas

הֲדַס שׁוֹטֶה
(*wild hadas*)

הֲדַס מְשׁוּלָשׁ
(*plaited* [*tripled*] *hadas*)

Untrimmed Hadas

2. **A** stolen myrtle twig or a dry one is invalid. [One] from an *asherah* or a city that was led astray is invalid.

If its top was broken off, [or] its leaves were severed, or its berries outnumbered its leaves, it is invalid.

If he decreased them it is valid, but we may not decrease them on *Yom Tov.*

YAD AVRAHAM

Shulchan Aruch (Orach Chaim 646:7) follows *Ravad's* view.

פָּסוּל — *is invalid.*

[As with the dry *lulav*, the invalidation here is for want of הָדָר, *beauty*.]

שֶׁל אֲשֵׁרָה וְשֶׁל עִיר הַנִּדַּחַת פָּסוּל. — *[One] from an asherah or from a city that was led astray is invalid.*

[See comm. to mishnah 1.]

נִקְטַם רֹאשׁוֹ, — *If its top was broken off,*

[See comm. on mishnah 1, s.v. נִקְטַם.]

In the use of the myrtle twig, the commentators are in almost total agreement that only if the top of the *stem* — not the leaves — is broken off is the myrtle invalid.

Meiri, however, holds that just as in the case of the *lulav*, the mishnah means that the tip of the leaf or leaves at the top of the stem are broken off. He states that if even a fraction of the top leaf is broken off, its הָדָר, *beauty*, is gone.

In mishnah 4, however, R' Tarfon holds that the invalidation of a broken tip does not apply to the myrtle twig (*Rav*). See commentary on that mishnah for a full discussion of the halachah.

נִפְרְצוּ עָלָיו, — *[or] its leaves were severed,*

Rashi comments that its leaves were severed; i.e., if a myrtle twig lost most of its leaves it is considered invalid.

Ran and *Ittur* disagree, citing the statement in the *Gemara* that even if a myrtle twig lost most of its leaves, it is considered valid if it maintains a plaited look. They conclude that our mishnah means the leaves are split. *Rosh* agrees

with *Rashi* and explains the *Gemara* differently. See below.

אוֹ שֶׁהָיוּ עֲנָבָיו מְרֻבּוֹת מֵעָלָיו, פָּסוּל. — *or its berries outnumbered its leaves, it is invalid.*

Hadas twigs sometimes produce a small berry-like fruit. As long as the berries are green like the leaves, there is no difficulty, even if they are more numerous than the leaves. If, however, the berries are black or red, and they outnumber the leaves, they create a spotted appearance that is inconsistent with the requirement of beauty. Thus the *hadas* is invalid (*Rav; Rashi* 11b s.v. עבר ולקטן).

וְאִם מִעֲטָן — *If he decreased them*

[I.e., he plucked off enough berries before *Yom Tov* so that they no longer outnumbered the leaves.]

כָּשֵׁר. — *it* [i.e., the *hadas*] *is valid,*

Since the invalidation of the excessive berries is one of הָדָר, *beauty*, it can be corrected by changing its appearance.

וְאֵין מְמַעֲטִין בְּיוֹם טוֹב. — *but we may not decrease them on Yom Tov.*

[I.e., on the first day of Succos or, where two days are observed as *Yom Tov*, on the second day.]

Since the presence of the berries disqualify the *hadas*, their removal in order to validate the twig is considered 'repairing,' and is prohibited on the Sabbath and *Yom Tov* (*Gemara* 33b).

But if one transgressed and removed the berries on *Yom Tov* the *hadas* remains valid (*Tif. Yis.; Orach Chaim* 646:2, see *Beur Halachah*).

[ג] **עֲרָבָה** גְזוּלָה וִיבֵשָׁה פְּסוּלָה. שֶׁל אֲשֵׁרָה וְשֶׁל עִיר הַנִּדַּחַת פְּסוּלָה.

נִקְטַם רֹאשָׁהּ, נִפְרְצוּ עָלֶיהָ, וְהַצַּפְצָפָה, פְּסוּלָה;

כְּמוּשָׁה, וְשֶׁנָּשְׁרוּ מִקְצָת עָלֶיהָ, וְשֶׁל בַּעַל, כְּשֵׁרָה.

[ד] **רַבִּי** יִשְׁמָעֵאל אוֹמֵר: שְׁלֹשָׁה הֲדַסִּים, וּשְׁתֵּי עֲרָבוֹת, לוּלָב אֶחָד, וְאֶתְרוֹג

יד אברהם

3.

⇐§ The Aravah

The third species required by the Torah is עֲרָבָה [aravah], willow twig. The Torah refers to it as עַרְבֵי־נָחַל, willows of the stream (Lev. 23:40) because it generally grows by a stream (Gemara 33b). Its identifying characteristics are a red stem, and elongated leaves with smooth edges (Gem. 34a).

עֲרָבָה גְזוּלָה וִיבֵשָׁה פְּסוּלָה. — A stolen willow twig or a dry one is invalid.

[See comm. to mishnah 1.]

שֶׁל אֲשֵׁרָה וְשֶׁל עִיר הַנִּדַּחַת פְּסוּלָה. — [One] from an asherah or from a city that was led astray is invalid.

[See comm. to mishnah 1.]

נִקְטַם רֹאשָׁהּ, — If its top was broken off,

[See comm. to mishnah 1.]

נִפְרְצוּ עָלֶיהָ — [or] its leaves were severed,

The majority of its leaves fell off, as in the case of the hadas (see comm. to mishnah 2).

Meiri, following his explanation of this term in the case of the lulav and the hadas, renders that the leaves were split.

וְהַצַּפְצָפָה, — or [it is] a tzaftzafah,

This is a mountain plant that resembles the aravah but its stem is white rather than reddish and its leaves are rounded with serrated edges, unlike the elongated, smooth leaves of the aravah (Gem. 34; Rambam, Lulav 7:4).

פְּסוּלָה. — it is invalid.

If the top is broken or severed, the aravah lacks beauty.

The tzaftzafah is invalid because it is a species other than the willow required by the Torah. The aravah is of the variety that generally grows by the water, while the tzaftzafah is found only in mountains and cannot be considered עַרְבֵי־נָחַל, willows of the stream (Gem. 34a; Shaar HaTziyun 647:3)

The Gemara (34a) discusses an aravah whose leaves are slightly serrated rather than completely smooth. This variety is considered valid, for it too grows by streams (Rambam, Lulav 7:4; Mishnah Berurah 647:6).

כְּמוּשָׁה, — [One whose leaves are] wilted,

[Though no longer fresh, the leaves not dried out.]

Obviously this condition is in contrast to the 'dry' willow which the mishnah invalidates. This contrast applies to the previous mishnayos as well: neither the lulav nor the hadas is invalid if it is merely wilted. The mishnah however mentions this rule only by the aravah for, as a species that grows by the water there would be more reason to believe that it should always be fresh (Ran).

Tiferes Yisrael adds that the willow is

3. A stolen willow twig or a dry one is invalid. [One] from an *asherah* or from a city that was led astray is invalid.

If its top was broken off, [or] its leaves were severed, or [it is] a *tzaftzafah,* it is invalid.

[One whose leaves are] wilted, or part of its leaves have fallen off, or [one] from a field, is valid.

4. R' Yishmael says: Three myrtle twigs, two willow twigs, one *lulav,* and one *esrog* [are

more likely to wilt than either the *lulav* or the *hadas,* and therefore the mishnah mentions this here rather than previously.

וְשֶׁנָּשְׁרוּ מִקְצָת עָלֶיהָ, — *or part of its leaves have fallen off,*

Only a minority of its leaves fell off. As long as the majority remained attached, it is still considered הָדָר, *beautiful,* in contrast to a twig from which most leaves were severed, which is invalid. This distinction applies to the *hadas* as well: only the loss of most of its leaves renders it invalid. This condition is mentioned here for this concludes the laws of the species to which the loss of leaves applies *(Rosh).*

וְשֶׁל בַּעַל, — *or [one] from a field,*

It grew in a rain-watered field, and not near a brook *(Rav; Ran).*

כְּשֵׁרָה. — *is valid.*

Although the willow did not grow by a stream, it is considered valid. The *Gemara* 33b explains that the phrase עַרְבֵי-נָחַל, *willows of the stream,* does not exclude willows that grew elsewhere. The intention is to identify the *aravah* as a species that *usually* grows by a stream. Any *aravah* with the characteristics of that species; i.e., reddish stems, and long, smooth leaves, is valid even if it grew in a desert *(Rambam, Lulav 7:3).* Accordingly, there is not even a preference for willows that grow by the water *(Taz 647:2).*

Some *Rishonim (Rashi, Tos.)* however, hold that although other willows are valid, there is a *mitzvah* to use those that actually grow by the water. *Rosh* and *Shulchan Aruch* (647:1) reject this view.

4.

Although it clearly indicates that the *mitzvah* of *lulav* involves four distinct species, the Torah is not explicit about the quantity needed of each species. Our mishnah discusses the amounts required to fulfill the *mitzvah.*

רַבִּי יִשְׁמָעֵאל אוֹמֵר: שְׁלשָׁה הֲדַסִּים, וּשְׁתֵּי עֲרָבוֹת, לוּלָב אֶחָד, וְאֶתְרוֹג אֶחָד; — *R' Yishmael says: Three myrtle twigs, two willow twigs, one lulav, and one esrog [are required];*

The *Gemara* (34b) explains that R' Yishmael derives these numbers from the wording of the verse *(Leviticus* 23:40):

עֲנַף עֵץ-עָבֹת — *branch of a plaited tree.* Each of these words indicates a quantity: עֲנַף, *branch,* is one; עֵץ, *tree,* is second; עָבֹת, *plaited,* is the third *(Rashi, ibid.).* Thus, three myrtle twigs.

עַרְבֵי-נָחַל — *willows of the stream.* The word עַרְבֵי is plural, *willows,* indicating no less than two twigs.

כַּפֹּת תְּמָרִים, — *branches of a date*

אֶחָד; אֲפִילוּ שְׁנַיִם קְטוּמִים וְאֶחָד אֵינוֹ קָטוּם.
רַבִּי טַרְפוֹן אוֹמֵר: אֲפִלוּ שְׁלָשְׁתָּן קְטוּמִים.
רַבִּי עֲקִיבָא אוֹמֵר: כְּשֵׁם שֶׁלּוּלָב אֶחָד
וְאֶתְרוֹג אֶחָד, כָּךְ הֲדַס אֶחָד וַעֲרָבָה אַחַת.

יד אברהם

palm. Even though the word כַּפֹּת is plural and means *branches,* since it is spelled defectively, כַּפֹּת instead of כַּפּוֹת, it may be read as a singular noun, כַּפֹּת, *"a" branch,* implying only one *lulav* (see *Gem.* 32a; *Meiri*).

— פְּרִי עֵץ הָדָר, *fruit of a beautiful tree,* implies a single fruit from such a tree.

אֲפִילוּ שְׁנַיִם קְטוּמִים וְאֶחָד אֵינוֹ קָטוּם. — *even if two are broken off and one is not broken off.*

Since this unidentified species totals three branches, it is obviously the myrtle twig of which R' Yishmael requires three. As long as one twig is intact, even if the other two have their tops broken off, one fulfills his obligation (*Rashi* 34b; *Rav*).

The *Gemara* points to the obvious contradiction: If clipped myrtle leaves are invalid (mishnah 2) then all three twigs must be whole. If, on the other hand, a broken twig *is* valid then why should even one have to be whole? The *Gemara* explains that R' Yishmael retracted his original view; initially he held that the *mitzvah* requires three myrtle twigs, but subsequently he held that one is sufficient. This explains why only one twig is sufficient. The other two have no halachic standing; even if one omitted them out entirely, he fulfills the *mitzvah* and certainly if they are merely broken.

The *Gemara's* explanation begs the question: If R' Yishmael meant to retract his original view, why did he not say simply that only one *hadas* is required rather than state that two of the three may be broken, as if to imply that their presence is necessary. *Ran* explains that although R' Yishmael holds that three twigs are preferable, only one is necessary for the *mitzvah.* The other two are

to enhance the *mitzvah* and therefore may be broken. See *Orach LaNer* for an alternate explanation.

— רַבִּי טַרְפוֹן אוֹמֵר: אֲפִלוּ שְׁלָשְׁתָּן קְטוּמִים. *R' Tarfon says: Even if all three are broken off.*

[I.e., if all three myrtle twigs are clipped at the top they are still valid.]

In R' Tarfon's view *three hadas* branches are required, but he holds that the *mitzvah* may be performed with a broken *hadas.*

R' Tarfon, in opposition to mishnah 2, validates a broken myrtle because he does not require הָדָר, *beauty,* for the myrtle or willow (*Rashi; Rav*).

Ramban (quoted by *Ran*) and R' *Yeshayahu* (quoted by *Rosh* 3:14) explain that since the leaves cover the twig all the way to the top, the missing tip is not noticeable, and the twig is therefore considered הָדָר, *beautiful* (*Mishnah Berurah* to 646.10, *Shaar HaTziyun ibid.* 32).

[*Meiri* adds however that R' Tarfon agrees with the invalidation of the dry myrtle (mishnah 2); since it can be crumbled with the fingers it is considered nonexistent.]

The *Gemara* (34b) quotes Shmuel, who rules according to R' Tarfon, in negation of mishnah 2. *Rif, Rambam* (*Lulav* 8:5) and *Rosh* (3:14) follow R' Tarfon and validate a *hadas* whose top has been clipped off.

Ravad (ibid.) strongly disagrees with *Rambam,* supporting his contention with the unusual statement כְּבָר הוֹפִיעַ רוּחַ הַקֹּדֶשׁ בְּבֵית מִדְרָשֵׁנוּ זֶה שָׁנִים רַבּוֹת, *the spirit of holiness was present in our Beis Medrash* [*study hall*] *many years.* *Ravad* concludes that the broken myrtle is invalid, in accordance with mishnah

required]; even if two are broken off and one is not broken off. R' Tarfon says: Even if all three are broken off.

R' Akiva says: Just as there is one *lulav* and one *esrog*, so [there is] one myrtle twig and one willow twig.

YAD AVRAHAM

2. He does not explain how he would reconcile that mishnah with R' Tarfon's statement here, though he suggests that such an explanation does exist.

Meiri and *Baal HaMaor* expound on *Ravad's* view. They explain that myrtle twigs grow in the form of a leaf-covered central stem from which grow smaller twigs that are, in turn, covered by their own leaves. The question in our mishnah does *not* concern a *hadas* whose top has been clipped — that has been invalidated in mishnah 2. Rather the discussion here concerns a *hadas* from which the smaller twigs have been trimmed or those twigs themselves. R' Yishmael rules that one of the three necessary myrtle twigs must be in its entirety — central stem and outgrowing twigs. The other two *hadas* twigs may be either a trimmed central stem or the outgrowing twigs that were removed from it. R' Tarfon disagrees, holding that any *hadas*, whole or trimmed central stem or its offshoot, is acceptable as long as it meets the other requirements of *hadas*. Concerning this dispute the *Gemara* rules like R' Tarfon.

R' Yosef Karo (Orach Chaim 646:1, 10) following the opinion of *Rif, Rambam*, and *Rosh*, validates a *hadas* whose top is clipped off. *Rama*, however, rules that wherever possible, one should fol-

low the *Ravad's* view and not use such a *hadas*.

רַבִּי עֲקִיבָא אוֹמֵר: כְּשֵׁם שֶׁלּוּלָב אֶחָד — וְאֶתְרוֹג אֶחָד, כָּךְ הֲדַס אֶחָד וַעֲרָבָה אַחַת.
R' Akiva says: Just as there is one lulav and one esrog, so [there is] one myrtle twig and one willow twig.

[Only one of each of the species is necessary to fulfill the *mitzvah*.]

R' Akiva addresses himself to R' Yishmael's opening statement concerning the number of each species that is required. In his view, one of each species is sufficient to fulfill the *mitzvah*. His reasoning is that all the species are compared to the *esrog*, of which the Torah certainly requires no more than one *(Aruch LaNer).*

Concerning the other aspect of R' Yishmael's statement that the *hadas* may not be clipped, *Ran* explains that R' Akiva is in agreement. In effect R' Akiva agrees with R' Yishmael's changed view (see comm. above). He argues with R' Yishmael, however, as to how many *hadasim* one should preferably take. R' Yishmael requires three even if two are cut off, for this enhances the *mitzvah*. R' Akiva, on the other hand, maintains that one *hadas* is sufficient.

5.

⇥§ The Esrog

Scripture requires the taking of פְּרִי עֵץ הָדָר, *fruit of a beautiful tree (Lev.* 23:40). The Sages teach (*Gem.* 35a) that by juxtaposing the word פְּרִי, *fruit*, with the word עֵץ, *tree*, the verse implies that the tree must be one whose *wood* [i.e., *tree*] tastes like its פְּרִי, *fruit*. This is the *esrog*.

R' Abahu (ibid.) interprets the word הָדָר as if it were pronounced הַדָּר, *which dwells* — i.e., a fruit which remains (dwells) on the tree from year to year. This is the *esrog*, which grows on its tree for a few years before it is fully developed.

It should be noted that the *esrog* is the only one of the Four Species that is edible. For that reason, laws relating to food will apply to it, though they are irrelevant to the other three species. Some of these laws are among the subjects of our mishnah.

[ה] **אֶתְרוֹג** הַגָּזוּל וְהַיָּבֵשׁ פָּסוּל. שֶׁל
אֲשֵׁרָה וְשֶׁל עִיר הַנִּדַּחַת
פָּסוּל.

שֶׁל עָרְלָה פָּסוּל.
שֶׁל תְּרוּמָה טְמֵאָה פָּסוּל. שֶׁל תְּרוּמָה טְהוֹרָה
לֹא יִטֹּל, וְאִם נָטַל, כָּשֵׁר.
שֶׁל דְּמַאי, בֵּית שַׁמַּאי פּוֹסְלִין, וּבֵית הִלֵּל
מַכְשִׁירִין.

אֶתְרוֹג הַגָּזוּל — *A stolen esrog*
[See *comm.* to mishnah 1.]

וְהַיָּבֵשׁ פָּסוּל. — *or a dry one is invalid.*
Ravad defines the degree of dryness
which invalidates an *esrog* as the complete lack of moisture, but as long as
moisture can be squeezed from it, it can
be regarded as הָדָר, *beautiful* (*Tur* 648
quoting *Raavad*).

שֶׁל אֲשֵׁרָה וְשֶׁל עִיר הַנִּדַּחַת פָּסוּל. — [One]
*from an asherah or from a city that was
led astray is invalid.*
[See *comm.* to mishnah 1.]

שֶׁל עָרְלָה — [One] *of orlah*
For the first three years after a tree's
planting, the fruit is forbidden for consumption and no benefit may be derived
from it (*Leviticus* 19:23). Such fruit
is called 'orlah' (restricted), and it must
be burned. As the only edible fruit
among the Four Species, an *esrog* is
subject to the laws of *orlah*, and no
benefit may be derived from it during
the first three years of its tree's existence.

פָּסוּל. — *is invalid.*
This invalidation stems from the requirement of לָכֶם, *for yourselves*, which

indicates that the species must be fit for
use. In the case of the *esrog*, which is a
fruit, it must be fit to be eaten. Since the
orlah esrog must be burned it is not considered 'yours' (*Gem.* 35a; *Rashi; Rav*).

Rambam (Comm.) adds that an *esrog*
which cannot be eaten is not considered
a 'fruit'and does not qualify for a *mitzvah* that calls for the 'fruit of a beautiful
tree'.[1]

Tosefos 35a and *Ran* point out that
since *orlah* must be burned, an *esrog* of
orlah will lack the required minimum
size in accordance with the principle of
כְּתוּתֵי מִכְתַּת שִׁעוּרֵיהּ, *its measurement is
pulverized.* See comm. to mishnah 1 s.v.
ושל עיר הנדחת

שֶׁל תְּרוּמָה טְמֵאָה פָּסוּל. — [One] *of contaminated terumah is invalid.*
Terumah, the tithe given to *Kohanim,*
must be kept in a state of purity. If it
becomes *tamei* [contaminated], it must
be burned. An *esrog* that had been
given to a *Kohen* as *terumah* and then
became contaminated is not considered
his property — as in the case of *orlah,*
above — because it is forbidden to him.

שֶׁל תְּרוּמָה טְהוֹרָה לֹא יִטֹּל — [If it is] *of
pure terumah he should not use* [lit.

1. If the invalidation stems from the requirement of ownership, then it is invalid only for the
first day, like a borrowed *esrog.* If, however, the reason is because of *Rambam's* explanation
that an inedible fruit is not considered a fruit then there is no difference between the first day
and the rest of the Festival.
Rambam's explanation is consistent with his ruling (*Lulav* 8:9) that any *esrog* that cannot
be eaten is invalid for the entire Festival (see *R' Manoach loc. cit.; Chasam Sofer* and *Meromei
Sadeh* 35a).

5. **A** stolen *esrog* or a dry one is invalid.

[One] from an *asherah* or from a city that was led astray is invalid.

[One] of *orlah* is invalid.

[One] of contaminated *terumah* is invalid. [If it is] of pure *terumah* he should not use it, but if he used it, it is valid.

[If it is] of *demai*, Beis Shammai invalidate it, and Beis Hillel validate it.

YAD AVRAHAM

take] *it*,

Although an uncontaminated *teru-mah-esrog* is valid according to the halachah, the Sages decreed that its use should be avoided. The basis for this law is that one is not allowed to con-taminate *terumah* or even make such contamination [*tumah*] possible. No food can accept *tumah* unless it first becomes wet (*Rambam, Tumas Ochlim* 1:2; see also *Orach Chaim* 158:4), therefore, one should not consciously make *terumah* wet, for that prepares it for *tumah*. Since *lulavim* and the other species are usually kept in water to keep them moist (see mishnah 15), the chances are that when the *esrog* is used with them, it too will become wet and thus become susceptible to *tumah*. Therefore, by using an *esrog* that is *terumah*, one would be increasing the likelihood of its becoming *tamei*, in violation of the Torah's injunction to 'safeguard' the *terumah* from contami-nation.

וְאִם נָטַל, — *but if he used it*,

[I.e., an *esrog* of *terumah*.]

כָּשֵׁר. — *it is valid*.

[Though it is forbidden to do so, the *mitzvah* is valid after the fact.]

The *terumah-esrog* may be consumed by a *Kohen*. And even an Israelite or Levite who acquired *terumah* from a *Kohen*, may feed it to his daughter's child by a *Kohen*. Consequently, it is considered fit to eat and therefore meets the requirements of לָכֶם (*Gem.* 35b; *Rashi*).

שֶׁל דְּמַאי, — [*If it is*] *of demai*,

According to the law of the Torah, no produce grown in *Eretz Yisrael* may be eaten, even by a *Kohen*, before the *terumah* and *maaser* tithes have been separated from it (*Makkos* 16b). When purchasing produce from an observant Jew, one can assume that *terumah* and *maaser* were already separated, for otherwise the produce would not be permitted for consumption. However, in the times of Yochanan, the High Priest, it was found that many un-learned people were careful to separate *terumah*, but were lax in separating *ma'aser*. As a result, an injunction was issued against the produce purchased from an עַם הָאָרֶץ, *unlearned person*, to the effect that the purchaser must separate *ma'aser* from it even if assured by the seller that he had already done. This produce is called דָּא מַאי [דְּמַאי, *what is this* — tithed or not?], *demai*. The Rabbis accorded it the status of סְפֵק אִיסוּר, *possibly forbidden*; i.e., one must consider it as questionable whether *ma'aser* was removed, and for that reason separate *ma'aser* to remove the doubt (*Sotah* 48a; *Rambam, Ma'aser* 9:1, 2).

בֵּית שַׁמַּאי פּוֹסְלִין, — *Beis Shammai in-validate it*,

Since the *demai* esrog may not be eaten until it is tithed, it lacks the neces-sary requirement of לָכֶם, *yours* (*Rav; Rashi* to 35b).

וּבֵית הֶלֵּל מַכְשִׁירִין. — *and Beis Hillel validate it*.

שֶׁל מַעֲשֵׂר שֵׁנִי בִּירוּשָׁלַיִם לֹא יִטֹּל, וְאִם
נָטַל, כָּשֵׁר.

‏[ו] **עָלְתָה** חֲזָזִית עַל־רֻבּוֹ, נִטְּלָה פִּטְמָתוֹ,
נִקְלַף, נִסְדַּק, נִקַּב וְחָסַר כָּל־
שֶׁהוּא, פָּסוּל.

יד אברהם

The *Gemara* (35a) explains the dispute between Beis Shammai and Beis Hillel on the basis of the law stated in *Demai* (3:1) concerning the feeding of the poor with *demai*. Since only a minority of unlearned people were lax in tithing, the Rabbis saw fit to waive the injunction against their produce in certain times of need, relying on the fact that the majority were sufficiently careful. Therefore one may feed the poor, who are supported from charity funds, with produce purchased from the unlearned.

Beis Hillel regards an *esrog* of *demai* as 'yours' because it is fit for consumption by the poor. Beis Shammai, on the other hand, forbids *demai* even to the poor. Accordingly, it follows that such an *esrog* is invalid for it cannot be eaten under any circumstances (*Ran*).

שֶׁל מַעֲשֵׂר שֵׁנִי בִּירוּשָׁלַיִם — [*If it is*] *of maaser sheni in Jerusalem*

In addition to מַעֲשֵׂר רִאשׁוֹן, *the first tithe*, which must be given to the Levite, the Torah requires מַעֲשֵׂר שֵׁנִי, *the second tithe*, which belongs to the owner of the crop, but can be eaten only in Jerusalem. Unlike the Levite's tithe, the second tithe, *ma'aser sheni*, is holy, and thus, like *terumah*, may be contaminated (*Lev.* 27:30). Our mishnah discusses an *esrog* of *ma'aser sheni* that is now in Jerusalem where it may be eaten.

לֹא יִטֹּל, — *he should not use* [lit. *take*] *it,*

As in the case of an *esrog* of *terumah* (see above s.v. טָהֳרָה שֶׁל תְּרוּמָה) the use of a *ma'aser sheni-esrog* would bring it into contact with water, thus making it susceptible to *tumah*.

וְאִם נָטַל, כָּשֵׁר. — *but if he used it, it is valid.*

After the fact, he has fulfilled the mitzvah. Since it is permissible to eat *ma'aser sheni* in Jerusalem it meets the requirement of 'yours' (Gem. 35b).

However, outside Jerusalem, where *ma'aser sheni* fruits may not be eaten, an *esrog* of *ma'aser sheni* would not be valid (*Rashi; Rav*).

According to *Ran*, however, an *esrog* of *ma'aser sheni* is valid anywhere; the fact that it can be brought to Jerusalem makes it *potentially* fit to eat and that is sufficient to satisfy the requirement. The mishnah merely mentions Jerusalem to teach that *even* in Jerusalem where it should be eaten, one should not use it (see also *Tos. Yom Tov*).

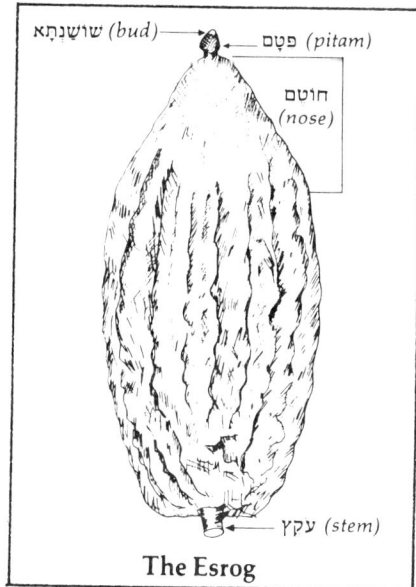

שׁוֹשַׁנְתָּא (bud)
פִּטָם (pitam)
חוֹטֶם (nose)
עֹקֶץ (stem)

The Esrog

If it is of *ma'aser sheni* in Jerusalem, he should not use it, but if he used it, it is valid.

6. **I**f a scab-like boil grew on most of it, [or] its *pitam* was removed, [or] it was peeled, [or] it was split, [or] it was punctured and is missing a slight portion, it is invalid.

YAD AVRAHAM

6.

עֶלְתָה חֲזָזִית — *If a scab-like boil grew*

Most commentators (including *Ran, Rav,* and *Rashi*) define חֲזָזִית as a small boil found on the rind of an *esrog.*

[In explaining the verse in *Leviticus* (22:22) that invalidates a *Kohen* whose skin develops boils, *Targum* renders the word יַלֶּפֶת, *boil,* as חֲזָזֵן. See *Rashi, ibid.*]

Rosh and *Tur* add that these boils are raised above the surface of the rind, and have a thickness that can be detected by touch *(Orach Chaim 648:13).*

Tosefos Yom Tov explains that these boils are caused by the rotting of the fruit, producing a mold-like effect. Insufficient exposure to air, even on one area of the *esrog's* surface may also cause this growth.[1]

An *esrog* with such a growth lacks beauty *(Rosh,* see comm. below s.v. פסול).

עַל־רֻבּוֹ, — *on most of it,*

Only if the boils cover the greater portion of the *esrog* is it considered invalid *(Rosh; Mishnah Berurah 648:37).*

The *Gemara* (35b) adds that even a small boil can invalidate the *esrog* if it is on its חוֹטֶם, *nose.*

Most commentators define the 'nose' as the narrowing part which rises upward from the thick waist of the *esrog* towards its peak. The importance attached to this part of the *esrog* is because any blemish there is immediately visible *(Rashi).*

Yerushalmi adds that the nose is tan-

tamount to the majority of the *esrog* [חוֹטְמוֹ כְּרֻבּוֹ].

נִטְּלָה פְטָמָתוֹ, — *[or] its pitam was removed,*

An *esrog* has two stem-like protrusions, one from its top [where the *esrog* becomes narrow] and the other from its base, from where it is cut off from the tree. The top stem is crowned by a rounded bud, while the bottom stem is flat. The פֶּטָם, *pitam,* is the short stem that protrudes from the nose of the *esrog.* It is also referred to as דַּד, *nipple* (*Rif; Rashi; Rambam; Rav; Ran*). The tip of this stem is called the שׁוֹשַׁנְתָּא, *bud.* The other stem is called the עֵקֶץ, *end* (see comm. later in this mishnah s.v. עוקצו). An *esrog* whose top stem, *pitam,* has been removed is invalid because it is חָסֵר, *deficient* (see comm. later in the mishnah s.v. פסול).

Rosh adds that this invalidation can apply only if the *esrog* had a *pitam* originally. Many *esrogim,* however, grow without a *pitam* and they obviously are not deficient *(Mishnah Berurah 648:32).*

The *Rishonim* discuss how much of the stem must be removed to invalidate it. In the view of most authorities, the entire stem must be missing. [This is based on the brief remark in the *Gemara* that compares the loss of the *pitam* to the removal of pestle from a mortar; i.e., removing the entire stem, leaving a cavity where the *pitam* was uprooted.]

Shulchan Aruch (648:7) follows this view, with the commentators adding that even if

1. Another type of imperfection on the *esrog's* peel is known as *blatt flek* [leaf spot] or *blettel.* This imperfection is not considered a boil *(Rama, Orach Chaim 648:13; Shaarei Teshuvah, ibid.* 23). The commentators differ regarding the criteria by which one may distinguish between a boil and a *blettel.* According to *Maharal,* a boil is slightly raised while a *blettel* feels

only a small tip of the *pitam* remains, the *esrog* is valid *(Taz; Magen Abraham, ibid.; see Mishnah Berurah 30).*

According to *Ran*, however, even if the rounded top of the stem (שׁוֹשַׁנְתָּא) is missing the *esrog* is invalid.

Rama (ibid.) concludes that if another *esrog* of equal overall quality is available with its tip completely intact, it is preferable to use it (see *Mishnah Berurah, ibid.* 31).

נִקְלַף, — [or] *it was peeled,*

An *esrog* has two peels: the thick yellow peel which some people eat, and a thin glossy skin on top of that.

The *esrog* in our mishnah is missing the thin outer peel, leaving the basic body of the *esrog* intact and not altering its color *(Ran).*

The *Gemara (36a)* distinguishes between an *esrog* that is completely peeled and one that is only partially peeled. Most commentators understand this to mean that only if the entire peel is missing is the *esrog* invalid *(Rif; R' Chananel; Rambam)*. *Rashi*, however, holds the opposite: if only part of the outer peel is left, the *esrog* lacks beauty because it appears spotted, while the absence of the entire peel does not affect the *esrog's appearance.*

Ran adds that if even a small part of the thick peel was missing then the *esrog* is חָסֵר, *deficient (Orach Chaim 618:6).*

See *Mishnah Berurah (ibid.* 26) for the law in case the peeling changed the coloration of the *esrog.*

נִסְדַּק, — [or] *it was split,*

Although no part of the *esrog* is missing the fact that it is split invalidates it as if it were deficient *(Orach Chaim 648:5).*

Ran explains that the crack must be

at least more than halfway through the thickness of the peel or else it is considered intact (see *Rama 648:5; Beur Halachah, ibid.* s.v. יכבל). *Rashi (36a)* and *Rosh* maintains that the crack must run the entire length of the *esrog* to render it invalid.

Ran holds that even a crack along the majority of the *esrog* is invalid. He also adds that even a small crack on the upper portion, the *nose* of the *esrog* would cause invalidation, just as a boil on that part invalidates it. (See *Shulchan Orach 645:5.*)

נִקַּב וְחָסֵר כָּל־שֶׁהוּא, — [or] *it was punctured and is missing a slight portion,*

Many commentators understand the mishnah to mean that the *esrog* was both punctured *and* made partially deficient *(Rashi; Ran; Ravad).* Accordingly a puncture invalidates an *esrog* only if it causes a deficiency in the *esrog*, no matter how minute. Later the mishnah states: נִקַּב וְלֹא חָסֵר כָּל־שֶׁהוּא, כָּשֵׁר, *if it was punctured and nothing was missing, it is valid.* Taken together these two laws teach that it is not a hole *per se* that invalidates the esrog, but a deficiency, even a minute one, *does* invalidate it.

The *Gemara (36a)*, however, adds a distinction between a hole that merely penetrates the *esrog*, and a נְקָב מְפוּלָשׁ, *a puncture that penetrates the esrog through and through.* A hole that penetrates completely, even if it is minute, invalidates the *esrog.* A partial puncture must be the size of an *issar* (a small Roman coin) to invalidate it. Accordingly, the *Gemara* adds to the mishnah: not only does a puncture invalidate an *esrog* when it causes a deficiency, but

indistinguishable from the *esrog's* surface. *Terumas Hadeshen* considers a *blettel* so common that it is part of an *esrog's* natural growth pattern, whether it is raised or not. The consensus of commentators is that except in emergency, one should be stringent and regard anything which is raised above the skin's surface as an inacceptable boil *(Mishnah Berurah, ibid.* 50).

Another distinction concerns the formation of the imperfection: if it is a growth such as a fungus or mold that results from the deterioration of the *esrog* it is a boil, but if it resulted from a scratch by a thorn or branch, it is a *blettel* [*Mabit* quoted by *Magen Avraham*; see *Shaarei Teshuvah*].

Citing *Tosefos Yom Tov*, *Bikurei Yaakov* adds that even a branch or thorn can cause the growth of an invalidating growth or fungus by laying upon the *esrog* so that part of it is not exposed to air *(Beur Halachah, ibid.* s.v. אבעבועות).

even if the *esrog* remains intact, a hole invalidates it if A) it penetrates it completely or B) it is as big as an *issar*, as in the case of a puncture made by a wide nail or spike which would leave a large hole, but not remove any part of the *esrog (Rashi)*.

Others incorporate the law of the *Gemara* into the text of the mishnah: they read *or it was punctured or it was missing a slight portion*. Accordingly the mishnah makes mention of two invalidations A) a puncture, B) a deficiency (*Rambam, Comm. to Mishnah;* see *Lechem Mishnah, Lulav* 8:7) *Ran; Rav;* see *Tos. Yom Tov.*

Ravad disagrees. He comments that the *Gemara* does not add a new law, but explains the mishnah's statement that a hole invalidates only if it creates a deficiency. The *Gemara* elaborates that the extent of the deficiency needed to invalidate depends on the depth of the hole. If it penetrates through and through, even a tiny deficiency is sufficient. If the hole does not penetrate, it does not invalidate unless the deficiency is as large as an *issar*.

Orach Chaim 648:2 concludes that one should be stringent and follow the views of *Rashi* and *Rambam* unless no other *esrog* is available. See *Mishnah Berurah* ibid 8.

According to *Bahag* (quoted by *Rosh* and *Rashi*), the hole must pass completely through the *esrog* from one side to the next to be considered מְפוּלָשׁ, *penetrating through and through.*

According to others, a hole that penetrates the thickness of the peel to the *esrog's* interior invalidates it *(Rosh; Ran)*.

פָּסוּל. — *it is invalid.*

[This applies to all the instances listed in the mishnah.]

The invalidations fall under two categories: הָדָר, *[lack of] beauty,* and חָסֵר, *deficient,* which stems from the requirement of לְקִיחָה תַמָּה, *a complete taking* [see introduction to this chapter].

In the case of an *esrog* with a boil and a peeled *esrog*, both of which are whole, the apparent reason for the invalidation is a lack of beauty (*Rosh* 3:15,17; *Meiri, Shulchan Aruch Harav* 648:14).

Tosefos (29b s.v. בעינן) and *Rosh* (3:2) say that this requirement is in force for the entire *Yom Tov.* Accordingly, an *esrog* with a boil or a peeled one is invalid for all seven days.

The other blemishes in the mishnah are invalid because they are considered deficient.

It is clear from the *Gemara* (36b) that the requirement of taking a complete *esrog* applies only to the first day of Yom Tov when the *mitzvah* is Scriptural (see introduction). Consequently, an *esrog* which is punctured, split or missing a *pitam* would be invalid only on the first day.

Magen Avraham 649:5,17, however, quotes authorities that consider an *esrog* without a *pitam* to be wanting in beauty. Accordingly it would be invalid for all seven days (see *Mishnah Berurah* 648:36).

Rambam (Lulav 8:9) maintains that beauty is required only on the first day. According to him, all the *esrogim* in our mishnah are valid for other days of Succos.

R' Yosef Karo (Orach Chaim 649:5) follows *Rambam* and validates such an *esrog* for the rest of Succos. *Rama (ibid.)* follows the view of *Tosefos* and *Rosh* and requires beauty for all seven days.[1]

1. There is a question about the status of the second day of Succos, which in the Diaspora is observed as *Yom Tov* (see *Rosh Hashanah* ch. 4 and appendix).

Ran cites two views: Some hold that since our calendar is accurate and we know that the second day of Succos is not *Yom Tov,* our observance is considered of Rabbinic status [מדרבנן] and as a result the requirements of *complete taking,* and according to *Rambam,* ownership — and beauty — do not apply.

Others maintain that since the Talmud ordained that the second Yom Tov day be observed as if there were still a question regarding the true date, we must judge all flaws in the Four Species as if it were the first day of Succos. Accordingly, they may be used only if no others are available and even then no blessing may be recited over them.

Shulchan Aruch (648:5) follows this later view and as a result one should not recite a blessing over a borrowed *lulav* or *esrog* on the second day Yom Tov (*Rama*).

עָלְתָה חֲזָזִית עַל־מְעוּטוֹ, נָטַל עֻקְצוֹ, נִקַּב
וְלֹא חָסַר כָּל־שֶׁהוּא, כָּשֵׁר.
אֶתְרוֹג הַכּוּשִׁי פָּסוּל. וְהַיָּרֹק כְּכַרְתִּי, רַבִּי
מֵאִיר מַכְשִׁיר, וְרַבִּי יְהוּדָה פּוֹסֵל.

[ז] **שִׁעוּר** אֶתְרוֹג הַקָּטָן — רַבִּי מֵאִיר
אוֹמֵר: כָּאֱגוֹז. רַבִּי יְהוּדָה אוֹמֵר:
כַּבֵּיצָה.

יד אברהם

עָלְתָה חֲזָזִית עַל־מְעוּטוֹ, — *If a boil covered
a minority of it,*

The first law of our mishnah states
that if a boil covers the greater part of
the *esrog* it is invalid. Conversely if it
covers only the lesser part it is valid.

The *Gemara* (35b) states that this distinction is true only regarding one boil;
if there are two or three boils, the *esrog*
is invalid in any case because the resultant spotted appearance is inconsistent
with the requirement of beauty *(Rashi).*

Ravad and *Rosh* hold that this is so only if
the spots are dispersed along both sides of
the *esrog*, but if they are concentrated in a
small area then it is not considered spotted.

R' Yitzchak Ibn Giath maintains that
anytime there are two or three boils it is invalid even if they are concentrated *(Tur,
Orach Chaim* 618).

נָטַל עֻקְצוֹ, — [*or*] *its stem was removed,*

The is the stem [עֻקְץ, grammatically
oketz, but popularly *ukatz*] at the base
of the *esrog* by which it was attached to
the tree.

This law is apparently the converse
of the earlier one: *if its pitam was
removed, it is invalid.* The contrast is
clear cut: an esrog without a *pitam* is invalid, but one without an *ukatz* is valid
(Rashi).

In the view of *Rambam (Lulav* 8:7)
and *Ran,* however, this is true only if
the *ukatz* is not completely removed,
but the total loss of the *ukatz*, resulting
in a cavity at the bottom of the *esrog*
would render it invalid as deficient.

נִקַּב וְלֹא חָסַר כָּל־שֶׁהוּא, — [*or*] *it was
punctured and nothing was missing,*

This law is in contrast to the law in
the first part of the mishnah that if it
was punctured and is missing even a
slight amount, it is invalid.

כָּשֵׁר. — *it is valid.*

In none of these cases is there sufficient lack of beauty to invalidate the
esrog. Nor do these deficiencies disqualify it as not being intact (see *comm.*
above s.v. פסול).

אֶתְרוֹג הַכּוּשִׁי פָּסוּל. — *An Ethiopian esrog
is invalid.*

According to *Rashi* (34b) the
reference here is to an *esrog* that actually comes from Ethiopia where *esrogim*
normally grow dark.

The *Gemara* (36a) adds that such *esrogim* are invalid only in areas like *Eretz
Yisroel* where *esrogim* do not grow that
color and people are unaccustomed to
seeing dark *esrogim.* In Ethiopia or
nearby, where a dark color is natural,
they are valid.

A non-Ethiopian *esrog* that by
chance grew dark is invalid for this is
not the natural color of *esrogim* in its
locale *(Rashi* 36a).

Rif and *Rambam (Lulav* 38:8),
however, explain that the term Ethiopian means dark, i.e., an *esrog* that has a
discoloration or tinge of darkness (not a
specific species of *esrog*). It is invalid
only in areas where such a color is unusual. However, if the *esrog* was very
dark or black, it is invalid everywhere.

וְהַיָּרֹק כְּכַרְתִּי, — *If one is green as a leek,*
Which resembles grass *(Rosh* 3:21).

If a boil covered a minority of it, [or] its stem was removed, [or] it was punctured and nothing was missing, it is valid.

An Ethiopian *esrog* is invalid.

If one is green as a leek, R' Meir validates it but R' Yehudah invalidates it.

7. **T**he minimum size of a *esrog* — R' Meir says: Like a nut. R' Yehudah says: Like an egg.

רַבִּי מֵאִיר מַכְשִׁיר, וְרַבִּי יְהוּדָה פוֹסֵל. — *R' Meir validates it but R' Yehudah invalidates it.*

The requirement of פְּרִי עֵץ הָדָר, *fruit of a beautiful tree,* implies a fruit that is ripe and full grown. R' Yehudah holds that a green *esrog* is unripe *(Gem.* 31b).

Rosh (3:21) quotes *Tosafos* (31b) that a green *esrog* that will turn yellow eventually is valid, because the fact that it

will eventually turn yellow is sufficient indication of its ripeness. This is also the view of *Orach Chaim* 648:21. Some views hold, however, that this is true only if the *esrog* is already partially yellow, for otherwise we cannot be certain that it will eventually change its color *(Maharil* quoted by *Magen Avraham* 648:23 and *Mishnah Berurah* 65; see *Aruch Hashulchan* 42).

7.

שִׁעוּר אֶתְרוֹג הַקָּטָן — *The minimum size of an esrog* —

[What is the smallest size *esrog* with which one may fulfill his obligation?]

רַבִּי מֵאִיר: אוֹמֵר כָּאֱגוֹז. רַבִּי יְהוּדָה אוֹמֵר: כַּבֵּיצָה. — *R' Meir says: Like a nut. R' Yehudah says: Like an egg.*

That an *esrog* has a minimum size stems from the requirement that it be a גְמַר פֵּירָא, *finished fruit,* i.e. fully grown *(Gem.* 31b).

R' Meir and R' Yehudah disagree on the minimum size at which *an esrog* can be considered full grown.

Tosafos (31b s.v. שיעור) makes a dis-

tinction between size and maturity: an *esrog* that is the minimum size is valid even if it is not yet ripe and would grow larger if left on the tree; on the other hand, an *esrog* that has attained its full potential growth but is smaller than the required minimum size is invalid, for it cannot be considered a fruit unless it has the minimum quantitative dimension (see Responsa *Chasam Sofer, Orach Chaim* 181, for a fuller explanation).

The halachah follows R' Yehudah that an *esrog* smaller than an egg is not valid *(Rambam* 7:8; *Rif; Meiri; Orach Chaim* 648:22).[1]

1. An *esrog* that grew to the proper size but had subsequently shrunk is considered invalid by some. Although it meets the condition of a finished fruit, a small *esrog* is not considered הָדָר, *beautiful (Chayei Adam* cited by *Beur Halachah* 648:21 s.v. פסול, *Chazon Ish, Orach Chaim* 148:2, disagrees).

Some hold that an *esrog* must be like an egg in both length and width; hence a long narrow *esrog* is invalid *(Beis Yitzchak, Yoreh Deah* 138). *Chazon Ish* rules that the criterion is weight or water displacement.

To fulfill the mitzvah according to all opinions of the minimum weight, one should use an *esrog* no less than 100 grams, 3.5 ounces.

וּבַגָּדוֹל—כְּדֵי שֶׁיֹּאחַז שְׁנַיִם בְּיָדוֹ אַחַת;
דִּבְרֵי רַבִּי יְהוּדָה. רַבִּי יוֹסֵי אוֹמֵר: אֲפִילּוּ אֶחָד
בִּשְׁתֵּי יָדָיו.

[ח] **אֵין** אוֹגְדִין אֶת־הַלּוּלָב אֶלָּא בְמִינוֹ;
דִּבְרֵי רַבִּי יְהוּדָה. רַבִּי מֵאִיר אוֹמֵר:
אֲפִילּוּ בִמְשִׁיחָה.

אָמַר רַבִּי מֵאִיר: מַעֲשֶׂה בְאַנְשֵׁי יְרוּשָׁלַיִם
שֶׁהָיוּ אוֹגְדִין אֶת־לוּלְבֵיהֶן בְּגִימוֹנִיּוֹת שֶׁל זָהָב.
אָמְרוּ לוֹ: בְּמִינוֹ הָיוּ אוֹגְדִין אוֹתוֹ מִלְמַטָּה.

יד אברהם

—וּבַגָּדוֹל — *And the maximum* —
What is the largest-sized *esrog* one
may use to fulfill his obligation (*Rashi*
34b)?

כְּדֵי שֶׁיֹּאחַז שְׁנַיִם בְּיָדוֹ אַחַת; דִּבְרֵי רַבִּי
יְהוּדָה. — *so that he can hold two*
[*esrogim*] *in one hand; these are the
words of R' Yehudah.*

According to the *Gemara* (31b), the
basis of this mishnah is the halachah the
lulav be taken in the right hand and the
esrog in the left. Sometimes people inadvertently take them in the wrong
hands and are forced to transfer them. If
an *esrog* is oversized, it may fall and
become invalid. If it is small enough for
two to fit into one hand, we do not fear
it falling.

Ran and *Ritva* prefer a different
reading of the mishnah. Instead of *so
that he can hold* שְׁנַיִם, *two* [*esrogim*] *in
one hand,* they read: *so that he can hold*
שְׁנֵיהֶם, *both of them* [i.e., the *lulav* and
the *esrog*] *in one hand.* This reading is
more consistent with the explanation of
R' Yehudah cited above.

רַבִּי יוֹסֵי אוֹמֵר: אֲפִילּוּ אֶחָד בִּשְׁתֵּי יָדָיו. — *R'
Yose says: Even one* [*that must be held*]
in both hands.

[I.e. R' Yose places no maximum on

the size of the *esrog*].

In R' Yose's view even if an *esrog* is
so large that it requires both hands to
hold it, it is valid. R' Yose does not
share R' Yehudah's fear that the *esrog*
will fall during a transfer as sufficient
grounds for proscribing the use of a
large *esrog* (*Tos. Yom Tov*).

The halachah follows R' Yose (*Rif;
Rambam, Lulav* 7:8; *Meiri; Rosh* 3:24;
Orach Chaim 648:22; 651:12).

According to *Ran,* the correct reading
is אֲפִילּוּ בִּשְׁתֵּי יָדָיו, *even with both
hands,* omitting the word אֶחָד, *one.* He
explains that R' Yose disagrees with R'
Yehudah in principle: there is no requirement to take the four species
together, even if he uses both hands for
the *esrog,* and picks up the other three
species separately he fulfills the *mitzvah.* Hence, there is no fear of dropping
the *esrog.* This is consistent with the
view of *Bahag* and others that the *mitzvah* can be performed by first picking
up the *lulav* and then the *esrog,* etc., as
long as he has all the species in front of
him, a view adopted by *Orach Chaim*
651:12.

R' Tam holds that the *mitzvah* cannot
be performed unless all the species are
held simultaneously, as all four are one
mitzvah (see *Tos.* 34b).

And the maximum — so that he can hold two [*esrogim*] in one hand; these are the words of R' Yehudah. R' Yose says: Even one [that must be held] in both hands.

8. **W**e do not bind the *lulav* except with its own kind; these are the words of R' Yehudah. R' Meir says: Even with cord.

R' Meir said: It happened that the men of Jerusalem would bind their *lulavim* with gold wire. The Sages said to him [in rebuttal]: They would bind it with its own kind underneath.

YAD AVRAHAM

8.

אֵין אוֹגְדִין אֶת־הַלּוּלָב — *We do not bind the lulav*

The *mitzvah* of the four species calls for the *lulav* to be bound together with the *hadasim* and *aravos* (*Gem.* 33a). Accordingly the reference to 'binding the *lulav'* means the binding together of all the three species (*Rashi* 31a).

אֶלָּא בְמִינוֹ; — *except with its own kind;*

Any part of the palm tree is considered material of its own kind — even strips of the bark or the vine-like material growing around the trunk (*Gem.* 36b).

Although such material is not beautiful, R' Yehudah holds that the requirement of beauty applies only to the *esrog* (*Gem.* 31a).

דִּבְרֵי רַבִּי יְהוּדָה. — *these are the words of R' Yehudah.*

According to R' Yehudah, the Torah ordains that לוּלָב צָרִיךְ אֲגַד, *the species of the lulav require binding*, together with the *hadasim* and *aravos*. Consequently, the binding is considered an essential part of the *mitzvah*, and the material used to effect it is an integral part of the Four Species. The use of any material other than the Four Species to bind the *lulav* would be tantamount to adding a fifth species to the four specified by the Torah, a violation of Torah's command *(Deut.* 13:1): לֹא תוֹסֵף, *you shall not add*, to any of the *mitzvos* (*Gem.* 31b; *Rashi ibid*).[1]

רַבִּי מֵאִיר אוֹמֵר: אֲפִילוּ בִמְשִׁיחָה. — *R' Meir says: Even with cord.*

[Even if he bound up the three species with a cord (which is actually made of a different species) it is valid.] R' Meir holds that לוּלָב אֵין צָרִיךְ אֲגַד, *the lulav does not require binding* [with the other two species], i.e., even if one takes the four species without tying them together he has performed the *mitzvah*. Accordingly, the binding material, because it is unessential, is not part of the *mitzvah*, so its material cannot be considered a forbidden addition to the *mitzvah*.

The Gemara (33a) adds that R' Meir agrees that the species should *preferably* be bound but this is only לְנוֹי, *for the sake of beauty*. It is not an essential part of the *mitzvah*.

1. The classical example of this prohibition, known as בַּל תּוֹסֵף, *not to add* , is the addition of a fifth compartment to the tefillin of the head or putting *tzitzis* on five corners of a garment, instead of four (*Sanhedrin* 88b; *Sifri Devarim* 13:1). According to *Rambam* (*Lulav* 7:7) it applies also to adding to the number of the individual species, i.e., two *lulavim* or two *esrogim*. *Ravad* (*ibid.*) holds that the prohibition applies only to adding an additional species, not increasing the number of each species prescribed by the Torah.

[ט] **וְהֵיכָן** הָיוּ מְנַעְנְעִין? בְּ,,הוֹדוּ לַה'', "
תְּחִלָּה וָסוֹף, וּבְ,,אָנָּא ה'
הוֹשִׁיעָה נָּא''; דִּבְרֵי בֵית הִלֵּל. וּבֵית שַׁמַּאי
אוֹמְרִים: אַף בְּ,,אָנָּא ה' הַצְלִיחָה נָּא''.

יד אברהם

אָמַר רַבִּי מֵאִיר: מַעֲשֶׂה בְּאַנְשֵׁי יְרוּשָׁלַיִם
שֶׁהָיוּ אוֹגְדִין אֶת-לוּלְבֵיהֶן בְּגִימוֹנִיּוֹת שֶׁל זָהָב.
— R' Meir said: It happened that the
men of Jerusalem would bind their
lulavim with gold wire.

They would bind the lulav, hadasim,
and aravos with bands made of golden
threads (Rashi 36b).

[R' Meir intended to prove his point
that one need not bind the lulav with its
own kind.]

אָמְרוּ לוֹ: בְּמִינוֹ הָיוּ אוֹגְדִין אוֹתוֹ מִלְמַטָּה.
The Sages [lit. they] said to him [in
rebuttal]: They would bind it with its
own kind underneath.

The noble Jews of Jerusalem first tied

together the lulav and the other species
with material of its own kind, and over
that they placed gold bands to glorify
the mitzvah. Thus, the mitzvah of
binding the species was accomplished
without adding a fifth species, for the
gold bands served only as adornment
and was not considered an essential part
of the mitzvah. In this way the prohibition against adding to the species was
not violated (Rashi to 36b; Rav; Tos.
Yom Tov).

Even though he was rebutted, the
halachah follows R' Meir (Rav; Rambam, Lulav 7:11,12; Orach Chaim
651:1).

9.

וְהֵיכָן הָיוּ מְנַעְנְעִין? — At which point [in
the Hallel service] did they wave [the
lulav]?

The Scriptural mitzvah of the Four
Species is accomplished by simply pick-

ing them up (Gem. 43a), but the Rabbis
instituted the procedure of נַעֲנוּעִים,
waving, which involves moving and
shaking the lulav in all four directions,
upward and downward.[1]

1. The actual נַעֲנוּעִים procedure is described by the Gemara (37b) simply as מוֹלִיךְ וּמֵבִיא מַעֲלֶה
וּמוֹרִיד — one brings it and retrieves it [i.e., a forward motion and a backward motion] raises it
and lowers it [i.e., moves it up and down]. This, the Gemara adds, symbolizes God's mastery
of all four directions, heaven, and earth, and it wards off harmful winds from all directions
and harmful rains or waters from above and below.

Yerushalmi adds that the movement in the six directions requires a back-and-forth motion
repeated three times. Based on Yerushalmi and the interpretations of the commentators (see
Rosh, Ran, and Meiri at length) two customs are cited by halachah:

R' Yosef Karo (Orach Chaim 651:9) rules that one makes one forward motion in each of six
directions and shakes the lulav three times.

Rama (ibid) holds that one makes a forward motion and shakes the lulav and then a
backward motion and shakes again. This process is repeated three times in each of the six
directions.

There are also two variant customs regarding the order of the directions in which the wav-
ings are made. According to Arizal: south, north, east, up, down, west. According to Vilna
Gaon: east, south, west, north, up, down. According to both customs one faces east when
waving (see Mishnah Berurah 651:47).

The commentators add that one also waves the lulav after reciting the blessing made over
the Four Species. Although the mishnah mentions only the waving at the time of the Hallel, it
goes without saying that waving is required when the primary obligation of the mitzvah is
fulfilled (Ritva; Rosh; Ran; Meiri).

9. At which point [in the *Hallel* service] did they wave the *lulav?* At *'Give thanks to HASHEM,'* at the beginning and end, and at *'Please HASHEM, bring salvation now;'* these are the words of Beis Hillel. Beis Shammai say: Also at *'Please HASHEM, bring success now.'*

YAD AVRAHAM

בְּ,,הוֹדוּ לַה' " תְּחִלָּה וָסוֹף, — *At 'Give thanks to HASHEM,' at the beginning and end,*

Psalm 118 begins and ends with the verse הוֹדוּ לַה' כִּי־טוֹב כִּי לְעוֹלָם חַסְדּוֹ, *Give thanks to HASHEM, for He is God, for His loving-kindness is eternal.* The waving of the *lulav* corresponds to the beginning and the end of the chapter (*Rashi* 37b).

וּבְ,,אָנָּא ה' הוֹשִׁיעָה נָא" — *and at 'Please HASHEM, bring salvation now;'*

Psalms 118:25 reads אָנָּא ה' הוֹשִׁיעָה נָא אָנָּא ה' הַצְלִיחָה נָא, *Please HASHEM, bring salvation now, please HASHEM, bring success now.* In the recitation of the *Hallel*, the verse is divided: first the phrase אָנָּא ה' הוֹשִׁיעָה נָא is said and repeated, and then אָנָּא ה' הַצְלִיחָה נָא is said and repeated.[1]

דִּבְרֵי בֵּית הַלֵּל. — *these are the words of Beis Hillel.*

Since the waving is based on the verse that refers to 'salvation' (see footnote), Beis Hillel holds that only the first part of the verse, which prays for salvation, required waving.

Since אָנָּא ה' הַצְלִיחָה נָא, *Please HASHEM, bring success now,* is recited separately, it is considered as if it were a separate verse and does not require waving.

וּבֵית שַׁמַּאי אוֹמְרִים: ,,אַף בְּ,אָנָּא ה' הַצְלִיחָה נָא" — *Beis Shammai say: Also at 'Please HASHEM, bring success now'* [One must also wave the *lulav* during this half of the verse].

Beis Shammai hold that although the requirement for waving is derived from the word הוֹשִׁיעֵנוּ, *help us,* one must wave during both halves of the verse from *Psalms* (*Tos. Yom Tov*).

The halachah of course, follows Beis Hillel.

1. A *Midrash* is cited as the source for the practice of waving, that also explains why these two verses were selected for waving during *Hallel.*

Scripture states (*I Chron.* 16:33-35): אָז יְרַנְּנוּ עֲצֵי הַיָּעַר מִלִּפְנֵי ה' כִּי־בָא לִשְׁפּוֹט אֶת־הָאָרֶץ. הוֹדוּ לַה' כִּי טוֹב כִּי לְעוֹלָם חַסְדּוֹ. וְאִמְרוּ הוֹשִׁיעֵנוּ אֱלֹהֵי יִשְׁעֵנוּ... *Then shall the trees of the forest sing joyfully before HASHEM for He will have come to judge the earth. Give thanks to HASHEM for He is good; for His loving-kindness is eternal. And say, 'Save us, O God of our salvation...'*

The Midrash comments: When Israel and the nations are brought to trial on Rosh Hashanah it is not known who is found innocent and who is found guilty. Therefore, the Holy One Blessed is He, granted this *mitzvah* to Israel — so that they rejoice with their *lulavim* as one who emerges innocent from before the judge.

This, then, is the meaning of the verse אָז יְרַנְּנוּ עֲצֵי הַיָּעַר, *then shall the trees of the forest sing.* The Jewish people will sing with the trees of the forest — i.e., holding their *lulavim* which came from date palms — by waving them when they emerge innocent from [לִפְנֵי ה'] *before God* [כִּי בָא לִשְׁפּוֹט הָאָרֶץ] *when He will have come to judge the earth.* And when do they wave? When they recite הוֹדוּ לַה', *Give thanks to HASHEM ...* and when they recited אָנָּא ה' וְאִמְרוּ הוֹשִׁיעָה נָא, *Please HASHEM bring salvation now* [which corresponds to the verse הוֹשִׁיעֵנוּ אֱלֹהֵי יִשְׁעֵנוּ, *And say: Save us, O God of our Salvation'*] (*Tos.* 37b; *Rosh* 3:26).

אָמַר רַבִּי עֲקִיבָא: צוֹפֶה הָיִיתִי בְרַבָּן
גַּמְלִיאֵל וְרַבִּי יְהוֹשֻׁעַ, שֶׁכָּל־הָעָם הָיוּ מְנַעְנְעִין
אֶת־לוּלְבֵיהֶן, וְהֵן לֹא נִעְנְעוּ אֶלָּא בְ,,אָנָּא ה'
הוֹשִׁיעָה נָּא''.

מִי שֶׁבָּא בַדֶּרֶךְ וְלֹא הָיָה בְיָדוֹ לוּלָב לִטּוֹל,
לִכְשֶׁיִּכָּנֵס לְבֵיתוֹ יִטֹּל עַל־שֻׁלְחָנוֹ.
לֹא נָטַל שַׁחֲרִית יִטֹּל בֵּין הָעַרְבַּיִם, שֶׁכָּל־
הַיּוֹם כָּשֵׁר לַלּוּלָב.

יד אברהם

אָמַר רַבִּי עֲקִיבָא: צוֹפֶה הָיִיתִי בְרַבָּן גַּמְלִיאֵל
וּבְרַבִּי יְהוֹשֻׁעַ, שֶׁכָּל־הָעָם הָיוּ מְנַעְנְעִין אֶת־
לוּלְבֵיהֶן, וְהֵן לֹא נִעְנְעוּ אֶלָּא בְ,,אָנָּא ה'
הוֹשִׁיעָה נָּא''. — Said R' Akiva: As I was
watching Rabban Gamliel and R'
Yehoshua, all the people were waving
their lulavim, but they did not wave except during 'Please, HASHEM, bring
salvation now.'

According to some commentators, R'
Akiva's statement is intended to cor-
roborate the view of Beis Hillel that one
waves the lulav only when saying אָנָּא
ה' הוֹשִׁיעָה נָא, Please HASHEM bring
salvation now, and not when saying
הַצְלִיחָה נָא, bring success now.
Although the people waved their
lulavim even during the second half of
the verse, following Beis Shammai's
view, Rabban Gamliel and R' Yehoshua
adhered to Beis Hillel's view indicating
that is indeed the halachah (Kappos
Temarim; Aruch LaNer based on Ritva.
See Meiri for variation of this explanation).

Rav's reading of the mishnah, however, adds a word: וְהֵן לֹא נִעְנְעוּ אֶלָּא
בְ,,אָנָּא ה' הוֹשִׁיעָה נָא'' בִּלְבָד, and they did
not wave except at אָנָּא ה' הוֹשִׁיעָה נָא only. Tosefos Yom Tov explains that according to this reading R' Akiva disagrees with the mishnah's version of
Beis Hillel. He testifies that he observed
Rabban Gamliel and R' Yehoshua who
were disciples of Beis Hillel, and they
waved only during אָנָּא ה', Please

HASHEM, and not during הוֹדוּ לַה', Give
thanks to HASHEM.

The halachah, Rav adds, follows the
tanna kamma's version of Beis Hillel
and not R' Akiva's.

In our custom the verse הוֹדוּ לַה', give
thanks to HASHEM ... is recited by the
congregation six times: once in reciting
Psalm 118, three times as a refrain in
response to the chazzan's recital of each of
the next three verses, twice more when
reciting the last verse of the psalm, which is
customarily repeated. Tosafos and Rosh
(3:26) followed by Rama (Orach Chaim
651:8), hold that each of the six times that
the הוֹדוּ is said by the congregation, the lulav
is waved.

In the opinion of Rambam (Lulav 7:10)
and Ran, followed by R' Yosef Karo (651:8),
the lulav is waved only when הוֹדוּ לַה', Give
thanks to HASHEM, is recited as the first and
last verses of the chapter, and not when it is
recited as a refrain. Accordingly one waves
the lulav three times: the first time the verse
is recited, and twice more when it is recited
and repeated.

מִי שֶׁבָּא בַדֶּרֶךְ וְלֹא הָיָה בְיָדוֹ לוּלָב לִטּוֹל —
One who arrived from a journey where
he did not have a lulav at hand to use,

I.e., during the Intermediate Days of
the festival when a trip is permitted
(Gemara 38a).

לִכְשֶׁיִּכָּנֵס לְבֵיתוֹ יִטֹּל עַל־שֻׁלְחָנוֹ. — when he
comes [lit. enters] home he should take
it at his table.

Our mishnah applies to the case of a

Said R' Akiva: As I was watching Rabban Gamliel and R' Yehoshua, all the people were waving their *lulavim*, but they did not wave except during *'Please HASHEM, bring salvation now.'*

One who arrived from a journey where he did not have a *lulav* at hand to use, when he comes home he should take it at his table.

If he did not take it in the morning he should take it in the afternoon, for the entire day is valid for the *lulav*.

YAD AVRAHAM

person returning from a trip, who began his meal in violation of the Rabbinic prohibition of eating before taking the *lulav*. The mishnah rules יִטֹּל עַל־שֻׁלְחָנוֹ, *he should take it by the table;* i.e., he should interrupt his meal to perform the *mitzvah*.

This Rabbinic prohibition is outlined in *Shabbos* 1:2 in connection with the *Minchah* [afternoon] prayer. It provides that no meal should be eaten before the performance of a time-related *mitzvah* for fear that one may become involved with his meal and forget to perform the *mitzvah* until its deadline has passed. This prohibition is applicable to any *mitzvah*, whether of Scriptural or Rabbinic origin which has a set time for its performance, for example, prayer, shofar, *lulav,* or *megillah.*

According to many commentators, the prohibition applies only to a סְעוּדַת קֶבַע, *fixed* [i.e., significant] *meal,* which means more than an egg's volume of bread or cake. Eating fruit or even meat is not prohibited (*Orach Chaim* 232:3). However, except in an urgent situation, one should eat nothing before taking the *lulav* (*Bikkurei Yaakov* 652:5).

The mishnah in *Shabbos* (1:2) teaches that the obligation to interrupt the meal applies only with regard to a Scriptural commandment such as *Shema,* but not to a Rabbinic commandment such as prayer. Since our mishnah is obviously speaking of the *mitzvah* of *lulav* on the Intermediate Days (when one may take a trip) which is only Rabbinic, why is he obligated to interrupt his meal?

The *Gemara* (38a) answers that our mishnah refers to one who began eating late in the day and would not have time to take the *lulav* before nightfall. He must, therefore, interrupt his meal and perform the *mitzvah.* On the first day, however, when the *mitzvah* is Scriptural he must interrupt his meal regardless of the time (*Ran; Orach Chaim* 652:2).

לֹא נָטַל שַׁחֲרִית — *If he did not take it in the morning.*

The time for the performance of the *mitzvah* of *lulav* begins at sunrise (*Megillah* 2:5).

Under certain circumstances, though, one may perform the *mitzvah* from when the first rays of dawn [עֲמוּד הַשַּׁחַר] appear over the horizon. This can be up to seventy-two minutes before sunrise (see *Orach Chaim* 529:1; and see *Beur Halachah* 89:1 for the exact time of עֲמוּד הַשַּׁחַר).

It is recommended that one perform the *mitzvah* as early as possible, in accordance with the *Gemara's* dictum: זְרִיזִין מַקְדִּימִין לְמִצְוֹת, *the zealous hasten to perform mitzvos* (*Pesachim* 4a). If, however, he did not have the opportunity to take the *lulav* in the morning then...

יִטֹּל בֵּין הָעַרְבַּיִם — *he should take it in the afternoon,*

[I.e., he should fulfill the *mitzvah* as soon as possible.]

שֶׁכָּל־הַיּוֹם כָּשֵׁר לַלּוּלָב. — *for the entire day is valid for the lulav.*

The *mitzvah* is valid only during the

[י] **מִי** שֶׁהָיָה עֶבֶד אוֹ אִשָּׁה אוֹ קָטָן מַקְרִין
אוֹתוֹ, עוֹנֶה אַחֲרֵיהֶן מַה שֶׁהֵן
אוֹמְרִין—וּתְהִי לוֹ מְאֵרָה! אִם הָיָה גָדוֹל מַקְרֵא אוֹתוֹ, עוֹנֶה אַחֲרָיו:
,,הַלְלוּיָהּ.''

יד אברהם

take for yourselves on the first "day" — the taking must be by day and not by night (Megillah 20b).

day, but not at night. This is derived from the verse (Leviticus 23:40): וּלְקַחְתֶּם לָכֶם בַּיוֹם הָרִאשׁוֹן, and you shall

10.

As we have seen in the previous mishnah there is a special relationship between the taking of the *lulav* and the recital of *Hallel* (see *Orach Chaim* 652:1 and *Aruch HaShulchan ibid.* 3). Therefore, after discussing the details of the performance of the *mitzvah* of *lulav*, the mishnah devotes its attention to the laws of *Hallel*.

Although it appears in the *siddur* as part of the Morning Prayer, *Hallel* is actually a separate *mitzvah*, independent of the *mitzvah* to pray daily, as evidenced by the fact that it requires a specific blessing prior to its performance.

In the times of the Mishnah, there were periods when not everyone was educated enough to read the *Hallel*. In order to insure that everyone fulfilled his obligation, the *chazzan* would recite the *Hallel* and the congregation merely listened, in much the same way that the Reading of the Torah and the *Megillah* are performed today (*Rashi*, 38b, s.v. ממינהגא).

This is based on the principle of שׁוֹמֵעַ כְּעוֹנֶה, *listening is equivalent to answering.* According to this principle one can fulfill his obligation of reciting such things as the *Megillah, Kiddush,* or blessings by listening to someone read for him. A prerequisite for this principle to be in effect is that the reader be obligated to perform the reading just as is the listener. A minor may not recite *Kiddush* or read the *Megillah* on behalf of an adult because, as a minor, he is not obligated to perform *mitzvos* (*Rambam, Hilchos Berachos* 1:11).

The *mitzvah* of *Hallel* is in the category of מִצְוֹת עֲשֵׂה שֶׁהַזְּמַן גְּרָמָא, *positive commands that are time related*, and as such are not obligatory for women, who are absolved from most time related *mitzvos* (*Kiddushin* 1:7), or for non-Jewish slaves, who are obligated only in the *mitzvos* that apply to women (*Chagigah* 4a). Accordingly, they cannot discharge males of their obligations in such categories of commandments.

Our mishnah begins by making a distinction between a case where the reader of the *Hallel* is obligated to read it for himself (i.e. an adult male) and where he is not obligated to do so.

מִי שֶׁהָיָה עֶבֶד אוֹ אִשָּׁה אוֹ קָטָן מַקְרִין אוֹתוֹ, — *If a [non-Jewish] slave, a woman, or a minor recited [Hallel] for someone,*

As explained above, the listener, as an

adult male, is obligated to recite the *Hallel*, but these three categories of people are not. If they read for him, in accordance with the custom of the time that

10. **I**f a [non-Jewish] slave, or a woman, or a minor recited [*Hallel*] for someone, he must repeat after them whatever they say — and let it be a curse upon him!

If an adult was reciting for him, he must respond after him, '*HalleluYah.*'

the *chazzan* read for the public (*Rashi* 38a; *Ran*), he cannot fulfill his *mitzvah* through mere listening.

עוֹנֶה אַחֲרֵיהֶן מַה שֶׁהֵן אוֹמְרִין— — *he must repeat after them whatever they say*—

By repeating each phrase after them, he reads the *Hallel* himself (*Rashi; Ran; Rav*). As described in *Sotah* 30b, in this form of responsive reading the *chazzan* would say a verse, and pause while the listeners repeated it, and so on. In this way even the illiterate could fulfill the *mitzvah*.

וּתְהִי לוֹ מְאֵרָה! — *and let it be a curse upon him!*

If he was compelled to resort to this form of *Hallel* reading because of his ignorance, let him be cursed for being so unlearned (*Rav*), for had he known how to read he would have recited the *Hallel* himself without resorting to such intermediaries. However, one who listens to the *chazzan* in the synagogue is not condemned for he is following the accepted practice (*Tos. Yom Tov*).

אִם הָיָה גָדוֹל מַקְרֵא אוֹתוֹ, — *If an adult was reciting for him,*

As was customary in those days, an adult male *chazzan* chanted the text of the *Hallel* to discharge his listeners (*Rav*).

עוֹנֶה אַחֲרָיו: ,,הַלְלוּיָהּ.'' — *he must respond after him, 'Hallelu Yah.'*

The *chazzan* would recite the entire first verse of *Hallel* and the congregation would respond הַלְלוּיָהּ [*HalleluYah*] *give praise to God;* the *chazzan* would recite the next verse, and the congregation would respond *HalleluYah,* and so

on throughout the entire *Hallel.* However even if he does not respond with *HalleluYah,* he fulfills his obligation, for it is the listening to the *chazzan* that is essential to the *mitzvah,* not the response (*Gem.* 38b).

Rashi and *Meiri* cite *Sotah* 5:4 that describes שִׁירַת הַיָּם, *the Song by the Sea,* in terms of the Reading of the *Hallel.* Moses acted as *chazzan,* reciting the song phrase by phrase and the children of Israel responded with the phrase אָשִׁירָה לַה' כִּי גָאֹה גָּאָה, *I shall sing to HASHEM for He has acted gloriously,* as a refrain. *Haamek Davar [Exodus* 15:21; *Numbers* 21:17] demonstrates that this use of a refrain was a common form of song in the Scripture.

The *Gemara* (38b) notes that this form of reading the *Hallel* was the custom in Mishnaic times, but by the time of *Rava,* every person read the *Hallel* for himself as we do it today.

Nevertheless, in certain parts of *Hallel,* the custom of responsive reading was continued in order to illustrate the law that the *chazzan's* reading can discharge the obligation of his listeners. In our custom there are two notable examples of this: Our way of saying הוֹדוּ לַה', *Give thanks to HASHEM,* where the *chazzan* says a verse and the congregation responds with the refrain הוֹדוּ, *Give Thanks...,* is patterned after the form of *Hallel* described in our mishnah, and our way of saying אָנָּא ה' הוֹשִׁיעָה נָּא, *Please HASHEM, bring salvation now,* when the congregation repeats the entire phrase after the reader, resembles the way of reciting *Hallel* when a minor was the *chazzan* (*Tos.; Ran; Gra; Mishnah Berurah* 422:20).

[יא] **מָקוֹם** שֶׁנָּהֲגוּ לִכְפֹּל, יִכְפֹּל; לִפְשֹׁט,
יִפְשֹׁט; לְבָרֵךְ אַחֲרָיו, יְבָרֵךְ
אַחֲרָיו—הַכֹּל כְּמִנְהַג הַמְּדִינָה.

יד אברהם

11.

מָקוֹם שֶׁנָּהֲגוּ לִכְפֹּל, — *In a place where they are accustomed to repeat,*

The custom was to repeat many verses in the *Hallel* prayer. It stems from *Psalm* 118, which forms a major part of the *Hallel*, many of whose verses have a repetitive character. For example, the chapter begins with four verses that end with the phrase כִּי לְעוֹלָם חַסְדּוֹ; *for His loving-kindness is eternal;* and the first verse ... הוֹדוּ לה', *Give thanks to HASHEM*, is repeated in its entirety at the end of the chapter. In other verses, too, individual phrases, are repeated — like יְמִין ה', *the right hand of HASHEM* (vs. 15-16; *Rashi; Ran; Meiri*).

According to *Rashi*, the Mishnaic custom was to repeat *every* verse in the entire *Hallel*.

According to *Rav*, the custom was to repeat the verses in chapter 118 that do not in themselves have a repetitive content beginning with v. 21 אוֹדְךָ כִּי עֲנִיתָנִי, *I thank you, HASHEM, though You have afflicted me*. Our practice follows this custom.

יִכְפֹּל; — *he repeats;*

The custom of the locality becomes an obligatory part of the performance of the *mitzvah* and must be followed. (See *Yevamos* 102a; *Yerushalmi, Bava Metzia* 7:1; *Rama, Orach Chaim* 690:17).

לִפְשֹׁט, יִפְשֹׁט; — [where the custom is] to *recite as is, he recites as is;*

If the custom of a particular place is to recite each verse only once, with no repetitions, that becomes the obligatory procedure *(Tif. Yis.)*.

לְבָרֵךְ אַחֲרָיו, יְבָרֵךְ אַחֲרָיו— — [where the custom is] *to recite a blessing after it, he recites a blessing after it—*

Many places have the custom in common use today of concluding the *Hallel* with a blessing that begins with יְהַלְּלוּךָ, *They shall praise You*, and ends with בָּרוּךְ אַתָּה ה' מֶלֶךְ מְהֻלָּל בַּתִּשְׁבָּחוֹת, *Blessed are You, HASHEM, King who is lauded with praises (Meiri)*.

The *Gemara* (39a) adds that only in regard with the concluding blessing is local custom the deciding factor. The blessing preceding the *Hallel* is obligatory, in accordance with the rule that all *mitzvos* require a blessing prior to their fulfillment.

Rambam's view is that a prefatory blessing is recited only on days when the full *Hallel* is recited, but not on the last six days of Pesach and Rosh Chodesh when parts of the *Hallel* are deleted. See *Orach Chaim* 422:2 for various customs on this point.

הַכֹּל כְּמִנְהַג הַמְּדִינָה. — *everything [must be done] in accord with the local custom* [lit. *the custom of the country*].

Tosafos (Yevamos 20b) declares, מִנְהַג אֲבוֹתֵינוּ תּוֹרָה הִיא, *the custom of our fathers [has the status of] Torah [law]*.

Rama (Orach Chaim 690:17) rules that we may not nullify any customs or amend them, for they were established with good reason.

❧§ Shemittah — Sabbatical Year

The next law in the mishnah involves the purchase of the Four Species during *Shemittah* year, the Sabbatical Year that concludes the recurring seven year cycle, when certain restrictions are imposed on agricultural activities and commerce, as outlined in numerous references in the Torah (*Ex.* 23:10, 11; 34:21; *Lev.* 25:1-13; *Deut.* 15:1-3). During the entire Sabbatical Year, also known as שַׁבַּת הָאָרֶץ, *the*

3
11

11. **I**n a place where they are accustomed to repeat, he repeats; [where the custom is] to recite as is, he recites as is; [where the custom is] to recite a blessing after it, he recites a blessing after it — everything [must be done] in accord with the local custom.

YAD AVRAHAM

Sabbath of the land (Lev. 25:6), the land lies fallow; plowing, planting, sowing, and harvesting are all forbidden *(Rambam, Shemittah V'Yovel* 1:1-3).

All produce which grew during *Shemittah* by itself or as a result of the previous year's cultivation may be eaten. These are called סְפִיחִין, *wild growths.* [There is a Rabbinic injunction, however, against eating most vegetables, for fear that the unscrupulous farmer may secretly plant them and claim they grew by themselves *(Rambam ibid.* 4:1-3).]

While growing, produce of *Shemittah* must be maintained in a state of הֶפְקֵר [*hefker*], *abandonment,* and must be left accessible to all who wish to take it. Any display of ownership on the part of the farmer, such as fencing off the field or gathering large amounts of crops into his warehouse, is prohibited *(ibid.* 4:24). Produce that had been 'protected' in violation of this prohibition is called מְשׁוּמָר, *guarded,* and may not be purchased from the farmer *(ibid.* 9:6, 7) and, according to some commentators, may not be eaten *(Rashi, Yevamos* 122 citing his teachers; *R' Tam* in *Tosafos* 39b).

Produce of *Shemittah* may be kept in one's private possession only as long as that particular crop is still available in the fields, i.e., figs may be kept in the house as long as figs are still growing on the trees; an apple for as long as its season lasts, and such produce should be consumed before the respective seasons are over. Once the season has ended, the ensuing period is called שְׁעַת הַבִּיעוּר, *the time of removal,* and all remaining produce must be removed from the home and placed at the disposal of people and animals *(Rambam, Shemittah V'Yovel* 7:1-3).

One may not engage in commerce with large quantities of *Shemittah* produce, but he may purchase small amounts for meals *(ibid.* 6:1).

Money used to purchase *Shemittah* produce has the sanctity of *Shemittah* produce itself and is subject to numerous restrictions. One may use it only to purchase food or products that may be used in accordance with the laws of *Shemittah,* but may not buy clothes or real estate, or use it to pay for services *(ibid.* 6:1; 10-11).

Money used to purchase *Shemittah* products is also subject to the time restriction imposed by the שְׁעַת הַבִּיעוּר, *the time of removal.* Accordingly the money must be spent by the time the product which was purchased is no longer available in the field *(ibid.* 7:7).

One may not purchase *Shemittah* produce from a person who is suspect of not being scrupulous to use the money in compliance with the laws of *Shemittah.* If, however, the price does not exceed the cost of three meals one may pay him for he will use the funds immediately *(ibid.* 8:10, 12).

There is a distinction between fruit and vegetables concerning the reckoning of the *Shemittah* year: fruits that reached a preliminary stage of growth (called חֲנָטָה, *budding)* before Rosh Hashanah of the seventh year have the status of sixth year produce and are not subject to *Shemittah* restrictions even if they were picked during *Shemittah.* Vegetables, however, that were picked during *Shemittah* — even if they were grown in the sixth year — are considered *Shemittah* products.

Regarding an *esrog,* there is a question whether it has the halachic status of a

הַלּוֹקֵחַ לוּלָב מֵחֲבֵרוֹ בַּשְּׁבִיעִית, נוֹתֵן לוֹ
אֶתְרוֹג בְּמַתָּנָה, לְפִי שֶׁאֵין רַשַּׁאי לְלָקְחוֹ
בַּשְּׁבִיעִית.

[יב] **בָּרִאשׁוֹנָה** הָיָה לוּלָב נִטָּל בַּמִּקְדָּשׁ
שִׁבְעָה, וּבַמְּדִינָה יוֹם

אֶחָד.

מִשֶּׁחָרַב בֵּית הַמִּקְדָּשׁ, הִתְקִין רַבָּן יוֹחָנָן בֶּּ־

יד אברהם

fruit or of a vegetable and therefore one must be stringent and apply all the laws of
Shemittah even if it was merely picked on Shemittah (ibid. 4:9, 12).

הַלּוֹקֵחַ לוּלָב מֵחֲבֵרוֹ בַּשְּׁבִיעִית, — If one
purchases a lulav from his friend during
Shemittah [lit. during the seventh],

Although the mishnah speaks of
purchasing a lulav, the problem of
Shemittah produce in this context applies only to the esrog that presumably
was purchased with the lulav. As noted
above, esrog has the status of the year in
which it was picked, not the year in
which it grew (Rashi).

The prohibition of Shemittah does
not apply to the lulav for it has the
status of a tree product, whose growth
is calculated according to its חֲנָטָה, budding. Since a lulav used on Succos of
Shemittah was obviously past its budding stage by Rosh Hashanah, it is considered as a product of the sixth year
(Gem. 39a; Rashi; Ran).

Rav offers another explanation: The lulav
is not considered produce but mere wood;
because it is inedible it is not subject to the
laws of Shemittah which apply only to
produce. (R' Akiva Eiger questions this explanation as apparently at variance with the
Gem. 40a. See also 40a; Bava Basra 102a with
Rashi; Rambam, Shemittah V'Yovel 5:11).

The seller here is an unlearned person
[am haaretz] to whom one may not give
money for Shemittah products for fear
he will not use them in accordance with
the halachah. Rashi suggests the text ac-

tually be emended to read מֵעַם
הָאָרֶץ, from an unlearned person, for
the term חֲבֵרוֹ, his friend, implies that
the seller, like the purchaser, is
scrupulous regarding the laws of
Shemittah. Tosafos (39a s.v. הלוקח) defends our reading, and maintains that
the word his friend, is often used to
refer to the ignorant and even non-Jews.

נוֹתֵן לוֹ אֶתְרוֹג בְּמַתָּנָה, לְפִי שֶׁאֵין רַשַּׁאי
לְלָקְחוֹ בַּשְּׁבִיעִית. — he must give him the
esrog as a gift, because it is forbidden to
purchase it during Shemittah.

Since the price of the esrog usually
exceeds the equivalent of three meals
one may not give the am haaretz money
for the purchase, for fear he will hoard
it past the time of בִּיעוּר, removal, when
it is forbidden to keep it (Rashi); or he
will spend it on products or services that
one is forbidden to purchase with
money of Shemittah (Gem. 39a; Tos.).

The Gemara (39a) adds that if the am
haaretz refuses to give the esrog as a
gift, then he may raise the price of the
lulav to cover the cost of the esrog so
that it is considered as if the money is
only in exchange for the lulav and thus
not subject to the restrictions of Shemittah. This procedure is called הַבְלָעָה, inclusion [of the esrog for the price of the
lulav].[1]

1. It should be noted that our mishnah discusses a case where the esrog was grown in confor-
mance with the laws of Shemittah and therefore is permitted to be eaten. There is no question
about the validity of such an esrog for the mitzvah; the only halachic problem is created by its

If one purchases a *lulav* from his friend during *Shemittah*, he must give him the *esrog* as a gift, because it is forbidden to purchase it during *Shemittah*.

12. **O**riginally the *lulav* was taken in the Temple seven [days], and in the provinces [it was taken] one day.

After the Temple was destroyed, Rabban

YAD AVRAHAM

12.

בָּרִאשׁוֹנָה — *Originally*
[In the years when the Temple stood.]

הָיָה לוּלָב נִטָּל בַּמִּקְדָּשׁ שִׁבְעָה, — *the lulav was taken in the Temple seven [days],*

The *mitzvah* of *lulav* was performed all seven days of Succos in the Temple. This Scriptural obligation, based on the verse *(Lev.* 23:40) which is the source of the *mitzvah* of *lulav*, stems from the words: וּשְׂמַחְתֶּם לִפְנֵי ה' אֱלֹהֵיכֶם שִׁבְעַת יָמִים, *And you shall rejoice before HASHEM Your God for seven days.* This 'rejoicing before HASHEM' means taking the Four Species in the Temple which is the seat of God's Presence *(Toras Kohanim, Lev.* 23:40). This, the Torah tells us quite clearly is to take place all seven days.

As we have seen throughout this chapter, the requirements for the Four Species are more stringent when their obligation is a Scriptural one. Accordingly, all the requirements of the Four Species, such as beauty, ownership, and deficiency, are required in the Temple throughout the seven days of Succos *(Tos.).*

In the opinion of *Ramban* and *Ritva* the requirement of ownership applies only on the first day, even in the Temple. Therefore, except for the first day, one may use a borrowed *esrog* in the Temple.

וּבַמְּדִינָה — *and in the provinces*
This includes all areas outside the Temple. Even Jerusalem is considered part of 'the provinces' in this context *(Rashi* 41a; *Rav; Ran).*

In the view of the *Rambam (Comm.* to *Mishnah* and *Shofar* 2:8) and *Aruch,* the entire city of Jerusalem is included in the category of the Temple, while everywhere outside of Jerusalem is referred to as the provinces. Accordingly the Scriptural requirement calls for the *lulav* to be taken in Jerusalem for seven days.

Bikkurei Yaakov 658:1 holds that even after the destruction of the Temple, the sanctity of Jerusalem remains unchanged. Therefore, in *Rambam's* view, even today in the old city of Jerusalem the *mitzvah* to take the *lulav* all seven days is Scriptural and as a result the requirements and invalidations connected with the Scriptural *mitzvah* apply for the whole Succos.

יוֹם אֶחָד. — *[it was taken] one day.*
Outside the Temple the Scriptural requirement for taking the Four Species is only one day, the first day of Succos. This is stated in the first segment of the

purchase from an *am haaretz.*

There is considerable controversy in the later commentaries about the validity of an *esrog* that was cultivated or even guarded on *Shemittah* in violation of the Torah law. According to some authorities such an *esrog* may not be eaten and is therefore invalid for the *mitzvah* (see comm. to mishnah 5, s.v. שֶׁל עָרְלָה). Other authorities permitted the use of these *esrogim.* See *Rambam* and *Ravad, Shemittah V'Yovel* 4:15, and commentaries ibid., *Chazon Ish, Sh'vi'is* 10:6; *Igros Moshe, Orach Chaim I* 18b; *Kuntreis Shalosh Teshuvos* and *Toras HaSh'vi'is*).

זַבַּאי שֶׁיְּהֵא לוּלָב נִטָּל בַּמְּדִינָה שִׁבְעָה זֵכֶר
לַמִּקְדָּשׁ; וְשֶׁיְּהֵא יוֹם הָנֵף כֻּלּוֹ אָסוּר.

[יג] יוֹם טוֹב הָרִאשׁוֹן שֶׁל חַג שֶׁחָל לִהְיוֹת
בַּשַּׁבָּת, כָּל-הָעָם מוֹלִיכִין אֶת-
לוּלְבֵיהֶן לְבֵית הַכְּנֶסֶת. לַמָּחֳרָת מַשְׁכִּימִין
וּבָאִין. כָּל-אֶחָד וְאֶחָד מַכִּיר אֶת-שֶׁלּוֹ וְנוֹטְלוֹ,
מִפְּנֵי שֶׁאָמְרוּ חֲכָמִים: אֵין אָדָם יוֹצֵא יְדֵי
חוֹבָתוֹ בְּיוֹם טוֹב הָרִאשׁוֹן שֶׁל חַג בְּלוּלָבוֹ שֶׁל

יד אברהם

same verse (ibid.): וּלְקַחְתֶּם לָכֶם בַּיּוֹם הָרִאשׁוֹן, *and you shall take for yourselves on the first day.*

מִשֶּׁחָרַב בֵּית הַמִּקְדָּשׁ, — *After the Temple was destroyed,*

[When the Scriptural obligation to take the *lulav* for seven days no longer applied.]

הִתְקִין רַבָּן יוֹחָנָן בֶּן-זַבַּאי שֶׁיְּהֵא לוּלָב נִטָּל בַּמְּדִינָה שִׁבְעָה, זֵכֶר לַמִּקְדָּשׁ; — *Rabban Yochanan ben Zakkai instituted that the lulav be taken in the provinces seven [days] in remembrance of the Temple;*

The *Gemara* (41a) explains that the concept of performing *mitzvos* in remembrance of the Temple was first expressed by Jeremiah (*Jer.* 30:17): צִיּוֹן הִיא דֹּרֵשׁ אֵין לָהּ, *she is Zion; she has no one inquiring about her.* The way to

show concern for Zion, the Sages determined, was to perform *mitzvos* in remembrance of the Temple.

[This mishnah appears in its entirety in *Rosh Hashanah* 4:3. See there for a full commentary.]

וְשֶׁיְּהֵא יוֹם הָנֵף כֻּלּוֹ אָסוּר. — *and that the entire Day of Waving be forbidden.*

The Day of Waving refers to the Omer offering which was brought in the Temple on the sixteenth of Nissan. When the Temple stood, all new grain crops were not permitted to be eaten until after the Omer service was complete. Following the Destruction, Rabban Yochanan decreed that new crops not be eaten until the sixteenth of Nissan was over.

This section of the mishnah, too, is found in *Rosh Hashanah* 4:3 and is explained there.

13.

יוֹם טוֹב הָרִאשׁוֹן שֶׁל חַג שֶׁחָל לִהְיוֹת בַּשַּׁבָּת, — *On the first day of the Festival that fell on the Sabbath,*

The *mitzvah* of *lulav* itself involves nothing that is in conflict with the Sabbath and, therefore, under Torah law, the *lulav* is taken even on the Sabbath. As explained in *Rosh Hashanah* (4:1), however, the Rabbis chose to nullify the *mitzvah* on the Sabbath, for fear that a person might inadvertently carry his *lulav* in the street to a learned person

that he may teach him how to perform the *mitzvah*, thus violating the prohibition of carrying in a public domain. When the first day of Succos occurred on a Sabbath, however, the Rabbis placed no restrictions on the *mitzvah* of *lulav*, for on the first day the *mitzvah* is מִדְּאוֹרַיְיתָא, *of Scriptural origin.*

The *Gemara* (43a) later adds that since the destruction of the Temple, the *lulav* is never taken on the Sabbath, even on the first day.

Yochanan ben Zakkai instituted that the *lulav* be taken in the provinces seven [days] in remembrance of the Temple; and that the entire Day of Waving be forbidden.

13. On the first day of the Festival that fell on the Sabbath, all the people would bring their *lulavim* to the synagogue. On the morrow they would awaken early and come. Everyone would recognize his own [*lulav*] and take it, for the Sages said: A man cannot fulfill his obligation on the first day of Succos with a *lulav* belonging to his friend; but on the other days of

YAD AVRAHAM

כָּל־הָעָם מוֹלִיכִין אֶת־לוּלְבֵיהֶן לְבֵית הַכְּנֶסֶת. — *all the people would bring their lulavim to the synagogue.*

They would do this on Friday before the commencement of the Sabbath. They had to bring the Four Species to the synagogue before the Sabbath began because, although the taking of the Four Species, *per se*, was not forbidden on the Sabbath, carrying them in a public domain (or from a private domain to a public domain) does not override the Sabbath (*Rashi* 41b; *Ran*; *Meiri*; see also comm. to 4:4).

לְמָחֳרַת מַשְׁכִּימִין וּבָאִין. — *On the morrow* [i.e., on the Sabbath morning] *they would awaken early and come.*

[The people who had brought their *lulavim* to the synagogue the day before would arise early so as to come to the synagogue and fulfill the *mitzvah* of taking the *lulav* as early as possible.]

כָּל־אֶחָד וְאֶחָד מַכִּיר אֶת־שֶׁלוֹ וְנוֹטְלוֹ, — *Everyone would recognize his own* [*lulav*] *and take it,*

Tiferes Yisrael (4:4:13) suggests that the *esrog* was entwined among the *lulav*, myrtles, and willow twigs (see also comm. to 4:4.)

מִפְּנֵי שֶׁאָמְרוּ חֲכָמִים: — *for the Sages said:*

In this context, the phrase *the Sages said* refers to their exegetical interpretation of the Scriptural requirements,

rather than to a Rabbinic enactment (*Tos. Yom Tov*; *Tif. Yis.*).

אֵין אָדָם יוֹצֵא יְדֵי חוֹבָתוֹ בְּיוֹם טוֹב הָרִאשׁוֹן שֶׁל חָג — *A man cannot fulfill his obligation on the first day of Succos*

[The day on which the taking of the *lulav* is דְּאוֹרַיְיתָא, a *Scriptural obligation.*]

בְּלוּלָבוֹ שֶׁל חֲבֵרוֹ; — *with a lulav belonging to his friend;*

As explained previously, this is derived from the word לָכֶם, *for yourselves*, which the Sages understand to mean מִשֶּׁלָכֶם, *of your possession*, i.e., belonging to you — neither borrowed or stolen.

The *Gemara* (41b) adds that although one may not borrow an *esrog* (or any of the species) to fulfill the *mitzvah* on the first day, one can use someone else's *esrog* if it is given him as a gift, even if the owner stipulates that the *esrog* be returned, for מַתָּנָה עַל־מְנָת לְהַחֲזִיר שְׁמָהּ מַתָּנָה, a gift [given] on the condition it be returned is considered a valid gift. Thus when 'lending' someone else an *esrog* on the first day(s) of *Yom Tov*, the intention must be to give it as a gift with the stipulation it be returned (*Orach Chaim* 658:3,4; see *Mishnah Berurah* 9).

Failure to return the *esrog*, even due to circumstances beyond the receiver's control (e.g., as the result of a theft or a fine), is considered as failure to comply with the stipulation and as a result the gift would become

חֲבֵרוֹ; וּשְׁאָר יְמוֹת הֶחָג אָדָם יוֹצֵא יְדֵי חוֹבָתוֹ בְּלוּלָבוֹ שֶׁל חֲבֵרוֹ.

[יד] **רַבִּי** יוֹסֵי אוֹמֵר: יוֹם טוֹב הָרִאשׁוֹן שֶׁל חַג שֶׁחָל לִהְיוֹת בַּשַּׁבָּת, וְשָׁכַח וְהוֹצִיא אֶת־הַלּוּלָב לִרְשׁוּת הָרַבִּים, פָּטוּר — מִפְּנֵי שֶׁהוֹצִיאוֹ בִרְשׁוּת.

[טו] **מְקַבֶּלֶת** אִשָּׁה מִיַּד בְּנָהּ וּמִיַּד בַּעְלָהּ וּמַחֲזִירָתוֹ לַמַּיִם בַּשַּׁבָּת.

יד אברהם

retroactively invalid, and the *mitzvah* unfulfilled (*Orach Chaim* 658:4).

וּשְׁאָר יְמוֹת הֶחָג אָדָם יוֹצֵא יְדֵי חוֹבָתוֹ בְּלוּלָבוֹ שֶׁל חֲבֵרוֹ. — *but on the other days of Succos a man can fulfill his obligation with a lulav belonging to his friend.*

According to *Tosafos* this is true only in connection with the Rabbinical obligation that the *lulav* be taken throughout the provinces as well in the Temple. In the Temple, one can never use someone else's lulav.

According to *Ramban* and *Ritva*, this applies even in the Temple, for the requirement of ownership is limited to the first day (see *Tosefos R' Akiva* here and on mishnah 1).

14.

רַבִּי יוֹסֵי אוֹמֵר: יוֹם טוֹב הָרִאשׁוֹן שֶׁל חַג שֶׁחָל לִהְיוֹת בַּשַּׁבָּת, — *R' Yose says: If the first day of Succos fell on the Sabbath,*

[During the time of the Temple when the *mitzvah* of lulav was observed on the Sabbath (see mishnah 12 and comm.).]

וְשָׁכַח — *and one forgot*

Involved in the detail of this *mitzvah*, he forgot that the day was also the Sabbath (*Rashi* to 41b; *Ran*).

וְהוֹצִיא אֶת־הַלּוּלָב לִרְשׁוּת הָרַבִּים, — *and carried the lulav out into the public domain,*

Thereby unintentionally performing the forbidden labor of transporting an object from a private domain to the public domain.

פָּטוּר — *he is exempt—*

Ordinarily when one violates the Sabbath unintentionally, he is obligated to bring a קָרְבַּן חַטָּאת, *sin offering*

(*Shabbos* 7:1). But in this case according to R' Yose, one is exempt from bringing a חַטָּאת, *sin offering* (*Rashi; Ran*).

מִפְּנֵי שֶׁהוֹצִיאוֹ בִרְשׁוּת. — *for he carried it out with permission.*

R' Yose holds that if the violation took place while one was engaged in performing a *mitzvah*, his involvement in the present *mitzvah* frees him from the need for expiation. Thus the performance of the *mitzvah* 'permitted' the unintentional transgression (*Rashi* to 41b).

Rambam (*Shegagos* 2:10; *Comm.*) and *Rav* rule according to R' Yosi. *Meiri*, however, states that most authorities do not follow R' Yose and require a sin offering even in this situation.

The *Gemara* (42a) adds that R' Yose exempts one from a sin offering only if his action was done in the course of fulfilling the *mitzvah*, not after the

Succos a man can fulfill his obligation with a *lulav* belonging to his friend.

14. R' Yose says: If the first day of Succos fell on the Sabbath, and one forgot and carried the *lulav* out into the public domain, he is exempt — for the carried it out with permission.

15. A woman may accept [a *lulav*] from her son or from her husband and return it to the water on the Sabbath.

YAD AVRAHAM

mitzvah was already fulfilled. Accordingly, in the specific case of our mishnah, one would be exempt from the sin offering only if he had not yet performed the *mitzvah* at the time he inadvertently carried out the *lulav*, but if he had already fulfilled the *mitzvah* at home, or carried the *lulav* home from synagogue, then he would be obligated to bring the sin offering, for such actions do not involve a *mitzvah*.

The *Gemara* raises the question of how this is possible, since one fulfills the *mitzvah* the moment he picks up the Four Species; consequently his carrying of them *always* constitutes a transgression whenever he carries it out, *after* the fulfillment of a *mitzvah*, and he should be obligated to bring the sin offering.

The *Gemara* offers two solutions to this problem: A) He carried the *lulav* upside down, for one can fulfill the *mitzvah* only if the species are held כְּדֶרֶךְ גְּדִילָתָן, *in their manner of growth*, and by holding it upside down he has not yet fulfilled the *mitzvah*; B) the

lulav was carried in a utensil, which, because it is not being held in the hands of the one doing the *mitzvah*, is not considered a legitimate form of לְקִיחָה, *taking*.

This brief *Gemara* is the basis of a discussion in the early commentators concerning the halachic problem of when to make the blessing on the *lulav*. If the blessing is made after one picks up the *lulav* then, in effect, the blessing was made after the fulfillment of the *mitzvah* — but this violates the dictum that a blessing on *mitzvos* must be recited עוֹבֵר לַעֲשִׂיָתָן, *prior to their performance*. Therefore, some *Rishonim* suggest that the *esrog* should first be held upside down, and then the blessing recited, following the *Gemara's* stipulation that the species must be held in their normal pattern of growth in order to fulfill the *mitzvah*. Then, after the blessing, the species should be turned right side up. This commonly practiced alternative is cited by *Shulchan Aruch (Orach Chaim* 651:5).

Other *Rishonim* argue that as long as the נַעֲנוּעִים, *waving process*, has not been performed, the *mitzvah* is not considered completed, and the blessing may be recited *(Rosh* 3:33; *Tosafos* 39a).

15.

מְקַבֶּלֶת אִשָּׁה מִיַּד בְּנָהּ וּמִיַּד בַּעְלָהּ — *A woman may accept [a lulav] from her son [lit. her son's hand] or from her husband [lit. her husband's hand]*

This mishnah addresses the question of *muktzah* [lit. *set aside*], the category of objects that, for various reasons,

were forbidden by the Rabbis to be moved. Since a woman is exempt from the *mitzvah* of *lulav*, as a result of her general exemption from *mitzvos* which are time-related, the *lulav* might be considered as an object with no useful purpose to her, and therefore should be

רַבִּי יְהוּדָה אוֹמֵר: בְּשַׁבָּת מַחֲזִירִין, בְּיוֹם טוֹב
מוֹסִיפִין, וּבַמּוֹעֵד מַחֲלִיפִין.
קָטָן הַיּוֹדֵעַ לְנַעֲנֵעַ חַיָּב בַּלּוּלָב.

[א] **לוּלָב** וַעֲרָבָה שִׁשָּׁה וְשִׁבְעָה. הַהַלֵּל
וְהַשִּׂמְחָה שְׁמוֹנָה. סֻכָּה וְנִסּוּךְ
הַמַּיִם שִׁבְעָה. וְהֶחָלִיל חֲמִשָּׁה וְשִׁשָּׁה.

יד אברהם

considered *muktza* for her.

Nevertheless, the *mishnah* teaches, the *lulav* is not *muktzah* and a woman may take the *lulav* from her husband or son and return it to its place in the water.

Rashi and *Ran* explain that since the *lulav* is considered an object of value to men, who are obligated to perform the *mitzvah*, it is not *muktzah* for anyone; as long as something is useful to some people it is not *muktzah* to others either.

Meiri and *Hagahos Asheri* (3:33) suggest that the *lulav* is considered an object of value to the woman because she too may perform the *mitzvah* and recite a *blessing* if she so desires [as indeed many women do today].[1]

וּמַחֲזִירְחוּ לַמַּיִם בְּשַׁבָּת. — *and return it to the water on the Sabbath.*

[I.e., to the same water from which it was removed] in order to keep it from withering (*Rashi* to 42a; *Rav*).

One may place cut branches into

water and there is no fear that he will also water his garden or his crops (*R' Chananel*).[2]

This mishnah was said in the time of the Temple, when the *lulav* was taken on the Sabbath. Nowadays, however, the *lulav* is never taken on the Sabbath. Consequently, the *lulav* is considered *muktzah* and may not even be handled on the Sabbath. If the *lulav* was inadvertently removed from the water on the Sabbath, it is forbidden to replace it (*Meiri; Ran; Orach Chaim* 658:2).

רַבִּי יְהוּדָה אוֹמֵר: בְּשַׁבָּת מַחֲזִירִין, — *Rabbi Yehudah says: On the Sabbath we return [it],*

[I.e. to the water from it was taken (see *comm. s.v.* וּמחזירתו, but), no fresh water may be added.]

בְּיוֹם טוֹב מוֹסִיפִין, — *on the Festival we add [water],*

On the first [and second outside of *Eretz Yisrael*] day of *Succos*, the only festival day on which the *lulav* is taken,

---

1. Performance of time related *mitzvos* by women who are not obligated to perform them is the subject of discussion among the *Rishonim*.

Rashi (*Eruvin* 96a) holds that since women are exempt from these *mitzvos*, their performance of the *mitzvah* is in violation of the Torah's command not to add to the *mitzvos* (בַּל תוֹסֵף).

Rambam (*Tzitzis* 3:9) holds that women may perform *mitzvos* from which they are exempt, but cannot pronounce the blessing; since they are not commanded to do the *mitzvah*, they cannot say וְצִוָּנוּ, *and [God] has commanded us.*

R' Tam (*Rosh Hashanah* 33a; *Eruvin* 96a) rules that a woman may perform the *mitzvah* and recite the blessing despite her exclusion from the command; her voluntary performance is also considered a *mitzvah*. *R' Yosef Karo* (*Orach Chaim* 589:6) follows the view of *Rambam*, but *Rama* (*ibid.*) rules like *R' Tam*. This is the source of the Ashkenazic custom that women recite blessings when taking the *lulav*, listening to the *shofar*, or sitting in a *succah*.

2. *Rama* (*Orach Chaim* 336:11 see *Mishneh Berurah*), however, forbids putting flowers with closed petals into water for that would make them open up.

3
15

R' Yehudah says: On the Sabbath we return [it], on the Festival we add [water], and during [the Intermediate Days of] the Festival we change [the water].

A minor who knows how to wave is obligated to take the *lulav*.

4
1

1. The [*mitzvos* of] *lulav* and the willow branch [are performed] six or seven [days]. The [recitation of] *Hallel* and the [*mitzvah* of] rejoicing [are performed] eight [days]. The [*mitzvos* of] *succah* and the water libation [are performed] seven [days]. And the flute [is played] five or six [days].

YAD AVRAHAM

one may *add* water to the vase where the *lulav* is kept, but may not replace the old water with fresh water, as this is considered undue exertion which is prohibited on a *Yom Tov* (*Rashi* to 42a; *Rav*).

וּבַמּוֹעֵד מַחֲלִיפִין. — *and during [the Intermediate Days of] the Festival we change [the water].*

It is advisable to replace the old water with fresh water during the Intermediate Days in order to keep the *lulav* fresh and beautiful (*Rosh* to 42a; *Rav*; *Ran*; *Orach Chaim* 654).

קָטָן הַיּוֹדֵעַ לְנַעֲנֵעַ — *A minor who knows how to wave*

He knows how the *lulav* should be raised and lowered, and waved back and forth [as described in comm. to mishnah

9] (*Magen Avraham* to *Orach Chaim* 657:1:1 quoting *Mordechai*).

חַיָּב בַּלּוּלָב. — *is obligated to take the lulav.*

This is due to the *mitzvah* of חִנּוּךְ, training, by which a father is obligated to induct his son into the performance of *mitzvos* (*Rashi*; *Rav*; *Ran*; *Meiri*).

Tur (*Orach Chaim* 657) and *Shulchan Aruch* [ibid.] state that the minor's father is required to purchase an extra *lulav* for his son.

Maharshal (as quoted by *Mishnah Berurah*, 657:1:4) and *Tosafos* (*Arachin* 2b s.v. אביו לוקח לו תפילין) disagree and state that the father need merely give his own *lulav* to his minor son (see also *Bach* to *Orach Chaim* 657; comm. end of 2:8).

Chapter 4

1.

This first mishnah introduces this chapter and the first four *mishnayos* of chapter 5. Each law mentioned here is reviewed in a subsequent mishnah and elaborated upon.

לוּלָב — *[The mitzvos of] lulav*

This refers to the taking of all Four Species for the performance of the *mitz-*

vah as set forth in *Lev.* 23:40 (*Rashi* to 42b; *Rav*).

וַעֲרָבָה — *and the willow branch*

This refers to the ceremony of marching around the altar after it was ringed with willow branches as described in mishnah 5 below (*Rav*; *Rashi* to 42b).

שִׁשָּׁה וְשִׁבְעָה. — [are performed] six or seven [days].

[The mishnah refers to the performance of these commandments in the Temple (see 3:12 and comm.).]

Since Succos is seven days long (Lev. 23:39), one of the days must always be a Sabbath. Our mishnah teaches that in some years the commandments of lulav and aravah are performed even on the Sabbath and are thus fulfilled for seven days. In other years, though, neither is performed on the Sabbath, and is thus performed on only six days. Mishnayos 2 and 3 explain these variations in detail (Rashi to 42b; Rav).

הַהַלֵּל — The [recitation of] Hallel

On each of the seven days of Succos and on the concluding holiday, Shemini Atzeres, the entire Hallel (Psalms 113-118) is recited [see mishnah 8]. This is in contrast to Pesach when the entire Hallel is recited only on the first day (and on the first two days outside of Eretz Yisrael). The Talmud (Arachin 10a-b) explains that this distinction between Succos and Pesach is based on the difference between their respective Mussaf offerings (Numbers 28:19-25; 29:13-34). During Pesach the Mussaf offerings consist of the same number of oxen, rams, sheep, and goats for each day. On Succos, although the numbers of rams, sheep, and goats, are the same every day, the amount of oxen is diminished by one on each successive day. Rashi (Taanis 28b s.v. יחיד) and Tosafos (loc. cit. s.v. ויום) explain that this changing number of offerings demonstrates that Succos should be considered a set of seven one-day festivals, each of which requires its own recitation of Hallel, whereas all seven days of Pesach should be regarded as a single festival spread out over a seven-day period, for which a single Hallel at the beginning of the festival is sufficient.

[Obviously the mishnah speaks about the law as it applies to Eretz Yisrael, where only one day of Yom Tov is observed. In the diaspora, where two days are held, Hallel is recited for nine days, including the second day of Shemini Atzeres, now known as Simchas Torah.]

[Although the entire Hallel is not recited on the last six days of Pesach, an abridged version which omits the first eleven verses of Psalms 115 and 116 is recited on these days. The same verses are omitted on Rosh Chodesh. This abridged form is popularly known as 'half Hallel.']

The universally accepted custom to recite 'half Hallel' on the remaining days of Pesach is patterned on the practice current in Babylon in Talmudic times on Rosh Chodesh (Taanis 28b). Then, too, the recital of Hallel is not obligatory (see Rambam, Chanukah 3:7), but it became customary to recite half Hallel. However, Ramban (cited by Maggid Mishneh, Chanukah 3:7; Ran to Rif, Shabbos, ed. Vilna p. 22, s.v. שאני) holds that the Hallel recital on the last six days of Pesach, though performed in the same abridged manner as our Rosh Chodesh, is nevertheless obligatory. His opinion is not accepted by Shulchan Aruch (490:4).

וְהַשִּׂמְחָה — and the [mitzvah of] rejoicing

The obligation to rejoice on all three annual festivals is stated in Deut. 16:14: וְשָׂמַחְתָּ בְּחַגֶּךָ, and you shall rejoice on your festival. This refers to the eating of peace offerings (or of other sacrifices; see Chagigah 8a and Rambam, Hil. Chagigah 2:9) on each day of the festival (see mishnah 8; see also Turei Even in Avnei Miluim to Chagigah 6b; Minchas Chinuch 488; She'elos U'Teshuvos Minchas Baruch p. 186). That it is obligatory to eat them is derived from וְזָבַחְתָּ שְׁלָמִים וְאָכַלְתָּ שָּׁם וְשָׂמַחְתָּ, And you shall slaughter peace offerings, and you shall eat [them] there, and you shall rejoice (Deut. 27:7). Clearly, by eating peace offerings one fulfills the commandment to rejoice (Pesachim 109a; Rashi to 42b; Rav).

Rambam (Yom Tov 6:17-18), however, in codifying our mishnah lists various forms of 'rejoicing' without mentioning sacrificial meat: children are given candies, women are given clothing and jewelry, and men are served meat and wine.[1]

The dispute between Rashi and Ram-

1. There is an obvious contradiction to Rambam's ruling from the Talmud's statement

bam is based on *Pesachim* 70b-71a where the Talmud inquires whether sacrifices which were offered before Yom Tov (such as שְׁלָמִים, *peace offerings*, which may be eaten for two days) can suffice to discharge the obligation of rejoicing. The *Gemara (ibid.)* endeavors to resolve this question in the affirmative from our mishnah: how can one perform the *mitzvah* of 'rejoicing' for eight days if the first day of Yom Tov falls on the Sabbath — when no private sacrifices may be offered — unless previously brought offerings are satisfactory? R' Papa rebuts that the *mitzvah* of 'rejoicing' alluded to in our mishnah may refer to other forms of 'rejoicing' such as wearing holiday dress (כְּסוּת נְקִיָּה) and drinking alcoholic beverages (יַיִן יָשָׁן). [Whether 'rejoicing' in this form is derived from the Torah or is of Rabbinic origin will be discussed below]. However, since the *Gemara (ibid.* כִּי אֲתָא רָבִין) seems to decide this question in the affirmative (see *Rambam, Hil. Chagigah* (2:12-13), R' Papa's rebuttal is rendered academic. Thus we revert to the original interpretation — i.e., 'rejoicing' refers only to eating sacrificial meat. This is *Rashi's* opinion, and the one offered in the commentary. Consequently this clause of the mishnah is applicable only in the Temple era when sacrifices were still offered.

Rambam, who defines 'rejoicing' without mention of eating sacrificial meat holds that while R' Papa's view is not incontrovertible, it is nevertheless the more *plausible* interpretation of the mishnah. Consequently, our mishnah refers to the forms of 'rejoicing' described by R' Papa, but not to the eating of sacrificial meat.

Rif and *Rosh*, whose codes include the clause about 'rejoicing', probably share *Rambam's* view because it is their practice to delete from their codes anything that applies only to the Temple-era. *Ran* (here) likewise understands the mishnah this way.

In conclusion it should be noted that the foregoing controversy pertains only to the interpretation of the term שִׂמְחָה, *rejoicing*, in our mishnah. Everyone agrees, however, that one should rejoice on the holidays even in our days in the absence of sacrificial meat; there is, however, a question whether this is a Torah-ordained or a Rabbinic *mitzvah*. From *Rambam (Yom Tov* 6:17 cited above; *Sefer HaMitzvos, Asseh* 54) and *Sefer HaChinuch* (488; see *Minchas Chinuch* there) one can deduce that it is a Torah obligation. However *Tosafos (Mo'ed Katan* 14b s.v. עשה) clearly holds it to be a Rabbinic *mitzvah*. (See *Sha'agas Aryeh* 65; *Sheilos U'Teshuvos Minchas Baruch* 77; *Orach Chaim* 529 with *Sha'arei Teshuvah* and *Mishnah Berurah*).

שְׁמוֹנָה. — [*are performed*] *eight* [*days*].

[These *mitzvos* are observed on the seven days of Succos and on Shemini Atzeres as is explained below in mishnah 8.]

סֻכָּה — *The* [*mitzvos of*] *succah*

I.e., the commandment to dwell in the *succah* (*Rashi* to 42b; *Rav*). See 2:9 with commentary.

וְנִסּוּךְ הַמַּיִם — *and the water libation*

This was a special ceremony performed only during the Succos festival. Water was poured on the altar during the service of the daily burnt offering every morning of Succos (*Rashi* to 42b; *Rav;* see comm. to *Yoma* 2:5).

שִׁבְעָה. — [*are performed*] *seven* [*days*].

[The *mitzvah* of *succah* and that of the water libation were performed all seven days of Succos as explained below in *mishnayos* 8 and 9.]

וְהֶחָלִיל — *And the flute* [*is played*]

Flutes and other kinds of musical in-

(*Pesachim* 109a) that 'In Temple-times rejoicing was accomplished only through [eating] meat, while in our days rejoicing is accomplished only through [drinking] wine.' This clearly indicates that there is no need for *both* wine and meat. *Yam Shel Shlomo (Beitzah* 2:5) responds that in Temple-times the uplifting spiritual experience of offering a sacrifice and partaking of it more than compensated for any lessening of rejoicing occasioned by the absence of wine. Only in post-Destruction times is it essential to add wine to the partaking of meat in order to effect rejoicing.

[ב] **לוּלָב** שִׁבְעָה כֵּיצַד? יוֹם טוֹב הָרִאשׁוֹן
שֶׁל חַג שֶׁחָל לִהְיוֹת בַּשַׁבָּת, לוּלָב
שִׁבְעָה; וּשְׁאָר כָּל־הַיָּמִים, שִׁשָׁה.

[ג] **עֲרָבָה** שִׁבְעָה כֵּיצַד? יוֹם שְׁבִיעִי שֶׁל
עֲרָבָה שֶׁחָל לִהְיוֹת בַּשַׁבָּת,

יד אברהם

struments were played to accompany
the night-long dancing and jubilation
which preceded the ceremony of water-
drawing for the 'water libation' as
described in 5:2-4 and commentary
there (Rashi; Rav).

[According to Rambam this jubilation was
not integrally connected to the water-
drawing ceremony, which followed it. Rather
these festivities were in observance of the
commandment to rejoice even more on Suc-

cos than on other festivals, as it is said (Lev.
23:40), ... and you shall rejoice before
HASHEM your God for seven days (Rambam,
Lulav 8:12; cf. Sefer HaMitzvos Asseh 54;
R' Sa'adiah Gaon, v. 3 p. 465-474; Sefer
HaChinuch 488; Chiddushei Maran Riz
HaLevi, Jerusalem 5721).

חֲמִשָּׁה וְשִׁשָּׁה. — five or six [days].

[The instruments were played
sometimes on five days, sometimes on
six, as explained in 5:1.]

2.

The mishnah now turns to examine in
detail each of the listed items, in the
order of their mention.

לוּלָב שִׁבְעָה כֵּיצַד? — How is [the mitzvah
of] lulav [performed] seven [days]?

[I.e., under what circumstances
would the mitzvah of taking the Four
Species be performed on all seven days
of the Festival?]

Mishnah 1 had stated that the mitzvah of
lulav is performed 'six or seven days.' Thus
we would expect our mishnah to begin its
discussion by repeating the phrase six or
seven [days], instead of omitting 'six'.
Tosefos Yom Tov cites Rosh who has the
reading six or seven and supports this
reading by pointing to 5:1 which reads five
or six regarding the flute-playing.

יוֹם טוֹב הָרִאשׁוֹן שֶׁל חַג שֶׁחָל לִהְיוֹת בַּשַׁבָּת,
לוּלָב שִׁבְעָה; — If the first day of the
Festival falls on the Sabbath, the lulav
[is taken] seven [days];

In the Temple era, the first day of the
Festival overrode the Sabbath insofar as
the taking of the Four Species is concerned — even in the provinces, where
the Torah ordained the mitzvah for only
one day (see above 3:13; Gem. 43a;
Rambam, Lulav 7:13). But if the Sab-

bath fell on any other day of the
festival, the lulav was not taken even in
the Temple where the taking of the
species was performed seven days in accord with Leviticus 23:40 (see above
3:12).

וּשְׁאָר כָּל־הַיָּמִים, שִׁשָׁה. — but [if it falls]
on any other days, [it is taken] six
[days].

If the first day of the Festival fell on
any other day of the week but the Sabbath, one of the Intermediate Days
would fall on the Sabbath, and the lulav
would not be taken. Thus is would be
taken only six days (Rashi 42b; Rav).

The Gemara (43a) explains that although the mitzvah of lulav in the Temple on the Intermediate Days is of equal
Torah status as is the mitzvah in the
provinces on the first day, nevertheless
the Sages instituted that it be waived
when the Sabbath occurs on any but the
first day of Succos. Because the mitzvah
on the first day applies in both the Temple and the provinces [and is therefore
to be considered of greater importance
(Meiri)], the Sages did not wish to
hinder the performance of this mitzvah.
On the Intermediate Days, however, the

2. How is [the *mitzvah* of] *lulav* [performed] seven [days]? If the first day of the Festival falls on the Sabbath, the *lulav* [is taken] seven [days]; but [if it falls] on any of the other days, [it is taken] six [days].

3. How is [the *mitzvah* of the] willow branch [performed] seven [days]? If the seventh day of [the] willow [ceremony] falls on the Sabbath, the

YAD AVRAHAM

Torah *mitzvah* applies only to the Temple [and is therefore judged to be of lesser importance] so the Rabbis had no qualms about banning it even in the Temple (cf. *Rambam, Lulav* 7:14).

Why should the taking of the *lulav* not override the Sabbath? The Sages banned the taking of the Four Species on the Sabbath (except on the first day of the Festival in the Temple) for fear that one might take his *lulav* and go to an expert in order to learn the laws concerning waving (נַעְנוּעִים) or the benedictions *(Ran)*. In the process of doing so, he may inadvertently carry the *lulav* four cubits through a public domain [רְשׁוּת הָרַבִּים] and thus desecrate the Sabbath *(Gem.* 43a).

Tosafos (43a s.v. ויעבירנו) and *Meiri* point out that the *Gemara* could also have said that he might carry the *lulav* from a private domain [רְשׁוּת הַיָחִיד] to a public domain or vice versa, both of them equivalent desecrations of the Sabbath.

Although, as a general rule, Rabbinical injunctions were not instituted in the Temple [אֵין שְׁבוּת בְּמִקְדָּשׁ] *(Pesachim* 65a), the *mitzvah* of *lulav* was not always fulfilled on the Sabbath in the Temple. Only *mitzvos* unique to the Temple were not subjected to Rabbinical injunctions, for the priests — who were responsible for the Temple procedure — were scrupulous and swift in performing their duties *(Eruvin* 103a). *Lulav*, however, is a *mitzvah* that is performed by everyone, not

only by the Kohanim in the Temple; so it is subject to Rabbinic restriction *(Meiri; Tif. Yis.).*

Nowadays, the *lulav* is not taken on the Sabbath even on the first day of the Festival *(Orach Chaim* 658:2).

Rambam (Lulav 7:17, 18 based on *Gem.* 43a-b; cf. *Tosafos* 43a s.v. אינהו; *Tos. Yom Tov)* explains that after the destruction of the Temple the Sages prohibited taking the *lulav* on the Sabbath even in *Eretz Yisrael,* because people living in places far from Jerusalem often did not know when the first day of the month of Tishrei [רֹאשׁ חֹדֶשׁ תִּשְׁרֵי] had been sanctified. As a result, they could not know with certainty which was the first day of *Succos,* but would have to observe two days as *Yom Tov .* If the first of their two days of *Yom Tov* fell on the Sabbath, they should not take the *lulav,* for *Yom Tov* might not begin until Sunday. Thus the Sages decreed that a *questionable mitzvah* of taking the *lulav* should not override the Sabbath.

The Sages then decreed that even in those parts of *Eretz Yisrael* where people knew with certainty which day of the month it was, no one was to take the *lulav* on the Sabbath in order to insure uniform observance and prevent a situation where some areas would observe the *mitzvah* and others would not.

Even though we nowadays rely on a universally accepted calendar, and all of Jewry knows the exact date of Rosh Chodesh Tishrei (Rosh Hashanah), the earlier custom still prevails [מִנְהַג אֲבוֹתֵינוּ בְּיָדֵינוּ] (see also *Rambam, Comm., Tos. Yom Tov).*

3.

עֲרָבָה שֶׁבְעָה כֵּיצַד? — *How is [the mitzvah of the] willow branch [performed] seven [days]?*

[When was the willow branch ceremony performed all seven days of Succos, even on the Sabbath?]

יד אברהם

יוֹם שְׁבִיעִי שֶׁל עֲרָבָה שֶׁחָל לִהְיוֹת בַּשַּׁבָּת,
עֲרָבָה שִׁבְעָה; — *If the seventh day of
[the] willow [ceremony] fell on the Sabbath, the willow [ceremony] is seven
[days];*

It is evident from the mishnah that
the *mitzvah* of the willow-branch is not
to be performed on the Sabbath except
on the seventh day of Succos, Hoshana
Rabbah. The *Gemara* (43b) explains
that the reason for prohibiting the taking of the *lulav* (see comm. to mishnah
2) on the Sabbath does not apply to the
mitzvah of the willow branch [*aravah*],
because, unlike the *mitzvah* of *lulav* and
its accompanying species, the *aravah*
was delivered by emissaries of the *beis
din* to the *Kohanim*, who were the *only*
ones who performed the *mitzvah* in the
Temple. The *Kohanim* could be relied
upon not to desecrate the Sabbath for
the sake of bringing *aravah* branches
(see *Rashi* and *Tosafos* 43b s.v. שלוחי;
Ran there).

Ran (citing other commentators) interprets
the pertinent passage of *Gemara* differently.
The willow-branches used in the Temple
ceremony were brought by emissaries of the
Beis Din (Sanhedrin) as set forth in mishnah
5, who could be depended upon to bring
them before the Sabbath. Since the populace
would receive the *aravos* directly from these
emissaries, they would not dare desecrate the

Sabbath, 'for the awe of Beis Din is upon
them.'[1]

In view of the foregoing, why is this
mitzvah prohibited on the Sabbath at
all? To this question the *Gemara* (43b)
replies that if the *mitzvah* of *aravah*
were permitted on the Sabbath while the
taking of the *lulav* were not, unknow-
ing people would come to the erroneous
conclusion that the *mitzvah* of *lulav*
was not done on the Sabbath because it
was less important than the *mitzvah* of
aravah. The Sages did not wish the
mitzvah of *lulav* to be held in such low
regard.

The *Gemara (ibid)* asks: Why does the
ceremony override the Sabbath on the
seventh day of Succos? [Just as *lulav* was set
aside on the Sabbath because the Torah *mitzvah* applies only to the Temple (see above,
mishnah 2), for the same reason the *aravah*
ceremony should not be performed on the
Sabbath *(Rashi).*] R' Yochanan said, 'In
order to publicize the fact that it [*aravah*] is a
Torah commandment [since this *mitzvah* is
not explicit in the written Torah, but was
transmitted orally to Moses (הֲלָכָה
לְמשֶׁה מִסִּינַי) it was necessary to make its
status known by having it done even on the
Sabbath *(Rashi).*] *Ritva* adds that the Sages
considered this publicity to be necessary to
counteract the influence of the Boethusians
[בַּיְיתוּסִים], heretics who did not recognize the
validity of the Oral Torah and did not prac-

---

1. An important halachic point is brought into focus by this disagreement.
As we will explain further (mishnah 5), the *aravah* was used in two ways: A) The altar was
ringed with these branches. It was obvious that this part of the *mitzvah* should not be
prohibited, for it was done by a select group of *Kohanim* at a pre-set time; B) According to
some, the branches were carried in the procession around the altar described in mishnah 5 (see
comm. there). It is about this facet of the *mitzvah* that explanations are given, for anyone
theoretically, might take part in this procession. According to *Rashi*, since only *Kohanim* were
permitted to enter the area between the altar and the Temple (see *Kelim* 1:8-9), this precluded
anyone not qualified to perform the Temple service [עֲבוֹדָה] from joining the procession.
Therefore even this facet of the *mitzvah* was permitted on the Sabbath for *Kohanim* are
zealous in the proper performance of their duties.
The commentators cited by *Ran*, while they might agree that the procession around the altar
is limited to *Kohanim*, hold that this is not sufficient reason to permit the taking of the *aravah*
because it would not account for another facet of the *aravah mitzvah*. They hold that all the
people in the Temple Court, Israelites included, held an *aravah* in hand during the *Kohanim's*
procession. This part of the mitzvah is analogous to the *mitzvah* of *lulav* and should be
prohibited on the Sabbath. In order to resolve this difficulty, these commentators advance the
principle that, 'the awe of Beis Din is upon them', thus removing the fear that people may carry an *aravah* in a forbidden manner as they might carry a *lulav*.

willow [ceremony] is seven [days]; but [if it falls] on any of the other days, [the ceremony is performed] six [days].

YAD AVRAHAM

tice this *mitzvah* (see comm. to mishnah 5).

The *Gemara (ibid.)* asks: Why does the willow ceremony not override the Sabbath as does the *lulav* if the first day of the Festival falls on the Sabbath? [Why did they pick the seventh day to publicize the Torah-origin of *aravah* unlike *lulav* which overrides the Sabbath when it falls on the first day of Succos *(Rashi)?*] The *Gemara* replies that if the *aravah* were taken on the first day, people would think that it is not the *aravah* ceremony, but the *lulav* that overrides the Sabbath. Onlookers would say that since the Sabbath prohibition had been waived for the sake of *lulav*, the *aravah* could be taken as well — but the *aravah* is not significant enough to justify a waiver of the Sabbath on its own account. Thus the need to publicize the Torah-status of this *mitzvah* would not be accomplished. The Sages, therefore, utilized Hoshana Rabbah to demonstrate the ceremony's power to override the Sabbath. *Rashi (ibid.)* adds that the first and last days are the most conspicuous and clearly defined, thus by overriding the Sabbath on the

seventh day the Sages achieved their goal.

וּשְׁאָר כָּל-הַיָמִים, שִׁשָׁה. — *but [if it falls] on any of the other days, [the ceremony is performed] six [days].*

[I.e., if the seventh day of Succos fell on any day of the week other than the Sabbath, so that the Sabbath would be another day of the Festival, the willow ceremony would be performed only six days, as the ceremony does not override the Sabbath unless it falls on the seventh day of Succos.]

Nowadays, the question is academic because the seventh day of Succos (21 Tishrei) can never fall on the Sabbath. This is due to our pre-calculated calendar system in which the first day of Tishrei can never fall on Sunday (*Orach Chaim* 428:1; see also the statement of Bar Hadya in *Gem.* 43b). And, because the *aravah* ceremony did not override the Sabbath in the Temple, we do not walk around the *bimah* [reading table] on the Sabbath (*Rama, Orach Chaim* 660:1; *Mishnah Berurah ibid.* 4).

◆§ The Aravah Ceremony as Practiced Today

Though it is not mentioned in Scripture, the willow ceremony in the Temple is nevertheless a Torah obligation because it was transmitted in the Oral Torah given to Moses at Sinai (see *Gem.* 44a, *Rambam, Lulav* 7:20; comm. above 4:2). However, the practice (not mentioned in the mishnah) of taking willow twigs (in addition to those taken together with the *lulav*) on the seventh day of Succos (Hoshana Rabbah) has no such basis. It was instituted in remembrance of the Temple observance (זֵכֶר לַמִּקְדָּשׁ; *Rambam, Lulav* 7:23, based on *Gem.* 44a), parallel to the similar institution requiring the taking of the *lulav* seven days in the post-Destruction era (3:12). The *Gemara* 44a presents two opinions about the authority for this practice. One is that the practice is יְסוֹד הַנְּבִיאִים, an *institution* [i.e., commandment] *of prophets.*[1] Another opinion is that it is a מִנְהַג הַנְּבִיאִים, a *custom of the prophets.* The difference between the opinions is whether a benediction must be recited before taking the willow. If the prophets *commanded* it, then it is proper to recite a blessing that included the word וְצִוָּנוּ, *and He commanded us;* if it is only a *custom* of the prophets, then it lacks the status of a command and no benediction is to be recited.

Our practice is to take a bunch of willow twigs (other than those bound with the

1. These prophets are Chaggai, Zachariah, and Malachi who were members of the Great Assembly (אַנְשֵׁי כְּנֶסֶת הַגְּדוֹלָה) and who were responsible for many Rabbinic Enactments (*Rashi* 44a; cf. *Tos. Yom Tov* here; *Rashi* 43b s.v. חאירדנא; *Tosafos* 44b s.v. כאן with *Maharshal;* *Tosafos* 43a s.v. והא with *Sfas Emes; Rambam, Comm.* and *Lulav* 7:199, 22).

[ד] **מִצְוַת** לוּלָב כֵּיצַד? יוֹם טוֹב הָרִאשׁוֹן
שֶׁל חַג שֶׁחָל לִהְיוֹת בַּשַּׁבָּת,
מוֹלִיכִין אֶת־לוּלְבֵיהֶן לְהַר הַבַּיִת, וְהַחַזָּנִין
מְקַבְּלִין מֵהֶן וְסוֹדְרִין אוֹתָן עַל־גַּב הָאִצְטַבָּא
— וְהַזְּקֵנִים מַנִּיחִין אֶת־שֶׁלָּהֶן בְּלִשְׁכָּה —

יד אברהם

lulav) on the seventh day of Succos without reciting a benediction (*Rav*; see also *Orach Chaim* 664:2).

In the words of *Rambam* (7:22): Since this willow twig is not specifically mentioned in the Torah, we do not take it all seven days in commemoration of the Temple ceremonies. Only on the seventh day alone do we take in present times. How does one perform it? He takes one twig, or many twigs, other than the ones bound to the *lulav*, and beats it two or three times on the ground or on a utensil without a benediction, as this ceremony is a custom of the prophets.

[See Overview to ArtScroll *Hoshanos* for an in-depth study of the present day *Hoshana* service.]

Though one willow twig suffices for this *mitzvah* (רב ששת in *Gem.* 44b; *Rambam, Lulav* 7:22; *Orach Chaim* 664:4) it is preferable to take at least three twigs to comply with R' Nachman's opinion (*Gem.* 44b; *Mishnah Berurah* 664:16 citing *Ohr Zorua*; cf. *Maharil*). The widely accepted custom to take five twigs has its origin in the procedure set forth by *Arizal* (*Mishnah Berurah* loc. cit.). Other customs are cited by *Magen Avraham* 664:8.

These twigs must meet all the halachic requirements of the *aravos* bound with the *lulav* (*Orach Chaim* and *Rama* 664:4; see also 3:3 with comm. for laws of the willow).

Chayei Adam (153:3) remarks that it is a great *mitzvah* to use long twigs as the branches used in the Temple were eleven cubits long. Even though one may not bind other species together with these twigs (*Tur* and *Orach Chaim* 664:5), it is customary to enhance the *mitzvah* by binding the twigs together with a strip of *lulav* leaf (*Chayei Adam,* ibid.).

There is a difference of opinion as to how this *mitzvah* is accomplished. *Rashi* (44b s.v. חביט) holds that the willow twig is held and waved. This has its counterpart in the Temple-ceremony where the willow branches were also waved [probably for the same reason as the waving of the *lulav* (see comm. to 3:9)] (according to *Rashi;* see comm. below s.v. בכל יום מקיפין). *Rambam* (*Lulav* 7:22) rules that the twigs should be beaten[1] on the ground, a utensil, or a piece of furniture two or three times. This also had its counterpart in the Temple procedure where the palm fronds were beaten on the earth (mishnah 6; see comm. there). R' Yosef Karo (*Orach Chaim* 664:4) rules that beating the twig upon the earth is sufficient, but *Rama* (ibid.) adds that the (Ashkenazic) custom is to do both — waving and beating.

---

1. An interesting interpretation of this practice is given in a responsum by *R' Zemach Gaon* (*Teshuvos HaGeonim Shaarei Teshuvah,* 340). The leaves of the willow are similar to lips and these twigs have the purpose of atoning for the sins of the lips. We beat them on the earth to symbolize our resolution that from now on we will not sin with our lips again but rather we will '*put his mouth to the dust...*' (*Lamentations* 3:29). R' Zemach cites a different interpretation in the name of the ancients. During the preceding holidays — Rosh Hashanah and Yom Kippur — Satan incites God's Attributes of Judgment against Israel. But now, after we have accumulated many *mitzvos*, we are confident that no-one's lips can harm us. So we beat the symbolic lips — the willow — to the earth.

4.

4. How is the *mitzvah* of *lulav* [performed]? If the first day of Succos falls on the Sabbath, they bring their *lulavim* to the Temple Mount, and the attendants receive [the *lulavim*] from them and arrange them upon the bench—but the elderly place theirs in a

After having explained when the *mitzvos* of *lulav* and *aravah* are performed on the Sabbath (*mishnayos* 2-3), the mishnah will now discuss how these *mitzvos* are accomplished in general, and the procedures instituted to insure that their observance will not lead to desecration of the Sabbath in the instances when the first day (in the case of *lulav*) or the seventh day (in the case of the *aravah*) fell on the Sabbath.

מִצְוַת לוּלָב כֵּיצַד? — *How is the mitzvah of lulav [performed]?*

I.e., how was the *mitzvah* of *lulav* fulfilled in the Temple when the first day of Succos fell on the Sabbath? (*Rashi* to 42b).

יוֹם טוֹב הָרִאשׁוֹן שֶׁל חַג שֶׁחָל לִהְיוֹת בְּשַׁבָּת, — *If the first day of Succos falls on the Sabbath,*

[So that the *mitzvah* of *lulav* overrides the Sabbath (see mishnah 2 and comm.).]

מוֹלִיכִין אֶת־לוּלְבֵיהֶן לְהַר הַבַּיִת, — *they bring their lulavim to the Temple Mount,*

The populace bring their *lulavim* to the Temple Mount on עֶרֶב שַׁבָּת, *the afternoon before the Sabbath (Rashi* to 42b; *Rav).* Although the actual *mitzvah* of taking the Four Species overrides the Sabbath, carrying them four cubits in the public domain or from a private domain to the public domain does not override the Sabbath because bringing them to the Temple is not a *mitzvah* itself, but only מַכְשִׁירֵי מִצְוָה, *preparation for a mitzvah (Rashi* to 41b; *Ran;* see also comm. to 3:13).

[The *lulav* could be carried on the Temple Mount which was considered רְשׁוּת הַיָּחִיד, *a private domain* — even

though it was open to the public — because it was surrounded by a wall (see *Middos* 1:3). The criterion by which an area is judged to be a private domain (pertaining to the Sabbath) is, not whether it is privately owned or inaccessible to the public, but whether it is surrounded by halachically recognized partitions (see *Shabbos* 6b).

The mishnah makes no mention of the *esrog. Tiferes Yisrael* suggests that the *esrogim* were intertwined with the myrtle and willow twigs. [See above 3:12 and 4:1-2 where the term *lulav* is used to include all Four Species. This is true also of the benediction recited before this *mitzvah* where only the *lulav* is mentioned.]

וְהַחַזָּנִין מְקַבְּלִין מֵהֶן וְסוֹדְרִין אוֹתָן עַל־גַּב הָאִצְטְבָא— — *and the attendants receive [the lulavim] from them and arrange them [i.e., the lulavim] upon the bench—*

The חַזָּנִים were people specially appointed to attend to the needs of the public (*Rashi* 42b; *Rav*).

As the Temple Mount ascended upward to the Temple, two long benches were built upon it, one higher and closer to the Temple than the other. These benches were covered by pillared canopies so that people could rest in the shade. The masses of *lulavim* were placed on the benches so that the roofs would shade them from the sun (*Rashi* to 42b, 45a).

וְהַזְּקֵנִים — *but the elderly*

I.e., people who were weak and old (*Rashi; Rav*).

מַנִּיחִין אֶת־שֶׁלָּהֶן בְּלִשְׁכָה— — *place theirs in a chamber—*

The elderly placed their *lulavim* in a

וּמְלַמְּדִים אוֹתָם לוֹמַר: ,,כָּל-מִי שֶׁמַּגִּיעַ לוּלָבִי
בְּיָדוֹ, הֲרֵי הוּא לוֹ בְּמַתָּנָה.''
לְמָחָר מַשְׁכִּימִין וּבָאִין. וְהַחַזָּנִין זוֹרְקִין
אוֹתָם לִפְנֵיהֶם וְהֵן מְחַטְּפִין, וּמַכִּין אִישׁ אֶת-
חֲבֵרוֹ. וּכְשֶׁרָאוּ בֵּית דִּין שֶׁבָּאוּ לִידֵי סַכָּנָה,
הִתְקִינוּ שֶׁיְּהֵא כָל-אֶחָד וְאֶחָד נוֹטֵל בְּבֵיתוֹ.

[ה] **מִצְוַת** עֲרָבָה כֵּיצַד? מָקוֹם הָיָה לְמַטָּה
מִירוּשָׁלַיִם וְנִקְרָא מוֹצָא. יוֹרְדִין

יד אברהם

Temple chamber set aside for this purpose *(Tif. Yis.)*. They were provided with a special room to prevent injury the next day when everyone was jostling for his *lulav* (*Rashi* to 42b; *Rav*).

וּמְלַמְּדִים אוֹתָם לוֹמַר: — *and they teach them to say,*
The *beis din* taught the entire populace (*Rashi* to 42b; *Rav*).

,,כָּל-מִי שֶׁמַּגִּיעַ לוּלָבִי בְּיָדוֹ, הֲרֵי הוּא לוֹ בְּמַתָּנָה.'' — *'My lulav is presented as a gift to whomever it may come'* [lit. *the one to whom my lulav will get into his hand; it is his as a gift*].
The reason for this declaration is that one cannot fulfill the *mitzvah* of *lulav* on the first day with a *lulav* that belongs to someone else (3:13), whether borrowed or stolen (see 3:1 and comm.). As a result of this statement, every *lulav* became the property of whoever had it (*Rashi* to 42b; *Rav*).
Why was this same statement not made also by people who brought their *lulavim* to the synagogue on Friday, as in mishnah 3:13? In the synagogues the number of people was small enough so that each person could recognize his own *lulav* on the Sabbath, but in the Temple, the throngs were so great that confusion was inevitable (*Tos. Yom Tov; Tif. Yis.* to 3:13).

לְמָחָר — *On the morrow*
[I.e., on the Sabbath.]

מַשְׁכִּימִין וּבָאִין. — *they arise early and come.*
[To הַר הַבַּיִת, *the Temple Mount.*]

וְהַחַזָּנִין זוֹרְקִין אוֹתָם לִפְנֵיהֶם — *the attendants throw* [the lulavim] *before them*
Tiferes Yisrael suggests that the esrogim were intertwined with the *lulav*, myrtle, and willow twigs. [They threw the *lulavim* into or in front of the throngs gathered on the Temple Mount.]

וְהֵן מְחַטְּפִין, וּמַכִּין אִישׁ אֶת-חֲבֵרוֹ. — *and they would snatch them* [i.e., *the lulavim*], *striking one another.*
[In their eagerness to retrieve their *lulavim*.]

וּכְשֶׁרָאוּ בֵּית דִּין שֶׁבָּאוּ לִידֵי סַכָּנָה, — *When the beis din saw that they were endangered* [lit. *they came to danger*],
[The jostling and striking grew intense enough to pose a threat to limb and perhaps to life as well.]

הִתְקִינוּ שֶׁיְּהֵא כָל-אֶחָד וְאֶחָד נוֹטֵל בְּבֵיתוֹ. — *they ordained that everyone should take* [his lulav] *at home* [lit. *in his house*].
[One should perform the *mitzvah* in his own house, rather than bring his *lulav* to the Temple Mount on Friday.]

5.

Mishnah 4, asked: *How was the mitzvah of lulav performed?* and limited its answer to a description of the *lulav*-

taking in the Temple when the first day fell on the Sabbath. There was no need to describe the daily procedure because

chamber—and they teach them to say, 'My *lulav* is presented as a gift to whomever it may come.'

On the morrow they arise early and come. The attendants throw [the *lulavim*] before them and they would snatch them, striking one another. When the *beis din* saw that they were endangered, they ordained that everyone should take [his *lulav*] at home.

5. How was the *mitzvah* of the willow [performed]? There was a place below Jerusalem called Motza. They descended there,

it was discussed in chapter 3. The identical question is asked in our mishnah about *aravah*, but since this *mitzvah* had hitherto not been mentioned in this tractate, the question is answered first with a description of how this *mitzvah* was observed every day. The procedure followed on the Sabbath is dealt with later (mishnah 6). According to those who hold that only the *lulav* was held while proceeding around the altar (see comm. below), the clause in our mishnah describing this procession actually belongs to the laws pertaining to *lulav*. Perhaps it was placed here because this procession followed immediately after the *mitzvah* of ringing the altar with willow-branches which is described here. It may also be argued that though the *lulav* was held during the procession, this procedure had no intrinsic connection to the *mitzvah* of *lulav*. Rather, the essence of the ritual was to circle the willow-ringed altar while holding a *lulav* — the core of the action was the willow-branches, not the *lulav*.

מִצְוַת עֲרָבָה בֵּיצַד? — *How was the mitzvah of the willow [performed]?*

[I.e., how was the special *aravah* ceremony performed in the Temple?]

Although not written explicitly in the Torah, this precept has the status of a Scriptural commandment, as discussed above.

According to *Abba Shaul (Gem. 34a;*

44a), the *mitzvah* is alluded to in *Lev.* 23:40. The word עַרְבֵי [נַחַל], *willows of [the stream]* appears in the plural form to signify that two willows, each serving a different purpose, are used on Succos. One, in twig form, is bound with the *lulav;* the other, in branch form, is used in this special ceremony around the altar.

The other Sages disagree with Abba Shaul's derivation, but state that the *aravah* ritual is a halachah given to Moses at Sinai [הֲלָכָה לְמשֶׁה מִסִּינַי].

מָקוֹם הָיָה לְמַטָּה מִירוּשָׁלַיִם וְנִקְרָא מוֹצָא. — *There was a place below Jerusalem called Motza.*

Willows grew there *(Rav).*

The *Gemara* (45a) explains that the actual name of this place was Kolonia (see *R' Chananel*), a name that was still retained during *Rav's* time. The *tanna* of our mishnah, however, refers to it by the descriptive title מוֹצָא, *Motza* [lit. *exempt*], since it was exempt from the king's tax (*Rashi* (45a) and *Rav*).

Ritva adds that this exemption from tax was to honor the inhabitants of this place for supplying the willows for the Temple.

יוֹרְדִין לְשָׁם, — *They descended there,*

[They went every day of Succos excluding the Sabbath.]

They — the emissaries of *beis din* — would go to Motza to bring the willows. This procedure survives in the custom that the synagogue attendant (שַׁמָּשׁ) brings willows for the congregants (*Ran* 43b).

סוכה לְשָׁם, וּמְלַקְּטִין מִשָּׁם מַרְבִיּוֹת שֶׁל עֲרָבָה,
ד/ה וּבָאִין וְזוֹקְפִין אוֹתָן בְּצִדֵּי הַמִּזְבֵּחַ, וְרָאשֵׁיהֶן
כְּפוּפִין עַל־גַּבֵּי הַמִּזְבֵּחַ.
תָּקְעוּ וְהֵרִיעוּ וְתָקְעוּ. בְּכָל־יוֹם מַקִּיפִין אֶת־
הַמִּזְבֵּחַ פַּעַם אַחַת וְאוֹמְרִים: ,,אָנָּא ה' הוֹשִׁיעָה

יד אברהם

וּמְלַקְּטִין מִשָּׁם מַרְבִיּוֹת שֶׁל עֲרָבָה, — *gath-ered from there large willow branches,*

Rav defines the word מַרְבִיּוֹת as *tall branches.* [They were, in fact, eleven cubits long; see comm. below s.v. וְרָאשֵׁיהֶן כְּפוּפִין עַל־גַּבֵּי הַמִּזְבֵּחַ.]

וּבָאִין וְזוֹקְפִין אוֹתָן — *and came and stood them up*

According to those who maintain that the willow was held while they walked around the altar, these branches were set up after a circuit had been made around the altar (*Tosafos* 45a; see also comm. below s.v. בְּכָל־יוֹם מַקִּיפִין אֶת־הַמִּזְבֵּחַ).

According to those who maintain that they walked around the altar while holding only the Four Species (see comm. below s.v. בְּכָל־יוֹם), the mish-nah's description follows the actual se-quence followed in the Temple. First the willows were set up next to the altar, and then the circuit was made with the Four Species (*Tos. Yom Tov*).

בְּצִדֵּי הַמִּזְבֵּחַ, — *against the sides of the altar,*

[They were placed on the base of the altar, leaning against its sides (*Gem.* 45a).]

וְרָאשֵׁיהֶן כְּפוּפִין עַל גַּבֵּי הַמִּזְבֵּחַ. — *with their tops drooping over the top of the altar.*

The tops of the willows drooped one cubit beyond the corners of the altar. The *Gemara* (45a) explains that in order for the willows to reach that far and droop down one cubit they had to be eleven cubits tall and be standing on the base of the altar.

[The altar was built in three square sections. The bottom section, called יְסוֹד, *base*, was 32x32 cubits. The mid-dle section, called סוֹבֵב, *circuit*, was 30x-30 cubits. The top section, called גג הַמִּזְבֵּחַ, *roof of the altar*, was 28x28 cubits. The base was one cubit high. Atop it was the circuit, which was five cubits high, and whose width was one cubit less than the base on each side. The top section was three cubits high and it too was drawn in a cubit on each side. On the four corners of the top were vertical projections forming the קְרָנוֹת, *corners*, of the altar, each of which was a cubit square. Thus slightly more than eight cubits (approx. 8.2 cubits) of the willow's length was needed to reach the top of the altar, leaving slightly less than three cubits

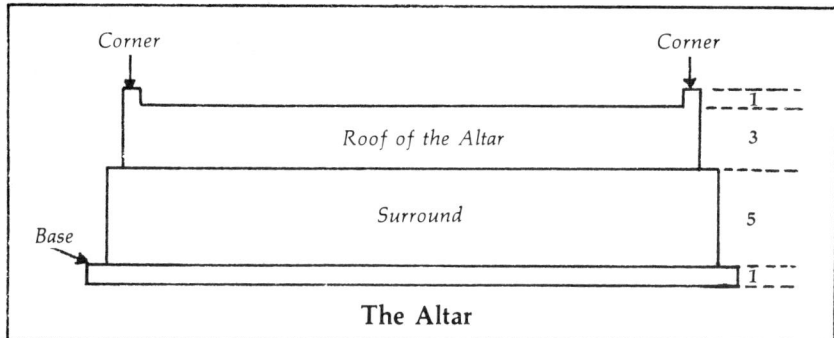

The Altar

(Diagram labels: Corner, Corner, Roof of the Altar, Surround, Base, 1, 3, 5, 1)

gathered from there large willow branches, and came
and stood them up against the sides of the altar, with
their tops drooping over the top of the altar.

They blew [on a trumpet] a *tekiah*, a *teruah*, and a
tekiah. Each day they would circle the altar one time
and say, '*Please HASHEM bring salvation now, please*

YAD AVRAHAM

(approx. 2.8 cubits). If we approximate
that half (or more) of this length continued in an upward direction, approximately one cubit (1.4 cubit or less) was
left to droop over the altar *(Rashi* 45a).]

תָּקְעוּ וְהֵרִיעוּ וְתָקְעוּ. — *They blew [on a*
trumpet] a tekiah, a teruah, and a
tekiah.

[A *tekiah* is an unbroken sound; a
teruah is a series of short (staccato)
sounds.] (See *Rosh Hashanah* 4:9 for a
detailed explanation.)

Rambam (Lulav 7:21) states that they
blew during the procession of bringing
the willow branches and while arranging them around the altar. In *Klei*
HaMikdash (7:6) he writes that they
blew on חֲצוֹצְרוֹת, *trumpets.*

בְּכָל יוֹם מַקִּיפִין אֶת הַמִּזְבֵּחַ פַּעַם אַחַת —
Each day they would circle the altar one
time

Only the *Kohanim* would walk
around the altar but not the general
public, because in order to make a circuit around the altar one had to pass
between the אוּלָם, *antechamber—* which
led into the interior of the Temple *Mid-*
dos 4:7) — and the altar, and only
Kohanim were allowed to enter this part
of the Temple (see *Keilim* 1:8,9; *Ram-*
bam, Beis HaBechirah, 7:19,20). Thus
only *Kohanim* were permitted to complete this circuit around the altar. *(Rashi*
to 43b s.v. שְׁלוּחֵי בֵית דִין, cf. *Tosafos loc.*
cit. s.v. שְׁלוּחֵי).

R' Sherira Gaon (in a responsum quoted by
R' Yitzchak ibn Giath, Meah Shearim part I
p. 114, *R' Yosef ibn Migash, Teshuvos* 43)
offers the novel interpretation that מַקִּיפִין
means not that they *walked* around the altar,
but rather that 'they *surrounded* the altar.'

Thus even Israelites could share in this
ceremony by standing on all sides of the altar
except the side that faced the Temple.
However, *R' Yitzchak ibn Giath* strongly
repudiates this opinion. He concludes that,
because of the *mitzvah,* even Israelites are
permitted to enter the space between the altar
and the Temple (see *Gem.* 44a כֹּהֲנִים בַּעֲלֵי
מוּמִין נִכְנָסִין בֵּין הָאוּלָם וְלַמִּזְבֵּחַ *Tosafos* there
s.v. והא with *Maharsha* and *Maharam;*
Yitzchok Yeranein to *Meah She'arim,* loc.
cit.).

The Sages (*Gem.* 43b) disagree about
the procedure of circling the altar. Some
maintain that the *Kohanim* walked
around the altar holding the *lulav* (and
the other species) after the willow
branches were set up around the altar
(see *Tosafos* 45a s.v. וזוקפין); others say
that only the willow branches (עֲרָבָה)
were held during this special ceremony
after which they were set up around the
altar.

Rashi (43b s.v. והביאום) explains, that
according to the view that the willow
branch was held during the procession
around the altar, the *Kohanim* first
'took' the branches, 'waved' them, and
then proceeded around the altar holding
these willows in hand, and only then
would they stand the willows up around
the altar (see comm. above s.v. ובאין
וזוקפין).

[I have not been able to find the view attributed to *Rashi* by *Mishnah Berurah* in
Sha'ar HaTziyun 664:6.]

Rambam, though ruling (*Lulav* 7:23) that
only the Four Species were held during the
procession, nevertheless holds that after the
procession, the people would come forward,
and hold the willow branches in their hands
(loc. cit. 7:22).

Ran (cited in comm. to mishnah 3) adduces
the opinion of 'some commentaries' that ac-

נָא, אָנָּא ה' הַצְלִיחָה נָא.'' רַבִּי יְהוּדָה אוֹמֵר:
,,אֲנִי וָהוּ הוֹשִׁיעָה נָא.'' וְאוֹתוֹ הַיּוֹם מַקִּיפִין
אֶת־הַמִּזְבֵּחַ שִׁבְעָה פְּעָמִים.
בִּשְׁעַת פְּטִירָתָן מָה הֵן אוֹמְרִים? ,,יָפִי לָךְ,
מִזְבֵּחַ! יָפִי לָךְ, מִזְבֵּחַ!'' רַבִּי אֱלִיעֶזֶר אוֹמֵר:
,,לְיָהּ וְלָךְ מִזְבֵּחַ! לְיָהּ וְלָךְ מִזְבֵּחַ!''

יד אברהם

cording to the view that the *Kohanim* held the willow branches while circling the altar, the Israelites in the Courtyard, too, held willow branches in their hands, albeit they could not join the procession around the altar.[1]

Ritva (who probably personifies the 'some commentators' mentioned by *Ran*) adds that the willow-branches were waved both by the *Kohanim* and the Israelites, and beat on the ground, the *Kohanim* doing so around the altar, and the Israelites in their place in the Temple Courtyard.

וְאוֹמְרִים: ,,אָנָּא ה' הוֹשִׁיעָה נָא אָנָּא ה' הַצְלִיחָה נָא'' — *'Please HASHEM bring salvation now, please HASHEM bring success now'* [*Psalms* 118:25].

Rambam (*Lulav* 7:23) states that when they circled the altar they said twice: אָנָּא ה', הוֹשִׁיעָה נָא, *please HASHEM, bring salvation now.* [Since he does not mention אָנָּא ה' הַצְלִיחָה נָא at all it seems that his text had אָנָּא ה' הוֹשִׁיעָה נָא, *please HASHEM bring salvation now,* two times, while deleting אָנָּא ה' הַצְלִיחָה נָא, *please HASHEM bring success now.* This is the version given in R.Y. Kafih's ed. of *Rambam's Commentary to Mishnah* which is assumed to be in *Rambam's* own hand and contains the text of the mishnah also). This seems to have been *Sefer HaManhig's* (*Esrog* 41) version. See *Shinuyei Nuschaos*.]

רַבִּי יְהוּדָה אוֹמֵר: ,,אֲנִי וָהוּ הוֹשִׁיעָה נָא'' — *R' Yehudah says: [They would say] 'ANI VAHO, bring salvation now!'*

Instead of saying אָנָּא ה', *Please*

HASHEM, the *Kohanim* said the words אֲנִי וָהוּ, *ANI VAHO.* The numerical value of both phrases is identical — 78 [which is three times the numerical value of HASHEM]. Furthermore, ANI and VAHO are two of the seventy-two Divine Names which are secreted in three verse in *Exodus* (14:19-21).

Each of these verses contains exactly 72 letters. 72 three-letter Divine Names are formed by taking one *consecutive* letter from each verse following a special sequence — i.e., the first verse read forward; the second read backward; and the third read forward. Thus, the first Name consisting of the ו of וַיִּסַּע; the ה of הַלַּיְלָה; and the ו of וַיֵּט — spells וָהוּ. Utilizing the same method, the thirty-seventh Name is אֲנִי.

If the seventy-two Names are divided into two groups of thirty-six, the first group begins with וָהוּ, *VAHO,* and the second with אֲנִי, *ANI.* The Name *ANI,* which begins the second group is recited before *VAHO* in conformity with the verse (*Isaiah* 44:6): אֲנִי רִאשׁוֹן וַאֲנִי אַחֲרוֹן, *I [ANI] am first and I [ANI] am last (Tos. Yom Tov).*

Tosafos (*ibid.*) explains why these two Names were chosen to be recited during the circling of the altar. *ANI* appears in the verse (*Ezekiel* 1:1): וַאֲנִי בְּתוֹךְ־הַגּוֹלָה, *and I [ANI] was among the exiles.* The name וָהוּ, *VAHO,* is found in *Jeremiah* (40:1): וְהוּא־אָסוּר בָּאזִקִּים, *and He (וָהוּ) was bound in chains. Eichah Rabbasi,* explains that the ttwo pronouns in these quotations allude to God — as if to say that God is also bound in chains and in exile

---

1. *Tosefos Yom Tov* (to mishnah 3) remarks that this is *Rambam's* opinion as well. However, this is only partially true. *Rambam* agrees that the people (i.e., those not in the procession) also took part in the *mitzvah* by 'taking' the willows. But where *Ran* holds that willows were distributed to the Israelites, who would only 'take' them, and to the *Kohanim* who would ring the altar with them, *Rambam* holds that except for those willows which ringed the altar, none more were brought. The people 'took' these after the procession.

HASHEM bring success now!' R' Yehudah says: [They would say] *'ANI VAHO, bring salvation now!'* But on that day they circled the altar seven times.

When they left what did they say? 'Beauty is yours, O altar! Beauty is yours, O altar!' R' Eliezer says: [They said,] 'To YAH and to you, O altar! To YAH and to you, O altar!'

YAD AVRAHAM

together with His People. *Rambam (comm.)* attributes a similar interpretation to the *Gaonim.* Thus the *Kohanim* were praying for God to "save" Himself and take Himself out of exile, as it were — i.e., that His sacred *Shechinah* [Divine Presence] shine forth and that the whole world accept and believe in Him. [See Overview and comm. to ArtScroll *Hoshanos.*]

Maharsha further adds that the idea of walking around the altar symbolizes the ultimate encirclement and destruction of our enemies. By walking around all sides of the altar we symbolize the downfall of the enemies who threaten us on all sides. The ceremony is completed by beating the willow on the floor and destroying it (see footnote end of mishnah 3). This signifies that our enemies will ultimately be beaten and destroyed.

וְאוֹתוֹ הַיּוֹם — *But on that day*

[I.e., the seventh day of Succos, Hoshana Rabbah.]

מַקִּיפִין אֶת־הַמִּזְבֵּחַ שִׁבְעָה פְעָמִים. — *they circled the altar seven times.*

Yerushalmi (4:3) states that this is in commemoration of the conquest of Jericho. Each day the Jewish People walked around the city one time, and on the seventh day they walked around it seven times. [See Overview to ArtScroll *Hoshanos.*]

Maharsha notes (see above s.v. רַבִּי יְהוּדָה אוֹמֵר) that the purpose of the circuits was to cause the downfall of our enemies. In Jericho after the Jews walked around the city seven times on the seventh day, the walls of the city sank into the earth and Israel conquered the city. We commemorate this on

Hoshana Rabbah by circling the *bimah* seven times in an act of prayer that our present enemies should be so demolished.

בִּשְׁעַת פְּטִירָתָן — *When they left*

[When they finished the circuits and left the altar.]

Meiri comments that this refers, not to the daily departure after each single circuit, but to the departure on the seventh day after they had completed the seven circuits and the entire yearly ceremony of the willow branches (see also *Tif. Yis.*).

מָה הֵן אוֹמְרִים? ,,יֹפִי לָךְ, מִזְבֵּחַ! יֹפִי לָךְ מִזְבֵּחַ!'' — *what did they say? 'Beauty is yours, O altar! Beauty is yours, O altar.'*

We have honored you so elegantly because you atone for us (*Rashi* 45b).

רַבִּי אֱלִיעֶזֶר אוֹמֵר: ,,לְיָה וְלָךְ מִזְבֵּחַ! לְיָה וְלָךְ מִזְבֵּחַ!'' — *R' Eliezer says:* [They said,] *'To YAH and to you, O altar! To YAH and to you, O altar.'*

The *Gemara* (45b) is concerned about the implication in R' Eliezer's phrasing that the altar is being deified to some degree alongside God. How can one say, 'To YAH [God] and to you, O altar!' when we have been taught that one who does so will be uprooted from the world, for it states (*Ex.* 22:19) בִּלְתִּי לַה' לְבַדּוֹ, *except unto HASHEM Himself!* The *Gemara* answers that their song meant: We believe in HASHEM and do not deny that He is our God — *Rashi*), and we praise the altar (which is so dear to God since it serves to atone for us (*Rashi*)].

[ו] **כְּמַעֲשֵׂהוּ** בְּחֹל, כָּךְ מַעֲשֵׂהוּ בַּשַּׁבָּת, אֶלָּא שֶׁהָיוּ מְלַקְּטִין אוֹתָן מֵעֶרֶב שַׁבָּת וּמַנִּיחִים אוֹתָן בְּגִיגִיּוֹת שֶׁל זָהָב כְּדֵי שֶׁלֹּא יִכְמֹשׁוּ.

רַבִּי יוֹחָנָן בֶּן בְּרוֹקָה אוֹמֵר: חֲרָיוֹת שֶׁל דֶּקֶל הָיוּ מְבִיאִין וְחוֹבְטִין אוֹתָן בַּקַּרְקַע בְּצִדֵּי הַמִּזְבֵּחַ. וְאוֹתוֹ הַיּוֹם נִקְרָא יוֹם חִבּוּט חֲרָיוֹת.

יד אברהם

6.

כְּמַעֲשֵׂהוּ בְּחֹל, — *Just as it was performed on the weekdays,*

[The same way the *aravah* ceremony was conducted on the weekdays of the festival (see previous mishnah)].

כָּךְ מַעֲשֵׂהוּ בַּשַּׁבָּת, — *so it was performed on the Sabbath,*

[The ceremony was conducted in exactly the same manner on the Sabbath.] As the phrase indicates this mishnah refers only to the seventh day of Succos that falls on the Sabbath, when the ceremony of the willow supersedes the Sabbath (*Meiri*; see also mishnah 4:3).

אֶלָּא שֶׁהָיוּ מְלַקְּטִין אוֹתָן מֵעֶרֶב שַׁבָּת — *except that they gathered them on the eve of the Sabbath*

[They gathered the willow branches on Friday and brought them to the Temple before the onset of the Sabbath.]

Tiferes Yisrael points out that for the first Festival day, too (when it did not fall on the Sabbath), they would cut the branches before the onset of the *Yom Tov* — why, then, does our mishnah single out the Sabbath? He explains that the mishnah wishes to tell us that it was permissible to *handle* these branches on the Sabbath in the same way as on *Yom Tov*. As to cutting them, however, no distinction between Sabbath and Festival is implied.

Lechem Mishneh suggests that there was a difference between the Sabbath and *Yom Tov*. On *Yom Tov* though the branches would be cut before sunset, they would be kept in a private house until the following

morning, when they would be brought to the Temple. Only because of the Sabbath, when the branches could not be carried through the streets, were they brought to the Temple on the previous day.

וּמַנִּיחִים אוֹתָן בְּגִיגִיּוֹת שֶׁל זָהָב כְּדֵי שֶׁלֹּא יִכְמֹשׁוּ. — *and placed them in golden vessels so that they should not wilt.*

The golden vessels were filled with water to prevent the leaves from withering (*Rav*).

Rashi (*Shabbos* 88a s.v. גיגית; see *Metargem* ibid) defines גיגית as a barrel or cask.

רַבִּי יוֹחָנָן בֶּן בְּרוֹקָה אוֹמֵר: חֲרָיוֹת שֶׁל דֶּקֶל הָיוּ מְבִיאִין — *R' Yochanan ben Berokah says: They brought date palm branches*

Not willow branches, as is the view of the first tanna.

R' Huna (*Gem.* 45b) explains R' Yochanan ben Berokah's reasoning: *Leviticus* (23:40) states, כַּפֹּת תְּמָרִים — *branches* (plural) *of a date palm*, which implies two — one branch to be used for the *mitzvah* of *lulav*, and one to be used for the altar. The first tanna however, notes that כַּפֹּת is spelled defectively without the plural ו, *vav*, to indicate that it should be interpreted as כַּפַּת, *a branch* (singular) — i.e., only one branch is to be taken and it is used for the *mitzvah* of *lulav* (see comm. to mishnah 4:1, s.v. עֲרָבָה).

R' Levi (*Gem.* 45a) offers a different reason for R' Yochanan ben Berokah's view: The Jewish People are compared

6. Just as it was performed on the weekdays, so it was performed on the Sabbath, except they gathered them on the eve of the Sabbath and placed them in golden vessels so that they should not wilt.

R' Yochanan ben Berokah says: They brought date palm branches and beat them on the ground at the sides of the altar. That day was called the day of the beating of the [date palm] branches.

YAD AVRAHAM

to the date palm *(Song of Songs* 7:8). Just as the date palm has one heart[1] i.e., its pith is found only in its central branch; so the heart of the Jewish People is one, i.e., it is dedicated totally to their Father in Heaven. That is why they use the symbolic date palm to praise God in the ceremony around the altar *(Rashi).*

וְחוֹבְטִין אוֹתָן — *and beat them*

[They beat the date palm branches.]

[It would seem that according to the first tanna the same was done with the willow branches. See *Gemara* (43b) לְפִי שֶׁאֵין בְּיְיסוּתִים מוֹדִים בְּחִיבּוּט עֲרָבָה, *because the Boethusians do not acknowledge the mitzvah of beating the aravah.* Hence our custom to do the same on *Hoshana Rabbah.* This would depend on the two opinions (cited above 4:3) regarding the procedure of Hoshana Rabbah. See *Ritva* to 43b s.v. אמר ר' יוסף.]

בַּקַּרְקַע בְּצִדֵי הַמִּזְבֵּחַ. — *on the ground at the sides of the altar.*

The mishnah text in *Talmud Yerushalmi* (4:4) reads עַל-גַּבֵּי הַמִּזְבֵּחַ, *on top of the altar.* [i.e., they beat the palm branches on the altar itself.]

וְאוֹתוֹ הַיּוֹם נִקְרָא יוֹם חִבּוּט חֲרִיוֹת. — *That day was called the day of the beating of the [date palm] branches.*

Rashi (45a), *Tosafos* (45b s.v. אחת) *Rav* and *Ritva* (in his second view) maintain that R' Yochanan ben Berokah disagrees with the first tanna regarding weekdays as well as the Sabbath. *Tosafos* (ibid.) accordingly points out

that the phrase וְאוֹתוֹ הַיּוֹם, *and that day,* must not be construed as referring to only one day, but that rather each day of the Festival was called "the day of the beating of the palm branches" (see also *Tos. Yom Tov).*

Ritva (in his first view) and *Meiri* hold that R' Yochanan ben Berokah disagrees with the first tanna only concerning the seventh day of Succos. This is why he called only the seventh day [וְאוֹתוֹ הַיּוֹם, *that* day], the day of the beating of the palm branches.

Tiferes Yisrael suggests that the reason R' Yochanan ben Berokah's view was not stated in mishnah 5 in immediate contrast to the view of the first tanna there, is because he disagrees with him only when the seventh day of Succos falls on the Sabbath. R' Yochanan maintains that since the branches had to be brought to the Temple on Friday, willows would not be fresh for the ceremony on the Sabbath, so the prophets ordained that palm branches, which do not wither quickly, be used since they would be fresh for the ceremony.

Lechem Shamayim and *Shoshanim L'David* contend that R' Yochanan disagrees with the first tanna regarding weekdays only in that he substitutes palm fronds for the first tanna's willow-branches. The *beating* of the palm fronds, however, was done only on the seventh day. Therefore the phrase 'that day' is correct in its single meaning.

Both *Tosafos* and *Ritva (ibid.)* suggest that

---

1. *Ritva* interprets the expression 'one heart' as meaning that the date palm has no bark, so its wood is the same inside and out. So, too, the actions and the thoughts of the Jewish People are as one in terms of their relationship to and belief in God. The Torah uses the words כפת תמרים, *branches of a date palm,* rather than *lulav,* to emphasize the symbolism.

[ז] **מִיָּד** הַתִּינוֹקוֹת שׁוֹמְטִין אֶת־לוּלְבֵיהֶן
וְאוֹכְלִין אֶתְרוֹגֵיהֶן.

[ח] **הֶהָלֵל** וְהַשִּׂמְחָה שְׁמוֹנָה כֵּיצַד? מְלַמֵּד
שֶׁחַיָּב אָדָם בַּהַלֵּל וּבַשִּׂמְחָה
וּבִכְבוֹד יוֹם טוֹב הָאַחֲרוֹן שֶׁל חַג, כִּשְׁאָר כָּל־
יְמוֹת הֶחָג.

יד אברהם

R' Yochanan ben Berokah did not mean that *only* palm branches were used, to the exclusion of willow branches. Rather, both palm *and* willow branches were used in the Temple ceremonies. The date palm branches however, were the more important.

The halachah does not follow R' Yochanan ben Berokah according to any of the above interpretations *(Rav; Rambam 7:20-22).*

7.

מִיָּד — *Immediately*

I.e., as soon as the *mitzvos* of the *lulav* and the willow branch had been performed [on the seventh day] *(Rosh 4:4; Rashi 465b*; s.v. מיד citing 'some commentators; *Tos.* 45a s.v. מִיָּד, according to second view; *Meiri).*

הַתִּינוֹקוֹת שׁוֹמְטִין אֶת־לוּלְבֵיהֶן — *the children loosened their lulavim*

They untied the festive bindings of the *lulav (Meiri).*

Rosh (4:4) defines the word שׁוֹמְטִין as *slip* or *slide out.* Thus, he states that the children would slip the *lulav* away from the willow twigs [to which it was bound], and they would then play with the *lulavim* since they are long and fun to play with. They would also make rings out of the *lulav* leaves and play with them.

Rashi (46b s.v. מיד) suggests that the word שׁוֹמְטִין means *put aside.* Thus, after fulfilling the *mitzvah* of *lulav* on the seventh day, the children would put aside their *lulavim* in a corner or [some other place].

וְאוֹכְלִין אֶתְרוֹגֵיהֶן — *and ate their esrogim.*

Even though there is a view that, throughout the seventh day, the esrog may not be used for any purpose but the *mitzvah* of the Four Species because it was set aside for *mitzvah* use for the whole seven-day period, nevertheless, the children ignored this law *(Rambam, Comm.; Meiri).*

Rashi (46b) suggests that the *esrogim* of children, unlike those of adults, were not set aside for a מִצְוָה גְמוּרָה, *complete mitzvah.* [Presumably, since children are required to take the Four Species only because of their parents' obligation to train them in the performance of *mitzvos* (חִנּוּךְ), their *esrogim* cannot be considered to be totally dedicated for the purpose of a *mitzvah.*] Therefore, the children were allowed to eat theirs on the seventh day when they completed the *mitzvah*, but the adults did not eat theirs.

In another exposition of this mishnah *(Rashi* 45a; *Tos.* ibid. in first view s.v. מיד) the word מִיָּד is rendered *from the hand of.* Thus the mishnah means: מִיָּד הַתִּינוֹקוֹת, *from the hand of the children,* שׁוֹמְטִין לוּלְבֵיהֶן, *they* [i.e., the adults] *snatched away their lulavim* — i.e., they snatched the *lulavim* from the hands of the children — וְאוֹכְלִין אֶתְרוֹגֵיהֶן, *and they ate their esrogim* — i.e., the adults ate the children's *esrogim.*

Rashi (45a) comments that although the adults took the children's *lulavim* and ate their *esrogim*, there was no question of גֵּזֶל, *theft*, as this custom was accepted as an expression of uninhibited שִׂמְחָה, *joy.*

7. **I**mmediately the children loosened their *lulavim* and ate their *esrogim.*

8. **H**ow are [the recitation of] the *Hallel* and the [*mitzvah* of] rejoicing [done for] eight [days]? This teaches that a man is obligated in [the recitation of] the *Hallel,* in the [*mitzvah* of] rejoicing, and in [the] honor of the last Festival day of Succos, like all the other days of Succos.

YAD AVRAHAM

As mentioned above,the children's *esrogim* could be eaten because they were set aside for the *mitzvah* only until it was completed on the seventh day.

Tosafos (45a s.v. מיד), expanding on *Rashi's* exposition, rules that youths who ride horses to greet a groom and act out mock battles with each other are exempt from payment if they damage one another's clothing or horses, because this custom was established as an expression of joy.

Rashi (46b) dismisses the first interpretation of the mishnah which states that the children put away their *lulavim* and ate their own *esrogim,* because of a Midrashic tale: A pious man always gave his money to charity. Once, when his wife had given him money to buy household necessities, he was approached for charity by a poor man to whom he gave away all his money. Fearing his wife's anger, he fled. Since it was the seventh

day of Succos [יוֹם שְׁבִיעִי שֶׁל עֲרָבָה], and he had no means of supporting himself (to pay his fare or to buy food) he snatched away *esrogim* from children until he had collected a sackful.[1]

This is a clear indication that מִיָּד הַתִּינוֹקוֹת שׁוֹמְטִין לוּלְבֵיהֶן וכו׳ means that the adults snatch the *lulavim* and *esrogim* from the hands of the children.

However, a different version of the same tale is found in *Vaykira Rabbah* (37:2) with the single change that after the pious man had fled he came to a synagogue and found the *esrogim* that the children had spoiled on Hoshana Rabbah and put aside. These he took and put into his sack. Accordingly, the correct interpretation of the mishnah is that the children ate their own *esrogim (Korban Nesanel* 4:200).

Thus, the Midrashim provide bases for both interpretations of the mishnah.

8.

הַהַלֵּל וְהַשִּׂמְחָה שְׁמֹנָה כֵּיצַד? — *How are [the recitation of] the Hallel and the rejoicing [done for] eight [days]?*

[This refers back to mishnah 1.]

מְלַמֵּד שֶׁחַיָּב אָדָם בַּהַלֵּל — *This teaches that a man is obligated in [the recitation of] the Hallel*

The difference between Pesach and

Succos is given in mishnah 1 s.v. ההלל.]

וּבַשִּׂמְחָה — *(and) in the [mitzvah of] rejoicing,*

'Rejoicing' here means eating the meat of peace offerings *(Rashi* to 48a).

R' Yehudah ben Beseira says בִּזְמַן שֶׁבֵּית הַמִּקְדָּשׁ קַיָּם אֵין שִׂמְחָה אֶלָּא בְּבָשָׂר, *when the Temple stands there* is no joy

---

1. The rest of the tale is recounted as follows:

He found himself at the seaport and sailed away on a ship. The ship took him to a certain city where the king, who was deathly ill, had been told by his doctors that only the *esrogim* used by the Jews on their Festival could effect a cure. The officers of the king searched everywhere but could not locate *esrogim.* Coming across the man they demanded to know what he carried in his sack. Opening the sack they saw that it was full of *esrogim.* They asked the pious man from where the *esrogim* came, and he answered 'from the Jews who use them on their Festival.' He was forthwith brought before the king and the king rewarded him handsomely. And so he traveled home a very wealthy person.

סֻכָּה שֶׁבְּעָה כֵּיצַד? גָּמַר מִלֶּאֱכוֹל, לֹא יַתִּיר
סֻכָּתוֹ; אֲבָל מוֹרִיד אֶת־הַכֵּלִים מִן־הַמִּנְחָה
וּלְמַעְלָה, מִפְּנֵי כְבוֹד יוֹם טוֹב הָאַחֲרוֹן שֶׁל חַג.

[ט] **נִסּוּךְ** הַמַּיִם כֵּיצַד? צְלוֹחִית שֶׁל זָהָב
מַחֲזֶקֶת שְׁלֹשֶׁת לֻגִּים, הָיָה מְמַלֵּא

יד אברהם

[on Festivals] *other than meat* [*of the peace offerings*] (*Pesachim* 109a).

[See comm. to mishnah 1 s.v. וְהַשִּׂמְחָה for the association of rejoicing with the eating of peace offerings.]

וּבִכְבוֹד יוֹם טוֹב הָאַחֲרוֹן שֶׁל חַג, — *and in* [*the*] *honor of the last Festival day of Succos,*

[Shemini Atzeres (*Gem.* 48a) is a holiday. Succos proper, which is only seven days, does not end with a holiday. But the day after Hoshana Rabbah is considered the last day of the Festival season even though it is not part of Succos. Thus the eighth day for *Hallel* and rejoicing is Shemini Atzeres.]

כִּשְׁאָר כָּל־יְמוֹת הֶחָג. — *like all the other days of Succos.*

The *Gemara* (48a) derives the obligation of rejoicing on Shemini Atzeres from *Deut.* (16:15) וְהָיִיתָ אַךְ שָׂמֵחַ, *and you shall be only joyful.*

This verse teaches that the *mitzvah* of rejoicing applies to the night of Shemini Atzeres as a continuation of the first seven days of Succos. Specifically, peace offerings were slaughtered in the Temple on the seventh day of Succos [since offerings may not be brought at night] to be eaten on the night of Shemini Atzeres. Logic also supports the idea that the verse comes to include Shemini Atzeres. The previous verse, which is directly connected to the Festival of Succos, already states וְשָׂמַחְתָּ בְּחַגֶּךָ, *and you shall be joyful in your festival.* For what purpose then is the idea of rejoicing repeated if not to include Shemini Atzeres in the *mitzvah* of rejoicing (*Rashi* 48a).

Rashi (ibid) and *Meiri* both point out that the commandment to rejoice on the night of Shemini Atzeres means that we are surely commanded to rejoice during the day, for that is the prime time for bringing offerings.

A question is raised by the commentaries: How can the Talmud derive an additional *mitzvah* — that of celebration on Shemini Atzeres — from the phrase וְהָיִיתָ אַךְ שָׂמֵחַ, *and you shall be only* [אַךְ] *joyful,* in view of the exegetical rule that the term אַךְ, *only,* indicates an exclusion rather than an inclusion. As *Yerushalmi* (*Berachos* 9:5) states the rule: אַכִּין וְרַקִּין מִיעוּטִין, *the words* אַךְ, *only, and* רַק, *but, come to exclude.*

Rashi and *Meiri,* cited above, explain that since the commandment to be joyous on Succos has already been given in the previous verses, there is no alternative but to refer this otherwise superfluous verse to Shemini Atzeres.

Meiri quotes authorities who answer that the word אַךְ in our connection comes to exclude anything which is *not* in the realm of joy. Consequently, joy is automatically included. He further states, however, that the primary answer is that the entire phrase is redundant since the previous verse had stated the *mitzvah* of joy on Succos.

Sefer HaMichtam answers in a similar vein. He states that we include Shemini Atzeres from the word שָׂמֵחַ, *joyful* and not from the word אַךְ, *only.*

The *Vilna Gaon* (as quoted by *Torah Temimah Deut.* 16:5) answers the question through a different approach utilizing אַךְ, *only,* as an exclusion in line with its traditional exegetical function. He says that on Succos there are many other *mitzvos* aside from joy, such as: *succah,* and the Four Species. Since the Torah mandates אַךְ שָׂמֵחַ — *"only" joyfulness* — this would mean that the term אַךְ comes to exclude all other *mitzvos* (e.g., *succah* and Four Species) so that *only* the mitzvah of joy will remain. Perforce, we must assign this *mitzvah* to the

4
9

How is [the *mitzvah* of] *succah* [observed for] seven [days]? When one has finished eating, he may not take apart his *succah*, but he may take down his utensils from Minchah time and later, in honor of the last day of Succos.

9. How is the water libation done? He filled a golden flagon holding three *lugim*, from the

YAD AVRAHAM

Shemini Atzeres to which the other Succos *mitzvos* do not apply; the only remaining *mitzvah* which it does have is that of joy.

סֻכָּה שִׁבְעָה כֵּיצַד? — *How is [the mitzvah of] succah [observed for] seven [days]?*

[I.e., what is the force of the commandment to dwell in the *succah* for seven days? (See comm. to mishnah 1 s.v. סֻכָּה).]

גָּמַר מִלֶּאֱכוֹל, — *When one has finished eating,*

On the seventh day of Succos, Hoshana Rabbah (*Rashi* to 48a).

לֹא יַתִּיר סֻכָּתוֹ; — *he may not take apart* [lit. *undo* (*Rashi; Rav*)] *his succah,*

Rav explains that he may not do so because the *mitzvah* of *succah* is still in force the entire day.

Rashi emphasizes that there is always the possibility that he will eat another meal that day — and it will have to be eaten in the *succah*.

Meiri adds that taking apart the *succah* would constitute בְּזוּי מִצְוָה, a shaming of the mitzvah; and would indicate that he seeks to unburden himself of the yoke of *mitzvos*, as soon as he can.

אֲבָל מוֹרִיד אֶת־הַכֵּלִים — *but he may take down his* [lit. *the*] *utensils*

Rashi (*Shabbos* 154b s.v. שְׁתַּיִם בִּידֵי אָדָם) points out that most people constructed *succos* on their roofs as we see from the phrase אֲבָל מוֹרִיד אֶת־הַכֵּלִים, *but he may take down his utensils.* (Cf.

Rabban Yochanan ben Zakkai and Rabban Gamliel in mishnah 2:5 who said, ''bring *them* up into the *succah*''; see also *Avodah Zarah* 3a).

The most beautiful utensils and couches were brought into the *succah* in fulfillment of תֵּשְׁבוּ כְּעֵין תָּדוּרוּ, *sit* [in the *succah*] *as you dwell* [at home], in order to make it as comfortable as home. One may not take them back into the home until the time stated by the mishnah (*Rashi; Rav*).

מִן־הַמִּנְחָה וּלְמַעְלָה, — *from Minchah time and later,*

I.e., from two and a half hours before the end of the day (*Ritva*). See comm. to *Rosh Hashanah* 4:4 for a full discussion of this time period.

מִפְּנֵי כְּבוֹד יוֹם טוֹב הָאַחֲרוֹן שֶׁל חָג. — *in honor of the last Festival day of Succos.*

One honors the approaching *Yom Tov* by preparing the place where he will eat his meal that night (*Rashi*).

Meiri says that he shows respect for the Festival by not exerting himself to bring in the utensils after dark.

Shulchan Aruch (666) cites these laws (that of not taking apart the *succah* and that of bringing utensils into the house) in the words of the mishnah, but adds that people who live outside *Eretz Yisrael* and consequently eat in the *succah* on the eighth day, do not bring in their utensils until they finish eating on the eighth day (cf. *Rama* in *Orach Chaim* 667).

9.

נִסּוּךְ הַמַּיִם כֵּיצַד? — *How is the water libation done?.*

[This special libation was performed

only during the seven days of Succos. All other libations in the Temple were of wine poured on the altar, but during

מִן־הַשִּׁלּוֹחַ. הִגִּיעוּ לְשַׁעַר הַמַּיִם תָּקְעוּ וְהֵרִיעוּ
וְתָקְעוּ. עָלָה בַכֶּבֶשׁ וּפָנָה לִשְׂמֹאלוֹ.
שְׁנֵי סְפָלִים שֶׁל כֶּסֶף הָיוּ שָׁם. רַבִּי יְהוּדָה
אוֹמֵר: שֶׁל סִיד הָיוּ, אֶלָּא שֶׁהָיוּ מֻשְׁחָרִין
פְּנֵיהֶם מִפְּנֵי הַיָּיִן.
וּמְנֻקָּבִין כְּמִין שְׁנֵי חֳטָמִין דַּקִּין, אֶחָד מְעֻבֶּה

יד אברהם

the seven days of Succos water was poured simultaneously with the wine libation appended to the daily burnt offering. This water pouring was only performed in the morning after the offering of the daily morning meal offering (*Yoma* 26b). (See comm. end of this mishnah s.v. וְרִגְּמוּהוּ כָּל־הָעָם בְּאֶתְרוֹגֵיהֶן].)

This water libation was commanded to Moses orally on Sinai [הֲלָכָה לְמֹשֶׁה מִסִּינַי] (*Gemara* 44a), and has the force of Scriptural law. It is, however, alluded to in the Torah for, as R' Yehudah ben Besaira noted, the Torah inserted an otherwise superfluous word מַיִם, *water*, into the section (*Numb.* 29) describing the *mussaf* sacrifices of Succos. Verse 19 uses the word וְנִסְכֵּיהֶם rather than וְנִסְכָּה which is written for all the other days except the second. Thus, there is an extra ם. For the sixth day the Torah uses וּנְסָכֶיהָ in verse 31, providing an extra י (over וְנִסְכָּה). And in verse 33, the Torah uses the word כְּמִשְׁפָּטָם rather than the word כַּמִּשְׁפָּט which appears on all the other days. Thus, again, an extra ם. The three extra letters spell מַיִם, *water*, in allusion to the Succos water-libation (*Taanis* 2b).

צְלוֹחִית שֶׁל זָהָב מַחֲזֶקֶת שְׁלֹשֶׁת לֻגִים הָיָה מְמַלֵּא — *He filled a golden flagon holding three lugim,*

Three *lugim* [singular, לֹג, *log*] is the measure of the smallest possible libation, the amount of wine that accompanies a sheep brought as a sacrifice (*Rashi* 48a; *Rav*). [Numbers 15:8 describes this libation as רְבִיעִית הַהִין, *a quarter of a hin*. A hin is twelve *lugim*, thus three *lugim* mentioned in our

mishnah are one quarter of a *hin* — the smallest libation mentioned in Scripture. Depending on the various opinions regarding the size of a *log*, it is approximately 36-67 fluid ounces.

מִן־הַשִּׁלּוֹחַ — *from the Shiloach.*

This is a fresh water spring near the Temple Mount (*Rashi*; *Rav*).

הִגִּיעוּ לְשַׁעַר הַמַּיִם — *When they reached the Water Gate*

[The *Kohanim*, the Levites and the accompanying populace arrived at the Water Gate with the flagon of water.]

The Water Gate was one the southern gates of the עֲזָרָה, *Temple Courtyard* (*Tos.* to 48a s.v. לְשַׁעַר הַמַּיִם; see *Midos* 2:6). It was given this name because the flagon for the water libation was brought into the Courtyard through it (*Rashi*; *Rav*; *Tos.* s.v. שער המים).

תָּקְעוּ וְהֵרִיעוּ וְתָקְעוּ — *they sounded a tekiah, a teruah and a tekiah.*

They did this in order to arouse happiness and joy as it is written (*Isaiah* 12:3) וּשְׁאַבְתֶּם־מַיִם בְּשָׂשׂוֹן, *and you shall draw water in joy* (*Rashi* based on *Gemara* 48b; *Rav*).

עָלָה — *He went up*

The *Kohen* chosen to carry the flagon of water went up the ramp (*Tif. Yis.*).

בַכֶּבֶשׁ — *the ramp*

The altar in the Temple Courtyard had a long ramp situated on its southern side (*Rashi*; *Rav*).

וּפָנָה לִשְׂמֹאלוֹ. — *and turned to his left.*

He turned left toward the southwestern corner of the altar where all

Shiloach. When they reached the Water Gate they sounded a *tekiah*, a *teruah*, and a *tekiah*. He went up the ramp and turned to his left.

There were two silver bowls there. R' Yehudah says: They were of plaster, but their surfaces were darkened from wine.

Each had a hole like a thin nostril, one wider and

YAD AVRAHAM

נְסָכִים, libations, were poured (Rashi; Rav).

Zevachim 6:3 states that all who ascend the altar must turn toward their right (i.e. eastward) and continue walking around the entire altar until they descend on the left (western) side [of the ramp]. There are, however, three exceptions one of which is נְסּוּךְ הַמַּיִם, the water libation.[1]

The Talmud (Zevachim 64a) explains why libations were exceptions. Had the Kohen walked to his right he would have walked more than a hundred cubits around the altar until he reached the place of the libation, the wine or water might become invalidated by the smoke of the fires burning on the altar. This invalidation is derived from the verse (Num. 28:31) תְּמִימִם יִהְיוּ לָכֶם וְנִסְכֵּיהֶם, without a blemish shall they be to you and their libations. Thus, even the libations must be without blemish (i.e., smoked).

In the performance of these exceptions, the Kohen would go up directly to his left (i.e., to the southwestern corner of the altar), and, when he finished the service, would step backwards to the ramp and then descend. [He did not walk all around the altar and then descend on the right side of the ramp] (Gem. 48b; Rashi ibid.).

שְׁנֵי סְפָלִים שֶׁל כֶּסֶף הָיוּ שָׁם. — There were two silver bowls there.

[On the southwestern corner] permanently cemented to the altar (Tosafos 48a s.v. שְׁנֵי).

One was for wine and the other for water (Tif. Yis.).

רַבִּי יְהוּדָה אוֹמֵר: שֶׁל סִיד הָיוּ אֶלָּא שֶׁהָיוּ מְשְׁחָרִין פְּנֵיהֶם מִפְּנֵי הַיַּיִן. — R' Yehudah says: They were of plaster, but their surfaces were darkened [lit. blackened] from wine.

On occasion a Kohen would inadvertently pour wine into the bowl reserved for water (Tos. Yom Tov and Tif. Yis. from Gemara 48b; see below s.v. ערה של מים).

Since both bowls came in contact with wine they darkened and took on a silvery appearance (Rashi; Rav).

וּמְנֻקָּבִין כְּמִין שְׁנֵי חֹטָמִין דַּקִּין, — Each had a hole like a thin nostril,

Beneath each bowl was a thin projection from which the liquid flowed through a hole. The Kohen would pour the wine and the water simultaneously into their respective bowls. The liquids would then flow through the projections onto the top of the altar, and then through a hole in the top of the altar, down into a deep cavity beneath the altar called the shissin (Rashi 48b; Rav; Tif. Yis.).

Tosafos (48b s.v. כמו) maintains that the חטמין were thin drain pipes built into the structure of the altar, leading from the bottom of the bowls straight to the shissin.

אֶחָד מְעֻבֶּה — one wider
[I.e., one of the two holes was wider than the other.]

1. The other two exceptions are נְסוּךְ הַיַּיִן, the wine libation, and עוֹלַת הָעוֹף, the burnt offering of a bird. The reason the Kohen turned to the left in the case of the wine libation is the same as the water libation (see comm.).

In the case of the burnt offering of a bird it should preferably be performed on the right side (i.e., the southeastern corner) of the altar. However, if there are already many Kohanim performing their sacrificial rites on the right side, there is a possibility that before it could be offered the bird might be choked by the smoke of the altar fires. In such an instance the Kohen ascended directly to the left, and performed the rites on the southwestern corner.

וְאֶחָד דַּק, כְּדֵי שֶׁיְּהוּ שְׁנֵיהֶם כָּלִין בְּבַת אַחַת.
מַעֲרָבִי שֶׁל מַיִם, מִזְרָחִי שֶׁל יַיִן. עֵרָה שֶׁל מַיִם
לְתוֹךְ שֶׁל יַיִן, וְשֶׁל יַיִן לְתוֹךְ שֶׁל מַיִם, יָצָא.
רַבִּי יְהוּדָה אוֹמֵר: בְּלֹג הָיָה מְנַסֵּךְ כָּל־
שְׁמוֹנָה.

וְלַמְנַסֵּךְ אוֹמְרִים לוֹ: ,,הַגְבַּהּ יָדֶךָ!" שֶׁפַּעַם
אַחַת נִסֵּךְ אֶחָד עַל־גַּבֵּי רַגְלָיו, וּרְגָמוּהוּ כָּל־
הָעָם בְּאֶתְרוֹגֵיהֶן.

[י] **כְּמַעֲשֵׂהוּ** בְחֹל, כָּךְ מַעֲשֵׂהוּ בַשַּׁבָּת,
אֶלָּא שֶׁהָיָה מְמַלֵּא מֵעֶרֶב

יד אברהם

The wine libation was poured into this bowl (Rashi; Rav).

וְאֶחָד דַּק, — and the other narrower,
The water libation was poured into the bowl with the narrower opening (Rashi; Rav).

כְּדֵי שֶׁיְּהוּ שְׁנֵיהֶם כָּלִין בְּבַת אַחַת. — so that both would drain out at the same time.
As mentioned above, both bowls were filled with their respective liquids simultaneously. Since water flows more freely than wine, the hole of the wine bowl was made wider so that the wine would flow out faster and both bowls would be empty at the same time (Rashi; Rav).
Tosafos (48b s.v. אחד) notes that the word מְעֻבָּה means thick, and suggests that the mishnah means that the bowl for the water had a thicker base than the other so that the water took longer to flow through it than the wine flowing through the bowl which had a thinner bottom.

מַעֲרָבִי שֶׁל מַיִם, מִזְרָחִי שֶׁל יַיִן. — The western one was for water; the eastern one was for wine.
[The water libation was poured into the bowl that lay toward the west and the wine libation was poured into the eastern one.]

Both bowls were situated at the southwestern corner of the altar, and stood side by side. Thus, the one that was closer to the western edge of the altar is referred to as the western one and the inner bowl as the eastern one (Rashi; Rav).

עֵרָה שֶׁל מַיִם לְתוֹךְ שֶׁל יַיִן, — If he poured the [flagon] of water into [the bowl] for wine,
If the Kohen erred and poured the water into the wrong bowl (Tif. Yis.).

וְשֶׁל יַיִן לְתוֹךְ שֶׁל מַיִם, — or [the flagon] of wine into [the bowl] for water.
If he mistakenly poured the wine into the wrong bowl (Tif. Yis.).

יָצָא. — he fulfilled the obligation.
[Although this is not the proper manner of fulfilling the mitzvah, as long as both libations were made, the mitzvah is considered fulfilled.]

רַבִּי יְהוּדָה אוֹמֵר: בְּלֹג הָיָה מְנַסֵּךְ כָּל־שְׁמוֹנָה. — R' Yehudah says: He would pour with one log all eight [days].
[I.e., he used a log measure for the water libation. The word log refers to the utensil used.]
R' Yehudah argues with the first tanna on two points: He maintains that the amount of water used in the water liba-

the other narrower, so that both would drain out at the same time. The western one was for water; the eastern one was for wine. If he poured [the flagon] of water into [the bowl] for wine, or [the flagon] of wine into [the bowl] for water, he fulfilled the obligation.

R' Yehudah says: He would pour with one *log* all eight [days].

To the pourer they would say, 'Raise your hand!' For once someone poured it over his feet, and all the people pelted him with their *esrogim*.

10. Just as it is performed on a weekday, so it is performed on the Sabbath, except that he

YAD AVRAHAM

tion was one *log*, while the first tanna holds three *lugim*. In addition, R' Yehudah says the water libation ceremony was performed all eight days — seven of Succos and one of Shemini Atzeres, but the first tanna holds that it was performed only during the seven days of Succos (*Rashi; Rav*).

The halachah does not follow R' Yehudah (*Rav*).

וְלַמְנַסֵּךְ אוֹמְרִים לוֹ: ,,הַגְבַּהּ יָדְךָ!" — *To the pourer they would say, 'Raise your hand!'*

They would ask the *Kohen* who performed the water-libation to keep his hands high as he poured so that all could see that he was pouring it into the bowl. Since the water libation is a הֲלָכָה לְמשֶׁה מִסִּינַי, *oral tradition transmitted to Moses at Sinai*, (as mentioned in *comm.* above s.v. נִסּוּךְ הַמַּיִם), the Sadducees denied its validity and refused to perform it properly (*Rashi; Rav*).

שֶׁפַּעַם אַחַת נִסֵּךְ אֶחָד עַל־גַּבֵּי רַגְלָיו, — *for once someone poured it over his feet,*

The *Kohen* performing the rite that time was a Sadducee and, instead of

pouring the water into the proper bowl, he poured it over his feet (*Rashi; Rav*).

וּרְגָמוּהוּ כָּל־הָעָם בְּאֶתְרוֹגֵיהֶן. — *and all the people pelted* [lit. stoned] *him with their esrogim.*

[Ever since that incident, they asked the *Kohen* to lift his hands so that they could see him pouring the water properly and thus be sure that no Sadducee would invalidate the libation.]

The Talmud (*Yoma* 26b and *Rashi* s.v. באתרוגיהן) notes that the phrase *with their esrogim* is superfluous; what halachic purpose is served by relating what was thrown? The Talmud explains that the mishnah used this phrase to teach that the water libation was performed in the morning when the *lulav* and *esrog* were taken (see comm. above s.v. נִיסוּךְ המים).

As related by *Josephus Flavius* (*Antiquties* 13:13, 5), the Hasmonean king Alexander Janneus was pelted with *esrogim* while engaged in the sacrificial service. (Apparently *Josephus* was not familiar with the exact circumstances of this event). The tragic sequel to this occurence (as related by *Josephus*) was that Alexander's soldiers massacred six thousand of the congregants in the Temple (cf. *Yossipon* ch. 33).

10.

בְּמַעֲשֵׂהוּ בְחֹל, כָּךְ מַעֲשֵׂהוּ בַשַּׁבָּת, — *Just as it is performed on a weekday, so it is performed on the Sabbath,*

[The procedure followed in performing the water libation on weekdays was followed on the Sabbath.]

שַׁבָּת חָבִית שֶׁל זָהָב שֶׁאֵינָה מְקֻדֶּשֶׁת מִן־
הַשִּׁלוֹחַ, וּמַנִּיחָהּ בְּלִשְׁכָּה.
נִשְׁפְּכָה אוֹ נִתְגַּלְּתָה, הָיָה מְמַלֵּא מִן־הַכִּיּוֹר,
שֶׁהַיַּיִן וְהַמַּיִם הַמְגֻלִּין פְּסוּלִים לְגַבֵּי הַמִּזְבֵּחַ.

[א] הֶחָלִיל חֲמִשָּׁה וְשִׁשָּׁה, זֶהוּ הֶחָלִיל
שֶׁל בֵּית הַשּׁוֹאֵבָה, שֶׁאֵינוֹ
דּוֹחֶה לֹא אֶת־הַשַּׁבָּת וְלֹא אֶת־יוֹם טוֹב.

יד אברהם

אֶלָּא שֶׁהָיָה מְמַלֵּא מֵעֶרֶב שַׁבָּת חָבִית שֶׁל זָהָב
שֶׁאֵינָה מְקֻדֶּשֶׁת — except that he would
fill an unconsecrated golden barrel on
the eve of the Sabbath

[Drawing water on the Sabbath from
the Shiloach required carrying it from a
public domain into the Temple area, a
private domain. Such carrying is forbidden on the Sabbath.]

[The barrel had not been sanctified
for the sacrifical service.] *Rashi* (48b)
quotes the *Yoma* 12b which states that
all utensils used by Moses in the holy
service of the מִשְׁכָּן, *Tabernacle*, were
anointed with special oil at the direct
command of God, and thus became holy. After that time new utensils were
consecrated by using them in the holy
service. [Hence the unconsecrated barrel
was one that had never been used before
in the Temple service.]

Why was a consecrated vessel not
used to store the water until the following morning? A כְּלִי שָׁרֵת, *sanctified vessel or utensil*, sanctifies what is put into
it and the contents attain the status of
קְדֻשַׁת הַגּוּף, *sanctified matter*. This is
derived from the verse (*Ex.* 30:29) כָּל־
הַנֹּגֵעַ בָּהֶם יִקְדָּשׁ, *whatever comes in contact with them shall become holy.* Sanctified matter becomes invalid by לִינָה,
being left overnight. Since they drew
the water on Friday for use the next
morning, it would have to remain overnight, but since it would become disqualified had it been consecrated, they
stored the vessel in an unconsecrated
golden barrel so that it could remain

overnight (*Gem.* 50a; *Rav*; *Rashi ibid.*;
see also *Yoma* 3:10 s.v. נפסלין בלינה
שלא יהיו מימין).

מִן הַשִּׁלוֹחַ — *from the Shiloach,*

[They filled the golden barrel with
water from the Shiloach spring. See
comm. to 4:9 s.v. מן השלוח.]

וּמַנִּיחָהּ בְּלִשְׁכָּה. — *and place it in a
chamber.*

[They put it in one of the Temple
chambers where it remained until the
Sabbath morning. Then the *Kohen*
would pour water from the barrel into
the gold flagon that was used on weekdays, and would continue the procedure
exactly as he did it on the weekdays (see
previous mishnah with comm.).]

נִשְׁפְּכָה אוֹ נִתְגַּלְּתָה, הָיָה מְמַלֵּא מִן־הַכִּיּוֹר —
*If they were spilled or uncovered, he
would refill it from the laver,*

The laver, situated in the Temple
Court, was a consecrated vessel that
held water. Through faucets the *Kohanim* released water from it for washing
their hands and feet before performing
any Temple service. (See *Ex.* 30:17-21
with *Rashi*.]

Even though the laver was a consecrated vessel and thus sanctified its
contents, a special device was invented
by a *Kohen Gadol* named Ben-Katin to
keep its water from being disqualified
by remaining overnight (*Yoma* 3:10 see
comm. there). He devised a wheel which
lowered the entire laver into a well.
There the water of the well and the
water of the laver merged and became

would fill an unconsecrated golden barrel on the eve of the Sabbath from the Shiloach, and place it in a chamber.

If they were spilled or uncovered, he would refill it from the laver, for uncovered wine and water are unfit for the altar.

1. The flute [is played] five or six [days], this is the flute of *Beis HaSho'evah*, which overrides neither Sabbath nor Festival.

YAD AVRAHAM

one [so that the water in the laver was considered part of the well rather than separate water stored in the laver]. Since the laver water was not disqualified, it could be used for the libation (*Rashi* 48b; *Rav*).

שֶׁהַיַּיִן וְהַמַּיִם הַמְגֻלִּין פְּסוּלִים לְגַבֵּי הַמִּזְבֵּחַ. — *for uncovered wine and water are unfit for the altar.*

But the laver was a *covered* vessel, and its water was therefore fit for the altar. Wine and water left uncovered for the amount of time it would take a snake to emerge from a nearby hole and drink, may not be drunk for fear that a snake may have drunk from them and left some of its venom behind (*Terumos* 8:4 and *Rav* ibid; see also *Chullin* 10a). They are then surely unfit for Temple

service (as explained below).

The *Gemara* 50a concludes that even if one strains out the venom[1] the water would still be unfit for use on the altar because of the verse in הַקְרִיבֵהוּ נָא לְפֶחָתֶךָ הֲיִרְצְךָ אוֹ הֲיִשָּׂא פָנֶיךָ אָמַר ה׳ צְבָאוֹת, *Present it to your governor, will he be pleased with you? Or will he favor you? said HASHEM of Hosts* (*Malachi* 1:8). In other words, "Would you offer to God that which is rejected by man?" The bringing of blemished animals is condemned by the prophet as unsuitable for God, for they would be rejected by mortal rulers. This applies to any offering that humans would reject, including a liquid into which a snake may have injected its venom, even if strained.

Chapter 5

1.

הֶחָלִיל חֲמִשָּׁה וְשִׁשָּׁה, — *The flute [is played] five or six [days].*

[The mishnah opens with a quotation from mishnah 4:1 and then explains it: The flute which was played in the Temple during the nights of Succos as musical accompaniment before the drawing of water for the libation (see above 4:9) was sometimes played for five days and sometimes for six.]

זֶהוּ הֶחָלִיל שֶׁל בֵּית הַשּׁוֹאֵבָה, — *this is the*

flute of Beis HaSho'evah [lit. *the Place of Water Drawing*],

Many other instruments besides the flute were played during the festivities (see mishnah 4). However, since the flute was the main instrument and its sound was heard above that of the other instruments, it was singled out to represent all the music played there (*Rav; Rambam, Comm.*).

This was the name given to the place

1. A snake's venom is sponge-like and floats on the surface of the water rather than mixing with it (*Gemara* 50a).

אָמְרוּ: ,,כָּל־מִי שֶׁלֹּא רָאָה שִׂמְחַת בֵּית
הַשּׁוֹאֵבָה, לֹא רָאָה שִׂמְחָה מִיָּמָיו."

יד אברהם

in the Woman's Court where special arrangements were made (see mishnah 2) for the joyous festivities of drawing the water *(Tif. Yis.)*.

[Since the water drawing ceremonies took place every morning of Succos, one could expect that the accompanying rejoicing would also be held every night of Succos. To dispel this notion the mishnah states that the playing of the flute (as well as the other festivities described in *mishnayos* 2-3), could override neither the Sabbath nor the Yom Tov. Accordingly, the water drawing on the first day of Succos was done without the accompanying 'rejoicing'. Thus the maximum amount of days allowed for 'the flute' was six.]

שֶׁאֵינוֹ דּוֹחֶה לֹא אֶת־הַשַּׁבָּת וְלֹא אֶת־יוֹם טוֹב.
— *which overrides neither Sabbath nor Festival.*

If the first day of Succos fell on the Sabbath, the flute would be played for all the remaining six days of festivities. If the first day of Succos fell on a weekday, one of the intermediate days would be a Sabbath and the flute would only be played for five days *(Rashi 50a; Rav)*.

The *Gemara* (50b) cites a dispute between R' Yose ben Yehudah and the Sages on whether instrumental music accompanying the Temple sacrifices overrides the Sabbath. R' Yose maintains that the essential feature of the Temple music which accompanied the wine libation of the two daily sacrifices was instrumental music, and therefore the instrumental music, like the sacrifice itself, overrides the Sabbath. But the other Sages (חֲכָמִים) regard only the vocal music as the essential feature of the Temple music accompanying the daily sacrifices (even though instrumental music, too, was played); therefore, instrumental music does not override the Sabbath. Nevertheless all agree that such music at the *Beis HaSho'evah* celebration does not override the Sabbath, as it was not essential to the celebration but served only to

enhance the rejoicing. *Rashi* (50b s.v. דברי הכל) adds that this particular 'rejoicing' is not obligated by Torah Law.

Tosafos (50a s.v. שֶׁאֵינוּ) asks: The prohibition against playing a flute on the Sabbath is Rabbinic, a precaution against the possible Scriptural transgression of repair of an instrument (see *Beitzah* 5:2 with comm.). Since Rabbinic prohibitions were not enforced in the Temple (אֵין שְׁבוּת בַּמִּקְדָשׁ) because the Kohanim, are scrupulous (*Beitzah* 11b; *Pesachim* 65a), why was the flute playing of the *Beis HaSho'evah* ceremony prohibited on the Sabbath? *Tosafos* answers (based on the *Gemara* quoted earlier) that the flute playing was merely *a means* of enhancing the joyousness of the festivities, but it was not an integral part of the service. *Tiferes Yisrael* elaborates: only when an action is necessary for the Temple service can it override a Rabbinic injunction. In this instance, the instrumental music was not part of the service, nor was it essential for the fulfillment of any service; it was only a means of enhancing the festivities.

אָמְרוּ: — *They said,*

[This word is deleted in the mishnah version printed in the *Gemara* (51a); there, this segment of the mishnah begins with the words כָּל־מִי, *Whoever*. 'They said,' implies that the tanna is quoting a statement by eyewitnesses, while deletion of the term may mean that the statement is the tanna's own understanding of the matter. Alternatively, this may be the verbatim statement of an early tanna who was himself an eyewitness.]

,,כָּל־מִי שֶׁלֹּא רָאָה שִׂמְחַת בֵּית הַשּׁוֹאֵבָה, לֹא
רָאָה שִׂמְחָה מִיָּמָיו." — *'Whoever did not see the rejoicing of the Beis HaSho'evah never saw rejoicing in his lifetime.'*

Rav comments that because the rejoicing which took place in the Temple on the nights of Succos was owing to the ceremony of drawing water, therefore this is noted in the title given this event: The Rejoicing of the Place of Drawing.

Some texts read בֵּית הַשְּׁאוּבָה which means

5
1

They said, 'Whoever did not see the rejoicing of
Beis HaSho'evah, never saw rejoicing in his lifetime.'

YAD AVRAHAM

''Place of Drawn Water (see *Shinuyei Nuschaos*).

Rambam (comm.) comments tersely that בֵּית הַשּׁוֹאֵבָה [lit. *the place of water drawing*] was the name of the place which was prepared for the rejoicing, apparently because the water drawing ceremony took place there (see mishnah 4). Thus שִׂמְחַת בֵּית הַשּׁוֹאֵבָה is rendered *the Rejoicing* [which was carried out] *in the Place of Water Drawing.* This is consistent with the view ascribed to *Rambam* (see comm. above 4:1 הֶחָלִיל) that the rejoicing which took place in the Temple was in honor of Succos, and was not integrally connected to the water drawing ceremonies, therefore, this particular rejoicing was identified according to the area where it took place. *R' Y.F. Perla (Sefer HaMitzvos, R' Saadiah Gaon v. 3)* points out that for this reason it is called שִׂמְחַת בֵּית הַשּׁוֹאֵבָה, *the Rejoicing of the 'Place of Water Drawing,'* rather than merely שִׂמְחַת

הַשּׁוֹאֵבָה, *the Rejoicing of the Water Drawing.*

Rashi (50a) points out that these extraordinarily joyous festivities fulfilled the verse in *Isaiah* (12:3): וּשְׁאַבְתֶּם־מַיִם בְּשָׂשׂוֹן — *And you shall draw water joyously.*

Yerushalmi cites R' Yehoshua ben Levi: Why was it called *Beis HaSho'evah?* Because, thanks to the intense joy of the occasion, they drew upon themselves רוּחַ הַקּוֹדֶשׁ, *the Spirit of Holiness,*[1] for the Divine Spirit rests only on one whose heart is full of joy. *Yerushalmi* cites another verse *(II Kings 3:15)* וְהָיָה כְּנַגֵּן הַמְנַגֵּן וַתְּהִי עָלָיו יַד ה', *And it was when the minstrel played that the hand of God was upon him.* [When the minstrel played his instrument for the prophet Elisha — thus bringing him into a state of joyousness — the Spirit of God rested upon him.]

---

1. King Solomon comments in *Koheles* 2:2, וּלְשִׂמְחָה מַה־זֹּה עֹשָׂה, *and of joy, what does it accomplish!* Further (8:15) he says, וְשִׁבַּחְתִּי אֲנִי אֶת־הַשִּׂמְחָה, *I praised joy.* The Talmud (*Shabbos* 30b) notes the apparent contradiction and explains that the latter verse refers to שִׂמְחָה שֶׁל מִצְוָה, *mitzvah-related joy,* while the former verse refers to שִׂמְחָה שֶׁאֵינָהּ שֶׁל מִצְוָה, *joy that is not mitzvah-related.* [Pure joy comes from total involvement in a *mitzvah,* in body and mind.]

Rambam writes *(Lulav* 8:15): The joy that a person feels when performing a *mitzvah* and when loving God as He commanded, is a great service. Whoever evades this joy deserves to be punished as it is written: *Because you have not served H ASHEM your God with joy and good heart* (Deut. 28:47).

Sfas Emes (on Torah, v. 5 p. 190 s.v. זמן) asks: Why did God give us the festival [season of joy] of Succos and Shemini Atzeres after Yom Kippur? He answers by explaining the verse *(Psalms* 97:11): וּלְיִשְׁרֵי־לֵב שִׂמְחָה, *and joy to the upright in heart:* only those whose hearts are upright in their beliefs and deeds (not distorted by misbelief and sin) are worthy and capable of true joy. In *Kiddush* and *Shemoneh Esrei* we describe these festivals as זְמַן שִׂמְחָתֵנוּ, *the season of our joy.* In order for the Jewish People to be worthy and capable of celebrating the festival with appropriate joy, God first provided us with the ten days time of penitence from Rosh Hashanah to Yom Kippur to make Jews upright of heart and worthy of celebrating the festival season of joy.

[When the Temple stood, the Jewish People were on so high a spiritual level after Yom Kippur that their joy was boundless. They even attained unusual levels of Divine Inspiration during the water drawing on Succos. *Mitzvos* were then performed out of אַהֲבַת ה', *love of God,* which is the highest level of serving Him. No wonder then that *whoever did not see the rejoicing of the Beis HaSho'evah never saw rejoicing in his life.!*]

Talmud *Yerushalmi* (*Succah* 5:1) relates that the prophet Yonah ben Amittai attended the *Beis HaSho'evah* celebration and it was there that the Holy Spirit descended upon him with the prophetic message to admonish the Assyrians to repent.

[ב] בְּמוֹצָאֵי יוֹם טוֹב הָרִאשׁוֹן שֶׁל חַג יָרְדוּ לְעֶזְרַת נָשִׁים, וּמְתַקְּנִין שָׁם תִּקּוּן גָּדוֹל.

וּמְנוֹרוֹת שֶׁל זָהָב הָיוּ שָׁם, וְאַרְבָּעָה סְפָלִים שֶׁל זָהָב בְּרָאשֵׁיהֶן, וְאַרְבָּעָה סֻלָּמוֹת לְכָל אֶחָד

יד אברהם

2.

בְּמוֹצָאֵי יוֹם טוֹב הָרִאשׁוֹן שֶׁל חַג — *At the conclusion of the first festival day of Succos*

[I.e., on the night preceding the first of the חֹל הַמּוֹעֵד, *Intermediate Days.*] The same procedure was followed each of the subsequent evenings (except the Sabbath) after the offering of the daily afternoon sacrifice (*Rambam, Lulav* 8:12).

יָרְדוּ לְעֶזְרַת נָשִׁים, — *they descended to the Women's Court,*

The *Kohanim* and Levites would descend from the Temple Courtyard to the Women's Court which was situated lower down on the slope of the Temple Mount (*Rashi* 51a).

Adjoining the Courtyard (עֲזָרָה) surrounding the Temple, was the עֶזְרַת נָשִׁים, *Women's Court.* This court, occupying an area of 135x135 cubits, was situated on the east side of the Temple Courtyard. Its width (135 cubits) corresponded to the width of the Temple Courtyard (see *Middos* 2:5 and 5:1) and the wall surrounding the Temple Courtyard separated it from the Women's Court (see *Middos* 1:4). Since the Temple stood on a mountain, the Temple Courtyard was higher than the Women's Court. One had to ascend fifteen steps to go from one to the other (*Middos* 2:5).

[It was called 'the Women's Court' probably because women would not, as a rule, enter the Temple Courtyard (see *Kiddushin* 52b; וְכִי אִשָּׁה בָּעֲזָרָה מִנַּיִן). The furthest they would advance on the Temple Mount would be this court.]

וּמְתַקְּנִין שָׁם תִּקּוּן גָּדוֹל. — *where they made*

a great improvement.

The *Gemara* 51b asks, ''What was this great improvement?'' and answers that originally the Women's Court had an unbroken expanse of wall going straight up, but later a balcony was built along it for the women to sit on while the men remained below, so that the men and women were separated from one another, thereby preventing frivolity. *Rambam (Comm.)* comments that the balcony was built to keep the men from looking at the women.

Rashi (ibid.) explains that projecting brackets were built into the walls all around the Court. Each year they would arrange planks of wood on the brackets [with a railing (*Tif. Yis.*)] to create a balcony from which the women could view the festivities. It was this great improvement that the mishnah implies was made every year.

The *Gemara (ibid.)* relates that originally the women were situated within the Women's Court and the men outside it [on the rest of the area encompassed by the wall surrounding the Temple Mount]. But as this caused levity, it was instituted that the women be outside the Women's Court and the men inside it. As this, however, still caused levity, it was instituted that the women should sit above in the gallery and the men below.

[The *mechitzah* or dividing wall separating the men and the women in synagogues is based on the separation of men and women in the Temple. The galleries of the large synagogues derive from the *great improvement* enacted in the Temple.]

The *Gemara (ibid.)* further asks how they were allowed to alter the structure of the Temple when Scripture (*I Chron.* 28:19) in-

2. At the conclusion of the first festival day of Succos they descended to the Women's Court, where they made a great improvement.

There were golden candelabra there with four golden bowls atop them, four ladders for each

YAD AVRAHAM

dicates that every detail of the construction of the Temple was Divinely ordained. The *Gemara* answers that they derived their authority from *Zechariah* (12:12-14) who in describing a period of mourning[1] in the future world says:

And the land shall mourn, every family separately; the family of the House of David separately and their women separately ... all the families separately and their women separately. The *Gemara* reasons, If in the future, [לְעָתִיד לָבֹא] when they will be engaged in mourning, and the Evil Inclination will have no power over them, men will mourn separately and women separately — how much more so in our days when they are engaged in rejoicing and the Evil Inclination has a hold over them.

Rambam (Lulav 8:12) says that the great improvement was actually made *before* Succos. According to this the mishnah's statement that, 'they made a great improvement' should not be treated as a continuation of the phrase, 'they descended to the Women's Court', but rather as a parenthetical clause. It is as if it said, 'At the conclusion of the first festival day of Succos they descended to the Women's Court where they had made a great improvement.' *Aroch LaNer* (51b) *Shoshanim L'David*, and *Mishneh Lechem* explain that the erection of a balcony in the Women's Court on the Intermediate Days would be a desecration of the festival.

וּמְנוֹרוֹת שֶׁל זָהָב הָיוּ שָׁם, — *There were golden candelabra there*

[In the Women's Court stood candelabra that were used only for the Water Drawing festivities.]

[See footnote to s.v. אַרְבָּעָה סֻלָּמוֹת, *below.*]

The mishnah does not tell us how many candelabra there were. *Aruch LaNer* derives from *Yerushalmi* that there were two. *Korban HaEidah* and *Pnei Moshe* state that *Yerushalmi* means merely that there were *at least* two candelabra. [The term מְנוֹרוֹת, candelabra, is plural, implying at least two].

Maharil (Hilchos Succos), states that there were four candelabra, but gives no source for his statement.

וְאַרְבָּעָה סְפָלִים שֶׁל זָהָב בְּרָאשֵׁיהֶן, — *with four golden bowls atop them,*

Each candelabrum had four golden bowls on top of it *(Rav; Rashi* 51a). Into these bowls were placed very thick wicks *(Tif. Yis.).*

וְאַרְבָּעָה סֻלָּמוֹת לְכָל אֶחָד וְאֶחָד, — *four ladders for each* [candelabrum],

The text of the mishnah in *Yerushalmi* reads וְאַרְבָּעָה סֻלָּמוֹת עַל־כָּל־מְנוֹרָה וּמְנוֹרָה, *and four ladders on each candelabrum*. This is also *Rambam's* (see comm. ed. Kafih) and *Meiri's* version. See *Shinuyei Nuschaos. Tiferes Yisrael* says there was one ladder for each bowl.

The *Gemara* (52b) states that each candelabrum was fifty cubits high, which is why the ladders were needed.

Yerushalmi (5:2) states that the candelabra

---

1. R' Dosa and the Sages offer different reasons for the future mourning mentioned in the verse. One explains the cause of the mourning will be the slaying of מָשִׁיחַ בֶּן־יוֹסֵף, *the Messiah of the House of Joseph*, the herald of the Messianic Age who will precede מָשִׁיחַ בֶּן־דָּוִד, *the Messiah of the House of David.*

   The other explains that the cause of the mourning will be the slaying of the יֵצֶר הָרַע, *Evil Inclination*. The righteous will perceive the inclination as a mighty mountain and they will weep, amazed that they were able to overcome 'such a towering hill!' The wicked will perceive the inclination as an insignificant obstacle, and they, too, will weep, perplexed that they were unable to 'overcome this insignificant thread!'

וְאֶחָד, וְאַרְבָּעָה יְלָדִים מִפִּרְחֵי כְהֻנָּה וּבִידֵיהֶם
כַּדִּים שֶׁל שֶׁמֶן שֶׁל מֵאָה וְעֶשְׂרִים לֹג, שֶׁהֵן
מַטִּילִין לְכָל סֵפֶל וָסֵפֶל.

[ג] **מִבְּלָאֵי** מִכְנְסֵי כֹהֲנִים וּמֵהֶמְיָנֵיהֶן מֵהֶן
הָיוּ מַפְקִיעִין וּבָהֶן הָיוּ
מַדְלִיקִין.

יד אברהם

were a hundred cubits high, and goes on to note that a structure that high must have a base of 33.33 cubits (one third its height) extending on all sides in order for it to stand securely. This implies that each candelabrum had a 67-cubit base. It is evident from *Yerushalmi* that the candelabra stood in the Temple Courtyard rather than the Women's Court. Since the entire Courtyard was 187 cubits by 135 cubits, of which the הֵיכָל, *Sanctuary*, occupied a hundred cubits and the area behind the Sanctuary another eleven cubits, only seventy-six cubits remained in which to place the four candelabra. Where could they be placed? And where did all the people stand?

Yerushalmi answers, 'It was a miracle.' Either the candelabra did not take up any space; or they stood securely on narrower bases (*Korban HaEidah; P'nei Moshe, ibid.* demonstrate that the candelabra could not have fit into the width of the עֲזָרָה)

Tiferes Yisrael suggests that the candelabra were not in actuality fifty cubits high for they would require an astronomical amount of gold. He therefore suggests that the candelabra were placed on a high platform or on the edge of the specially constructed balcony, and that is why the ladders were necessary as a means of reaching the barrels on top of the candelabra.

וְאַרְבָּעָה יְלָדִים מִפִּרְחֵי כְהֻנָּה — *and four youths from [among] the young [lit. blossoms] priests*

Rashi (51a) defines the word יְלָדִים, *youths*. Each youth was assigned a lad-

der which he climbed to light a wick in one bowl. Consequently, four youths were assigned for each candelabrum.

In *Tamid* (1:1) the phrase פִּרְחֵי כְהֻנָּה is defined by the commentators as young *Kohanim* whose beards had just begun to sprout (פרח, *to bloom*). See also *Aruch* s.v. פרח; *R' Chananel* cited by *Tosafos, Berachos* 47b, s.v. קטן; *Rashi loc. cit.*

Tiferes Yisrael points out that the words פִּרְחֵי כְהֻנָּה, *young priests*, adds two dimensions to the term יְלָדִים, *youths*.

The word פִּרְחֵי has the connotations *flower* (פֶּרַח) and *to fly* (פּוֹרֵחַ). This teaches that they chose young priests who were comely and handsome like beautiful *flowers*, and light and swift in their actions like a bird that *flies*. All this was to enhance the joy of the occasion.

וּבִידֵיהֶם כַּדִּים שֶׁל שֶׁמֶן שֶׁל מֵאָה וְעֶשְׂרִים לֹג, — *holding* [lit. *in their hands*] *pitchers of oil containing one hundred and twenty log,*[1]

Each held a pitcher that contained thirty *lugim* (*Gem.* 52b).

In praising their physical prowess, the *Gemara (ibid.)* states that they were superior in strength to the son of Marta daughter of Baitus.[1] He was a *Kohen* who was capable of carrying two sides of a huge ox, and walking with them in a slow, dignified manner [up the ramp of the altar] to deposit them on the altar. In fact, the other *Kohanim* did not permit him to do so because of the verse (*Prov.* 14:28) בְּרָב עָם הַדְרַת מֶלֶךְ, *in the mul-*

---

1. *Tosefos Yom Tov* suggests that the mishnah does not simply state thirty *log* per Kohen, but gave the total of 120 *log*. The total was meant to allude to Moses who lived that many years, thus suggesting that the light of the Torah he transmitted shines upon the Jewish People as did the light of the candelabra.

Aruch LaNer notes another allusion here. The number 120 alludes to the concept of repentance, which was the number of years God granted the דוֹר הַמַּבּוּל, *Generation of the Flood*, to repent while the ark was being built. Repentance is in fact mentioned during the festivities

[candelabrum], and four youths from [among] the young priests holding pitchers of oil containing one hundred and twenty *log*, which they poured into each bowl.

3. From the worn-out trousers of the *Kohanim* and their belts they made wicks and they would kindle them.

YAD AVRAHAM

titude of people is the king's glory. Therefore, fifteen priests were assigned to carry the limbs of one ox up to the altar (*Yoma* 2:7).

In what way were these young *Kohanim* superior to the son of Marta who could bear a much greater weight than any of them? The *Gemara* answers that Marta's son walked up the altar ramp, which was on an incline; the total length of the ramp was thirty-two cubits going up the nine-cubit height to the roof of the altar. The young priests, however, ascended ladders that stood almost perpendicular to the ground so that their climb required greater physical strength.

שֶׁהֵן מַטִּילִין לְכָל סֵפֶל וָסֵפֶל. — *which they poured into each bowl.*

3.

מִבְּלָאֵי מִכְנְסֵי כֹהֲנִים וּמֵהֶמְיָנֵיהֶן — *From the worn-out trousers of the Kohanim and their belts*

Both these garments were purchased from communal funds and were worn by the *Kohanim* when they performed the Temple service (*Rashi* 51a; see *Yoma* 7:5).

מֵהֶן הָיוּ מַפְקִיעִין וּבָהֶן הָיוּ מַדְלִיקִין. — *(from them) they made wicks and they would kindle them.*

[The wicks were placed in the bowls atop the candelabra.]

Rashi (51a) and *Rav* define the word מַפְקִיעִין as *tearing* — they would tear up these garments in order to make wicks.

A footnote in some editions of Mishnah suggests that the word מַפְקִיעִין stems from the word פְּקַעַת, *a coil*, thus מַפְקִיעִין would mean *to coil* or *twist into a wick* (see also *Shabbos* 3:2). This interpretation is also indicated in *Yoma* (23a: מאי פקיע פליתא). Cf. *Aruch* s.v. פקע (4).

Tosafos (51a s.v. מבלאי) asks why the worn-out כְּתָנוֹת, *tunics*, which were also made of linen and worn by the *Kohanim* were not used.

Likewise *Tosefos Yom Tov* asks why the worn-out מִצְנֶפֶת, *turbans*, worn by the *Kohanim* were not used.

Tiferes Yisrael suggests that trousers and belts are more likely to wear out than tunics or turbans. Although all the garments would be made into wicks when they wore out, the mishnah names the commonest. He also suggests a second approach: the Talmud *(Shabbos* 21a) states that the worn-out clothing of the *Kohanim* was made into wicks for the menorah in the Sanctuary. This clothing does not include trousers which are not regarded as respectable for use in the Sanctuary itself. The belts could not be used because the significant amount of wool they contained made them unsuitable for use in

(see below 5:4,. s.v. וְאוֹמְרִים לְפָנֶיהָ) to indicate that they should repent fully before the one hundred and twenty *lugim* of oil were used up.

To the saintly men and the men of good deeds who were present, the one hundred and twenty *lugim* of oil represented Moses' lifespan (as explained above). For the penitents who were present (see comm. to mishnah 4) the oil represented the time allotted for repentance.

That the candelabra were fifty cubits high alludes to the חֲמִשִּׁים שַׁעֲרֵי בִינָה, *fifty gates of understanding*, which are illuminated by the light of the Torah.

וְלֹא הָיָה חָצֵר בִּירוּשָׁלַיִם שֶׁאֵינָהּ מְאִירָה מֵאוֹר בֵּית הַשּׁוֹאֵבָה.

[ד] **חֲסִידִים** וְאַנְשֵׁי מַעֲשֶׂה הָיוּ מְרַקְּדִים לִפְנֵיהֶם בַּאֲבוּקוֹת שֶׁל אוֹר שֶׁבִּידֵיהֶן וְאוֹמְרִים לִפְנֵיהֶן דִּבְרֵי שִׁירוֹת וְתִשְׁבָּחוֹת; וְהַלְוִיִּם בְּכִנּוֹרוֹת וּבִנְבָלִים וּבִמְצִלְתַּיִם וּבַחֲצוֹצְרוֹת וּבִכְלֵי שִׁיר בְּלֹא מִסְפָּר, עַל-חֲמֵשׁ עֶשְׂרֵה מַעֲלוֹת הַיּוֹרְדוֹת

יד אברהם

the menorah where an even flame was required (see *Shabbos* 21a), but they were ideal for the thick wicks needed for the candelabra of the *Beis HaSho'evah* (cf. *Aruch LaNer; Lechem Shamayim; Shoshanim L'David;* see *Rambam, Klei HaMikdash* 8:6 and *Kessef Mishneh*).

וְלֹא הָיָה חָצֵר בִּירוּשָׁלַיִם שֶׁאֵינָהּ מְאִירָה מֵאוֹר בֵּית הַשּׁוֹאֵבָה. — *There was not a courtyard in Jerusalem that was not illuminated by the light of the Beis HaSho'evah.*

Since the fifty-cubit-high candelabra rose up above the eastern wall of the Temple, and the Temple Mount was higher than the rest of Jerusalem — the light shone out over the whole city (*Rashi* 51a; *Rav*).

The *Gemara* (53a) states that women could sift wheat kernels by the light of the *Beis HaSho'evah*. *Tosafos* (ibid.) comments that the *Gemara* does not mean that women *actually* sifted wheat by this light, because deriving personal benefits from these lights would constitute מְעִילָה, *unlawful use of sacred property*. Rather the *Gemara* means that the illumination was so great that they *could* have selected grain by it.

4.

חֲסִידִים — *Devout men*

חֲסִידוּת, *devoutness*, is explained by a saying of our Sages (*Berachos* 17a): אַשְׁרֵי אָדָם שֶׁעֲמָלוֹ בַּתּוֹרָה וְעוֹשֶׂה נַחַת רוּחַ לְיוֹצְרוֹ, *fortunate is the man whose labor is in the study of Torah and who provides his Creator with a feeling of satisfaction.* One who loves the Creator, blessed be He, with a true love will not be content to fulfill his duties only through those obligations that are binding on all Jews; he will act like a son who truly loves his father. If his father merely suggests a particular desire, the son will do all he can to fulfill his father's wish. Even if the father mentioned the matter only once and then only implicitly, that is enough for the son to understand what his father means and he thus makes it his mission to do even what was not stated explicitly. All because the son concludes that by doing these things immediately and not waiting to be told more explicitly or even a second time he gives his father great pleasure and contentment. To sum up, the principle of חֲסִידוּת, *devoutness*, widens the scope of the fulfillment of the *mitzvos* with all their possible ramifications under all possible conditions. By doing much more than what is expressly commanded, our additional actions will bring great joy and contentment to Him, Blessed be He (*Mesillas Yesharim,* ch. 19).

וְאַנְשֵׁי מַעֲשֶׂה — *and men of [good] deeds* [Those men who occupy themselves

There was not a courtyard in Jerusalem that was not illuminated by the light of the *Beis HaSho'evah.*

4. Devout men and men of [good] deeds would dance before them with the flaming torches [that were] in their hands and would utter before them words of songs and praises; and the Levites with harps, lyres, cymbals, trumpets, and countless musical instruments [stood] on the fifteen steps that

YAD AVRAHAM

in communal matters, such as the collection of charity, raising orphans, helping brides and so on.]

הָיוּ מְרַקְּדִים לִפְנֵיהֶם — *would dance before them* [i.e., the assembled people *(Tos. Yom Tov; Tif Yis.)*]

Rambam (Lulav 8:4) comments that it is a *mitzvah* to rejoice greatly in this celebration. But it was not for the common men, but rather for the outstanding scholars of Israel, the heads of the yeshivos, the Sanhedrin, and the pious men and men of good deeds. They would dance and clap and sing and act joyously in the Temple during the days of Succos. But the general populace, both men and women, would come to watch and listen.

בַּאֲבוּקוֹת שֶׁל אוֹר שֶׁבִּידֵיהֶן — *with flaming torches [that were] in their hands*

They would throw them up in the air and then catch them. Some were expert enough to juggle four torches and some could juggle eight *(Rashi* 51b; *Rav).*

The *Gemara* (53a) relates that R' Shimon ben Gamliel, when rejoicing at the *Beis HaSho'evah,* juggled eight burning torches without any of them touching another.

וְאוֹמְרִים לִפְנֵיהֶן דִּבְרֵי שִׁירוֹת וְתִשְׁבָּחוֹת; — *and would utter before them words of songs and praises;*

[They recited or sang songs of praise.]

The Sages taught that some would praise God by saying, 'Happy is our youth that has not shamed our old age'

— i.e., we did not transgress in our youth and, as such, are not ashamed in our old age. These were the men of piety and of devoutness and of good deeds who were devout all their lives *(Rashi).*

Penitents used to say, 'Happy is our old age which has atoned for our youth.'

All of them would say together, 'Happy is he who did not sin, but if he has sinned let him repent and He will forgive him.'

וְהַלְוִיִּם בְּכִנּוֹרוֹת וּבִנְבָלִים וּבִמְצִלְתַּיִם וּבַחֲצוֹצְרוֹת וּבִכְלֵי שִׁיר בְּלֹא מִסְפָּר, — *and the Levites with harps, lyres, cymbals, trumpets, and countless musical instruments*

There was no set number *(Tif. Yis.; Rashash).*

Aruch LaNer points out that הֶחָלִיל, *the flute,* is conspicuously absent from this list of musical instruments. Perhaps the tanna felt that it did not have to be mentioned, since it has already been mentioned in mishnah 1. There, only the flute was mentioned because it was the main instrument (see comm. there). *Rambam (Lulav* 8:13) mentions the flute together with the instruments mentioned here.

However *Rambam (ibid.)* omits the stipulation set forth here that the Levites play these instruments.

Aruch LaNer suggests that the laws governing instrument playing for the *Beis HaSho'evah* should surely not be more stringent than those of the music accompanying the wine libation. The *Gemara* (51a) states that according to those tannaim holding the view that the essential feature of Temple music was vocal, even Israelites

מֵעֶזְרַת יִשְׂרָאֵל לְעֶזְרַת נָשִׁים — כְּנֶגֶד חֲמִשָּׁה
עָשָׂר שִׁיר הַמַּעֲלוֹת שֶׁבַּתְּהִלִּים. שֶׁעֲלֵיהֶן לְוִיִּם
עוֹמְדִין בִּכְלֵי שִׁיר וְאוֹמְרִים שִׁירָה. וְעָמְדוּ שְׁנֵי
כֹהֲנִים בַּשַּׁעַר הָעֶלְיוֹן שֶׁיּוֹרֵד מֵעֶזְרַת יִשְׂרָאֵל
לְעֶזְרַת נָשִׁים, וּשְׁתֵּי חֲצוֹצְרוֹת בִּידֵיהֶן. קָרָא
הַגֶּבֶר, תָּקְעוּ וְהֵרִיעוּ וְתָקְעוּ.

יד אברהם

could play the instruments. Thus Israelites could surely play instruments for the *Beis HaSho'evah* festivities which were not a part of sacrificial service. Only according to the view that instrument music *was* an essential feature which had to be performed by Levites, can there be a stipulation that the Levites play for the *Beis HaSho'evah*. Therefore, our mishnah which requires Levites for the *Beis HaSho'evah*, must be of the view that only Levites were qualified to play at the wine libation. *Rambam*, who rules that everyone may play at the wine libation (*Klei HaMikdash* 3:3), is justified in deleting this requirement.

עַל־חֲמֵשׁ עֶשְׂרֵה מַעֲלוֹת — [stood] *on the fifteen steps*

[This is where the Levites stood while they played their instruments.]

The steps ran across the width of the Court. Each step was half a cubit deep and half a cubit high (*Rashi* 51b; *Middos* 2:3).

Rashi's words here should not be taken literally. The implication that these steps were straight and ran alongside the whole wall separating the Women's Court from the Temple Courtyard, is dispelled by *Middos* 2:3 which states clearly that these steps were circular. Thus the top step was fifteen cubits shorter than the bottom step. Also when *Rashi* says that these steps were as long as the width of the Women's Court, he cannot mean that, like the Women's Court, they were 135 cubits long, for the following reasons: A) Because of their circular shape these steps would take up a substantial part of the 135x135 area (if each step formed a half circle); B) the mishnah (*Middos* 2:3)

relates that in each corner of the women's court there was a chamber (לִשְׁכָּה) of 40x40 cubits. Since eighty cubits of the court's width were taken up by these two chambers, only fifty-five cubits remained available for steps. The diameter of the circular bottom step measured fifty-five cubits across, while the top step measured forty cubits across.

However *Tosefos Yom Tov* and *Tiferes Yisroel* in their diagrams of the Temple (*Middos*) seem to assume that the top step was only as wide as the eastern gate of the Temple court — ten cubits — with the consequence that the bottom step measured only twenty-five cubits across (cf. *Teshuvos VeChidushei Maharit HeChadashim* p. 283).

Tiferes Yisrael (*Middos* 2:3) surmises that the reason for the circular shape of these steps (a departure from the shape of other steps in the Temple) was so that more Levites could stand on the steps during the *Beis HaSho'evah* festivities.

הַיּוֹרְדוֹת מֵעֶזְרַת יִשְׂרָאֵל לְעֶזְרַת נָשִׁים — *that descend from the Court of the Israelites to the Women's Court—*

כְּנֶגֶד חֲמִשָּׁה עָשָׂר שִׁיר הַמַּעֲלוֹת שֶׁבַּתְּהִלִּים. — *corresponding to the fifteen Songs of Ascent in Psalms.*[1]

[The fifteen steps corresponded to the fifteen Songs of Ascent (*Psalms* 120-134), each of which begins with the words שִׁיר הַמַּעֲלוֹת, *A Song of Ascents*, or *Steps*.

שֶׁעֲלֵיהֶן לְוִיִּם עוֹמְדִין בִּכְלֵי שִׁיר וְאוֹמְרִים שִׁירָה. — *Upon them the Levites would stand with musical instruments and chant [lit. recite] songs.*

1. In explaining why King David composed the fifteen Songs of Ascent, the *Gemara* (53a) relates: David prepared the pits beneath the altar into which the wine and water libations would flow (See comm. to 4:9 s.v. שְׁנֵי חֲטָמִין דַּקִּין). The תְּהוֹם, *deep*, arose and threatened to overflow the world. David inscribed the Divine Name upon a shard and cast it into the deep

descend from the Court of the Israelites to the Women's Court — corresponding to the fifteen Songs of Ascent in *Psalms*. Upon them the Levites would stand with musical instruments and chant songs. Two *Kohanim* stood at the Upper Gate that descends from the Court of the Israelites to the Women's Court, with two trumpets in their hands. When the crier called out, they sounded a *tekiah*, a *teruah*, and a *tekiah*.

YAD AVRAHAM

They performed on the steps only during the *Beis HaSho'evah* festivities. Throughout the rest of the year when they sang and played for the daily sacrifices, they stood on a דּוּכָן, *platform*, near the altar (*Rashi 51b; Rav*).

וְעָמְדוּ שְׁנֵי כֹהֲנִים בְּשַׁעַר הָעֶלְיוֹן — *Two Kohanim stood at the Upper Gate*

This gate was also known as שַׁעַר נִקָּנוֹר, *Gate of Nicanor* (see *Yoma* 38a). It was called the Upper Gate because it stood higher on the Temple Mount than the Women's Court (*Rambam, Klei HaMikdash* 7:6; *Tos. Yom Tov*).

This gate was situated in the wall separating the Temple Courtyard from the Women's Court.

שֶׁיּוֹרֵד מֵעֶזְרַת יִשְׂרָאֵל לְעֶזְרַת נָשִׁים, — *that descends from the Court of the Israelites to the Women's Court,*

[The Temple Courtyard between its eastern wall and the altar was divided into two areas. A) The area immediately adjacent to the eastern wall, measuring eleven cubits from east to west and occupying the entire width of the court from north to south — 135 cubits. This was called עֶזְרַת יִשְׂרָאֵל, *Court of the Israelites*, because the Israelites were permitted to stay there; B) The area adjacent to the Israelites' Court having the altar as its western boundary. This area, too, measured eleven cubits east-west and 135 cubits north-south. This area which Israelites were forbidden to enter, was called עֶזְרַת כֹּהֲנִים, the *Kohanim's Court*.]

Consequently, the two *Kohanim* stood on a spot which overlooked the dancing and rejoicing (*Tif. Yis.*).

וּשְׁתֵּי חֲצוֹצְרוֹת בִּידֵיהֶן. — *with two trumpets in their hands.*

קָרָא הַגֶּבֶר, — *[When] the crier called out,*

This was *Gevini*, the Temple Crier (*Shekalim* 5:1), who called out every morning at daybreak (or according to *Tosafos* at some time prior to it) 'Arise *Kohanim* to perform your service; *Levites* to your platform; and Israelites to your stations' (*Yoma* 20b; see *Yoma* 1:8).

תָּקְעוּ וְהֵרִיעוּ וְתָקָעוּ. — *They sounded a tekiah, a teruah, and a tekiah.*

The two *Kohanim* sounded a *tekiah*, a *teruah*, and a *tekiah* [on their trumpets] as a signal to proceed toward the Shiloach spring to draw the water for the water libation (*Rashi 51b; Rav; Tif. Yis.*). (For definitions of *tekiah* and *teruah* see 4:5, 9 s.v. תָּקְעוּ וְהֵרִיעוּ וְתָקָעוּ).

According to *Rambam* (*T'midin U'Mussafin* 2:11 with *Kessef Mishneh*), this moment is apparently identical with daybreak. However, *Tosafos* (here 51b s.v. קרא; *Yoma* 27b s.v. איכא;

which then receded sixteen thousand cubits. When he saw that it had receded so far he said, 'The nearer it is to the earth's surface the moister the land will be' (and thus produce better crops — *Rashi*). He, thereupon recited the fifteen 'Songs of Ascent' and the deep rose fifteen thousand cubits to remain one thousand cubits beneath the earth's surface.

הִגִּיעוּ לְמַעֲלָה עֲשִׂירִית, תָּקְעוּ וְהֵרִיעוּ
וְתָקְעוּ. הִגִּיעוּ לָעֲזָרָה, תָּקְעוּ וְהֵרִיעוּ וְתָקְעוּ.
הָיוּ תּוֹקְעִין וְהוֹלְכִין עַד שֶׁמַּגִּיעִין לְשַׁעַר
הַיּוֹצֵא מִזְרָח. הִגִּיעוּ לְשַׁעַר הַיּוֹצֵא מִמִּזְרָח,
הָפְכוּ פְּנֵיהֶן לַמַּעֲרָב, וְאָמְרוּ: אֲבוֹתֵינוּ שֶׁהָיוּ
בַּמָּקוֹם הַזֶּה אֲחוֹרֵיהֶם אֶל־הֵיכָל וּפְנֵיהֶם
קֵדְמָה, וְהֵמָּה מִשְׁתַּחֲוִים קֵדְמָה לַשָּׁמֶשׁ. וְאָנוּ
— לְיָהּ עֵינֵינוּ.״

רַבִּי יְהוּדָה אוֹמֵר: הָיוּ שׁוֹנִין וְאוֹמְרִין ,,אָנוּ
לְיָהּ, וּלְיָהּ עֵינֵינוּ.״

יד אברהם

see *Yoma* 1:8) holds that it was before daybreak.

Tosafos, however, agrees that before they returned with the water and consecrated it in a sacred vessel, dawn had already broken. Otherwise the water, once consecrated, would become disqualified with daybreak according to the rule that all consecrated objects (except vessels) become disqualified when held overnight (פְּסוּל לִינָה). Before consecration in the vessel, the water would not yet have attained the degree of consecration (קְדוּשַׁת הַגּוּף) which could become disqualified from being kept overnight.

הִגִּיעוּ לְמַעֲלָה עֲשִׂירִית, — [When] they reached the tenth step,

The *Gemara* (53b) asks: Did they descend five of the fifteen steps and stand on the tenth step from the bottom? Or did they descend ten steps and stand on the fifth from the bottom? The *Gemara* does not resolve the question.

תָּקְעוּ וְהֵרִיעוּ וְתָקְעוּ. — they sounded a tekiah, a teruah, and a tekiah.

[See comm. mishnah 5 s.v. וְשָׁלֹשׁ לַשַּׁעַר הַתַּחְתּוֹן.]

הִגִּיעוּ לָעֲזָרָה, — [When] they reached the Court,

When the two *Kohanim* reached the floor of the עֶזְרַת נָשִׁים, Women's Court (*Rashi* 51b; *Rav*).

The version of the mishnah printed in the

Gemara (51a) has the reading הִגִּיעוּ לַקַּרְקַע, they reached the ground [of the Women's Court]. This reading, preferred by *Vilna Gaon*, substitutes for the phrase הִגִּיעוּ לָעֲזָרָה, they reached the Courtyard, in our versions (see *Hagahos HaGra* loc. cit.). [One can surmise that this reading is preferred because as soon as they stood upon the top step, they were technically already in the Women's Court, rendering the phrase, 'they reached the Court incorrect.

תָּקְעוּ וְהֵרִיעוּ וְתָקְעוּ. הָיוּ תּוֹקְעִין וְהוֹלְכִין — they sounded a tekiah, a teruah, and a tekiah. They would continue sounding tekiah

They would prolong these last three blasts (*Rashi* 51b; *Meiri*).

עַד שֶׁמַּגִּיעִין לְשַׁעַר הַיּוֹצֵא מִזְרָח. — until they reached the gate leading out [to the] east.

That gate led from the Women's Court to the eastern slope of the Temple Mount. This gate faced the Upper Gate mentioned above. Their route of descent was from west to east. When they entered the Temple, they ascended from east to west (*Rashi* 51b).

According to *Rambam*, these two sets of shofar blasts — one sounded when the *Kohanim* stood in the Upper Gate, and the second sounded until they reached the Lower Gate, the gate that leads out to the east — were sounded every festival when these gates were opened in the morning (see mishnah 5;

5
4

[When] they reached the tenth step, they sounded a *tekiah*, a *teruah*, and a *tekiah*. When they reached the Court, they sounded a *tekiah*, a *teruah*, and a *tekiah*. They would continue sounding *tekiah* until they reached the gate leading out [to the] east. When they reached the gate leading out to the east, they turned to the west and said, 'Our forefathers who were in this place [with] their backs toward the Sanctuary and their faces toward the east, and they bowed eastward toward the sun. But as for us — our eyes are toward YAH.'

R' Yehudah says: They repeated and said, 'We are for YAH and toward YAH are our eyes.'

YAD AVRAHAM

Klei HaMikdash 7:6). On Succos they would sound a third set of blasts when those bearing the flask with the water for the libation reached the Water Gate (above 4:9).

הִגִּיעוּ לַשַּׁעַר הַיּוֹצֵא מִמִּזְרָח — [When] they *reached the gate leading out to the east,*

When the entire gathering of people led by the two *Kohanim* reached this gate... (*Tif. Yis.*).

הָפְכוּ פְּנֵיהֶן לַמַּעֲרָב — *they turned* [lit. their faces] *to the west*

I.e., the entire group [which was about to exit] turned toward the Temple Courts and the more sanctifed portions of the Temple (*Rashi* 51b; *Rav*).

וְאָמְרוּ: ,,אֲבוֹתֵינוּ שֶׁהָיוּ בַּמָּקוֹם הַזֶּה — *and said, 'Our forefathers who were in this place*

Some of the Jews at the end of the First Temple era were sun worshipers (see *Ezekiel* 8:16) and would deliberately turn their backs to the Temple in an obscene gesture of derision (see *Yoma* 77a) while bowing down eastward toward the rising sun (*Rashi* 51b).

אֲחֹרֵיהֶם אֶל-הֵיכַל ה' וּפְנֵיהֶם קֵדְמָה, וְהֵמָּה מִשְׁתַּחֲוִים קֵדְמָה לַשָּׁמֶשׁ. — [with] *their backs toward the Sanctuary and their faces toward the east, and they bowed eastward toward the sun.*

This entire clause starting with

אֲחֹרֵיהֶם, *their backs,* and concluding with לַשָּׁמֶשׁ, *toward the sun,* is a verbatim quote from *Ezekiel* 8:16. The only variation is that where the mishnah has הֵיכַל, *Sanctuary,* *Ezekiel* (8:16) states הֵיכַל ה', *HASHEM's Sanctuary* (there is also a variation in the spelling of מִשְׁתַּחֲוִים). Some texts of the mishnah also include the word ה' (see *Shinuyei Nuschaos*).]

וְאָנוּ לְיָה עֵינֵינוּ.'' — *But as for us —our eyes are toward YAH'.*

In the First Temple period the sin of idol worship was prevalent, but in the Second Temple period the temptation to worship powers other than Hashem was removed. [So they could truly state 'our eyes are toward Hashem'] (*Yoma* 9b).

רַבִּי יְהוּדָה אוֹמֵר: הָיוּ שׁוֹנִין וְאוֹמְרִים ,,אָנוּ לְיָה, וּלְיָה עֵינֵינוּ.'' — *R' Yehudah says: They repeated and said, 'We are for YAH and toward YAH are our eyes.'*

The *Gemara* (53b) asks how the name of God may be repeated in this way, for we learned in *Berachos* (5:3, 33b) that if one says שְׁמַע שְׁמַע, *Shema Shema,* while reciting the *Shema,* he must be silenced, since the repetitious expression suggests חִ"ו dualism (two deities).

The answer is that each time the word

[ה] **אֵין** פּוֹחֲתִין מֵעֶשְׂרִים וְאַחַת תְּקִיעוֹת
בַּמִּקְדָּשׁ, וְאֵין מוֹסִיפִין עַל־אַרְבָּעִים
וּשְׁמוֹנֶה.

בְּכָל־יוֹם הָיוּ שָׁם עֶשְׂרִים וְאַחַת תְּקִיעוֹת
בַּמִּקְדָּשׁ: שָׁלֹשׁ לִפְתִיחַת שְׁעָרִים, וְתֵשַׁע
לְתָמִיד שֶׁל שַׁחַר; וְתֵשַׁע לְתָמִיד שֶׁל בֵּין
הָעַרְבַּיִם. וּבַמּוּסָפִין הָיוּ מוֹסִיפִין עוֹד תֵּשַׁע.
וּבְעֶרֶב שַׁבָּת הָיוּ מוֹסִיפִין עוֹד שֵׁשׁ: שָׁלֹשׁ
לְהַבְטִיל הָעָם מִמְּלָאכָה; וְשָׁלֹשׁ לְהַבְדִּיל בֵּין
קֹדֶשׁ לְחֹל.

יד אברהם

לְיָהּ, *for YAH*, is used, it is in a different
context and is not a dualistic repetition.
The meaning of our mishnah is that
they would say, 'They worshiped the
sun but as for us [מִשְׁתַּחֲוִים] אָנוּ לְיָהּ],
we bow to YAH; וְעֵינֵינוּ לְיָהּ
[מְיַחֲלוֹת], *and our eyes look forward to
YAH.'*

R' Yehoshua ben Chananiah said: When
we used to rejoice at the *Beis HaSho'evah*
festivities, our eyes saw no sleep. How was
this? The first hour we were involved with
the תָּמִיד שֶׁל שַׁחַר, *daily morning offering;*
afterwards, we recited תְּפִלָּה, *prayer;*
afterwards we were involved with the קָרְבָּן
מוּסָף, *mussaf offering;* then we went to the
house of study; from there we went to eat
and drink; from there we went to the
תְּפִלַּת מִנְחָה, *afternoon prayer;* from there to
the תָּמִיד שֶׁל בֵּין הָעַרְבַּיִם, *afternoon daily of-*

fering; from there we [again] rejoiced at the
Beis HaSho'evah (Gem. 53a).

[Though the mishnah concludes the
description of the water drawing ceremony
here, the picture is yet far from complete.
The narrative is to be filled in with what is
related above (4:9). Our mishnah means only
to supply the information not given above.]

According to *Rambam's* view (see comm.
to 4:1 s.v. וְהִחֵל), the breakup of the narrative into two parts is logical and apparent.
In 4:9 the mishnah discusses the procedure
essential for the water drawing. Here the
mishnah describes only the (unrelated)
festivities preceding the water drawing. We
have already pointed out (above s.v. עַד
שֶׁמַּגִּיעִין) that according to everyone, the
shofar blasts described here were not integrally connected to the water drawing service, and were sounded on every festival at
the opening of the upper and lower gates.

5.

אֵין פּוֹחֲתִין מֵעֶשְׂרִים וְאַחַת תְּקִיעוֹת בַּמִּקְדָּשׁ,
— *They make no fewer than twenty-one
trumpet blasts in the Temple,*

The term *tekios* here, literally *long,
unbroken blasts,* refers also to *teruos,*
broken sounds, for every sounding of
the trumpet was a set of three blasts — a
tekiah, a *teruah* and another *tekiah.* On
any given day in the Temple, there were
never less than seven sets, a total of
twenty-one trumpet sounds (Gem. 53b
with *Rashi* and *Tos.*).

וְאֵין מוֹסִיפִין עַל־אַרְבָּעִים וּשְׁמוֹנֶה. — *and no
more than forty-eight.*

[Every day a minimum of twenty-one
blasts was sounded in the Temple, and
on specific occasions as many as forty-
eight. The mishnah proceeds to explain.] (See last comm. to our mishnah.)
בְּכָל־יוֹם הָיוּ שָׁם עֶשְׂרִים וְאַחַת תְּקִיעוֹת
בַּמִּקְדָּשׁ: שָׁלֹשׁ לִפְתִיחַת שְׁעָרִים; — *Every
day there were twenty-one trumpet
blasts in the Temple: three for the opening of the gates;*

5. **T**hey make no fewer than twenty-one trumpet blasts in the Temple, and no more than forty-eight.

Every day there were twenty-one trumpet blasts in the Temple: three for the opening of the gates; nine for the daily morning burnt offering; and nine for the daily afternoon burnt offering. With the *mussaf* offerings they added another nine. And on the eve of the Sabbath they added another six: three to stop the people from work; and three to distinguish between the sacred and the secular.

YAD AVRAHAM

When they opened the gates of the Temple Courtyard each morning, they sounded three blasts: *tekiah, teruah,* and *tekiah* (Rashi; Rav).

וְתֵשַׁע לִתְמִיד שֶׁל שַׁחַר; — *nine for the daily morning burnt offering,*

Each morning when they poured the נִסּוּךְ הַיַּיִן, *wine libation,* on the altar as part of the morning burnt offering service, the Levites would chant the שִׁיר שֶׁל יוֹם, *Psalm-song of the day.* This daily psalm was divided into three parts. Before each part, the *Kohanim* sounded a *tekiah-teruah-tekiah* on their trumpets and the people bowed, for a total of nine blasts (*Tamid* 7:3; Rashi 53b; Rav).

וְתֵשַׁע לִתְמִיד שֶׁל בֵּין הָעַרְבַּיִם. — *and nine for the daily afternoon burnt offering.*

[The trumpet-blowing was performed here in precisely the same way as at the daily morning burnt offering. This brought the minimum number of daily trumpet blasts to twenty-one.]

וּבַמּוּסָפִין — *With the mussaf offerings*

[On those days when an additional offering is brought, specifically: the Sabbath, all Festival days including the Intermediate Days, Rosh Chodesh, Rosh Hashanah, and Yom Kippur.]

הָיוּ מוֹסִיפִין עוֹד תֵּשַׁע, — *they added another nine.*

Accompanying all the sacrifices (see mishnah 6) of the additional offering,

they would blow three sets of *tekiah — teruah — tekiah* during the wine libation (*Tif. Yis.*). [Consequently, on a day when there was a *mussaf* offering, the sum total of blasts was thirty: the daily twenty-one plus the additional nine.]

The *Gemara* (55a) concludes that even when there is more than one additional offering (e.g., when a festival falls on the Sabbath — one for the festival and one for the Sabbath) they blew only nine blasts for all of them.

Tosefos Yom Tov uses the above conclusion of the *Gemara* to explain why Rosh Hashanah which falls on the Sabbath is not cited by our mishnah as an example of a day when forty-eight blasts were sounded. For on Rosh Hashanah which falls on the Sabbath three additional offerings are brought: one for Rosh Hashanah, one for the Sabbath, and one for Rosh Chodesh. If they sounded nine blasts separately for each of the three offerings that would be twenty-seven blasts. Adding these to the basic twenty-one gives a total of forty-eight. However, since the *Gemara* concludes that even for all three additional offerings, they still sounded only nine blasts it is clear why the mishnah did not use it as an example of a forty-eight-blast day.

וּבְעֶרֶב שַׁבָּת הָיוּ מוֹסִיפִין עוֹד שֵׁשׁ: שָׁלֹשׁ לְהַבְטִיל הָעָם מִמְּלָאכָה; — *And on the eve of the Sabbath they added another six: three to stop the people from work;*

The Talmud (*Shabbos* 35b) explains that the first *tekiah* signalled the stoppage of all work in the fields, upon

עֶרֶב שַׁבָּת שֶׁבְּתוֹךְ הֶחָג, הָיוּ שָׁם אַרְבָּעִים
וּשְׁמוֹנָה: שָׁלֹש לִפְתִיחַת שְׁעָרִים; שָׁלֹש לַשַּׁעַר
הָעֶלְיוֹן; וְשָׁלֹש לַשַּׁעַר הַתַּחְתּוֹן; וְשָׁלֹש לְמִלּוּי
הַמַּיִם; וְשָׁלֹש עַל־גַּבֵּי מִזְבֵּחַ; תֵּשַׁע לְתָמִיד שֶׁל
שַׁחַר; וְתֵשַׁע לְתָמִיד שֶׁל בֵּין הָעַרְבַּיִם; וְתֵשַׁע

יד אברהם

which, those in the fields would return to the city. The second blast, a *teruah*, was a signal for all the shops to close and lock up. The third blast, a second *tekiah*, was the signal to remove all the boiling pots from the fire, to store the hot food in the oven, to seal the oven, and to light the Sabbath candles. (See *Rashi*; *Tos. s.v.* רבי).

וְשָׁלֹש לְהַבְדִּיל בֵּין קֹדֶשׁ לְחֹל — *and three to distinguish between the sacred and the secular.*

After pausing long enough to roast a small fish or to attach an unbaked bread to the side of an oven, they sounded a second set of *tekiah-teruah-tekiah*. This set signaled the arrival of the holy Sabbath. All work was forbidden from that moment on (*Shabbos* 35b), and the applicable punishment was in effect (*Rashi* 53b).[1]

[Accordingly, if an additional offering was brought on Friday (on Rosh Chodesh, for example) they would sound thirty-six blasts: the daily twenty-one, nine with the additional offering, and the standard six Friday afternoon blasts.]

Tiferes Yisrael notes that these six Friday blasts were blown in all the cities of the Holy Land, not solely in Jerusalem. Since they were not part of the Temple trumpeting, why are they included in the mishnah's total of blasts?

He concludes that these blasts had a special significance even in the Temple. They highlighted the distinction between the Tem-

ple Service which overrides the Sabbath, and all other labor which does not override the Sabbath even in the Temple.

עֶרֶב שַׁבָּת שֶׁבְּתוֹךְ הֶחָג — *On the eve of the Sabbath during Succos* [lit. *the Festival*],

[The name חָג, *Festival*, throughout Mishnah refers to Succos.]

הָיוּ שָׁם אַרְבָּעִים וּשְׁמוֹנָה: — *there were forty-eight:*

[Sixteen sets of *tekiah — teruah — tekiah* were sounded.]

שָׁלֹש לִפְתִיחַת שְׁעָרִים; — *three for the opening of the gates;*

[Those are the three blasts blown every day when the gates of the Court-yard were opened.]

שָׁלֹש לַשַּׁעַר הָעֶלְיוֹן; — *three for the Upper Gate;*

[These were blown at the outset of the procession led by two *Kohanim* (mishnah 4) from the Upper (Nicanor's) Gate to the Shiloach to draw water.]

(See 5:4 comm. s.v. וְעָמְדוּ שְׁנֵי כֹּהֲנִים בְּשַׁעַר עֶלְיוֹן ... קָרָא הַגֶּבֶר, תָּקְעוּ וְהֵרִיעוּ וְתָקְעוּ.)

Presumably these blasts were blown only after the opening of the Upper Gate. Thus six blasts were blown in connection with the Upper Gate (which was also the principal gate to the Temple Courtyard): three every day when the gates were opened, and an additional three on Succos, when the *Kohanim* stood within this gate. *Rambam (K'lei HaMikdash* 7:6) maintains that on festivals the three for the Upper Gate were sounded at its opening. This, however, seems to be dif-

1. [Since it is clear from *Shabbos* 35b that these three blasts were sounded before sundown, one cannot take literally *Rashi's* statement here that after these blasts the punishment of stoning was in effect. Even at sundown there is still some time until צֵאת הַכּוֹכָבִים, *the emergence of the stars*, which is the harbinger of the most stringent period of the Sabbath — when stoning is the punishment for intentional desecration. Perhaps *Rashi* means that from the moment of the blast, one most beware of the *possibility* of incurring the penalty for transgressing.]

On the eve of the Sabbath during Succos, there
were forty-eight: three for the opening of the gates;
three for the Upper Gate; three for the Lower Gate;
three at the filling of the water; three on top of the
altar; nine for the daily morning burnt offering; nine
for the daily afternoon burnt offering; and nine for

YAD AVRAHAM

ficult: since the Upper Gate is also the gate to
the Courtyard, how can we say that on
festivals they blew three blasts at the opening
of the Upper Gate *in addition* to the three
blasts at the opening of the gates — when
these two events were one and the same?
Aruch LaNer suggests that 'opening of the
gates' refers to *all* the gates to the Temple
Courtyard (there were seven of these; *Middos* 1:4). He bases this on *Rashi* (53b s.v.
שלש לפתיחת שערים) who comments the
phrase 'three for the opening of the gates':
there were seven gates to the Courtyard,
implying that the opening of only one gate
was not sufficient to require the blowing of
the shofar. Thus when all seven gates were
opened they sounded the three blasts. On
festivals, however, three blasts would be
blown upon the opening of the Upper gate
followed by another three blasts when they
had opened all the remaining gates.

וְשָׁלֹשׁ לְשַׁעַר הַתַּחְתּוֹן; — *three for the
Lower Gate;*

[This was the gate which led out from
the Women's Court to the eastern slope
of the Temple Mount.]

The mishnah states that the blasts
were made as soon as the procession
reached the floor of the Courtyard,
which was before they arrived at the
Lower Gate. However, as noted there,
they prolonged the blasts until they
reached the gate of the Women's Court,
which was known as the Lower Gate.
Because this series of blasts was
stretched out until the *Kohanim* arrived
at the gate, the blasts are identified with
the Lower Gate *(Rashi* 53b; *Rav;* see
also comm. to mishnah 4).

The *Gemara* (54a) notes that the tanna of this mishnah disagrees with the
tanna of mishnah 4 and therefore omits
the three blasts which the latter said
were sounded on the tenth step; the tanna of that mishnah disagrees with the

tanna of this mishnah and therefore
omits the three blasts which the latter
said (below) were sounded at the altar.

As already mentioned (above mishnah 4
s.v. עד שמגיעין), *Rambam* holds that these
blasts at the Upper and Lower gates were
sounded every festival. Succos is singled out
only because on it there was yet an additional
set of three blasts for the filling of the water,
so that only on this festival was there a total
of forty-eight blasts.

וְשָׁלֹשׁ לְמִלּוּי הַמַּיִם: — *three at the filling
of the water;*

After filling the gold flask with water
they returned to the Temple and entered
the Court through the Water Gate as
described above (4:9). It was at this gate
that they sounded three blasts *(Rashi*
53b; *Rav;* see comm. to 4:9 s.v. הגיעו
לְשַׁעַר הַמַּיִם תָּקְעוּ וְהֵרִיעוּ וְתָקְעוּ).

וְשָׁלֹשׁ עַל־גַבֵּי מִזְבֵּחַ; — *three on top of the
altar;*

This took place when the willow
branches were set up against the side of
the altar as described in 4:5 *(Rashi;
Rav;* see comm. to 4:5 s.v. וְזוֹקְפִין
אוֹתָן בְּצִדֵּי הַמִּזְבֵּחַ ... תָּקְעוּ וְהֵרִיעוּ וְתָקְעוּ).

Rambam (Klei HaMikdash 7:6) and an
opinion quoted by *Ritva* maintain that these
three blasts *on top of the altar* were blown
when the water libation was poured on the
altar.

Meiri disagrees with this view. If three
blasts were blown when the libation was
poured, then the three blasts of 4:5 are omitted from our mishnah. If we consider them,
too, we are left with a total of fifty-one
blasts, not forty-eight.

[It might be possible to reconcile the view
of *Rashi* and *Rav* with that of *Rambam.
Tiferes Yisroel* (4:5:24) states that after they
set up the willow branches at the side of the
altar they performed the water libation. Accordingly, *Rambam* may mean that when
they blew upon setting the willows along the
side of the altar, it was all in honor of the

לַמּוּסָפִין; שָׁלֹשׁ לְהַבְטִיל אֶת־הָעָם מִן־
הַמְּלָאכָה; וְשָׁלֹשׁ לְהַבְדִּיל בֵּין קֹדֶשׁ לְחֹל.

[ו] **יוֹם** טוֹב הָרִאשׁוֹן שֶׁל חַג הָיוּ שָׁם שְׁלֹשָׁה
עָשָׂר פָּרִים, וְאֵילִים שְׁנַיִם, וְשָׂעִיר
אֶחָד; נִשְׁתַּיְּרוּ שָׁם אַרְבָּעָה עָשָׂר כְּבָשִׂים
לִשְׁמוֹנָה מִשְׁמָרוֹת.
בַּיּוֹם הָרִאשׁוֹן שִׁשָּׁה מַקְרִיבִין שְׁנַיִם שְׁנַיִם,
וְהַשְּׁאָר אֶחָד אֶחָד. בַּשֵּׁנִי חֲמִשָּׁה מַקְרִיבִין
שְׁנַיִם שְׁנַיִם, וְהַשְּׁאָר אֶחָד אֶחָד. בַּשְּׁלִישִׁי

יד אברהם

water libation, and the blasts were considered as having been blown in connection with the water libation.]

תֵּשַׁע לְתָמִיד שֶׁל שַׁחַר; וְתֵשַׁע לְתָמִיד שֶׁל בֵּין הָעַרְבַּיִם; וְתֵשַׁע לַמּוּסָפִין; שָׁלֹשׁ לְהַבְטִיל אֶת־הָעָם מִן־הַמְּלָאכָה; וְשָׁלֹשׁ לְהַבְדִּיל בֵּין קֹדֶשׁ לְחֹל. — *nine for the daily morning burnt offering; nine for the daily after-noon burnt offering; and nine for the mussaf offerings; three to stop the peo-ple from work; and three to distinguish between the sacred and the secular.*

[These passages were explained at the beginning of this mishnah. All in all, the sum of all the blasts sounded on Friday during Succos is forty-eight.]

The *Gemara* (54b) wonders why our mish-

nah says וְאֵין מוֹסִיפִין עַל־אַרְבָּעִים וּשְׁמוֹנָה, [*they never blow*] *more than forty-eight*, since, in fact, if the day before Pesach fell on the Sab-bath, the total number of blasts would be fifty-seven: in addition to the twenty-one daily blasts and the nine Sabbath blasts, there were another twenty-seven connected with the Pesach sacrifice. The multitudes bringing their offerings were divided into three groups, each of which recited the *Hallel* three times during the course of the slaughter. Each time the *Hallel* was begun (three times), three blasts were sounded — for a total of twenty-seven. Why then does the mishnah state that forty-eight was the max-imum? The *Gemara (ibid.)* answers that since the day before Pesach rarely falls on the Sab-bath, that case is omitted by the mishnah. Obviously the mishnah's statement is not meant categorically.

6.

◆§ Twenty-four Temple Watches

The Talmud (*Taanis* 27a) states that Moses established a system of dividing the *Kohanim* into eight מִשְׁמָרוֹת, *watches*, four from the family of Elazar and four from the family of Issamar. The eight watches took turns being responsible for the ser-vice in the Tabernacle.

Samuel and David further divided the *Kohanim* into twenty-four watches. Each watch had a leader in charge of seeing that his watch came up to Jerusalem for its appointed period of service. A watch would be in charge of the Temple service for one week after which another watch would take its place. This continued until each of the twenty-four had a turn and then the rotations would begin again. [Thus a watch generally served in the Temple twice a year for a week.] (*Rambam, K'lei HaMikdash* 4:3).

On the three pilgrimage festivals of Pesach, Shavuos, and Succos, however, all the watches shared in the service of the festival *mussaf* offering (*Deut.* 18:7-8 with

5
6
nine for the *mussaf* offerings; three to stop the people from work; and three to distinguish between the sacred and the secular.

6. On the first festival day of Succos there were thirteen bullocks, two rams, and one he-goat; there remained fourteen yearling sheep for eight watches.

On the first day six [of the watches] offered up two each, and the rest [offered] one each. On the second [day] five offered up two each, and the rest one

YAD AVRAHAM

Rashi; mishnah 7; Rambam, ibid. 4). However, the regular daily service, as well as sacrifices offered by individuals, belonged to the *Kohanim* in whose watch the festival fell. Our mishnah explains how the *mussaf* offerings were divided among the watches on Succos.

יוֹם טוֹב הָרִאשׁוֹן שֶׁל חַג הָיוּ שָׁם שְׁלֹשָׁה עָשָׂר פָּרִים, וְאֵילִים שְׁנַיִם, וְשָׂעִיר אֶחָד; — *On the first festival day of Succos there were thirteen bullocks, two rams, and one he-goat;*

The entire *mussaf* offering specified by Scripture for the first day of Succos (Numbers 29:12-16) is: *And on the fifteenth day of the seventh month...you shall offer [as] a burnt offering...thirteen bullocks, two rams, fourteen yearling sheep and one he-goat for a sin offering.* Our mishnah lists sixteen of them, which were offered by sixteen different watches, leaving fourteen yearling sheep not accounted for (*Rashi* 55b; *Rav*).

נִשְׁתַּיְּרוּ שָׁם אַרְבָּעָה עָשָׂר כְּבָשִׂים לִשְׁמוֹנָה מִשְׁמָרוֹת. — *there remained fourteen yearling sheep for eight watches.*

[Of the twenty-four watches mentioned in the introduction to this mishnah, sixteen had offered the bullocks, the rams, and the he-goat, leaving eight watches to offer the remaining fourteen lambs.]

בַּיּוֹם הָרִאשׁוֹן — *On the first day*

[The eight watches divided the fourteen lambs as follows:]

שִׁשָּׁה מַקְרִיבִין שְׁנַיִם שְׁנַיִם, — *six [of the watches] offered up two each,*

Each watch would offer two lambs, for a total of twelve lambs (*Rashi* 55b; *Rav*).

וְהַשְּׁאָר אֶחָד אֶחָד. — *and the rest [offered] one each.*

The last two watches (*Rashi; Rav*) [by offering one lamb apiece, brought the number of lambs to fourteen].

בַּשֵּׁנִי — *On the second [day],*

Scripture (*Num.* 29:13-32) requires one bullock less on each successive day of Succos: twelve for the second day, eleven for the third day, and so on, together with the constant two rams and single he-goat. Thus on the second day there was a total of fifteen animals requiring fifteen watches. That left nine watches to offer up the fourteen lambs (*Rashi* 55b; *Rav*). [They divided up the lambs as follows:]

חֲמִשָּׁה מַקְרִיבִין שְׁנַיִם שְׁנַיִם, — *five offered up two each,*

Each of these five watches offered two lambs for a total of ten lambs (*Rashi; Rav*). [The four remaining lambs were offered as follows:].

וְהַשְּׁאָר אֶחָד אֶחָד — *and the rest one each.*

The last four watches (*Rashi; Rav*) [by offering up one apiece, brought the total to fourteen.]

אַרְבָּעָה מַקְרִיבִין שְׁנַיִם, וְהַשְּׁאָר אֶחָד
אֶחָד. בָּרְבִיעִי שְׁלֹשָׁה מַקְרִיבִין שְׁנַיִם שְׁנַיִם,
וְהַשְּׁאָר אֶחָד אֶחָד. בַּחֲמִישִׁי שְׁנַיִם מַקְרִיבִין
שְׁנַיִם שְׁנַיִם, וְהַשְּׁאָר אֶחָד אֶחָד. בַּשִּׁשִּׁי אֶחָד
מַקְרִיב שְׁנַיִם, וְהַשְּׁאָר אֶחָד אֶחָד. בַּשְּׁבִיעִי כֻּלָּן
שָׁוִין.
בַּשְּׁמִינִי חָזְרוּ לְפַיִס כְּבָרְגָלִים.
אָמְרוּ: ,,מִי שֶׁהִקְרִיב פָּרִים הַיּוֹם, לֹא יַקְרִיב
לְמָחָר;'' אֶלָּא חוֹזְרִין חֲלִילָה.

יד אברהם

בַּשְּׁלִישִׁי — *On the third [day]*
One less bullock was offered as
Numbers (29:20) specifies eleven bullocks, two rams, and a he-goat for the
third day, for a total of fourteen offerings requiring fourteen watches. That
left ten watches for the fourteen daily
lambs (*Rashi; Rav*). [They divided up
the lambs as follows:]

אַרְבָּעָה מַקְרִיבִין שְׁנַיִם שְׁנַיִם, — *four offered up two each,*
Each offered two lambs for a total of
eight (*Rashi; Rav*).

וְהַשְּׁאָר אֶחָד אֶחָד. — *and the rest one
each.*
The last six watches (*Rashi; Rav*) [by
offering one lamb apiece, brought the
total to fourteen].

בָּרְבִיעִי — *On the fourth [day]*
[One less bullock was offered as
Numbers (29:23) specifies ten bullocks,
two rams, and a he-goat for the fourth
day, a total of thirteen offerings requiring thirteen watches, leaving eleven
watches to offer the fourteen lambs.
They divided up the lambs as follows:]

שְׁלֹשָׁה מַקְרִיבִין שְׁנַיִם שְׁנַיִם, — *three offered up two each,*
[Each offered two for a total of six.]

וְהַשְּׁאָר אֶחָד אֶחָד. — *and the rest one
each.*
[The last eight watches, by offering
up one lamb apiece, brought the total to
fourteen.]

בַּחֲמִישִׁי — *On the fifth [day]*
[One less bullock was offered, as
Numbers (29:26) specifies only nine
bullocks, two rams, and a he-goat for
the fifth day, a total of twelve offerings
requiring twelve watches. Twelve
watches remained to offer the fourteen
lambs, which they divided as follows:]

שְׁנַיִם מַקְרִיבִין שְׁנַיִם שְׁנַיִם, — *two offered
up two each,*
[Each offered two lambs for a total of
four.]

וְהַשְּׁאָר אֶחָד אֶחָד. — *and the rest one
each.*
[The last ten watches, by offering up
one lamb apiece, brought the total to
fourteen.]

בַּשִּׁשִּׁי — *On the sixth [day]*
[One less bullock was offered as
Numbers (29:29) specifies only eight
bullocks, two rams and a he-goat for the
sixth day, for a total of eleven offerings
requiring eleven watches. Thirteen
watches were left to offer the fourteen
lambs as follows:]

אֶחָד מַקְרִיב שְׁנַיִם, — *one offered up two,*
[Only that watch offered two lambs.]

וְהַשְּׁאָר אֶחָד אֶחָד. — *and the rest, one
each.*
[The remaining twelve watches, by
offering up one lamb apiece, brought
the total to fourteen.]

בַּשְּׁבִיעִי — *On the seventh [day]*
[One less bullock was offered as

each. On the third [day] four offered up two each,
and the rest one each. On the fourth [day] three offered up two each, and the rest one each. On the fifth
[day] two offered up two each, and the rest one each.
On the sixth [day] one offered up two, and the rest,
one each. On the seventh [day] all were equal.

On the eighth [day] they reverted to [casting] lots
as on the [other] festivals.

[The Sages] said, 'Whoever offered up bullocks today should not offer them tomorrow;' but they took
turns in rotation.

YAD AVRAHAM

Numbers (29:32) specifies only seven
bullocks, two rams, and a he-goat for
the seventh day, a total of ten offerings
requiring ten watches. Fourteen Watches were left to offer fourteen lambs.]

כֻּלָּן שָׁוִין. — all were equal.
Since each of the remaining fourteen
watches offered one lamb, every one of
the twenty-four watches offered only
one animal that day (Rashi; Rav).

בַּשְּׁמִינִי, — On the eighth [day]
[Shemini Atzeres, though not part of
Succos, is the eighth consecutive Festival day. Numbers (29:35-38) requires
one bullock, one ram, one he-goat, and
seven lambs to be offered.]

חָזְרוּ לְפַיִס — they reverted to [casting]
lots
Since there were only ten offerings
that day, all twenty-four watches par-
ticipated in the casting of lots to determine which ones would participate in
the ten offerings (Rashi 55b; Rav; Tif.
Yis.).
In view of the fact that twenty-two
watches had three turns during Succos, while
two watches had had only two turns (see
below s.v. אֶלָּא חוֹזְרִין), the Gemara (55b)
debates whether the lots were cast among all
twenty-four watches or whether the two
watches were given preference and cast lots
only among themselves.

כְּבָרְגָלִים. — as on the [other] festivals.
On the other festivals the small
number of offerings required the

casting of lots among the watches to
determine which of the twenty-four
would perform the service for that particular festival (Rashi). The method of
casting lots is described in Yoma (2:1).

אָמְרוּ: ,,מִי שֶׁהִקְרִיב פָּרִים הַיּוֹם, — They
[the Sages] said, 'Whoever offered up
bullocks today;
I.e., on one of the seven days of Succos (Tif. Yis.).

לֹא יַקְרִיב לְמָחָר;" — should not offer
them tomorrow;'
The Kohanim would not allow any
watch to offer bullocks on two consecutive days (Rashi; Rav).

אֶלָּא חוֹזְרִין חֲלִילָה. — but they took turns
in rotation.
The rotation system was as follows:
First day: 13 bullocks — watches 1-
13.
Second day: 12 bullocks — watches
14-24;1.
Third day: 11 bullocks — watches 2-
12.
Fourth day: 10 bullocks — watches
13-22.
Fifth day: 9 bullocks — watches 23-
24; 1-7.
Sixth day: 8 bullocks — watches 8-15.
Seventh day: 7 bullocks — watches
16-22.
On each of these days the remaining
watches offered the rams, he-goat and
lambs as explained above.
The above list makes it clear that

[ז] **בִּשְׁלשָׁה** פְּרָקִים בַּשָּׁנָה הָיוּ כָל-
מִשְׁמָרוֹת שָׁווֹת בְּאִמוּרֵי
הָרְגָלִים וּבְחִלּוּק לֶחֶם הַפָּנִים.
בַּעֲצֶרֶת אוֹמְרִים לוֹ: ,,הֵילָךְ מַצָּה, הֵילָךְ
חָמֵץ!"
מִשְׁמָר שֶׁזְּמַנּוֹ קָבוּעַ — הוּא מַקְרִיב תְּמִידִין,

יד אברהם

watches 1-22 had three turns at offering the bullocks, whereas watches 23 and 24 had only two turns each (Rashi 55b).

The total number of bullocks offered during Succos was seventy, while only one bullock was offered on Shemini Atzeres.

R' Elazar said (Gem. 55b): To what do those seventy bullocks offered during the seven days of Succos correspond? To the seventy nations. (These offerings were brought on behalf of the seventy nations to atone for their sins so that they would merit proper rainfall throughout the year [cf. Zechariah 14:17-18]. For it is on Succos that the world is judged on the year's water supply (Rashi).

To what does the single bullock offered on Shemini Atzeres correspond? To the unique nation [Israel]. This may be compared to a mortal king who said to his servants, 'Prepare for me a great banquet'. But on the last day he said to his favorite, 'Prepare for me a simple feast, so that I may derive pleasure from you. [I can have pleasure and satisfaction only from you (Israel) and not from them]' (Rashi, ibid.).

Maharsha suggests that the diminishing number of bullocks on Succos represents the idea that the seventy nations will diminish. Those that oppressed the Jews will become fewer and fewer until the Jewish people alone will reign supreme under the direct guidance of God. See Overview to ArtScroll Hoshanos.

7.

בִּשְׁלשָׁה פְּרָקִים בַּשָּׁנָה — *During three periods of the year*

These were the שָׁלשׁ רְגָלִים, three pilgrimage festivals — Succos, Pesach and Shavuos (Rashi 55b).

הָיוּ כָל-מִשְׁמָרוֹת שָׁווֹת — all [twenty-four] watches were equal

They are equal regarding their participation in the sacrificial service and in dividing the Kohanim's share of these offerings (Gem. 56a). These include the breast and thigh of שַׁלְמֵי חֲגִיגָה, festival peace offerings, brought by every adult male and the hides of the עוֹלוֹת רְאִיָּה, personal festival burnt offerings, and of the festival additional offerings (Rashi 55b).

בְּאִמוּרֵי הָרְגָלִים — in the prescribed offerings of the festivals

The term אִימוּרִים, [emurim] usually refers to those portions of the animal that are burned on the altar (Tif. Yis. to Zevachim 2:2; 2:7). The language of the mishnah implies that the emurim, like the Panim Bread is divided among the Kohanim to be eaten. But, the Gemara (55b) asks, are not the emurim offered on the altar? It answers that our mishnah uses the term emurim in a different sense. As used in this mishnah it is derived from the word אָמַר, to say, or state, and it refers to all the festival offerings that are 'stated' in the Torah, many which have parts that are eaten by the Kohanim.

וּבְחִלּוּק לֶחֶם הַפָּנִים. — and in the division of the Panim Bread.

Every Sabbath, twelve fresh breads, the Panim Breads, were arranged on the table in the Sanctuary (Lev. 24:5-9), and the previous week's breads removed and divided between the incoming and the outgoing watches, for it was on the Sabbath that the watches would relieve

7. **D**uring three periods of the year all [twenty-four] watches were equal in the prescribed offerings of the festivals and in the division of the *Panim* Bread.

On Shavuos they would say to him, 'Here is matzah for you; here is chametz for you!'

The watch whose time [of service] was fixed — [only] it offers the daily burnt offerings, vow offer-

YAD AVRAHAM

each other (mishnah 8). The mishnah informs us here that on a festival Sabbath the *Panim* Bread was divided equally among all twenty-four watches.

Tosafos (55b s.v. וּבְחִילּוּק) points out that this sharing of the breads on a festival was only in regard to apportioning it for eating. But the Temple service of removing the previous week's breads, arranging the fresh ones on the table, and burning the accompanying frankincense on the golden altar was carried out only by the designated watch of that particular Sabbath day, as were all the daily and Sabbath services (Cf. *Tos. Yom Tov*).

בַּעֲצֶרֶת — *On Shavuos*

When Shavuos falls on the Sabbath (*Rashi; Rav*), all watches shared not only the *Panim* Bread, but also the שְׁתֵּי הַלֶּחֶם, *Two Loaves*, that were brought as a special offering from the חָדָשׁ,[1] *new wheat* that grew after Pesach (*Lev.* 23:16; *Rashi ibid. Menachos* 9:1). While the *Panim* Bread was מַצָּה, *unleavened* (*Men.* 52b; *Tos.* s.v. מִנַּיִן), the Two Loaves, on the other hand, were חָמֵץ, *leavened bread* (*Lev.* 23:17; *Menachos* 5:1). Thus, on a Shavuos-Sabbath, the service included both *chametz* and matzah (*Rambam, Comm.*).

אוֹמְרִים לוֹ: — *they would say to him,*

Those who distributed portions from these two kinds of breads would say to each *Kohen* who received a portion (*Tif.*

Yis.), when they gave him his portions of the *Panim* Bread and the Two Loaves (*Rashi; Rav*):

,,הֵילָךְ מַצָּה, — *'Here is matzah for you* [i.e., *Panim* Bread];

הֵילָךְ חָמֵץ!'' — *here is chametz for you* [i.e., *Two Loaves*]!'

The reason each *Kohen* was told, 'Here is *chametz*; here is *matzah*' was so that he would receive some of each kind rather than a double portion of one and none of the other. (See also *Kiddushin* 53a; *Menachos* 73a; *Rashi* to 53b; *Rav*).

Tosefos Yom Tov explains that matzah was mentioned before *chametz* because of the principle — תָּדִיר וְשֶׁאֵינוֹ תָּדִיר, תָּדִיר קוֹדֵם, *between the constant and the occasional, the constant takes precedence.* Since unleavened *Panim* Bread was brought every Sabbath, it preceded the leavened Two Loaves which were brought only on Shavuous.

מִשְׁמָר שֶׁזְּמַנּוֹ קָבוּעַ — *The watch whose time [of service] was fixed —*

The watch whose turn it was to serve in the Temple on the week of the festival (*Rashi 55b; Rav*).

הוּא מַקְרִיב — *[only] it offers*

All the offerings that were not brought specifically because of the festival (*Rashi; Rav*). [These included:]

תְּמִידִין, — *the daily burnt offerings,*

These were the daily burnt offerings of the morning and afternoon, for these

1. The two loaves offered on Shavuos were a counterpart to the *omer* offering brought on the second day of Pesach. Just as the *omer* offering (of barley) permitted the general use of all חָדָשׁ, *new grains*, that had grown since the previous Pesach, the offering of the two loaves permitted the new grains to be used in the Temple for meal offerings (*Menachos* 10:6,7).

נְדָרִים, וּנְדָבוֹת, וּשְׁאָר קָרְבְּנוֹת צִבּוּר, וּמַקְרִיב
אֶת־הַכֹּל.
יוֹם טוֹב הַסָּמוּךְ לַשַּׁבָּת, בֵּין מִלְּפָנֶיהָ בֵּין
לְאַחֲרֶיהָ, הָיוּ כָל־הַמִּשְׁמָרוֹת שָׁווֹת בְּחִלּוּק
לֶחֶם הַפָּנִים.

[ח] **חָל** לִהְיוֹת יוֹם אֶחָד לְהַפְסִיק בֵּינָתַיִם,
מִשְׁמָר שֶׁזְּמַנּוֹ קָבוּעַ הָיָה נוֹטֵל עֶשֶׂר
חַלּוֹת, וְהַמִּתְעַכֵּב נוֹטֵל שְׁתָּיִם. וּבִשְׁאָר יְמוֹת

יד אברהם

offerings are not related to the festival
(Rashi; Rav).

נְדָרִים, וּנְדָבוֹת — *vow offerings, freewill offerings,*

Various personal offerings were pledged during the year and brought to the Temple in fulfillment of the pledges during the festival. The watches whose turns were not fixed for this week did not share in these offerings, for they were entitled to share only in offerings that were directly connected with the festival (*Rashi 55b; Rav*).

A נֶדֶר, *vow offering*, is an obligation undertaken when a man vows to bring an offering without designating a specific animal. A נְדָבָה, *freewill offering*, is an obligation when a person designates a specific animal and states 'This one is an offering', without, however, explicitly obligating *himself* to bring an offering. Accordingly, in the case of the vow offering if the eventually chosen animal dies or is stolen, it must be replaced, because the obligation to bring an offering is a personal one and remains incumbent upon him. In the case of a free will offering, however, if the animal dies or is stolen, its owner is exempt from offering a different one, because his sole obligation was to offer the specifically designated animal (*Kinnim 1:1*).

וּשְׁאָר קָרְבְּנוֹת צִבּוּר — *the remaining public offerings,*

This term includes the bullock brought by each tribe in the rare instance when a majority of the entire Jewish People sinned following an erroneous ruling of the *Beis Din* which permitted a transgression whose מֵזִיד, *deliberate violation*, would result in כָּרֵת, *spiritual excision* [פַּר הֶעְלֵם דָּבָר]. If the *Beis Din* erred in permitting idol-worship, then a he-goat must accompany the bullock (*Gem. 56a; Rambam, Shegagos, 12:1; Rashi 56a; Rav*).

Tosafos (55b) notes that the *mussaf* sacrifice of the Sabbath is also offered by the watch 'whose time was fixed' as *Tosefta* (4:11) clearly states. The other *Kohanim* had rights only insofar the sacrifices integrally connected to the festivals were concerned, and in regard to eating the *Panim* Bread.

וּמַקְרִיב אֶת־הַכֹּל — *and [this watch] offers everything.*

This phrase includes קֵיץ הַמִּזְבֵּחַ [lit. *dessert of the altar*]. When there were not enough private sacrifices to keep a steady flow of offerings coming to the altar, communal funds were made available to purchase animals for burnt offerings so that the altar would not remain idle. It was as if the altar was being given a 'dessert' once the regular 'meal' of offerings was completed. Only the watch whose turn it was on that Sabbath would perform this service (*Gem. 56a with Rashi; Rav*).

יוֹם טוֹב הַסָּמוּךְ לַשַּׁבָּת בֵּין מִלְּפָנֶיה — *If a*

5
8

ings, free will offerings, the remaining public offerings, and [this watch] offers everything.

If a festival fell near a Sabbath, either before it or after it, all the watches shared equally in the division of the *Panim* Bread.

8. If one day intervened between them, the watch whose time was fixed took ten loaves, and the one that stayed behind took two. But during the rest

festival fell near a Sabbath, either before it

For example, if a festival fell on Friday so that all the *Kohanim* who were not part of the regular watch could not leave for home until after the Sabbath *(Gem.* 56a and *Rashi; Rav).*

בֵּין לְאַחֲרֶיהָ, — *or after it,*

If a festival fell on Sunday, all the *Kohanim* coming to serve during the festival had to arrive before the Sabbath *(Gem.* 56 and *Rashi; Rav).*

הָיוּ כָל־הַמִּשְׁמָרוֹת שָׁווֹת בְּחִלּוּק לֶחֶם הַפָּנִים. — *all the watches shared equally in* [lit. *were equal*] *the division of the Panim Bread.*

In both cases the *Kohanim* who came to serve in the Temple during the festival were compelled to spend an additional Sabbath in the Temple, so the Sages provided for all the *Kohanim* to share the *Panim* alike *(Gem.* 56a; and *Rashi; Rav).*

[The mishnah mentions only the division of the *Panim* Bread, because all the other services performed for the Sabbath belonged to the 'watch whose time was fixed,' even if the Sabbath fell on *Yom Tov* itself. So on a festival which fell next to a Sabbath, when only the daily and Sabbath services were performed, the only thing that could be offered to the other *Kohanim* was a portion of the *Panim* Bread.]

8.

חָל לִהְיוֹת יוֹם אֶחָד לְהַפְסִיק בֵּינָתַיִם — *If one day intervened* [lit. *fell to intervene*] *between them,*

If either the first day of a festival was Monday, in which case Sunday intervened between the Sabbath and *Yom Tov,* or the last day of a festival was Thursday, in which case Friday intervened between the festival and the Sabbath, in either case, in addition to the designated watches that were assigned to the Temple service, there are large numbers of *Kohanim* who came for the festival. If the festival was to begin on Monday, many *Kohanim* would arrive on Friday instead of Sunday, and if the festival ended Thursday, many *Kohanim* would remain for the Sabbath rather than leave for home on Friday *(Rashi* 56a; *Rav).*

מִשְׁמָר שֶׁזְּמַנּוֹ קָבוּעַ נוֹטֵל עֶשֶׂר חַלּוֹת, — *the watch whose time was fixed took ten loaves,*

On an ordinary Sabbath, two watches would be at the Temple since that is the day when the watches were changed. Thus *the watch whose time was fixed* refers to both the incoming and the outgoing watches. Below, the mishnah tells us that on a regular Sabbath, the twelve *Panim* Breads would be divided equally between these two watches, six for each. If the Sabbath occured as near to *Yom Tov* as described here, only ten loaves are given to the fixed watch, five for the outgoing watch and five for the incoming *(Rashi; Rav).*

וְהַמִּתְעַכֵּב — *and the one that stayed behind*

Those were the *Kohanim* who came

[143] **THE MISHNAH** / SUCCAH

הַשָּׁנָה, הַנִּכְנָס נוֹטֵל שֵׁשׁ וְהַיּוֹצֵא נוֹטֵל שֵׁשׁ.
רַבִּי יְהוּדָה אוֹמֵר: הַנִּכְנָס נוֹטֵל שֶׁבַע וְהַיּוֹצֵא
נוֹטֵל חָמֵשׁ.
הַנִּכְנָסִין חוֹלְקִין בַּצָּפוֹן וְהַיּוֹצְאִין בַּדָּרוֹם.
בִּלְגָּה לְעוֹלָם חוֹלֶקֶת בַּדָּרוֹם, וְטַבַּעְתָּהּ
קְבוּעָה, וְחַלּוֹנָהּ סְתוּמָה.

יד אברהם

to the Temple on Friday and remained over the Sabbath, even though they could have come on Sunday, or the *Kohanim* who could have gone home on Friday but decided to stay over the Sabbath (*Rashi; Rav;* see *comm.* in beginning of mishnah s.v. חל להיות).

Tosefos Yom Tov challenges the above interpretation. If the term וְהַמִּתְעַכֵּב, *the one that stayed behind*, is referring to all of the *Kohanim* who decided to come early or to stay on for the Sabbath, the mishnah should have used the plural term וְהַמִּתְעַכְּבִים, *those who ...*, rather than the singular form. Citing *Kessef Mishneh*, he further points out that term *stayed behind* could refer only to the case where the festival ended on Thursday and, instead of departing on Friday, they decided to remain at the Temple, but in the case where the festival began on Monday and some *Kohanim* came ahead of time, the proper term would be וְהַמַּקְדִּים, *and the one who arrived early*.

Rambam's view is (*T'midin U'Mussafin* 4:13; *Comm.*) that the term וְהַמִּתְעַכֵּב stems from an Aramaic root meaning *linger* or *delay*, in the sense that one is reluctant to do what is expected of him. [In the case of Lot, who was reluctant to leave Sodom even when its destruction was imminent, *Onkelos* translates וַיִּתְמַהְמָהּ, *he lingered* (Gen. 19:16), as וְאִתְעַכַּב. Thus, *Rambam* applies the term וְהַמִּתְעַכֵּב to the incoming watch. Since the members of this watch knew that they would have to share the festival service with huge numbers of other *Kohanim*, and would have only the Sunday service completely to themselves, many of them would be reluctant to come, they would *linger* at home. Since, relatively few of them would arrive for the Sabbath before the Festival, they did not require the normal quota of six loaves. Consequently, it was sufficient to give them only two.

According to *Rambam*, the mishnah is explained as follows: If one day intervened between the Sabbath and the festival — whether the festival began on Monday or ended on Thursday — the watch of that week would have only one day, either Sunday or Friday, when it would have the exclusive right to the service. Consequently, many of its members would linger at home and the watch is described as מִתְעַכֵּב, *the lingering watch*, with the result that no more than two loaves were required to satisfy their needs.

נוֹטֵל שְׁתַּיִם — *took two.*

[Its members divided up two of the twelve breads among themselves.].

וּבִשְׁאָר יְמוֹת הַשָּׁנָה — *But during the rest* [lit. *the other days*] *of the year,*

[I.e., on Sabbaths that were not festival days.]

הַנִּכְנָס נוֹטֵל שֵׁשׁ וְהַיּוֹצֵא נוֹטֵל שֵׁשׁ — *the incoming [watch] took six [loaves] and the outgoing [watch] took six.*

The watches changed on the Sabbath. The outgoing watch offered up the תָּמִיד שֶׁל שַׁחַר, *daily morning burnt offering,* and the מוּסָף, *additional [Sabbath] offerings.* The incoming watch offered up the תָּמִיד שֶׁל בֵּין הָעַרְבַּיִם, *daily afternoon burnt offering,* and the two spoonfuls of frankincense which lay on the table together with the loaves of *Panim* Bread. Four *Kohanim* would enter the Courtyard, two from one watch and two from the other, and they apportioned the breads (*Gem.* 56b; and *Rashi*).

It is not clear, according to this, whether these four *kohanim* merely took the six loaves for their respective 'watches', leaving the apportionment among the individual members of each watch (described below in our mishnah) to others, or whether these four *Kohanim* were responsible to apportion them among the individuals.

of the year, the incoming [watch] took six [loaves] and the outgoing [watch] took six. R' Yehudah says: The incoming [watch] took seven and the outgoing [watch] took five.

The incoming [watch] divided [the bread] in the north and the outgoing [watch] in the south.

[The watch of] Bilgah always divided [the bread] in the south, its ring was permanently affixed, and its window was sealed.

YAD AVRAHAM

רַבִּי יְהוּדָה אוֹמֵר: הַנִּכְנָס נוֹטֵל שֶׁבַע — *R' Yehudah says: The incoming [watch] took seven*

The incoming watch is entitled to seven of the breads. The *Gemara* (56b) explains that it receives an extra loaf because that evening it will close the Temple gates which had been opened that Sabbath morning by the outgoing watch.

Meiri is at loss to understand this explanation. Why does closing the gate entitle the incoming watch to an advantage? After all the outgoing watch had to open these doors in the morning. *Rashi* (56b s.v. בשכר) implies that those who opened the gates in the morning should have had the duty of completing their task by closing them at night. Since the incoming watch· did the closing, its seems as though it were doing the work of the outgoing watch. Therefore it behooves the outgoing watch to yield one of its loaves in payment of this service.

Meiri suggests that the incoming watch assisted in *opening* the gates in the morning.

The *Gemara* (ibid.) notes that on the next Sabbath, this same watch would only receive five loaves since then it would be the outgoing watch, so the net result would be the same as if the loaves had been divided equally at the outset. But, comments the *Gemara*, one prefers to receive tangible benefits immediately rather than to have them deferred.

וְהַיּוֹצֵא נוֹטֵל חָמֵשׁ. — *and the outgoing [watch] took five.*

[Having already received seven loaves the previous Sabbath for closing the Temple gates that night, they this time received only five.]

הַנִּכְנָסִין חוֹלְקִין בַּצָּפוֹן — *The incoming [watch] divided [the bread] in the north*

[They divided their six or seven loaves among themselves (Rashi; Rav)... in the section of the Courtyard north of the altar (see Yoma 36a; comm. to Yoma 3:8) where קָדְשֵׁי קָדָשִׁים, *offerings of highest sanctity*, were slaughtered. This, symbolized that the incoming watch was dedicating itself to serve in the Temple (Gem. 56b; Rashi to 56a; Rav; Rambam, Comm.).

וְהַיּוֹצְאִין בַּדָּרוֹם — *and the outgoing [watch] in the south.*

They divided their share of the loaves among themselves in the least important area of the Courtyard, where no particular service was designated to be performed, thus symbolizing that they were the outgoing watch (Gem. 56b; Rashi to 56a· Rav).

בִּלְגָּה — *[The watch of] Bilgah*

This was the name of the fifteenth watch. Each watch was named after one of its ancestors (I Chron. 24:7-18; Rashi Rav).

לְעוֹלָם חוֹלֶקֶת בַּדָּרוֹם — *always divided [the bread] in the south,*

Even when it was the incoming watch, Bilgah was required to divide its share in the southern part of the Courtyard; consequently, Bilgah always seemed to be leaving the Temple (Rabbeinu Chananel). This was a fine imposed upon the Bilgah watch, as will be explained below (Rashi, 56a; Rav).

וְטַבַּעְתָּהּ קְבוּעָה, — *its ring was per-*

manently affixed,

Twenty-four rings were affixed to the floor of the Temple Courtyard where the slaughtering was done. The rings were stapled to the floor at one point, and were raised so that the animal's head could be inserted in them and locked in place during the slaughtering so as not to invalidate the slaughtering. The ring assigned to Bilgah, however, was permanently stapled to the floor at two points so that it could not be raised. This, too, was a fine imposed on Bilgah, forcing it to use the ring of another watch and thus suffering embarrassment (Rashi; Rav; Tif. Yis.).

Rambam (comm.) suggest that the rings were affixed to the wall and were used to hang the carcasses after slaughtering to facilitate the skinning process.

וְחַלוֹנָה סְתוּמָה. — and its [Bilgah's] window was sealed.

As described in Middos, the אוּלָם, antechamber, of the Temple was thirty cubits wider than the Temple proper, and there were rooms at its northern and southern extremities. These were called בֵּית הַחֲלִיפוֹת, the knife room(s). Each of the watches had a window through which it would deposit its knives in the room (Rav; Rashi see Meiri).

Tiferes Yisrael maintains that these חַלונות were alcoves (cf. Tosefos Yom Tov, Meilah 6:1 s.v. מן החלון). The Kohanim entered the knife rooms by way of a door. The wall of these rooms contained twenty-four indentations or alcoves which could be closed, (like a built-in closet. The window or closet of Bilgah was permanently sealed.

Bilgah was penalized in the three

ways described because of an unfortunate incident. A woman named Miriam [from the family of Bilgah (Rashi)] became an apostate and married a Greek officer. When the Greeks entered the Sanctuary [during the time of Mattisyahu the son of Yochanan (Rashi)], she stamped with her sandal upon the altar crying out, "Lukos, Lukos,[1] how long will you consume Israel's money and yet not stand by them in the time of oppression!'

When the Sages heard of this they made Bilgah's ring immovable, blocked up its window [and permanently designated the southern section of the Temple Courtyard for its division of the breads] (Gem. 56b).

Others (ibid.) however, say that the reason for the penalties was the fact that Bilgah's watch was tardy in coming and so Yeshevav, one of its fellow watches, replaced it. [In the sequence of the watches Bilgah was number fifteen, following Yeshevav, which was number fourteen, so Yeshevav was always the outgoing watch when Bilgah was the incoming watch.) Whenever Bilgah was tardy Yeshevav stayed on to replace it — (Rashi 56b; I Chron. 24:13,14).]

The Gemara notes that according to the view that the whole watch of Bilgah was tardy, it was understandable why the whole watch was penalized. But according to the view that Miriam left the fold, why did the Sages penalize a family on account of one of its daughters?

Abaye replied: As the saying goes, 'The child's statement in the marketplace is either of his father or of his mother,' and 'Woe to the wicked and woe to his neighbor; bounty to the righteous and bounty to his neighbor,' as is written (Isaiah 3:10): אִמְרוּ צַדִּיק כִּי טוֹב כִּי־פְרִי מַעַלְלֵיהֶם יֹאכֵלוּ, Say of the righteous that it shall be well with him for they shall eat the fruit of their deeds."

סליק מסכת סוכה

---

1. Rashi (56b) notes that 'Lukos' is a Greek term meaning 'wolf.' The wolf is known to devour sheep. She abused the altar, upon which two sheep are offered every day by calling it 'wolf' (Maharsha).